Nebraska
Symposium on
Motivation
1975

Nebraska Symposium on Motivation, 1975, is Volume 23 in the series on CURRENT THEORY AND RESEARCH IN MOTIVATION

University of Nebraska Press
Lincoln/London 1976

Nebraska Symposium on Motivation 1975

Conceptual Foundations of Psychology

James K. Cole	*Series Editor*
William J. Arnold	*Volume Editor*
Joseph R. Royce	*Director, Center for Advanced Study in Theoretical Psychology University of Alberta, Canada*
Willard F. Day	*Professor of Psychology University of Nevada, Reno*
Theodore Mischel	*Professor of Philosophy State University of New York at Binghamton*
Joseph R. Rychlak	*Professor of Psychology Purdue University*
Amedeo Giorgi	*Professor of Psychology Duquesne University*
Klaus F. Riegel	*Professor of Psychology University of British Columbia, Canada*
Carol F. Feldman	*Associate Professor of Psychology University of Houston*
Stephen Toulmin	*Professor of Philosophy University of Chicago*
Sigmund Koch	*Professor of Psychology Boston University*

Contents

Introduction

*W*illiam Blake once asked, "What may man be?" and answered, "Who can tell?" Today there are those among us who are asking what psychology may be, and an echo from Blake might be heard to reply, "Who can tell?"

Perhaps it will be seen as a paradox by future historians that for so many years psychology guided itself by a model of physics long outmoded in its own field of inquiry. As Oppenheimer (1956) has observed, physics, at the beginning of this century, "inherited a notion of the physical world as a causal one, in which every event could be accounted for if we were ingenious, a world characterized by number, where everything interesting could be measured and quantified, a determinist world, a world in which the object of study was simply there and how you studied it did not affect the object. . . . It was just the given real object; there it was, and there was nothing for you to worry about of an epistemological character." But with quantum mechanics, Heisenberg's principle of uncertainty, etc., the old Newtonian model of physics was profoundly changed. As Bronowski (1973, p. 340) writes in *The Ascent of Man*, "When we step through the gateway of the atom, *we are in a world which our senses cannot experience.* There is a new architecture there, a way that things are put together which we cannot know: we only try to picture it by analogy, a new act of the imagination. . . . [Thus] *all our ways of picturing the invisible are metaphors, likenesses that we snatch from the larger world of eye and ear and touch*" (italics added). As a product of this revolutionary change in its conception of the world, physics found itself confronted with epistemological questions regarding the foundations of knowledge and the nature of knowing. And in its effort to deal with these questions, physics came to recognize the degree to which its theoretical conceptions and empirical definitions are inextricably bound with its philosophical assumptions about the world of nature and human observation.

To the extent, therefore, that psychology has been committed to an older, Newtonian conceptual system (and its interlocking philosophical assumptions), it becomes apparent that we, in our domain, have been guiding ourselves by a limited conception of science and, accordingly, by a restricted conception of the human being. Nonetheless, in recent years many psychologists have been acquiring a sharper perception of the mutable, evolutionary character of all theoretical conceptions—including the regnant conceptions in psychology. As a consequence psychology appears to be in a period of transition or "crisis." Like physics before it, psychology is engaged in a critical reappraisal of its fundamental assumptions concerning the nature of knowledge and the very nature of the events it observes. For if, as Bronowski and other "new physicists" have perceived, we live in a world which cannot be directly known through the senses alone, and if we must expand our conceptual framework in ways that will include the *invisible architecture of relationships* within and between observable events, then psychology, too, finds itself confronted with epistemological questions of knowing. And it is the search for answers to these questions that is leading psychology, again like physics, to recognize its ineluctable relationship with philosophy.

It is against this background that we chose *Conceptual Foundations of Psychology* as the topic for the 1975 Nebraska Symposium. Because the questions being asked in psychology today have created a need for greater communication between psychology and philosophy, the notion of providing a forum for such an exchange of thought became one of our primary objectives. In effect, this is a symposium on metatheoretical psychology, that is, on theories regarding the kinds of theories or explanatory systems psychology should have. As we shall see, such questions are not answered merely by running more experiments and gathering more "facts." Rather, they are questions of choice among differing conceptual frameworks where the decisions that we make will define what are to be regarded as psychological "facts," how they are to be determined, and what they mean.

So if we ask once more what psychology may be, we might suggest a new interpretation of Blake's reply, "Who can tell?" To some extent *we* can tell as we track the thoughts of theorists who are currently articulating themselves into the already begun of psychology's past and moving toward the yet-to-be-thought-of in psychology's future. True, we will discover no final answers. But what we find here are eight extraordinary theorists who are in the process of transforming the conceptual framework of psychology. In no way are we suggesting that these eight theoretical papers can be fused into a single perspective. Yet, as some of these papers show, the existence of these alternatives becomes a part of our available potential for reappraising our conceptions of psychology. In this continuing process of structuring and restructuring our theoretical conceptions, we all become explorers at the edge of uncertainty. And if in this process, we are, as Sherif (1970) suggests, "groping toward the shape of the future," then we are groping toward the shape of a future whose shape is being shaped by the groping!

The following are abstracts of each of the symposium papers, but—like any abstraction—these are incomplete and limited statements of the richness and complexity of argument to be discovered in reading the papers themselves.

Royce. In his paper Royce first recognizes the "multi" nature—or the conceptual pluralism—of contemporary psychology, and then asks the critical question, "Where do we go from here?" His own position is that the multiperspectivism of psychology calls for "a massive onslaught of theoretical synthesizing and philosophical analysis." We need a dialogue between psychology and philosophy that will examine our conceptual foundations (philosophical assumptions, epistemologies, etc.) and develop a metatheoretical framework appropriate to the "multi" nature of contemporary psychology.

On the basis of his analysis, Royce sees the greatest obstacle to the advancement of our discipline in an empiricist epistemology "which has been so focused on data gathering that theory has been neglected." Nevertheless, he is convinced that the philosophy of logical positivism which supported this empiricism is moribund and is being replaced by a new philosophy rooted in the writings of Polanyi, Toulmin, Feyerabend, Radnitzky, and others. Royce refers to this new philosophy as a "theory-laden constructivism" which claims, in part, (a) that *theory* is crucial in the doing of science; (b) that all observations are theory-laden, that is, each observation is made within an overall conceptual framework and may, accordingly, have different meanings if embedded in different theoretical contexts; (c) that the basic concepts of a theory are *constructed* by the investigator, and thus, (d) that scientific findings are, in some sense, *man-made inventions or constructions* rather than discoveries.

If this shift in the philosophy of science from the superempirical bias of logical positivism to theory-laden constructivism constitutes a more adequate metatheory, then it follows that scientific advancement in our understanding of psychological phenomena is more dependent upon theory construction per se than was heretofore realized. Indeed, a major point made by Royce is that viable theory is the ultimate goal of science because, as he notes, theory in its best sense constitutes an "explanation" of the phenomena within a universe of discourse. But, in urging that a greater emphasis be placed upon theory construction and metatheory, Royce is careful not to underestimate the critical role of an empirical data base in the never ending process of science. From his viewpoint, empirical observation and conceptual synthesis are not mutually exclusive but *complementary.*

As his title suggests, Royce conducts an extensive examination of the ways in which the study of psychology is multimethodological, multivariate, multiepistemic, multitheoretic, multiparadigmatic, and even multidisciplinary. Once we recognize the broad range, complexity, richness, and surface contradiction of psychological phenomena, we can hardly expect that the study of "total man" could be accommodated by one theory, one paradigm, or one world view. In the past, Royce notes, we have tended to view such pluralism as a sign of theoretic weakness and immaturity. Yet recent developments in the history and philosophy of science suggest that, on the contrary, "the prolific spinning of alternative theoretical constructions is a more accurate reflection of the typical situation in science." Still, for Royce it does not follow that some theoretical unification is impossible. His point, quite simply, is that we must strive for as much theoretical synthesis as possible while respecting the full range and complexity of psychological phenomena.

In the final section of his paper, Royce explores the possibility of developing a philosophy of psychology which could take psychology's "multi" nature into account. From his analysis of the current trends in (a) scientific psychology toward a "cognitive psychology" and in (b) humanistic psychology toward an "interpretive hermeneutics," Royce sees the possibility of a metatheoretical convergence in the epistemic and theoretic frameworks of both traditions. In his view this metatheoretical convergence may develop from the emerging dialecticism and constructivism that are becoming apparent in both scientific and humanistic psychology. Therefore Royce suggests that a truly indigenous philosophy of psychology will appear as some form of "constructive dialecticism" within which the term *dialectic* refers to an acceptance of the tension of contradiction between viable conceptual alternatives, and the term *constructive* refers to the theoretical constructions which are created or invented by investigators. In this framework, constructive dialecticism is seen by Royce as a philosophy which can deal with the multiperspectivism of "mind *and* behavior." Epistemologically, it implies an "integrative dialectic"— the attempt to sort out the complementary roles of each of the three epistemological ways of knowing, namely, empiricism, rationalism, and metaphorism. Theoretically, it implies an "interpretative dialectic"—the attempt to sort out the complementary roles of the many theories of mind and behavior. Within a philosophy of constructive dialecticism, each of the several methods, epistemologies, and theories should be exploited for whatever truths it can reveal. Although Royce is doubtful that the end product of a constructive dialecticism in psychology will be *one* integrated theory, he does anticipate that this approach would promote a significant development in the direction of theoretical synthesis and unification.

Day. Day's paper on contemporary behaviorism and the concept of intention is presented in two parts. In the first Day seeks to define "contemporary behaviorism," primarily by contrasting it with "methodological behaviorism." In the second he attempts to clarify the position of contemporary behaviorism with respect to the concepts of intention and intentionality.

Turning first to the contrast between the two behaviorisms, Day argues that methodological behaviorism refers to the conceptual framework which is widely accepted in academic experimental psychology as "establishment tradition." Contemporary behaviorism, he contends, differs from traditional methodological behaviorism in two important ways: (a) in the nature of its stance in opposition to mentalism, and (b) in the nature of its treatment of private events. In dealing with these issues, Day discusses both Skinner's position and his own personal point of view. On the first issue, Day points out that Skinner defines mentalism as taking feelings and inner states to be the *causes*—or explanations—of behavior. From his standpoint, methodological behaviorism is intrinsically mentalistic because it characteristically makes use of mental or cognitive states to explain behavior. For Skinner, it is "tragic" for us to use mentalistic explanations because "they mistakenly identify the causes actually at work in governing our behavior." In his view the only acceptable explanation is "causal explanation"—and he stipulates that fundamentally only two kinds of causes operate in the determination of behavior: contingencies of reinforcement and contingencies of survival. In sum, Day states that contemporary behaviorism attempts to explain behavior in the light of these causal contingencies and is likely to regard any deviation from such an analysis as an invitation to mentalism.

Turning to the second issue, Day notes that Skinner views the treatment of private events as the central factor distinguishing contemporary behaviorism (or what Skinner calls "radical behaviorism") from methodological behaviorism. Methodological behaviorism, like some versions of logical positivism, rules private events out of bounds as "unobservables" because there can be no public agreement about their validity. Contemporary behaviorism, in contrast, does not insist upon "truth by agreement" and can, accordingly, take into consideration the events that occur in the private world within the skin. It does not call these events unobservable. But neither does it consider events that "are felt or introspectively observed" to be the *causes* of behavior. In Day's own view of contemporary behaviorism, private events are regarded as playing a "controlling" role in behavior. Thus an organism can indeed respond discriminatively to stimuli arising within the skin, but such discriminative responding can never be taken as the cause of behavior. It might be noted that in this section Day gives special consideration to the way in which "interpretation" has gained respectability within contemporary behaviorism.

In part two Day discusses the concepts of intention and intentionality in a manner that will allow psychologists and philosophers to assess the position of contemporary behaviorism in relation to these concepts. In this discussion Day refers to what Skinner calls "the misguided charge that behaviorism has no place for intention or purpose." He then quotes Skinner's counterargument that "operant behavior is the very field of purpose and intention. By its very nature it is directed toward the future: a person acts *in order that* something will happen." Nonetheless, Skinner maintains that "when a person is 'aware of his purpose,' he is feeling or observing introspectively a condition *produced by reinforcement*." Thus what he rejects is the "causal efficacy" of such a "felt purpose." Again, Skinner's central concern is with the reinforcement contingencies which have "caused" us to feel the condition we call a purpose.

Day concludes his paper by responding to a set of ten questions regarding intention and intentionality. In part, Day maintains that the feelings or inner conditions which can set the occasion for talk of "feelings of intending to do something" *do* occur in us, and are spoken of by behaviorists as part of the private events of our conscious experience. In his view it is *not* always maladaptive to speak of our intentions. Yet even when we seem to find it helpful to hear what someone's intentions are, this intentionalistic talk is helpful simply because it has altered the discriminative control over our behavior in such a way that more productive behavior becomes possible. Thus Day maintains that if we *really* want to make sense out of the behavioral scene, we should spend our time thinking about the causes of behavior. This means that we should be making an assessment of "the reinforcers that are actually operating to make us say we have the intentions that we do." In this sense the humanistic injunction to "do your own thing" fails to take into consideration how the feelings and intentions (of your particular thing) have been "set up by reinforcement" in the first place.

Mischel. As a philosopher, Mischel is concerned with the disagreements among psychologists regarding the definition of their subject matter and hence "the nature of a psychological explanation." From his perspective, the questions that are raised with respect to alternative forms of explanation involve choice: "these matters cannot be settled by just taking another look at the facts, or by running some more experiments." Thus Mischel suggests that it may be useful to examine some of the vicissitudes which psychological explanations have suffered under the impact of changing philosophical assumptions regarding the nature of mind, mechanism, and science. In the course of his analysis, Mischel focuses primarily on what is currently at issue between radical behaviorists and cognitive psychologists.

According to Mischel, behaviorism has its philosophical roots in men like Hobbes, who assumed that a human being can only be a material system and that the explanation of his behavior must, therefore, have the same form as mechanistic explanations in the physical sciences. He contends that this mechanistic form of explanation is epitomized in Skinner's radical behaviorism, which sees the task of psychology as that of discovering laws or "functional relations" between external inputs and outputs that will allow us to predict and control human behavior without bringing in notions of mind, intention, or purpose.

Cognitive approaches, in contrast, have their roots in the philosophical assumptions of men like Kant and Brentano. For Kant, there are two very different points of view which we can take toward human behavior, and "an adequate conceptualization of human behavior must have room for both." From one point of view behavior must be explained by the laws of the physical sciences. The second point of view sees human beings as agents who are faced with choices and who have the capacity to formulate plans and act accordingly. In this sense the conceptions of human beings—the "meanings" which situations have for them in virtue of the way they construe them—can make a difference to their actions. Thus a cognitive approach which is based on these assumptions seeks to explain behavior by showing how people acquire conceptions and how these conceptions enter into the generation of behavior. Behavioral outputs are *not determined simply* by physical inputs impinging upon sense receptors, but depend rather on the selection, transformation, and use of information extracted from stimuli. Because the experiences that shape us are also shaped by our own selective and transformational activities, the reality to which we respond—"things as they appear to us"—is, in part, our own construction.

However, what is important for Mischel's purposes is that Kant recognized the validity of both of these points of view and that his approach "makes it possible to separate claims about the distinctive features of psychological explanations from claims about the existence of immaterial minds." In terms of this approach, the peculiar features of psychological explanations are due to the fact that these explanations are taking the intentionalistic point of view of agents. As Mischel explains, if we individuate behavior at the psychological level by relating it to the agent's conception of what a situation means, then "the agent's interpretations will enter into the definition of the phenomena under study" and "psychology will involve interpretation in a way that the physical sciences do not." He concludes, therefore, that when the data of psychology are characterized intentionalistically, psychology cannot be a science on all fours with the physical sciences. "Psychological explanations" will be of a different type from the "causal explanations" given by physical scientists who characterize behavior purely from the spectator's point of view. But the central point is that psychological and physical explanations of behavior differ because they are concerned with answering different sorts of questions: they deal with the same behavior from different points of view within a framework where *both* points of view are essential for an adequate conceptualization of human behavior.

Because the "causal explanations" of behavioristic approaches like Skinner's have met with such small success in dealing with "complex human behavior," many psychologists have been turning to the "intentionalistic explanations" of cognitive approaches. At one point Mischel directs his attention to Skinner's fears that such intentionalistic explanations of behavior—which assume agents who have cognitive powers—will somehow involve a commitment to the "ancient notion of a homunculus." Historically, such fears may well have been justified, but now, as Mischel demonstrates, even the *explanations* of complex computer behavior share the features that are characteristic of our intentionalistic explanations of human actions! Thus the power to guide behavior by means of thought is not "occult," Skinner to the contrary. Instead, Mischel argues that our cognitive powers have evolved as a part of the "natural design" of the organism because, as he points out, these powers have clearly had survival value. It is Mischel's position, therefore, that psychological phenomena are to be explained intentionalistically from the point of view of agents in whom one presupposes these species-specific, cognitive powers.

Rychlak. For three generations, Rychlak informs us, psychology has been dominated by a behavioristic tradition hostile to the teleological descriptions of behavior that are fundamental to a humanistic psychology. As a means of understanding his "modest proposal" for a revolution in theory that would admit such descriptions, Rychlak examines the historical issues that have divided behavioristic—or mechanistic—psychology from humanistic psychology. He indicates first that mechanists and humanists differ on the nature of causation. The explanations of mechanistic psychologists, he asserts, are couched exclusively in terms of Aristotle's material and efficient causation. Humanists, on the contrary, maintain that the explanation of behavior is *not completely determined* by past inputs. Instead, how the individual conceptually organizes, "frames in" and "comes at" a life situation makes a difference in the course of events. Humanists have accordingly expanded their explanations to include both Aristotle's formal cause, which specifies the form, structure, or system of organization that exists, and his final cause, which specifies the purpose for which something was made or "that for the sake of which" something exists. Thus humanists are seeking teleological explanations of human behavior and experience where the primary emphasis is placed upon the purpose or intention of a human being.

Rychlak also maintains that humanistic and mechanistic psychologists differ with respect to the process of generating scientific knowledge. Mechanists, he notes, are Lockean empiricists. They are committed to a realism—to a study of "what is" rather than "what is not." Moreover, they restrict themselves to what Rychlak refers to as "demonstrative reasoning," that is, reasoning by a method of demonstrating whether a theoretical conception is true or false on the basis of independent empirical evidence. Humanists, in contrast, are more likely to be Kantian. They believe that human beings are also open to "dialectical reasoning"—by which they mean a capacity to reason to the opposite of environmental inputs. In this sense a humanistic theory is fundamentally concerned with the processes which can account for "human choice." It recognizes that individuals will not always behave "rationally" according to "demonstrated probabilities." Because of their capacity to reason dialectically, people can create alternative possibilities, they can transcend existing realities, they can be unpredictable, they can opt against the odds, and, it must be added, they can be in error.

Now for Rychlak, the generation of scientific knowledge depends on both demonstrative and dialectical reasoning or, to be more specific, on a sequence that, of necessity, goes from theoretical speculation to methods of demonstrating the validity of a theoretical implication, and back again to theory. However, his central point is that in the history of science, a masking of the distinction between theory and method prevailed among the mechanistic Newtonian scientists until the Einsteinian revolution in thought clarified a role for theory independent of method. As a result of this revolution in thought, today's theoretical physicist is no longer restricted to a single efficient-cause explanation of the course of observed events. Indeed, many philosophers of science now believe that for any research sequence of events, there are, in principle, N potential theories to account for the observed regularity.

Yet despite these changes in the philosophy of science, Rychlak contends, psychology continues to be dominated by a mechanistic and Lockean efficient-cause paradigm. And he argues further that psychology, like the older Newtonian model of science, has confounded theory with method so that most psychologists have mistakenly believed that the evidence gathered by their methods supports *only* the mechanistic Lockean account of behavior. Therefore Rychlak is calling for a revolution, not, it must be noted, in the scientific method of validating a theoretical implication, but a revolution on the side of theory which will open up alternative theoretical explanations of the same data collections. Psychology too must recognize that, in principle, there are N potential theories to account for our empirical observations. Within this expanded theoretical framework, the mechanistic Lockean model would no longer be viewed as the *only* acceptable theoretical paradigm for a science of psychology, and simultaneously, the teleological descriptions of a Kantian-humanistic model—which emphasize the purpose or intention "for the sake of which" we act—would be admitted. As an exemplar, Rychlak presents his own humanistic theory and research program. And finally, in reemphasizing the crucial role of theory in the generation of scientific knowledge, Rychlak warns in his "humanistic manifesto" that we must never foreclose on theoretical speculation. If we restrict ourselves to one and only one theoretical formulation, we seek only the kind of data that seem likely to support such a formulation, and in this process, we restrict our conception of the nature of man.

Giorgi. Giorgi conceives of the current "crisis" in psychology in terms of three theoretical problems: a lack of unity in the sense that psychology has yet to find a unifying paradigm, a lack of relevance in the sense that it has not clarified its intentions, and a deficiency in its understanding of psychology as a science itself. According to Giorgi, the theoretical problems of psychology are generated by assumptions rooted in a narrow, restrictive conception of science. He argues that, for the most part, psychologists have uncritically accepted the existing natural scientific conception of a science and rigidly imposed its methodological criteria on our psychological conception of man.

In his view the problem is not in the natural scientific conception when used within its own framework to study the phenomena of nature, but in the extension of this conception to the study of the qualitatively different phenomena of human experience and behavior. To the extent that psychology has conformed to a natural scientific conception, it has emphasized observable phenomena and an external viewpoint while it has neglected—and often denied—the importance of such phenomena as the intentionality, internal viewpoint, experience, and meanings of the human being. What Giorgi proposes is that we extend the notion of science itself so that we can develop a "human scientific paradigm" that will be relevant to the phenomena of human experience and behavior. Significantly, our notion of science remains open to reconsideration and modification, in Giorgi's view, since he perceives science as being, in principle, both "evolutionary and dialectical." Indeed, "to claim that our current understanding of method or theory is the final one is to give an unjustifiable privilege to the present."

As a means of moving toward a notion of the "human sciences," Giorgi turns first to Husserl's philosophy of phenomenology. He argues in part that phenomenology is important because it is concerned first and foremost with the study of "the phenomena of the world as experienced by man." It is, moreover, concerned with "intentionality" in the sense that consciousness is perceived as a *process* rather than a substance—as a stream of activity which is directed toward and related to the world. In addition, phenomenology is a *method* for studying the phenomena of experience: it begins by describing the phenomena of experience as precisely as possible and without presuppositions, and then by interrogating this description, it seeks to understand and emphasize the *meaning* of these phenomena. Using guidelines from phenomenology, Giorgi explains just how he would enlarge the procedures of the natural sciences—procedures which he reminds us were developed originally in dialogue with the phenomena of nature. Within his larger framework, he contends that we can make use of the phenomenological method of asking questions and developing the procedures that seem appropriate *in dialogue with the particular human phenomena being studied.* As a result, Giorgi claims, we would be able to describe a wider range of human phenomena and discover their meaning in ways that will produce systematic, rigorous, and intersubjective psychological knowledge.

With the further aim of discovering what kind of "scientific praxis" human psychological phenomena might demand, Giorgi turns to Merleau-Ponty and his phenomenologically based critique of scientific praxis in traditional psychology. The force of Merleau-Ponty's argument is directed against the exclusive acceptance of (a) scientific reductionism, (b) the analytic method, (c) scientific realism, (d) mechanistic explanations, and (e) the positivism of laws. However, Giorgi's central point is that Merleau-Ponty simultaneously supports a critical shift toward (a) phenomenological description, (b) a structural approach which emphasizes the *system of relationships* among the parts of the phenomenon, (c) an analysis of the "meaning" of an experience for the subject, (d) an emphasis on our existential relations by which he means the totality of our *conscious and behavioral* relations to the world, to ourselves and to others, and (e) a recognition of dialectical thinking as a source of change and development.

In his final section, Giorgi articulates the beginnings of a "human scientific conception of psychology" based on the key phenomenological concepts of Merleau-Ponty. He also indicates how such a human scientific paradigm could provide a theoretical unity within psychology and resolve the remaining aspects of our current crisis. According to Giorgi, a human scientific psychology is still in the process of defining itself and a number of different influences and traditions are contributing to this process. Among these he describes Radnitzsky's "hermeneutic-dialectic tradition," which conceives of man as interpretational—as an inquirer in search of the significant meaning of a situation. This tradition would also subscribe to a "dialectical model of knowledge" whereby "totalizations" from various perspectives are developed, come into conflict, and become "retotalized." In Giorgi's view a hermaneutic-dialectic tradition converges with a phenomenologically based conception of science and is, at the same time, compatible with the essential ideals of science in general.

Riegel. In moving beyond the concepts of stable traits and static equilibrium, Riegel argues that a comprehensive view of development can be realized only through a dialectic conception of man as "a changing being in a changing world." Riegel begins his presentation with a historical overview in which he criticizes the abstract concepts of stable traits and abilities. He is also critical of developmental theories such as Piaget's that emphasize the stable over the unstable, the static over the changing. As Riegel shows, this emphasis is clearly evident in the Piagetian conception of development as a succession of stages where equilibrium or balance is achieved at each stage.

In contrast, a dialectic theory of development conceives of the individual as being in a continuous process of change brought about by the successive interactions of concrete events over time. Dialectical theory is fundamentally concerned with the question of how individuals and groups transcend existing conceptions, actions, and feelings, and how they generate new developments. As Riegel points out, theories of development which emphasize equilibrium over change fail to recognize that any change must be preceded by a state of imbalance which then serves as the basis for further development. In a dialectic conception, conflict and contradiction are perceived as the source of every new developmental achievement, and "stability" appears only as a transition—a temporary marking—in the stream of ceaseless changes.

For Riegel, the basic distinction between formal and dialectic logic lies in the latter's recognition of contradiction as a basic operation of thinking. Thinking, in a dialectic sense, is "the process of transforming contradictory experience into momentary stable structures." While these "stable" structures do in fact consolidate the contradictory evidence, they do not represent the *process* of thinking but merely the *products* of thinking. The critical dialectic conception is that every new product or achievement of man's thinking, action, and feeling "gives rise to new questions and contradictions." Thus each new achievement becomes an integral part of a *developing* "reality" in the continuing process of change: it is both an actual, objectified development relative to past achievements and, at the same time, a part of the available potential for all future achievements. In this sense there are no finished products of man's thinking, no fixed and final answers that can be laid down once and for all. Within this process of change, a dialectic theory sees the contradictions and questions raised by each new achievement as *the means by which* an existing achievement can be reappraised and transformed into an achievement of still greater comprehension. From this perspective, the dialectics of development are perceived as a ceaseless flux of contradictions and the synchronizing of new developmental achievements.

Riegel shows that such a theory must embrace both short-term situational changes—exemplified by what he calls a "complex dialogue"—and long-term individual and cultural developments. A dialectic theory is also concerned with "inner" and "outer" dialectics but, more specifically, with their *dynamic interdependence*. Inner dialectics is expressed by Piaget's account of the development of an individual's cognitive structure through the operations of assimilation and accommodation. But Riegel contends that developmental psychologists have failed to conceptualize an outer dialectics, that is, the existence of other individuals intimately related to those under concern who, like them, are simultaneously engaged in their own process of transformation and change. Nevertheless, the key to a dialectic theory of development is found in the realization that development occurs neither in the individual alone nor in the social or cultural group alone but "is constituted by the dialectic interactions of both in conjunction."

In the last section of his paper, Riegel summarizes his position in a way that reveals the significance and implications of dialectic thinking for psychological research and theory. He argues, for instance, that the strength of dialectic theory is founded both in its commitment to the study of activity and change, and in its ability to "encompass a manifold of contradictory conceptions." Finally, Riegel reemphasizes his point that a dialectic theory conceives of man as "a changing being in a changing world." In this relationship of change, individual and cultural changes are inextricably linked. Although each individual coordinates and transforms the conflicting events of his experience into his own sequence of development, no individual creative achievement occurs in isolation from the changing developments in other individuals. The achievements of an individual are, in other words, individually created but created in a "collective dialogue" with the significant others of his cultural group. In this dynamic conjunction of individual change and social-historical change, it becomes apparent that as man creates and transforms himself, he not only transforms the outer world in which he lives but is himself transformed by the world which he and others have created.

Feldman and Toulmin. Toulmin, who presented this paper at the Nebraska Symposium, and his coauthor, Feldman, have sought to show how certain problems of empirical corroboration—which must be faced by *any* scientific theory—arise with particular force for current structuralist theories in psychology. By introducing "formal representations" (derived from symbolic logic, group theory, etc.) as a means of describing the systematic relations between their hypothetical "mental structures," these structural psychologists have taken on the epistemological problems that arise inescapably for any theory that tries to provide a "formal representation of authentic empirical phenomena." There is, they note, always the danger of confusing the character of the representation with the character of the empirical structures it supposedly represents.

In facing these epistemological problems, the authors have set out to do three things. First, they identify the chief points at which difficulties arise with structuralist theories such as Piaget's when the formal representations are to be corroborated against the empirical observations of actual performance. Second, they consider some episodes in the history of other sciences—theoretical physics, structural chemistry, and evolutionary biology—that have made the difficult transition from operating in a purely empirical and de-scriptive manner to the development of theoretical concepts and representations on a more formal, abstract level. And third, they use the lessons of these historical examples to formulate a number of proposals designed to remove some of the confusions associated with structuralist theories in psychology.

Using the problems that scientists have faced in dealing with the "invisible entities" of atomic theory as one exemplar, the authors ask, "To what extent do the 'formal structures' captured in a logical representation [e.g., atomic theory] presuppose the *actual existence* of corresponding, isomorphic empirical 'structures' in the natural phenomena that they are used to represent? . . . To what extent is it legitimate to operate with theoretical representations having formal features for which *no* identifiable correlate can be found in the empirical phenomena?" In summing up the lessons they have learned for the structuralist theories of cognitive psychology, they state that timeless, formal "structures" can safely be put to use in the context of "theoretical representations" of cognitive capacities only if care is taken not to assume automatically that those "formal structures" must mirror exactly corresponding, empirical "mental structures" in the individuals concerned. In the absence of very specific empirical evidence of such an "isomorphism," we should presume that these "formal structures" represent at best a theoretical idealization of any corresponding empirical features. This amounts to a warning that "any use we make of formalism in our attempts to develop theories about some aspect of reality—whether physical or psychological—requires us either to provide direct empirical verification of the existence of any 'entities' referred to in the theory, or else to admit frankly that no such empirical objects or structures should be expected to correspond to these 'entities.' "

For the time being, the authors conclude, we shall do better if we respect the epistemological "distance" between Piaget's formal theories and their empirical application to psychological reality. As we avoid importing the merely *formal* features of Piagetian theory into our descriptions of *substantive* psychological phenomena, we can see just how much can be done "by using a terminology and mode of description that remains closer to the temporal and empirical realities of the phenomena in question." If this view appears more complex by comparison with the seeming exactness and conciseness of current theoretical terminology, the authors counter that "this *complexity* has had to be accepted in other sciences—theoretical physics, structural chemistry, organic evolution—as the price of achieving a genuine measure of methodological sophistication and self-understanding."

Koch. In his paper Koch puts forward a perceptual theory of definition—or, alternatively, a psychological theory of meaning. Prior to presenting this theory, however, Koch develops his argument for the noncohesiveness of psychology and against the search for a single paradigm. He also cites the ways in which the many misreadings of Thomas Kuhn have given psychologists a false optimism concerning the prospects for an integral discipline.

As one segment of his argument, Koch maintains that "man's stipulation that psychology be adequate to *science* outweighed his commitment that it be adequate to man." From this perspective he criticizes both the notion of considering psychology as an extension of the natural science methods and—perhaps of even greater significance—the supposition that knowledge based on inquiries not saturated with the iconology of a Newtonian science is worthless. In his counterargument he contends that the complexity, lability, and mutual interdependencies now apparent in the functioning of the human cortex suggest orders of complexity in human action and experience that have been grossly slighted in the scientific conceptions of behavioral psychology. According to Koch, insufficient concern has been given to the possibility that at some point of "internal complexity" or "system openness," the totally ordered and sequential analytic patterns of Newtonian mechanics may no longer apply. This is not to say that Koch is arguing against tough-minded empirical analyses of the interdependencies among significant events, but he is convinced that in many fields of human inquiry, the "psychological studies" must become more adequate to the complexities of man: they must range over an immense and disorderly spectrum of human activity and experience with "methods of inquiry that are both contextual and flexible," and with "anticipations of synoptic breakthroughs held in check."

In the last half of his paper, Koch presents his psychological theory of definition and meaning which, he notes, has a strong consonance with Polanyi's view that "explicit knowledge is always, if in varying degree, founded on extra-articulate or 'tacit' knowing." Koch begins by describing the problems of communicating meaningfully in terms of the definitional criteria of logical positivism. As an exemplar he shows that a concept such as *dignity* cannot be fully specified or "reduced" to an operational language or physical-thing observation base. Instead, he proposes a psychological or perceptual theory of definition which, because it sees all linguistic meaning as having a *perceptual* basis, might well be called a "psychological theory of meaning." More specifically, Koch contends that definition is based on a perceptual discrimination of an often subtle, embedded, or delicately contoured relation or property of the "world flux." The relations or properties that are discriminated by such a perception are in the strictest sense the "meanings" that are conveyed by words. For Koch, a perceptual frame reminds us that the discrimination of a new relation or property of the world must be made *within* the "crucibles" of man's *discriminative capacities and sensibilities.* Yet because he assumes that human beings "perceptually interact with an external world," definition is for him empirical: that is, definition is *about something*—however embedded or intricately contoured that something may be.

In the ideal case, Koch sees definition as a form of "ostension" that seeks to direct perception to the relevant relations or properties of world events via a "perceptual display" which exhibits these qualities in their purest, most sharply contoured form. (Scientific experiments can be seen in this context.) In actual definitional practice, however, it is often difficult to approximate the ideal form of definition. Still, as Koch illustrates with the word *dignity*, many terms in the natural language—and in science—can "tag" and preserve perceptual discriminations of great specificity.

A notable conception within Koch's theory appears in his statement that the differentiation and extension of meaning can, under some circumstances, occur through man's "capacity for inventive metaphor." For Koch, the creative use of metaphor may involve an effortful perceptual search in new contexts for subtle relational qualities which overlap (or are similar to) the contours of meaning already tagged by an "old" term. And when in fact the perceptual discriminations governing a term are enriched or refined by perceiving an "overlapping" relational quality in some new—and perhaps less masked—world context, then knowledge has been extended.

After presenting his perceptual theory of definition, Koch considers its implications for the study of psychology. He shows, for instance, that the observation base of psychology must become a far more extensive domain than is ordinarily thought. Within his framework it is literally meaningless to talk about an observation base to and from which definitions of higher-order terms are "reduced" or "constructed." Thus Koch contends that the universe of what used to be called "direct observables" must be vastly expanded, and many "theoretical" terms must be seen to discriminate definite, though highly embedded, relations of events and things—and to do so in a direct way. "To insist on fixing the definition of a term, via a standard linkage relation, to some tightly restricted observation . . . would be to sacrifice the possibility of precise or subtle communication. *Far worse, it would eliminate much meaning and knowledge from the universe.*"

Koch also unpacks the implications of his analysis of definition for—as his title indicates—"language communities, search cells, and the psychological studies." On the basis of an extended discussion that takes note of the polymorphous character of the phenomena in our domain and the essential noncohesiveness of the activities within our specialized research groups, he proposes replacing the term *psychology* by an expression like the *psychological studies*.

Still further, Koch's theory of definition and meaning tends to destroy certain of the traditional bases for a sharp separation between the sciences and the humanities. In some of its reaches he is convinced that psychology must turn to "modes of inquiry"—and to the "cumulation of knowledge" derived from these modes of inquiry—more like those of the humanities than the sciences. To make his point, Koch provides an elegant example of sensibility-dependent, multiperspectival inquiry within the humanities and suggests by analogy that the existence of several different perspectives within some field of psychological inquiry does not mean that these perspectives can be combined into a single integrating framework, but it does mean that the availability of these different perspectives to other inquirers creates a potential for extending and enriching our understanding of that particular domain. With respect to the knowledge derived from such inquiry, Koch asserts, "That, too, is cumulation—and in a more subtle sense than mere 'heaping up.' "

Finally, Koch raises the great question of how one can appraise and choose between contending theories or conceptual templates. The complexities of his response reveal that there may be no ultimately "satisfying" answer. Nonetheless, Koch contends that perhaps his position suggests an "outline of an 'answer.'" For there is a sense in which both a theory of truth and a theory of error are built into the perceptual theory of definition that he has put forward. Our perceptual frame, he observes, reminds us that language is *about something*. And once we appreciate the vast resources of psychological knowledge coded within the natural language and *internalized in the discriminative capacities and sensibilities* of those who use it well, we can see that this internalized knowledge gives us a kind of *ontology of the human universe*. Accordingly, one decision basis for theory appraisal is found in the degree to which a theory is what Koch describes as ontology-distorting, ontology-respecting, or ontology-revealing and enriching. But where, he asks, are the "rational" safeguards against deception and error in making these appraisals? Where are the "decision rules" that guarantee forward movement? "But, of course, there are none. We are *on our own*—as we have always been. Yet mankind has managed to learn a thing or two." And Koch's perceptual theory of definition and meaning can be viewed as a theory of our *capacity* for defining the real and of our *capacity* to detect error in the light of the vast resources of knowledge internalized in the human sensibility. "What safeguards we have, then, against irrationality, imprecision, error, must be situated within ourselves. History and any individual biography will show these safeguards to be grotesquely fragile and tenuous, but they are there."

In closing I want to express my appreciation first to James K. Cole, whose support and advice as the Nebraska Symposium series editor made this particular volume possible. And I'm sure I speak for all those associated with the symposium in expressing our thanks to the National Institute of Mental Health and the University of Nebraska for their continued support of the series. Finally, I am profoundly grateful to each of the participants of the 1975 Nebraska Symposium for the way in which they rose to the occasion and created what I believe to be a landmark contribution to the symposium itself and to the field of psychology as a whole.

WILLIAM J. ARNOLD
Professor of Psychology

REFERENCES

Bronowski, J. *The ascent of man.* Boston: Little, Brown & Co., 1973.
Oppenheimer, R. Analogy in science. *American Psychologist*, 1956, **11**, 127–135.
Sherif, M. On the relevance of social psychology. *American Psychologist*, 1970, **25**, 144–156.

Psychology Is Multi-: Methodological, Variate, Epistemic, World View, Systemic, Paradigmatic, Theoretic, and Disciplinary[1]

Joseph R. Royce
University of Alberta

THE PRESENT SITUATION

*T*hose of us with a theoretical bias in our scholarly efforts are of the opinion that philosophic or metatheoretic issues simply cannot be avoided. They can be evaded by the individual scientist qua scientist, but the issues won't go away; they will not be resolved unless somebody takes them on. And while it is true that they can be left to the philosophers, it is also true that work on the philosophic foundations of a discipline needs the thoughtful participation of at least a few of its practitioners. Furthermore, some scholars simply find these issues interesting and worthy of study regardless of official titles and formal background. I'm one of those people. Thus, a portion of my total effort has been devoted to such theoretical-philosophical issues. But I come to such efforts as an amateur—in the original sense of amateur—namely, as one who loves or cares about the issues in question rather than as a scholar with a degree in philosophy. Thus, although I'll not provide you with the meticulous argumentation of the language analyst, in what follows I hope to develop the thesis

1. The preparation of this manuscript was partially supported by Canada Council grants S–70–0433 and S–70–0544. In particular, the writer wishes to acknowledge the assistance of Steve Nicely, graduate assistant at the Center for Advanced Study in Theoretical Psychology. Mr. Nicely tracked down and summarized background material at selected points, such as Kuhn's concept of paradigm. However, I particularly wish to acknowledge his help in the section on the logic of discovery. He reviewed the relevant literature and helped clarify my thinking on this issue.

that psychology is necessarily pluralistic. More specifically, my thesis is that contemporary psychology is multimethodological, multivariate, multiepistemic, multi-world view, multiparadigmatic, multisystemic, multitheoretic, and multidisciplinary. However, before elaborating on these specific issues, I should like to offer some general comments on the present situation in theoretical and philosophical psychology.

The Need for Dialogue between Psychology and Philosophy

Most psychologists probably agree that twentieth-century psychology has been dominated by an empirical epistemology (Royce, 1964, 1965a, 1970a). Furthermore, most of us probably agree that the accumulation of the currently available storehouse of empirical data was a necessary antidote to the nineteenth-century and pre-nineteenth-century commitment to vacuous philosophizing and specious speculation concerning man and his mind. The disagreement comes when we ask, "Where do we go from here?" The answers range all over the map, but the full spectrum is captured if we contrast the ultraempiricism of the Skinnerians with the ultrarationality of the math-modelers on the one hand, and if we introduce the extreme forms of antirationality and subjective phenomenology of some existentialists and other "humanists" on the other hand.

Once we have opened the Pandora's box of "total man," that is, seeing man as unconscious as well as conscious, man as irrational and emotive as well as rational, man as cognitive as well as conditionable, man as motivated, curious, creative, and contemplative, and man's "being" as well as his "doing"—once we go beyond simplistic conceptions of "behaving" to the complexities of "mind"—it seems ridiculously obvious that we will be forced into more sophisticated philosophic-conceptual analyses of what we are doing and why. In short, the full weight of our subject matter is upon us, and the gambit of overly simplistic assumptions just won't be adequate for the task before us. Thus, like it or not, from here on in we psychologists are going to have to *think*. We shall have to go beyond the mere gathering of data and its attendant hope that insightful concepts and principles will automatically ride in on the coattails of super-empiricism. This is not to deny the theoretical value of inductive generalizations and functional relationships, but rather, to underline the fact that such activities constitute one form of conceptual analysis, and that more sophisticated *thought* about data, even if it is limited to relatively simple inductions, will be required to move us beyond the tons of uninterpreted data which are currently inundating us. Furthermore, we shall have to think about all manner of things, not just the meaning of data. We shall have to think about what it means to be human, what it means to talk about "mental illness," and the relevance of values. We shall have to get down to cases about such hoary issues as freedom and determinism, and the mind-body problem. And we must at least not add to the muddying of the conceptual waters by confusing ideological and political polemics with scholarly analysis, as seems to have been the case in the recent outpourings on the role of heredity and environment in accounting for observed differences in human intelligence.[2]

Having made the point that psychologists will benefit by the philosopher's skill in conceptual analysis, I now wish to add a caveat. But first a word of clarification concerning the terminology "conceptual analysis." The focus of conceptual analysis is on concepts and ideas rather than data gathering. Furthermore, it does not refer to the approach of a particular philosopher, such as Kant, nor does it refer to a school of thought, such as the early Vienna Circle. Rather, the primary concern is with conceptual foundations (i.e., logic, language, epistemology, and philosophic assumptions)—for example, clarification of the multiple meanings of theoretical concepts and the "precising" of language usage. While the psychologist should have no argument with such analysis qua philosophy, he is on firm ground, in my opinion, when he says that such a concern can easily miss the main point of the psychologist's enterprise—namely, to understand psychological phenomena. Thus, the psychologist will continue to see the typical philosopher as merely playing a "language game" as long as philosophers refuse to put their analyses in the context of empirical findings. Why should the psychologist care, for example, about the logicality or the semantics of the ordinary language usage of terms like *perception, intelligence,* and *motivation* in the face of his concern for making

2. Witness the current polemical writings which have resulted in an incredible political polarization of hereditarian and environmental camps. Such writings are blatantly contaminated by implied or crudely articulated ideological assumptions which must be made more explicit. With even minimal skills in conceptual analysis, scholars could clarify their ideas about this issue rather than merely conveying feelings and ideologies.

conceptual sense out of the observables of perceptual, intelligent, and motivated behavior which are reported in literally thousands of experimental papers? Thus, if the philosopher wants to have a meaningful dialogue with the psychologist he will have to do it on the psychologist's turf. Given this context, I'm convinced the psychologist will eventually see the value behind the fine-grained linguistic analyses of the philosopher. However, as matters now stand, philosophers simply do not appreciate substantive psychology on the one hand, and contemporary psychologists are undisciplined in the skills of conceptual analysis on the other hand.

The Current Scene in Theoretical Psychology

Unfortunately, the gulf between unifying thought and viable data is not confined to the gap between philosophy and psychology. Nor is this philosophy-psychology gap the crucial obstruction to the advancement of our discipline. As I see it, the psychology zeitgeist has been so focused on data that theory has been neglected. This has resulted in a general level of sophistication in theory construction within the psychology community of scholars which simply has not kept pace with our competence in experimentation and statistical-methodological analysis. If the reader doubts this conclusion, he should ask such questions as these:

1. How many departments of psychology permit theoretical (i.e., no new data) theses?
2. How many departments of psychology have professors of theoretical psychology (as in physics)?
3. How many theoretical (i.e., no gathering of data) research grants have been awarded?
4. How many departments offer a degree-granting graduate program in theoretical psychology?

Furthermore, the state of affairs is amplified by the fact that psychology is in the midst of significant paradigm shifts which will *demand* conceptual-philosophical analysis by scholars with formal training in theory construction and metatheory. For example, it is now abundantly clear that the philosophy of logical positivism is moribund (e.g., see Koch, 1964) and that it is being replaced by what I will refer to as *theory-laden constructivism*. Theory-laden constructivism claims that:

1. Theory is more crucial in the doing of science than was heretofore realized.
2. All observations are theory-laden; that is, an observation is made within an overall conceptual framework. Thus, the same observation might have different meanings if embedded in different theoretical contexts.
3. Furthermore, the basic concepts of a theory are *constructed* by the investigator.
4. Thus, scientific findings are, in some sense, man-made inventions or constructions rather than discoveries.
5. We choose between competing theories primarily on theoretical grounds, only secondarily on empirical grounds, via such criteria as exhaustiveness, reliability, fruitfulness, and interpretability (hermeneutics).
6. The role of observation is not that of arbitration between competing theories, as was claimed by the logical positivists and others. In fact, historical analysis shows that no theory has ever been dropped because of a so-called crucial experiment or because of inadequate or insufficient data.
7. The primary role of empirical observation is to provide the empirical correlates of one or another theory-laden construct; that is, observation provides the substantive content of the conceptual abstraction of the theoretician.

Although earlier forms of the new philosophy occurred in the writings of Polanyi (1958), Toulmin (1960), and Kaplan (1964), and the kernel of the new thinking is apparent in the traditional views of instrumentalism (e.g., see Nagel, 1961), the major proponents of a theory-oriented view are contributors such as Feyerabénd (1965, 1970) and Wartofsky (1968), and the hermeneuticists (e.g., Habermas, 1971, and Radnitzky, 1970). Furthermore, the historians of science, such as Hanson (1961), Kuhn (1962), and Butterfield (1951), have provided what we might refer to as a weak form of empirical (i.e., historical-factual, or how science was actually done) support for this new view. Schmidt (1957), for example, in a beautifully cogent and unusually clear article which I recommend to you, points out that the history of scientific ideas shows a progressive movement away from concrete, physical models toward abstract, formal (i.e., mathematical) constructions. The implication is, of course, that the earlier physical modeling was consistent with a traditional realist view, whereas the more contemporary formal models (i.e., having no concrete physical analogy) which contain no substance per se, are more consistent with a "constructionist" view. And, although I'll develop the point more completely in later sections, it should be mentioned in passing that there have been parallel developments in substantive, psychological theory. I am thinking of psychology's current massive movement away from classical behaviorism toward cognition. Furthermore, the empirical findings of psychology, as exemplified by the "new look" work in perception and motivation, and investigations such as Piaget's, have had a direct impact on the thinking of philosophers (e.g., Polanyi, 1958) and the scientific historians (e.g., Kuhn, 1962).

If we assume that the current shift of the philosophy of science toward theory-laden constructivism constitutes a more adequate metatheory, what are its implications for the advancement of psychology? The most obvious implication is that *scientific advancement is more dependent upon theory construction per se than was heretofore realized*. If our understanding of psychological phenomena is crucially dependent upon adequacy of conceptualization, then it is obvious that our present overcommitment to empiricism (Royce, 1970a) is blatantly in error! That is, if the theory-laden view of doing science is correct, then we are clearly not engaged in the most crucial research activities, nor are we providing the appropriate training in our graduate programs for the investigators of tomorrow. Thus, the implied message from contemporary metatheory is that scientists need to become more sophisticated in *theory-construction skills*. This means, among other things, providing advanced training in empirically oriented conceptual analysis and synthesis and providing (at least) an introduction to philosophy of science and epistemology.

Let me elaborate on what this kind of training entails, but before I do, I will comment briefly on a common attitude which has been the source of some harassment for the serious theoretician. I am referring to that very pervasive and insidious notion in much of the academic community, and to some extent in the culture at large, that theory construction is the harebrained activity of far-out, "fringe" persons, or that it constitutes a symptom of the early senility of loose thinkers who irresponsibly spin out "bull" from the easy comfort of the armchair.[3] Unfortunately, there is some justification for this

3. What about the role of speculation? The dangers of unfounded speculation lie behind the attitude expressed in the text. Although empirically anchored

view. Much of what passes for theoretical and philosophical psychology, for example, falls into this category. But, of course, a major reason for this is that so few psychologists have received formal training in theory construction and conceptual analysis. Furthermore, our experience at the Center for Advanced Study in Theoretical Psychology at the University of Alberta is that this kind of know-how is *definitely not acquired* via the typical department of psychology doctoral program, and that little is known about how to go about developing these skills.

Ten years of experience at the center has involved the training of a handful of doctoral students, interaction with several dozen postdoctoral fellows and research associates, and working sessions with around 100 advanced researchers, a good 50% of the latter including the leading theorizers of our discipline. Here are some impressions based on this experience:

1. Very few individuals, whether predoctoral, postdoctoral, or senior research men, are effective in doing theory construction.
2. In general, theoretical psychology involves two large classes of activity: (a) critical analysis, and (b) creative synthesis.
3. In general, psychologists and psychology students are particularly unimpressive in the synthesis and/or creative aspects of theory construction. This is true at all levels, including senior researchers.
4. In general, psychologists are highly critical of other psychologists. Unfortunately, however, this criticalness is rarely constructive in the sense of astute analysis, rigor, wisdom, or, most important, providing increments in the viability of the theory in question. Usually the criticism merely points up obvious methodological or research design inadequacies, or it is simply ad hominem. (At its worst we get the typical APA Division 3 convention conversation which says, in effect, that my work is what's important and all these other twits are just wasting their time.)[4]

---

and formally stated theory is clearly to be preferred, it is also obvious that these constraints frequently cannot be met. What then? Bakan (1975) argues that speculation is necessary for the development of a truly robust science (i.e., a science with explanatory power and the power to predict and control behavior), and further, that it opens up new possibilities.

4. Although I recognize that the truly insightful critical analyst is as rare as the creative synthesizer, my sympathies are with the producers of theory rather than the critics of theory. This is due to my bias that our biggest advances in most fields are due to creative production rather than critical analysis. That is, it is more important to write plays than it is to be a drama critic, it is more important to write novels and poems than it is to be a literary

8

ON METHOD

On the Many Methodolatries of Psychology;
or, The One-Trick Expert

Psychology is a deceptive field of study. It is obvious that our field is of very great importance, but it is equally obvious that the most important issues go begging. I have a rough rule of thumb which says "the more important the problem, the less we know about it." How much do we really know about the brain correlates of behavior, for example? And what can we do for the mentally retarded, the emotionally confused, the neurotic, and the psychotic?

My point is that psychology looks easy, but it is hard. It looks easy to the outsider because of its everyday-ness, because "everyman" sees himself as something of a psychologist. And it is relatively easy to get into problems, including socially relevant ones—but coming up

---

critic, and it is more important to produce the theoretical synthesis which provides an "explanation" for a segment of the observable world than it is to demonstrate the inadequacies of that "explanation." The point is that were it not for the artistic and scientific constructions of the creative synthesizers, the critics would have nothing to say.

On the other hand, the scholarship demands which confront the serious critic are mind-boggling. For the "compleat" critic is a scholar whose knowledge transcends, at least to some degree, the contradictory requirements of breadth versus depth. For both depth and scope are required in order to get beyond superficial commentary to the deeper level of either providing metatheoretic insights or advancing the construction of substantive theory. Omitting consideration of current contributions (on the grounds that more time is needed for perspective), examples of what I'm alluding to can be found in the writings of Egon Brunswik, Paul Meehl, and Sigmund Koch. Brunswik's (1952) monograph, for example, stands in a class by itself as a statement of psychology's conceptual foundations circa 1940. Similarly, Sigmund Koch's various analyses, particularly his epilogue (1959) in Volume 3 of the six-volume compilation of psychological theory (Koch, 1959), provide a more recent landmark statement of the state of our discipline. And Meehl provides us with a variety of ideas which have had a germinal impact on substantive theory construction. These include, for example, the distinction between intervening variables and hypothetical constructs (MacCorquodale & Meehl, 1948), and the concept of construct validity (Cronbach & Meehl, 1955). There are, of course, many more examples of individually important analytic papers (e.g., see Marx, 1963), but psychology has never produced more than a handful of scholars who have maintained a full-time, life-long program of metatheoretic analysis. I suspect one reason is that there is, in fact, a strong component of creativity along with gargantuan requirements of scholarship in those cases.

with convincing answers is something else. And, unfortunately, we've come up with relatively few answers to the big questions. Furthermore, we've developed elaborate, holier-than-thou escape hatches for our failures.

Consider, for example, the physiological psychologist who starts out by looking for the biological correlates of behavior, discovers that he needs to know more biochemistry and neurophysiology, and ends up looking for neurochemical transmitters at the synaptic junction of individual cells. Or, consider the gung-ho laboratory man who gets so intrigued by his latest electronic gadgetry that he literally spends years in the defensible (and frequently defensive) position of having to work out the bugs in his equipment before he can attack his original problem. Or, consider the math-modelers. How many of them have taken on the big theoretical problems in psychology? Or, for that matter, how many of them even pretend to be interested in substantive issues? Lest you think this is all old hat, let's look at the latest knights in shining armor—such items as the computer, information theory, and behavior genetics. The demands and intrigues of computer and information technology have lured many a psychologist into prolonged conversations with Illiacs, Johniacs, "Shakey," and other robots rather than with people and other living organisms. And the behavior geneticists, now that they have demonstrated that genes make a difference, are beginning to realize that continuation of their present research strategies may provide more details regarding gene loci and hereditary mechanisms, but that a new orientation is required if the field of behavior genetics is to be of direct assistance in the resolution of psychological questions. My point is that, while we must grant the relevance of all manner of other-disciplinary expertise, the extent to which interdisciplinary psychologists have thereby been lured into side issues and/or psychological trivia is symptomatic of how difficult scientific problem solving is in psychology.

Another observation regarding our discipline is the fact that 90% of all psychological publications are produced by around 10% of the professional psychology community. If we assume there are around 50,000 psychologists on a worldwide basis circa 1975, we might well ask what the 45,000 nonproducing psychologists are doing. It won't do to say that they are teaching and doing applied work such as clinical and industrial psychology. If each psychologist came up with as few as two or three significant contributions of a theoretical and/or empirical nature during his entire professional career it would result in an increase in the *quality*[5] of the current outpouring of articles and books on psychology.

Finally, we have the symptom of overextension of a particular concept, theory, method, or research strategy—what I call the one-trick expert. What happens in these cases is that we get too much of a good thing. Thus, both psychoanalysis and behaviorism made very important contributions in their time, but it is now clear that continued overcommitments to these approaches would actually obstruct theoretical advancements. Take the powerful concept of reinforcement, for example. This concept, along with its varieties of contingency schedules, can account for an impressive range of learned phenomena. But its recent overextensions (e.g., see Skinner, 1953) are like the earlier overextensions of psychoanalysis—in both cases too much is "explained." There are also many examples of misuse of methodology. The most obvious example from the first half of this century was making a career out of administering *one* test, such as the Binet, the Wechsler, or the Rohrshach. The most obvious contemporary example is the almost indiscriminate use of analysis of variance, as if it were the only research design worth consideration.

What do these symptoms—the symptoms of (a) being lured into other specialties, (b) highly trained professionals (e.g., most doctorates) having nothing significant to say, (c) other highly trained professionals having too much to say (i.e., being "too productive" and/or persuasively claiming more than is justified), and (d) the one-trick expert—have in common? I think they are indicative of the sheer difficulty of our subject matter. I think they point, in a rather dramatic way, to how tough it is to say something significant and enduring about behavior. Three of the four indicators, all but the second, exemplify one form or another of "methodolatry." The first group, which we can call the *Big Scientist* group, does it by adopting a holier-than-thou attitude. They simply flee the field by hiding

5. This point is predicated on the assumption that scholarly inputs from the total range of potential contributors would thereby provide a greater range of innovative inputs as well. It is assumed that the equally greater range in the direction of low-quality inputs would be taken care of by the usual selection process (i.e., those manuscripts would be rejected). It is also assumed that the consequent general increase in manuscript volume would also result in a tougher manuscript selection ratio for all potential contributors (i.e., the poorer manuscripts of each contributor, including the more prolific writers, would also be rejected).

behind *Science,* or by *Technological Tinkering.* The last two groups, the *Overextenders,* constitute examples of the cultist's commitment. Apparently we have "true believers" (Hoffer, 1951) in all walks of life, whether it is "everyman" living in southern California or the scientific "followers" of "great men." Perhaps our biggest hope lies with the second group, the *Silent Majority,* for hope springs eternal with the young and/or the uncommitted. While it might be argued that this group at least shows the good taste of not forcing itself upon that apathetic community of scholars called one's peers, I fear it is more accurate to conclude that the difficulty of the task has, in fact, rendered them speechless. However, as an antidote to the ever present threat of "academic methodolatry," it may be desirable to introduce machinery for "quantity control" in addition to "quality control." For example, perhaps we psychologists should subsidize a small segment of each professional journal for unpublished authors (say, at age 40 or beyond). And perhaps "prolific" authors should be guided by some kind of "asymptotic upper limit," say around 100 to 200 papers per professional career. I realize there is potential danger in this last suggestion, but we need some kind of "productivity equilibrium" mechanism on the one hand, and a control (since a cure is impossible) for verbal diarrhea on the other hand.

Why Have We Been So Blind to the Obvious Multidimensionality of Psychology?

Any psychologist worth his salt knows that most behavioral phenomena are multiply determined. Why, then, has he contributed so vehemently and persistently to the myth of univariate determination? I suspect the answer is to be found in the history of our discipline, and that it is traceable to the fact that scientific development began with such closed-system phenomena as mechanics and planetary motions. The point is that, even though physical systems are also multivariate, because of the highly nomothetic, predictable character of these simpler, closed systems, it was, indeed, possible to control experimentally (or otherwise) the most pertinent variables, and make accurate assessments of functional relationships via the traditional bivariate laboratory procedures. Thus it was natural for the new discipline of psychology to latch on to established scientific method in the solution of its problems. However, as psychology moved into more complex and more socially relevant areas, such as intelligence and temperament, it became apparent that the traditional methodology wasn't working. In short, such inadequacies constituted the necessity for the invention of the current bag of multivariate strategies like multiple, partial, and canonical correlation; analysis of variance; discriminant function, pattern and profile analysis; path analysis; diallel analysis; multidimensional scaling; cluster analysis; and factor analysis.

Although these multivariate methods have enjoyed wide application in the research contributions of the past two decades, they have made relatively little impact on the theoretical products of the discipline as a whole. A major exception to this is the factor analytic model (e.g., see Royce, 1973a), but even here there has been a fundamental ignorance and mistrust of this approach on the part of the general psychology community. Since a minimal technical proficiency in factor methodology is limited to a small proportion of the professional community, it is not surprising that it has had relatively little impact on mainstream psychology. The reasons for this are many, and they are complex, but they can be briefly summed up as follows:

1. *Technical problems indigenous to factor analysis.* The most obvious problem in this category has been the transformation or rotational problem; that is, indeterminacy in locating the reference frame. This was the major problem with the formal model from about 1930 to 1960, but with the advent of the computer, this issue has been basically resolved, particularly if the investigator follows up computerized solutions with graphic rotations when needed. The current technical deficiency in factor methodology is the problem of factor invariance, which is a special case of the general scientific problem of the boundary conditions of a scientific construct. Although the rotational and invariance problems have been very difficult to resolve, the fact of these difficulties does not thereby constitute an invalidation of the method. It is unfortunate that so many nonexpert "critics" have misunderstood this situation and inappropriately rejected factor analysis on these grounds.

2. *Issues indigenous to the psychology zeitgeist.* The almost reflex response of the typical scientist confronted with a scientific problem is to proceed via *the* scientific method, meaning the traditional controlled, bivariate laboratory experiment. Furthermore, most psychological scientists of the past few decades have been committed to such philosophic assumptions as operationism, behaviorism, and

logical positivism. Such radical empiricism has left little room for factorially identified concepts such as traits, or other not directly observed (i.e., inferred) theoretical constructs.

3. *The primitive state of contemporary psychological theory.* Overall, psychology is in a relatively primitive state as a theoretical science (Royce, 1975b). This includes multivariate theoretical psychology, which has just begun to apply itself to substantive problems (e.g., see Cattell, 1966; Royce, 1973b).

In short, the blindness of mainstream psychology to the obvious multidimensionality of the discipline is primarily a matter of the relative immaturity of the field as a theoretical science, combined with its relatively simplistic, and largely imported, philosophic commitments to date. If and when psychology develops a more indigenous philosophy (see pp. 47–57, below), multivariate analysis will be firmly integrated with other approaches within the discipline.

Factor Analysis and the Logic of Discovery[6]

In this section we are concerned with the logic of factor analysis—not in terms of the mathematics of the model, but rather in terms of its logical character as a general scientific method. Let me begin by assuming that doing science involves something like Cattell's inductive-deductive spiral (see Figure 1). The lower segment of this figure, the portion up to the term "Hypothesis," describes what I call the empirico-inductive-hypothesis-generating aspect of science, and the upper segment of the first loop of the spiral describes what has been generally referred to as the hypothetico-deductive aspect. The ascending spiral implies a never ending process of empirico-inductive-hypothetico-deductive refinement which need not occupy us at this time.

Although we have just initiated the inquiry, we have already come in contact with the first of several difficulties—namely, that although most practicing scientists spend most of their time at the empirico-inductive end of Cattell's spiral exploring possibilities via a varied bag of laboratory and other observation techniques, the typical philosopher of science has spent most of his time analyzing the

6. Although my ultimate goal is to offer a statement on the psycho-logic of factor analysis, and although this section deals primarily with the logic of discovery, the beginnings of a psycho-logic are implicit in Table 2 and the portion of text relevant to that table.

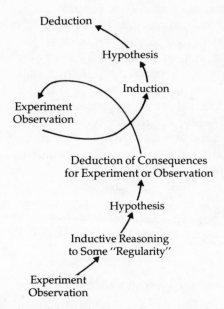

FIG. 1. Cattell's inductive-hypothetico-deductive spiral (Raymond B. Cattell, "Psychological Theory and Scientific Method," in Raymond B. Cattell [Ed.], *Handbook of Multivariate Experimental Psychology*, © 1966 by Rand McNally & Co., Chicago, Fig. 1–1, p. 16. Adapted by permission of Rand McNally College Publishing Co.).

logical implications of hypothetico-deduction. The latter is called the logic of justification and the former is called the logic of discovery, and unfortunately, the philosophers have had too much to say about justification and practically nothing to say about discovery.

Although the recent statements by a small number of historians of science such as Kuhn (1962) and Hanson (1961) are relevant and, in fact, are of more intrinsic interest to the psychologist, they are not directly on target. For these statements are focused on what scientists do, as is also the case for Polanyi (1958), whereas our primary concern is with what is logically possible regardless of what scientists do. Thus, research on the logic of discovery seems to have been neglected by the philosophers—in fact, I have been led to believe that, except for the contributions of two of my colleagues at the center, W. W. Rozeboom (1961, 1971) and Charles Morgan (1973), the last philosopher to give the matter serious attention was C. S. Peirce (1931–1935).

An oversimplified summary of Morgan's (1973) analysis includes the following points: (a) Given a formal language and a specifiable set of rules for generating sentences, it is possible to write a computer program which will generate hypotheses concerning the domain in question. (b) However, in its initial form, the program generates an infinite number of hypotheses; so it is desirable to provide a set of criteria for determining which hypotheses are preferrred. (c) Thus, hypothesis generation, combined with hypothesis selection, results in the identification of a relatively short list of hypotheses. In brief, Morgan ends up with a subset of algorithmically generated "plausible hypotheses," where "plausibility" is necessarily very much context dependent.

How does factor analysis fit into this picture? The most obvious point to be made is that the identification of factors is a problem in the logic of discovery. At least I have presumed that its fundamentally exploratory role, and its data-to-inferred-factor character, are familiar to most psychologists. While it is true that it is possible to employ factor analysis for the purpose of confirming what is already known, or to make deductions via the use of a criterion variable (e.g., see Eysenck, 1950), it is also obvious that there are more powerful and efficient deductive strategies available. On the other hand, the utilization of massive matrices of empirical variables to cover a previously unexplored terrain, or a terrain where the covariations are blurred, particularly if the analyses constitute an orderly and insightful progression of planned investigations, constitutes a powerful means for getting a handle on potentially useful theoretical constructs in complex domains where observables are confusedly interrelated (Royce, 1963).

My experience in the substantive application of the factor model indicates that there are two phases of scientific inference in the typical exploratory factor investigation. The first phase is focused on the identification of *replicable patterns* of observables, and the second phase is concerned with the identification of *latent unknowns*. Mere factoring, which is all there was to factor analysis up to around 1930, was unable to achieve the pattern replicability demand of Phase I. Hence, the importance of the matrix algorithm and, in particular, the availability of matrix transformations. That is, with the introduction of rotation to simple structure, it became possible to replicate the patterns of observable covariations. The essence of what is involved in a Phase I inference can be captured via the following case of simple structure—a case involving ones and zeros in the appropriate

Table 1

An Idealized Simple Structure Matrix

Variables ($n = 12$)	Factors ($m = 3$)		
	I	II	III
1	1	0	0
2	1	0	0
3	1	0	0
4	1	0	0
5	0	1	0
6	0	1	0
7	0	1	0
8	0	1	0
9	0	0	1
10	0	0	1
11	0	0	1
12	0	0	1

cell entries, combined with overdetermination of each column (i.e., factor) entry. This is exemplified in Table 1, an n (variables) by m (factors) matrix (where $m < n$). In this example the common factor variance for each row vector (i.e., test variable) is completely accounted for in terms of one column vector (i.e., factor). Furthermore, each column vector is (minimally) overdetermined— that is, it is identified by several high-loading (i.e., .30 or more by convention) variables. This is, of course, a highly idealized case of simple structure—a case where we have a factorial complexity of one for each test in the battery, and collinearity between a given test vector and its appropriate factor vector. Furthermore, in this example, we shall assume this finding has been found repeatedly over a series of analyses (involving the same test battery and "similar" or "same" populations). Thus, the *replicable patterns* are now obvious—namely, that three subsets of variables, 1–4, 5–8, and 9–12, always cluster. Although there are a variety of technical-methodological problems, Phase I inferences are, in principle, and, circa 1975, in practice, essentially algorithmic.

Further exposition of the two phases of scientific inference in factor analysis will be facilitated by reference to Table 2. In this table I have juxtaposed the critical elements of Cattell's induction process,

Table 2

*The Empirico-inductive Generation of Hypotheses
in Empirical Science*

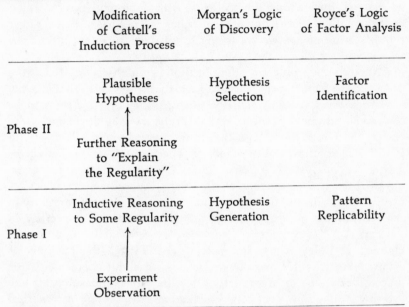

	Modification of Cattell's Induction Process	Morgan's Logic of Discovery	Royce's Logic of Factor Analysis
Phase II	Plausible Hypotheses ↑ Further Reasoning to "Explain the Regularity"	Hypothesis Selection	Factor Identification
Phase I	Inductive Reasoning to Some Regularity ↑ Experiment Observation	Hypothesis Generation	Pattern Replicability

Morgan's analysis of the logic of discovery, and Royce's analysis of the logic of factor analysis. Reading from left to right and from the bottom up, we have a simple two-phase sequence involving inductive reasoning to some regularity for Phase I in Column 1, paralleled by the generation of hypotheses in Column 2 and pattern replicability in Column 3. The implication is that factor solutions, which include replicable vector patterns or replicable clusters of variables, can be cranked out via specifiable computer programs (e.g., see Harman, 1967, and Royce, 1973b), and that the underlying logic is similar or parallel to Morgan's algorithmic generation of hypotheses. Furthermore, such generation of hypotheses is seen as the first step in the empirico-inductive portion of Cattell's spiral.

It will be recalled that Morgan had no trouble generating hypotheses—his problem occurred in selecting *the* hypothesis. And his answer lay in putting a filter into the computer program so that he could come up with a subset of plausible hypotheses. Since the testing of a multiplicity of (usually plausible) hypotheses constitutes a more accurate representation of what scientists actually do, I have modified the Cattell spiral accordingly. Therefore, in Table 2 I have labeled that aspect of the Cattell spiral as Phase II. And, parallel to Morgan, the more difficult factor analytic scientific inference also lies in Phase II, for we must now come up with *the* hypothesis regarding factor *x* rather than *a* hypothesis. That is, in Phase II, the *factor interpretation* phase, we are trying to uncover the *latent unknowns which have resulted in the observed covariations*.

Although the problem of identification is widely recognized as *the* problem in factor analysis, the fact that there are two general strategies for providing *plausible hypotheses* does not seem to be common knowledge. One of these strategies was developed from within the factor model and the other evolved via an alliance with traditional experimental psychology. The internal strategy involves *invariance analysis* (e.g., see Cattell [1966] and Royce [1973a, 1973b] for a broad coverage of the theoretical and empirical aspects of this approach; my own contributions in this area are primarily in the comparative-physiological domain [Royce, 1966], especially in the area of behavior genetics [Royce, Poley, & Yeudall, 1973; Royce, Holmes, & Poley, 1975; Poley & Royce, 1973])—the business of establishing whether or not we are talking about the same factor despite variations in investigators, test batteries, and subjects. The external strategy involves *experimental manipulation of factors* (e.g., the effect of such variables as brain damage [Mos, Lukaweski & Royce;[7] Royce, Yeudall, & Bock[8]] electric shock and drugs [Satinder, Royce, & Yeudall, 1970], maternal stimulation [Poley & Royce, 1970], early stress [Mos, Royce, & Poley, 1973], and the effect of light [Mos, Vriend, & Poley, 1974] and height [Royce & Poley, 1976]) via the usual laboratory techniques. In both strategies the ultimate goal is to establish the "boundary conditions" (e.g., Factor A is functional up to age 15, but does not account for any observable covariation for the remainder of the human life span, etc.) or the range of effectiveness for each factorially identified unknown. Although the *intent* of current efforts to find a mathematical solution to the invariance problem is to extend the *algorithmic* character of the factor model to a Phase II inference, current opinion (e.g., from direct conversation with Ledyard Tucker, Henry Kaiser, and Owen

7. L. P. Mos, R. Lukaweski, & J. R. Royce, The effect of septal lesions of factors of emotionality in two inbred strains of mice. In preparation.

8. J. R. Royce, L. T. Yeudall, & C. Bock, Factor analytic studies of human brain damage: I. The factors and their brain correlates. *Multivariate Behavioral Research* (in press).

White, among others) is that a mathematical solution is not possible in principle, because of insufficiency of necessary information (e.g., consider the difficulty of estimating factor invariance in the situation where two entirely different subsets of variables are involved; the problem becomes even more horrendous if we introduce the complication of administering the test battery to two entirely different populations, etc.). Thus, the factor approach will probably not be able to circumvent completely the subjective input of the investigator at the level of *factor identification*.[9] However, it seems reasonable to conclude that as factor investigators increase their knowledge of the "boundary conditions" of factors, these empirical constraints will increase the probability that the nth interpretation of factor x is a *more plausible* (if not *the*) *hypothesis*.

We can regard the two strategies just described as having *empirical tenability*; that is, plausibility in terms of the weight of the empirical evidence. But there is one more plausibility criterion available to us, namely, *theoretical tenability*, or the weight of the theoretical evidence. Examples of this from factor theory include the empirical search for missing entries in a taxonomic table, such as Guilford's (1967; Guilford & Hoepfner, 1971) (periodic-like) cubic table of cognitive elements. Other examples include the usual

---

9. The theory-laden constructivist view (see pp. 4–5) of doing science provides an insight at this juncture, namely, that no observation is devoid of an "interpretive context." In short, part of the subjective aspect of the factor identification problem is the conceptual framework which the investigator brings to bear in making a Phase II inference. Thus, the same factor solution may elicit different conceptualizations for a given factor because of differences in world view, paradigm, and other cognitive commitments. This point is of particular importance in Phase II, for it is at this juncture that the factor analyst provides his "theoretical construction" as to the nature of a given factor. While this "inventive" interpretation is offered within the constraints of the pattern replicability provided by Phase I, thereby delimiting the number of "plausible hypotheses," the fact that Phase II involves cognitive constructions, and that more than one construction is feasible, suggests that it is not possible, in principle, to generate *the* hypothesis to explain data. That is, we cannot "discover" *the* hypothesis because a Phase II scientific inference actually involves generating a "construct"—a man-made "invention." While it is true that such plausible hypotheses are subsequently empirically tested via hypothetico-deductive procedures, and thereby receive further confirmation or disconfirmation, the constructivist or interpretive input remains.

Thus it would appear that "discovery," at least as it applies to the logic of factor analysis, involves interpretation or cognitive construction in addition to pattern replicability.

deductions from a theoretical structure, such as Eysenck's (1967, 1970, 1973) many deductions involving the higher-order dimension of introversion-extroversion.[10]

How can we briefly recapitulate the logic of factor analysis? I believe a convincing case has been put forward for factor analysis as an empirico-inductive-hypothesis-generating method, and further, that such hypotheses are, in fact, generated algorithmically. Moreover, it would appear that both empirical and theoretical considerations provide sufficient constraints for identifying a subset of plausible hypotheses regarding the interpretation of a factor. However, there seems to be little hope, on either logical or experimental grounds, for algorithmically generating *the* hypothesis regarding factor identification. But, to my knowledge, such certainty is not possible for *any* scientific method, even for the case of the highly esteemed hypothetico-deductive method.[11]

10. At this juncture, I recognize that I have moved into, or at least toward, the hypothetico-deductive portion of Cattell's spiral, and that deductive inferences have been analyzed in the context of justification. This was done by design in order to at least allude to the fact that, in practice, scientific inference typically involves mixtures of empirico-induction and hypothetico-deduction. This is also true in the case of factor analysis in ways that are of considerable interest, as in the following instances (which cannot be developed because of space limitations): (a) the fact that factor analysis has a highly formal model (i.e., matrix algebra) on the one hand, but is focused on letting the data generate hypotheses on the other hand; and (b) the fact that the variables which constitute a test battery represent a limited sampling of the test universe, and thereby constitute a not-well-understood, a priori, theory-laden specification of the factors to be identified. Although this state of affairs would appear to negate the empirico-inductive nature of factor analysis, it does not do so in the same sense that the usual sampling problems also do not negate the inductive process. Also, in spite of the limitations of test sampling, the conceptual context of the variables in a test battery is not equivalent to the deductive procedures of the hypothetico-deductive method.

11. This statement is based on the idea that no knowledge claim, regardless of its epistemic norm, is incorrigible (e.g., see Royce, 1974, and Royce & Tennessen, in preparation). This view seems intuitively obvious in the case of empirical science because of the inherent "dirtiness" of data, whether the data precedes theory (induction) or is gathered subsequent to theoretical deduction. For the purpose of the statement above, pure logic and pure mathematics (i.e., no data) are meant to be excluded. However, it is my understanding that the incorrigibility claim holds for formal systems as well (e.g., it is always possible to raise objections about the adequacy of the axioms for a given formal system).

PSYCHOLOGICAL EPISTEMOLOGY

Three Ways of Knowing

In this and the remaining sections we come to the heart of what I have to say about the major concern of this symposium—the conceptual foundations of psychological theory. While there is more to metatheory than epistemology, my approach to these foundational issues is primarily epistemological. This means I will leave most of the philosophic questions to my more philosophically astute colleagues in this symposium, Professors Mischel, Toulmin, and Koch.

In several recent publications (Royce, 1964, 1965a, 1967, 1970a, 1974, 1975a; Royce, Mos, & Kearsley, 1975), I have outlined a psycho-philosophical scheme for ways of knowing. In particular, I posit three ways of knowing: empiricism, rationalism, and metaphorism. These three "isms" are regarded as basic because of their dependence upon various cognitive processes on the one hand, and their epistemological justifiability on the other hand. This view can be briefly summarized by reference to Figure 2. The implication here is that each of these "isms" represents a legitimate approach to reality, but that different criteria for knowing are involved. Rationalism, for example, is viewed as being primarily dependent upon logical consistency. That is, this approach says we will accept something as true if it is logically consistent, and we will reject something as false if it is illogical. Empiricism says we know to the extent we perceive correctly, and metaphorism says that knowledge is dependent upon the degree to which symbolic cognitions lead to universal rather than idiosyncratic awarenesses. While each of these cognitive processes may lead to error, the implication is that each is also capable of leading to truth. The possibilities of perceptual error, for example, are readily apparent. The errors of the thinking process are probably more subtle, but I have been led to believe that they have plagued the efforts of the logicians and mathematicians. And the errors of symbolizing are even more elusive, primarily because of the sheer difficulty of providing an adequate articulation of metaphoric knowing (e.g., the problem of what symbols "mean"; what qualifies as "universal"?). Furthermore, I realize that none of these psychological processes operates independently of the others. That is, we do not conceptualize independently of sensory inputs

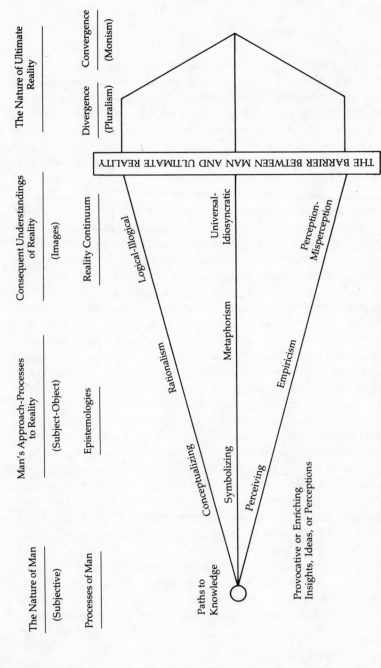

FIG. 2. The basic paths of knowledge (modified version of Royce, 1964, p. 12. By permission of Litton Educational Publishing International).

and the process of symbol formation; nor do we perceive independently of concepts. In short, although the correspondences indicated in Figure 2 are oversimplified for purposes of analysis and exposition, they represent the best fit between a given cognitive class and its parallel epistemological criterion.

Although psychologists have just begun the task of evolving an adequate cognitive psychology, it is incumbent upon me at least to indicate what I am alluding to when I employ such terms as "conceptualizing," "perceiving," and "symbolizing." Working definitions of these terms follow.

Conceptualizing: Cognitive processes which focus on concepts —their formation, elaboration, and functional significance to the organism; more deductive than inductive; focus is on the logical consequences of information currently available to the organism.

Perceiving: Cognitive processes which focus on observables— sensory inputs and their "meaning"; more inductive than deductive; focus is on the processing of sensory information.

Symbolizing: Cognitive processes which focus on the formation of symbols—"constructed productions" offered as representations of reality; analogical rather than deductive or inductive; focus is on the processing of "new-formation" (i.e., internally generated forms) rather than "in-formation."

In Figure 2 I have attempted to show the relationships between man, the knower, and the nature of reality via three ways of knowing. The two columns to the extreme right are separated from the other three columns by a barrier between man and ultimate reality. That which is epistemologically untestable lies to the right of this barrier and constitutes unknowable ultimate reality. That which is testable by some criterion for knowing lies to the left of the epistemological barrier and leads to "reality images" which are "true" or "real." Despite the efforts of great thinkers to circumvent somehow the epistemological limits involved, the only valid assessments open to finite man necessarily lie to the left of the barrier.

Such efforts to find truth have presumably been going on since man first made his appearance in the universe, and they have slowly evolved to the current special disciplines of knowledge such as history, literature, and biology.[12] By definition, such specialties

---

12. I view the various special disciplines as further differentiations or subcategories of Cassirer's symbolic forms. According to Cassirer, all knowledge

provide a highly selective view of reality, and lead to divergent world views. The psycho-epistemological basis for this state of affairs is depicted in Figure 3. For present purposes I suggest we ignore the right half of this figure[13] and that we focus on the left side. It is to be understood that all three epistemologies are involved in each of the three representative disciplines of knowledge, but it is also clear that each discipline gives greater credence to one or more of them. The scientist, for example, "conceptualizes," "symbolizes," and "perceives" as scientist, but he maximizes the rational and empirical ways of knowing and minimizes metaphoric symbolizing as final judge. Conversely, the artist, who also invokes his entire cognitive repertoire, maximizes the symbolizing process at the expense of the conceptualizing and perceptual processes. There are, of course, wide variations in the possible combinations of epistemological profiles; this brief exposition should be taken as relative and typical rather than as absolute and general.

---

manifests itself in one symbolic form or another. The earliest form was the myth, followed by certain primitive art forms, such as the dance and ritualistic drama; primitive scientific forms, such as early astronomy and astrology; and simple number systems, such as Roman numerals. One of Cassirer's major theses is that in the course of cultural evolution there has been increasing elaboration of these early manifestations of knowledge. With the increase in elaboration over the centuries there has also been a corresponding differentiation, culminating in the multitude of arts and sciences which are the essence of twentieth-century culture. For various historical and other reasons, these have been codified into special disciplines which we can think of as a more differentiated taxonomy of symbolic forms. It is in this sense that I would argue for beginning any analysis of knowing with its products—namely, knowledge. And I have adopted Cassirer's approach as the most adequate basis for such an analysis because his philosophy of symbolic forms (Cassirer, 1953, 1955, 1957) deals with the full spectrum of knowledge.

13. In seminar and lecture presentations of this material I have been asked why I include the right-hand section of the diagram, particularly since it deals with unknowable reality. The major reason is for the sake of completeness. For example, much of the metaphysical history of philosophy is alluded to via the right-hand portion of Figure 2. A second reason is that the omission of that portion of the diagram invariably leads to questions about ultimate reality. Psychologically, I have come to think of reality projections to the right of the epistemic barrier as a kind of cosmic Rorschach test. Ontologically, I see no way to circumvent, pole vault, go under, or pass through the barrier, and I hereby challenge anybody to demonstrate that this can be done (e.g., some mystics and/or drug takers have made such claims, but so far as I know, such claims have not been successfully demonstrated).

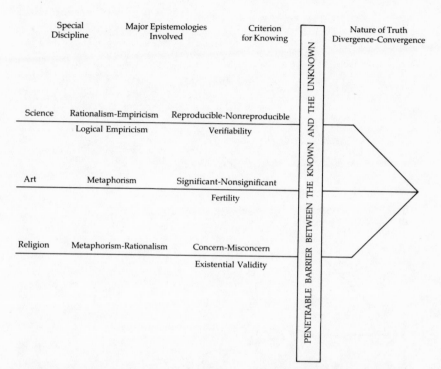

FIG. 3. Representative special disciplines of knowledge (modified version of Royce, 1964, p. 20. By permission of Litton Educational Publishing International).

Epistemic Styles, Individuality, and World View

How can we account for differences in world view, where *world view is defined as "an organism's organized set of personal cognitions which constitute a model or image of reality"* (Royce, 1974)? The answer I come up with involves a synthesis of two projects already alluded to—the development of a general theory of individual differences (Royce, 1973a; Royce[14]), and the development of a psychological theory of knowledge (Royce, 1974, 1975a; Royce & Tennessen;[15] Royce et. al.[16]). The essence of the knowing project

14. J. R. Royce, *A multi-factor theory of individuality.* In preparation.

15. J. R. Royce & H. Tennessen (Eds.), *Inquiries into a psychological theory of knowledge.* In preparation.

16. J. R. Royce, H. Coward, E. Egan, F. Kessel, & L. P. Mos, *Psychological epistemology: A critical review of the empirical literature and the theoretical issues.* In preparation.

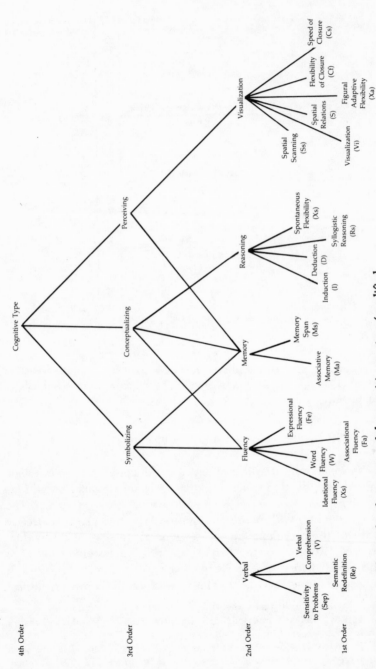

FIG. 4. The revised hierarchical structure of the cognitive system (modified version of Royce, 1973).

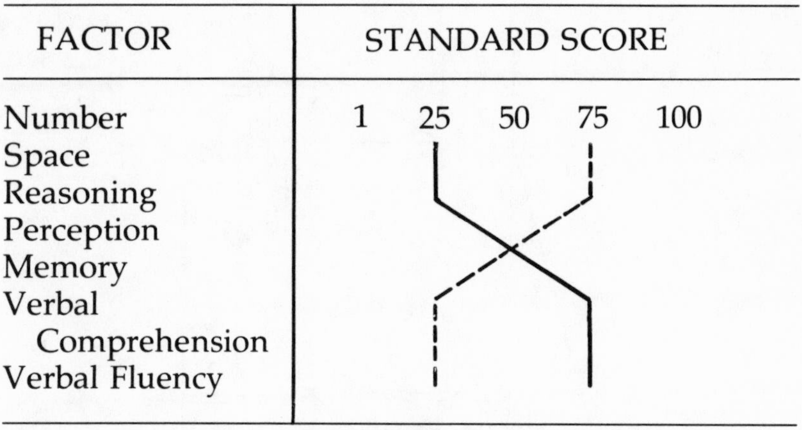

FACTOR	STANDARD SCORE
Number	1 25 50 75 100
Space	
Reasoning	
Perception	
Memory	
Verbal	
Comprehension	
Verbal Fluency	

FIG. 5. Showing two persons, A (solid line) and B (dotted line), with the same IQ, but with opposite mental ability profiles (Royce, 1957).

has just been reviewed in terms of the three ways or styles of knowing—empiricism, rationalism, and metaphorism. The essence of the theory of individuality, which takes it point of departure from factor theory, is that a person's psychological makeup is an organized, multidimensional system. However, the total psychological system subsumes six subsystems, designated as sensory, cognitive, affective, style, evaluative, and motor. Highly oversimplified, the key idea is that individuality can be portrayed by subprofiles of the multidimensions for each of the six subsystems.

What are these dimensions, where did they come from, and how might they be organized? So far the theory includes some 30 cognitive dimensions and around 35 affective dimensions which appear to be hierarchically arranged. And they have emerged inductively from the hundreds of empirical reports in the factor analytic literature. Let us look at cognitive structure as paradigmatic for each of the six subsystems (see Figure 4).[17] What we have here is around twenty first-order factors, five second-order factors, three third-order factors, and a fourth-order construct labeled cognitive type. The key concept here is *cognitive type*, for it reflects individual profiles for the entire hierarchy of traits. I now refer the reader to Figure 5 for two simplified (i.e., showing only seven primary factors)

17. Except for styles, we shall omit the other four systems because of limitations of space and time.

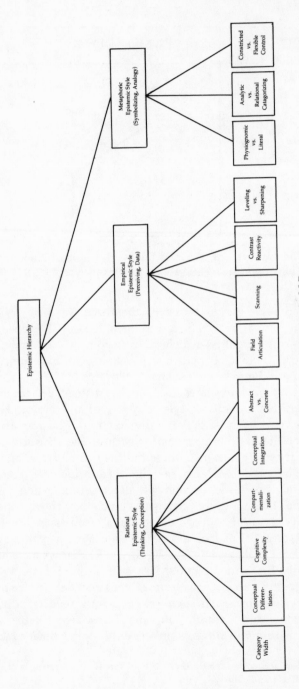

FIG. 6. Hypothesized epistemic style structure (Royce, 1973, p. 38). N.B.: The specific linkages of each epistemic style to cognitive abilities and affective traits remain to be spelled out. However, it is anticipated that epistemic styles will be primarily cognitive in nature (i.e., with few affective linkages).

cognitive profiles, A (solid line) and B (dotted line). The profiles show the relative strengths and weaknesses of two cognitive types, indicating which cognitive dimensions are optimally available to the subject in his interactions with the environment. Thus, the verbal type (A) will do better with "verbal tasks" and the quantitative type (B) will do better with "quantitative tasks."

However, in this context we are more concerned with style structure and epistemic hierarchy. Thus, we will define the style system as *"a multidimensional, organized system of processes (subsumes cognitive, affective, cognitive-affective, and epistemic styles) by means of which an organism manifests cognitive and/or affective phenomena"* (Royce, 1973a). Although the cumulative data base in the style domain is such that it is not possible to present an empirically anchored picture at the present time, we can offer a hypothesized style structure which shows one logically possible hierarchical arrangement.[18] This is summarized in Figure 6. Most of you are aware of the concept of *style as a characteristic mode or way of manifesting cognitive and/or affective phenomena*, and of *cognitive style as a style construct which is limited primarily to cognitive processes*. The construct of *epistemic style* is a new one, however, and it is defined as *a style construct which simultaneously invokes a valid truth criterion (i.e., leads to a justifiable knowledge claim in addition to being a characteristic mode or way of interacting with the environment)*. The important concept here is *epistemic type*, which is a profile or a hierarchy of all style constructs, but especially the three epistemic styles indicated at the second level. The grounds for conceptualizing the three previously discussed ways of knowing as epistemic styles should now be obvious. Although I cannot take the time to develop the point, I have also hypothesized that higher-order factors, such as epistemic style, are personality integrators (Royce & Buss, 1976).

If we now embed both the cognitive and the style systems within the total psychological system,[19] the individuality basis for world

18. Although a more adequate conceptualization is now available (see D. Wardell & J. R. Royce, A multifactor theory of styles. In preparation), it is nevertheless probable that major modification will be required in the light of subsequent empirical findings.

19. The sensory and motor systems have been omitted for purposes of simplification.

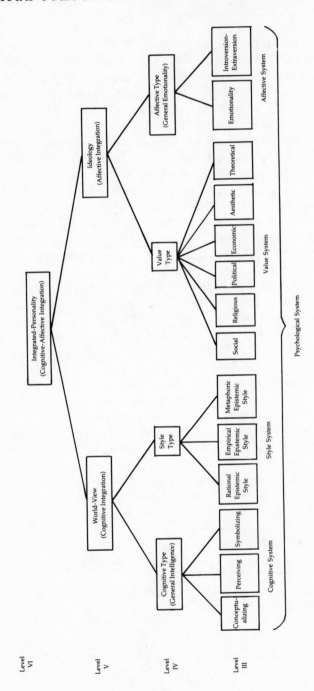

FIG. 7. The hierarchical structure of personality (modified version of Royce, 1973, p. 39).

view should become more apparent (see Figure 7). Our focal point is on world view at Level V. According to the hierarchical structure on the left side of this figure, differences in world view can be accounted for in terms of variations in cognitive and epistemic type. That is, the "rationalist" (in varying degrees of purity, of course) will manifest a typical style profile, as will the "empiricist" and the "metaphoric." And because there are also (unknown) relationships between styles and cognitive abilities, it is to be expected that different subsets of these dimensions will also be part of the total (i.e., including affective and value dimensions) psychological profile of the "metaphoric," the "rationalist," and the "empiricist." The main point is that it is this epistemic hierarchy, combined with cognitive profile, which determines world view.

THEORY AND METATHEORY

The Behaving Organism Is Multisystemic

A major deterrent to the advancement of viable theory has been the psychologist's inability to come to grips with "organized complexity." The gestaltists raised the right questions, and they even provided some answers, but they never developed an adequate methodology. The behaviorists developed an impressive methodology, and they also provided some answers, but they never got around to the questions. And the psychoanalysts seemed, at least for a while, to have *all* the answers, but now there is nothing but questions, including questions about their scientific charade. And, although a broad spectrum of subsequent theories have had their successes in accounting for behavioral phenomena, it is clear that their theoretical scope has been relatively narrow-gauged, and further, their depth of penetration along the complexity dimension has not been great (Royce, 1970a). In short, the problem of units, parts, and wholes continues to plague the efforts of psychological theorists, whether they are operating at the relatively molecular level of the conditioned response and physiological psychology, or the more molar levels of perception and social psychology. Thus, while there have been noticeable improvements in the isolation and understanding of many of the parts, nobody has ever succeeded in putting Humpty Dumpty together.

I have recently run into this problem head-on in connection with the general theory of individual differences alluded to in the last section. While I have found factor theory to be invaluable for providing a multivariate, taxonomic point of departure, I have also become aware of the limitations of the factor model at the more molar levels of part-whole interactions and integrations.

Although I've been flirting with the possibilities of general systems theory for many years, including interacting directly with von Bertalanffy (a former colleague who is one of the innovators of general systems theory), it was not until the appearance of J. G. Miller's (1973) recent monograph that I became convinced of its relevance to behavior. In particular, I became convinced that an amalgamation of factor theory and Miller's general systems behavior theory holds exciting prospects for bridging the gap between the multivariate level of traits and the level of the total organism. The bridging is accomplished via the interactions and integrations of subsystems combined with ancillary concepts and principles from information and feedback theory (Royce & Buss, 1976).

Miller's overall theory is a brilliant tour de force. Its panoramic range from cell to society is breathtaking; and its depth of penetration is mind-boggling. While it may require some time before we get beyond mere programmatic possibilities, it is my guess that general systems theory has the potential for a Kuhnian (1962) paradigmatic revolution, particularly in the nonphysical sciences. Furthermore, Miller's inventory of explicit hypotheses constitutes an impressive demonstration that information-systems behavior theory can, indeed, go beyond its long-recognized programmatic possibilities. It must be granted, however, that the total theory is so grand in scope that it will require decades before we can adequately assess (i.e., both conceptually and empirically) its potential.

The Major Paradigms of Psychology

"Paradigm" is one of those fad terms which has caught the fancy of academia. So, in spite of considerable confusion as to what the term means, we ought to do what we can with it because it is probably here to stay. Certainly Kuhn's original document (1962), although very provocative and insightful about the social psychology of knowledge, was not clear on the metatheoretic status of a paradigm. For example, do terms such as "pattern," "model," or "conceptual system" constitute adequate synonyms? Is "scientific paradigm" meant to be a more inclusive term than "theory" or "school"? Just where does it fit in the verbal jungle of metatheoretic terminology?

In his 1970 postscript to the second edition of *The Structure of Scientific Revolutions* Kuhn replies to his critics by focusing on two key characteristics of a paradigm. These are (a) the constellation of group commitments, and (b) problem solving via specific exemplars. The first point has to do with the social fact that a paradigm is shared by a community of scholars. What is shared are philosophic assumptions, subcultural values and/or prescriptions (e.g., see Watson, 1967), problem-solving methods, and conceptual models. The latter phrases come closest to what Kuhn is alluding to in his second point, namely, the sharing of exemplars. For it is in the solving of "typical problems" (or exemplars) that the novice acquires in-group know-how so that future problems can be resolved. Furthermore, it is these paradigms or exemplars which Kuhn says are given up or transformed when a scientific revolution occurs. Of course, changes at this substantive, specific problem level could not occur without changes in the background "disciplinary matrix" (Kuhn's terminology for the theoretical-philosophic group commitments) as well. With these two points in mind, I will now elaborate on one possible way to retain Kuhn's term without loss of his original intent. Since Kuhn originally developed the concept in the context of "the scientist doing his thing," it seems appropriate to bring in the concept of world view. You will recall that I defined world view as "a person's organized set of personal constructions or cognitions which constitutes a model or image of reality." I propose that when a world view transcends the individual—that is, when it becomes an image of reality for a community—we refer to it as a *conceptual framework.* Since a communal world view or conceptual framework can refer to any domain of discourse, such as the arts, the sciences, or the occult, we require an additional constraint for the concept of paradigm. I suggest, therefore, that we simply limit the technical usage of the term "paradigm" to cases when the communal world view refers to the scientific segment of the subculture. Putting all this together, a *paradigm is a scientific community's organized set of constructions or cognitions which constitutes a model or image of reality.* The "constructions and cognitions" refer to such matters as the paradigm's nomological network (i.e., variables and their relationships), plus specifiable philosophic assumptions (i.e., such notions as causality, probability, organismic or mechanistic philosophic presuppositions, etc.).

Since contemporary psychology is undergoing visible conceptual changes, including a paradigm shift, the question arises: just what is occurring? The major claim about current events is that we are shifting from a "neobehavioristic" to a "cognitive" paradigm. While I am in agreement with the basic claim, it does contain certain complexities which I should now like to bring to the surface. We begin with what I will call the explanatory status of a paradigm. Imagine a "paradigmatic maturity continuum" with the descriptive term "programmatic" at the left end of the scale and the term "explanatory" at the right end. Furthermore, let us characterize the continuum in two ways: (a) degree of inclusiveness of the scientific community, and (b) degree of conceptual explicitness. The polar coordinates in this scheme are summarized in Figure 8 below. Thus, a programmatic paradigm is one whose nomological network and/or philosophic assumptions are merely vaguely alluded to, in contrast to an explanatory paradigm, which is highly explicit on these matters. Furthermore, an explanatory paradigm also reflects a high epistemic correlation between empirical observables and formal (i.e., mathematical, in its most rigorous form) structure (Royce, 1970a). And on the issue of the sharing community, the explanatory paradigm captures most or all of the active participants of the discipline. The programmatic paradigm, on the other hand, is limited to a relatively small subcommunity of scholars.

What about psychology's paradigms? There has been confusion as to whether it would be accurate to ascribe paradigmatic status to its schools of thought. However, Kuhn's recent revisions, as exemplified by the following quotation, make it clear that psychological schools qualify.

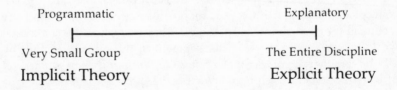

FIG. 8. The paradigmatic maturity continuum.

> That change just outlined in my text deprives me of recourse to the phrases "pre-paradigm period" and "post-paradigm period" when describing the maturation of a scientific specialty. In retrospect that seems to me all for the good, for, in both senses of the term, paradigms have throughout been possessed by any scientific community, including the schools of what I previously called the "pre-paradigm period." [Kuhn, 1970]

However, since Kuhn has dropped the distinction between pre-paradigmatic and paradigmatic, and further, since most schools which occur early in the history of a science are programmatic, I have introduced the metatheoretic notion of "paradigmatic maturity." My intent here is to provide a basis for making qualitative distinctions between more or less developed scientific paradigms. Thus, both gestalt psychology and psychoanalysis are highly *programmatic*, having captured relatively small segments of the relevant community of scholars, and neither having been very successful in spelling out the details of the implicit nomological network. Behaviorism has been the most advanced of psychology's three major paradigms, for it has dominated the field for the past fifty years, and it has been reasonably explicit about its nomological network and its philosophic assumptions.

However, in spite of the behavioristic flavor of 20th-century psychology, it is my opinion that it would be more accurate to describe the discipline-wide paradigm of the past 50 years as a combination of surface behaviorism and underground structuralism-functionalism.[20] What I'm alluding to in this claim is that some form

20. The terms "structuralism" and "functionalism" cover such a wide range that most writers will not specify what they mean. This, of course, merely adds to the confusion. On the other hand, it is true that the issues involved are so numerous and complex that it will require an extensive conceptual-historical analysis in order to come up with an adequate definition. For example, the structuralism of Piaget has little in common with the structural thinking of factor analysts, and the structuralism of neoassociationism would not be viewed as structuralism by the gestaltists. It would be inappropriate, therefore, to attempt a comprehensive definition in a footnote. What I will attempt, however, is a statement which is meant to convey the minimal meaning of these two terms. Furthermore, it is hoped that what is put forward will at least provide an accurate basis on which to build. Thus, my tentative, working definitions follow. By *structuralism* I mean the approach to understanding psychological phenomena in terms of a set of elements and their relationships. And by *functionalism* I mean the approach to understanding psychological phenomena in terms of their adaptive or functional significance.

of structuralism-functionalism is not only common to the areas of investigation covered by the three major 20th-century paradigms, but to the remaining domains of study as well. For example, in the domain I know best, individual differences, it is clear that the factor model is *the* conceptual framework. Furthermore, it is a model with considerable explanatory power. The point is that the factor analytic focus on psychological *functioning* and the *structural* organization of factors (e.g., see Cattell, 1966, and Royce, 1973a, 1973b) leaves little doubt as to its stuctural-functional paradigmatic nature. And the obvious commitment of biology to the premise that "function is dependent upon structure" points to a similar paradigmatic commitment for the domain of physiological psychology.

Thus, I am suggesting that we would be more accurate in our description of the psychology-wide paradigm of roughly the past 50 years if we include structuralism-functionalism as part of the characterization. This raises the question of the paradigmatic maturity of structuralism-functionalism. However, since this conceptual approach has been "underground," it is obviously difficult to make a judgment. It is my guess that, in general, it has been more programmatic than explanatory, and that recognition of this fact by its proponents is a major reason for its underground character. However, psychology is in the midst of conceptual upheaval, and I suspect the paradigm change currently under way involves several shifts, the major ones being (a) a current decline in behaviorism, (b) a current rise of cognitive psychology, and (c) a subsequent surfacing of an implicit but persistent structuralism-functionalism. While a thorough historical analysis will eventually be required concerning psychology's current paradigm shift, it is my guess that the emergence of cognitive psychology constitutes the beginning of

---

In the case of structuralism the implication is that the various manifestations of this viewpoint share a common concern for elements or units, and that the wide variety of structural theories are due to variations in such criteria as the relative molarity of units (e.g., the micro units of the neobehaviorists versus the molarity of the more rational structuralists such as Chomsky and Piaget), and how units are organized (e.g., the gestaltist's insistence on nonreducible wholes). And in the case of functionalism the implication is that its various forms share a concern for action or dynamics, and that its manifestations range from the specification of functional (e.g., as in a mathematical function or equation) relationships and the spelling out of underlying psychobiological mechanisms to attempts to deal with purpose (e.g., cybernetics, information theory, and systems theory).

a more explicit and articulate structuralist-functionalist psychology. Thus, if this guess is correct, the immediate future points to the emergence of some form of *constructive-structural-functionalism*.

But what about third-force psychology? This movement has been hailed as a Kuhnian revolution in psychology. The first point to be made regarding this claim is that its relevant subculture is to be found in the arts and the humanities, *not* science. That is, the humanistic world view, as I see it, is defined in terms of the organized cognitions or constructions of various "humanistic-artistic" subcommunities. The point is that scientific conceptual paraphernalia, such as paradigm and nomological network, are irrelevant to this approach. Thus, it is misleading to refer to third-force psychology as a paradigm shift, since humanistic psychology is, according to the conception just described, *nonparadigmatic*. It is appropriate, however, to refer to the development of third-force psychology in terms of a *shift in conceptual framework* and, more specifically, a *shift in epistemology*. For it is the epistemology of metaphorism which is crucial in humanistic endeavors, not the scientific epistemologies of rationalism and empiricism (Royce, 1967, 1972). This implies, for example, an ideographic rather than a nomothetic endeavor, communicating via a symbolic rather than a prose language, and working toward metaphoric patterns (i.e., the various artistic forms such as poetry and paintings) rather than *scientific theories* (Royce, 1965a; for more on this see Figure 9 and and p. 53, below). In the present context the major point is that humanistic psychology does *not* constitute a paradigm shift. Rather, it constitutes a different world view (e.g., see Royce, 1964, 1974, 1975). With this understanding of the situation, it comes as no surprise that the humanistic psychologist's view of man and his nature is radically different from that of the scientific psychologist.

The Inevitability of Psychology's Theoretical Pluralism

A case can be made that any scientific discipline, including a relatively integrated, monolithic field such as physics, can be characterized as "theoretically pluralistic." This is due to (a) the "theory-laden constructivism" of all observables—that is, the idea that all facts or observations are cast within the context of a subset of theoretical constructions and metatheoretic presuppositions; and

(b) the multiplicity of conceptual frameworks which are potentially relevant to the same subset of observables.

If we now add the previously developed points regarding the psychological bases for different world views, the evidence that there are at least three epistemic styles or ways of knowing, and the old saw of cultural relativism, the case for some form of theoretical monism is considerably weakened. And finally, if we consider the complexity of what is to be theoretically accommodated, especially as we move from the relative simplicity of physical phenomena to the complexity of behavioral and social phenomena, the demand that one theory cover the entire universe of scientific discourse seems downright bizarre, or, at best, a manifestation of an extreme form of religious commitment. From this perspective, it would indeed be a miracle if the range, complexity, and richness of psychological phenomena were to be accommodated by one world view, one conceptual framework, one paradigm, or one theory. Rosenzweig's (1937) analysis of psychology's early schools of thought and Brunswik's (1939, 1952, 1956) analyses of the conceptual focus of psychological theories demonstrate that no one school or theoretical viewpoint was able to encompass the totality of psychology. And my own (Royce, 1970a) recent analysis of the epistemic foundations of psychological theories concludes that most contemporary efforts are, in fact, area rather than general theories of behavior. Furthermore, the point is made that variations in "epistemic commitments" are at least partially responsible for variations in theoretical outputs. For example, the radical empiricism of a Skinnerian will result in a theory which is different in form and content from the kind of theory we could expect from mathematical-modeling approaches.

The considerations described above, plus recent developments in the history and philosophy of science, call for a reevaluation of the meaning of our multitheoretic situation. In the past, probably under the influence of some form of monistic realism, we have tended to view such pluralism as a sign of theoretic weakness and immaturity.[21] There is considerable counterthought on the

21. The recommendation of theoretical pluralism appears to be in conflict with the concept of paradigmatic maturity summarized in Figure 8. Although this point is beyond the present scope, the following are two possibilities for its resolution: (a) Theoretical pluralism per se does not rule out the possibility of overall theoretical integration; it merely calls for the explicit formulation of several alternatives, followed by selective retention of the most viable

contemporary scene (e.g., Radnitzky, 1970, and Naess, 1971) to the effect that an objective, integrated science à la the laws of mechanics is part of the simplistic methodology of now outmoded philosophies of science, and that the prolific spinning of alternative theoretical constructions is a more accurate reflection of the typical situation in science. The major point in this context is that we not be overly distressed about the *number* of theoretical alternatives which are available to us. In fact, the current prescription is that we should elicit even more alternatives (Naess, 1972). Our problem, according to this view, is not with theoretical pluralism, but rather with a *paucity of sophisticated theoretical productions.* The corrective recommendation calls for the creation of more, and more adequate, theory in the first place, followed by critical evaluation and selective elimination of inadequate theoretical structures (Popper, 1959).

Strategies for Advancing Theory Construction

The most obvious step for alleviating psychology's deficiencies in theory construction is to provide such training for future generations. Since our center at the University of Alberta is the only existing institutionalized academic unit with direct experience in this matter, the reader might be interested in a brief summary of our activities. The center's program includes: (a) various standard departmental seminars in psychological theory (i.e., theories of perception, theories of learning, etc.); (b) a center-staffed, inter-disciplinary seminar in philosophy and psychology; (c) a center-staffed seminar in theory construction; (d) a center-sponsored

---

candidates and the attempt to synthesize these as special cases of (one or) a relatively small number of more comprehensive theories. (b) The concept of paradigmatic maturity may have to be revised in the light of organized complexity; that is, further analysis may reveal that organized complexity involves attempts to integrate several subdomains whose boundary conditions are such that subsumability under one overall theory is impossible in principle. Thus, it may be necessary to modify the concept of paradigmatic maturity in terms of the boundary conditions of scientific domains. For example, if theory x accommodates all the possible phenomena of subdomain x, and makes no claim beyond subdomain x, then it would constitute a fully explanatory paradigm for subdomain x; ditto for theory y in its accommodation of sub-domain y. Furthermore, it may be impossible, in principle, for either theory x or theory y to subsume the other, or for a more general theory, z, to subsume theories x and y as special cases.

seminar in theoretical psychology (this involves year-round visiting scholars, center staff, and local scholar seminars-in-the-round, plus other working seminars on a wide range of theoretical-philosophical issues); (e) center-sponsored Banff Conferences (these are week-long mountain retreat working conferences on an annual theme; they occur around every third year); (f) participation in theory construction and/or metatheoretic analysis as part of a staff-directed research project.

A major step we have taken is the sponsoring of theoretical dissertations. While data gathering is permissible, the primary focus is on the development of psychological theory. It may involve new theory, the modification or extension of existing theory, and/or conceptual analysis of important theoretical-philosophical issues. The student works out the details of his program via one of two routes: (a) the departmental route, where the student meets the usual departmental requirements and simply elects theoretical psychology as his specialty, or (b) the interdisciplinary route, where a tailor-made program is put together in terms of the special interests of the student.

I should add that we are primarily a research institute, a think tank. From the outset our primary target has been to advance the conceptual aspects of psychology. And, because of the difficulty of the task, our focus has been primarily on postdoctoral personnel—the local center staff, postdoctoral fellows and research associates, and visiting scholars. Our reasoning was that we would be more likely to make headway by taking advantage of the know-how of mature scholars. Thus, the Distinguished Visiting Scholars Program and the Banff Conferences have been a vital aspect of our operation. These efforts have resulted in three books to date, with several more in the works. The point is that the training of doctoral students has been a secondary target so far. Although we have admitted a small quota of students into the program, only a handful have survived the subsequent ordeal. There are easier routes to the doctorate!

Although nobody knows how to train theoretical psychologists, as a result of several years of teaching and research in this area we know a little more now than when we started. Here are some tentative impressions:

1. Doing theoretical psychology is very difficult. It requires special skills, and it probably requires a certain kind of temperament as well.

2. In general, it is easier to criticize the work of others than it is to produce viable, substantive theory.

3. Furthermore, critical analysis is easier to teach than creative synthesis. For example, increments in analytic skill are demonstrable as a consequence of critically examining existing theories. It should be noted that tutelage by a skilled formalist is crucial. It should also be noted that this approach, while valuable, has an (unknown) asymptotic point of diminishing returns (perhaps it should be studied for a quarter or a semester). The analytic skills of the philosopher are relevant (i.e., the philosopher can teach us how to do conceptual analysis, especially if it is done in the context of empirical findings).

4. Creative synthesis may be impossible to teach; that is, we can teach the neophyte how to go about synthesizing, but it is improbable that we can do much about improving creativity. This aspect of teaching theory construction is more like the problems involved in teaching creative writing, and I suspect the answers on how to teach creativity are similar. Thus, in general, the idea is to provide an atmosphere where theory construction is encouraged, followed by constructive (i.e., both reinforcing and critical) feedback regarding such effort. We know very little regarding the point of diminishing returns; however, it is highly probable that a minimum of one year is essential.

5. We have found value in each of the following procedures: (a) analyzing case studies in "how I did it" (e.g., examining the biographies of successful theorists); (b) "exercises" covering various components of the total theory-construction enterprise (e.g., producing an inductively generated empirical generalization, producing a hypothetical framework, curve fitting, etc.); (c) producing a "modification" (replacing an axiom, adding a new concept, deriving new theoretical consequences, extending the theory, etc.) in an existing theory; (d) finally, making a full-blown attempt at constructing a segment of a theory, a theorette, or a more encompassing theory (this will usually be in a subdomain of greatest interest to the student, and requires the cooperation of a knowledgeable, theory-oriented staff colleague).

6. The master-apprentice relationship is of special value in theory construction, but it is my guess that results will be optimized if this occurs *after* the student has received formal training; and further, that payoff will be most likely if there is true interaction

on real problems-in-progress (this requires true collaborative effort on the part of both participants).

7. Our experience with postdoctoral fellows and research associates who come to us with no previous formal training in theoretical psychology (which is most of them) is that they are of little or no help in actually constructing theory (i.e., in solving real theoretical problems). They can contribute as research assistants, but they rarely come up with viable, autonomous, creative inputs, even after one or two years of "grooming." We've had best results to date with either (a) the occasional postdoctoral fellow or research associate who had received formal training in conceptual analysis elsewhere (e.g., the most obvious cases are those who have had direct experience doing theory or those who had a formal background in some aspect of mathematics or philosophic analysis), or (b) graduates from our own program. However, regarding the former, our biggest difficulty has been that pure formalists frequently do not know enough psychology, and regarding the latter, it should pointed out that only three doctoral-level students have completed our program in a period of eight years.

8. With respect to the production of substantive theory, we find that the potential theoretician in psychology needs to combine two relatively rare qualities: (a) he must be *thoroughly immersed* in empirical psychology; this immersion must be at that level which is described as having a feel for the discipline, or at least the subdomain of investigation; and he must be able to resolve apparent paradoxes (e.g., empirical findings which appear to be contradictory); and (b) he must have advanced skills in conceptual analysis (e.g., training in formal methodology) and creative synthesis (i.e., he must be an imaginative, innovative synthesizer).

9. Metatheoretic content per se is relatively easy to convey, as this is primarily concerned with developments in the philosophy of science, epistemology, and the history of science. However, while we believe this kind of knowledge is valuable, especially in doing metatheoretic analysis, we simply do not know how much it helps in the construction of theory per se.

A major point in my presentation is that viable theory is the ultimate goal of science. Stated another way, theory in its best sense constitutes an "explanation" of the phenomena of a universe of discourse. And while I agree that it was necessary for psychology to go through a period of "empirical imperialism," there is now reason to believe that the current stockpile of empirical observables is inundating us, and that the discipline is in dire need of conceptual compression. I presume, furthermore, it is obvious that the activities of empirical observation and conceptual synthesizing are not mutually exclusive—that, in fact, they are complementary activities of any mature science. Thus, the idea that the psychology zeitgeist needs a "think input" as a complement to its heretofore super-empirical bias in no way implies a weakening of its empirical data base. But where do we go from here? If there's anything to what I've been saying, we must proceed in the context of "conceptual pluralism." For I have been arguing that the study of mind and behavior is multimethodological, multivariate, multiepistemic, multiparadigmatic, multi–world view, multisystemic, and multi-disciplinary. The point is that no *one* conceptual framework is likely to accommodate such an obviously pluralistic situation. However, it does not follow from this that theoretical synthesis is impossible, nor does it follow that we should give up a priori on the goal of overall integration.[22] The point, very simply, is that we must strive for as much theoretical unification as possible if we want to understand mind and behavior. But we must take on this overwhelming task in the context of the full complexity of the psychological beast rather than provide yet another inadequate Procrustean model in that long, tedious, and, by now, absurd parade of mythological simplifications which have plagued so much of our theory to date. In a recent analysis of contemporary theory I came up with four prescriptions for action (Royce, 1970a, pp. 25–26). They can be summarized briefly as follows:

1. That we inductively generate, from within the storehouse of existing psychological data, an inventory of basic concepts, functional relationships, and principles.
2. That we make greater use of multivariate methods of problem solving in addition to the continued use of traditional bivariate analyses.
3. That conceptual schemes, both those developed within psychology

22. The juxtaposing of conceptual pluralism with the demand for theoretical unification seems to pose an unabridgeable paradox, or at least conceptual difficulties, for some psychologists. See, for example, Robert Shaw's (1972) review of the center's first Banff Conference book, *Toward Unification in Psychology*. Incredible and naive as it may seem, we were rebuked by the reviewer for having failed to integrate psychology during that three-day conference!

and those imported from outside, be screened very critically in terms of their appropriateness to the particular area of study in question.

4. That we focus more on area rather than general theories of behavior, with subsequent linkages between area theories as a basis for moving toward further theoretical unification in psychology.

The last point concerning area theory deserves further elaboration, particularly in the context of conceptual pluralism. A major implication of psychology's theoretical pluralism is that the field is so complex that it simply cannot be accommodated by any one conceptual framework. I suspect that this limitation of any one approach is traceable to the grass-roots level of behavioral empirical regularities. For example, is there a problem area in psychology where the empirical findings are not contradictory? I'm not thinking of the occasional contradictory finding—I'm referring to massive cumulations of data which simultaneously say up-down. This state of affairs is too ubiquitous to be explained away on the grounds of poor experimental controls, differences in method, etc., with the implication that the mere accumulation of better and more data will eventually clear it all up. While better data always help, they will not, in my opinion, get to the source of this particular difficulty. For I suspect the source of the difficulty has to do with the generalizability of psychological regularities. It is my observation that the boundary conditions for any one of psychology's observable regularities are relatively narrow-gauged. This means that very few psychological relationships (i.e., laws, principles, regularities) are universal across time and space (e.g., hold for all individuals in all cultures and in all epochs of time). It follows, therefore, that specification of the range (over time and space) of effectiveness for a given regularity should be a major preoccupation of the psychological researcher. Until this task is effectively carried out—and this is an argument in favor of what I would like to think of as the thinking man's version of empiricism—psychology will continue to be harassed by the ubiquitous situation of empirically contradictory findings.

If this assessment of the situation is correct, it means that the production of a massive inventory of low-level empirical regularities (e.g., see Berelson & Steiner, 1964, and Prescription 1, above) should receive immediate and sustained attention. For it would appear that only with this kind of firm empirical basis will it then be possible to analyze the enormous behavioral complexities and surface contradictions which are a consequence of the interactions and integrations of these low-level and relatively narrow-gauged concepts and principles. It also follows that, because of the relatively narrow range of psychology's empirical regularities, immediate progress in theory construction is more likely to occur to the degree that generalizability is consistent with underlying empirical regularities.

On the other hand, while most theorists will have their hands full trying to come up with an adequate mini-theory, and while I wish to underscore the need for focusing most conceptual efforts on area theory, I see no reason to rule out the development of a small band of theoretical generalists who will focus their energies on understanding interarea and interdisciplinary interactions and integrations. In fact, there are weighty arguments which demand this kind of commitment, not the least of them being the general fragmentation which characterizes so much of twentieth-century life. Thus, there are legitimate demands from the culture at large and from within academia for the broad-scoped education of generalists. Psychology is, of course, an obvious candidate for interdisciplinary discourse, for it involves alliances with representatives from the natural sciences (e.g., physics, biochemistry and pharmacology, genetics and neurology), mathematics, the social sciences (e.g., anthropology, sociology, and others) (Royce, 1957), and, with the advent of humanistic psychology, possibly the humanities (e.g., religion, drama, literature; see Royce, 1959, 1961a, 1962, 1964, 1965a, 1967, 1968, 1970a). The need for various combinations of interdisciplinary expertise is obvious. For example, speaking out of my own lifetime experience, when I started doing research in behavior genetics some 25 years ago, the Watson-Crick double helix paper had not yet been written, the diallel cross design hadn't been hatched, and, in fact, except for Tryon's classical selective-breeding experiments on bright versus dull rats and a variety of twin studies, behavior genetics didn't exist as a specialty. A young person going into this area now must learn both psychology and genetics equally well, otherwise he'll not be in a position to advance knowledge in this interdisciplinary specialty. This is equally true for other combinations of disciplines, such as neuropsychology, social psychology, psychometric theory, and mathematical psychology. In addition, the demand for increasing expertise also occurs within various subsegments of the discipline. In short, theoretical-empirical psychology requires all manner of specialist-generalist expertise, depending upon the interests of the individual and the scope of the questions being asked. Thus, specialist-specialists include the intradisciplinary experts in areas such as learning and perception. These are the traditional specialists whose energies are focused on relatively narrow-scoped problems within a given area of the discipline. The specialist-generalists include the interdisciplinarians, such as social psychologists and biopsychologists, with a specialty in psychology, but with generalist leanings in the direction of one or more adjacent disciplines. Finally, we have the generalist-generalists, whose scope either spans the various areas of a discipline, or, in extreme cases, cuts across several disciplines. While the demands being placed on the general-generalist are becoming increasingly impossible to meet, I presume it is obvious that society's *need* for such people is overwhelming. However, in spite of society's obvious need for generalists, it is equally obvious that today's institutions of higher learning are *not* producing the inter- and intradisciplinary generalists society will need tomorrow (Royce, 1961b, 1964). And this includes psychology, despite its rich, multidisciplinary connections.

My final recommendation concerning the advancement of theory construction is the proliferation of psychology think tanks, both inside and outside the groves of academe. Most think tanks, especially those established within the administrative structure of the university, are relatively inexpensive to maintain, since there are few hardware and software needs beyond the key personnel who constitute the core group. A natural cluster of related interests include (a) theory construction, (b) the philosophy of psychology, and (c) the history of psychology. A given think tank can focus on any combination of these broad interests, or it can specialize in a variety of ways. An example of the latter would be an institute on perception or neuropsychology which includes all three of the area interests indicated above. In the case of specialized domains of investigation, such as perception or neuropsychology, it would probably make more sense to establish the theoretical program as a part of its overall operation, including empirical investigations. But we also need institutionalized units of broad scope—think tanks and/or programs on cognition, for example.[23] Or a think tank and/or

23. There are, of course, many programs and/or institutes devoted to the advancement of this or that aspect of psychology. My point, however, is that most of these approaches are long on data and short on conceptual analysis.

program covering all aspects of any one of these topics, or all three of them. As is generally known, there is one institutionalized doctoral program in the history of psychology at the University of New Hampshire under the leadership of Robert I. Watson, and although the University of Alberta program and center covers all three areas in principle, we have done very little with history. There are, however, a considerable number of programs in philosophic psychology looming on the horizon. These include a variety of humanistically oriented experiments at such places as Sonoma State College and West Georgia College, the phenomenologically oriented programs at Duquesne and Dallas, and the recently established interdisciplinary programs in the history and philosophy of the social and behavioral sciences at the State University of New York, Binghamton.

Toward an Indigenous Philosophy of Psychology

I have attempted to show that psychology is multimethodological, multivariate, multiepistemic, multi–world view, multiparadigmatic, multisystemic, multitheoretic, and multidisciplinary. In short, my position is that contemporary psychology is *conceptually pluralistic*, and further, that a philosophy of psychology cannot be characterized as truly indigenous unless it takes psychology's "multi" nature into account.

Psychology's pluralism is a complex product of history—the history of psychology per se and the history of psychology as part of world, but primarily Western, culture. A recent input into psychology from the broader culture in which it is embedded has been referred to as third-force or humanistic psychology. Just as earlier historical movements, such as behaviorism and psychoanalysis, came into being in reaction to limitations of the established theoretical paradigm of the time (introspective structuralism), so have subsequent intellectual movements come into being. However, while the main job of the twentieth-century psychologist was to demonstrate that scientific psychology was a viable enterprise, this goal has been so convincingly demonstrated that a twenty-first-century issue might well be whether humanistic

---

I would argue that such units would profit by the addition of formal programs (or at least the addition of one investigator with a formal background) on the theoretical, philosophical, or historical aspects of their enterprise.

Table 3

The Major Metatheoretic Trends in Scientific Psychology

Time Periods

	1860	1900	1940	1980
Epistemic Paradigm		Empiricism	Logical Empiricism	Integrative Dialecticism
			Logical Positivism	
		(————Empiricism–Rationalism————)		
Theoretic Paradigm		Introspective Structuralism		Cognitivism
			Mediational Behaviorism	
		Watsonian Behaviorism		
		(Functionalism)	(Structuralism-Functionalism)	

psychology is viable. The underlying epistemological question is whether psychology will build its conceptual foundations on the broadest possible "truth base" or whether its truths will be limited to scientific truths. Furthermore, the case can be made that most of psychology's foundational problems emerge from the fact that we do not have an articulated theory of man. For example, if we take man as machine, then a philosophy of psychology based on "science only" would be appropriate. If, on the other hand, we take man as "existential being," then a "philosophy of science only" approach is clearly inappropriate. And if we adopt the view that both scientific and humanistic approaches to man are relevant, then psychology becomes a crossroads for a dialogue between humanistic and scientific psychology and philosophy. This means that psychologists will be directly confronted with such hoary philosophic enigmas as the mind-body problem and determinism-indeterminism. These issues will have to be dealt with head on rather than avoided, as in the past. These and other relevant philosophic problems are intractable and overwhelming, but they are crucial to the direction our discipline will take. Furthermore, there are so many signs that the psychology zeitgeist is shifting toward at least regaining its "mind," if not its "soul," that the time is also ripe for at least initiating the conscious articulation of a more indigenous philosophy of psychology. I propose that each of the following will be required in such an endeavor: (a) a philosophy of science to accommodate scientific psychology, (b) a humanistic philosophy to accommodate humanistic psychology, and (c) a dialogue between scientific and humanistic psychology as precursor to a possible synthesis.

Toward an Indigenous Philosophy of Scientific Psychology. I have summarized the major metatheoretic historical and contemporary trends in scientific psychology in Table 3. According to this analysis, the dominant epistemology from psychology's scientific beginnings (1860) until around 1940 was highly positivistic, but the epistemic framework since 1940 has grown increasingly rationalistic (note the parentheses in Table 3). The primary theoretical paradigms within psychology during this time were introspective structuralism and behaviorism.[24] And the currently emerging epistemic framework has been described in Table 3 as integrative-dialectic. Because we are in the midst of the "new" psychology and philosophy, my descriptive terms may not be quite accurate. However, the important point about the metatheoretic term "integrative dialecticism" is the acceptance of the "constructive" or "interpretive" nature of scientific theory on the one hand, and the "dialectic" analysis of viable alternatives on the other hand. The "cognitive" counterpart within psychology reflects the commitment to "constructivism," but because of the superempiricist domination of the psychology zeitgeist (Royce, 1970a), contemporary psychology has lagged behind the more rational focus of contemporary philosophy of science. It is, therefore, difficult to say whether or not psychology is ready for the extensive conceptual commitment which a dialectic analysis of alternatives would require. However, if the major point of this paper is correct—namely, that psychology's underlying epistemology is becoming more rationalistic and, further, that psychology is conceptually pluralistic—then scientific psychology either will fail because of

24. The terms in parentheses, functionalism and structural-functionalism, represent potential theoretical paradigms which may eventually emerge in more articulate form. Thus, a case can be made that somewhat amorphous versions of both structuralism and functionalism have been crucial to the development of psychology since its inception. The hindsights of history will be necessary for a better vision of which currents of thought are surface ripples and which ones run deep.

Table 4

The Major Metatheoretic Trends in Humanistic Psychology

Time Periods

	1860	1900	1940	1980
Epistemic Framework		Intuitionism	Subjectivism	Interpretive Dialecticism
				(Metaphorism)
			("Inter-Subjective Perspective")	
Theoretic Framework		Verstehende Psychology	Phenomenology	Hermeneutics
			Existentialism	

conceptual inadequacy or it will eventually cope with the issue of viable conceptual alternatives. In short, I am suggesting that current developments will force psychology to make heavier commitments to theoretic and metatheoretic analysis and that such analytic-synthesizing efforts will involve some form of structural-cognitive-functionalism. Furthermore, as I see it, these conceptual developments in scientific psychology are definitely in the direction of a more indigenous philosophy of psychology.

Toward an Indigenous Philosophy of Humanistic Psychology. Although the situation is more blurred, we can also summarize the major metatheoretic trends in humanistic psychology (see Table 4). Here we see intuitionism and subjectivism as the early epistemic frameworks, *verstehende* psychology as the earliest theoretical counterpart, and phenomenological and existential psychology as more recent conceptual developments. With such apparently weak epistemological foundations as intuitionism and subjectivism, it is no wonder that humanistic psychology has had its "conceptual confusions" (see Royce, 1972). It is, of course, conceivable that some form of "intersubjective perspective" can emerge from the humanistic approach, but this claim has been difficult to demonstrate. It takes the form of "conceptual bracketing" in the case of phenomenology and "existential validity" in the case of existential psychology. However, the most convincing developments along these lines have recently emerged from the European continent under the banner of hermeneutics. Hermeneutics is concerned with textual interpretation, and, in fact, it is a term which originally had reference to biblical interpretation. Thus, although its recent applications (e.g., see Habermas, 1971; Radnitzky, 1970) have been primarily in such areas as history, the social sciences, and psychoanalysis, it has an important lineage in the humanities. "Metaphorism" has a similar humanistic affinity. In both cases there is a concern for transcending subjectivity—"universal significance" via the concrete case for metaphorism and via an interpretive dialectic for hermeneutics.

I have taken the view that failure to examine epistemological foundations has resulted in conceptual confusion in the writings of humanistic psychologists (Royce, 1972). For example, many humanistic psychologists talk about a "scientific humanistic psychology," which strikes me as a contradiction in terms, and according to my analysis, it certainly is a contradiction of epistemologies. This kind of linguistic usage blurs the epistemological differences between art and science, as in the following examples: "Exemplary biography, autobiography, and fiction, it seems to me, are human *science* at its best" and "advances in humanistic psychology, or a human science of psychology, will consist in perfecting the *art* of biography and autobiography" (italics mine) (Jourard, 1972, pp. 373–374). It is probable that writings of this sort reflect a concern for a more complete psychology—a psychology with more of the human being in it and less of the animal. (Rychlak's paper in this volume is an example of this view of humanistic psychology.) As I see it, the demand is to deal with the total complexity of our subject matter—but from a broadened conception of science. If this is an accurate portrayal, I see no need for the term "humanistic," for, in epistemic terms, these psychologists still want to do science (i.e., their endeavor "reduces" to science on the grounds of methodological-epistemological reductionism). Furthermore, there is nothing new in this kind of demand. It has been with us from the beginning of modern psychology, and in fact, psychology has, indeed, expanded its horizons in the direction of complexity in spite of the restrictive assumptions of radical behaviorism and other overly simplistic approaches. Thus, I see merit in the concerns of humanistic

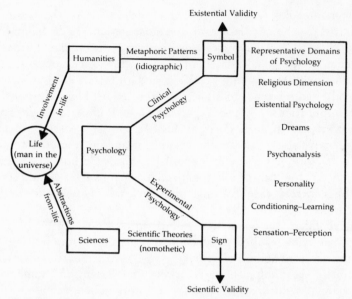

FIG. 9. Psychology at the crossroads (from J. R. Royce [Ed.], *Psychology and the Symbol*, p. 17, © 1965 by Random House, Inc. Used by permission).

psychology, but its conceptual foundations (logical, linguistic, epistemological) are in serious need of extended diagnosis and repair.

Another concern of humanistic psychology has to do with helping people. Thus we have transactional analysis, encounter groups, and self-actualization and gestalt therapies. But these are merely new therapies, part of the armamentarium of the clinical psychologist. Once again there is nothing new in principle. Just as there has been a historical trend calling for a broadening of the conception of science, so has there been a historical trend calling for more humane treatment of the person.

My argument is that an epistemological analysis of humanistic psychology shows that (a) to the extent it is, in principle, a scientific approach, "humanistic" psychology thereby reduces to science (and hence it follows that the term "humanistic" is simply not needed in the context of evolving a broadened conception of science); and (b) it would be more accurate to put the helping concern of humanistic psychology in the perspective of psychotherapy and clinical psychology, thereby seeing it in the context of the humane or humanitarian concerns of psychologists. In short, it is my view that the relevant epistemology of humanistic psychology is probably at hand in the form of interpretive dialecticism and/or metaphorism. If this is true, humanistically oriented psychologists should be exploring the methodological and conceptual implications of psychology's alliances with the arts and the humanities (Royce, 1965a, 1967, 1970a).

The Dialogue between Scientific and Humanistic Psychology. Although the philosophic issues concerning the arts and the sciences are old, they have not been adequately joined in the context of modern psychology. Furthermore, a thorough scientific-humanistic psychology confrontation will not be possible until there is an adequate articulation of their separate philosophies. However, the kind of analysis which is required can be briefly alluded to by way of Figure 9. On the left side of this figure we see the humanities as concretely involved *in* life, as opposed to scientific abstractions, which are derived *from* life. And parallel to the ultimate theoretical goal of science, we see that the humanistic disciplines are also ultimately beamed at making overarching statements (i.e., metaphoric-rational) regarding man-in-the-universe. However, and this is the main point, the humanities speak through a symbolic rather than a sign language. Hence, the emerging statements take the form of meta-phoric patterns or symbol systems rather than scientific theories, and the truth-giving quality of such statements follow the epistemological criteria of symbols rather than signs (e.g., see Figure 3 on p. 25 and note the fertility criterion of art and the criterion of existential validity for religion). As used in this context, the essence of the sign-symbol distinction is that the sign reveals a one-to-one correspondence (that is, A means B, and not C, D, and E), whereas the symbol provides a one-to-many relationship (that is, A may mean B, C, D, or E, or any combination thereof).

We can also juxtapose the major metatheoretic trends summarized in Tables 3 and 4 above (see Table 5). The major conclusion to be drawn from Table 5 is that the historical development of these two traditions is widely divergent in their theoretic and epistemic frameworks as well as in their content. The gap is particularly obvious for the late middle period, from about 1920 to 1960, for here we have the contrast between logical positivism and subjectivism on the one hand, and the contrast between behaviorism and

Table 5
The Metatheoretic Trends in Scientific–Humanistic Psychology

		Time Periods			
		1860	1900	1940	1980
Epistemic Framework	Scientific Psychology	Empiricism	Logical Positivism	Logical Empiricism	Integrative Dialecticism
			(———— Empiricism—Rationalism ————)		
	Humanistic Psychology	Intuitionism		Subjectivism	Interpretive Dialecticism
			(———— Intersubjective Perspective ————)		(Metaphorism)
Theoretic Framework	Scientific Psychology	Introspective Structuralism	Watsonian Behaviorism (Functionalism)	Mediational Behaviorism	Cognitivism (Structuralism-Functionalism)
	Humanistic Psychology	Verstehende Psychology	Phenomenology	Existentialism	Hermeneutics

phenomenology-existentialism on the other hand. However, one cannot help but be struck by a contemporary convergence, namely, the "dialecticism" of both the scientific and the humanistic approach, and the "constructivist" aspects of interpretive hermeneutics in the case of the humanistic approach and the current movement of scientific psychology toward cognition.

It is my view that psychology lies peculiarly at the crossroads between the two cultures, and further, that it is from this dialogue that a truly indigenous philosophy of psychology will eventually emerge, for such a dialectic contains the full range of complexities and contradictions of our subject matter.

The Emergence of Constructive Dialecticism. My answer to the question of what a more indigenous psychological philosophy will look like is now apparent. It will take some form of what I will call *constructive dialecticism*, where the term *dialectic* has to do with maintaining the tension between viable conceptual alternatives, and the term *constructive* refers to the "theoretical constructions" of investigators. The full realization that scientists "create" or "invent" potentially useful theoretical concepts and principles rather than "discover" them is one of the most important insights to emerge from the recent analyses of the philosophers and historians of science (i.e., Feyerabend, Kuhn, Hanson, Polanyi, et al.). But it is the growing convergence of these philosophic insights with the insights of such divergent philosophies as those of the Continental hermeneuticists (e.g., Habermas, Radnitzky) and the symbol-metaphor orientation of Langer (1942) and Cassirer (1953, 1955, 1957), along with the empirical findings of cognitive and epistemological psychology (e.g., see the summary by Royce & Tennessen, cited in footnote 15), which makes the commitment to constructivism so palatable. And it is the overwhelming reality of psychology's conceptual pluralism which makes the demand for some form of dialectic so compelling. Thus, the philosophy of constructive dialecticism takes its point of departure from the following:

1. Simplistic philosophies and theories are not adequate accounts of the overall complexity. Rather, a given perspective is limited to a subsegment of the complex totality.
2. Conceptual pluralism is taken as a given. Therefore, a major conceptual preoccupation will involve elaboration of the assets and limitations (e.g., the boundary conditions) of each of the several methods, epistemologies, paradigms, theories, world

views, and philosophies. In short, each viable approach should be exploited for whatever truths it can reveal.[25]

3. Apparent contradictions and paradoxes must be accepted, and in appropriate instances highlighted, as a necessary characteristic of mind and behavior. This point has to do with maintaining a proper tension and an exhaustive dialectic among the viable alternatives as opposed to the inappropriate subsumption or suppression of viable alternatives. However, a crucial aspect of this critical dialectic involves continued attempts to resolve such contradictions. Thus, the intent is to reach for unambiguous unification in the face of paradoxical contradiction.

Constructive dialecticism is seen as a philosophy which can deal with the multiperspectivism of mind and behavior. Epistemologically it implies an *integrative dialectic*—the attempt to sort out the complementary roles of each of the epistemologies of empiricism, rationalism, and metaphorism. In terms of psychological theory it implies an *interpretive dialectic*—the attempt to sort out the complementary roles of the many theories which deal with limited aspects of mind and behavior.

While it is doubtful that the end product of constructive dialecticism, or any other theoretical-philosophical approach in psychology, will be *one* integrated theory, it is anticipated that there will be a payoff in the direction of theoretical unification. For example, within the broad framework of constructive dialecticism it is anticipated that various manifestations of constructive-structural-functionalism will constitute a particularly viable segment of the dialectic synthesis. This prediction is based on the historical trends summarized in Tables 3, 4, and 5, as well as currently viable theoretical efforts (e.g., the varieties of cognitive psychology, biopsychological theory, developmental theory, and differential theoretical psychology).

Finally, it is appropriate to point out that fragmentation of different approaches such as scientific and humanistic psychology into separate disciplines, each with its indigenous philosophy, is a viable alternative. In fact, it has been convincingly argued that differential development and specialization of function is the usual result of growth—in disciplines of knowledge as well as the development of organisms (see Klüver, 1949). Furthermore, there is

25. See, for example, Mario Bunge's (1969) recent elaboration and defense of "integrated pluralism."

no question that intradisciplinary communication is easier when there is a common underlying metatheoretic framework and metalanguage. Thus, fractionation or separatism would at least simplify the situation within a given specialty. But conceptual pluralism would not thereby be eliminated, for the task of synthesizing our knowledge of mind and behavior would still have to be done, albeit under different specialist rubrics. While it is impossible to predict the future, it seems reasonable to suggest that fragmentation will increase to the extent the ratio of factual knowledge to conceptual synthesis decreases. Stated inversely, unless theoretical synthesis keeps up with factual tonnage, there will be further fragmentation. Whether psychology continues as a single discipline or fractionates is partly a political issue. The more important issue is the scholarly one of providing theoretical synthesis in this enormously complex domain.

RECAPITULATION AND CONCLUSIONS

I have argued that the psychology zeitgeist has been so focused on data that theory has been neglected, resulting in a general level of sophistication in theory construction within the psychology community of scholars which has not kept pace with our competence in experimentation and statistical-methodological analysis. Furthermore, if the current shift in the philosophy of science from logical empiricism to what I have called *theory-laden constructivism* constitutes a more adequate metatheory for doing science, then it follows that *scientific advancement is more dependent upon theory construction than was heretofore realized.* If these claims are valid, they carry with them several practical implications concerning the future of psychology and how we should train future generations of investigators. The major implication is that our present overcommitment to empiricism is blatantly in error, and that psychological scientists need to improve their *theory-construction skills.* This means, among other things, providing advanced training in empirically oriented theoretical analysis and synthesis, and providing (at least) an introduction to the philosophy of science and epistemology.

The essence of my thesis is contained in the title of this

address—namely, that contemporary psychology is multimethodological, multivariate, multiepistemic, multi—world view, multiparadigmatic, multisystemic, multitheoretic, and multidisciplinary. In short, my position is that contemporary psychology is *conceptually pluralistic*, and that an adequate unraveling of where we've been, where we're at, and where we're going will require a massive onslaught of theoretical synthesizing and philosophic analysis.

Finally, I have argued that the time is ripe for psychology to develop its own philosophy, but that the evolution of a psychological philosophy will not be truly indigenous unless it takes psychology's "multi" nature into account. I have suggested that we launch this effort under the banner of *constructive dialecticism*, where the term "dialectic" requires maintaining a sustained tension between viable conceptual alternatives, and where the term "constructive" refers to the theoretical "inventions" or "constructs" of investigators. Constructive dialecticism is seen as a philosophy which can deal with the multiperspectivism of mind and behavior. Epistemologically it implies an *integrative dialectic*—the attempt to sort out the complementary roles of the epistemologies of empiricism, rationalism, and metaphorism. In terms of substantive psychological theory it implies an *interpretive dialectic*—the attempt to sort out the complementary roles of the most viable theories of mind and behavior.

While it is doubtful that the end product of constructive dialecticism, or any other theoretical-philosophical approach in psychology, will be one integrated theory, it is anticipated that there will be a payoff in the direction of theoretical unification. For example, it is anticipated that various manifestations of *constructive-structural-functionalism* will constitute a particularly viable segment of the dialectic synthesis.

It has been said that nothing is more practical than good theory. Personally, I know of no greater scholarly challenge, nor am I aware of an endeavor with more potential for resolving so many of the (man-caused) ills of mankind, than our common effort to develop viable psychological theory.

REFERENCES

Bakan, D. Speculation in psychology. *Journal of Humanistic Psychology,* 1975, **15**, 17–25.

Berelson, B., & Steiner, G. A. *Human behavior.* New York: Harcourt, Brace & World, 1964.

Brunswik, E. The conceptual focus of some psychological systems. *Journal of Unified Science,* 1939, **8**, 36–49.

Brunswik, E. The conceptual framework of psychology. *International Encyclopedia of Unified Science,* 1952, **1** (10).

Brunswik, E. Historical and thematic relations of psychology to other sciences. *Scientific Monthly,* 1956, **83**, 151–161.

Bunge, M. The metaphysics, epistemology and methodology of levels. In L. L. Whyte, A. G. Wilson, & D. Wilson (Eds.), *Hierarchical structures.* New York: American Elsevier Publishing, 1969, pp. 17–28.

Butterfield, H. *The origins of modern science—ca. 1300–1800.* London: Bell, 1951.

Cassirer, E. *The philosophy of symbolic forms.* Vol. 1. New Haven, Conn.: Yale University Press, 1953.

Cassirer, E. *The philosophy of symbolic forms.* Vol. 2. New Haven, Conn.: Yale University Press, 1955.

Cassirer, E. *The philosophy of symbolic forms.* Vol. 3. New Haven, Conn.: Yale University Press, 1957.

Cattell, R. B. (Ed.) *Handbook of multivariate experimental psychology.* Chicago: Rand McNally, 1966.

Cronbach, L. J., & Meehl, P. E. Construct validity in psychological tests. *Psychological Bulletin,* 1955, **52**, 281–302.

Eysenck, H. J. Criterion analysis: An application of the hypothetico-deductive method of factor analysis. *Psychological Review,* 1950, **57**, 38–53.

Eysenck, H. J. *The biological basis of personality.* Springfield, Ill.: Charles C. Thomas, 1967.

Eysenck, H. J. *The structure of human personality.* London: Methuen, 1970.

Eysenck, H. J. *Eysenck on extraversion.* New York: Wiley, 1973.

Feyerabend, P. K. Problems of empiricism. In R. G. Colodny (Ed.), *Beyond the edge of certainty.* New York: Prentice Hall, 1965. Pp. 145–260.

Feyerabend, P. K. Against method. In M. Radner & S. Winokur (Eds.), *Minnesota studies in the philosophy of science,* Vol. 4. Minneapolis: University of Minnesota Press, 1970. Pp. 17–130.

Guilford, J. P. *The nature of human intelligence.* New York: McGraw-Hill, 1967.

Guilford, J. P., & Hoepfner, R. *The analysis of intelligence.* New York: McGraw-Hill, 1971.

Habermas, J. *Knowledge and human interests.* Boston: Beacon Press, 1971.

Hanson, N. R. *Patterns of discovery.* Cambridge: University Press, 1961.

Harman, H. *Modern factor analysis.* (2nd ed.) Chicago: University of Chicago Press, 1967.

Hoffer, E. *The true believer: Thoughts on the nature of mass movements.* New York: Harper, 1951.

Jourard, S. Men are like me, not like rats. *Contemporary Psychology,* 1972, **7,** 373–374.

Kaplan, A. *The conduct of inquiry.* San Francisco: Chandler, 1964.

Klüver, A. On the impending dismemberment of psychology. *Journal of Psychology,* 1949, **28,** 383–410.

Koch, S. (Ed.) *Psychology: A study of a science.* 6 vols. New York: McGraw-Hill, 1959–1963.

Koch, S. Psychology and the emerging conceptions of knowledge as unitary. In T. N. Wann (Ed.), *Behaviorism and phenomenology.* Chicago: University of Chicago Press, 1964. Pp. 1–81.

Kuhn, T. S. *The structure of scientific revolutions.* Chicago: University of Chicago Press, 1962.

Kuhn, T. S. *The structure of scientific revolutions.* (2nd ed.) Chicago: University of Chicago Press, 1970.

Langer, S. K. *Philosophy in a new key.* New York: Mentor, 1942.

MacCorquodale, K., & Meehl, P. E. On a distinction between hypothetical constructs and intervening variables. *Psychological Review,* 1948, **55,** 95–107.

Marx, M. H. *Theories in contemporary psychology.* New York: Macmillan, 1963.

Miller, J. G. Living systems: The organism. *Quarterly Review of Biology,* 1973, **48,** 92–276.

Morgan, C. G. On the algorithmic generation of hypotheses. *Scientia,* 1973, **108,** 583–598.

Mos, L. P., Royce, J. R., & Poley, W. The effect of post-weaning stimulation on factors of mouse emotionality. *Developmental Psychology,* 1973, **8,** 229–239.

Mos, L., Vriend, J., & Poley, W. Effects of light environment on emotionality and the endocrine system of inbred mice. *Physiology and Behavior,* 1974, **12,** 981–989.

Naess, A. *The pluralist and possibilist aspect of the scientific enterprise.* Oslo: Universitetsförlaget, 1972.

Nagel, E. *The structure of science.* London: Routledge & Kegan Paul, 1961.

Peirce, C. S. *Collected Papers.* Ed. by C. Hartshorne & P. Weiss. Cambridge, Mass.: Harvard University Press, 1931–1935.

Polanyi, M. *Personal knowledge.* Chicago: University of Chicago Press, 1958.

Poley, W., & Royce, J. R. Genotype, maternal stimulation, and factors of mouse emotionality. *Journal of Comparative and Physiological Psychology,* 1970, **71**, 246–250.

Poley, W., & Royce, J. R. Behavior genetic analysis of mouse emotionality: II. Stability of factors across genotypes. *Animal Learning and Behavior,* 1973, **1**, 116–120.

Popper, K. R. The logic of scientific discovery. London: Hutchinson, 1959.

Radnitzky, G. *Contemporary schools of metascience.* Göteborg: Akademiförlaget, 1970.

Rosenzweig, S. Schools of psychology: A complementary pattern. *Philosophy of Science,* 1937, **4**, 96–106.

Royce, J. R. Psychology in the mid-twentieth century. *American Scientist,* 1957, **45**, 57–73.

Royce, J. R. The search for meaning. *American Scientist,* 1959, **47**, 515–535.

Royce, J. R. The problem of encapsulation. *Journal of Existential Psychiatry,* 1961, **1**, 426–440. (a)

Royce, J. R. Educating the generalist. *Main Currents of Modern Thought,* 1961, **17**, 99–103. (b)

Royce, J. R. Psychology, existentialism, and religion. *Journal of General Psychology,* 1962, **55**, 3–16.

Royce, J. R. Factors as theoretical constructs. *American Psychologist,* 1963, **18**, 522–528.

Royce, J. R. *The Encapsulated Man.* Princeton, N. J.: Van Nostrand, 1964.

Royce, J. R. Psychology at the crossroads between the sciences and the humanities. In J. R. Royce (Ed.), *Psychology and the symbol: An interdisciplinary symposium.* New York: Random House, 1965. Pp. 3–25. (a)

Royce, J. R. (Ed.) *Psychology and the symbol: An interdisciplinary symposium.* New York: Random House, 1965. (b)

Royce, J. R. Concepts generated from comparative and physiological psychological observations. In R. B. Cattell (Ed.), *Handbook of multivariate experimental psychology.* Chicago: Rand McNally, 1966, Pp. 642–683.

Royce, J. R. Metaphoric knowledge and humanistic psychology. In J. F. T. Bugental (Ed.), *Challenges of humanistic psychology.* New York: McGraw-Hill, 1967. Pp. 21–28.

Royce, J. R. (Collaborator), with J. Havens (Ed.), *Psychology and religion: A contemporary dialogue.* Princeton, N. J.: Van Nostrand, 1968.

Royce, J. R. The present situation in theoretical psychology. In J. R. Royce (Ed.), *Toward unification in psychology: The first Banff conference on theoretical psychology.* Toronto: University of Toronto Press, 1970. Pp. 10–52. (a)

Royce, J. R. (Ed.) *Toward unification in psychology: The first Banff conference on theoretical psychology.* Toronto: University of Toronto Press, 1970. (b)

Royce, J. R. On conceptual confusion in humanistic psychology. *Contemporary Psychology,* 1972, **17**, 704–705.

Royce, J. R. The conceptual framework for a multi-factor theory of individuality. In J. R. Royce (Ed.), *Multivariate analysis and psychological theory.* London: Academic Press, 1973. Pp. 305–407. (a)

Royce, J. R. (Ed.) *Multivariate analysis and psychological theory.* London: Academic Press, 1973. (b)

Royce, J. R. Cognition and knowledge: Psychological epistemology. In E. C. Carterette & M. P. Friedman (Eds.), *Handbook of perception.* Vol. 1. *Historical and philosophical roots of perception.* New York: Academic Press, 1974. Pp. 149–176.

Royce, J. R. Epistemic styles, individuality, and world-view. In A. Debons & W. Cameron (Eds.), *Perspectives in information science.* Pp. 259–296. Leyden: Noordhoff, 1975. (a)

Royce, J. R. How we can best advance the construction of viable theory in psychology, Center paper in progress, 1975. (b)

Royce, J. R., & Buss, A. R. The role of general systems and information theory in multi-factor individuality theory. *Canadian Psychological Review,* 1976, in press.

Royce, J. R., Holmes, T. M., & Poley, W. Behavior genetic analysis of mouse emotionality: III. The diallel analysis. *Behavior Genetics,* 1975, **5**(4), 351–372.

Royce, J. R., Mos, L. P., & Kearsley, G. P. *Test manual for the psycho-epistemological profile.* Edmonton: University of Atlanta Printing Office, 1975.

Royce, J. R., & Poley, W. Acrophobia factor scores as a function of pole height. *Multivariate Behavioral Research,* 1976, in press.

Royce, J. R., Poley, W., & Yeudall, L. T. Behavior genetic analysis of mouse emotionality: I. The factor analysis. *Journal of Comparative and Physiological Psychology,* 1973, **1**, 116–120.

Rozeboom, W. W. Ontological induction and the logical typology of scientific variables. *Philosophy of Science,* 1961, **28**, 337–377.

Rozeboom, W. W. Scientific inference: The myth and the reality. In S. R. Brown & D. J. Brenner (Eds.), *Science, psychology, and communication: Essays honoring William Stephenson.* New York: Teachers College Press, 1971. Pp. 95–118.

Satinder, K. P., Royce, J. R., & Yeudall, L. T. Effects of electric shock, D-amphetamine sulphate, and chlorpromazine on factors of emotionality in inbred mice. *Journal of Comparative and Physiological Psychology,* 1970, **71**(3), 443–474.

Schmidt, P. F. Models of scientific thought. *American Scientist,* 1957, **45**, 137.

Shaw, Robert. Towards continued disunity in psychology. *Contemporary Psychology,* 1972, **17**, 75.

Skinner, B. F. *Science and human behavior.* New York: Free Press, 1953.

Toulmin, S. E. *The philosophy of science: An introduction.* New York: Harper & Row, 1960.

Wartofsky, N. W. *Conceptual foundations of scientific thought.* London: Macmillan, 1968.

Watson, R. I. Psychology: A prescriptive science. *American Psychologist,* 1967, **22**, 435–443.

Contemporary Behaviorism and the Concept of Intention

Willard Day
University of Nevada, Reno

*T*his paper has two parts. In Part 1 the central aim is to make a major contrast between *contemporary behaviorism,* an expression I shall use to refer to practices derived from the intellectual outlook of B. F. Skinner, and *methodological behaviorism,* by which expression I shall refer to a certain outlook toward the nature of scientific inquiry that has been widely accepted in professional psychology for the past forty years. In an overview of the current situation in psychology, I argue that contemporary behaviorism is only one of a number of areas of professional activity which severely challenge the reasonableness of the assumptive view generally respected as methodological behaviorism.

In a variety of ways people often distinguish between different "kinds" of behaviorism. "Classical" behaviorism is commonly distinguished from "neobehaviorism," or even "neo-neobehaviorism" (e.g., Koch, 1964), when the interest is on certain historical developments in modern psychology. "Metaphysical" behaviorism is often distinguished from "methodological" behaviorism, when the effort is to separate out what are taken to be offensive philosophical theses from talk which is otherwise commendable for its relation to research practices which are widely admired (e.g., Marx & Hillix, 1963). "Radical" behaviorism is distinguished from what is presumably "ordinary" behaviorism in a variety of ways which differ greatly depending on the particular verbal subcommunity involved (e.g., Day, 1969b, and Skinner, 1974, as opposed to Feigl, 1958, or Kaufman, 1967). However, in what follows I will make little systematic use of any of these distinctions, for even my interest in methodological behaviorism is not to make a contrast with the common objection to metaphysical theses.

In the second part of this paper I argue that, if it is true that at the moment we stand in a period of conceptual crisis in psychology, then it is appropriate to focus on the concept of intention in attempting to assess both the sources and the structure of that crisis. In an introduction to certain fairly recent developments within philosophy, I try to indicate the special contemporary relevance of an interest in the concept of intention. However, my chief aim in Part 2 is to clarify as explicitly as possible precisely how the conceptual practices of contemporary behaviorism actually engage interest in psychological phenomena generally taken to involve either intention or intentionality.

CONTEMPORARY BEHAVIORISM CONTRASTED
WITH METHODOLOGICAL BEHAVIORISM

An Overview of the Situation

One way to talk about the history of modern psychology is to force upon it at the outset, as I shall be doing, a distinction between structural and functional orientations. In this way we can impose upon the intellectual realities of the nineteenth century a contrast between, on the one hand, the experimental psychology of Wundt, and on the other, the thought of Brentano in Germany and of James in the United States, perceived even at the time as oppositional to Wundt in a variety of senses. Contrasts of this kind are, of course, frequently made in textbooks on the history of psychology. Thus we commonly speak of the contrast between the work of Wundt and of Brentano as a distinction between psychologies of content and of act, and of the contrast between Wundt and James as a difference between structural and functional approaches. I freely use such strong metaphors as "forcing" or "imposing" in speaking of the way in which any such distinctions are brought to bear upon the intellectual realities of a period, because I think they are helpful in keeping close to the surface our recognition that we can never bring to the interpretation of history anything other than the discriminations which our contemporary verbal community enables us to have, and that one should not be embarrassed by this fact.[1] I

1. For further discussion of at least one way of bringing behaviorist methodological considerations to bear on the analysis of historical material, see Day (1973).

might also only mention that one of the central values of true scholarship in history is the way it often functions to break down the rigid lines of demarcation that get established when distinctions formulated in textbooks act to shape the discriminative capacities of the ensuing verbal community.

A second contrast I shall ask the reader to bear deals with academic realities which we frequently conceptualize in such notions as the politics of academic power, the fashions and canons of professional respectability, and the dignity generally associated with conservative traditions. Also involved in the special case of psychology are notions of the inherent superiority of "science" to "philosophy," where science means conformity to certain respected traditions in one's approach to experimental work, and philosophy is regarded as a type of thinking intrinsically riddled with an unmanageable proportion of "speculation," into which the insufficiently wary is ever likely to fall. In a way I suppose I am talking about academic "Ins" and academic "Outs" within psychology, but that is far too simple. A good example of the kind of thing I am thinking of is the conflict between academic psychology and psychoanalysis in the first half of this century. On the one hand there was establishment psychology, with its tacit commitment to the respectability of experimental method. On the other there was the irrepressible popular conviction that there was something of enormous value in the Freudian and post-Freudian way of looking at things. The situation was unique in that an overwhelmingly significant, yet new, psychology had been produced by a tradition—the medical—over which the usual moves acting to protect the traditions of academic psychology had no control. When the inevitable "victory" of certain aspects of psychoanalytic modes of thinking could no longer be doubted in academic circles, efforts to "legitimize" the new discipline were unavoidable, as in such studies during the forties as Mowrer's (1940) efforts to demonstrate regression experimentally in the laboratory rat.

The contrast I want to make is between the conception of psychology as an experimental science that was forged and fought for by Wundt and his followers, and the "loyal" and respectable opposition within the profession to that conception. On the one hand there came to be carved out an establishment tradition in academic psychology, fundamentally identified with experimental psychology, which gradually came to be accepted as the backbone of the discipline. Thus we have come to have a core of professional values, preferences, orienting attitudes, and verbal clichés to which assent is generally given tacitly and from which too extreme a departure is not tolerated. On the other hand there have been the professional fashions, movements, schools, or what you will, that have the common property of being in opposition to the establishment outlook in one or another of its dimensions, even though at the same time they do not stray too far from the patterns of professional functioning tacitly endorsed by the Mother-tradition.[2] The heart of the Mother-tradition is of course commitment to the notion that psychology is, and always is to be, science. Consequently, deviations or innovations within the field generally attempt to legitimize themselves either by extensive discussions of the nature of "true" method in science or by criticizing the then reigning conception of what the nature of science is.

If you will allow me to draw a contrast of this nature, then I believe I am in a position to make the following claim, which will be useful to me as I proceed. If our professional history can be viewed in the light of the preceeding distinction, then I would claim that there has been only one significant readjustment of in-group or establishment professional values throughout the ninety-year history of our discipline. I would want to make an exception of the exciting developments that have taken place over the past ten years. However, the single, major readjustment I am speaking of was, of course, the massive reorientation of the profession toward its own subject matter that was accomplished, let us say, by 1940. Up through the time of Titchener the presumption of the professional establishment was that the focus of research should be toward constructing an account of the realities of conscious mental functioning. Thereafter, and the situation remains so to this day, the establishment presumption is that our subject matter is in at least some way publicly observable behavior. Thus it is not uncommon for us to agree that as psychologists we are all at least to *some* extent behaviorists, quite independently of the strong emotional reactions

2. A beautiful illustration of the reluctance of deeply innovative psychologists to stray too far from the establishment tradition is Carl Rogers's (1964) contribution to the Rice Symposium on Behaviorism and Phenomenology (Wann, 1964). In this paper Rogers sadly pays lip service to operationism and positivistic philosophy of science before an audience at least some of whom had reason to hope that he would take a strong, "revolutionary" stance for the "third force," then relatively new.

that we may have to the sorts of things "behaviorists" happen to be saying at the moment.

However, my purpose here is not primarily to call attention to how deeply the establishment commitment to experimental method has been connected with values historically derived from behaviorism as a tradition within the field. I would like instead now to call upon the first distinction I imposed upon this overview of professional history at the beginning of this paper, namely, the distinction between structural and functional orientations. If both the earlier German professional conceptualizations centering on mental functions and the subsequent largely American readjustment in terms of behaviorally oriented concepts are regarded as phases of a single commitment to a particular kind of science as a locus of professional self-identity, then that tradition must also be seen as essentially structuralist in nature. I argue that, whatever the particular set of concepts may be that are employed in trying to make a distinction between structural and functional orientations within the history of psychology, the basic values of the dominant tradition from which we find it difficult to stray too far in our thinking remain today largely and deeply structuralist.

This is not to say that all significant professional opposition to the early German structuralism of Wundt should be regarded as primarily functional in spirit. I say this in spite of the fact that the relations between Brentano's thought and contemporary functionalism are very important, and relations between what anyone would regard as functionalism and the work of the Würzburg school and the nineteenth-century psychologies of act are obvious. However I might say something here in particular about relations between functionalism and behaviorism, since they are commonly discussed (e.g., Boring, 1950, pp. 505 f., 642 f.; Misiak & Sexton, 1966, p. 345; Murphy, 1949, p. 223; Wolman, 1960, p. 32; Woodworth, 1948, p. 71). Much of this discussion, concentrating as it does on the widespread functionalist climate in this country at the time of Watson's objectivist stance, can be seriously misleading to the student of the professional situation in psychology in 1975.

The thing about behaviorism that has been endorsed by the professional establishment over the past thirty years is its objective stance, not its early historical connections with functionalism. The aspect of early functionalism which has been carried through to the present, and indeed is coming even now to play an increasingly significant role in contemporary thought, is the importance of Darwinian notions of natural selection and of the adaptation of species to the environment. The conspicuous example here is Skinnerian functional analysis; yet this orientation is, of course, profoundly antiestablishment. On the contrary, what I urge on the reader is that he bring to the fore of his thinking, as we proceed, the close ties between the legacy of behaviorism and *structuralism*. The structural similarities between structuralism and the standard image of behaviorism have been noted from time to time, but perhaps most trenchantly by R. S. Peters (1962). The context surrounding the following quotation develops the point.

> Thus Watson, in his main theoretical concepts, was very much in the old associationist tradition. He substituted "behaviour" for "consciousness" as his starting-point or subject-matter, analysed it into the Behaviouristic version of simple units, and postulated connections between the units built up in accordance with old associationist principles. His actual theory of behaviour became outmoded nearly as quickly as Descartes' theory of vortices, but his methodological advice, like Descartes', provided inspiration to many who followed him. [P. 698]

I have felt it necessary to make these observations on the history of our profession because I cannot escape the conclusion that at the moment psychology is in a situation which the historian of the future is likely to regard as of exceptional significance. I am not entirely sure that "crisis" is the best word to use to describe the current situation. Yet basically what I see is that the long-established and respected assumptive view of the inherent nature of the profession is being severely challenged by a rather large number of essentially independent developments. I am led to this perspective simply by looking at where currently in the field we clearly have a sense of vigorous accomplishment and new achievement. To me the most conspicuous of these seem to be (1) physiological research in nervous-system functioning; (2) research in animal and human ethology; (3) comparative research on higher primates; (4) the scarcely believable phenomenon of the humanistic psychologies; (5) the revival of interest in psychoanalytically derived therapies; (6) the heavy interest in group processes; (7) phenomenological psychology; (8) philosophical psychology, in the English sense; (9) contemporary behaviorism in the Skinnerian sense; and now (10) continental and dialectical psychology. Indeed the very nature of this symposium is symptomatic of the unusual professional situation of which I speak.

Yet my point is that this range of vigorous professional activity is not merely interesting in its own right. It seems to me that each of these activities in its own way constitutes a threat to something deep in the heart of psychology's concept of itself. My purpose here is of course to talk about *contemporary behaviorism*. But the very first thing I would want to say about contemporary behaviorism is that it is one of a variety of contemporary developments in the field which challenge the traditional and established set of values that have constituted the identity of the discipline from the outset. Yet it is also the case that frequently this multifaceted challenge to the traditions of experimental psychology is verbally articulated as an attack on *methodological behaviorism*. I shall have occasion shortly to discuss methodological behaviorism in some detail. However my purpose in this will be to try to set off methodological behaviorism very sharply from the vigorous current interest in Skinnerian thinking, a point of view to which I shall refer as contemporary behaviorism. As I proceed to contrast *contemporary* behaviorism with *methodological* behaviorism, please keep in mind that I am at the same time trying to clarify how contemporary behaviorism stands in marked contrast to the traditions of mainstream experimental psychology.

Methodological Behaviorism

In this section I do three things. First, I illustrate professional usage of the expression "methodological behaviorism" by extracting a certain amount of material from the relevant literature. Second, I briefly discuss a sample of previous verbal behavior of my own that directly concerns methodological behaviorism and that was emitted by me not too long ago in preparation for teaching a specific class. I do both of these things primarily in order to set up one pole of the major contrast drawn in this paper, namely, the contrast between what I call methodological behaviorism and what I call contemporary behaviorism. Third, I discuss in some detail certain methodological aspects of a book by T. A. Ryan entitled *Intentional Behavior*. In this, the reader should keep in mind that the analysis of intention is the central topic of this paper. I make use of Ryan's book in this section largely to illustrate a professional psychological analysis of intention that is interestingly and deeply representative of current methodological behaviorism.

Let me set the stage for sampling relevant professional usage of "methodological behaviorism" by asking the reader to attend first to the following commentary by Sigmund Koch (1964), which is taken from the introduction to his contribution to the Rice Symposium on Behaviorism and Phenomenology. I begin with this statement by Koch not only because, even though it is strongly expressed, I am deeply sympathetic with it personally, but also because it illustrates, more clearly than any other statement I know, why it is important to draw clearly the lines that distinguish methodological from contemporary behaviorism.

> Behaviorism has been given a hearing for fifty years. I think this is generous. I shall urge that it is essentially a role-playing position which has outlived whatever usefulness its role might once have had. . . . More than this, I think that for both metaphysical and methodological variants of behaviorism (and I am not convinced that the methodological variety is quite so "uncontaminated" with metaphysics as stereotype would have it), the following can be said: These are essentially irrational positions (like, e.g., solipsism) which start with a denial of something much like a foundation-tenet of common sense, which *can*, in the abstract, be "rationally" defended for however long one wishes to persist in one's superordinate irrationality, but which cannot be *implemented* without brooking self-contradiction. [P. 6]

I would agree with Koch in his assessment of methodological behaviorism as an inherently restrictive and unrealistic framework within which to conceptualize those research strategies that are actually productive in professional psychology. However, I would disagree with Koch that the central tenets of Skinner's thought should be included in this general indictment.

If I were to put Koch's statement at one extreme of a complex continuum of usages involving "methodological behaviorism," I would want to put something like the following remarks of Misiak and Sexton (1966) at the other.

> The issue of behaviorism was the subject of heated debates for about two decades. Its tenets were continually examined,

reviewed, and modified. New formulations were proposed, and thus new varieties of behaviorism developed. The naive behaviorism of Watson, or so-called "muscle-twitch psychology," was replaced by more sophisticated forms. But while the original form of behaviorism gradually declined and differences among behaviorists grew wider, the basic conception of an objective psychology of behavior gained strength and remained the common denominator of various groups. On this important point, it is well to note the words of Walter S. Hunter's *Autobiography:*

> The fundamental issue in behaviorism is not, and never was, the particular speculations of any one behaviorist—of Watson for example. Behaviorism is the point of view in psychology which holds that an adequate account can be given of psychological problems without reference to the term consciousness and introspection.

In this sense it is truly said that American psychology has become behavioristic. [P. 333]

Since this statement concerns the nature of the major change in professional orientation and values that is generally attributed historically to behaviorism, I regard the statement as a comment about methodological behaviorism, even though it does not contain that expression as such. However, the thing that I find so fascinating about this passage is concentrated in the last sentence: "In this sense it is truly said that American psychology has become behavioristic." This sentence has the form of a factual claim, the truth of which is strongly asserted. I doubt that very much of anything is actually *described* in this sentence. Yet I find the sentence striking because I read it as a strong expression of professional *values*. It seems to me that where what "is truly said" has an actual referent is in an area that has to do with widespread professional agreement about values and orienting attitudes. What it is that can be truly said of "American psychology" is not accurately identified by referring specifically to use of the term "consciousness" or to "introspection." What it is that can be truly said of "American psychology" that is historically derived from behaviorism is a particular set of orienting attitudes and values toward the nature and conduct of psychological research. It is this set of orienting attitudes and values that I have prominently in mind in speaking of "methodological behaviorism."

However, what strikes me so much about that single sentence is the simplicity, naturalness, confidence, indeed almost innocence, with which Misiak and Sexton appear to take for granted that it will be easily understood. It is as if they assumed that surely any psychology student who happens to read their book is by now clearly familiar with *one* way in which psychology has been influenced by behaviorism, namely, that the subject matter of psychology is properly behavior, or at least human behavior. It is as if it were *obviously* true. I regard the fact that it is still widely possible for psychologists to assume that it is *obviously* true that psychology is the study of behavior as an excellent illustration of the tenacious hold that methodological behaviorism continues to exercise over the mentality of establishment psychology at the present time.

Actually, in my opinion, it is *not* obviously true that the proper subject matter of psychology is the study of behavior. Introductory psychology students have to be trained with some persistence if they are actually to "get the idea." Psychological talk has now filtered down to the lay verbal community so that there is indeed little difficulty in getting beginning students to accept comfortably the intraverbal "Psychology is the study of behavior." Yet considerable training is required before it is "obvious" to them that "playing the piano," for example, is largely a behavioral matter.

Moreover, not only is it not obvious that the proper subject matter of psychology is the study of behavior; for anyone to attempt to describe what it is that *is* "obvious" to most psychologists in this way is to make a misdescription. It is not easy to say even what we mean by "behavior."[3] Behavior is presumably some characteristic of the functioning of organisms. Yet the contingencies which established the meaning of "behavior" for the psychological community had importantly to do with the conviction that it was not possible to do science with data that were not "publicly observable." When we say that it is obvious that psychology is the study of behavior, what we actually mean is that it is difficult to take anyone seriously who does not realize that one cannot do science unless he is

3. See, for example, Kaufman's discussion of problems involving the definition of behavior in the *Encyclopedia of Philosophy* (1967, p. 269 f.). This discussion is not an example of a philosopher quibbling about the meaning of ordinary words. The discussion takes its technical philosophical form for the sake of professional efficiency. If it were at all clear that psychologists speak of "behavior" in a coherent sense, the philosophers would be the first to recognize it.

going to be objective about it, where "being objective" means relying fundamentally on data that are in some sense publicly verifiable. This is methodological behaviorism. It implies a professional stance with respect to the philosophy of science, involving attitudes towards the proper way to carry out research. It is not at all obvious; it is very sophisticated. *It is also, in my view, quite mistaken.*

The issue is important to our concerns here because of the contrast I must make between methodological and contemporary behaviorism. As we shall see, Skinner sees at the heart of methodological behaviorism (or more precisely, associated philosophies of logical positivism and operationism) epistemological commitment to what he calls "truth by agreement" (e.g., 1974, p. 14; 1945, p. 294). I delay further reference to Skinner's use of the expression until the next section of this paper on contemporary behaviorism, where I go into the matter in some detail. However, my point here is that what we in psychology are likely to regard as obviously true as the legacy of classical behaviorism in methodological behaviorism is something that has to do with a particular stance taken toward what is "obviously" the only respectable way to do science in psychology. Yet this position is by no means *obviously* true. Even to be able to hold the view is to have been nicely sophisticated. I will later want to go on to argue that the perspective of *contemporary* behaviorism toward the analysis of behavior, which is epistemologically quite different from that of methodological behaviorism, is also not obviously true. On the contrary, it is even more sophisticated, specialized, and unique in its orientation toward "behavior" than the outlook we tend so much to take for granted at the present time.

About as respectable a source as one can find for the relatively recent professional socialization of psychologists in matters related to systematic issues are the textbooks *Systems and Theories in Psychology* by Marx and Hillix (1963, 1973). Let us take a look, then, at what these authors have to say about methodological behaviorism. The 1963 edition contains a glossary, where we find, in part, the following:

> Specifically, 1. *methodological* (empirical) behaviorism: the view that behavior is all that scientists can study and that strictly objective techniques are therefore required, as in all other natural science; 2. *metaphysical . . . behaviorism: . . .* [P. 380]

Actually, the entire glossary is dropped in the 1973 edition, yet both editions devote some five or six pages to discussion of methodological behaviorism in the body of the text. The treatment in the 1973 edition is substantially the same as in the earlier edition, there being slight changes in organization for increased clarity of exposition and additional quotations from more recent references. The authors discuss methodological behaviorism in a section of the chapter on behaviorism entitled "Watsonian Behaviorism: Criticisms and Replies." The following material extracted from it is relevant to our purposes here, where I provide the first paragraph only to give the context of discussion:

> On a somewhat different level of argument, Boring has also criticized Watson for his acceptance of verbal report (1950, p. 645): [Watson] wished to let in discriminatory verbal report when it was accurate and verifiable, as it is, for instance, in the observation of difference tones, and to rule it out when it was unverifiable, as it is when it consists of statements about the nature of feeling or about the impalpable contents of imageless thinking. . . . The admission or verbal report was a damaging concession, for it made it appear that behaviorism was asking only for verbal changes and not for a reform in scientific procedures.
>
> The modern behaviorist's answer to Boring's objection is simply agreement [sic.] The point basic to the whole behaviorist revolution was to use only verifiable, accurate data in psychology. The thing that furnishes such data is behavior and only behavior. Verbal behavior is behavior and constitutes valuable data if it is verifiable and repeatable. Not all behavior, and hence not all verbal behavior, furnishes useful data; the behaviorist is not obliged to accept data indiscriminately. [Pp. 190, 191]

In a text competitive with those of Marx and Hillix, B. B. Wolman (1960) discusses methodological behaviorism in the following way:

> It seems advisable to distinguish between the methodological approach of behaviorism and behaviorism as a theory of human behavior. The first insists on avoiding statements which cannot be proved by controlled experiments or observation. This kind of behaviorism must reject introspection, psychoanalysis, Rorschach, etc., as unscientific methods.
>
> One may accept the first sort of behaviorism without approving of the second. Watson tried to combine both and hence the

apparent weakness of his system. Not all data are observable, and nonobservable data are not necessarily the same as observable ones. Any scientific inquiry comes to grip with nonobservable data; Watson and Bekhterev went about it in rather a crude and naive way. . . . One must ask at this point: What is the methodological advantage of shifting away from one kind of unobservable facts in an area under consideration [as Wolman claims was the case with Watson and Bekhterev] to another unobservable group of facts without making sure that these two groups form a continuum? But Watson was not the first and maybe not the last to believe that inner secretion or electric waves are more self-explanatory than feelings or thinking and that physiological facts could be substituted for mental processes and everything would be explained in a scientifically satisfactory manner. [Pp. 84, 85]

Let me complete this selected sampling of professional usages of the expression "methodological behaviorism" by some quotation from a paper, "The Contribution of John B. Watson," by Gustav Bergmann (1956). Since Bergmann is a philosopher,[4] his usage can be expected to differ in certain respects from that of many psychologists, and in this case it is clearly connected with vested professsional interests on his part in the philosophy of science of the period. In the paper Bergmann not only endorses methodological behaviorism but *physicalistic* behaviorism as well. However, I display this usage of Bergmann's in particular because I will make reference to it later on in connection with my discussion of Ryan's approach to the analysis of intention. The fact is that Ryan simply accepts Bergmann's account of the nature of methodological behaviorism and finds it professionally unobjectionable.

Speaking very directly of methodological behaviorism as he sees it, Bergmann has the following to say:

The contribution was not, as probably Watson thought, his materialism or *metaphysical behaviorism*—i.e., that there are no minds—but, rather, his *methodological behaviorism.* Let me then for a moment disregard history and present what I take to be a correct and defensible statement of this thesis. Consider

4. For further examples of professional philosophical usage of "methodological behaviorism," see Sellars (1956, p. 314 f.) or Feigl (1958, p. 429).

three kinds of variables; call them behavioral, physiological, and environmental, respectively. Behavior and, therefore, the behavioral variables are physical. Smiling, frowning, talking, and so on, whatever else they may be or betoken, are certainly also physical events. . . . The nature of the physiological variables I shall take for granted. They describe, for the most part though not exclusively, the stuffings of the organism. The environment in which we move is to a very large extent social. This, however, means merely that it contains, in addition to other kinds of physical objects, other people. Thus the environment could in principle be described in terms of physical, physiological, and behavioral variables. Notice, incidentally, that I just used "physical" in a narrower sense which is quite customary. Notice, furthermore, that I did not claim that these three kinds of variables are independent of each other. Combine, next, Watson's good thesis, that there are no interacting minds, with the great Functionalist truism about process. What follows is the thesis of methodological behaviorism. It must *in principle* be possible to predict future behavior, including verbal behavior, from a sufficiency of information about present (and past) behavioral, physiological, and environmental variables. . . .

As I have just cautiously formulated it, methodological behaviorism, like Functionalism, has conquered itself to death. It, too, has become a truism. Virtually every American psychologist, whether he knows it or not, is nowadays a methodological behaviorist. [Pp. 269, 271]

Let me now ask the reader to look at a précis of a sample of my own verbal behavior that deals with methodological behaviorism. The reason that I do this is precisely *not* that I consider it in some sense to be superior to the samples of professional discussion of methodological behaviorism that I have given above. The verbal material simply differs in its control from the other samples of professional usage in an especially interesting way. The material was generated in about twenty minutes off the top of my head in an effort to pull together in a concise way what I had been saying about methodological behaviorism in a history of psychology class in April, 1974. I felt that what I had been saying had been somewhat over the heads of the students, and I needed something concrete that organized the material in a unified way, and which the students could be asked to study. Thus there is an innocence and an honesty about the material that I like. Actually, in the outline that I produced I was contrasting methodological behaviorism with classical, or Watsonian, behaviorism; but the précis which follows is restricted to a summary of the seventeen propositions originally listed in outline form under the heading "Methodological Behaviorism."

I have said that what follows is a précis or summary of the original outline. This means that the reader will not have as accurate an access to the factors which actually governed the way in which I put my conceptualization of methodological behaviorism together, as he would have if I were simply to reproduce the original outline. However, the outline itself is too cumbersome to have to deal with here. Even so, since the original outline is the dominant factor governing construction of the précis, what I regard as the interesting thing about the control of the commentary on methodological behaviorism is indirectly preserved. What I like about the original outline is precisely that it lacks those sources of control which are generally present in the preparation of material for professional publication. In writing for professional purposes one generally has a different sort of axe to grind than that which may be involved in simply trying to make one's understanding of something clear to students. The outline really was simply a statement of what I understood methodological behaviorism to be a year ago, and it was uninfluenced by any special reading on the topic such as that involved in preparation of this paper for the symposium. Thus its sources of control lie mainly in the realities of the course of my professional development in general and are consequently very complex and diverse. In this way they make contact more readily with the general patterns of professionalization which the readers of this paper are likely to have, than they would were the sources of control more specialized and technical.

Here is the précis:

To think in roughly the following way is to manifest what I take to be the heart of methodological behaviorism. Psychology is to a certain extent inherently behaviorist whenever it makes use of experimental (i.e., control-group) method, since the independent variable is always capable of being conceptualized as a stimulus, the dependent variable as a response. However, if one looks at it in a certain way, *all* psychology of whatever kind is inevitably the study of "behavior," since the only thing about people one can observe is what they do, that is, behavior. Consequently, psychological knowledge of any kind is always an inference from behavior. This explains why the central effort in psychological explanation is always to construct theories, even though they may not be formal. What one does with theories is to try to subject them to testing. The most important psychologists become important because of their theories.

Psychological phenomena are lawful. What theories really do is to codify the inherent lawfulness of behavior. In clarifying the lawfulness of human functioning, the major research problem is to design experiments in such a way that confounding variables are controlled. There is great interest in simply getting the facts of lawfulness straight first, by patient, plodding, experimental, laboratory labor. The precise relation between knowledge of such laws and the practical realities of *explaining* behavior is a matter of logical deduction from theories. There is little respectable interest in practical application of experimental findings. To be sure, it is all right to be interested in applied research, but the real psychology in it has to be extracted out of it.

It is taken for granted that psychology as science fits in with a more specialized "philosophy of science," where it is all at least crudely worked out by philosophers. We make contact with that philosophy of science in our commitment to operationism. What operationism boils down to is that one should clearly describe one's experimental manipulations and dependent measures. Yet operationism also means that professionally useful concepts should always be carefully defined. It is certainly reasonable to regard science as inherently concerned in some sense with "prediction and control," since any experiment gives you this.

Knowledge claims are not in the realm of science if they are not "in principle" capable of verification by others. Hence science is always inherently interested in public, not private, data.

Let me only call the attention of the reader to the way in which this summary mixes together beliefs and values which sometimes would be regarded as precepts from the philosophy of science and at other times as prescriptions for respectable conduct on the part of properly professionalized experimental psychologists.

Finally, in this section I will consider the treatment that T. A. Ryan gives to the problem of intention and intentionality in his book *Intentional Behavior* (1970). In view of the title of this symposium it is perhaps appropriate to call attention to the fact that Ryan's book carries the subtitle: *An Approach to Human Motivation*. My chief objective in examining Ryan's work at this point is to draw from it samples of his reasoning which exemplify methodological behaviorism as a current professional reality much more vividly than any of the preceding talk I have displayed that is *about* methodological behaviorism as a particular point of view. However, the reader should keep in mind that this material illustrates a methodological-behaviorist treatment of *intention*, the central topic of this paper.

My purpose here is to look only for certain things having to do with methodological behaviorism in Ryan's treatment of intentional behavior. However, for me to concentrate solely, as I shall, on certain aspects of Ryan's approach to the psychology of intention would be likely to give a misleading impression of the book to someone who has not read it. Perhaps I can correct the imbalance of impression created by my interest in only certain aspects of the nature of his approach by letting Ryan speak for himself regarding his chief aims in the book.

> The systematic study of intention as a potent controlling factor in behavior has been neglected. . . . The purpose of this book is to bring together as much dependable information as possible concerning the role of intention in behavior and its relations to other factors.
>
> A further aim is to develop a point of view or approach (not a theory) for organizing the information. Progress in this area, as in any other, must be based upon facts that can be obtained only by controlled research, either in the laboratory or outside in "real life"; we cannot depend upon casual observation and personal experience to give us dependable and representative information. Moreover, it is not enough to have a heterogenous collection of facts; we also need a coherent set of principles that fits the facts together, and the principles themselves need to be tested by further controlled research. Speculation and hypothesis that intentional and unintentional activities are different must be tested by finding ways of comparing them experimentally, of measuring or recording the characteristics of the activities, and of manipulating intention as an experimental variable. This book attempts to point out avenues and neglected areas of research through which these goals might be attained.

Let me call attention here to how clearly Ryan makes his commitment to methodological behaviorism. Progress is viewed as contingent upon "facts that can be obtained only by controlled research." Casual observation and personal experience are regarded as generating information which is neither dependable nor representative. Being in possession of the relevant facts is regarded as not enough: "We also need a coherent set of principles that fits the facts together." Once the principles are somehow extracted from the facts "the principles themselves need to be tested by further controlled research." Hypotheses are tested by making experimental comparisons, involving techniques of measurement and recording, and "of manipulating intention as an experimental variable." The commitment is clearly to *experimental* research.

In the preface of his book (pp. v–vi) Ryan continues to clarify its aims by specifying "the principle questions to be considered." For my own purposes, let me simply extract these questions from their context and give them numbers:

1. Is intention (along with similar terms such as task, purpose, desire, and goal) a legitimate and useful explanatory concept to be used in psychology?
2. If intention is used as an explanatory term, what is its relation to other terms and concepts used in explaining behavior?
3. Where does intention fit into a general scheme for explaining human behavior?
4. What other factors operate along with intention in controlling behavior?
5. What relation do they (factors such as needs, drives, and motives) have to intention?
6. How is intention itself formed or produced?
7. What is responsible for a particular intention being formed or a particular decision being made?

At least in the way I read the book, the questions do indeed receive answers in the body of the book. However, we should look at the *nature* of the way in which these questions are answered. In general, answers are given to these question within the book in either of two ways. The first three questions and the fifth are answered by argument and constitute the professional stance taken in the book that is of interest to us here as an example of methodological behaviorism. The fourth, sixth, and seventh questions are answered by an appeal to the status of experimental work in specific research areas, the relevance of which is apparent from "common sense," and we will not be further concerned with them. In many of these research areas—for example, post-Lewinian research on "task-tension" and the effect of interruption (p. 95 ff.)—concrete conclusions of substantial bearing on our knowledge of what intention is and how it works get lost in the shuffle of conflicting experimental findings and the details of efforts to exercise satisfactory experimental control. It seems to me that such a situation is highly characteristic of much of the current research in psychology, and I trust that it is apparent that I attribute this to the general expectations of psychological research that are characteristic of methodological behaviorism.

The first question Ryan answers by argument is, "Is intention (along with similar terms such as task, purpose, desire, and goal) a legitimate and useful explanatory concept to be used in psychology?" The answer is given in the preface itself: "The author believes that intention is a legitimate explanatory term, although it is not claimed that it is the only useful one nor that other approaches to explanation are erroneous and valueless." Let us sample his reasoning in the argument. Actually, the argument is preceded in the first chapter by a discussion of relations between the notions of causal explanation, prediction, and understanding (pp. 4–8), all of which can be taken as nicely illustrative of "reasonable" professional thinking tightly governed by the values of methodological behaviorism. However, the argument itself is equally illustrative, and is cast as an objection to S-R psychology:

> S-R psychologists have for many years insisted that terms involving conscious experience or awareness are not suitable explanations of behavior, on the ground that experience is not scientifically observable. Contrary to the S-R position, this book supports the use of experiential concepts in explanation. . . .
>
> It will be argued that there is no *a priori* reason for rejecting the use of any concepts so long as they refer to something which can be observed and manipulated in research. . . . In other words, we do not believe that there are logical, epistemological, or metaphysical reasons for rejecting these concepts as legitimate explanatory concepts. This is a radical thesis not only because it is opposed to the dominant S-R orientation in present-day psychology, but also because even "cognitive" theorists have not gone this far. [Pp. 8, 9]

The significant thing about this passage for our present purposes is that in it Ryan takes his stance against something—"the dominant S-R orientation in present-day psychology"—which many psychologists would regard as methodological behaviorism, yet I offer his book as one of the best examples of methodological behaviorism that I can find. If the reader has accepted the statement of the nature of methodological behaviorism presented above as the handout to my students, then I am confident he will find little defection from these standards on Ryan's part throughout his book. To my mind the important thing about methodological behaviorism is not any rigid prescription against the use of certain kinds of concepts; it is a matter of the way in which research problems, formulated in the concepts of ordinary language, are brought under investigation in the laboratory. Ryan believes that "the Watsonian approach and its descendants have not displayed notable success in explaining human behavior." Yet in my assessment the chances are that Ryan's approach can expect "notable success in explaining" intentional behavior in roughly comparable measure, and for essentially the same reasons.

Let me close this section by giving information concerning Ryan's own view of methodological behaviorism. Ryan severely challenges the adequancy of any account of intention that is couched in S-R language, and in so doing he regards himself as denying the possibility of any adequate behavioristic treatment. However, methodological behaviorism, taken in what is regarded as Bergmann's sense and as something that "has become a truism in present-day psychology," is viewed as essentially harmless.

> In much of the current writing which uses the S-R language there is little more than an acceptance of familiar terms. As Bergmann puts it, *methodological behaviorism* has become a truism in present-day psychology and merely means the acceptance of the thesis: "It must *in principle* be possible to predict future behavior, including verbal behavior, from a sufficiency of information about present (and past) behavioral, physiological, and environmental variables" (1956, p. 270). Since behavior means "smiling, frowning, talking, and so on" it could include "introspective reports" and would not rule out any point of view in experimental psychology. If using the S-R language means only this, then there is no general theoretical issue left. There are specific problems to be solved, of course, such as how well behavior can be predicted from the verbal reports of a subject under a given condition, and how much knowledge about the past history of the individual is needed to be able to predict a given kind of behavior, but these are empirical questions.
>
> In many instances, however, the use of the S-R language implies more than this general acceptance of "methodological behaviorism"; it implies certain kinds of hypotheses about principles of behavior or learning. [P. 77]

Contemporary Behaviorism

In this section I shall focus my discussion of contemporary behaviorism largely on the consideration of only one question: How does contemporary behaviorism differ from methodological behaviorism? Moreover, in dealing even with this question I shall restrict my major attention to only two of the most important differences.

However, first I want to say something about what I mean by "contemporary behaviorism." I am afraid that the expression can be misleading in a number of ways. One thing that contemporary behaviorism might mean would be the professional behavior of psychologists currently at work that has been significantly influenced by verbal and research practices derived from classical behaviorism. I do not use the expression in this way, for it would then include methodological behaviorism. Nor do I mean the behavior of professional psychologists currently at work who regard themselves as behaviorists. That would also be too broad, for it would include experimental and applied psychologists whose work is connected to associationist learning theory. Nor do I mean simply the thought of B. F. Skinner: that would be too narrow, since it would not take into account the relevance of an enormous amount of experimental and applied activity.

What I am trying to engage by the expression "contemporary behaviorism" has the dimensions of a social and intellectual movement. The movement exists largely within professional psychology, yet it extends (to a certain extent) out into the paraprofessional and lay community as well. Although the movement is highly controversial, it seems to me that it is growing, and that is why it is important to talk about it.

As something of a movement, it has a variety of facets. It is not consistently manifest in the behavior of any single individual. I also believe that it is correct to say that the movement has no codification within what one might want to call a firm "intellectual position" that is generally accepted. Perhaps the closest one could come to such a codification of contemporary behaviorism as a "position" would be Skinner's new book, *About Behaviorism* (1974). In any case, the conception of contemporary behaviorism that I have is strictly controlled by the personal interactions I have had with various representations of that movement.

One thing can be said definitely about the current movement in behaviorism: the movement is a product of Skinner's verbal behavior. But it is a misdescription to say that this product consists significantly of people simply believing "what is said" in Skinner's verbal behavior, although a certain amount of that undoubtedly occurs. The basic difficulty with mentalism (as it would be mentalistic, for instance, to think that anyone's verbal behavior, including Skinner's, has its constructive effect largely in its being believed) is that it is contrary to fact. Contemporary behaviorism is something that has happened to people when they have come in contact with Skinner's verbal behavior, or that of others significantly influenced by it. Being a contemporary behaviorist does not consist fundamentally of having certain beliefs or of holding a certain professional "position," although it is again true that many behaviorists rattle off chains of intraverbals that others respond to as tantamount to their "having" an apparently very rigid position. Mentalism is rampant among contemporary behaviorists; such mentalism is easy to generate by asking applied behaviorists to consider the ethical issues involved in certain practices associated with behavior modification. Behaviorists are always susceptible to mentalism where they face behavioral situations in which they have never specifically attempted to assess operating contingencies. It is only when people attempt to deal with behavior in the light of suspected controlling contingencies that they function as contemporary behaviorists.

Since contemporary behaviorism is a matter of specific people dealing (sometimes) with behavior in a particular way, and since it is not primarily a matter of stereotyped intraverbal chains that can be regarded as beliefs, reacting to what people have to say about behaviorism as a systematic intellectual position is perhaps not the best way to try to come to grips with contemporary behaviorism as a professional reality. It is true that I will be asking the reader to do just that for the remainder of this paper. Even so, let me point the reader toward published material that I regard as representative of contemporary behaviorist thinking at its best.

Whenever I am asked to suggest representative material of this kind I invariably think first of Skinner's book *Verbal Behavior* (1957), where the nontheoretical parts of it provide example after example of the interpretative analysis of contingencies of which I shall have occasion to speak later. Representative of the experimental analysis of controlling contingencies is Ferster's book, with Skinner, *Schedules of Reinforcement* (1957). What one needs to do with experimental work of this kind is not simply to "trust" or "believe" the specification of controlling relations identified throughout the book simply because they are made in association with conditions of experimental control characteristic of laboratory work. Instead it is important to focus on the interpretative behavior of Ferster and Skinner as it manifests its particular form of control by the perceptual properties of the rate-of-response curves under inspection.

To move away from Skinner's own verbal behavior, the paper "Chomsky's Formal Analysis of Natural Languages: A Behavioral Translation" by A. C. Catania (1972) is valuable because it puts the functional approach of contemporary behaviorism in explicit contrast to a structural approach to the same material. Goldiamond's important paper "Toward a Constructional Approach to Social Problems" (1974) is in my opinion one of the finest examples of behaviorist thinking that exists, since it shows how ethical issues, exceedingly difficult for most people to discuss without mentalizing, can be clarified largely through a display of operating controlling contingencies. The exceedingly important social and intellectual relevance of current developments in contemporary behaviorism are very clearly manifest in David Wexler's comment (1975) on the significance of Goldiamond's paper for the legal profession. The forthcoming proceedings of the Behavioral Analysis and Ethics Conference held at West Virginia University in June, 1975, are throughout an excellent example of the current social and intellectual relevance of strictly behaviorist thinking.

Let me finally call attention to the central importance of the most recent work of Skinner himself, the books *Beyond Freedom and Dignity* (1971) and *About Behaviorism* (1974). I have tried to discuss the importance of the former work in a review of my own (Day, 1972), and there is an instructive review of *About Behaviorism* by Roger Schnaitter (1975). Schnaitter's review is of independent interest here because it is itself an excellent example of behaviorist thinking, even to the point of manifesting insecurity in regard to the realities of behaviorist interpretative behavior.

However, the fact that we now have *About Behaviorism* from Skinner will play an important part in the structure of the remainder of this paper in a fashion that I need now to make clear. In dealing with the central topic of this paper, namely, the problems of intention and intentionality in behavior, it would be relatively easy simply to extract the relevant material from *About Behaviorism*, where fairly explicit discussion of these problems is available for anyone who will read it. Actually, I will want to do a certain amount of that for the assistance of the reader of this paper. But perhaps the most useful thing that I can do in considering contemporary behaviorism and issues related to intention is to look, not so much to Skinner's efforts at systematic formulation, but to the actual analytical practices which constitute contemporary behaviorism at work. Consequently my method in the remainder of this paper will be to approach the matter at two levels. First I will consider appropriate verbal material from Skinner which reflects his efforts at relevant systematic treatment. Then I will say what I myself have to say about the matter, which will involve discussion stemming from what I take to be the realities of the professional practices which actually constitute contemporary behaviorism as a vigorous movement within the field.

In this section I will focus my discussion on the following question: How does contemporary behaviorism differ from methodological behaviorism? Concisely, contemporary behaviorism differs very importantly from methodological behaviorism (a) in the nature of is stance in opposition to mentalism, and (b) in the nature of its treatment of private events. Let me turn at once to the issue of mentalism.

Differences with Respect to Mentalism. First, I will discuss Skinner's treatment of mentalism in *About Behaviorism.* Actually, in view of the centrality of Skinner's concern with mentalism, almost everything that goes on in the book sheds light in one way or another on his conception of mentalism. Basically, for Skinner, mentalism is taking feelings and inner states to be the causes of behavior. Skinner gives countless illustrations throughout the book of how we all call upon feelings and mental states to explain the facts of our daily and professional lives, but let me offer the following as representative. The passage is concerned chiefly with mentalism as it often gets involved in explaining the facts of operant conditioning:

> The view that mental activity is essential to operant behavior is an example of the view that feelings or introspectively observed states are causally effective. When a person replies to the question "Will you go tomorrow?" by saying, "I don't know, I never know how I will feel," the assumption is that what is in doubt is the feeling rather than the behavior—that the person will go if he feels like going rather than that he will

feel like going if he goes. Neither statement is, of course, an explanation.

There are other words referring to mental activities said to be more specifically required by behavior. People must "judge" what will or will not occur if they do or do not act in certain ways. The dog in the Pavlovian experiment salivates in anticipation of food or because it "expects" food. In operant experiments a rat presses a lever because it "anticipates" that food will be delivered when it does so. "In social learning theory the potential of the occurrence of a behavior is considered to be a function of the expectancy that the behavior will lead to a particular reinforcement or reinforcements and the value of these reinforcements in a given situation." [Pp. 69–70]

In another passage Skinner richly illustrates the range of concepts that can be involved in mentalism, since they are often regarded as the *causes* of behavior. The passage is also interesting because it has been constructed to produce a direct contrast with a behaviorist analysis:

A behavioristic analysis rests on the following assumptions: A person is first of all an organism, a member of a species and a subspecies, possessing a genetic endowment of anatomical and physiological characteristics, which are the product of the contingencies of survival to which the species has been exposed in the process of evolution. The organism becomes a person as it acquires a repertoire of behavior under the contingencies of reinforcement to which it is exposed during its lifetime. The behavior it exhibits at any moment is under the control of a current setting. It is able to acquire such a repertoire under such control because of processes of conditioning which are also part of its genetic endowment.

In the traditional mentalistic view, on the other hand, a person is a member of the human species who behaves as he does *because of* [italics added] many internal characteristics or possessions, among them sensations, habits, intelligence, opinions, dreams, personalities, moods, decisions, fantasies, . . . [and so on for a list of some sixty more terms]. [P. 207]

It is important to realize that it is not simply the use of any of the preceding long list of terms *per se* that involves one in mentalism. Mentalism becomes involved only when there are grounds for believing that the expression is used to serve the function of explanation. Thus when Skinner says in the first sentence of the preceding quotation, "A behavioristic analysis rests on the following assumptions," he is open to the charge of talking mentalistically in this instance. Actually, of course, there is no question here but that this sentence was emitted as a compositional device giving form to the construction of the paragraph, and not as a statement of any "belief" on Skinner's part that the practices of behavioral analysis involve "assumptions" (a term which might well have been included in the list) upon which the analysis "rests." Similarly, if the reader will look back over the material in this paragraph he will find the expression "grounds for believing that." Even though I have used the expression "grounds for believing" I have not given evidence of mentalism. The term "occasions" substitutes nicely for "grounds" within the expression, and "occasions" maps directly on to the behaviorist concept of discriminative stimulation, a type of variable to which Skinner refers in the first of the above paragraphs which manifests "the control of a current setting."

It is necessary here to call attention only to two other features of the conception of mentalism developed by Skinner in *About Behaviorism*. First, Skinner does not, of course, deny that mentalistic explanations are generally taken as successful explanations in our culture. The force of his opposition to mentalism is that it is "tragic" (p. 195) for us to do so. The objection is that although we generally regard mentalistic explanations as adequate and successful, it is inappropriate for us to do so, since they mistakenly identify the causes actually at work in governing our behavior. The position taken by Skinner in the book is that there are basically only two kinds of causes that operate in the determination of behavior, contingencies of survival and contingencies of reinforcement. The perspective of behaviorism as a scientific outlook that is developed in *About Behaviorism* is one that restricts applicability of the concept of causation to organism-environment interaction.

Another feature of Skinner's treatment of mentalism in *About Behaviorism* is that it contains an answer to this question: If mentalistic explanations do not really explain behavior, how is it that we have come to adopt the practice and continue to employ it? Briefly, Skinner's response to this question is that certain natural contingencies, largely irrelevant to what would be revealed in a causal analysis of the behavior at issue, have acted to shape these explanatory practices in us. Having been shaped by natural contingencies, mentalistic explanations are adaptive in various ways; however, when viewed in the light of the advantages for prediction, control, and interpretation which follow from a truly causal account, the essentially fictional nature of mentalistic explanations is apparent.

Let me comment only briefly on the issue of mentalism as it pertains to contemporary behaviorism as a reality of professional practices, rather than as an aspect of the integrated position set forth in *About Behaviorism*. As I have said before, it seems to me that most people who at times function most successfully as contemporary behaviorists can at other times be led into mentalistic practices. When they do so, of course, they fail to function as behaviorists. An important circumstance in which this often seems to occur is when behaviorists involve themselves in expounding or defending in professional situations what they take to be the behaviorist position. Instead of trying to call attention to whatever contingencies they believe may be operating in the situation at hand, it is easy to fall into practices of *explaining the reasons why* one should or should not approach a particular problem in a given way. If the reasons are generated self-consciously in knowledge of their likely controlling consequences, then there is little to quibble about. However, serious problems of inherent mentalism can be present for any behaviorist who *believes* his reasons, or who takes his reasons seriously to himself as legitimate *grounds* for his professional behavior. If one may not have a very clear notion of what the *causes* happen to be for his behavior, that is perhaps a particularly appropriate occasion for him to begin the effort to assess what they are. In no way can contemporary behaviorism avoid the challenge of identifying and assessing what the variables actually are that govern and control ongoing human behavior.

In sum, then, how does contemporary behaviorism differ from methodological behaviorism in its stance in opposition to mentalism? From the standpoint of contemporary behaviorism, methodological behaviorism is intrinsically mentalistic to begin with. This is because, in spite of the great concern of methodological behaviorism for experimental rigor and for theoretical sophistication in moving from some sort of established "base" in publicly observable data to whatever inferences are necessary to make contact with psychological reality, methodological behaviorism characteristically makes central use, in the work of professional explanation, of the concepts already dominant in the popular account of behavior. Contemporary behaviorism, on the other hand, objects to *any* use of popular psychological concepts for robustly explanatory purposes, and it is likely to regard any deviation from a strict concentration on the analysis of controlling contingencies as an invitation to mentalism. Consequently, Ryan's treatment of the problem of intention is, for contemporary behaviorists, an example *par excellence* of methodological behaviorism. In Ryan's formulations the intention at the outset is to show how the concept of intention can be productively regarded as a major factor in the causation of behavior.

Differences with Respect to Private Events. I turn now to a consideration of the second of the two major ways in which contemporary behaviorism differs from methodological behaviorism, namely, in its stance toward private events. First, I consider relevant material taken from *About Behaviorism* that is representative of Skinner's position. Second, I respond for myself, in connection with this issue, to the situation as I take it to exist in contemporary behaviorism as a professional reality.

Skinner views the treatment of private events as the central factor that distinguishes "radical behaviorism" (an expression Skinner uses to characterize his own point of view) both from mentalism and from methodological behaviorism. Actually the entire first chapter of *About Behaviorism* is set up to show how mentalistic psychology, structuralism, methodological behaviorism, and radical behaviorism involve different approaches to the problem of behavioral causation. The contrast of radical behaviorism with methodological behaviorism centers around the issue of private events. The following material is representative, and it contains the heart of the discussion:

> Methodological behaviorism might be thought of as a psychological version of logical positivism or operationism, but they are concerned with different issues. Logical positivism or operationism holds that since no two observers can agree on what happens in the world of the mind, then from the point of view of physical science mental events are "unobservables"; there can [thus] be no truth by agreement, and we must abandon the examination of mental events and turn instead to how they are studied. . . . [P. 14]
>
> Methodological behaviorism and some versions of logical positivism ruled private events out of bounds because there

could be no public agreement about their validity. . . . Radical behaviorism, however, takes a different line. It does not deny the possibility of self-observation or self-knowledge or its possible usefulness, but it questions the nature of what is felt or observed and hence known. It restores introspection but not what philosophers and introspective psychologists had believed they were "specting," and it raises the question of how much of one's body one can actually observe. . . . [P. 16]

Radical behaviorism restores some kind of balance. It does not insist upon truth by agreement and can therefore consider events taking place in the private world within the skin. It does not call these events unobservable, and it does not dismiss them as subjective. . . . The position can be stated as follows: what is felt or introspectively observed is not some nonphysical world of consciousness, mind, or mental life but the observer's own body. This does not mean, as I shall show later, that introspection is a kind of physiological research, nor does it mean (and this is the heart of the argument) that what are felt or introspectively observed are the causes of behavior. An organism behaves as it does because of its current structure, but most of this is out of reach of introspection. [Pp. 16, 17]

The reader may well inquire, then, what does all this amount to in practice? From a philosophical standpoint, this is basically an endorsement of central state materialism. Psychologically, this says that we can respond discriminatively to stimulation that arises within the skin, but that such discriminative responding can never itself be the *cause* of behavior. However, as I shall discuss in detail in Part 2 of this paper, private events can participate in the functional control of behavior, as when they set the occasion discriminatively for self-descriptive verbal behavior.

It is, however, hardly the function of *About Behaviorism* to concentrate on the role of private events in the control of behavior. The point is repeatedly stressed that private events *play no part* in the *causation* of behavior. It is also stressed that our knowledge of private events is singularly unreliable because of their relative inaccessibility to the verbal community which enables us to make the discriminations involved and to talk about our experiences. Even so the topic of private events is pursued in *About Behaviorism*—and it is simply the case that Skinner's discussion of the problem is pushed further in this book than in any other of his writings—in the second chapter, which essentially updates the analysis of how the verbal community enables us to talk about our experiences from Skinner's earlier treatment in the Symposium on Operationism (1945). However, most of the new discussion is in the penultimate chapter, "What Is Inside the Skin?," from which the following material is relevant to the issue of what all this amounts to in practice:

> *Use in Prediction.* A decision between radical behaviorism and the traditional view is perhaps more difficult if we simply want to predict behavior. What a person feels is a product of the contingencies of which his future behavior will also be a function, and there is therefore a useful connection between feelings and behavior. It would be foolish to rule out the knowledge a person has of his current condition or the uses to which it may be put. He may say that he does what he "feels like doing" without asking why he feels that way, and we may ask him to tell us what he feels like doing and use his answer without further inquiry, as we prepare for his behavior. In casual discourse the limits of accuracy noted in Chapter 2 are not necessarily serious, but we can nevertheless predict behavior more accurately if we have direct knowledge about the history to which feelings are to be traced.
>
> Attitudes, opinion, or intelligence, as states inferred from behavior, are also useless in control, but they permit us to predict one kind of behavior from another kind known to be associated with it, presumably because of a common cause.
>
> *Use in Interpretation.* When human behavior is observed under conditions which cannot be exactly described and where histories are out of reach, very little prediction or control is possible, but a behavioristic account is still more useful than a mentalistic one in interpreting what a person is doing or why he behaves as he does under such circumstances. A listener usually has no trouble in identifying the ideas a speaker is expressing, although he has no independent evidence, but if we are going to guess, it is more helpful to guess about genetic endowment and environmental history than about the feelings which have resulted from them. [Pp. 209, 210]

I find these last passages particularly interesting as we turn now to my own comments on the interests of contemporary behaviorists at large in the analysis of private events. In this connection, one thing is certain: the role of private events in the control of behavior has not been a focal area for extensive research in the field, although there are currently indications of increasing interest (see, e.g., Kanfer, 1973). That private events *do* function in the control of behavior is clear from the fact that we can talk about them: one way private events enter into the control of behavior is in the discriminative control of verbal behavior.[5] This is not to say that people's talk about their feelings is the most interesting aspect of their behavior that could be investigated. However, feelings are amenable to external manipulation. If one truly abandons an epistemology of "truth by agreement," then feelings are as observable as anything else: that is, they are capable of governing differential responding. However, the importance of the fact that feelings can enter into the control of verbal behavior lies in the fact that the challenge of their experimental investigation raises an enormously more important problem of the same kind: the investigation of the control of verbal behavior in general.

It has been my experience to find that one of the most embarrassing questions a contemporary behaviorist can be asked is how to account for the facts of most of Skinner's published verbal behavior. With the exception of the first book, *The Behavior of Organisms* (1938), and of course the work with Ferster on *Schedules of Reinforcement* (1957), Skinner's books rarely contain any experimental data at all. The problem was particularly acute with *Verbal Behavior* (1957), which was clearly not intended simply for use as a textbook. However, in *Verbal Behavior* itself Skinner spoke of the nature of the material in the book as an "exercise in interpretation." The expression stuck, and since that time the professional behaviorist community has increasingly tended to rely on the concept of "interpretation" in trying to find a place for the large amount of Skinner's talk that is clearly highly significant for behaviorists but which is far removed from controlled experimental investigation. However Skinner himself is not so loose in his conceptualization. Skinner speaks of the internal coherence of the verbal material in *About Behaviorism*, not as "interpretation," but as "philosophy." Nonetheless, there is clearly a considerable amount of what Skinner would regard as interpretation within the body of the book.

---

5. I am not thinking here of talk about, or expressive of, beliefs, attitudes, and opinions. Such expressions generally do not refer to occurrent events; hence they are not private events.

I think it is fair to regard as exemplary of interpretation the intellectual moves Skinner so frequently makes and speaks of as "translations." Directly illustrative of "translations," and indirectly of what I take Skinner to mean by "interpretation," is the following:

Multiple Translations. Conditions relevant to behavior are reported according to the circumstances in which they have been acquired, and this means that an expression may be translated in several ways. Consider the report "I am, was, or will be hungry." "I am hungry" may be equivalent to "I have hunger pangs," and if the verbal community had some means of observing the contractions of the stomach associated with pangs, it could pin the response to these stimuli alone. It may also be equivalent to "I am eating actively." A person who observes that he is eating voraciously may say, "I really am hungry," or, in retrospect, "I was hungrier than I thought," dismissing other evidence as unreliable. "I am hungry" may also be equivalent to "It has been a long time since I have had anything to eat," although the expression is most likely to be used in describing future behavior: "If I miss my dinner, I shall be hungry." "I am hungry" may also be equivalent to "I feel like eating" in the sense of "I have felt this way before when I have started to eat." It may be equivalent to "I am covertly engaged in behavior similar to that involved in getting and consuming food" or "I am fantasying eating" or "I am thinking of things I like to eat" or "I am 'eating to myself.'" To say, "I am hungry," may be to report several or all of these conditions. [Pp. 28, 29]

The practice of regarding the achievement in Verbal Behavior as largely "an exercise in interpretation" was initiated by the following statement in the book:

The emphasis is upon an orderly arrangement of well-known facts, in accordance with a formulation of behavior derived from an experimental analysis of a more rigorous sort. The present extension to verbal behavior is thus an exercise in interpretation rather than a quantitative extrapolation of rigorous experimental results. [P. 11]

The vagueness and insecurity within the contemporary behaviorist community about practices of interpretation undoubtedly cannot be traced to the lack of explicitness many readers are likely to sense in the quoted material. The difficulty can perhaps be pinpointed at the apparent vagueness of the expressions "in accordance with" and "derived from," that appear in the phrase "in accordance with a formulation of behavior derived from an experimental analysis of a more rigorous sort." However, in material that is too extensive to be reproduced here, there is what I regard as a sufficiently explicit description of the behavioral practices involved in "interpretation," both for a bird in a laboratory and a human outside the laboratory, on pages 88 through 90 of *Science and Human Behavior* (1953). Coincidentally, this passage constitutes the bulk of a section entitled, "Goals, Purposes, and Other Final Causes"; it is thus relevant to our primary concern with the analysis of intention, a topic to which I turn shortly. I make this reference here largely to encourage confidence on the part of contemporary behaviorists in the "respectability" of interpretative practices as an important and legitimate aspect of their professional behavior. Skinner makes moves in the organization of *About Behaviorism* that should have a similar effect. Throughout the book interpretation is treated on an equal footing with traditional canons of prediction and control, as in the following: "The things which make us happy are the things which reinforce us, but it is the things, not the feelings, which must be identified and used in prediction, control, and interpretation" (pp. 70, 71). The two paragraphs quoted above, one with the heading "Use in Prediction" the other with "Use in Interpretation," are preceded by a paragraph having the heading "Use in Control." I heartily recommend to the behaviorist who is skittish about the realities of behaviorist interpretation the pages cited in the index of *About Behaviorism* under "Interpretation."

Undoubtedly, the discomfort among behaviorists about interpretative practices is associated with their outspoken "faith" in science. Yet the conception of "science" popular among contemporary behaviorists is often an exceedingly narrow and rigid one, derived without question from the success of the procedures of exceptional environmental control that are necessary in the experimental analysis of behavior. There is less consensus among applied behavior analysts as to what the appropriate "standards" for "research" should be, and this is in part associated with their awareness of the centrality of interpretative practices in their own work. However in general the commitment is to the notion that there can be no research without explicit environmental manipulation and control. The connection with values associated with epistemologies of "truth by agreement," and hence methodological behaviorism, is obvious.

However, I think it is a mistake to concentrate too heavily on the interpretative aspect of *Verbal Behavior*. In my opinion the great achievement in the book lies in the extraordinary range of discriminations concerning verbal behavior which the book displays. The extraordinary thing about the book is Skinner's *sensitivity* to verbal behavior, not the occasional translations that it makes into possible reinforcement histories. The *power* of the book lies not in the interpretative "knowledge" that it contains, but in the work that it does upon the reader in extending his discriminative capacities with respect to what is going on in language. Skinner beautifully discusses his behavior in generating the book, not in the quoted remark on the book as "an exercise in interpretation," but in an added "personal epilogue" entitled "The Validity of the Author's Verbal Behavior." The following material from the epilogue is relevant:

> What effect may I presume to have had on the reader? . . . I have, as it were, put the reader through a set of exercises for the express purpose of strengthening a particular verbal repertoire. Stating the matter in the most selfish light, I have been trying to get the reader to behave verbally as I behave. What teacher, writer, or friend does not? And, like all teachers, writers, and friends, I shall cherish whatever I subsequently discover of any "influence" I may have had. If I have strengthened the reader's verbal behavior with spurious devices of ornamentation and persuasion, then he will do well to resist, but I plead not guilty. If I had been solely interested in building a verbal repertoire I should have behaved in a very different way.
>
> But a repertoire is not enough. The responses which I have tried to get the reader to make function by singling out events or aspects of verbal behavior which should make his subsequent behavior more expedient. I have emphasized certain facts and ignored others. . . .
>
> In many ways, then, this seems to me to be a better way of talking about verbal behavior, and that is why I have tried to get the reader to talk about it in this way too. But have I told him the truth? Who can say? A science of verbal behavior probably makes no provision for truth or certainty (but we cannot even be certain of the truth of that). [Pp. 455, 456]

What I am myself doing in the profession right now is trying to stimulate my fellow contemporary behaviorists to join me in taking steps to realize such a science of verbal behavior. The aim of such a science, to paraphrase Skinner's words above, would simply be to make our subsequent behaving with respect to verbal behavior more expedient. More concretely, the aim of such a science would be to bring the behavior of the scientist, especially in its discriminative aspects, more directly under the control of the behavioral facts. This is not much different from saying that if one messes around with something he is going to find out more about it. Another way of saying this is that the aim of science is *knowledge*, where I do not mean by knowledge anything more than repertoires of responding. Would such a science make any provision for truth or certainty? Actually, the way in which any scientific activity makes provision for Truth or Certainty is not at all clear, but I am sure that a science of verbal behavior would involve use of new and innovative methods which would not fit well the conception of science as exclusively a matter of manipulation and control. Such a science would approach interests in truth and certainty by means of an analysis of behavior. Skinner clearly points the way to such an enterprise in the following material from the chapter "Logical and Scientific Verbal Behavior":

> When new verbal behavior has been constructed, it must often be "confirmed." The process is not limited to constructed sentences. We confirm any verbal response when we generate additional variables to increase its probability. Thus our guess [sic] that something seen at a distance is a telescope is confirmed by moving closer until the weak response *(I think) it's a telescope* may be replaced by the strong *(I know) it's a telescope*. Similarly our guess that a rather unfamiliar object is a *kind* of telescope is confirmed if we find that it can be used as such. In using it successfully we provide additional stimulation for the unextended tact *telescope*. . . .
>
> Empirical science is only in part concerned with the construction and confirmation of verbal behavior. In broader terms, it is a set of practices which are productive of behavior. . . .
>
> An important part of scientific practice is the evaluation of the probability that a verbal response is "right" or "true"—that it may be acted upon successfully. . . . The verbal processes of logical and scientific thought deserve and require a more precise analysis than they have yet received. One of the ultimate accomplishments of a science of verbal behavior may be an

empirical logic, or a descriptive and analytical scientific epistemology, the terms and practices of which will be adapted
to human behavior as subject matter. [Pp. 425–431]

The steps I have taken personally toward such a science of verbal
behavior are modest indeed, mostly involving professional activity
at conventions. I have a relevant paper, delivered at an APA
symposium on private events in the control of behavior, that carries
the title "Methodological Problems in the Analysis of Behavior
Controlled by Private Events" (1971). I distribute copies of this
paper privately upon request. In it I distinguish two methods for
collecting data which we have been exploring at the University of
Nevada, Reno. One of these involves isolating a subject in an
experimental room, getting him simply to generate verbal behavior
in whatever way he will, looking for consistent patterns in the verbal
material he emits over a number of sessions, and then introducing
new stimulation into the situation to see if we can detect significant
deviation from the baselines previously established. The second
method involves getting a group of behaviorist students together
where we actually try to assess the variables controlling samples of
verbal material generated both by members of the group themselves
or verbal material picked up elsewhere. Then we make primitive
steps toward confirmation of the assessment by discussion. I also
regard the analysis of historical material (1973) to which I have
already made reference in a footnote as having methodological
significance; however I would imagine that most psychologists
would find the analysis in this paper too esoteric for their tastes. In
this paper I describe a very self-conscious attempt to do little more
than to place myself under the control of the verbal artifacts being
analyzed and then simply to respond under their control with the
discriminative repertoires that I have. However my assessment of
the current situation is that an increasing number of contemporary
behaviorists are coming to appreciate the need for explicit attention
to the problem of identifying variables in the control of verbal
behavior. Representative of this interest are the papers presented as
an informal symposium, "The Analysis of Verbal Behavior," at the
APA Convention in Chicago (1975) by Brian Lahren, Diane
Spooner, and Robert Hemenway, all of the University of Nevada,
Reno.

Be all that as it may, I close the first part of this paper with the
summary statement that in contemporary behaviorism, private

events are regarded as playing only a controlling, rather than a causative, role in behavior. Even this controlling function is regarded as contributing only in a relatively minor way to those major aspects of human functioning of most professional interest to psychologists, being obvious largely in the control of self-descriptive verbal behavior. Methodological behaviorism, on the other hand, generally deals with private events reductively in some sense, if at all. Professor Ryan's treatment of intention would be an exception to this rule, since he argues that under certain circumstances intentions can be directly observed. However, it is much more common for methodological behaviorism simply to take at face value psychological concepts which function in the lay vocabulary (e.g., beliefs, ideas, and opinions), to regard these concepts as referring to "private events," even though they rarely can be seen to have such ontological status, and then to deal with these concepts reductively through operational definition.

INTENTION, INTENTIONALITY, AND CONTEMPORARY BEHAVIORISM

My aim in this section is largely to help the reader appreciate why it is important at this time for a behaviorist to speak directly to contemporary professional interest in the concepts of intention and intentionality, for the two concepts are different. First, however, let me say something about the problem of getting into the relevant literature. In my opinion, the most efficient thing to do is to consult the entries under "Intention" and then under "Intentionality" in the relatively recent and utterly contemporary *Encyclopedia of Philosophy*, edited by Paul Edwards (1967). If the busy psychologist finds his appetite whetted by this experience, then he might want to proceed directly to the use of recent issues of *The Philosopher's Index*, an international index to the philosophical periodicals, published quarterly, and containing abstracts. In using the *Index* he should seek information under the same two headings: "Intention" and "Intentionality," under which references appear regularly in the *Index*.

In a number of ways, contemporary interest in the concepts of intention and intentionality stems indirectly from the *Philosophical Investigations* of Ludwig Wittgenstein (1953), a work of enormous

significance in contemporary philosophy.[6] The book *Intention*, by
G. E. M. Anscombe (1957), was one of the first examples of the new
direction taken in philosophy as a consequence of the problems
raised in the *Philosophical Investigations*, and in it we have a
germinal source for subsequent philosophical interest in what our
intentions are. In general, interest in the concept of intention is an
interest in what our intentions are, in their general characteristics,
and in the role they play in our behavior.

Interest in the concept of intentionality is quite different. One
aspect is that we are interested in the problem of reference. A central
concern here is the problem of how language involving words can be
taken to refer to things. Quine (1960, 1969), for instance, is led to a
view in which the ultimate achievement of reference is invariably
restricted to something shaped by cultural interactions with the
environment. Thus, when certain philosophers are interested in
intentionality they are primarily interested in the *nature* of
language. However, the focus of interest in this philosophy is
generally the problem of how we refer to *things*, and it is clearly of
interest whether we happen to regard the things that we actually

6. *Philosophical Investigations* bears important connections with contemporary Skinnerian behaviorism in work that is just now coming to the
fore (e.g., Zuriff, 1975; Day, 1969a). However, much more important is the
relevance of the *Philosophical Investigations* to methodological behaviorism
and the logic of the traditional values in experimental psychology. Very simply,
the connection can be put this way. The adoption of methodological behaviorism in the 1930s was accompanied by a general advocacy of operationism, which
in its turn was widely given partial justification by an endorsement of the
variety of logical positivism dominant at the time (see Boring, 1950, pp. 653 f.,
661 f.). While the values of the professional establishment in its new orientation
toward behavior as subject matter became deeply hardened in this intellectual
climate, technical professional philosophy went its own way, making what
psychologists regarded as exceptionally promising philosophy quickly out of
date. During the forties and fifties, and largely in England, there took place
in philosophy something that looked like a complete turning of things upside
down, so that what psychologists regarded in operationism as clearly most
respectable methodology came to be viewed among philosophers as clearly
most suspicious (see Urmson, 1956; Warnock, 1958). At the time, the change
in philosophical climate appeared most vivid in the thought of Wittgenstein,
who to all intents and purposes seemed completely to have reversed himself,
in the contrast between his earlier *Tractatus-Logico-Philosophicus* (1922) and
the later *Philosophical Investigations*. Yet the earlier *Tractatus* had been
enormously influential in the thinking of the Vienna Circle (see Passmore,
1967), which was the avenue through which logical positivism operated in
the formation of methodological behaviorism.

refer to as real or not. As we shall see, the very source of the problem of intentionality lies in a concern with the reality status of such things, for example, as unicorns, which we can think about but which we do not regard as being real.

Issues of this kind are precisely the sort of issues that are opened up by Skinner in *Verbal Behavior* (1957). This book of Skinner's engages the most vigorous current philosophical concerns at the outset by its immediate claim to have taken a radically new direction in abandoning conventional notions of reference (1957, p. 9). All this is of course very different from the matters of concern to methodological behaviorists, who hardly seem to suspect that there is any problem at all in what we normally take to be the referring properties of language.

The second aspect of interest in the concept of intentionality that I shall mention here stems from the claim by Franz Brentano that a criterion for distinguishing the mental from the physical could be found in intentionality. In a significant way Brentano held that only

---

Precisely in what way, and to what degree, the professional philosophical impact of the *Philosophical Investigations* can be taken to have implications in regard to the conduct of science remains an issue hotly debated to this day. So clear-cut confidence in this matter is out of line. The issue appears to engage philosophical thinking about science at every level. However, let me urge the interested psychologist not to fail to take a look at Bruce Aune's book, *Knowledge, Mind, and Nature: An Introduction to Theory of Knowledge and the Philosophy of Mind* (1967), particularly the last chapter, which is an overview of the situation. Psychologists might be tempted to move at once to the highly innovative direction taken by Harré and Secord in *The Explanation of Social Behaviour* (1972). However, much more representative of the kinds of implication that might be thought to be immediately obvious are those found in Charles Taylor's book, *The Explanation of Behaviour* (1964). The similarity in titles of these books seems intended to convey an interest in analogous implications of post-Wittgensteinian philosophy for the conduct of professional psychology. The import of Taylor's book is to manifest the inherent futility of behaviorism as an outlook in psychology, and indeed it is a valuable professional philosophical companion to Koch's (1964) contributions to the Rice Symposium, published in the same year. It seems to me that the force of Taylor's argument can be extended to the broad perspective that I speak of as methodological behaviorism in this paper with only slight extension. Considering my own purposes here, however, I should call attention to the fact that Taylor in his book does not attempt to deal significantly with the work of Skinner. For discussion of similar issues from a somewhat different perspective, *Between Science and Philosophy* by J. J. C. Smart (1968) is much to be recommended. See particularly his suggestions for further reading on pp. 19–20 and 119–120. For relevant hot debate, see Chihara (1973).

the psychological, as opposed to the physical, possessed the property of intentionality. In this he called attention to what he regarded as the common property of all psychological concepts, namely, their capacity to contain within them a reference toward something else. Brentano's view has led to philosophical activity that engages contemporary behaviorism in a number of ways. Basically the issue here is the extent to which behavior is inherently *purposive* in nature. Thus discussions of intentionality often have to do with what we mean by purpose, in what ways behavior can be regarded as purposive, and how we account for the purposive quality that is so apparent in much of human and animal functioning. Many important discussions center around the role of "reasons" versus "causes" in the explanation of behavior. Basically the issue here is whether what can be regarded as essentially *causal* accounts are adequate to the task of explaining psychological functioning, or whether we in some sense *always* need the reference to wants, motives, and beliefs (i.e., purposes of some kind) that we characteristically give in stating the *reasons* for what we do. For entry into this literature let me suggest the paper "Reasons and Causes" by Stephen Toulmin (1970), the paper "Actions, Reasons, and Causes" by Donald Davidson (1963), or the book *Content and Consciousness* by D. S. Dennett (1969).

Actually, one of the truly interesting things about the book *Intentional Behavior*, which we have already considered as a representative example of methodological behaviorism, is that in it Ryan attempts to engage this recent philosophical literature on intentionality, something which strikes me as a remarkably heroic thing for an experimental psychologist to do. Ryan specifically enumerates five philosophical problems related to intentionality and discusses their relevance to a scientific interest in a causal account of intention. Representative of the philosophical claims he considers are the following:

> An intention cannot be defined independently of the action itself, while the concept of cause involves at least the interrelationship between two independently definable events. An intention is a characteristic of an action, not a cause of that action. . . .
>
> Even if we assume that intention can be separated from the behavioral event we wish to explain, it cannot be a cause in that a cause must be a *sufficient* condition for what it explains. [Pp. 9, 10]

I cannot review here Ryan's treatment of the issues he discusses. In general, however, he develops the following position:

> I believe that these problems and objections are surmountable. The exact logical status of causal explanations may still be in doubt as Louch and others suggest, yet physics seems to be a healthy science in spite of these ambiguities. Psychology's problems are different and our methods of explanation must be different from those of physics, but we can proceed in a similar fashion to work out our own scheme of explanation and to test it by its ability to manage facts and make predictions, even if our philosophy of science is questioned by philosophers. [P. 10]

Reasoning of this sort is likely to seem both intelligible and reasonable to many successfully professionalized psychologists. Ryan's ideas do not involve esoteric or eccentric notions that other psychologists might want to take serious issue with; instead they represent the kind of things that in one way or another many psychologists would be inclined to say. In my view they thus cast light upon the realities of the values and beliefs which hang together loosely as main-stream professional thought and which constitute the sense in which I speak of methodological behaviorism in this paper. I also happen to believe that Ryan's discussion does not engage at all effectively the patterns of professional philosophical thinking which make these issues important to philosophers and relevant in their eyes to practices in our field. Yet I regard the fact that Ryan takes the trouble to speak to these problems as an indication of his intellectual integrity and responsibility.

A Statement "In My Own Words" of the Upshot of the Current Interest in Intention and Intentionality

My major aim in this section is to make a statement, in my own words, of what the range of issues are which, from a psychological perspective, are engaged by the current philosophical interest in the concepts of intention and intentionality. The conceptualization of intention and intentionality that I verbalize in this way will be the cluster of problems with which I am largely concerned to deal as a behaviorist in the remainder of this paper. What do I mean, however, when I say that this will be a conceptualization "in my own words?" I am calling attention to the character of the particular verbal subcommunity that has strengthened the material that will come out. Thus when I say what I have to say "in my own words," I will manifest operants presumably strengthened in a fashion similar to that involved when people ask someone who has been talking about technical material to say the same thing "in his own words." This means that I will be speaking largely under the control of the general literate public at large, and quite a bit less under that of the professional psychological and philosophical communities. Even so, the fact that I have done a certain amount of reading in the philosophical literature will, I hope, ensure that what I am "talking about" will be genuinely relevant to current philosophical concerns.

Let me introduce this statement by showing you how Aune and Chisholm introduce the topics of intention and intentionality in the *Encyclopedia of Philosophy* (1967). I do this in part to strengthen relevant operants on the part of the reader, who will then have to deal with the sense of what I say. I also do this so that the contrast between the philosophical talk and my own way of putting things into words may be appreciated. A psychologist is likely to find even the discussion in the *Encyclopedia* difficult to follow without much rereading. Yet I can hardly overstate the strength of my view that this encyclopedia is that place for psychologists to start who want to learn where the ball park is in connection with specific contemporary philosophical issues.

Aune (1967a) begins his discussion in the following way:

INTENTION. The concept of intention relevant to modern philosophy (in contrast to the medieval notion of the first and second intention of a term) is usually discussed under four chief headings: (1) expressions of intention—"I shall (am going to) do A in circumstances C"; (2) ascriptions of intention— "Jones has the intention of doing A and C"; (3) descriptions of the intention with which some action is done—"His intention in saying that was to embarrass her"; and (4) classifications of actions as intentional or as done with intention—"She shot him intentionally." That these headings are logically related may be seen in the schema "In saying 'I shall do A in C,' Jones expresses the intention that is ascribed to him by 'Jones intends to do A in C'; if having honestly expressed his intention, Jones then does A in C (without changing his mind), he does it intentionally, and the intention with which he does it is that of doing *A* in *C*." This schema also makes it clear that the word "intention" is ambiguous in the way, for example, that the word "belief" is ambiguous, for like "belief" the word may refer either to a state or episode (in this case, intending) or to the intentional object of such a state or episode—that is to that which is intended.

Disposition to action. The basic philosophical problem about intention concerns the sort of state or episode that an intention is and also the manner in which such episodes are related to intentional actions. A fair diversity of opinion has been generated by this problem, but there is marked agreement on one point—namely, that at least one of the things "expressed" by remarks of the sort "I shall (am going to) do *A* in *C*" is, other things being equal, a readiness to do, or try to do, things that (one believes) will realize the object or state of affairs intended. [P. 198]

Chisholm (1967) for his part, introduces his discussion of intentionality in the following way:

INTENTIONALITY. The term "intentionality" was used by Jeremy Bentham to distinguish between actions that are intentional and those that are not. It was reintroduced by Edmund Husserl in connection with certain doctrines set forth in Franz Brentano's *Psychologie vom empirischen Standpunkt* (1874). The word is now used primarily in this second sense.

Brentano wrote:

Every mental phenomenon is characterized by what the scholastics of the Middle Ages called the intentional (and also mental) inexistence of an object, and what we would call, although not in entirely unambiguous terms, the reference to a content, a direction upon an object (by which we are not to understand a reality . . .), or an immanent objectivity. Each one includes something as an object within itself, although not always in the same way. In presentation something is presented, in judgement something is affirmed or denied, in love [something is] loved, in hate [something] is hated, in desire something is desired, etc.

This intentional inexistence is exclusively characteristic of mental phenomena. No physical phenomenon manifests anything similar. Consequently, we can define mental phenomena by saying that they are such phenomena as include an object intentionally within themselves. (*Op. cit.*, Vol. 1, Book II, Ch. 1)

This passage contains two different theses: one, an ontological thesis about the nature of certain objects of thought and of other psychological attitudes; the other, a psychological thesis, implying that reference to an object is what distinguishes the mental or psychological from the physical. These two theses are the subject matter of the present article. It should be noted, however, that "intentionality" is also used in connection with certain other related theses of phenomenology and existentialism. [P. 201]

My own statement of the range of problems to which I shall be speaking will attempt to cover issues which, in my treatment of them, will allow philosophers to assess where contemporary behaviorism stands with respect to intention and intentionality. As philosophers, of course, they will want to look at my treatment in their own way. However, the context within which I will be speaking is much simpler than theirs. I will be speaking to people whose concern with the stance of behaviorism toward intention and intentionality is likely to involve the predisposition that a truly behaviorist outlook and any interest in concepts like intention and intentionality are intrinsically incompatible. Contemporary behaviorism is historically connected with methodological behaviorism and, behind that, to the classical behaviorism of Watson. Consequently, psychologists not deeply involved in contemporary behaviorism are likely to have such broad attitudes as that behaviorists believe that there are no such things as intentions, that to speak of intentions is to be mentalistic, that purposive explanations are teleological and hence unscientific, that intentions, wants, needs, and beliefs must be operationally defined to be professionally intelligible,[7] and so forth. In my own statement I will

7. I am not thinking here of the conception of operational definition which was advocated by Skinner in the Symposium on Operationism (1945) and was essentially nonreductive in nature. To my knowledge, Skinner's radically original conception of operationism has played no part in establishing the extensive talk within professional psychology about the virtues of operational definition, so very characteristic of methodological behaviorism. For current discussion of what operational definition amounts to for contemporary behaviorism, see Moore (1975).

be speaking to an audience which asks of behaviorism such questions as these, rather than being concerned with how Skinnerians "deal with" the specific issues engaged among philosophers in their own discussions of the topic.

What I will try to do in the remainder of this paper is to open up for discussion the question whether or not behaviorism has any place for intention and purpose, and if it does, precisely in what way. The statement that I have to make in my own words of the upshot, for psychological purposes, of the current interest in intention and intentionality consists of the following set of questions. In the concluding section of this paper I respond as a contemporary behaviorist to each of these numbered questions in order.

(1) Is it helpful under certain circumstances to say that we have intentions? (2) If so, what are these circumstances? (3) In such circumstances what are intentions? Are they occurrent, dispositional, or what? (4) Obviously there are problems with the concept of intention. What are they? (5) How is it that we most commonly explain what we do by stating our intentions? (6) Can intentions act as causes of behavior? (7) In what sense does a behaviorist look for causes in making a functional analysis? (8) Is it true that the best way to find out a person's intentions is simply to ask him? (9) Whenever we act, or do something meaningfully, do we in some sense do so intentionally? (10) If we are not conscious of any intention when we do things, are we then being motivated by intentions that are unconscious?

These questions will function to shape my discussion of intention in what follows. I trust the reader will keep in mind as I do so that I am speaking not as a philosopher, but as a behaviorist.

The Place of Intention and Intentionality in
Contemporary Behaviorism

Skinner's Discussion of Intention in About Behaviorism. In this part of the paper I confine myself to discussion of certain material concerning intention and intentionality in *About Behaviorism*. Skinner sets the stage for relevant discussion in the introduction to the book. Here he lists 20 "things commonly said about behaviorism," which represent in his view "an extraordinary misunderstanding of the achievements and significance of a scientific enterprise." Of the 20 he says, "They are all, I believe, wrong." Fifth in the list is the contention, simply expressed, "that [behaviorism] has no place for intention and purpose" (1974, pp. 4, 5). In the final chapter, which is a summing up of the book, Skinner returns to the 20 charges he regards as mistakenly applied to behaviorism, and he briefly states there the essence of his position with respect to them. His response to the misguided charge that behaviorism has no place for intention or purpose is as follows:

5. Evolutionary theory moved the purpose which seemed to be displayed by the human genetic endowment from antecedent design to subsequent selection by contingencies of survival. Operant theory moved the purpose which seemed to be displayed by human action from antecedent intention or plan to subsequent selection by contingencies of reinforcement. A person disposed to act because he has been reinforced for acting may feel the condition of his body at such a time and call it "felt purpose," but what behaviorism rejects is the causal efficacy of that feeling. [P. 224]

In *About Behaviorism* Skinner specifically discusses intentionality in a special section entitled "Purpose and Intention." The section occurs in a chapter broadly titled "Operant Behavior," and the structure of the book makes it clear that this chapter functions as an introduction to the whole field of study that is of concern primarily to psychologists, in contrast with the preceding chapter, "Innate Behavior," of concern primarily to ethologists. Clearly everything in the chapter on operant behavior pertains in one way or another to interest in intention and intentionality; I will reproduce here the section "Purpose and Intention" in its entirety. I have numbered the paragraphs for my own use in what follows immediately.

[1] Possibly no charge is more often leveled against behaviorism or a science of behavior than that it cannot deal with purpose or intention. A stimulus-response formula [as in associative learning theory] has no answer, but *operant behavior is the very field of purpose and intention. By its nature* it is directed toward the future: a person acts *in order that* something will happen, and the order is temporal. "Purpose" was once commonly used as a verb, as we now use "propose." "I propose to go" is similar to "I intend to go." If instead we

speak of our purpose or intention in going, it is easy to suppose that the nouns refer to things.

[2] A good deal of misunderstanding has arisen from the fact that early representations of purpose were spatial. The racer's purpose is to reach the goal, and we play Parcheesi with the purpose of bringing our pieces home. In the mazes in which purposive behavior was once studied, organisms moved toward the place where reinforcement was to occur. To use goal for purpose ("What is his goal in life?") is to identify it with a terminus. But it is meaningless, for example, to say that the goal—let alone the purpose—of life is death, even though the ultimate termination is death. One does not live in order to die or with the purpose of dying, whether we are speaking in terms of natural selection or operant conditioning.

[3] Goals and purposes are confused in speaking of purpose in a homing device. A missile reaches its target when its course is appropriately controlled, in part by information coming from the target during its flight. Such a device is sometimes said "to have purpose built into it," but the feedback used in guidance (the heart of cybernetics) is not reinforcement, and the missile has no purpose in the present sense. (Feedback may be used in a kind of explicit goal-seeking behavior to be discussed in Chapter 8.)

[4] Not all consequences are reinforcing, and much of the effect of those which are depends upon the contingencies. Psychoanalysts have often said that the gambler's true purpose is to punish himself by losing. It is almost always the case that the gambler eventually loses, and the behavior therefore has that consequence, but it is not therefore reinforcing. Gambling can be demonstrated in many other species and is explained by a special schedule of reinforcement to be noted in a moment. The ultimate loss (the "negative utility") does not offset the effect of the schedule.

[5] The Utilitarians supposed that it might be possible to measure quantities of pleasure and pain in such a way that the pleasure generated by socially objectionable behavior could be offset by a calculated amount of pain in the form of punishment. Unfortunately, the condition generated by a reinforcer and felt as pleasure is relatively insignificant in determining the quantity of behavior produced compared with the schedule of reinforcement.

[6] A valid distinction lies back of the statement "Motives and purposes are in the brain and heart of man, whereas consequences are in the world of fact." Remove the gratuitous physiologizing, and the point is made that motives and purposes are in people while contingencies of reinforcement are in the environment, but motives and purposes are at best the effects of reinforcements. The change wrought by reinforcement is often spoken of as "the acquisition of purpose or intention," and we are said to "give a person a purpose" by reinforcing him in a given way. These are convenient expressions, but the basic fact is that when a person is "aware of his purpose," he is feeling or observing introspectively a condition produced by reinforcement.

[7] Seeking or looking for something seems to have a particularly strong orientation toward the future. We learn to look for an object when we acquire behavior which commonly has the consequence of discovering it. Thus, to look for a match is to look in a manner previously reinforced by finding matches. To seek help is to act in ways which have in the past led to help. If past consequences have not been very explicit, we are likely to look in vague and unproductive ways. People can usually say what they are looking for and why they are looking in a given place, but like other species they also may not be able to do so.

[8] Many features of the debate about purpose in human behavior are reminiscent of the debate about purpose in evolution. As the *Columbia Encyclopedia* puts it:

> A still prevalent misunderstanding of evolution is the belief that an animal or plant changes in order to better adapt to its environment; e.g., that it develops an eye for the purpose of seeing. Since mutation is a random process and since most mutations are harmful rather than neutral or beneficial to the organism, it is evident that the occurrence of a variation is itself a matter of chance, and that one cannot speak of a will or purpose on the part of the individual to develop a new structure or trait that might prove helpful. (Pp. 55–57)

In the material quoted above I have added the italics in *"operant behavior is the very field of purpose,"* and in *"By its nature* it is directed toward the future." The italics of *"in order that"* are Skinner's, and the function is to get the reader to see the connection between the purposive expression "in order to" and usages of "order" in a temporal sense, as in "putting things in order," or "In what order did they arrive?"

Let me help the reader get into this material closely. I have found that people who do not follow Skinner's writing sufficiently closely often end up feeling that nothing very important has been said, or that it is mostly common sense riding on uncommon sense in a jargonistic way. Contrariwise, there are those who mentalize the argumentation as it proceeds and wind up with a hornet's nest of fictional distinctions. I will go over the paragraphs in numerical order.

The important matter in Paragraph 1 is the tight identification of purpose and intention with the whole range of operant behavior *in their nature*. In what sense intention is connected with operant behavior in its nature I will go into shortly. However one aspect of this connection is specified in this paragraph: the purposive expression "in order to" (then "purpose," and then "intention") is linked to the inherent temporality of behavior that *functions* in any way, or that achieves anything.

In Paragraph 2 a contrast begins to be developed between purposes and goals, and the spatiality of important uses of "goals" is capitalized upon. Racers go outward from their starting point, and Parcheesi players try to bring their pieces back. The food for rats in mazes is at the end of the maze. The inherent temporality of purpose—the topic of concern—is obscured when "goals" is used to mean "purpose." Goals and purposiveness (our problem here) are different.

In Paragraph 3 the central notion is that the confusion between goals and purposes can lead people pointlessly to wonder whether homing devices have purposes in some sense, or to try to deal with the inherent "purposiveness" of operant behavior by models patterned after electronic homing devices. The contrast between the concept of "control" and the purpose-cause nexus is important in the paragraph. The *goal*-reaching performance of homing devices does not engage the purpose-cause problem in behavior, hence neither do feedback psychologies such as cybernetics, because the *controlling* relation of such setting variables as discriminative stimuli which "guide" behavior is not the same as the *causal* function of reinforcement. The linkage between purposiveness and the causal concept of reinforcement begins to be made in this paragraph. There is this contrast: information-control is different from purpose-cause.

In Paragraph 4 the temporality inherent in purposiveness engages the concept of "consequences" in the sense of "what comes after" behavior. But many consequences of behavior have nothing to do with purpose: only sometimes is the purpose side of the purpose-cause nexus involved in the consequences of behavior, and that is when the cause side of the nexus is manifest in reinforcement. The *persistence* of behavior, which we connect with the conspicuous purpose evident when we really "try," is not purposive in the causal sense, because it is the product of the schedule of reinforcement, not the reinforcement itself (that kind of consequence that is genuinely related to purposiveness in its inherent causality).

This same concern with the *amount* of behavior we manifest conspicuously in "trying hard" is the focus of Paragraph 5. The argument does not advance in this paragraph.

In Paragraph 6, movement in the argument occurs at the clause "but motives and purposes are at best the effects of reinforcement." What we discriminate as motives and purposes in behavior does not manifest directly the inherent "purposiveness" of behavior, which lies in the causal efficacy of reinforcement as it is related to behavior, in time. The causal action of reinforcement changes behavior, and we are led into commentary on talk about the acquisition of "purposes," "motives," "intentions," and the like. The last sentence is not about purposiveness—or intentionality, in the philosophical sense—but about intention, also in the philosophical sense.

Paragraph 7 is largely a commentary on the behavior of searching, looking for things, trying to find things, and seeking things. It is important to mention this kind of behavior in particular because it is purposive in the descriptive sense. There is no further discussion of intentionality, in the philosophical sense, in the paragraph. The behavior of seeking is no more intentional than, and it is intentional in precisely the same manner as, any other piece of operant behavior.

In Paragraph 8 the reference is to the fact that in Skinner's position there are two distinct kinds of causal action, both involving contingencies: contingencies of survival and contingencies of reinforcement.

In the above material we have the Skinnerian treatment of the philosophical problem of intentionality, not of intention. It is important to note, in my opinion, that the field of psychological concern with operant behavior coincides precisely with that of the philosophical concern with intentionality. Any aspects of human functioning that raise the philosophical problem of intentionality are likely to be regarded by behaviorists as operant behavior. Where then, for Skinner, does the intentionality of behavior come from? Intentionality arises from the inherently functional nature of behavior. Behavior is followed by consequences. Some of these consequences (reinforcers) act biologically to change the organism, causing it to be more likely to emit similar behavior under similar controlling circumstances. Whenever behavior points forward, it always points forward to consequences that have been reinforcing in the past.

However, intentionality is connected with explanatory practices, and the "reasons versus causes" issue is raised. I trust it is clear that for Skinner there is only one kind of explanatory practice that can be regarded as interestingly explanatory, and that is *causal* explanation. Other kinds of explanatory activity, like the offering of reasons, function only in the service of whatever reinforcement is appropriate to a behavioral analysis of the situation. "We must remember that mentalistic explanations explain nothing" (p. 224). "It must be remembered that mental or cognitive explanations are not explanations at all" (p. 103).

In *About Behaviorism,* from which the preceding quotations are taken, there is a chapter entitled "Causes and Reasons"; however, it does not deal with the problem of intentionality except in the following section on "Reason and Reasons":

> Possibly the most admired cognitive or mental process is reason. It is said to be a thing of the mind which distinguishes man from the brutes. It was once thought of as a possession, "an essence of innate ideas, granted anterior to experience, by which the absolute being of things is disclosed to us." But by the eighteenth century, according to Cassirer, reason "is much less a possession than it is a mode of acquisition. Reason is not the area, the treasury of the mind, in which truth, like a minted coin, lies protected. Reason is rather the principle and original force of the mind, which impels to the discovery of truth and to the defining and assuring of it." The reference to an impelling force suggests that we are still a long way from a behavioral definition.
>
> We often speak of the consequences of behavior as *reasons*. We cite them in explaining our own behavior: "The reason I went to the bank was to get some money." The term seems more suitable than cause, especially if we have not understood

the process of selection, because anything which follows behavior does not seem to be in the right place to be the cause of it. Nevertheless, a reason which lies in the future is no more effective than any other future event. It does not become effective because a person "keeps it in mind" or "thinks of it" or "knows the probability that it will occur," for expressions of this sort merely reflect an effort to find a prior representative of a future consequence.

The consequences described or implied in advice, warnings, instructions, and laws are the *reasons why* a person takes advice, heads warnings, follows instructions, and obeys laws. People are not born with a readiness to follow advice or heed warnings. Stimuli having the status of advice and warnings must play a part in a long history of conditioning before a person can be induced to behave by being given reasons. To give a student reasons why something is worth learning is to point to possibly reinforcing consequences, but they may be long deferred, and the student's behavior will change as a result of the pointing only if the teacher has been part of effective contingencies in the past. When a therapist points to reasons why his patient's behavior is costing him friends, he can be said to "clarify a relation between behavior and certain aversive consequences," but the patient will change only if the therapist makes remarks effective in other ways. [Pp. 128, 129]

In these paragraphs Skinner is saying basically that the reasons people give, either by way of explaining why they have done something or why others should do something, often point to relevant contingencies. "When you give a person a reason, you describe contingencies. If he behaves for a reason it is because he is reacting to a description of contingencies. He will do so only if there are supporting sanctions. If he is responding simply because of the contingencies, another person may speak of his reasons, but he is responding simply because of the contingencies."[8] All this seems to be clear enough. However, it is important to keep in mind that by no means all reasons are "good" reasons, of the sort that Skinner is

8. Personal communication, December, 1974. For a more detailed discussion of these issues, see Chapter 6, "An Operant Analysis of Problem Solving," in Skinner's book *Contingencies of Reinforcement* (1969).

speaking of here. One of the reasons why the reasons and rationalizations people so frequently offer are notoriously unreliable is that they bear little relation to realistically adaptive contingencies, but reflect instead contingencies functioning largely in the service of self-protection.

With this I complete my discussion of Skinner's position as it bears upon the problems of intention and intentionality.[9] However, we are fortunate to have independent behaviorist discussion of issues tightly connected with the problems of intention and intentionality in a paper by G. E. Zuriff, "Where Is the Agent in Conditioning?" (1975). The paper is important because it has its sources not so much in intraverbal responding to Skinner's position as in the current professional practices which I have spoken of as the realities of contemporary behaviorism.

Contemporary Behaviorism and the Concept of Intention. I conclude this paper by responding to the set of questions concerning intention and intentionality which I raised earlier in this paper "in my own words."

9. It is difficult for me to write a paper on the technical aspects of Skinner's thought without making at least some reference to Verplanck's exceptionally able, insightful, and professionally constructive analysis of Skinner's *The Behavior of Organisms*. This analysis was prepared as a follow-through to the Dartmouth Conference, held in the summer of 1950, and is published in *Modern Learning Theory* by Estes, et al., (1954), a book which I regard as one of the singular achievements of professional psychology. The utility of Verplanck's analysis was obscured by Koch's monumental achievement in the analysis of Hull's theoretical work, which represented so clearly the methodological-theoretical aspirations of the period. As a historical document, *Modern Learning Theory* is of inestimable value in giving precise definition to the complex of values which we identify as the logical-positivist, operationist, and methodological-behaviorist influence on our discipline. However, with the widespread professional disenchantment with methodological behaviorism, and the concurrent increasing interest in Skinner's thought, Verplanck's analysis of *The Behavior of Organisms* assumes importance as a careful analysis of the very foundations of what I have called contemporary behaviorism in this paper. I also think it is important for contemporary behaviorists, especially those interested in methodological innovation, to study *The Behavior of Organisms* again, now, with Verplanck's analysis as a companion piece. Although the structuralist climate of the period prevented Verplanck from dealing explicitly with the inherently functional nature of Skinner's work, he does call attention to the affinities of Skinner's behaviorism with the position of Tolman and Lewin, generally taken by the professional community of the time as significantly "purposive" in structure (e.g., 1954, p. 307–308).

1. Is it helpful under certain circumstances to say that we have intentions? The behaviorist characteristically answers this question strongly in the negative. Briefly put, even though the behaviorist may acknowledge in his own way the inherent "intentionality" of behavior, this does not imply for him that man has intentions. The easiest way to comprehend the force of his perspective is to consider the situation as it pertains to animals somewhat lower than man on the phylogenetic scale. Consider the horse as a representative example. We do not regard horses as machinelike beings, any more than we do people. We regard the functioning of horses as in some sense "purposive," and hence we find the issue of intentionality nicely engaged in that species. Yet I do not believe that many psychologists view horses as having intentions, in any robust sense of that term. Most of us are aware of the conceptual inadequacies we face in interpreting animal behavior after the model of the mental life we commonly attribute to man, and we identify the danger of doing so as anthropomorphizing. It is to anthropomorphize to say that animals have intentions. Yet it is in precisely the same sense that the behaviorist says that humans do not have intentions. The simplest way to put the behaviorist's far-reaching objection to mentalism is to say that we should not anthropomorphize human behavior. The interesting thing about behaviorism, in my view, is that it succeeds, in its resistance to mentalism, in achieving a coherent perspective toward human functioning that avoids those very dangers we are so well aware of when it comes to anthropomorphizing the functioning of lower animals.

Presumably the horse goes about its business in a fashion that is amenable to investigation by the variety of techniques employed in ethological research. The behaviorist argues that the functioning of human beings should be studied in essentially the same way. In *About Behaviorism* Skinner restricts ethology to the study of contingencies of survival, from which contingencies of reinforcement have been separated out as the special province of psychology. However, this is to misdescribe the practice of ethologists. Ethologists are just as interested in the role of "learning" as anyone else, even though in the Skinnerian experimental analysis of behavior attention is given much more explicitly to the functioning of environmental contingencies in the control of behavior acquired in restricted laboratory situations. I think it is unfortunate that behaviorists, in their outspoken advocacy of science, so often turn to the experimental analysis of behavior as the model of relevant research rather than to the more flexible practices of ethologists, as a rule more conscious of the aim of giving an account of the functioning of an animal in its natural setting.

It may be granted that there is something wrong with looking at horses as having intentions. But is not the case different with humans? To be sure, people have their own way of going about their business, just as horses have theirs. However, people have extensive repertoires of talking, and these verbal repertoires can be connected with other aspects of their differential responding in a variety of ways serving a variety of functions. Differential reinforcement can make people conscious of environmental differences to which they respond differentially, although it is quite clear that only a very small portion of the environmental differences which actually control responding are the kinds of things we can normally attend to or be conscious of. Presumably the situation is much the same with respect to stimulation arising within our own bodies, consciousness of which we generally verbalize as knowledge of our feelings or our inner states. From time to time, and for certain people, the verbal community may function in particular cases to lead people to speak of certain feelings within them as "feelings of intention." However, most talk among humans of their intentions is not primarily under the discriminative control of various feelings within the body. Talk about intentions serves many different functions, ranging from making excuses to trying to impress people, and such talk is only quite rarely the kind of simple report analogous to what we do when we say "I have a sinking feeling in the pit of my stomach." If a person's interaction with the verbal community is such as to lead him to respond to certain inner feelings as feelings of intention, then so be it. As people go about their business they are often led to have all sorts of feelings, some more of interest to the community than others. Personally, I am inclined to find that people who spend a great deal of time talking about their feelings are likely to be tiresome.

However, since we find ourselves talking from time to time about our having intentions, it must in some sense be helpful for us to do so. The next question deals with this matter.

2. *If it is helpful under certain circumstances to say that we have intentions, then what are these circumstances?* One of the things we may mean when we regard things as *helpful* is that they are *adaptive.* Since it is on the whole at least *meaningful* to say that we have intentions, then in at least some sense it must be *adaptive* to do so. It is not so much that because we find it meaningful to say that we have

intentions it must therefore be adaptive for us to do so, as that because the expression exists in the language it must have some function, and be adaptive in that sense. For the behaviorist, what the function is of any particular talk about our intentions will vary from circumstance to circumstance and is a matter of empirical investigation.

It is important to recognize that the adaptive functioning of talk about our intentions is not restricted to situations tied tightly to use of the word "intention" itself. The functioning of talk about our intentions often does not differ substantially from the function of many motivational words in many different contexts, as for example when we speak of our wants, our needs, our hopes, our desires, our plans, and so forth. We need to give explicit attention to identifying the range of functions that are served by talk involving motivational expressions as it actually occurs in ordinary life. Once again we face the need for practice and experience in the assessment of variables controlling ongoing human behavior. Knowledge of the variables controlling ongoing verbal behavior is of course critical in this, if our interest is in human functioning. However, the problem here is not so much one of coming to know the variables controlling language as a special area of study as it is of coming to understand the functioning of language as just another aspect of ongoing behavior. To the behaviorist, all the problems we face in giving a professional account of what is involved in saying "Open the door, please" are equally present in giving an adequate account of someone's simply reaching for a door and opening it.

It would be possible for me to spin off the top of my head samples illustrating the range of circumstances in which we find it adaptive to talk about what our intentions are. It comes first to mind that we are a notoriously self-deceptive species. Undoubtedly the enormous long-range maladaptibility of our adaptive capacities to conceptualize our intentions for self-protective purposes is related to the fact that we so rarely think it appropriate to try to assess the reinforcers that are actually operating to make us say we have the intentions that we do. Frequently we seem to have feelings which some would verbalize as "feelings of intention" when changes in the environment suddenly alter the accessibility of reinforcement, as when we are forbidden to engage in patterns of behavior we had more or less taken for granted. We can also have similar feelings when sources of aversive control are suddenly removed and we realize what our intentions have been all the time. Skinner's writings are full of claims like these I have just been making, and they are typical of the behavioral "interpretations" he provides in making "translations" of common mentalistic terms. However, if Skinner-like "interpretations" and "translations" of mentalistic expressions can be haphazardly generated simply by thinking about specific behaviorial circumstances in which such expressions occur, then the time is all the more clearly ripe for systematic efforts to bring the analysis of such circumstances self-consciously under explicit empirical control.

However, for the behaviorist, even though talk about our intentions is always adaptive in the sense that it always serves one or another adaptive function, it remains largely maladaptive when the needs for a realistic assessment of what is actually taking place in human interaction are brought to the fore. Still, even in this sense it is not always maladaptive to speak of our intentions. Yet even when we do actually seem to find it helpful to hear some assessment of what someone's intentions are, it is helpful simply because the intentionalistic talk has altered the discriminative control over our behavior so that more productive behavior becomes possible for us. Mentalistic talk is not always maladaptive. It is sometimes meaningful in a sense that we find genuinely helpful. However, when it is so, I believe that it is helpful simply because the mentalistic talk has succeeded in manipulating verbal repertoires so that new discriminative capacities are set up.

3. *In such circumstances, what are intentions? Are they occurrent, dispositional, or what?* I have already argued that most of the time when we discuss our intentions, no intentions are actually "there." For example, we generate talk about our intentions when our ongoing behavior, guided by discriminative control and set up by reinforcement, is interrupted, often by an occasion for some explanation of what we are doing. In these situations an ontology of intentions is misplaced: instead, ontological interest should be brought to bear on the realities of the adaptive functioning of the intentional talk.

However, the feelings or inner conditions which from time to time can set the occasion for talk of "feelings of intending to do something" are occurrent. This means that they actually occur in us, and they are spoken of by behaviorists as part of the "private events" which, if responded to discriminatively, constitute aspects of our conscious experience. These feelings and inner conditions have the same ontological status as our experience of external stimulation;

that is, we are conscious of our feelings in precisely the same way that we can be said to be conscious of the environment. In all cases, what is involved is responding to stimulation: in one class stimulation arises in the environment, in the other, within the skin. Just as we do not respond to all stimulation from the environment, we do not respond to all stimulation arising from within the body. An important consideration is that in order for us to be able to be conscious of anything, differential reinforcement must be associated with the responding involved. Thus people can be expected to vary greatly in the extent to which they can "have" feelings of intention. Some people "pay more attention to," "are more responsive to," or "are more sensitive to" their feelings than others. How all this gets connected to talk about feelings is a matter of the practices of the specific verbal community in which a person functions. The feelings that control our talk when we say we have feelings of intention are not dispositional in nature. Interest in behavioral dispositions is connected entirely with the effects of reinforcement, or with the inherent intentionality of behavior, if you will.

4. *Obviously there are problems with the concept of intention. What are they?* To put the matter simply, people waste a lot of time, and get each other in too much trouble, by trying to make sense of behavior in terms of intention. People waste a lot of time worrying about what in the world the intentions of other people could be that would make them act the way they do. They also waste a lot of time trying to discover motives within themselves that would help them both understand themselves and proceed to do something about it.

If one wants to make sense out of the behavioral scene, as we all do, then we should spend our time thinking about the causes of behavior. That means that we should spend our time looking for operating contingencies of reinforcement. This does not mean taking people's intentional talk and simply "translating" it into reinforcers that might be teased out of it by a kind of intraverbal implication. One has to make an assessment of the contingencies that are *actually* operating. People's talk about their intentions may be largely under the control of aversive conditions, perhaps no longer critically present, which have set up self-deceptive repertoires that provide not even an indirect intraverbal clue to relevant reinforcement. Moreover, a great deal of professional talk about intentions seems to be largely intraverbal anyway. One must try to get to the root of the problem of what the operating contingencies actually are. How does one do this?

Frankly, what one has to do now, in view of the state of our knowledge of these things, is to guess. Some people make more informed guesses than others, and presumably the amount of experience one has had in assessing contingencies, either within the laboratory or outside it, is relevant here. However, in the social world where the confusion associated with efforts to find intentional explanations is the most painful to see, we cannot escape the business of making guesses about operating contingencies if we are to behave rationally and relevantly at the same time.

Once one has made his guesses, there may be opportunities at hand for various steps one might make at confirmation. To act on the basis of even very partially confirmed guesses is presumably better than to act on guesses with respect to which absolutely no attempt at confirmation has been made. I have advocated at many points in this paper professional effort toward developing something of a methodology that one might look to for help in the assessment of variables controlling ongoing behavior. However, in the social situations within which most of us function, the opportunity for confirming the guesses we make may be very small indeed.

My own views on this subject are so strong that I am inclined to think that almost anything else is better to do than to intentionalize human situations. One can, of course, resort to following rules as a guide to behavior, where we are clearly ignorant of controlling contingencies. Yet some rules are more productive than others, and different rules become relevant at different times. However, in view of the enormous proportion of behavior within our society that appears to have been set up in response to aversive situations, a good rule to keep in mind might be to try to do what one can to minimize whatever aversive elements can be seen in the social situation involved. Then, too, rather than trying desperately to "psychoanalyze" one's situation by resorting to whatever intentions one can read into it, there is much to say for simply behaving spontaneously. If one cannot see rationally what to do on the basis of an assessment of causes in which one has some confidence, then rather than intentionalize the situation, perhaps the best thing to do is to behave spontaneously, and let the consequences follow. Some of the consequences may be reinforcing in some way, and then behavior will change.

5. *How is it that we most commonly explain what we do by stating our intentions?* In certain cases our expressions of intending, wanting, needing, hoping, and so forth can point fairly directly to

reinforcers that are actually operating, as often in such usages as "I would like a good night's sleep," or "I intend to marry that girl," or "What I need is a good book." It is at least plausible that the widespread cultural practices of explaining behavior by offering what we regard as reasons for it may have had their origins in this way. However, the behaviorist regards the basic issue here as a largely empirical matter. That the problem is empirical follows from the view that explanatory practices are aspects of behavior and, as such, are shaped up within the culture as a product of natural contingencies. In any case, progress in discussion of this issue, critical in systematic psychology, would be greatly facilitated by systematic empirical investigation of the range of verbal practices we actually engage in by way of offering explanations of things. Piecemeal conceptual work along this line is undertaken from time to time among philosophers, yet the behaviorist would call attention in this work to how critically such analyses depend on contact with the realities of verbal practice. Explicit attention to the problem of assessing the control of such explanatory verbal practices could be expected to enrich deeply professional discussion in this area.

6. *Can intentions act as causes of behavior?* The behaviorist response to this question is direct: No. To answer this question in the affirmative would be to move outside the conceptual practices constituting the behaviorist perspective. This follows from the centrality of its opposition to mentalism. I might point out that, so far as I can see, when the behaviorist denies that intentions can act as causes of behavior he does not make use of a notion of cause that is in the least way esoteric or especially sophisticated. The same cannot be said of the concept of reinforcement. In my view, the extraordinary innovation contained in the Skinnerian perspective centers around the unusual and powerful conceptual work accomplished by the concept of reinforcement, with respect to which intensive conceptual clarification would be particularly productive.

7. *In what sense does a behaviorist look for causes in making a functional analysis?* A major difficulty here is that so few psychologists, other than those directly involved in behaviorist work, have an accurate conception of what the behaviorist means by the concept of "control," as in the expression "controlling variable." The aim of any functional analysis of behavior is the specification of controlling contingencies. Yet the relations which the behaviorist actually discriminates as controlling relations in observable behavior would not ordinarily be regarded as "causal" relations in any robust sense.

The situation is complicated by the moves behaviorists generally make in presenting their perspective as a systematic position. Characteristically, Skinner follows the practice of defining an operant contingency as a relation involving three terms: discriminative stimulation, response, and reinforcement. The nature of the interrelation among these terms is usually clarified by saying that "the discriminative stimulus sets the occasion for the response to be followed by reinforcement." Such a statement works well both as a description of a prototypical experimental arrangement in the laboratory and as a model for the functional interpretation of behavior in fairly simple situations. No conception of cause is significantly engaged in these paradigmatic usages.

However, in other contexts behaviorists often attribute robustly causal properties to reinforcement. Reinforcement is widely taken to have the power to cause behavioral repertoires to change, and claims as to the existence of relevant reinforcement are regarded as sufficient to do the real work of explanation whenever coherent explanatory accounts of behavior are attempted. The reliance upon a strongly causal conception of reinforcement for systematic purposes is particularly evident in the systematic position taken by Skinner in *About Behaviorism*, where the only causal agency relevant to behavioral matters is explicitly restricted to contingencies of reinforcement plus contingencies of survival.

However, the empirical work of behaviorism is achieved, not in the intraverbal efforts to give a systematic account of behaviorism as a philosophy of psychology, but in the realities of functional analysis itself. It is important to recognize the fact that here, in the interpretative and experimental practices of functional analysis, causal concepts are characteristically not brought into play. What is involved is the specification of antecedent occurrent events which are discriminated as bearing a "controlling" relation to responding, where the responding is then taken to bear a "functional" relation to some consequent state of affairs specified as reinforcement. The realities of these discriminative practices on the part of behaviorists as they actually engage in functional analysis clearly stand much in need of empirical clarification.

8. *Is it true that the best way to find out a person's intentions is simply to ask him?* In a sense, yes; in a sense, no. If one asks a person what his intentions are in a particular situation, what he says by way of reply can be controlled by any of a number of quite different contingencies that are conceivable, many of which may have nothing to do with what might easily be taken as the reinforcement toward

which the stated intention points. Only in the situation where we are dealing with occurrent states verbalized as intentions can a person "report" his intention "as he feels it." There is nothing epistemologically heavy in asking people to tell you their feelings, provided that they are actually feeling something and that you are interested in dealing with the verbal behavior as it happens to come out. However, one should keep in mind that even in those cases where one is interested only in feelings verbalized as intentions, the verbal comment on the feelings may or may not point to controlling reinforcement very well.

9. *Whenever we act, or do something meaningfully, do we in some sense do so intentionally?* Yes. For the behaviorist, action is connected to reinforcement, and in this sense behavior always engages directly the philosophical notion of intentionality, as I have discussed above. However, in any other sense than this, the behaviorist answers this question in the negative.

10. *If we are not conscious of any intention when we do things, are we then being motivated by intentions that are unconscious?* The behaviorist would reply: Most certainly not. We are not even motivated by intentions that are conscious. At issue here is the business of psychoanalytic psychotherapy. This is not the place to discourse on the conceptual equipment employed by psychoanalysts. However, the behaviorist would argue that whenever psychoanalytic therapy works, it does so because relevant operating contingencies have somehow been manipulated. The behaviorist does not disengage himself from knowledge of the mushrooming range of therapeutic practices which now so conspicuously play their own part in the current conceptual crisis in psychology, simply because they do not have the form of behavior-modification. There is new life now even in the most classic of the psychoanalytic approaches, and practitioners in these fields now approach their work with a sense of new confidence in their knowledge. For the behaviorist, any claims to genuine knowledge concerning human functioning are of intrinsic interest. The theoretical or semi-theoretical formulations of such knowledge claims provide an intriguing pocket of material within the larger problem area of the functional analysis of verbal behavior. To the extent that the knowledge claims have substance, the behaviorist would want to urge explicit clarification of the discriminative repertoires which, at least for him, must constitute the behavioral reality of whatever knowledge is involved. To the extent that such therapeutic ap-

proaches appear to be successful as avenues to treatment, then to that extent the behaviorist would want to inspect the actualities of the interaction between therapist and patient in an effort to pinpoint the manipulation of contingencies which, he would hold, must necessarily be involved.

Of particular interest to the behaviorist should be the practices of the humanistic therapies of the day, which as a rule advocate getting to know what one's feelings actually are, and openly and unselfconsciously expressing one's feelings as an avenue to personal health. By appearing in this way to emphasize the causal role of the knowledge of feelings in the control of behavior, the slogans of humanistic psychology seem to challenge directly the behaviorist's central objection to mentalism. To the behaviorist, the conspicuous growth of the humanistic movement indicates clearly that powerful reinforcers are being manipulated. What are they? The humanistic interest in facilitating the "expression" of sexual "feelings" is undoubtedly only a superficial place to start. It would seem more likely that interest in developing verbal discriminations concerning one's feelings is reinforced as a side effect of the increased availability of affectional reinforcers associated with humanistic practices, and possibly that contingencies based ultimately on the generally aversive repertoires so commonly involved in social interaction are in part reduced.

Yet the total elimination of aversive repertoires is no workable social goal, and it is unfortunate that the humanistic psychologies are taken so frequently to encourage rule-following behavior in accordance with the injunction, "Do your own thing." Responsible man has a "bit" of aversive control in him, just like a horse that can be ridden. Behaviorism does not deny the relevance of the concept of responsibility to an assessment of human affairs. Yet if social responsibility is in some sense important for successful social organization, the behaviorist insists that the concept is no more than a description of patterns of behavior. These patterns are capable of analysis in terms of contingencies actually operating in the control of a person's behavior, and they are based upon repertoires of responding set up by the action of positive and negative reinforcement. Similarly, there is a distinctly conspicuous component of aversive control in the behavior patterns we sometimes admire so much as manifestations of human dignity. But on this note, then, let me conclude my discussion of contemporary behaviorism and the concept of intention.

128

NEBRASKA SYMPOSIUM ON MOTIVATION, 1975

Anscombe, G. E. M. *Intention*. Oxford: Blackwell, 1957.

Aune, B. Intention. In P. Edwards (Ed.), *The encyclopedia of philosophy*, Vol. 4. New York: Crowell-Collier & Macmillan, 1967. Pp. 198–201. (a)

Aune, B. *Knowledge, mind, and nature: An introduction to theory of knowledge and the philosophy of mind*. New York: Random House, 1967. (b)

Bergmann, G. The contribution of John B. Watson. *Psychological Review*, 1956, **63** , 265–276.

Boring, E. G. *A history of emperimental psychology*. (2nd ed.) New York: Appleton-Century-Crofts, 1950.

Catania, A. C. Chomsky's formal analysis of natural languages: A behavioral translation. *Behaviorism*, Fall 1972, **1**(1), 1–15.

Chihara, C. Operationalism and ordinary language revisited. *Philosophical Studies*, 1973, **24**, 137–156.

Chisholm, R. M. Intentionality. In P. Edwards (Ed.), *The encyclopedia of philosophy*, Vol. 4. New York: Crowell-Collier & Macmillan, 1967. Pp. 201–204.

Davidson, D. Actions, reasons, and causes. *Journal of Philosophy*, 1963, **60**, 685–700.

Day, W. F. On certain similarities between the *Philosophical Investigations* of Ludwig Wittgenstein and the operationism of B. F. Skinner. *Journal of the Experimental Analysis of Behavior,*1969, **12**, 489–506. (a)

Day, W. F. Radical behaviorism in reconciliation with phenomenology. *Journal of the Experimental Analysis of Behavior,*1969,**12**,315–328. (b)

Day, W. F. Methodological problems in the analysis of behavior controlled by private events: Some unusual recommendations. Paper presented at the annual meeting of the American Psychological Association, Washington, D.C., September 1971.

Day, W. F. Beyond bondage and regimentation. *Contemporary Psychology*, 1972, **17**, 465–469.

Day, W. F. A behaviorist looks at the surviving work of Justin Martyr. Paper presented at the annual meeting of the American Academy of Religion, Chicago, November 1973.

Dennett, D. C. *Content and consciousness*. New York: Humanities Press, 1969.

Edwards, P. (Ed.) *The encyclopedia of philosophy*. New York: Crowell-Collier & Macmillan, 1967.

Estes, W. K., Koch, S., MacCorquodale, K., Meehl, P. E., Mueller, Jr., C. G., Schoenfeld, W. N., & Verplanck, W. S. *Modern learning theory*. New York: Appleton-Century-Crofts, 1954.

Feigel, H. The "mental" and the "physical." In H. Feigel, M. Scriven, & G. Maxwell (Eds.), *Minnesota studies in the philosophy of science*, Vol. 2. Minneapolis: University of Minnesota Press, 1958. Pp. 370–497.

Ferster, C. B., & Skinner, B. F. *Schedules of reinforcement.* New York: Appleton-Century-Crofts, 1957.

Goldiamond, I. Toward a constructional approach to social problems. *Behaviorism,* 1974, **2**, 1–84.

Harré, R., & Secord, P. *The explanation of social behaviour.* Totowa, N.J.: Rowman & Littlefield, 1972.

Hemenway, R. The controlling relationship between antecedent events and verbal behaviors. Paper presented at the annual meeting of the American Psychological Association, Chicago, 1975.

Kanfer, F. H. Self-regulation: Research, issues and speculations. In M. R. Goldfried & M. Merbaum (Eds.), *Behavior change through self-control.* New York: Holt, Rinehart & Winston, 1973. Pp. 397–406.

Kaufman, A. S. Behaviorism. In P. Edwards (Ed.), *The encyclopedia of philosophy,* Vol. 1. New York: Crowell-Collier & Macmillan, 1967. Pp. 268–273.

Koch, S. Psychology and emerging conceptions of knowledge as unitary. In T. W. Wann (Ed.), *Behaviorism and phenomenology.* Chicago: University of Chicago Press, 1964. Pp. 1–45.

Lahren, B. Analysis of the discriminative control of controlling variable statements. Paper presented at the annual meeting of the American Psychological Association, Chicago, 1975.

Marx, M. H., & Hillix, W. A. *Systems and theories in psychology.* New York: McGraw-Hill, 1963.

Marx, M. H., & Hillix, W. A. *Systems and theories in psychology.* (2nd ed.) New York: McGraw-Hill, 1973.

Misiak, H., & Sexton, V. S. *History of psychology: An overview.* New York: Crune & Stratton, 1966.

Moore, J. On the principle of operationism in a science of behavior. *Behaviorism,* 1975, **3**, 120–138.

Mowrer, O. H. An experimental analogue of "regression" with incidental observations on "reaction formation." *Journal of Abnormal and Social Psychology,* 1940, **35**, 56–87.

Murphy, G. *Historical introduction to modern psychology.* (Rev. ed.) New York: Harcourt, Brace & World, 1949.

Passmore, J. Logical positivism. In P. Edwards (Ed.), *The encyclopedia of philosophy,* Vol. 5. New York: Crowell-Collier & Macmillan, 1967. Pp. 52–57.

Peters, R. S. *Brett's history of psychology.* New York: Macmillan, 1962.

Quine, W. V. *Word and object.* Cambridge: Massachusetts Institute of Technology Press, 1960.

Quine, W. V. *Onotological relativity and other essays.* New York: Columbia University Press, 1969.

Rogers, C. R. Toward a science of the person. In T. W. Wann (Ed.), *Behaviorism and phenomenology.* Chicago: University of Chicago Press, 1964. Pp. 109–140.

Ryan, T. A. *Intentional behavior: An approach to human motivation.* New York: Ronald Press, 1970.

Schnaitter, R. Between organism and environment: A review of B. F. Skinner's *About Behaviorism. Journal of the Experimental Analysis of Behavior,* 1975, **3**, 297–307.

Sellars, W. Empiricism and the philosophy of mind. In H. Feigl & M. Scriven (Eds.), *Minnesota studies in the philosophy of science,* Vol. 1. Minneapolis: University of Minnesota Press, 1956. Pp. 253–329.

Skinner, B. F. *The behavior of organisms.* New York: Appleton-Century-Crofts, 1938.

Skinner, B. F. The operational analysis of psychological terms. *Psychological Review,* 1945, **52**, 270–277, 291–294.

Skinner, B. F. *Science and human behavior.* New York: Macmillan, 1953.

Skinner, B. F. *Verbal behavior.* New York: Appleton-Century-Crofts, 1957.

Skinner, B. F. *Contingencies of reinforcement.* New York: Appleton-Century-Crofts, 1969.

Skinner, B. F. *Beyond freedom and dignity.* New York: Knopf, 1971.

Skinner, B. F. *About behaviorism.* New York: Knopf, 1974.

Smart, J. J. C. *Between science and philosophy.* New York: Random House, 1968.

Spooner, D. The identification of controlling variables: An analysis of some recorded verbal material. Paper presented at the annual meeting of the American Psychological Association, Chicago, 1975.

Taylor, C. *The explanation of behaviour.* New York: Humanities Press, 1964.

Toulmin, S. Reasons and causes. In R. Borger & F. Cioffi (Eds.), *Explanation in the behavioural sciences.* Cambridge: Cambridge University Press, 1970. Pp. 1–26.

Urmson, J. O. *Philosophical analysis: Its development between the two world wars.* Oxford: Clarendon Press, 1956.

Verplanck, W. S. Burrhus F. Skinner. In W. K. Estes, S. Koch, K. MacCorquodale, P. E. Meehl, C. G. Mueller, Jr., W. N. Schoenfeld, & W. S. Verplanck, *Modern learning theory.* New York: Appleton-Century-Crofts, 1954. Pp. 267–316.

Wann, T. W. (Ed.) *Behaviorism and phenomenology.* Chicago: University of Chicago Press, 1964.

Warnock, G. J. *English philosophy since 1900.* London: Oxford University Press, 1958.

Wexler, D. The surfacing of behavioral jurisprudence. *Behaviorism,* 1975, in press.

Wittgenstein, L. *Tractatus-logico-philosophicus.* Trans. by C. K. Ogden. New York: Harcourt, Brace, 1922.

Wittgenstein, L. *Philosophical investigations.* Trans. by G. E. M. Anscombe. Oxford: Blackwell, 1953.

Wolman, B. B. *Contemporary theories and systems in psychology.* New York: Harper & Brothers, 1960.

Woodworth, R. S. *Contemporary schools of psychology.* (Rev. ed.) New York: Ronald Press, 1948.

Zuriff, G. E. Where is the agent in conditioning? *Behaviorism,* 1975, 3, 1–22.

Psychological Explanations and Their Vicissitudes

Theodore Mischel

*State University of New York
at Binghamton*

THE PROBLEMATIC STATUS OF PSYCHOLOGICAL EXPLANATIONS

*W*hat is a chemical, or a mechanical, explanation? We can answer such questions by examining the way in which the concepts and theoretical formulations of chemistry, or mechanics, are deployed by scientists in order to account for chemical, or mechanical, phenomena. But we cannot elucidate the nature of psychological explanations in this way because, as one distinguished psychologist has put it,

> There is no concord among psychologists about what the facts they have accumulated are evidence for. This does not mean that they are merely in disagreement about the edifice they wish to erect; they have not even decided what constitutes a building. That is, not only do they disagree about the explanation of their findings, but they are not clear about what it would be to explain them. As a result, it is not sufficient only to put forward a theory to explain the facts; it is also necessary to put forward a theory to justify the type of theory put forward. [Deutsch, 1960, p. 1]

Perhaps we should not be surprised by this lack of concord about the nature of the basic concepts that should be deployed in psychological explanations. For psychology, so it is often said, is a young science and science never begins with

> clear and sharply defined basal concepts. . . . The true beginning of scientific activity consists rather in describing

phenomena and then in proceeding to group, classify and correlate them. Even at the stage of description it is not possible to avoid applying certain abstract ideas to the material in hand, ideas derived from various sources and certainly not the fruit of the experience alone. . . . we come to an understanding about their meaning by repeated reference to the material of observation, from which we seem to have deduced our abstract ideas, but which is in point of fact subject to them. Thus, strictly speaking, they are in the nature of conventions; although everything depends on their being chosen in no arbitrary manner, but determined by the important relations they have to the empirical material. . . . It is only after more searching investigation of the field in question that we are able to formulate with increased clarity the scientific concepts underlying it. [Freud, 1915, p. 60]

But this passage, used by Freud to introduce the "still rather obscure basal concept" of instinct, appeared in 1915; Deutsch's book was published in 1960. And, as the topic chosen for this year's Nebraska symposium shows, disagreement about foundational issues in psychology is increasing rather than diminishing; the participants in this symposium are doing metapsychology, they are presenting theories to justify the type of theory they think psychology should develop.

It should also be noted that while there is a sense in which Deutsch can rightly say that, in spite of disagreement about what counts as psychological explanation, "a large mass of scientifically impeccable evidence has been built up and the pile is daily augmented" (1960, p. 1), what is being accumulated is not really "evidence" but a mass of information of various sorts whose significance is far from clear. For a consequence of radical disagreement about the nature of psychological explanation is a corresponding uncertainty about what constitutes evidence, about what sorts of data under what sorts of descriptions are *relevant* to the science of psychology. This uncertainty is reflected in the almost totally vacuous way in which textbooks of psychology define its subject matter as "the behavior of organisms." This not only fails to differentiate psychology's subject matter from that of animal physiology, or ethology, but since humans are organisms it does not do much to distinguish the subject matter of psychology from that of sociology, linguistics, economics, jurisprudence, or history. Again, during the first stages in the development of a science some uncertainty about its subject matter is to be expected. It was only after Newtonian mechanics had begun to develop that one had a basis for claiming that in spite of the many "surface" differences between, for example, apples, billiard balls, satellites, or tides, some of their behaviors could be characterized as motions that can be explained in terms of the principles of mechanics. And once a science of mechanics has developed, the fact that a certain phenomenon cannot be explained in terms of its concepts and principles becomes a reason for thinking that the phenomenon in question is not "purely mechanical," and thus, for looking to other sciences for part of its explanation.

The point is that what counts as a psychological phenomenon is not independent of what counts as a psychological explanation. Psychology can delimit its subject matter in useful ways only insofar as it can find effective explanatory concepts, concepts which are "chosen in no arbitrary manner, but determined by the important relations they have to the empirical material." For it is only if the employment of these concepts in "more searching investigation of the field" shows that they enable us to structure that field in theoretically interesting and fruitful ways—so that we can say, with some confidence, that these are "the scientific concepts underlying it"—that we can be in a position to identify those theoretically important similarities between phenomena in virtue of which they are "psychological phenomena" to be explained by this, rather than some other, science. Given the uncertainty about the subject matter of psychology which follows from lack of agreement about the conceptual basis of psychological explanations, it is not too surprising to find an article entitled "What Psychology is About" in a recent issue of the *American Psychologist* (Hebb, 1974)—though one can hardly imagine a distinguished physicist writing an article for his professional colleagues under the title "What Physics is About."

Now while some uncertainty about foundational questions is to be expected in the early states of a developing science, psychology is no longer all that young. Leaving aside Freud's metapsychological papers of 1915, there was Watson's behaviorist "revolution" in 1913, Wundt's founding of "experimental" psychology in 1879, Herbart's attempt to make psychology a mathematical science in 1824—and this geneology could easily be continued. If, following the standard histories, we take 1879 as the year in which psychology was established as an independent science, it seems clear that compared to the cumulative theoretical progress other sciences have made in about a hundred years, psychology is a slow starter. Perhaps, then, there is another explanation for the conceptual uncertainties that have impeded the development of the science of psychology. Perhaps the development of an adequate framework of explanatory concepts has been hampered because psychological theorists have subjected the field under investigation to "ideas derived from various sources and certainly not the fruit of the experience alone"—in particular, philosophical ideas about the nature of mind, of mechanism, of science, and the like.

Studies of the history of the physical sciences have shown that even their development is often marked by arguments about what concepts, methods, and forms of explanation are appropriate for engaging in a program of empirical research, and about whether the subject matter under investigation should be defined in one way rather than another. They have shown that such background assumptions for empirical research are not unambiguously determined by observation and experiment but involve choice, and that the choices made can make an very important difference to the body of science actually developed; different commitments on such foundational issues lead to different research programs and to different theories (cf., e.g., Hanson, 1958; Kuhn, 1962; Toulmin, 1961). In the end the success or failure of a research program employing certain concepts and methods will show that the choices made were, or were not, justified. But such ultimate considerations are not available to scientists initiating a program of empirical research; in the beginning, what is at issue is the *plausibility* of trying one approach rather than another. At that point, the appeal can only be to considerations which are "philosophical" in the innocent sense that conceptual analysis and argument must be used to resolve disagreements; these matters cannot be settled by just taking another look at the facts or by running some more experiments.

Now one should certainly expect choices of this sort to play an even more crucial role in the development of scientific psychology. For insofar as psychology is concerned with the investigation of high-grade human behavior, it has to deal with the behaviors of conscious language users who can give accounts of their own behavior. No doubt, the concepts people use to characterize physical phenomena are acquired from their culture. But while it makes sense to suppose that what physical phenomena really are does not depend on what concepts we have for characterizing them, there seems to be a much more intimate relation between what concepts we possess and what intentions, emotions, motives, thoughts, and perceptions we can have. At least some of our psychological states and processes appear to depend essentially on our conceptual resources, and this endows such psychological phenomena with characteristics that appear to differ radically from those of physical phenomena.

To illustrate, consider the emotions. The very attempt to individuate emotional phenomena raises peculiar problems.[1] A psychologist interested in studying the emotions might, initially, be inclined to construe them as states of the organism. But even if, contrary to fact, certain physiological, or "feeling," states were to occur when, and only when, a certain emotion occurs, one would still need some independent way of identifying the emotion before one could show that just these states occur in the organism when that emotion is present. Nor could we get far in identifying the emotions in terms of specific behaviors, since it is far from clear what, if anything, a person does when, and only when, he feels, for example, guilt. It all seems to depend on the person, the circumstances, and what it is he is feeling guilty about. That, of course, brings up another crucial issue: to feel guilt is, normally, to feel guilty about something. That is, emotions are directed toward objects in a way in which physical processes are not; a physical state is not about something, as guilt is about having done something that is, or is believed to be, wrong. Analysis of our ordinary conception of the emotions indicates that we individuate the emotions in terms of appraisals of objects, actions, or situations with which different emotions are characteristically connected (cf. Peters, 1969). Guilt, for example, is connected with the judgment that one has failed to do what is right, and we differentiate that emotion from the related, but different, emotion of shame on the ground that the latter involves a

1. These problems may be pushed into the background when psychologists who want to study the emotions focus on, for example, fear in the rat. For it is not hard to set up a laboratory situation in which a rat brought up in the laboratory will exhibit behaviors which psychologists can agree to identify as fear. But once we move out of controlled laboratory environments to the behavior of animals in natural settings, and from the very limited range of emotions of lower animals to those of higher ones, especially the rich range of emotions of which people are capable, the problems I am talking about become central.

negative appraisal of some aspect of oneself; one becomes ashamed if in some way one has failed, or thinks one has failed, to be the sort of person one should, or wishes, to be. This is also why a person may feel guilt, or shame, when he has no real reason for feeling that way. Consequently, emotions, unlike physical states, can be appraised and judged to be reasonable or unreasonable, justified or unjustified. Moreover, if something like our ordinary way of individuating the emotions is right, then it follows that there is an irradicably cognitive element in the emotions, so that we cannot intelligibly attribute an emotion to someone who lacks the conceptual apparatus needed for making the appraisal with which the emotion is connected; we could not say of a being that has no understanding of what it is to do, or to be, wrong that it feels guilt or shame.

These remarks are, of course, extremely sketchy and I will return to a more detailed discussion of the peculiar features of our ordinary conceptualization of psychological states and processes. For the moment, I only want to call attention to the way in which, for example, attributing an emotion to someone involves supposing that he has certain beliefs and desires and makes certain judgments and appraisals, all of which may, or may not, be reasonable in light of his actual situation. In other words, the attribution of a psychological state or process to a person is typically linked to the attribution of other relevant psychological states and processes; it assumes that the person is a subject who perceives, believes, desires, and intends various things in ways that are interconnected, and that may be peculiar and idiosyncratic. As a result, the behavior of persons, as we normally understand it, is described in ways that differ radically from the descriptions we use to characterize the behavior of merely physical things. To put the same point in another way, since the objects of human psychology are, at least prima facie, conscious subjects who can give accounts of what they are doing, psychology must deal with the behaviors possible for concept-using beings, whose behaviors seem to be such that they can be affected by the conceptual distinctions they are able to make and the subjective perspective on the world they can thus develop. And it is certainly not clear a priori that such "behaviors" must be on all fours with the behavior of inanimate objects, or even the behavior of lower animals.

Consequently, there is much more room in psychology for disagreement about the way the subject matter under investigation is to be defined, about appropriate methods and explanatory concepts, and about the conditions psychology must satisfy if it is to be a genuine science. Under these circumstances, it would be surprising if assumptions about the nature of mind and the nature of science, borrowed from philosophy, had not exercised a profound influence on theorists who were seeking to formulate the conceptual foundations of psychological explanation. Questions concerning the "definition" of psychology, about proper methods, and about the general conditions psychology must satisfy if it is to be a science were, in fact, hotly debated in the nineteenth century, when psychology was trying to become an empirical science; and after a behavioristic interlude during which most psychologists thought that all the fundamental questions had been settled, we now seem, once again, to be in a situation where psychologists do not agree on what background assumptions can provide a reasonable foundation for fruitful empirical investigations of high-grade human behavior.

It may, therefore, be useful to examine some of the vicissitudes which psychological explanations have suffered under the impact of philosophical assumptions about the nature of mind, mechanism, and science. If we can disentangle some of the basic characteristics and functions of psychological explanations from extraneous assumptions with which they have often been combined, we may have a basis for assessing the merits of the metatheories psychologists are now advancing in order to justify the competing types of psychological explanation they favor. I want to focus primarily on what is currently at issue between radical behaviorists and cognitive psychologists, but I must begin with some historical considerations because these current controversies can be properly understood only in the light of the historical background that informs them.

HISTORICAL ROOTS IN PHILOSOPHICAL ISSUES

Psychological Explanation and Ontological Commitments: Descartes and Hobbes

Much as the child begins by conceiving inanimate objects on the model of persons (Piaget, 1929), so early attempts at a rational understanding of nature sought to provide something like a psychological explanation for all behaviors. For example, Aristotle's analysis of natural processes in terms of their four causes —corresponding, roughly, to the answers to the following questions: What was it made out of? Into what was it made? By what was it made? For what purpose was it made?—can be seen as an attempt to employ the sort of analysis that enables us to understand what is done intentionally by a craftsman as a model for understanding all natural processes. This is not to suggest that Greek though was childish, but rather that there is something very natural about attempts to extend the background assumptions in terms of which we structure our understanding of ourselves and our fellows to the understanding of all phenomena. But no matter how plausible attempts to understand nature in this anthropomorphic way may have been initially, their success was, in fact, quite limited. In sharp contrast, the very different background assumptions for scientific research that came to be accepted with the development of Galilean physics led to very rapid and cumulative theoretical progress in that science.

The dramatic success of the scientific revolution lent plausibility to attempts to extend the background assumptions of mechanics to the investigation of other domains, and theorists soon attempted to construct mechanical explanations for the behavior of living organisms. That Galileo's "new method" could be applied not only to the motions of inanimate objects but also to organic processes was shown by his contemporary Harvey, and Descartes held that all animal behavior could be explained as nothing more than the operation of various bodily mechanisms. Even some human behaviors—for example, withdrawing one's hand from a flame, or even blind flight when one is overcome by fear—could, as Descartes (1649) recognized, be plausibly construed as reactions caused by physical stimuli which set off the operation of various bodily mechanisms.

But not all human behaviors are like that. When people "act from knowledge," or when they "arrange different words together, forming of them a statement by which they make known their thoughts" (1637, pp. 116–117), there is, so Descartes thought, no way of explaining what they do in terms of physical mechanisms. Mechanisms, after all, are (or rather were, in Descartes's day) arrangements of gears, springs, levers, and the like. But in order to explain what people do when they "act from knowledge" one appeals to their beliefs, aims, and desires, the rules or norms they follow, etc., and these "considerations," which guide intelligent actions in ways appropriate for achieving the agent's goals, appear to be "things" of an entirely different kind from the physical events and structures on which the operation of mechanisms depend. Further, we are conscious through introspection of our own thoughts, aims, etc., and, at least in one's own case, the conviction that we really have thoughts, etc., seems to be quite unshakable. Though Descartes managed, in the course of his systematic doubt, to produce reasons for being uncertain even about the existence of his own body, the one thing he found impossible to doubt was that he is "a thing which thinks" (1641, p. 152).

Questions about the nature and status of psychological explanations thus were linked for seventeenth-century theorists to the ontological question: What sort of a thing is man? Those like Descartes, who found mechanism inconceivable because they could see no way in which our intelligent, self-initiated actions and the thoughts, etc., of which we are introspectively aware, could be generated by the operation of bodily mechanisms, insisted that man cannot just be a material thing, he must also be a nonmaterial thinking thing; in addition to a body he must have a mind. The possibility of distinctively psychological explanations, different in kind from the mechanical explanations of the physical sciences, was thus made dependent on the existence of nonmaterial minds.

On the other hand, those like Hobbes (1641), who found the idea of immaterial minds that act on material bodies inconceivable, concluded that man can only be a material system and that the explanation of his behavior must, therefore, have the same form as mechanistic explanations in physics. Action, according to Hobbes, can be understood as nothing but the communication of motion, and an agent can be nothing more than a body that sets another body in motion because it has itself been moved (1655, chap. 10). In order to explain actions, which we seem to initiate and guide in light of our desires, purposes, and beliefs, in a mechanistic framework that appeals only to bodily motions and their efficient causes, Hobbes sketched a theory according to which our "voluntary" actions are really initiated by external stimuli which propogate motions that interact with the autonomic "vital motions" within the organism; the resulting internal motions are then amplified by various bodily mechanisms into motion of the organism toward, or away from, the stimulus object. On this view, psychological explanations of actions in terms of thoughts, aims, and the like—for example, he went to the kitchen in order to get a sandwich—are simply prescientific myths;

for what really explains the behavior is not the man's thought or aim, but a story about how motions coming from the sandwich cause other motions which cause him to move toward it. It seems, says Hobbes, "as if we draw the object to us, whereas the object rather draws us to it by local motion" (1630, p. 179). This analysis rules out the possibility of distinctively psychological explanations on the ground that there are no immaterial minds, and so no psychological states or processes that can enter into the causal explanation of behavior.[2]

The Mechanization of Mind and the Concept of Agency:
Association Psychology versus Kant

Though the conceptualization of man as essentially a machine continued in writers like Holbach and de la Mettrie, mainstream theorizing during the eighteenth and nineteenth centuries was firmly Cartesian. Man, it was assumed, is essentially a center of consciousness that is somehow linked to a material body. Only mental states can be directly present to us, so that the mind is populated by ideas to which each of us has direct and privileged access; these ideas were construed as nonmaterial entities which are the referents of our words and the immediate objects of our knowledge. "Empiricists" did not dispute the Cartesian picture of the mind held by "rationalists," but differed from them primarily about whether the mind contains "innate ideas" or whether it is initially a "tabula rasa," so that all mental contents derive ultimately from external objects which "occasion" the occurrence of mental states in us.

"Association psychology" was developed in the empiricist tradition that runs from Locke and Hume through the Mills, and these philosophers certainly thought of themselves as in the business of developing psychological explanations. But the important thing to see is that this only meant that the entities whose behavior they were trying to explain were construed as mental rather than physical; the *form* of explanation which they tried to deploy in order to account for the workings of the mind was taken over directly from the new science. Hume (1739) explicitly sought to "introduce the

2. For a more detailed discussion of the views of Descartes and Hobbes in relation to psychological theory, see Mischel (1969).

experimental Method of Reasoning" (i.e., Newton's method) into the mental sciences in order to "discover, at least in some degree, the secret springs and principles by which the human mind is actuated in its operation" (1748, p. 24). The laws of the association of ideas were to explain the operations of the mind in much the same way as Newton's laws explained the operations of bodies: here, says Hume thinking of Newton, is "a kind of *attraction* which in the mental world will be found to have as extraordinary effects as in the natural" (1739, pp. 12–13).

The psychological explanations sketched by Hume and his successors thus took the form of quasi-mechanical explanations for the behavior of immaterial entities. That is, ideas became the analogue of material particles, and the principles of association the analogue of the principles of mechanics. The result is a picture of mental life purely from the point of view of a privileged spectator of "inner" conscious phenomena, an account from which all notions of agency have been eliminated, much as such "occult powers" had been eliminated from Galilean physics. Talk about mental activities, which we have the power to initiate and perform, is replaced by an account of how the "forces" of association make ideas move through the mind. Herbart (1824), who wanted to borrow mathematical equations from dynamics in order to chart the movement of ideas through consciousness, gave explicit expression to the notion that psychology is the "mechanics of ideas," much as physics is the mechanics of bodies. But that notion, in less extreme from, was implicit in all of association psychology.

Descartes had distinguished the "actions" of the soul, which are initiated and produced by it, from the "passions" which come over the soul, being caused to occur in it (1649, p. 331), thus appealing to the mind as an active principle that explains our self-initiated, intelligent actions. But since thinking and other mental activities were not construed by association psychology as actions which we have the power to perform—instead, we get the spectator's explanation of the occurrence of thoughts, etc., in terms of mental mechanisms—the appeal to the mind could no longer distinguish agency from passivity, what it is in our power to do from what happens to us but is not our doing. By adopting the Cartesian picture of the mind while borrowing the mechanical form of explanation from the new sciences, association psychology developed an account of the workings of the mind which made it little more than an essentially private, inner mirror of outer contingencies. Since the nature and order of our ideas simply mirrors the nature and order of external events that have impinged on us—Hume's "pre-established harmony between the course of nature and the succession of our ideas" (1748, p. 67)—there is no room for any internal ordering or direction of behavior. Because the mind thus failed to do any explanatory work, it was easy for behaviorists to lop off the mind (or rather this version of the nature of mental processes) and to replace association psychology with a theory about the association of stimuli and responses. The development of S-R behavior theory was, as Hull himself pointed out, "a genuine and perfectly natural evolution of English associationism" (1934, p. 382).[3]

A very different approach to the understanding of human agency was suggested by Kant. For according to Kant (1781), we must start by recognizing that there are two very different points of view which we can take toward human behavior, that neither of these points of view can be rejected, and that an adequate conceptualization of human behavior must have room for both. One point of view is that of theoretical sciences like physics. Whatever else we may want to say of persons, they surely are material organizations, and as such, the laws of physics, chemistry, etc. must apply to them; whatever else we may want to say of human actions, they are, at least if we are talking of overt actions, events in space and time and so presumably caused by other events in space and time. So actions can, for Kant, be viewed as physical phenomena whose explanation must be found in other physical phenomena in the brain and nervous system. The possibility of a neurophysiological explanation for all human behaviors is implicit in the point of view adopted by sciences like physics.

A very different, but equally indispensable, point of view is that of the agent who is faced with choices, deliberates, makes decisions, and tries to act accordingly. Central to Kant's analysis of this point of view is his claim that human beings can have a *conception* of what it is they want and what they should do in order to get what they want, and that their conceptions—the meaning which situations and behaviors have for them in virtue of the way they construe them—can make a difference to their actions. Rational beings "have a faculty of taking a rule of reason for the motive of an action" (Kant,

3. For a detailed discussion of conceptual issues in the development of association psychology in the English tradition, see Mischel (1966a). On the relation between association psychology and behaviorism, see Mischel (1969, pp. 26 ff.).

1788, p. 151), they have the capacity to formulate plans, policies, or rules, and they can follow these rules—they have the power to act from the "mere conception" of a rule. "Everything in nature works according to laws," says Kant, but only rational beings "have the faculty of acting according to *the conception* of laws" and, therefore, have a will (1785, p. 29).

Seen in this way, the claim that people are agents is not a Cartesian claim about the role played by introspectable inner states as causal antecedents of outer bodily movements, but is the claim that we have the power to act according to our conceptions, so that what we do depends, at least in part, on the way we understand our situation. We cannot eliminate the notion that we are agents because it is central to our conception of what it is to be a person who can engage in practical life. But I can also look at myself from a purely external point of view, as an object in nature, and that my behavior must then be seen as caused by other events in nature is central to our conception of physical science.

What is important, for our purposes, is that Kant recognized the validity of both of these points of view and that his approach makes it possible to separate claims about the distinctive features of psychological explanations from claims about the existence of immaterial minds. For on this approach, the peculiar features of psychological explanations are due to the fact that in giving such explanations we take the point of view of agents. When we characterize behavior from that point of view, our descriptions and explanations deploy the network of concepts which agents use in their commerce with each other. In this context, we describe behaviors as actions by characterizing the goal which we take the agent to intend, or aim at, in what he is doing; and we try to explain what he is doing in terms of his conception of things—by identifying those of his beliefs and desires, those rules or maxims which he follows, etc., that can make his aim and the way he is trying to achieve it intelligible to other agents. Of course, such descriptions and explanations will be of a very different type from those given by physical scientists who characterize behavior purely from the spectator's point of view by deploying the network of concepts used to identify various sorts of bodily processes and their causes. But the crucial point is that psychological and physical characterizations of behavior differ, not because they describe the operations of ontologically different substances, but because they are concerned with answering different sorts of questions, they are informed by different sorts of interests—in this sense, they deal with the same behavior from "different points of view."

The physical sciences identify human behaviors as physical events and look for their causes in other physical events. Psychology differs from the physical sciences, not because it is concerned with minds rather than bodies, but because it is concerned with how it is that people (and perhaps, though Kant would have denied this, higher animals) acquire conceptions of their engagement in the world, conceptions which may or may not be justified by the facts, and with how these conceptions enter into the generation of their behavior. The physical sciences operate with a conceptual framework in which there is no room for appeal to agents and the perspective they have on things because of their conceptions; but that appeal is central to the conceptual framework used by agents (including physical scientists) in their commerce with each other. Since neither point of view can be legitimately rejected, the question becomes: How can psychological explanations, given from the point of view of agents who have the capacity to act in light of their conceptions (plans, rules, beliefs, etc.), and the very different explanations of that behavior given by the physical sciences, *both be true*? The issue is not how there can be minds in addition to bodies, but how these different types of explanations, both of which are valid, can be related to each other.[4]

The Nineteenth-Century Divide: Wundt's "Experimental" Psychology versus Brentano's "Intentionalistic" Psychology

Kant, perhaps because his identification of science with Newtonian physics led him to deny that psychology could ever become a "science properly so called" (cf. Mischel, 1967), had little influence on the way in which Wundt sought to establish psychology as an experimental science. To be sure, Wundt made the subject's point of view central to psychology, but his understanding of what is involved in taking that point of view was Cartesian rather than Kantian. Where Kant links the agent's point of view to our capacity for acting on rules and plans, our ability to act purposefully and intentionally in light of the meaning things have for us when we

4. For a detailed discussion of Kant's views on psychology and its relation to other sciences, see Mischel (1967).

engage in practical life which is public and social, Wundt, Titchener, and other introspectionists linked the subject's point of view to Descartes's conception of the mind as a center of consciousness which is accessible solely through introspection. Given the point physiology had reached by the middle of the nineteenth century, Wundt did, of course, reject Descartes's notion that there are mental substances which can exist independent of the body; instead, he espoused "psycho-physical parallelism," a theory according to which physical processes always "run parallel to" the psychological processes of which we are conscious. But the key point is that Wundt and his followers shared Descartes's conception of psychological phenomena as conscious states or processes to which each of us has privileged access through introspection, but which can never be witnessed from "outside."[5] Indeed, this Cartesian picture of what it is to be a "psychological phenomenon" was the basis for Wundt's "definition" of psychology, which attempted to show that, even though all organic processes can, in principle, be explained in terms of physics and chemistry, there is still room for psychology as an experimental science that has its own subject matter and methods. Wundt's definition, which became the accepted background for some 50 years of experimental introspective psychology, held that psychology studies experience solely from the inside, "from the point of view of the perceiving, feeling and willing subject," while physiology and other natural sciences can study experience only from the outside, "purely from the point of view of objects" (Wundt, 1908–11, Vol. 3, p. 744). There is no limit to what physiology can explain, since it can take all of outer experience for its subject matter, but there is always room for psychology, because it alone takes the point of view of the experiencing subject, the center of consciousness for whom alone there can be ideas, feelings, and the like. Psychological explanation thus came to be construed as an attempt to analyze mental phenomena, which can be present only to the subject's own consciousness, into their elements and to discover the laws that govern them. And the doctrine of psychophysical parallelism was to provide the rationale for the use of experimental methods in psychology. Since mental phenomena are always paralleled by physical ones, laboratory procedures that

5. As Titchener put it, "vital processes may be viewed from the outside, and then we have the subject matter of physiology, or they may be viewed from within, and then we have the subject matter of psychology" (1929, p. 14).

control the occurrence of certain physical processes could, so Wundt thought, be used to control the occurrence of the "parallel" mental processes; in this way psychology could become a science that uses laboratory experiments "in order to deliberately produce psychological processes, to repeat them or to change them in ways precisely determined in advance" (Wundt, 1908, p. 167). The idea was that this would make it possible for psychologists to describe and analyze mental states and processes "objectively," much as natural scientists describe and analyze physical states and processes by means of repeated observation under controlled conditions.[6]

But this Cartesian identification of the subject matter of psychology, which made introspection its indispensable method —"the direct object of psychological study" says Titchener, "is always a consciousness" (1916, p. 19)—broke all conceptual links between "inner" mental states and "outer" circumstances and behaviors; any objective description of the latter fell, by definition, under the point of view of sciences other than psychology. As a result, there was nothing against which one could check the "descriptions" of inner states and processes given by subjects in the experiments conducted by introspective psychologists, no way of really identifying these Cartesian "inner" phenomena, and no possibility of developing an objective science of psychology. The philosophical assumptions about the nature of psychological phenomena, which informed the research program of introspective psychology, made its debacle a foregone conclusion.[7]

A very different characterization of mental phenomena had been suggested by Brentano in 1874, the year in which the first edition of Wundt's *Physiological Psychology* was also published. According to Brentano,

> Every mental phenomenon is characterized by what the
> Scholastics of the Middle Ages called the intentional (or mental)
> inexistence of an object, and what we might call . . . reference
> to a content, direction toward an object . . . or immanent ob-

6. Titchener, expounding Wundt, again, puts this very clearly: "The results of inner observation are surest when the appliances of external observation, the procedures of physiology, are pressed into psychological service. . . . [Wundt's] primary aim in all cases is to describe the phenomena of mind as the physiologist describes the phenomena of the living body, to write down what is there, going on observably before him" (1929, p. 19).

7. For a more detailed discussion of these issues, see Mischel (1970).

jectivity. . . . In presentation something is presented, in judgment something is affirmed or denied, in love loved, in hate hated, in desire desired and so on. . . . This intentional inexistence is characteristic exclusively of mental phenomena. No physical phenomenon exhibits anything like it. [Pp. 88–89]

Though Brentano appealed to the rather obscure scholastic notion of "intentional inexistence"—and the question of how this is to be understood immediately became,[8] and indeed continues to be,[9] a matter of dispute—for our purposes Brentano's approach can be linked to Kant's characterization of the different points of view from which agents and spectators describe behavior. For the intentionalistic "act-psychology" of Brentano and his followers (e.g., Meinong, Stumpf, Lipps, Külpe) attempted to distinguish mental from physical phenomena on the ground that the former are always acts directed to some content, and therefore inherently relational in a way in which physical phenomena are not.[10] But since physical phenomena can and do stand in all sorts of relations to each other, for example, spatial or temporal, it could not be simply their relational character that distinguishes the mental from the physical. Rather, the distinguishing feature had to be the special sort of relation into which only mental phenomena can enter—namely, the relation of being intended, or meant, by someone (cf. McAlister, 1974). One stick may be bigger than, or to the left of, another, but one stick cannot be "directed toward" (mean, intend, refer to) another as my thought of a particular stick is directed toward it, or my desire for a particular stick intends that stick and no other.

8. Titchener reviews the different interpretations of the nature of mental phenomena in the work of such nineteenth-century theorists as Meinong, Husserl, Münsterberg, Stumpf, Lipps, Messer, and Witasek, all of whom drew on Brentano's criterion (1929, pp. 196–251).

9. Chisholm, the leading contemporary philosophical exponent of Brentano, develops the criterion in terms of the different truth conditions for "sentences that are intentional" and sentences that are not (1957, p. 170), a difference linked, very roughly, to an interpretation of Brentano's criterion according to which mental experiences have objects that may or may not exist, while physical experiences have objects that must exist. Other philosophers have developed counterexamples in response to which Chisholm has tried to reformulate his criteria (cf. Chisholm, 1967); and the translator of Brentano's *Psychology* has recently argued that Chisholm "gives a misleading impression of what Brentano's views actually were" (McAlister, 1974, p. 329).

10. See Titchener's characterization of Brentano's views (1929, pp. 12–13).

Indeed, the intentional object of my mental act can be individuated only as that which is intended by the act. What I desire when I desire beer or immortality, what I think of when I think of men or ghosts, is different; but the difference can only be specified in terms of the different descriptions of the content of my thought or desire. Since the individuation of the object of my desire, thought, feelings of guilt, and the like, depends essentially on my characterization of what it is I intend, it cannot matter one way or the other whether there really exists anything that has the features described in the characterization of my desire, thought, or guilt. So the criterion of "intentional inexistence" seems to draw the line between mental and physical phenomena, since the latter, unlike the former, can be individuated without reference to what someone intends.

But in a very similar way, we characterize actions in relation to what the agent intends. "He is looking for his glasses" is a description that individuates an action in terms of an intention he is taken to have, and not in terms of his bodily movements. It matters not which of the indefinite range of bodily movements that may be involved in looking for one's glasses occurs, and the only thing that can individuate whatever bodily movements do occur as the act of "looking for his glasses" is the agent's intention. The movements which his hands, for example, perform are intentional because they can be related to his intention of looking for his glasses; but what he intends is to look for his glasses, not to move his hands in this way or that. And he may move his hands in various ways with the result that his glasses turn up, but one could not characterize what he was doing as "looking for his glasses" unless that was what he intended—for he might, for example, be looking for his keys, or just nervously shuffling papers on his desk, and in the process accidentally turn up his glasses. But in such cases, he certainly was not looking for his glasses. Similarly, what someone does in looking for his glasses may have all sorts of other results—for example, some papers get pushed off the desk, air molecules get disturbed, etc.—but we could not say, without qualification, that this is what he is doing; his action is intentional under the description "he is looking for his glasses," but not under the description "he pushed some papers off the desk" (cf. Anscombe, 1957). Since actions, the things a person does, as contrasted with bodily reactions (e.g., reflexes) that may be elicited in him, are normally individuated in relation to the agent's intentions—what he aimed at in what he was doing, what meaning or significance it had for him—such bodily actions share the characteristic of "intentional inexistence" by which Brentano sought to distinguish mental and physical phenomena: looking for Shangri-la is just as much an action as looking for one's glasses.

Brentano, like Wundt and most other theorists of the time, assumed that all sciences start from "phenomena" given by experience, so that the job of differentiating psychology from other sciences must be the job of providing some criterion by which "physical phenomena," which are the province of the natural sciences, can be distinguished from "mental phenomena," which are the subject matter of psychology. But we can now see that Brentano's criterion can serve to distinguish, not two different kinds of phenomena, but two different ways of individuating and describing phenomena. Brentano's important insight pertains, not to the difference between physical and mental phenomena *qua* "things" of a different sort, but to the difference between physical and psychological descriptions of behaviors, whether these be intentionalistically characterized bodily acts, like "looking for one's glasses," or such "mental acts" as thinking of, or hoping for. Psychological characterizations always presuppose an agent, they appeal to what he means or intends, they describe behavior from his point of view. And so we are back to something like Kant's centrally important distinction between the different ways in which behaviors are described from the point of view of agents in their interactions with other agents, on the one hand, and the "external" point of view of the natural sciences, on the other.

Something like this version of Brentano's way of distinguishing psychological from physical characterizations of behavior may have been operative in Freud, who found himself in the difficult position of trying to develop descriptions and explanations which were neither physiological nor psychological in Wundt's sense, since they involved appeal to unconscious mental states and processes.[11] In order to distinguish the psychoanalytic approach both from that of physiology and from that of the "experimental psychology" of his time, Freud repeatedly appeals to the fact that both dreams and

11. Wundt rejected "unconscious" mental processes as "mystical metaphysics"—"since the 'unconscious' does not belong to immediate experience, it cannot belong to the subject matter of psychology" (1896, pp. 34–35). A direct historical connection between Brentano and Freud has been suggested by P. Merlan (1945, 1949).

symptoms (which may, of course, be bodily acts) "have meaning" (e.g., 1914, p. 75), as do at least some errors and slips—"the slip itself makes sense [and so can be regarded] as an expression having content and meaning" (1914, p. 33). But Freud was outside the mainstream of academic psychology.

Titchener, on the other hand, thought that Wundt rather than Brentano had pointed to the direction in which psychology must go if it is to become a science. To be sure, Titchener admitted that "intentionalism is as durable as common sense" because

> the psychologist of intention means to take mind as he finds it, and . . . like all the rest of the world, who are not psychologists, he finds it in use; he finds it actively at work in man's intercourse with nature and with his fellow-man, and in his discourse with himself. [1929, P. 254]

Something like a "functionalist" approach to psychology was emerging in the work of the act psychologists who were drawing on Brentano's theory around the turn of the century. But Titchener (1929, pp. 193–251) pointed up differences in their analyses, and argued that if psychology takes Wundt's direction[12] it

> can follow methods and achieve results that are not unique and apart but, on the contrary, of the same order as the methods and results of physics and biology; then, by sheer shock of difference, the act-systems . . . will no longer venture to offer themselves as science. [P. 256]

Wundt held out the hope of making psychology a science "parallel" to the natural sciences; but the trouble with intentionalistic psychology, says Titchener, is that "if intentionalism is scientific, then science can no longer be called impersonal" (p. 252).

There is an important sense in which that is true. If the data of psychology are characterized intentionalistically, then psychology cannot be a science on all fours with the physical sciences. For if we individuate behavior at the psychological level by relating it to what

12. The division between Wundt and Brentano was actually not as sharp as Titchener made it out to be, because Wundt's efforts to distinguish "psychological causality" from physical causality hinge upon the notion that psychological phenomena are always acts (see Mischel, 1970). But it is Titchener's version of Wundt that became part of psychology's tradition, and standard histories like Boring's speak of "Wundt's mental chemistry" (1950, p. 336).

meaning the situation to which the agent is responding, and the response he is making, have in light of his conceptions, then his own interpretations will enter into the definition of the phenomena under study. If psychological characterizations of what a person is doing, as contrasted with physical characterizations of his movements, depend essentially on what he intends to be doing in relation to a situation he construes to have a certain meaning, then psychology will involve interpretation in a way in which the physical sciences do not. For though interpretation may be involved in the physical sciences in relation to the practices of the scientific community—for example, the physicist may say, on the basis of his theory, that the perturbation of the planet's orbit means that another force is acting—there is no room for asking what the behavior means from the planet's point of view, what the planet intended by it. The data of the physical sciences are individuated without reference to intentions, or point of view, on the part of the phenomena under investigation. In contrast, the agent's own interpretation will be constitutive of the data studied by psychology, insofar as these data are characterized from the agent's point of view. In this sense, a science whose data are intentionalistic characterizations of behavior cannot be "impersonal."[13]

CAN INTENTIONALISTIC EXPLANATIONS BE ELIMINATED FROM PSYCHOLOGY?

Methodological, Purposive, and Radical Behaviorism

Behaviorism can be seen as an attempt to eliminate from psychology the agent's point of view and the intentionalistic organization of the data which it entails. When the hollowness of Titchener's claim that introspective psychology "can follow methods and achieve results . . . of the same order" as the natural sciences became painfully apparent, psychologists came to agree that the subject matter of

13. The sense Titchener had in mind is somewhat different, since he was thinking primarily about the way the need for interpretation led different act psychologists to differ: "there is no psychology of act, there are only psychologies . . . on the basis of intentionalism there will only be psychologies" (1929, p. 253).

psychology could only be behavior. Having accepted the same Cartesian picture of the mind, early behaviorists like Watson concluded, quite properly, that the mind cannot be studied scientifically. Since the subject's point of view, as conceptualized in introspective psychology, could not even provide data on which psychologists could agree, the only alternative seemed to lie in conceptualizing the data of psychology as behavior seen from an "objective," that is, external, point of view; in this way psychology could, it was thought, become a science of behavior whose methods, concepts, and explanatory laws would not differ, in principle, from those of the natural sciences. Of course, the definition of behavior, the attempt to distinguish the behavior psychology studies from the behavior studied by physiology without reintroducing mental terms, ran into tricky problems. Since Watson's characterization of behavior as whatever movements occur in response to stimuli—"the response may confine itself to a change in respiration . . . or blood pressure . . . or [there may be] movements of the whole body, movements of the arm, leg, trunk, or combinations of all the moving parts" (1924, p. 14)—simply failed to distinguish the responses studied by psychology from those studied by physiology, the concept of "behavior" soon became amazingly elastic and vague. But most psychologists did not worry too much about this because genuine progress was being made in laboratory studies of the behavior of lower animals, and between, say, 1920 and 1950, most psychologists were convinced that such studies of animal "learning" provided the indispensable precondition and foundation for any science of human behavior.

There wasn't much justification for that conviction. It was simply assumed that complex human behavior can be reduced to elements found in exactly the same form in lower animals, and that all learning can be conceptualized as an association of stimuli and responses that are measurable by instruments which record overt behavior, or are hooked up to muscles and glands, so that stimuli and responses can be characterized in physical terms (cf. Segal & Lachman, 1972). The notion that the species-specific capacity to use language might make a real difference to the sort of behaviors human beings are able to acquire and display just was not seriously entertained. Instead, an implicit faith that the concepts and methods that had proved effective in the laboratory study of animals simply had to yield results when applied to people, led behaviorists to justify their research program by developing a picture of people such as they would have to be if they were to be understood by means of the research methods they had in hand.

E. C. Tolman did worry about the fact that "Watson has in reality dallied with two different notions of behavior," namely, the molecular definition in terms of "physical and physiological details" and the "molar definition of behavior" (1932, p. 6). Tolman saw clearly that the behavior which concerns psychology is molar and that "behavior as behavior, that is, as molar, *is* purposive and *is* cognitive" (p. 12). But his identification of the mental with the private (p. 3), together with the then prevalent philosophical doctrine of "logical positivism," led him to suppose that if concepts like "purpose" and "cognition" were to have a place in a science of psychology, then their meaning had to be operationally defined in terms of a "physical thing" language which does not require interpretation from the agent's point of view.

Since Tolman was, as he later put it, "trying to rewrite a common-sense mentalistic psychology . . . in operational, behavioristic terms" (1959, p. 94), he was trying to have it both ways. On the one hand, our ordinary intentionalistic characterizations of actions in terms of the agent's purposes and cognitions must be used to identify molar behavior: the "descriptive identification of any behavior-act per se requires descriptive statements [which] identify behaviors in terms of goal-objects, and patterns of commerce with means-objects [and this implies] something perilously like purposes and cognitions. . . . And yet, there seems to be no other way out" (Tolman, 1932, p. 12). On the other hand, "purposes and cognitions . . . are wholly objective as to definition" (p. 13) and it is "we, the outside observers, who discover—or, if you will, infer or invent—them as immanent in, and determining behavior" (p. 19). Since purposes and cognitions can, according to Tolman, be defined by an "outside observer" who does not take the agent's point of view into account—that is, purposes, etc., can be defined in a nonintentionalistic language—they can be "intervening variables" in causal chains that lead from"initiating causes" (environmental stimuli and physiological conditions), through inner determinants including "objectively defined purposes and cognitions," to overt behavior (pp. 20–21).

But this attempt to develop a "purposive behaviorism" by translating our "common-sense mentalistic language," which presupposes the point of view of agents in deploying intentionalistic concepts like purpose and cognition, into an interpretation-free, extensionalistic "physical thing" language acceptable to behaviorism, seems hopeless. The reasons for this become apparent when we look at the nature of the behavioral evidence which the outside observer can use in order to "discover," or "infer," someone's purpose or belief. The fact that someone tells us, for example, that he believes the glass in front of him contains water is excellent evidence for ascribing that belief to him, but only if he does not aim to deceive us by his remark. The fact that he drinks it when thirsty is good evidence, but only if his aim was to quench his thirst with water—it would not be evidence if, for example, what he intended was to drink wine. And just as the ascription of beliefs to someone on the basis of his behavior depends essentially on assumptions about the aim or purpose of his behavior, so the ascription of purposes or intentions to his behavior depends essentially on assumptions about his beliefs. So the fact that he drinks the glass of water allows us to characterize his behavior intentionalistically in relation to his goal object—that is, allows us to claim that what he is doing is "drinking water"—only on the assumption that he believes that what is in the glass is water. But we could not conclude from the fact that, for example, he is thirsty and refuses to drink the water, that it is not his aim to drink water—for he might, for example, believe (falsely) that the water is poisoned. This systematic interconnection between an agent's purposes, beliefs, and desires is an essential feature of intentionalistic characterizations of behavior,[14] and it is what makes Tolman's attempt to define intentionalistic concepts in terms of extensional characterizations of behavior, which do not require interpretation from the agent's point of view, hopeless. For the outside observer's behavioral evidence for the ascription of purposes, beliefs, and desires is good evidence only "other things being equal," and when we try to unpack what must be equal we are forced to reintroduce the intentionalistic, psychological concepts which these operational definitions in behavioral terms were supposed to avoid.

But this, it must be emphasized, does not imply that the outside observer can never have conclusive evidence for ascribing purposes, beliefs, and desires to someone. It is by no means a return to the introspectionist conception of the mental as that which is inherently "inner" because it has no conceptual links to "outer" circumstances

14. Chisholm (1957, chap. 11) provides a number of arguments to show that attempts to provide a behavioral analysis of "believing" and "intending" are caught in a vicious circle.

and behaviors. In reacting against this Cartesian picture, which had brought introspective psychology to naught, Tolman argued that purposes and cognitions "are wholly objective as to definition"; he tried "to show that immanent in any behavior there are certain immediate 'in-lying' purposes and cognitions" (1932, p. 19), and he contrasted his view with that of McDougall, for whom purpose seems to be "something other, and more than, the manner in which it appears in behavior; it is a 'psychic,' 'mentalistic' somewhat behind such objective appearances and to be known in the last analysis through introspection only" (1932, p. 16). But these are not the only alternatives. For one can hold, in opposition to introspectionism, that there are conceptual links between psychological concepts and behavioral dispositions which will be manifested in certain circumstances, and even that this must be so if psychological concepts are to have commonly agreed meanings in our language. And one can, at the same time, deny that a purpose or cognition must be so transparent that we can recognize it from nothing more than "the manner in which it appears in behavior" and paraphrase it in purely extensional terms. For even though psychological concepts can be analyzed in dispositional terms, and so have conceptual links to outer circumstances and behaviors, the dispositions in question are dispositions to act in ways that are appropriate from the agent's point of view. But such dispositions are not transparent in behavior; they require interpretation and cannot be cashed without appealing to the meaning situations and behaviors have for the agent.

To illustrate, consider fear. One could define "fear of X" as a disposition to behave in ways appropriate to seeing X as a danger of some sort; but we could not decide what counts as "appropriate behavior" without knowing a great deal about the agent. Without such knowledge, we cannot conclude from the fact that, for example, he avoids X, that he avoids it intentionally, let alone that he avoids it because he sees it as a danger. But if we know enough about a person, his system of beliefs, purposes, coping styles, and the like, his behavior may provide us with conclusive evidence for claiming "he is afraid of X." Indeed, the evidence may be so strong that we may overrule his sincere claim that he is not conscious of any fear of X—for example, his psychotherapist may, on the basis of a good deal of evidence, construe his denial of that fear as "resistance." So "fear of X" may be conceptually linked to outer circumstances and be-haviors, and yet not be such that it can be defined in extensional terms which make no appeal to the meaning which situations and behaviors have for the agent to whom we ascribe that fear.

Even in the case of lower animals, where the complexities of human purposes and cognitions do not arise, Tolman's analysis of "the rat expects food at location L" is not a definition of "expects" but a (usually) reliable test condition for the truth of that proposition, and in theory there is no way of specifying all the imaginable circumstances under which the test would fail (cf. C. Taylor, 1964, pp. 79–82). In practice, the experimenter can, of course, have the strongest reasons for claiming that the test condition does hold in a given case. Similarly, even in the much more complex human case, our background knowledge of relevant social practices, rules, roles, and the like often enables us to read the meaning of someone's behavior from the context—I can see that she is cooking dinner, that he is tackling the opposing player, that the conductor is collecting tickets on the train. But, in the first place, even in such standardized situations what the other person says about his intentions may lead us to change our mind; if, for example, we believe his story about really being a detective disguised as a train conductor, then we will redescribe what he did. And beyond these standardized situations there is a range of increasingly problematic ones, where we need to know a great deal about the other person's conceptions and the meanings which things have for him in virtue of these conceptions, before we can decide how what he is doing should be characterized. Is he really angry with his wife, or is he venting his anger on her when he is really angry with someone else, or is he trying to win points in an argument with her? Given sufficient background knowledge of the person and his circumstances, we may have excellent evidence for answering such questions one way or the other; we may even claim, in the face of his sincere denial of being conscious of having any such purpose, that we must dig deeper into the meaning various things really have for him in order to see whether the aim of which he is conscious is what really motivates him. But what is at issue is not whether we can have excellent evidence for intentionalistic characterizations of behavior—indeed, we can—but whether such characterizations can be translated into extensional ones which make no reference to how things appear to be from the agent's point of view. The answer to that, most philosophers would now agree, is no, and that rules out the "purposive behaviorism" Tolman envisaged.

Skinner's radical behaviorism continues the attempt of earlier behaviorists to make psychology a science which eliminates the agent's point of view from descriptions and explanations of behavior, but radical behaviorists have a much clearer idea of what such a science would have to be like than did behaviorists like Watson. For classical behaviorism was wedded to the Pavlovian model of conditioning, in which a physical excitation impinging on receptors (the sound of the bell) comes, as a result of association with an unconditioned physical stimulus (the smell of food), to elicit *in* bodily organs the same pattern of movements (salivation) that was originally elicited by the unconditioned stimulus because of a reflex arc. Thus behaviorists, though they were, in fact, trying to investigate actions, that is, responses *on the part* of organisms to various complex situations, committed themselves to conceptualizing their investigations on the reflex-arc model, as if there were no difference between their investigations and those of physiologists who study movements elicited in organisms by physical excitations (cf. Hamlyn, 1970). Tolman's purposive behaviorism sought to provide criteria for distinguishing the level at which, and the parameters in terms of which, psychological, as opposed to physiological, data could be identified and discriminated. But, as we have just seen, one cannot identify behavior intentionalistically, in terms of purposes and cognitions, and at the same time satisfy the conceptual and methodological restrictions behaviorists had imposed on themselves.

The problem is, however, overcome in Skinner's operant conditioning paradigm. Operants, far from being movements elicited in glands and muscles by physical stimuli, are simply "emitted" by organisms; they are responses on the part of the organism and are defined as a class of behaviors in terms of the effect they produce— a bar press is any behavior that gets the lever down. Consequently, operant conditioning deals with molar behavior acts, while the basic stance of behaviorism is maintained since operants are defined from an external point of view, by the experimenter who does not raise any questions about what the situation may mean from the organism's point of view. And though the manipulation of schedules of reinforcement can bring operant behavior under the control of a discriminative stimulus, operant conditioning differs sharply from classical conditioning. For in classical conditioning the new stimulus comes to elicit the respondent by being paired with an unconditioned stimulus which is linked to the respondent by a *prior* reflex-arc, while in operant conditioning everything depends on the *consequences* which the emission of the operant produces. It is not the built-in physiology of the dog, but the fact that his sitting on command is followed by the reinforcement, that brings his sitting under the control of the stimulus "sit!"

This makes it possible for Skinner to claim that "the distinction between voluntary and involuntary behavior is a matter of the kind of control. It corresponds to the distinction between eliciting and discriminative stimuli. . . . voluntary behavior is operant and involuntary behavior reflex" (1953, p. 112). Since operants are controlled by the consequences they produce, Skinner can provide a sketch of how the behaviors we normally talk about as purposive or intentional actions can be handled within his paradigm. He suggests that we can treat individual purposes in the way evolutionary theory treated phylogenetic purposes when it moved " 'seeing better' from the future into the past" by showing that the eye developed, not in order to see better, but as a result of consequences for survival which followed certain biological changes (Skinner, 1966, p. 13). Similarly, says Skinner,

> only a slight change is required to bring [purposes] within the framework of natural science. Instead of saying that a man behaves because of the consequences which *are* to follow his behavior, we simply say that he behaves because of the consequences which *have* followed similar behavior in the past. [1953, p. 97]

Consequently there is, according to Skinner, no basis for the charge that "behaviorism has no place for intention or purpose" (1974, p. 4); far from it, "operant behavior is the very field of purpose and intention" (p. 55).

Similarly, Skinner rejects the "methodological behaviorism" of Watson and others which "ignores consciousness, feelings, and states of mind" on the ground that they cannot be studied scientifically, because this merely avoids the mentalistic problem instead of dealing with it (1974, pp. 4, 13 ff.). In contrast, "the heart of radical behaviorism," according to Skinner, is its ability to deal with "what is inside the skin," and in so doing radical behaviorism "provides an alternative account of mental life" (pp. 211–212). A great deal of Skinner's writing is devoted to attempts "to interpret a wide range of mentalistic expressions" (p. 17)—"I consider scores, if not hundreds, of examples of mentalistic usage. . . . Many of these expressions I 'translate into behavior' " (p. 19).

Central to Skinner's "translations" is the notion that mental states and processes can be construed as felt bodily states which are private, in the sense that only the person himself can, normally, feel or observe what is going on "inside his skin." People and other animals are conscious of stimulation in the environment, as well as inside the skin, because evolution has provided them with an appropriate nervous system. A person also "becomes conscious in a different sense when a verbal community arranges contingencies under which he not only sees an object but sees that he is seeing it. In this special sense, consciousness or awareness is a social product" (1974, p. 220). In introspection we are conscious, in this second sense, of conditions in our body associated with seeing, or wanting (p. 50), or being worried or anxious (p. 63), or happy (p. 70). One may also "feel or otherwise observe some of the conditions associated with the probability that he will behave in a given way" (p. 72), for example, when one is "inclined" to act one way rather than another. Someone who is aware of his purpose "is feeling or observing introspectively a condition produced by reinforcement" (p. 57), and a person may even "feel conditions associated with 'judging,' 'anticipating,' and 'expecting,' but he does not need to do so" (p. 69). But "no special kind of mind stuff is assumed. A physical world generates both physical action and the physical conditions within the body to which a person responds when a verbal community arranges the necessary contingencies" (p. 220). So "radical behaviorism . . . does not deny the possibility of self-observation or self-knowledge" (p. 16), but "interprets" introspective knowledge as the observation of bodily states inside the skin that are associated with behavior.

This "translation" of mentalistic concepts provides Skinner with a justification for bypassing the inner states to which they refer in the scientific analysis of the causes of behavior. For if desires, purposes, and other so-called "mental states" are really physical states inside our own bodies, then they cannot initiate or direct behavior but must themselves be caused by other physical states and conditions. This is why Skinner argues that

> The objection to inner states is not that they do not exist, but that they are not relevant in a functional analysis. . . . [For though we can distinguish three links in our causal chain: (1)

"an operation performed on the organism from without," (2) "an inner condition," and (3) "a kind of behavior" (cf. p. 34)], unless there is a weak spot in our causal chain so that the second link is not lawfully determined by the first, or the third by the second, the first and third links must be lawfully related. . . . we may avoid many tiring and exhausting digressions by examining the third link as a function of the first. [1953, p. 35]

Again, in his most recent book, Skinner says that "the objection to the inner workings of the mind is not that they are not open to inspection but that they have stood in the way of the inspection of more important things" (1974, p. 165). The reason why these inner states are not important for the explanation of behavior is that they have the same cause as the behavior they are supposed to explain. Thus "motives and purposes are in people while contingencies of reinforcement are in the environment, but motives and purposes are at best the effects of reinforcements" (p. 56). . . ."His behavior does not change because he feels anxious; it changes because of the aversive contingencies which generate the condition felt as anxiety. The change in feeling and the change in behavior have a common cause" (pp. 61–62; see also pp. 158–165).

Now if "states of mind . . . may be interpreted as collateral products of the contingencies which generate behavior" (1974, p. 68), then it would be a mistake to cite them as causes of the behavior we are trying to explain, especially in view of the fact that "the private world within the skin is not clearly observed or known" (p. 31). The reasons for that are: first, our "rather primitive nervous systems," which are not suited for introspective observation of "an important part of the physiology which fills the temporal gap" between past external circumstances and present behavior (pp. 31, 216); second, the difficulties which the verbal community faces when it tries to arrange contingencies under which a person will respond to "private" stimuli inside his skin (pp. 23, 31). So while introspection may be able to provide someone with "clues" about his own behavior—in this sense "stimulation arising inside the body plays an important part in behavior" (p. 219)—these "inner states" are hard to spot and do not cause behavior. Moreover, we distract attention from what is important when we focus on inner conditions because external circumstances, unlike inner states, are readily accessible: "we cannot anticipate what a person will do by looking directly at his feelings *or* his nervous system, nor can we change his behavior by changing his mind *or* his brain" (p. 11). That is why "the experimental analysis of behavior goes directly to the antecedent causes in the environment" (p. 30).

What emerges from Skinner's "translations" and "interpretations" of mentalistic concepts is a biologized version of the passive organism of association psychology, a picture according to which we never act, but always react to external contingencies. Seemingly future-oriented activities are interpreted as behaviors controlled by past contingencies—for example, "to look for a match is to look in a manner previously reinforced by finding matches" (1974, p. 57)—and the translation of "purpose" and "reason for action" turns them into "felt" conditions "inside the skin" that are caused by the same contingencies which cause the behavior they are supposed to explain (pp. 129, 224). It could not be otherwise, since the adoption of the explanatory framework of the physical sciences excludes the agent's point of view, and thus also the framework of concepts in which we can distinguish actions, which are initiated and directed by someone, from reactions that are caused to occur in him. As Skinner puts it, "there is no place in the scientific position for a self as a true originator or initiator of action" (p. 225).

If Hume fancied himself the Newton of our mental life, Skinner seems to fancy himself as its Darwin. In order to explain the development of more adaptive forms biologists had appealed to purpose, but "it remained for Darwin to discover the selective action of the environment, as it remains for us to supplement developmentalism in behavioral sciences with an analysis of the selective action of the environment" (1974, p. 68). Skinner's theoretical achievement lies in showing how behavior *might* be due to the action of external contingencies even when it does not have any obvious environmental cause. In the case of respondent (reflex) behavior the cause, that is, the eliciting stimulus, is obvious enough; but operants are not elicited by any known environmental cause—they are just "emitted" by the organism—and "the principal feature is that there seems to be no necessary prior causal event" (p. 53). But, and this is Skinner's practical achievement, when pigeons and the like are put in a Skinner box, one can show that the operants they emit can, in fact, be controlled and shaped by manipulating their schedules of reinforcement. And Skinner's contention is that we call the operants which human beings emit in complex, uncontrolled natural situations "voluntary" because "the cause is simply harder to spot" (p. 54), so that "operant behavior is felt to be under the control of the behaving person" (p. 40). The absence of a conspicuous cause for such behavior leads "to the invention of an initiating event" (p. 53), and because "feelings appear at just the right time to serve as causes of behavior" (p. 10), they become the "inner causes" to which we mistakenly appeal. That is, we do not know the reinforcement history which is causally responsible both for what is felt and what behavior is emitted, but "associated bodily conditions can be felt or observed introspectively, and they are often cited as the causes. . . . the behavior is erroneously attributed to the feelings rather than to the contingencies responsible for what is felt" (p. 58).

This, according to Skinner, explains why we are inclined to develop mentalistic pseudo-explanations in terms of purpose, intention, and the like. But just as Darwin showed that we can explain the evolution of more adaptive species in terms of past contingencies of survival, without bringing in purpose as a future goal, so Skinner purports to show that we can explain the adaptive and purposive behavior of individual members of a species in terms of past contingencies of reinforcement, without bringing in purpose (in the intentionalistic sense). "The environment made its first great contribution during the evolution of the species, but it exerts a different kind of effect during the lifetime of the individual and the combination of the two effects is the behavior we observe at any given time" (1974, p. 17). Just as genetic endowment is "the product of the contingencies of survival," so the behavior repertoire acquired by the individual organism is the product of "the contingencies of reinforcement to which it is exposed during its lifetime" (p. 207).

Now if it is really true that complex human behaviors can be predicted and explained in terms of the operant paradigm, then Skinner's claim that mentalistic explanations are just "inventions" (1974, p. 104), that to explain behavior one "must look to the constructing environment, not to a constructing mind" (p. 117), will have real force. The objection that what is important is not the physical stimulus, or the topography of the behavior, but their meaning, will then be beside the point. For the intentionalist appeals to the meanings things have from the agent's point of view in order to establish explanatory relations between current settings and behaviors, when there do not seem to be any such relations between settings and behaviors that are described in physical terms. But if Skinner is right, then these relations become apparent in the experimental analysis of behavior when we look at the re-inforcements the organism has previously received in similar settings. The "meaning of a response," says Skinner, ". . . is to be found in its antecedent history. . . . the meaning [of a situation] is not in the current setting but in a history of exposure to contingencies in which similar settings have played a part" (p. 90). If a rat has been reinforced with food in the presence of a flashing light, but with water when the light is steady, then it will respond differentially to the lights and "it could be said that the flashing light means food and the steady light means water" (p. 91). Similarly, the behavior of two rats may be topographically indistinguishable, but if one has been reinforced for this behavior with food and the other with water, then their responses "may be said to differ in meaning: to one rat pressing the lever 'means' food; to the other it 'means' water" (p. 90). But obviously this way of distinguishing the meaning of situations and behaviors does not involve interpretation from an agent's point of view.

This construal of "meaning" as a matter of causal history, rather than intentionality, is extended to the human case when Skinner claims that, in addition to describing a man's behavior "in fully objective terms" (i.e., in terms of a physical thing language),

> we may also "interpret" his behavior or "read a meaning into it" by saying that "he is looking for something" or, more specifically, that "he is looking for his glasses." What we have added is not a further description of his behavior but an in-ference about some of the variables responsible for it. There is no *current* goal, incentive, purpose, or meaning to be taken into account. This is so even if we ask him what he is doing and he says "I am looking for my glasses." This is not a further description of his behavior but of the variables of which his behavior is a function; it is equivalent to "I have lost my glasses," "I shall stop what I am doing when I find my glasses," or "when I have done this in the past, I have found my glasses." These translations may seem unnecessarily round about, but only because expressions involving goals and pur-poses are abbreviations. [1953, pp. 89–90]

It is not hard to ridicule this, as Malcolm (1964) does, on the ground that it confuses the logic of first- and third-person psychological statements. Of course, Skinner has not provided anything like a translation of what we ordinarily mean. But to say this in criticism of Skinner is to miss the mark. Since Skinner's aim is to make psychology a natural science, he must find a way of discriminating its data so that they will be interpretation-free; consequently, the assimilation of first-person to third-person psychological statements, the conflation of the agent's point of view with that of the observer is, for Skinner, not a liability but part of the project of making psychology a natural science. Indeed, Skinner conceptualizes the reports I make about the behavior of others, as well as my self-reports, merely as "verbal behavior"—they are simply data for psychology, behaviors whose emission must be explained in terms of past and present environmental variables and reinforcements, so that neither type of statement is really a "statement" or "report" in the ordinary sense. Language itself is for Skinner something that psychology must explain without bringing in meaning in the intentionalistic sense (e.g., 1974, p. 91 ff.).

One cannot argue against Skinner's contention that "behaviorism . . . profiting from recent advances in the experimental analysis of behavior . . . can now analyze, one by one, the key terms in the mentalistic armamentarium" (1974, p. 32), that his "analyses" do not provide "translations" of our ordinary mentalistic concepts. As I suggested earlier, it does not seem possible to translate intentionalistic expressions into a purely extensional language, but Skinner himself recognizes that his translations may not be exact, "that there are perhaps no exact behavioral equivalents" for our mental concepts (p. 19). Though Skinner's "interpretations" violate the logic of our ordinary concepts, that does not matter much since psychology can no more be required to confine itself to our ordinary concepts than any other science. As Skinner rightly points out, the modern physicist may not be able to provide exact translations for "ether, phlogiston, or *vis viva*" either (p. 19). If Skinner can show that his conceptualizations of "purpose," "meaning," and the like allow us to formulate empirical laws that can be used to predict, explain, and control human behavior more effectively than we can do on the basis of our ordinary mentalistic conceptions, then he will have all he needs. He has shown how molar behavior acts can be conceptualized on his paradigm; if he can also show that our actions are, in fact, under the control of environmental variables in the way in which the pigeon's bar-pressing in the Skinner box is under the control of stimuli and reinforcements, then he will have discovered nonmentalistic laws that apply to human actions, laws which allow us to predict and control human behavior without bringing in meaning or intentionality, so that the laws of psychology will not differ from those of the physical sciences.

It is easy to understand why Skinner thinks that the establishment of such laws, or "functional relations," is the sole aim of psychology, why he holds that psychology does not need "theory" in the sense of "any explanation of an observed fact which appeals to events taking place somewhere else, at some other level of observation, described in different terms and measured, if at all, in different dimensions" (1961, p. 39). Theoretical mediators can have no place in Skinner's science of behavior, because any attempt to explain his functional relations must lead either in the direction of cognitive mediation or in the direction of physiological processes. But Skinner rejects the former as mentalistic pseudo-explanation that appeals to "thought processes," which "are real enough at the level of behavior, but merely questionable metaphors when moved inside" (1974, p. 218). Thus "the cognitive psychologist talks about various systems of access borrowed from the filing systems of libraries, computers, . . . [but] the contingencies which affect an organism are not stored by it. They are never inside it; they simply change it" (p. 109). The changes involved are physiological and will, presumably, be explained some day. But the important physiological changes involved are not open to introspection, and their discovery is the business of physiology rather than psychology. In the meantime, the behavioral psychologist can get on with his business without worrying about what the physiologist of the future may discover, since that "cannot invalidate the laws of a science of behavior, but it will make the picture of human action more nearly complete" (p. 215) by filling the physiological gap between past environmental contingencies and present behavioral outputs.

While Skinner has, I think, succeeded in sketching coherent background assumptions for a possible program of psychological research, he talks of "laws of the science of behavior" and "recent advances in the experimental analysis of behavior" *as if* laws of the appropriate type had, in fact, been established for complex human behavior. But Skinner's claim that "it is in the nature of an experimental analysis of human behavior that it should strip away the functions previously assigned to autonomous man and transfer them one by one to the controlling environment" (1971, p. 189) is certainly not supported by evidence showing that such an experimental analysis can, in fact, be carried through for complex human behavior. What Skinner has shown is that a surprising amount of animal behavior in the Skinner box, and a very limited range of human behavior, can be predicted and controlled in terms of the operant conditioning paradigm. Behavior modification is the only area in which there has been a serious attempt to apply Skinnerian principles to human behavior, though Skinner claims that "the extensive experiments by cognitive psychologists on accessibility can all be reinterpreted" (1974, p. 109) in terms of operant conditioning. But even if that should be true, it works both ways: cognitive psychologists can, and do, argue that what happens when behavior modification is effective is best reinterpreted in cognitive terms (cf. Breger & McGaugh, 1965). So at least with respect to human behavior, Skinner's talk about "advances in the experimental analysis of behavior" is a promissory note, and what is at issue is the plausibility of thinking that it can be cashed.

For example, Skinner's *Verbal Behavior* (1957) is most charitably read, not as an attempt to show that verbal behavior is, in fact, a function of operant conditioning, but as an attempt to show the plausibility of a Skinnerian "interpretation" of verbal behavior. Chomsky's (1959) criticisms show that Skinner's basic concepts lose their exact meaning when they are extrapolated from animal laboratory experiments to ordinary verbal behavior, so that it becomes impossible to falsify these extrapolations. This does not really refute Skinner, since the Skinnerian psychologist can always follow the methodological injunction "Keep looking for explanations in terms of operant conditioning!"; he can continue to hope that the promissory note will, some day, be cashed. But it is hard to see why people like MacCorquodale (1970) should take comfort in the fact that Chomsky has not refuted Skinner. There is no a priori reason why the attempt to show that all behavior is a function of operant conditioning *must* fail; equally, there is not a priori reason why it must succeed. It is, after all, a question of fact whether or not we succeed in finding lawful relations about behavior when we confine ourselves to interpretation-free data characterized from the outside—that is, when we set out to discover laws that hold between operants, identified by the investigator who takes no account of what the behavior may mean from the agent's point of view, and stimuli and reinforcements that are characterized in physical terms. Though the success of this enterprise has, so far, been minimal, it is not logically impossible, and consequently no philosophical argument can show that it can never be done.

Skinner himself seems to recognize this difference between program and results when he distinguishes "the science of human behavior" from "behaviorism [which] is the philosophy of that science" (1974, p. 3), and admits that "much of the argument goes beyond the established facts. I am concerned with interpretation rather than prediction and control" (p. 19). It may well be that Skinner has devoted so much of his effort throughout his career to behavioristic "interpretations" of mental concepts in order to make his program plausible as a research strategy for developing a psychology of human behavior. But all Skinner's "interpretations" can do is sketch the form which the explanation of complex human behavior *could* take, if we had the science of behavior he envisages. Since "advances in the experimental analysis of behavior" have, in spite of much time and effort, established very little by way of incontrovertible positive findings about complex human behavior, the support for Skinner's program has to rest mainly on arguments *against* other approaches—arguments against "mentalism," "theoretical mediators," "cognitive explanations," and the like. In other words, the plausibility of Skinner's program for developing a science of human behavior that is free of intentionalistic descriptions and explanations depends, almost entirely, on whether his arguments succeed in showing that "no matter how defective a behavioral account may be," it is still our best bet because "mentalistic explanations explain nothing" (p. 224). Unless Skinner can make that contention stick, there is very little to recommend his behaviorist program over other approaches to the development of a science of human behavior.

Skinnerian and Philosophical Arguments against Mentalistic Explanations

Before turning to Skinner's arguments, it should be noted that they are not peculiar to behaviorists but have close analogues in arguments deployed by some contemporary philosophers. This coincidence is not a matter of mutual influence, but is due to the fact that much as behaviorism is a reaction against introspective psychology, so a good deal of contemporary philosophy of mind is a reaction against Descartes's dualism. Ryle's highly influential *Concept of Mind* (1949) was designed to explode "Descartes's myth"; but since getting rid of the "ghost in the machine" required abandoning the notion that psychologists can have special "proprietary data on which to found their theories," Ryle found it hard to see how there could be any such thing as a special empirical science called "psychology" (p. 320 ff.). Similarly, a recent paper by Malcolm (1971), entitled "The Myth of Cognitive Processes and Structures," argues that the psychologist's appeal to such inner processes and structures rests on confusion. Quite a few contemporary philosophers talk as if they can see the point of physiology, on one side, and of ordinary common-sense explanations on the other, but can see no room in between for a science of psychology; like Skinner, they seem to think that the notion of a science which deals with inner mental processes must involve some sort of confusion.

What then are the arguments against theories that appeal to mental organization, cognitive processes, and the like? Why do "mentalistic explanations explain nothing"? One argument used by Skinner is that there simply are no such inner processes: "mental life and the world in which it is lived are inventions. They have been invented on the analogy of external behavior occurring under external contingencies" (1974, p. 104). For example, the fact that people can make physical copies of things in the outside world, store them, and on "a future occasion such a record can evoke behavior appropriate to an earlier occasion . . . has led to the elaboration of a cognitive metaphor" (p. 108). Psychologists proceed to talk about what is "stored in memory, later to be retrieved or recalled and used" in behavior (ibid.). "But," asks Skinner, "what is the mental parallel of physical search? How are we to go about finding an item in the storehouse of memory? . . . If we can remember a name, we have no need to search our memory; if we cannot remember it, how do we go about looking for it?" (pp. 108–109). Similarly, Malcolm points out that though I may do various things when I am *trying* to remember something, there is very often "*no* process of remembering"—asked what novel I read last week, I just remember and give its title without any process of remembering at all; he suggests that it is simply a muddle to suppose that when I just remember, or recognize, something, "the process of recognition is *hidden*" and has to be discovered by psychologists (1971, pp. 385–386).

Malcolm's contention is that when I remember, or recognize, something without consciously doing anything, there is no call for "inventing" explanations in terms of "hidden" (nonconscious) psychological processes. Skinner sees no room for explanations of behaviors like remembering, or recognizing, in terms of either conscious or nonconcious "mental" processes. He claims to have no difficulty with such "higher mental activities" as searching, etc., provided that what we are talking about is "simply behaving [or at least] behaving covertly." What Skinner rejects is "the assumption that comparable activities take place in the mysterious world of the mind" (1974, p. 223). Skinner's substitution of "covert behavior" for "mental activities" seems to be nothing more than a verbal device for avoiding the appearance of talk about the "mysterious world of the mind," since it is not clear that, for example, my "overt" search for my briefcase has anything in common with my "covert search" for it—that is, trying to remember where I left it by thinking about when I last had it, where I went from there, etc.—except perhaps that they have a similar intent or aim: to locate the briefcase. And "aim" is, of course, an intentionalistic concept. But leaving that aside, it is clear that when cognitive psychologists talk about information storage and retrieval and the like, they are talking neither about (observable) behavior nor about psychological operations which we consciously perform. Whether or not their theories are justified by the facts, the point is that these clearly are *theories* about nonobservable processes which are assumed in order to explain and predict some of the facts we can observe when people remember, recognize a visual pattern, etc. Consequently the objection that we don't observe any "mental parallel of physical search," that there may be no conscious "process of remembering," has as little force as the objection that we can't observe the subatomic particles of modern physics. One could, of course, fall back on the Descartes-Wundt tradition and hold that a nonconscious psychological process is a contradiction in terms. But that, as the work of Freud might suggest, is not a profitable move. (I will return to this point in the next section.)

Another argument often used by Skinner is that talk about mental states and processes can be eliminated from the explanation of behavior because these "inner" states are always inferred from observed behavior. Thus,

> when we reinforce a person we are said to give him a motive or incentive, but we infer the motive or incentive from the behavior. We call a person highly motivated when all we know is that he behaves energetically. [1974, p. 51] . . . Many sup-

posed inner causes of behavior, such as attitudes, opinions, traits of character, and philosophies, remain almost entirely inferential. [P. 59] . . . [Cognitive psychologists claim that languages have invariant features because "that is the way the brain is wired," but] a conceptual nervous system cannot, of course, be used to explain the behavior from which it is inferred. [P. 213]

The mistake, Skinner argues, is like that involved in saying that a fluid that is observed to flow slowly "possesses viscosity," and then "explaining" that it "flows slowly because it is viscous. . . . A state or quality inferred from the behavior of a fluid begins to be taken as a cause" (1974, p. 161). But that would be a good argument only if there could be no evidence for the postulated "inner" states or processes other than the evidence which initially led to their postulation. We know that in developed sciences such postulations have proved very fruitful in producing new predictions and explanations, and it is not clear why it should be different in psychology.

Now Skinner says that "a science of behavior must eventually deal with behavior in its relation to certain manipulable [i.e., external] variables" (1961, p. 61), and that may be true. But what is at issue is whether behavior is *solely* a function of external variables so that the appeal to internal processes can be eliminated. He tells us that "we observe that a person responds to a current setting ('the evidence of his senses') because of his exposure to contingencies of which the setting has been a part. We have no reason to say that he has stored information which he now retrieves in order to interpret the evidence of his senses" (1974, p. 78). But whether or not we have reason to say this depends on whether or not we can really explain what he perceives solely in terms of past contingencies of which the present setting has been a part.

An analogue to Skinner's argument that psychology should stick to correlations between "what we can observe" is made by Malcolm in relation to the meaning of mental concepts. He suggests that since there is no way in which we could introspectively name the occupants of an inner mental realm, the meaning of mental concepts must depend on external circumstances and behavior. And he argues that once we see that, contrary to the Cartesian picture, there is no introspectable inner state in virtue of which something is a recognition, memory, or thought, we should also see that there is nothing "inner" for psychology to investigate. In Malcolm's words, if psychologists would recognize that what makes something, for example, a case of recognition, is not "something that goes on inside," then "they would no longer have a motive for constructing models for recognition, memory, thinking, problem solving, and other 'cognitive processes' " (1971, p. 387).

These arguments are versions of the operationalist notion that because the meaning of theoretical concepts must be cashed in terms of observable circumstances and behavior, science should only concern itself with empirical correlations between external circumstances and behaviors. The move is even less plausible in psychology than in physics. For the lack of isomorphism between, for example, physical inputs and what a person perceives, is just what led psychologists since Helmholtz to develop explanations which appeal to "inner" processes (e.g., "unconscious inferences"). But while physicists, who had been using theoretical concepts to develop powerful explanatory and predictive theories, never took operationalism seriously in their work, psychologists took it very seriously because they had not succeeded in constructing such theories. If talk about atoms never got further than the empirical correlations in connection with which the concept was first introduced, there would, of course, be force to the claim that talk about atoms is unnecessary because the concept can be completely cashed in terms of operational definitions. But psychology's lack of success in constructing powerful theories may not show that all behavior is a function of external variables so that psychology can do without theory, but rather that the background assumptions which have informed psychological research programs have put unreasonable constraints on the sort of concepts which psychologists have allowed themselves to use, thus preventing the introduction of concepts that might be more appropriate for the development of powerful psychological theories of high-grade human behavior.

In sum, Skinner claims that a science of behavior can do without theories about underlying "inner" processes because it can establish empirical generalizations which link behavior to the external variables of which it is a function. But all he has really established is that when pigeons or rats are confined in a Skinner box one can discover empirical generalizations relating, for example, rate of response and contingencies of reinforcement. Skinner simply assumes that the same *must* be true for all other behaviors, including complex human behavior, when he says, for example,

A person is changed by the contingencies of reinforcement under which he behaves; he does not store the contingencies. . . . there are no "data structures stored in his memory"; he has no "cognitive map". . . . He has simply been changed in such a way that stimuli now control particular kinds of perceptual behavior. [1974, p. 84] . . . Techniques of recall are not concerned with searching a storehouse of memory but with increasing the probability of responses. [Pp. 109–110] . . . It is said that there are rules and instructions which govern the use of language and which we obey without being aware of them. . . . But it is the contingencies which "govern the use of language," not rules, whether or not they are extracted. [Pp. 127–128]

One cannot argue with Skinner when he says "there is no *a priori* reason why a complete account is not possible without appeal to processes in other dimensional systems" (1961, p. 67); one can only point out that there is also no a priori reason why such an account must be possible.

Skinner simply begs all the relevant questions when he replies to the objection that behaviorism neglects "what meaning a situation has for a person" by saying that

to investigate how a situation looks to a person, or how he interprets it, or what meaning it has for him, we must examine his behavior with respect to it, including his descriptions of it, and we can do this only in terms of his genetic and environmental histories. [1974, p. 77]

Since a person's genetic and environmental histories include everything that could (logically) be relevant to understanding his behavior, that is obvious enough. But how is that history to be studied? The issue is not whether we find out what a situation means to someone from his behavior ("including his descriptions of it"), but how we can plausibly proceed with the examination of that behavior: can we understand and predict it when we attempt to establish empirical generalizations between stimuli, responses, and reinforcements characterized from the outside in physical terms? Or can we find lawful relations only between stimuli and responses that have been interpreted in terms of the meaning they have from the agent's point of view? In the latter case, we will have to know how he selects, codes, stores, interprets, and uses information from the environment before we can find lawful relations between environmental situations and behavioral responses, and there will be no way of avoiding theory that appeals to "other dimensional systems."

Further, Skinner's arguments for the elimination of theoretical concepts depend on his "interpretation" of mental concepts, an interpretation according to which they always refer to "felt" states, or events, inside the skin. For on this interpretation the referents of our mental concepts are, at best, internal states that mediate between external variables and overt behaviors. And since these internal ("theoretical") states are themselves functionally dependent on external variables, they are, so Skinner argues, eliminable in a functional analysis—recall the passage quoted earlier about the eliminability of the internal middle term in our causal chains. (In much the same way, when association psychology construed what goes on "in the mind" as a reflection of contingencies imprinted from outside, the mind, as we noted earlier, ceased to do any real work in the explanation of behavior and became eliminable.) But this argument fails for at least two reasons. First, even if one were to accept the Skinnerian "interpretation" of the meaning of our mental concepts, and construe their referents as events or states inside the body which are functionally dependent on external variables, it does not follow that these "mediators" must be eliminable. For suppose that, for example, having a motive, or an attitude, were contingently identical with the occurrence of some inner state which is a function of external variables; it might still be the case that we do not know the external variables of which this state is a function, and at the same time we might have good evidence for attributing this inner state to an organism—for example, on the basis of what the person tells us, or on the basis of inferences from some of his behaviors, or even on the basis of neurological evidence (cf. Lacy, 1974, pp. 30–32).

Second, but more important, there is no reason to accept Skinner's "interpretation" of the meaning of our mental concepts. We have already seen that mental concepts are used to characterize behavior intentionalistically, in relation to what various situations mean to the agent and what he intends, or aims at, in what he is doing; and it is far from clear that "meaning," "aim," "intention," and the like refer to *any* states or events, be they internal or external. Such concepts are embedded in a different explanatory framework, the one used by agents in their commerce with each other, and the attempt to fit aims, meanings, etc., into causal chains by making them intermediate links in a series of events that runs from external variables to overt behaviors does violence to the logic of intentionalistic explanations. Skinner keeps arguing that "felt" states of, for example, anxiety do not cause a person's behavior, but that simply is not what is at issue. The question is not whether "feelings," either qua mental or bodily states, cause behavior, but rather whether we have to know what a person feels anxious, or guilty, *about*, as well as other related beliefs, attitudes, and the like, in order to understand and predict his behavior.

Put another way, intentionalistic explanations which deploy such mental concepts *presuppose* agents who have the power to act in light of their conceptions. But Skinner rules out the possibility of such explanations—that is, I think, the most basic reason for his contention that "if a behavioristic interpretation of thinking is not all we should like to have, it must be remembered that mental or cognitive explanations are not explanations at all" (1974, p. 103). Skinner's argument here is that "both the mind and the brain are not far from the ancient notion of a homunculus" (1974, p. 117). That is, "we attribute the visible behavior to another organism inside—to a little man or homunculus. . . . the explanation is successful, of course, only so long as the behavior of the homunculus can be neglected" (1964, pp. 79–80). According to Skinner, "information theory, with respect to the behavior of the individual, is merely a sophisticated version of copy theory" (1974, p. 143), and the trouble with the copy theory of perception is that it "makes no progress whatsoever in explaining" what it is supposed to explain (p. 81). The objection Theophrastus raised to Greek versions of the copy theory more than two thousand years ago—if we try to explain perception by assuming inner copies of outer stimuli we still have to explain how we perceive the copy, so that "the old problem would still confront us" (p. 81) —is, so Skinner suggests, applicable to "the metaphor of storage in memory. . . . the computer is a bad model. . . . We do make external records for future use . . . but the assumption of a parallel inner record-keeping process adds nothing to our understanding of this kind of thinking" (p. 110).

A similar argument is developed by Malcolm, who claims that cognitive psychologists, like philosophers in the classical tradition, make the mistake of thinking that if it is to be possible for me to recognize something, as for example a dog, then I must be guided in this activity by an inner representation or idea. But in order to see that the idea really fits the thing before me, I will need a "model of fitting," a second-order idea which guides me, and this will in turn have to be guided by a third order of idea, and so on (Malcolm, 1971, pp. 389–391). Different versions of this infinite regress argument can, of course, be found in Ryle.

The point of such arguments seems to be that when we appeal to cognitive processes in order to explain a person's ability to do something, we are not explaining anything, because we are merely postulating another ability which is just as much in need of explanation as the behavior we are trying to explain. When cognitive psychologists talk about the extraction, coding, storage, or use of information, they are, as Skinner sees it, appealing to a homunculus, which possesses these unexplained abilities, in order to explain what a person does when he remembers or recognizes something, or acts purposefully in light of his conceptions. Persons are organisms which are changed by contingencies of reinforcement so that they behave differently in the future, and physiology will some day tell us what causal mechanisms mediate that change. But we explain nothing and distract attention from what is important (i.e., behavior and external variables of which it is alleged to be a function), when we appeal to cognitive powers, as, for example, in Kant's notion that we have the ability "to act from the mere conception of a rule" and so can *use* information and the like to guide our behavior. In Skinner's view, "we do not act by putting knowledge to use" (1974, p. 139); indeed, we do not "possess" knowledge, or even behavioral capacities, except in the sense in which an organism may be said to " 'possess' a system of immune reactions" (p. 137). For Skinner, as for Hume, all talk about mental powers or cognitive abilities is occult:

> Behavior exists only when it is being executed. [1974, p. 137] . . . Human thought is human behavior. [P. 117] . . . By attempting to move human behavior into a world of nonphysical dimensions, mentalistic or cognitive psychologists have cast the basic issues in insoluble forms. [P. 118] . . . [If we suppose that the organism can respond to a physical environment with mental activities] the puzzling question of how a physical event causes a mental event, which in turn causes a physical event, remains to be answered. [P. 211]

We will see whether explanations which appeal to the cognitive powers and processes of agents must involve occult homunculi and threaten the return of Cartesian dualism, as we turn to an examination of the type of explanation cognitive psychologists are trying to develop.

COGNITIVE PSYCHOLOGY AND THE NATURE OF PSYCHOLOGICAL EXPLANATIONS

There are many differences between various types of cognitive models now being developed, including the different ways they conceive the relation between cognitive processes and consciousness. Some models attempt to account for perceptual phenomena in terms of psychological processes which neither are, nor could become, conscious. For example, though linguistic rules are thought to integrate acoustic signals in speech perception (Fodor & Bever, 1965; Garrett, Bever, & Fodor, 1966), there is no suggestion that a person consciously uses these rules when he hears a sentence in a language he knows. Similarly, Dodwell's (1970) model of visual pattern recognition postulates a "coder" which is basically an information reduction device, a "recognizer" which notes the occurrence of particular temporal patterns and the like, without any suggestion that these psychological processes are, or could become, conscious. Others, like Kelly's (1955) theory of personal constructs or Ryan's (1970) treatment of intentional behavior, deal with ways of categorizing situations and behaviors of which the person is, or can usually become, conscious. In some theories (e.g., Irwin, 1971; Boneau, 1974) the question of whether cognitive processes are conscious or not is regarded as having no importance. Still others, for example, some versions of psychoanalytic theory, can be seen as dealing with the role played in behavior by cognitive processes that are "dynamically unconscious"—that is, processes which the person is motivated to keep himself from consciously knowing, but which can be brought to consciousness through psychotherapy. Piaget's developmental account of how "schemas," which are initially organized motor dispositions, gradually develop into strategies, plans for action, or conscious schemas is probably the most ambitious cognitive theory.

In spite of the differences between them, cognitive theories share a common emphasis on the notion that behavioral outputs are not simply determined by physical inputs that impinge on sense receptors, but rather depend on the selection, transformation, and use of information extracted from stimuli. On this view, the reality to which we respond—"things as they appear to us"—is, in part, our own construction. Experience then cannot be characterized as the passive reception of inputs, because the experiences that shape us are also shaped by our own selective and transformational activities. This emphasis on the subject's constructive activities gives cognitive psychology a Kantian flavor, though the ways such theories differ from Kant is obvious enough: where Kant attempted a transcendental deduction of the unchanging principles of the human mind as such, these are empirical theories dealing with the activities of actual subjects, and the constructive principles involved are seen as conditioned by evolution, culture, and history. The contrast between such theories and behavioristic ones is equally obvious: the aim of cognitive theories is to discover *psychological* processes that explain behavior by telling us something about "how the mind works" (Neisser, 1967, p. 8), rather than to find "functional relations" between external inputs and outputs that can be characterized without bringing in the mind.

It is important to notice, first, that the psychological processes assumed in models of, for example, pattern or speech recognition are *nonconscious*. They are neither conscious, nor unconscious in the Freudian sense, because there is simply *no way* in which these psychological processes could be brought to consciousness. The activities attributed to the coder and recognizer are simply not activities which we can be said to perform at all; nor could we be said to be applying those rules which cognitive psychologists postulate to explain speech perception. In effect, such models exploit an analogy with persons when they postulate these activities. They treat the behavior of, for example, the coder or recognizer *as if* it were the behavior of a person who can select information, notice the occurrence of certain patterns, etc.—they talk *as if* there were an agent who applies these rules. The reason they do so is that they see no way, for example, of accounting for differences between specifiable characteristics of past and present physical stimuli and contingencies, on the one hand, and what is perceived (informational content), on the other, without hypothesizing some sort of nonconscious data processing. Since the postulated activities are nonconscious, the value of these postulations has to be established in much the same way in which one evaluates models in other sciences that deploy an analogy in order to postulate unobservable processes that may account for what we observe: does the model which postulates these unobservable processes succeed in predicting and explaining what we observe and is it fruitful? If the answer is yes, the theory will have all the empirical justification it needs, even if it cannot answer a further question that moves us to a different level of explanation: for example, from How is information from physical inputs selected and organized in pattern recognition? to What is it about the structure of the human organisms that makes it possible for them to select and organize information in these ways?

Now one could refuse to call the processes postulated in such models "psychological" or "mental" on the ground that they are nonconscious, much as Wundt ruled Freudian theory out of psychology solely on the ground that it appealed to processes which are not conscious. To be sure, the processes postulated in such cognitive models are neither physiological processes nor processes that have been incorporated into our common-sense knowledge of people and their behavior because we are conscious of them. But what area should one expect psychological theory to explore, if not just this area between physiology and common sense? Further, as Fodor has pointed out, "it seems clear that *only* consciousness is at issue" (1968, p. 87). That is, the processes postulated in such models differ sharply from, for example, an organism's immune reactions, because they are such that if they were conscious, one would not hesitate to call them mental; moreover, the behavior to which they lead is clearly intelligent—understanding a language, or recognizing a visual pattern, is an intelligent performance. So it hardly seems a useful move to rule such processes out of the domain of psychology solely on the ground that they are nonconscious.

Indeed, one of the most interesting features of cognitive psychology is that it uses concepts rooted in the conceptual framework employed by agents, in order to develop empirical theories that can tell us something about the behavior of agents that is not already available to common sense. Since the meaning of these psychological concepts is rooted in their application to persons, to language-using beings who can consciously self-monitor their behavior and give accounts of what they are doing, talk about nonconscious psychological operations performed by the recognizer, or about nonconscious rule following, is, of course, anthropomorphic. But that such anthropomorphism is innocent of dualism should be clear from the fact that it is involved in all program-level talk about computers; and models of the sort we are considering are intended to provide explanations at a level analogous to that at which program talk about a computer's subroutines can explain what it is up to.

The development of modern computers is, of course, what made the appeal to rule following, instructions, information processing, and the like, respectable and so led to the rapid development of cognitive psychology over the last ten or so years. Once such computers were developed, one could hardly avoid being struck by the importance of distinguishing the abstract structure of a system from its material embodiment; a program could, after all, not only be run on differently constructed machines, it could also be written by a programmer who knows nothing about computer hardware. Those who work with such machines had to recognize the different levels at which their behavior could be described, and the very different sort of explanations and predictions that are relevant to our interests and concerns at different levels. As Deutsch puts it:

> Clearly, the question about what the actual physical change is which occurs during learning in the machine is the wrong type of question to ask and to attempt to answer. For, whatever the answer, we still do not understand how the machine learns. . . . The precise properties of the parts do not matter; it is only their general relationships to each other which give the machine as a whole its behavioral properties. These general relationships can be described in a highly abstract way. . . . This highly abstract system thus derived can be embodied in a theoretically infinite variety of physical counterparts. Nevertheless, the machine thus made will have the same behavioral properties, given the same sensory and motor side. Therefore, if we wish to explain the behavior of one of these machines, the relevant and enlightening information is about this abstract system and not about its particular embodiment. Further, given the system or abstract structure alone of the machine, we can deduce its properties and predict its behavior. On the other hand, the knowledge that the machine operates mechanically, electrochemically, or electronically does not help us very much at all. [1960, Pp. 12–13]

Thus, even though a computer is certainly a physical system, if it is sufficiently complex and well designed, then there will be a level at which it will have "behavioral properties" that can be usefully described and explained as the behavior of a system that uses information in order to achieve its goals.

It is important to appreciate this point, because it has often been argued that, though mechanisms can serve the purposes of their designers, there is no sense to the supposition that mechanisms can be purposive systems that act to achieve goals of their own. For example, Richard Taylor argues this thesis, on the ground that "any purely behavioral conception of a goal [is] utterly inadequate" (1966, p. 235) for three reasons. (a) The fact that a process "culminates in some final state . . . is not a defining condition of its being purposeful. One must add that the behaving object behaves as it does *in order* that such a final state . . . may result" (p. 236). (b) Two "processes or activities which are behaviorally and physically identical may nevertheless be directed toward entirely different ends or goals"—for example, the behavior of the man who aims at a bird, fires and misses, hitting a nearby tree, and that of the same man who, on another occasion, aims at the tree and hits it while the bird is flying by (p. 237). (c) "The end or goal of purposeful activity sometimes does not exist" (ibid.). Taylor points out that a little old lady on an assembly line might be able to thread a needle most of the time but might, perhaps because of a grudge against the company, miss half the time on purpose; the difference between her missing half the time on purpose and her just missing half the time is intelligible, but no such distinction, Taylor argues, could be made for a needle-threading machine. For

> suppose an engineer were told to construct *two* needle-threading machines. . . . one of them would be such that it simply missed half the time, the other would be such that, like the lady, it missed half of the time on purpose. How would the two machines differ? What could the engineer *add* to the second to achieve such a difference? It seems perfectly obvious that there would be nothing whatever to add. [P. 241]

Taylor's arguments are closely related to the distinction between intentional and extensional characterizations of behavior which we discussed earlier. His three criteria for distinguishing between genuinely purposive behavior and behavior that only seems purposive can be satisfied by behavior that is characterized in intentional terms, but not by characterizations given in "purely behavioral" (i.e., extensional) terms. He sees no difficulty in constructing a machine that will emit behaviors characterized in extensional terms (e.g., a needle-threading machine that misses half the time), but sees no way in which intentional characterizations (e.g., missing half the time on purpose) could be applicable to a machine. The argument assumes that since there are causal mechanisms which produce the behavior of a machine, the notion that the machine's behavior may or may not be appropriate to the realization of its goals (as contrasted with the goals of its designer) makes no sense. For example, if a "target-seeking" torpedo fails to "function 'correctly'"—for example, hitting a school of fish instead of an enemy ship—it is still "behaving exactly as it was designed to behave, namely to move in the direction of certain sources of sound" (p. 231); the "mistake" was the designer's, not the missile's. Since mechanisms are causal systems whose behavior can be explained by laws of the physical sciences which make no reference to agents and their point of view, intentionalistic concepts like "mistake," "purpose," "appropriate behavior," and the like cannot, as Taylor sees it, be properly applied to them.

Taylor is right in thinking that we are stretching concepts if we think of such simple mechanisms as needle-threading machines, or a torpedo guided by feedback from sound waves, as purposive systems. In order for a system to be really purposive it must be able to *use* information to generate behaviors *appropriate* to the achievement of its goals. What is needed is not merely "information storage," in the sense of inputs that somehow contribute causally to later outputs; rather, the system must be capable of what Dennett calls "intelligent storage," which is

> storage of information that is *for* the system itself, and not merely *for* the system's users or creators. For information to be *for* a system, the system must have some *use* for the information, and hence the system must have needs. The criterion for intelligent storage is then the appropriateness of the resultant behavior to the system's needs given the stimulus conditions of the initial input and the environment in which the behavior occurs. [1969, Pp. 46–47]

The torpedo that changes direction in response to changes in sound waves does not use this information any more than a parrot that can be made to emit "Fire hurts" on presentation of some stimulus can use that information. The parrot, like the torpedo, can be used by an agent to achieve his purpose, but the purpose in question is not the parrot's or the torpedo's. In order for talk about a system's "using information to attain its goals" to get a foothold, the input must have a significance for the system (rather than its designer), which requires that the input be connected with behavioral outputs that are *appropriate* to an input having that meaning for a system with certain goals. Unless, for example, an input with the informational content "Fire hurts" will lead to behaviors that are appropriate in relation to the system's circumstances and goals, there is no basis for talk about "intelligent storage" (cf. Dennett, 1969, pp. 47 ff., 72 ff.).

But there are machine programs that can be naturally described as using information to achieve goals. This, for example, is the way Newell and Simon's General Problem Solver is characterized: "Basically, the GPS program is a way of achieving a goal by setting up subgoals whose attainment leads to the attainment of the initial goal" (Reitman, 1966, p. 184). Given a problem to solve, GPS employs a series of subroutines, one after the other, and checks the results of a completed subroutine against the specified goal; partial success is recognized as progress towards the goal, and the result is put to further use.[15] Though GPS does not have much by way of heuristics to generate elegant solutions, it does use a repertoire of alternate behaviors until it succeeds in bringing about a certain end result. And this is, after all, the only *sort* of evidence we can have for attributing purposive behavior to animals. Whether or not we decide to regard the behavior as purposive will depend, in both cases, on a judgment about how appropriate the behavior seems for achieving the goal (e.g., how successful is the system in recognizing partial progress and using that in subsequent behavior?). What is at issue in such cases is whether or not it is *useful* to think of the system as a purposive system when we are trying to explain and predict its behavior.

We expect more in the human case, because people can often tell us what they are aiming at and why. This suggests that they must somehow be able to develop internal representations of the environment and their own behaviors, but the notion of such

15. For example, to transform object A into object B, GPS matches the objects element by element. If the match reveals a difference D, a subgoal of reducing the difference is set up. This is done by searching for an operator Q that is relevant to the difference, subjecting it to a preliminary test of feasibility, and if it passes the test a subgoal is set up to apply Q to the object, thus producing a new object, A', which is a modification of the original one in the direction of reducing the difference. Then a new subgoal is set up to transform A' into B. Cf. Reitman (1966, pp. 185 ff.).

internal models is now being applied to computers. For example, Minsky (1965) sees no difficulty in a computer that can "answer questions about the world" because it has an internal mechanism that enables it to model that world, or about its having higher level models that can be used to answer higher order questions like "What sort of a thing are you?" as well as special models that enable the machine to represent and analyze its own goals and resources (pp. 45–48). Indeed, "there seems to be no logical limitation to the possibility of a machine understanding its own basic principles of operation" (p. 48).

Two points are important for our purposes. First, there is no difficulty in principle about a machine whose behavior is guided, in part, by internal models of its world, including itself and its behaviors, or even about the machine's having models of its own models. Second, when the behavior of computers is described in this way, our descriptions are intentionalistic. For, as Minsky points out, "The model relation is inherently ternary. Any attempt to suppress the role of the intentions of the investigator, B, leads to circular definitions" (1965, p. 45). That is, in order for something to be a model, it must be not only a model of something, but also a model for someone—it must be used as a model of something by someone who has some purpose, or intention, in using it. The model is realized in some extensionally specifiable mechanism, but qua model it is not an extensionally specifiable "copy" of something in the environment; it is an abstract relation of resemblance in certain respects which is used by the system to serve its interests and needs. Since the model is a model only insofar as it is used by the system for some purpose, the only way in which it is possible to specify what model of the environment a system (B) has is to specify the way B uses that model in its commerce with the environment. So the concept of "model," like that of "intelligent storage," is an intentionalistic concept that is intelligible only in relation to the use which the system makes of the model for its own purposes, interests, or needs. In attributing a model to a system we are thus attributing a "point of view" to it, and in explaining its behavior in relation to its internal model we are explaining it from the system's "point of view."

If the nature of a mechanical system is such that its behavior outputs are mediated and controlled by internal models, then its behavior will exhibit features that can be characterized in ways that are analogous to intentionalistic characterizations of human behavior. For the peculiar features of such characterizations, suggested by Brentano's notion of "intentional inexistence" and exploited by Taylor in his arguments against the notion that mechanisms can be purposive, are that they are given from the agent's (system's) point of view, so that their truth does not depend on extensional characterizations of the way things are, but on what the agent (system) takes them to be, on what he (it) intends, aims at, etc. As Boden (1970) has pointed out, if we suppose that the behavior of a physical system is not controlled by environmental stimuli, but is largely mediated and controlled by "internal—and often idiosyncratic—representations of the environment," then "being mediated by them, behavior will naturally reflect their features as well as environmental conditions. It is this which accounts for the intentional characteristics of behavior and which underlies the logical features remarked upon by Chisholm and others" (p. 212).

This is not to say that people are really very much like complex computers. The point is rather that the question of whether or not intentionalistic characterizations of behavior can be usefully applied to a system is independent of ontological questions about what the nature of the system really is, what stuff it is made out of. Whatever the practical difficulties may be, there is no logical problem about the possibility of a complex mechanical system whose behavior depends on such "control functions" as input classifications ("perceptions" which have a meaning for the system), internal models ("beliefs" and "concepts"), problem-solving strategies, and goal-states ("purposes" and "desires"). Such a system would be a mechanical system whose behavior can, in principle, be explained in terms of the laws of the physical sciences. At the same time, the system would be such that a useful strategy for predicting and explaining its behavior would be to take its "point of view" into account, attribute some of its behaviors to "mistakes" (e.g., internal representations which do not correspond to the way things are), or to the attempt to attain goals which do not exist (but are represented in the system), and the like. Kant's "two points of view" would be applicable to such a system. It is, therefore, evident that, Skinner to the contrary, explanations that are given from the agent's point of view and appeal to his cognitive powers and activities need not involve any commitment to dualism or occult homunculi.

Such explanations do, however, deploy a system of explanatory concepts which differs sharply from that of the physical sciences. For descriptions and explanations of behavior which appeal to the meaning things have for the system (or agent), to the system's internal representations and goal states (the agent's beliefs, aims, and desires), and the like, are such that they can only be understood, and the connections between them can only be grasped, by taking up the point of view of the system (or agent) to which these psychological states or processes are ascribed. This difference is often marked by contrasting psychological explanations in terms of beliefs, purposes, and intentions with causal explanations in the physical sciences. Though philosophers do not agree on the analysis of the concept of "cause," if we choose to identify causal explanations with explanations of the Humean type which require that cause and effect be atomistically identifiable, that is, that causality be construed as a purely contingent "regular conjunction" of two events that can be identified without reference to each other, then such psychological explanations differ from causal explanations.

This claim needs to be unpacked, because discussions of this matter have sometimes failed to be clear about just what is at issue.[16] First, it is clear that cause and effect may be atomistically identifiable even if there are some descriptions under which they are conceptually linked. Since descriptions in the physical sciences are typically "theory-laden," the description of a physical effect often individuates it by reference to its cause—for example, we distinguish a strep throat from a mere sore throat in terms of their different causal history. Again, at a certain stage in the development of a physical science, we may be able to specify a cause only by referring to the effect it is presumed to have: at one point in the history of genetics, one could identify genes only as "whatever it is that causes" plants to be tall, and the like (cf. Fodor, 1968, p. 36). So what is at issue cannot be whether cause and effect may be conceptually linked under some descriptions; for even if they are, they can satisfy the Humean requirement as long as there is some other description under which they are independently identifiable. If, as in the example

16. The thesis that psychological explanations cannot be Humean causal explanations is developed in detail by Melden (1961) and Taylor (1964, 1970a). For criticisms of Melden's arguments, see Davidson (1963) and Fodor (1968, pp. 32 ff.).

of genes, we are not in a position to provide an independent description of the cause, we can still regard the explanation as potentially a Humean causal explanation, but only on the assumption that an independent description of the cause will eventually be provided. The real question then is whether the intentions, beliefs, desires, aims, etc. cited in psychological explanations are of the right logical type to allow a characterization of them that is logically independent of the actions they explain.

The answer to that seems to be no, because, as we have already seen, psychological characterizations are intentionalistic and resist translation into an extensional language. That is, our intentionalistic descriptions of psychological states and behaviors depend on systematic conceptual links between an agent's purposes, beliefs, desires, etc. and his (intentional) actions. We characterize a psychological state in relation to the intentional object to which it is directed—what the desire is for, what the belief or guilt is about. And the only way we can individuate a psychological state as, for example, a desire for X, is to take the agent's point of view and grasp the noncontingent connections between what he desires, and what behaviors can be appropriate expressions of what he desires. The trouble with finding an atomistic characterization of the desire for X (e.g., to get a promotion) is that a characterization of a psychological state which does not link it noncontingently to what are, for this agent, appropriate behavioral expressions of that desire (e.g., doing, other things equal, what he believes is likely to get him promoted, talking and daydreaming in ways which express his desire for promotion, and the like) would not be a characterization of the "desire to get a promotion."

The point is that there is no way of identifying a desire for X atomistically at the psychological level, because it is only in virtue of the (noncontingent) intentional connection between the desire and behaviors which can be interpreted, in relation to the agent's relevant beliefs, his other desires, and the like, as expressions of his desire, that we can have any basis for saying that this agent has a "desire for X." No atomistic, extensional characterization of psychological states can preserve the noncontingent links between desires, beliefs, and appropriate behaviors that are characteristic of the conceptual framework deployed by agents. And it is only in virtue of these noncontingent links that desires, intentions, etc. can be individuated as the desire for X, the intention to Y, etc. Similarly, behaviors that are characterized in psychological rather than physical terms are identified in relation to what the agent intends, aims at, wants. "Looking for his glasses" is, as we have seen, an action that can be individuated only in relation to the agent's intention; no extensionally characterizable pattern of movements can be identified with that act. So action descriptions, like characterizations of psychological states, can only be given in relation to the agent's point of view and are not independent of his psychological states; behavioral evidence for action attributions is good evidence only "other things equal," and what has to be equal cannot be unpacked without appealing to the agent's intentions, beliefs, and desires.

Consequently, our evidence for saying that an agent "desires X" is that, other things equal, he is disposed to behave in ways which, from his (possibly idiosyncratic, confused, etc.) point of view, give expression to the desire for X. But our evidence for saying that the things he is disposed to do can be characterized as behaviors of the appropriate sort is that they can be interpreted, in relation to his point of view, as expressions of his desire for X. The link between desire and behavior cannot be established externally, but requires taking up the agent's point of view and appealing to intentions, beliefs, and the like. The evidence that someone desires a promotion may thus be that he writes articles and serves on committees; that he talks and daydreams about getting a promotion may also be evidence. But his writing of articles is evidence of that desire only insofar as he intends it as a step toward promotion. Similarly, his talk and daydreams are evidence only insofar as they can be regarded as expressions of that desire—for example, his talking about it would not be evidence if it was intended to deceive the listener, or his daydreams would not be evidence if they are intended to avoid thoughts about some unpleasant family problem. So the evidence for attributing a desire for X to an agent is not logically independent of the evidence for attributing actions of the relevant sort to him; it is only in virtue of the noncontingent links between desires and actions that are, from his point of view, appropriate to the desire that we can have evidence for attributing to him both the desire and the (intentionalistically characterized) actions or action dispositions. Put another way, both the desire and the action can be characterized intentionalistically only by being interpreted so that their noncontingent connection is intelligible in relation to that same wider context of systematically connected aims, beliefs, and the like which constitutes the agent's point of view. This is why no logically independent characterizations of desires and actions can be given at the psychological level. A similar argument could be developed for motives, emotions, and other psychological "states."

But while psychological explanations are not Humean causal explanations, we cannot conclude that such explanations are incompatible with the possibility of causal explanations of behavior. For even if actions cannot be individuated without reference to the agent's intentions, desires, and the like (and these in turn cannot be individuated without reference to his action dispositions), should it turn out that sufficient conditions for having a desire or intention can be specified at the neurophysiological level, and linked contingently to the motions performed when the system is in that state, then there would be causal explanations at that level (cf. Fodor, 1968, p. 45). Of course, we could not identify desires or intentions with neural states, or actions with movements; these concepts belong to different conceptual frameworks and there is no equivalence of meaning. But no a priori arguments can show that an empirical, as opposed to logical, reduction might not be carried through; equally, there are no a priori reasons for thinking that such an empirical reduction must be possible, since the question at issue is empirical rather than conceptual (cf. Taylor, 1970b).

Further, though psychological explanations are not Humean causal explanations, they certainly do tell us something important about what it is that brings about behavior. What they tell us about is the agent's intentional world: the way he perceives things (the meanings they have for him), the structure of his beliefs, desires, and preferences, and the strategies and tactics he uses to pursue his goals. Such explanations enable us to understand what Boden (1973) calls the "structure of intentions," that is, the complex interrelations between a goal and the hierarchically structured "action-plans" that are generated as appropriate for achieving it in relation to the agent's perceptions and preferences, his sociocultural constraints and opportunities, motivations, and the like. The way in which such action-plans guide behavior "is closely analogous to the sets of instructions comprising procedural routines within a computer program, for such routines also specify certain operations and control the order of their execution" (p. 24). Such structured and intentionalistically characterized "action-plans" bring about behavior because they "guide" it, in much the same sense in which a program may be said to "guide" the machine which executes it.

Neither provides a Humean causal explanation; but both provide explanations of behavior at the psychological, or program (procedural subroutine) level.

Of course, such explanations, like all others, do not explain everything. They assume that the system has the power to act intentionally, that is, to guide its behavior by means of action-plans that are appropriate in relation to the information it has and the goals it is pursuing, but they do not explain what it is in the nature of the system in virtue of which it has that power.[17] In giving such explanations one takes what Dennett (1971) calls the "intentional stance." That is, one tries to predict and explain the behavior of the system by assuming that its design is optimal, so that it will behave rationally—that is, it will use the information it has to achieve its goals in appropriate ways. The conceptual relations between intentionalistic concepts like desire, belief, and action, which allow us to judge certain actions as appropriate from the agent's point of view, are thus used as a heuristic device for the investigation of the system's behavior. The decision to adopt this strategy will be justified pragmatically if it pays off, because the system does, in fact, behave, at least a good part of the time, as one expects it to behave in adopting this stance. But what one expects is not "perfect rationality"; rather, empirical investigation will, on this approach, be used in order to explain and predict deviations from this heuristic ideal in terms of "blind spots" in the system's perceptions of certain sorts of things, false beliefs (or internal representations), misleading or self-defeating strategies, and the like (cf. Mischel, 1964, 1966b). If these departures become sufficiently large and frequent, we may, of course, conclude that there is no point in trying to explain and predict the system's behavior by adopting the "intentional stance" toward it.

One of Skinner's objections to explanations of this sort is that the only reason we appeal to "competences" (powers) of the organism, which are presumed to be due to its "structure" (nature), is that we have not succeeded in fully explaining and predicting its behavior (1974, pp. 66 ff.). He is right, in the sense that if a system, be it mechanical or organic, is so simple that one can fully understand the

17. The "power"/"nature" distinction is borrowed from Harré (1970), who defends the explanatory role of ascriptions of specific powers to systems whose nature cannot, at a given stage of scientific inquiry, be specified, whether the systems be material things, animals, or people.

steps leading from input to output at the hardware or physiological level, then there is no call for developing explanations of its behavior in terms of procedural subroutines or the structure of its intentions (action-plans). But while there is no point to adopting the intentional stance toward such simple systems, the fact is that we are unable to understand human behavior at the physiological level, and even computers are now so complex that "intentional explanation and prediction of their behavior is not only common but works when no other sort of prediction of their behavior is manageable" (Dennett, 1971, p. 91). In light of this, what is wrong with adopting the intentional stance toward such systems?

Skinner might reply that we have as little justification for supposing that people "really" have desires, beliefs, and the like as did those Aristotelean philosophers who sought to provide psychological explanations for all natural phenomena by talking about, for example, the stone's "desire" to return to its natural place. Further, so Skinner might argue, the analogy to explanations in terms of program subroutines and the like does nothing to rid such explanations of "animism" and "anthropomorphism," since talk about such subroutines, about "intelligent storage" and the computer's "internal models," is itself based on an analogy with persons and deploys the intentionalistic psychological concepts we ordinarily use to talk about their actions.

But such ontological worries are simply beside the point, since what is at issue is the heuristic value of treating people (or complex mechanisms, or other animals) as intentional systems. As Minsky points out, the "distinctly bipartite structure" of our world model, which assigns mechanical and physical matters to one domain, and goals, meanings, and social matters, to another (1965, p. 46), would be theoretically unified in a single model if researchers in artificial intelligence, cybernetics, and neurophysiology all reach their goals. But

> such a success might have little effect on the overall form of our personal world-models. . . . for practical, heuristic reasons, these would still retain their form of quasi-separate parts. . . . The primitive notions of physics, or even neurophysiology, will be far too remote to be useful in accounting, *directly*, for the mental events of everyday life. [P. 47]

The point is that the interests and concerns which inform the questions we ask about behavior at the psychological level are such that these questions would not be answered by neurological considerations. At the psychological level we may be interested in why a person (or certain classes of persons) behaves in certain ways in certain situations, and the answer may make reference to some goal or intention. This in turn may be explained in relation to how the situation is perceived (the meaning it has for the person), the person's anticipations about the likely outcome of various ways of behaving, self-concepts, self-regulatory plans, values, and anticipations about the expectations of others. These in turn may be explained by reference to the psychological genesis of these perceptions, expectations, strategies, self-conceptions, motivations, construction-competences, and the like.[18] Such questions, including the general questions that arise at each level about the saliency and role of these psychological factors for different sorts of people in various sorts of situations, are psychological questions, and they would not be answered by a neurophysiological story, even if we could tell it. That story is just "far too remote to be useful" as an answer to the questions we ask about behavior at the psychological level.

Put another way, psychology, like other disciplines, derives its identity from research problems, interests, and concerns that are grouped together for practical reasons, and these would not disappear even if the empirical reduction of the discipline to neurophysiology were carried through—think, for example, of the relation between chemistry and quantum physics. Since attempts to answer psychological questions by means of a Skinnerian "experimental analysis of behavior" have not met with great success, especially with respect to complex human behavior, increasing numbers of psychologists are turning to cognitive approaches. But old allegiances linger on, and so we get talk about "cognitive behaviorism" (Boneau, 1974), "cognitive social learning theory" (W. Mischel, 1973), and the like. Psychologists who use such locutions seem to think that cognitive processes can be introduced into theories that remain essentially behavioristic by "liberalizing" those theories so as to include some "cognitive variables"; they talk as if introducing cognitive processes were simply a matter of adding some new "independent variables" to the old type of theory, and fail to

18. See Ryan (1970, chap. 2) for a discussion of these successive "levels" of psychological explanation, and W. Mischel (1973) for a catalogue of the "person variables" that must be taken into account in personality theory.

recognize that the appeal to cognitive processes involves adopting a new type of theory which conceptualizes the nature of persons, and the contribution they make to behavior, in a very different way.

Specifically, both Ryan and Boneau see that the reasons for adopting a cognitive approach are pragmatic. Ryan focuses on psychological investigations of the role of "intention, task, purpose or goal" in behavior because he believes that such investigations "have the greatest likelihood of 'paying off' with tested explanations of practical usefulness" (1970, p. 21); "another and different tack is being tried here only because the Watsonian approach and its descendants have not displayed notable success in explaining human behavior" (p. 8). Similarly, Boneau holds that the individual "can create for itself a model of [the] environment [IME] containing information" about both the environment and the likelihood of certain outcomes if certain actions are performed, and then tries to explain and predict behavior on the assumption that these out-comes are "evaluated" and that the individual "performs the action necessary to produce the highest expected hedonic value" (1974, p. 303). But he explicitly points out that the only way of testing his theory is to explore "the heuristic value of the theory as a pointer to truly important areas of research" (p. 308). So the reason for empirical investigations of the role of intentions and purposes, or of IMEs, in behavior is that these may be more effective approaches to the prediction and explanation of complex behavior than Skinner's "functional analysis." But both Ryan and Boneau think their approach leads to causal explanations of behavior; they construe psychological states and processes as "independent variables" which are Humean causes of behavior (the dependent variable). Ryan says that "it will be assumed that something which an individual experiences (perceives, understands) can . . . cause behavior" (1970, p. 8); "it is useful to think in terms of a causal chain in which intentions exert an immediate influence on activity" (p. 23). And Boneau says that his "conceptual scheme based on information-processing notions" describes "the variables of which behavior is assumed to be a function and the way they combine to produce behavior" (1974, p. 298).

Such attempts to combine cognitive and behavioristic approaches leave themselves open to two very different, but related, objections. On the one side, Skinnerians can accuse Ryan of "mentalism" (cf. Day, this volume). For talk about how "the experienced intention . . . is related to movements" (Ryan, 1970, p. 10) in a causal chain raises the old ontological issues, even if one adds the ingenuous disclaimer that "intentions, images, or other 'mental events' are in the same organism in which we can measure changes in electrical potential" (p. 12). On the other side, humanistic psychologists can accuse Boneau of serving old wine in new bottles. For if explanations in terms of the IME are construed as causal explanations which exhibit the dependence of behavioral outputs on independent variables, then it looks like the IME is only an (eliminable) internal mediator which is itself the effect of prior external contingencies. The explanation then is really a Humean causal explanation rather than a purposive, or intentionalistic, explanation. This is why Rychlak argues that Boneau really gives us "two sensory inputs, situation and outcome, and one output feature, the action, all of which are rolled up into a continuing model of the environment" (this volume, p. 245); in Rychlak's view, Boneau's IME is just a version of Locke's notion of "an idea . . . as a mapping of reality" (ibid., p. 248).

Humanistic psychologists like Rychlak are worried about whether cognitive theories really allow for purpose, meaning, choice, and the like. Thus Rychlak does not think that the "internal processes" to which Boneau, and cognitive theorists in general, appeal show that "the person as psychological identity can contribute anything to the determinate inputs" (ibid., p. 250). But this objection simply does not apply once it is recognized that cognitive explanations in terms of purposes, internal models, and the like are intentionalistic rather than causal explanations. For whether or not the person can be said to "contribute anything" to his behavior depends on whether or not that behavior is brought about (i.e., guided) by his beliefs, desires, etc.; if it is, then he can be influenced by rational considerations, he can make choices and act purposefully and appropriately in light of the meaning situations have for him. The worry that beliefs, desires, internal models, and the like may themselves turn out to be Humean efficient causes in disguise can be laid to rest by recognizing that since characterizations of such psychological states and processes are intentionalistic, they cannot be identified at the psychological (as opposed to neurological) level with extensionally characterizable states of affairs that could themselves have Humean causes. Even explanations of computer behavior which treat the system as an "information-processing system" share, as we have seen, the features characteristic of our ordinary intentionalistic explanations of human actions. And it is in this intentionalistic framework that our conceptions of agency, self-direction, choice, purpose, and meaning are rooted. Since the behavior of such systems is largely mediated and controlled, not by external stimuli, but by the use of internal models and the like, they do not just react passively to external contingencies in the way imagined by associationists like Locke and his behavioristic descendants; rather, such systems can act intentionally and their behavior can be described and explained in relation to what Kant called "the agent's point of view."

Of course, the concepts deployed when we take that point of view may drop out when we take the point of view of neurophysiology (or machine hardware) and try to explain behavior at that level. But this in no way shows that there is something illusory about intentionalistic characterizations given from the agent's point of view, that we are not really dealing with an agent capable of intentional action. For in a similar way, one can study, for example, respiration as a physiological function in relation to the contribution it makes to the life of the organism, or one can study the physiochemical processes respiriation calls into play. In the latter case, physiological considerations and categories, talk about the "function" of respiration, will drop out; but this does not make characterizations of physiological functions illusory, it does not show that respiration does not really make a contribution appropriate to the life and survival of the organism (cf. Toulmin, 1974, pp. 198 ff.). Analogously, systems which are designed in such a way that their behavior can be guided by internal models and the like, in ways appropriate to their goals or needs and the information they have, are systems that really have the power to act purposively and intentionally; their behavior is not just a reaction to environmental stimuli and contingencies. And that will be true no matter how "mechanistic" the explanation of these cognitive powers, that can be given at a different level, may turn out to be.

This in turn suggests the way in which Skinnerian worries about "mentalism" can be allayed. What is required for the applicability of intentionalistic descriptions and explanations is not a system composed of mind-stuff in addition to physical-stuff, but that the system be designed in such a way that it can employ internal models of its environment and of its own behaviors, problem-solving strategies, goals, and the like to guide what it does in ways that are, by and large, appropriate. Of course, organisms, unlike computers, are not designed by anyone. But there is a clear sense in which organisms are "natural designs." From the point of view of evolutionary theory, the development of organisms which have such cognitive powers can hardly be miraculous, since such powers would clearly have survival value.[19] Skinner may fail to recognize this because he thinks that "no one has ever shown that the covert form [of behavior] achieves anything which is out of reach of the overt" (1974, p. 103). But that is simply false. The advantage gained by the power to guide overt behavior by means of thought (i.e., "covert behavior") is, as Popper pointed out, that it "permits our hypotheses to die in our stead."

Clearly, the development of a "mental apparatus" which, other things equal, makes for optimal recognition of the significance of environmental inputs and enables the organism to use that information to guide behavior effectively toward optimal satisfaction of its needs is biologically adaptive. We can, therefore, look to the physical sciences for an explanation of the development and material embodiment of such a mental apparatus. In other words, the mental apparatus is not a nonphysical addition to the organism, but consists of those species-specific mental, or cognitive, powers which organisms have in virtue of their biological nature. The explanation of the development and physical basis of these mental powers is the business of the biological sciences, and our intentionalistic descriptions and explanations of behavior presuppose the existence of such mental powers. But the cognitive powers assumed in such explanations are not "occult," because we presume that they will, some day, be explained from the point of view of extensional, physical theory in a way that may make no reference to agents and their powers.

The fact that we do not, at present, have such explanations has bred fear of occult powers, of mentalism, and homunculi; it made theorists uncertain of the scientific status of psychological explanations, and this has had an unfortunate effect on the development of psychological theory. For it has misled some psychologists into attempts to link their theories to biology in a way that is far too direct. Species-specific cognitive powers do, indeed, have a biological basis and contribute to biological goals like survival, reproduction, and growth. But the powers involved are of a very general kind and their contribution to biological goals is

19. See Dennett (1969, especially chap. 3) for some interesting speculations about how a "useful brain," that is, one that can produce environmentally appropriate behavior because it can discriminate inputs according to their environmental significance for the organism, might be evolved.

indirect because it is mediated by a particular way of life. That is, the cognitive powers which are biologically conditioned are such general "control functions" for action as perception, internal models of the environment (beliefs and concepts), heuristic strategies, and goals (needs, desires, purposes). The specific form which all of these functions take—the meaning which various sorts of perceptions have, the content of the internal models, the structure of "action-plans," etc.—will, therefore, depend to a large extent, not on biology but on culture and individual experience. This is why we can get a great deal of explanatory mileage out of intentionalistic accounts which presuppose these species-specific, cognitive powers without explaining them. And this is what gets lost when psychologists attempt to bypass the intentionalistic level and to connect their theories directly to biology.

Freud can serve to illustrate this point. For he assumed the existence of a "mental apparatus," but was unclear about the level at which it was supposed to describe and explain behavior. On the one hand, Freud clearly recognized the idea-dependent character of neurotic symptoms, the fact that they have meaning for the neurotic, and that psychoanalytic interpretation and theory are intelligible only in relation to this intentionalistic context. But Freud was concerned about the scientific status of his theories and sometimes sought to make them respectable by grounding them directly in biological considerations; so he attempted to find support for his metatheoretical discussions of the workings of the mental apparatus in speculations about energy exchanges (cathexes and anticathexes) derived from the physiology of his day (cf. Mischel, 1974).

But the link between psychological and biological functioning need not be that direct. To be sure, there is, as Freud saw, an analogy between "mental disease" and "physical disease." For much as physical health and disease are best understood in relation to the way biological organisms function as natural designs (cf. King, 1945)—physical disease is a state of the organism's bodily structures or processes which is inappropriate to the continued performance of its natural functions—so the notion of mental disease (or health) is rooted in the biological contribution which an organism's cognitive powers make to its functioning as a natural design. That is, cognitive functioning is biologically adaptive when an organism's internal representations correspond to the significance things really have and when it uses that information to satisfy its needs, or achieve its goals, in appropriate ways; such a condition of the organism's mental apparatus constitutes "psychological health" and corresponds, pretty much, to "rationality." Disruptions of such cognitive functioning—for example, large-scale distortions of the significance of external inputs, misperceptions of other people's intentions, beliefs about oneself and others that are not grounded in the way things are but in the way one wishes them to be, or conflicting desires which paralyze appropriate action,—interfere with the continued performance of natural functions and constitute "psychological disease."

Such malfunctioning may, of course, be due to hormonal imbalance, neurological damage, and the like; but if it is, then we have diagnosed a physical rather than a mental disease. The disease is mental only insofar as its etiology is not rooted in physical conditions that impair the general powers of perception, internal representation, and action but in the specific ways in which an organism that has these powers exercises them in certain contexts. That is, the neurotic's general power to guide his behavior by means of "action-plans" has not been biologically impaired, but there is something very wrong with the way in which he generates action-plans to guide his behavior in certain situations. To identify something as a mental disease is to claim that its etiology lies in inappropriate internal models, in internal representations of self and others that are systematically distorted; and the explanation for cognitive malfunctionings that are diagnosed in this way is not to be found in biology but in the organism's intentionalistically characterized psychological interactions with the environment. Mental disease is thus diagnosed by means of the framework of intentionalistic concepts which agents use in their psychological commerce with each other. And it is "treated" by restructuring the agent's intentional world: by helping him to become aware of conflicting desires he has refused to face consciously, or of self-defeating strategies he has been employing; by making it possible for him to correct motivated distortions in his perceptions and beliefs about himself and others, thus enabling him to guide his behavior by means of more appropriate and effective action-plans.[20]

20. This is, of course, greatly oversimplified. For a more detailed interpretation of psychoanalytic theory along these lines, see Mischel (1974). It should also be noted that nothing I have said implies that there are no neurological changes in neurosis; my point pertains to the level at which, and the concepts in relation to which, neurosis is identified and dealt with.

Put another way, an organism which is capable of purposive activities because evolution has provided it with a mental apparatus that can model the environment internally and guide behavior in ways appropriate to the achievement of its desires is also an organism capable of conflicting purposes, erroneous perceptions, false internal representations, misleading strategies, and the like. And this is the level at which psychology is concerned with "abnormal behavior." As a contribution to psychological theory, Freud's "mental apparatus" has to be related to issues about specific forms and manifestations of cognitive functioning that arise at this intentionalistic psychological level, and physiological considerations, pertaining to the material conditions in virtue of which the exercise of these mental powers is possible, are not directly relevant to these concerns.

Like abnormal behavior and personality, perception, motivation, learning, and the like can be investigated at different levels and from different points of view. But the point of view that can be naturally characterized as psychological is, so at least I have been suggesting, the point of view of agents, which carries with it intentionalistic identifications and explanations of behavior. In giving such characterizations and explanations, one presupposes agents who have cognitive powers. My aim has been to show that the suspicion of such powers, which psychologists have harbored, is intelligible in relation to the historical and philosophical background out of which empirical psychology developed, but that it is no longer justified. At this point in history, it should be possible for psychologists to stop worrying about mentalism, homunculi, and the scientific status of their discipline, and to proceed with the business of developing psychological theories that can help explain complex human behaviors.

REFERENCES

Anscombe, G. E. M. *Intention.* Oxford: Blackwell, 1957.
Breger, L., & McGaugh, J. L. Critique and reformulation of "learning-theory" approaches to psychotherapy and neurosis. *Psychological Bulletin,* 1965, *63,* 338–358.
Brentano, F. *Psychology from an empirical standpoint.* 1874. Ed. by L. L. McAlister. New York: Humanities Press, 1973.

Boden, M. A. Intentionality and physical systems. *Philosophy of Science,* 1970, **37**, 200–214.

Boden, M. A. The structure of intentions. *Journal for the Theory of Social Behavior,* 1973, **3**, 23–46.

Boring, E. G. *History of experimental psychology.* New York: Appleton-Century-Crofts, 1950.

Boneau, A. C. Paradigm regained? Cognitive behaviorism restated. *American Psychologist,* 1974, **29**, 297–309.

Chisholm, R. M. *Perceiving.* Ithaca: Cornell University Press, 1957.

Chisholm, R. M. On some psychological concepts and the "logic" of intentionality. In H. Castaneda (Ed.), *Intentionality, minds, and perception.* Detroit: Wayne State University Press, 1967. Pp. 11–35.

Chomsky, N. Review of B. F. Skinner's *Verbal behavior. Language,* 1959, **35**, 26–58.

Davidson, D. Actions, reasons, and causes. *Journal of Philosophy,* 1963, **60**, 685–700.

Dennett, D. C. *Content and consciousness.* New York: Humanities Press, 1969.

Dennett, D. C. Intentional systems. *Journal of Philosophy,* 1971, **68**(4), 87–106.

Descartes, R. Discourse on method. 1637. In *Philosphical Works,* Vol. 1. Trans. by E. S. Haldane & G. R. T. Ross. New York: Dover, 1955.

Descartes, R. Meditations on first philosophy. 1641. In *Philosophical Works,* Vol. 1. Trans. by E. S. Haldane & G. R. T. Ross. New York: Dover, 1955.

Descartes, R. The passions of the soul. 1649. In *Philosophical Works,* Vol. 1. Trans. by E. S. Haldane & G. R. T. Ross. New York: Dover, 1955.

Deutsch, J. A. *The structural basis of behavior.* Chicago: University of Chicago Press, 1960.

Dodwell, P. *Visual pattern recognition.* New York: Holt, Rinehart & Winston, 1970.

Fodor, J. *Psychological explanation.* New York: Random House, 1968.

Fodor, J., & Bever, T. The psychological reality of linguistic segments. *Journal of Verbal Learning and Verbal Behavior,* 1965, **4**, 414–420.

Freud, S. *General introduction to psychoanalysis.* 1914. New York: Garden City Publishing Company, 1943.

Freud, S. Instincts and their vicissitudes. 1915. In *Collected Papers,* Vol. 4. London: Hogarth Press, 1956. Pp. 60–83.

Garrett, M., Bever, T., & Fodor, J. The active use of grammar in speech perception. *Journal of Perception and Psychophysics,* 1966, **1**, 30–32.

Hamlyn, D. W. Conditioning and behavior. In R. T. Borger & F. Cioffi (Eds.), *Explanation in the behavioral sciences.* London: Cambridge University Press, 1970. Pp. 139–152.

Hanson, N. R. *Patterns of discovery.* London: Cambridge University Press, 1958.

Harré, R. *Principles of scientific thinking.* Chicago: University of Chicago Press, 1970.

Hebb, D. O. What psychology is about. *American Psychologist,* 1974, **29,** 71–79.

Herbart, J. F. Psychologie als Wissenschaft. In *Sämmtliche Werke,* Vols. 5 & 6. Ed. by G. Hartenstein. Leipzig: Voss, 1850.

Hobbes, T. A short tract on first principles. 1630. In R. S. Peters (Ed.), *Hobbes: Body, man and citizen.* New York: Collier, 1962.

Hobbes, T. Third set of objections urged by a celebrated English philosopher [i.e., Hobbes]. 1641. In Descartes, *Philosophical Works,* Vol. 2. Trans. by E. Haldane & G. R. T. Ross. New York: Dover, 1955. Pp. 60–78.

Hobbes, T. De Corpore. 1655. In W. Molesworth (Ed.), *English works,* Vol 1. London: Bohn, 1839.

Hull, C. L. Learning. In C. Murchinson (Ed.), *Handbook of general experimental psychology.* Worcester, Mass.: Clark University Press, 1934. Pp. 382–455.

Hume, D. *Treatise on human nature.* 1739. Ed. by L. A. Selby-Bigge. Oxford: Clarendon Press, 1888.

Hume, D. *Inquiry concerning human understanding.* 1748. Ed. by C. W. Hendel. New York: Liberal Arts Press, 1955.

Irwin, F. W. *Intentional behavior and motivation.* New York: J. B. Lippincott, 1971.

Kant, I. *Critique of pure reason.* 1781. Trans. by N. Kemp Smith. London: Macmillan, 1929.

Kant, I. Fundamental principles of the metaphysics of morals. 1785. In *Critique of practical reason and other works.* Trans. by T. K. Abbott. New York: Longmans, 1909.

Kant, I. Critical examination of practical reason. 1788. In *Critique of practical reason and other works.* Trans. by T. K. Abbott. New York: Longmans, 1909.

Kelly, G. A. *The psychology of personal constructs.* New York: Norton, 1955.

King, C. D. The meaning of normal. *Yale Journal of Biology and Medicine,* 1945, **17,** 493–501.

Kuhn, T. S. The structure of scientific revolutions. In O. Neurath, R. Carnap, & C. W. Morris (Eds.), *International encyclopedia of unified science,* Vol. 2, No. 2. Chicago: University of Chicago Press, 1962.

Lacey, H. M. The scientific study of linguistic behavior: A perspective on the Skinner-Chomsky controversy. *Journal for the Theory of Social Behavior,* 1974, **4**(1), 17–51.

MacCorquodale, K. On Chomsky's review of Skinner's *Verbal behavior. Journal of the Experimental Analysis of Behavior,* 1970, **13,** 83–99.

Malcolm, N. Behaviorism as a philosophy of psychology. In T. W. Wann (Ed.), *Behaviorism and phenomenology.* Chicago: University of Chicago Press, 1964. Pp. 141–155.

Malcolm, N. The myth of cognitive processes and structures. In T. Mischel (Ed.), *Cognitive development and epistemology.* New York: Academic Press, 1971. Pp. 385–392.

McAlister, L. Chisholm and Brentano on intentionality. *Review of Metaphysics,* 1974, **28**(2), 328–338.

Melden, A. I. *Free action.* New York: Humanities Press, 1961.

Merlan, P. Brentano and Freud. *Journal of the History of Ideas,* 1945, 6(3), 375–377.

Merlan, P. Brentano and Freud, a sequel. *Journal of the History of Ideas,* 1949, **10**(3), 451.

Minsky, M. Matter, mind and models. In *Proceedings of the International Federation of Information Processing Congress,* Vol. 1. Washington, D.C.: Macmillan, Spartan Books, 1965. Pp. 45–49.

Mischel, T. Personal constructs, rules and the logic of clinical activity. *Psychological Review,* 1964, **71**(3), 180–192.

Mischel, T. "Emotion" and "motivation" in the development of English psychology: Hartley, J. Mill, Bain. *Journal of the History of the Behavioral Sciences,* 1966, **2**, 123–144. (a)

Mischel, T. Pragmatic aspects of explanation. *Philosophy of Science,* 1966, **33**, 40–60. (b)

Mischel, T. Kant and the possibility of a science of psychology. *Monist,* 1967, **51**, 599–622.

Mischel, T. Scientific and philosophical psychology: A historical introduction. In T. Mischel (Ed.), *Human action.* New York: Academic Press, 1969. Pp. 1–40.

Mischel, T. Wundt and the conceptual foundations of psychology. *Philosophy and Phenomenological Research,* 1970, **31**(1), 1–26.

Mischel, T. Understanding neurotic behavior: From "mechanism" to "intentionality." In T. Mischel (Ed.), *Understanding other persons.* Oxford: Blackwell; Totowa, N.J.: Rowman & Littlefield, 1974. Pp. 216–259.

Mischel, W. Toward a cognitive social learning reconceptualization of personality. *Psychological Review,* 1973, **80**(4), 252–283.

Neisser, U. *Cognitive psychology.* New York: Appleton-Century-Crofts, 1967.

Peters, R. S. Motivation, emotion, and the conceptual schemes of common sense. In T. Mischel, (Ed.), *Human action.* New York: Academic Press, 1969. Pp. 135–165.

Piaget, J. *The child's conception of the world.* London: Routledge & Kegan Paul, 1929.

Reitman, W. *Cognition and thought.* New York: John Wiley, 1966.

Ryan, T. A. *Intentional behavior.* New York: Ronald Press, 1970.

Ryle, G. *The concept of mind.* London: Hutchinson's University Library, 1949.

Segal, E. M., & Lachman, R. Complex behavior or higher mental process: Is there a paradigm shift? *American Psychologist,* 1972, **27**, 46–55.

Skinner, B. F. *Science and human behavior.* New York: Macmillan, 1953.

Skinner, B. F. *Verbal behavior.* New York: Appleton-Century-Crofts, 1957.

Skinner, B. F. Are theories of learning necessary? In *Cumulative record.* New York: Appleton-Century-Crofts, 1961. Pp. 39–69.

Skinner, B. F. Behaviorism at fifty. In T. W. Wann (Ed.), *Behaviorism and phenomenology.* Chicago: University of Chicago Press, 1964. Pp. 79–97.

Skinner, B. F. Operant behavior. In W. K. Honig (Ed.), *Operant behavior.* New York: Appleton-Century-Crofts, 1966. Pp. 12–32.

Skinner, B. F. *Beyond freedom and dignity.* New York: Alfred A. Knopf, 1971.

Skinner, B. F. *About behaviorism.* New York: Alfred A. Knopf, 1974.

Taylor, C. *The explanation of behavior.* New York: Humanities Press, 1964.

Taylor, C. Explaining action. *Inquiry,* 1970, **13**(1–2), 54–89. (a)

Taylor, C. The explanation of purposive behavior. In R. Borger & B. Cioffi, (Eds.), *Explanation in the behavioral sciences.* Cambridge: Cambridge University Press, 1970. Pp. 49–79. (b)

Taylor, R. *Action and purpose.* Englewood Cliffs, N.J.: Prentice-Hall, 1966.

Titchener, E. B. *Textbook of psychology.* New York: Macmillan, 1916.

Titchener, E. B. *Systematic psychology.* New York: Macmillan, 1929.

Tolman, E. C. Principles of purposive behavior. In S. Koch (Ed.), *Psychology: A study of science,* Vol. 2. New York: McGraw-Hill, 1959. Pp. 92–157.

Tolman, E. C. *Purposive behavior in animals and men.* 1932. New York: Appleton-Century-Crofts, 1967.

Toulmin, S. E. *Foresight and understanding.* Bloomington: Indiana University Press, 1961.

Toulmin, S. E. Rules and their relevance for understanding human behavior. In T. Mischel (Ed.), *Understanding other persons.* Oxford: Blackwell; Totowa, N.J.: Rowman & Littlefield, 1974. Pp. 185–215.

Watson, J. B. *Behaviorism.* 1924. Chicago: University of Chicago Press, 1963.

Wundt, W. Über die Definition der Psychologie. *Philosophische Studien,* 1896, pp. 1–66.

Wundt, W. *Grundzüge der phyciologischen Psychologie.* 1874. 3 vols. (6th ed.) Leipzig: Engelmann, 1908–1911.

Wundt, W. *Logik.* 1883. Vol. 3. (3rd ed.) Stuttgart: Enke, 1908.

Psychological Science as a Humanist Views It

Joseph F. Rychlak
Purdue University

*T*hree generations have now passed since John B. Watson (1913) published his monumental paper, "Psychology as the Behaviorist Views It." This paper made explicit certain attitudes which had been germinating in earlier schools of thought, including both American structuralism and functionalism. It delineated an approach to psychological science which was to dominate in our academic centers down to the very present. There have been refinements in the outlook, of course, but behaviorism and the learning theories it was to spawn have never given up or otherwise changed on one significant point. Since Watson's call to action, a psychologist who considers himself rigorous has been—whether he is consciously aware of this or not—martialed *against* the teleological description of human behavior. This is understandable, because one of the explicit reasons cited as a *need* for behavioristic interpretations of psychology by men like Watson (1913), Weiss (1919), and Kuo (1928) was the supposedly unscientific usage of terms like soul, spirit, ego, consciousness, intention, and purpose. These terms are all based on a teleological description of behavior, which in turn is fundamental to a humanistic psychology.

The attack on humanism was therefore pressed in the name of scientific rigor, with psychologists in this behavioristic tradition framing the backbone conceptions of what most consider to be psychological science today. Watson (1913, 1917) called our attention to the "control and prediction" of lawful behavioral relations. Calverton (1924) stressed the importance of measurement and the objectivity to be achieved when statistics were applied to the data under our observation. Stevens (1935) called for operational definitions of our terms, since ultimately the meaning of our concept is in the environment and not in any self-induced "mental" factor. Hull (1937) next popularized this empiricism by referring to logical positivism, and he devised his hypothetico-deductive method to ensure that theory would not stray too far from the hard data of observation. Behavior was equated with experimental fluctuation, so that Bergmann and Spence (1941) could speak of experimentally manipulated responses, rather than experimentally manipulated variables.

When the more humanistically inclined psychologists spoke in opposition to the role this view of science was fostering for psychology, charging that this easy equation of experimental manipulation and human-behavior control was suppressing of man's intellectual potentials, a not uncommon retort suggested that mental conceptions were anathema to the deterministic position of a proper science (Boring, 1946). Thought is not reality and all we can observe as proper scientists is reality. Theory is a product of thought, and though it is necessary at times, there is no doubt but that intervening methodological variables are superior to hypothetical theoretical constructs (Meehl & MacCorquodale, 1948). Anyone who would argue for humanistic conceptions is probably misguided in his profession, if not a little "light" in intellectual baggage. Scientific knowledge is simply different from the sorts of knowledge one gets in the arts (Spence, 1944, 1948). Speculations on human nature in the arts have been "made up," and these fanciful illusions of humanity may have no relevance to "the facts" whatsoever. Indeed, it might be feasible for the science of psychology to do without theory of *any* sort (Skinner, 1950). Observed reality is before us, and manipulations are predictable. Why then concern ourselves with archaic notions about human nature?

In the more humanistic line of descent, we find McDougall (1922) early opposing Watson, and calling for a purposive description of behavior. Fernberger (1922) argued that psychology might have to split into two wings, one devoted to the study of behavior and the other to the study of consciousness. Interestingly, some years later the eminent experimentalist Yerkes (1933) concurred, suggesting that we divide into the two wings of psychology (study of consciousness) and psychobiology (study of behavior). Yerkes freely admitted that he had never been a true "psychologist" (ibid., p. 211). Adams (1928, 1937) offered many fine arguments for why a concept of mind was necessary to the proper conceptualization of human behavior. Skaggs (1934) observed that the contrived laboratory procedures being used by psychologists of his time bore little relevance to life outside the lab. And Winter (1936) pointed to the outmoded Newtonian science on which behavioristic psychology was basing its claim to legitimacy (a theme which was mentioned again a generation later by the physicist Oppenheimer, 1956).

Waters (1939, 1948) argued that thanks to behaviorism's great commitment to "Morgan's canon" (operational parsimony), a logical error of failing to anthropomorphize the "anthrop-" (i.e., man) had developed. In place of this more humanistic conceptualization, psychologists were "mechanico-morphizing" *all* behavior. Allport (1940) decried this mechanical image of man, tracing it at least in part to the fact that psychologists had made "science" into a "purr word" (Allport, 1946, p. 132). Miller (1946) added that the prediction of behavior in an experimental context does not necessarily mean that a scientist understands "why" this regularity is the case. Hence, "control and prediction" is not an infallible guide to the genuine understanding of behavior. Bakan (1953a) carried on a spirited counter to the Bergmann and Spence (1941) denigration of psychological theory, and he also showed how the Hullian hypo-thetico-deductive method informally presumed certain humanistic conceptualizations which it denied existence to in its formal statement (Bakan, 1953b).

This half-century review provides us with the major parameters along which most current humanism-mechanism debates are framed. There is a noteworthy contrast to be seen in this running exchange between our two camps. By and large, the behavioristic psychologist is seen to argue from *method* while the humanistic psychologist argues from *theory*. In so doing, the humanist suffers a great disadvantage. Even if he believes in the logic of scientific methodology, his very tactic of trying to show that such methods are *also* predicated on certain arbitrary (hence, "metatheoretical") assumptions stamps him as in some way an anti- or nonscientist. Sometimes this may be true, of course, but often it is not and it *was not* true of the humanists cited above. By continually speaking of methodological data first, and either ignoring or admitting to theoretical issues secondarily, the behavioristic psychologist has preempted the title of "scientific psychologist." One of the aims of the present effort is to show how fallacious this preemption is.

Those humanistic psychologists who have indeed turned their attention away from "scientific method" have sought or held out hope of finding some equally viable alternative. This dream of find-ing a properly scientific method which can retain the rigor of science and yet capture the richness of lived experience began in the late nineteenth century with Husserl (1965) and in more recent years has been advanced with considerable sophistication by van Kaam (1969) and Giorgi (1970). While sympathizing with this hope to revise method to match humanism, the present humanistic position will make no call for a change in the scientific method now employed.

This treatise is written in hopes of clarifying the technical reasons why a humanism-mechanism controversy occurs in the first place, and then to offer some recommendations which might well end the tension that now exists between outlooks. Nothing can end the conflict in outlook short of having one side or the other give up its theoretical biases—and this we do *not* wish to see. Indeed, it would be quite impossible! We shall begin with a review of some basic issues in the humanism-mechanism controversy, including the nature of causation, bipolarity in meaning, scientific theory versus method, and the theoretical perspective taken in scientific explanation. This will permit us to define humanism and mechanism in a purely technical fashion. We then go on to a discussion of knowledge as requiring a bifurcation into method and theory, and call for a revolution in psychology *only* in terms of the latter. This "revolution" is not one of displacing the currently accepted model in psychology *entirely*, but rather to sophisticate psychologists in the realm of theory so that they might stop *seeing* one thing (a particular theory) in another (a method of validation).

Our proposed revolution is therefore fairly modest, calling for greater variation in scientific explanation rather than—as now—a tightening of description into what has come to be an almost boring "theme and variations" on one set of technical jargon. We next take up a few examples of humanistic "methods" and try to show why they tend to fail as science. We also take up mediational and related "cognitive" models that are now appearing on the scene, to show why they tend to fail as humanistic theories. The writer's humanistic theory is then given a brief overview, and some 15 years of experimental evidence in detailed support of one theoretical extension from this paradigmatic style of thought is reviewed. Finally, we end with seven suggestions as a "humanistic manifesto" which, if followed, would be likely to open up psychology to humanistic formulations *in the laboratory!* This we feel would be different enough from what is now practiced to deserve the term *revolution* being applied to it.

BASIC ISSUES IN THE HUMANISM-MECHANISM
CONTROVERSY

In order to clarify just what it means to be a mechanist or a humanist we must first review a number of technical points in theory construction. This puts us in that realm of mere "talky talk" which has so handicapped the humanist in the past, but the reader may be assured that we will follow this up below with a consideration of some hard data which emanated from the more liberal view of scientific description which our metatheoretical presentation will generate.

The Nature of Causation

Since the time of Aristotle, scientists have endeavored to explain events in terms of causes. Yet, it is possible to ask what this word *cause* really means. If one looks it up in the dictionary, or if he asks the average person what it means, he is likely to get something like "a cause is that which brings about an effect," so that the typical definition places emphasis on the impetus, the action, the flow of events over time which bring something about. In psychology we think of this time flow in terms of antecedent events leading to consequent events. But the causal construct was not always conceived of so narrowly.

It is often said that scientific thought begins in the early speculations of Thales (of Miletus), who departed from mythological and quaintly anthropomorphic accounts of nature to suggest that the world was made up of a uniform substance. He felt this was water, but his student, Anaximander, referred to this universal substance as the "boundless." Heraclitus and Parmenides later raised the issue of change, of whether anything really happened in this world of days and nights, and thus brought forward a concern with the "fabric of movement," or impetus of events across time. Heraclitus was also instrumental in bringing another notion to the fore, dealing with the *logos* or *Rationale* by which events flowed. The movement of time was patterned into a rational order which was therefore not happenstance; and reasoning from this assumption, Democritus was later to say that there was no such thing as "chance" in the universe, for everything is subject to patterned laws making for predictability in events.

Aristotle was to take these conceptual models of substance, impetus, and pattern and add to them the notion of a reason or a "that for the sake of which" events came about. The resulting combination was his profoundly influential theory of knowledge based upon what he called the *causes*, and we now state this in plural for there were *four* such causes to be isolated in showing that one had a true grasp of experience.

What are these four causes? The first Aristotle called the *material* cause, which was tantamount to Thales' and Anaximander's attribution of a pervasive substance to the world. In describing a chair we can say we know it is a chair because, like most chairs, it is made of wood, or iron, or marble; not many chairs are made of cotton or of ice cream! Another cause of the chair is the fact that someone or some machine "made" it, or put it together. This Aristotle termed the *efficient* cause, and we can see here the matter of flux and change which so fascinated Parmenides and Heraclitus. Events change, things get done, some form of energic propulsion seems evident in the flow of events. Chairs also take on certain patterned outlines; they meet our blueprint conceptions of what chairs "look like." Chairs look more like chairs than they look like tricycles or apple trees. This usage, drawn from the logos conception of Heraclitus and Democritus, Aristotle termed the *formal* cause.

It is important to appreciate that Aristotle did not think it advisable to *limit* the number of causes one might use in describing the nature of anything. It is possible to have formless substances, as in a "blob" of mud, and we can even think of formless movements, such as the impact of a breeze which wafts against our face. But mud can be shaped and baked into statues and dinnerware, and breezes can be elevated and patterned into an easily recognizable tornado. In like fashion, Aristotle believed, the enlighted physicist can bring to bear more and more causes to enrich his descriptive account of *natural* events. There is no Morgan's canon or principle of parsimony in the Aristotelian theory of knowledge. Adding causal description is like cutting additional facets on a diamond; the result is always a descriptive enrichment.

But Aristotle would have held that a rendering of the causes of the chair would not be complete until we had cited the *purpose* of the chair's existence. This notion of a purpose or an intentionality in events Aristotle subsumed under his fourth cause—the *final* cause. A final cause is "that for the sake of which" something exists, is happening, or is about to take place. The "sake" for which a chair is constructed might be termed "utility" in eating, writing, relaxing, and so forth.

The chair need not *itself* decide to "come about" or "to be." It is the human being who obtained the wood (material cause) and made it (efficient cause) into a chair matching his physiognomy (formal cause) so that he might live more comfortably (final cause) who may be said to have a purpose or intention in his behavior. However, in point of fact, Aristotle was not above adding in such final-cause terms to his descriptions of what today we call "inanimate nature." For example, in his *Physics* (1952), Aristotle theorized that leaves exist for the sake of providing shade for the fruit on trees, and he concluded thereby "that nature is a cause, a cause that operates for a purpose" (pp. 276–277). What this amounted to was the assignment of a teleology to nature (*telos*, from the Greek word meaning "goal," or "that for the sake of which" events are changing, aiming toward, and so on). Aristotle was thus advocating a natural teleology, and when we substitute God for Nature we have a *deity* teleology. Such theorizing was to bring much heartache to science, but before we consider this aspect of history we must take up a second technical issue in theory construction, having to do with the nature of meaning.

The Nature of Meaning

As noted in the introduction, behavioristic psychologists essentially denied that anything like a meaning construct (stated as "consciousness") is needed in the description of behavior. The concept is certainly elusive. What is the meaning of meaning? If we apply Aristotle's theory of knowledge to the term we would subsume it under the final cause designation, for it takes roots from "to wish" and "to intend." Assuming we take the term seriously, it is then proper to ask: Is this a *unipolar* or a *bipolar* conception? Do meanings always express unidirectional designations as stimuli? For example, when a person's sense of sour taste is stimulated on his tongue, the stimulus message carried by this receptor is presumably *only* sour. We have named this unipolar sensory experience "sour." But in so naming it, and though the receptor is definite in its meaningful message, can anyone deny that to know the meaning of sour also implies an oppositional inference—that of sweetness? In the realm of mind, therefore, where meanings are said to play a role in behavior, is it ever possible to know only one end of a bipolarity or an opposition? And if not, what might this imply concerning the organism which reasons according to bipolar knowledge? When we multiply these bipolarities and think of congeries of meanings "all at once," such bipolarities would deal with the relational, the totality, the "field" of interlacing meanings that might confront an individual's awareness as he comes at experience. The cognitive-phenomenological tradition has tended to emphasize the complex *interrelations* of these congeries without explicating the fact that only in a world of bipolar meanings would it be possible to achieve that totality we know of as the "phenomenal field" (Rychlak, 1973, pp. 500–526).

This is precisely how the early Greeks viewed their world—as composed of a host of interlacing meanings, each joined ultimately into a totality (one in many) thanks to the *dialectical* nature of experienced events. Anaximander maintained that the elements of the universe were held together by an opposition—air is cold, fire is hot, and so forth. Heraclitus found oppositional "strife" to be the principle by which events moved over time. Empedocles argued that "love and strife" were the antagonists which moved events. And we hardly need recite the extreme importance which both Socrates and Plato placed upon man's capacity to know truth by way of a dialectical method, or, as Aristotle was to call it, *dialectical reasoning* (Rychlak, 1968, pp. 256–264).

The celebrated Grecian mind was a Universal Mind at least in part thanks to the fact that it presumed all events to be ultimately united in opposition. This meant that "truth" was simply the other side of "error," and that by beginning in the latter we could come to know the former. Implications and possibilities which were not intended by the meanings as framed could be extracted through subsequent dialectical analysis. A host of meanings could be extracted in this fashion until what was being meaningfully conveyed by the dialectical analysis might bear no clear resemblance to what was initially expressed. Discovery was thus to be seen as an act of free intellect.

It was Aristotle (1952, p. 142) who led the first attack on dialecticism as the proper method of a science. He equated it with sophistry where, as in the Socratic Dialogues, two men could talk and talk, and rather than moving from error to truth, they simply perpetuated the erroneous opinions with which they had begun their discourse. Aristotle held that one has to begin with premises which are "primary and true" in order to develop further knowledge which is also true. He called this more rigorous style of thought *demonstrative reasoning*. A premise which is primary and true is essentially *unipolar*. It is either a kind of operational definition, as when we say "procedure X *is* my construct X," or it is a summary of the "facts" as observed empirically. A fact is not to be tampered with and twisted into its opposite designation. Aristotle founded biology because he wanted science to rest upon such facts and clear-cut (tautological) definitions, even though he *also* held that men could and often must reason dialectically. Experimentation for Aristotle, who was very toughminded in outlook, was principally a question of rigorous observation. And as we have seen in his natural teleology, the theories which issued from this observation were framed by Aristotle in what today we call an anthropomorphic fashion. This takes us into the next technical point.

Scientific Theory versus Scientific Method

The innovations of Aristotle in the history of scientific thought essentially dealt with the nature of evidence, or the willingness to check one's thinking against some independent (from mind) standard of "truth." Demonstrative reasoning is essentially a *methodological* point of order. A "method" is the means or manner of determining whether a postulated theoretical conception is true or false (however tentatively and lightly one wears these truth-value designations). The dialecticians were using common sense. They failed to go out and gather proper empirical evidence, and consequently their theories were not to be trusted. Of course, even a method must rely upon certain common sense assumptions, and to that extent method is ultimately confounded with "meta-" theoretical questions. Philosophical points of view are surely theoretical questions of the most subtle variety.

It was just such a philosophical subtlety in the history of science which led to a monumental masking of the theory-versus-method distinction which we can easily make in any theory of knowledge. This masking was accomplished by the British empiricists. Sir Francis Bacon (1952) gave it philosophical birth by going beyond Aristotle to claim that there was no rationality "for the sake of which" leaves shaded fruit or bones held up muscle (ibid., p. 44). This is the way theologians had spoken about the universe, adapting Heraclitus's logos to a Divine Plan conception, and Bacon wanted no part of it. As scientists, we must explain things in *only* material and/or efficient cause terms—even if this means reducing concepts below what they seem to be in common sense. It is difficult to underestimate the suspicion with which natural science has viewed humanistic theories, dating from the turn of the seventeenth century when Galileo and others were forced by religious Inquisitors to recant or face serious reprisals. One would be either naive or ingenuine if he did not honestly admit that to "anthropomorphize" means for many to "sanctify" the human image. The science-religion antinomy can be traced to a debate over causal description. Since the 1600s a scientific account of the universe had to be framed in *only* material and efficient-cause terms. Even when a formal-cause concept is introduced, it is assumed that some underlying substance or thrust of lawful events is "actually" the cause of the pattern.

Since the research paradigm of William Gilbert was patterned on the "practical machines" of manual workers (Zilsel, 1957, p. 233), it was easy to equate the scientific theories of a Baconian efficient-cause cast with the efficient cause-effects of the newly proposed research experiment. The upshot was that the theories of nature were rigidly brought into line with the evolving research methods of natural science on the matter of causal description. The natural scientist in the Newtonian mold thus consciously sought to explain things and then to test these explanations within a single causal framework. It was necessarily the outcome that his theories of nature *would* be proven. They could not be disproven, really, until the Einsteinian and Machian revolutions in thought of the late nineteenth century forced the physicist to think more creatively about the possible bifurcation of scientific knowledge into theory *and* method. As Burtt (1955) has observed, the Newtonian scientist was to make a metaphysic of his method—which is to say, he turned his mechanical apparatus into a world view, thanks to the easy equation of two forms of efficient causality.

The confounding of theory and method was to fix for all time a demonstrative image of man in natural science (Giorgi, 1970). Thomas Hobbes (1952) viewed man's thoughts as directly analogical to mathematical calculation, a theory we see continued in today's information-processing and related cybernetic models. John Locke (1952) held that "ideas" were like "primary and true" copies of an immutable (input) reality, to which man's mind responded passively. Each "simple" idea was thought to embody a *unipolar* building-block meaning. These simple ideas were said to combine into more complex ideas in a quasi-mathematical fashion, but in no case could they be generated anew through dialectical examination as the Greeks had claimed. British empiricism thus succeeded in placing man's intellect on the effect side of the cause-effect tandem we recognize as the efficient cause.

The dialectical tradition was not lost to history entirely, however. We see it in the more Continental Philosophy of someone like Kant (1952). Unlike Locke, who viewed meanings as issuing "from below," from the input of efficient causes out of our experience, Kant stressed man's "categories of the understanding," which were like *intellectual spectacles* (formal causes) framing in meaning "from above." Though he, like Aristotle, was distrustful of the dialectic as a method of arriving at truth, Kant considered *free thought* to be dialectical in its essence. Whereas Locke felt that we could not—as human beings—subdivide, frame, or invent one "new" simple idea in mind, Kant recognized that in free thought or "imagination" man could and often did see the opposite implication of these Lockean inputs.

But how does one bring this maverick dialectic into the "control and prediction" strictures of Gilbert's machinelike research methodology? Well, one *cannot* do so. If you remove that often miniscule element of arbitrariness from dialectical reasoning—to do or to think the opposite of what is called for in the meaning of stimulus input or "environmental influence"—then you are no longer dealing with the dialectic. You have a theory of opposites, but these are not truly dialectical opposites. Well, if this is the case, why should a science aiming at the (methodological) *truth* become bogged down in the (theoretical) *error* term? As anyone who reads history can properly determine, with the rise of modern natural science these past 350 years we have witnessed a steady decline in the *formal* use of dialectical conceptions. There have been many informal applications of dialectical conceptions in psychological theory, however (see Rychlak, 1973).

Theoretical Perspective in Scientific Explanation

The wedding of theory and method in natural science had a profound influence on the kind of theory which was to be written. The logic of methodology, in which the scientist assumed the attitude of an observer, demanded theoretical explanation of such "facts" in a third-person or *extraspective* sense (Rychlak, 1968, p. 27). The Newtonian scientist took the machine analogue of Gilbert's method and, remaining within the efficient-cause strictures of Bacon, turned his world into a huge, predictable, efficient- and material-cause reality (Burtt, 1955). To think about the course of events from the vantage point or "slant" of the item under observation promoted anthropomorphic explanation, and therefore we find the scientist removing *himself* as analogue from the theory he was propounding. This is proper, of course, because in inanimate and subhuman events it does seem illogical to use an animate or human analogue to account for the regularities to be seen in such events.

It was not until the rise of psychology—both in the academic centers and in the "applied" settings of psychiatric medicine—that a new form of theoretical challenge faced the scientist. In this case, since the item under observation was animate and human, and it purported to know things about its existence which seemed difficult to capture theoretically in other than teleological terms, a kind of theorizing was called for which would send the account into an *introspective* theoretical perspective (Rychlak, 1968, p. 27). This requires a first-person account, a recognition that the identity under observation is making a contribution to the course of events in some formal-final-cause sense which is not itself *only* efficiently caused! In this case, it is perfectly logical to employ oneself as human analogue for the items (human beings) under description. Unfortunately, because of identification of method with theory, it seemed as if any scientist who performed this division of one (theory) from the other (method) was in violation of proper scientific procedure. This has proven to be a major stumbling block to psychology, but thanks to the rise of modern science the appreciation of a role for theory independent of method is now general. The eminent physicist Oppenheimer (1956) once encouraged psychologists to begin using themselves as analogue for descriptions of other human beings, and that included teleological description as well.

Humanism versus Mechanism

It is now possible to distinguish mechanistic psychology from humanistic psychology in purely technical terms. Mechanists continue in the time-honored natural science tradition of accounting for events extraspectively, following the admonitions to find supposedly basic, underlying material and especially efficient causes in events. Occasionally you will get some patterning conception—such as the organization of a cell assembly system, or the schedules of reinforcement—but in *no* case do you see a final-cause concept being used. Terms like *purpose* are redefined so that they lose a true "that for the sake of which" meaning and are instead said to be *observed* improvements in trial-and-error responsiveness (Tolman, 1967, p. 14) or *observed* consequences of operant responses which may or may not lead to contingent reinforcement (Evans, 1968, p. 19). Yet a true purpose is simply inexplicable in extraspective terms. Purposes are not ascribed by an observer to an actor without some imputation regarding the actor's strategy of behavior. The behaviorists do not feel they are twisting meaning in their account. They feel behaviorism clarifies *new* aspects of older conceptions by taking a more scientific view of things. We find that a considerable amount of the behaviorist's time is spent in asking questions like "how can we account for this behavior [purpose] in other, more scientific [efficient cause] terms?"

Mechanists are Lockeans. They want to build up the person from a substrate of factors which constitute his totality. The reverse logic calls for a reductionism in scientific theoretical accounts. These which translates into the "what is" rather than the "what is not" theorists are committed to the study of the "primary and true" (i.e., possibilities, dreams, playful ideas, etc.). Dialectic is taken to be error, and error as such is not considered an active principle worthy of scientific study. Error is something to be removed or ignored. Indeed, thanks to the underlying commitment to realism, the Lockean theorist views error—like creativity—as a naive characterization of what *really* moves events over time from a substrate fabric of efficient causality. The mechanistic image of man is therefore completely demonstrative. Primary and true bits of information are put in, mediated and totaled in some fashion, and then put out—all in a completely (in principle) observable fashion of cause-to-effect (efficient causation). Chimerical factors of the human condition like wishes, ideas, or fantasies are given no credence short of accidental functions or peculiar illusions of the higher nervous systems to be found in nature.

In technical language, humanism is the theoretical description of behavior falling back on formal and final causality as a major explanatory strategy—which, of course, results in teleological accounts written from the introspective perspective. This is the tie binding all humanists. Whatever their terminology, an impartial analysis of the claims they make will convince one that humanists are seeking for a telic explanation of human behavior (see Giorgi, 1970, or van Kaam, 1969). Humanists do not want a substitute language. They do not ask, "How can we account for what used to be called purpose?" but rather, "How can we convince our peers that purpose in human affairs does exist?" As introspective theorists, humanists are likely to fall into the Kantian line of descent, seeing something like the categories of understanding "framing-in" experience as the mentally alive organism "comes at" life rather than "responds to" life (Rychlak, 1973, pp. 500–527). Talk of phenomenal fields, world views, and personal constructs fills their accounts—all of which are introspectively conceived theoretical terms, serving as the "that" against which behavior is therefore being carried out. Humans are not only or merely "responding" to antecedent pushes called "stimuli." They are also *precedently* arraying events "for the sake of which" they will *sequaciously* behave.

The humanist substitutes for the Lockean tabula rasa conception of mind a pro forma conception of the mind bringing to bear influence from the outset of life. Learning is more than simply input, because even simple ideas are not so "simple." This gives the humanistic introspective account a more idealistic coloring. As with Kant, the humanist believes that in free thought the individual can "cook up" all sorts of possibilities, some of which he can then bring creatively to bear in life while others end up on the trash heap as mistakes. In so behaving, the human reflects an ability to transcend reality or the "facts" of life as input from reality. Kant based his concept of transcendence on the functioning of an underlying "transcendental dialectic." Though not all humanists are aware of the reliance they place on dialectical logic, *some are* (e.g., Binswanger, 1963, p. 313; Jung, 1953, p. 4). Dialectical conceptions permit us to say how it is that the unidirectional control over mind which mechanists believe to be the case is *not* the case.

The dialectic provides us with a rationale for conceptions of psychological freedom. In the computer, which reasons only demonstratively, information that is fed into the machine has a unipolar, "primary and true" acceptance by the machine. The computer never receives "two meanings" as one or the other of the binary-information "bits" it is considering. It receives either-or, and proceeds in a uniform and predictable course of demonstrative logic which culminates in an iron-clad conclusion without the possibility of true error *or* creativity being attributed to the thinking of the machine. This machine is not *free* to contemplate alternatives. But is this true of the human person? If we are now standing at the base of a mountain, looking upward to the summit, the indisputable facts are that we are "here," and "there" is the summit. But is it not true that, as dialectically reasoning animals, we realize—in that chimerical-phantasy sense if nothing else—that we "could be up there!" Aspirations to achieve and to create (telic factors) spring from such realizations.

The humanist believes that it is this facility to see open alternatives in all meaningful understandings which stamps human intelligence as fundamentally different from the efficient-cause "thinking" of a machine. If a machine were programmed to think dialectically (assuming that this were possible) it would no longer have that iron-clad, predictable quality in its conclusions. It would begin to suggest (create) alternatives to the input which the operator is sending "primarily and truly" into its hopper for consideration. The other side of this is that it would begin to project error, or come up with hunches and notions which would prove erroneous. Who would want such a machine, one which is no more predictable than the human being who made it? One could not run an actuarial business using it. One could not assess scientific data using it. This machine would be free in a way that the mechanistic philosophy has no inkling of. Hence, to the humanist, freedom is the capacity which certain animals have to reason to the opposite of environmental-input meanings and thereby to affirm more than one predication "for the sake of which" they then have a possibility (choice) of behaving.

Because teleology has been associated in the history of thought with conceptions of freedom, free will, and so forth, an unfortunate development we see taking place in the present is the presumption that a humanist *must* argue for the more uplifting, quasi-religious side to man. Some psychologists who might honestly prefer to give a humanistic theory serious consideration in their work are dissuaded from doing so because of the goody-goody connotation that humanism has taken on. Humanism has been identified with en-counter groups and social reform of various types. It therefore appears that a related admonition of the humanistic approach is to "see thy brother human being as worthy of respect and help" or some such. Desirable as this might be for a general approach to human relations, such ethical pronouncements are unquestionably harmful to an objective assessment of the data we must examine as scientists. They arise as shortcut solutions to the problems being discussed in the present paper. Not understanding that man's dehumanization is a function of the cementing of method to theory in science, the humanist thinks he can *force* his fellow psychol-ogist into presenting mankind teleologically by going to telic pronouncements on how one "ought" to view man as a higher being.

This is a misguided effort. Much better to follow the Jungian insight that human beings are no more elevated than they are submerged.

If a psychologist is really theorizing in order to raise man's dignity, as Rogers (1961) seems to do, or, if he is pitching his psychology at an application to human welfare, as Skinner (1972) seems to be doing, then *both* such theorists might be said to be *humanitarian* in outlook. The former is a humanistic humanitarian and the latter, a mechanistic humanitarian. This distinction between humanitarian and humanist has the advantage of removing those unfair ad hominems which Skinner and other behaviorists have had to confront, such as "fascist" or "cruel" or "enemy of man's dignity." One may disagree with the image of man underlying behavioral modification, but surely the intent of such efforts is no less humanitarian than encounter-group "marathons" or dances around a park bench! It is possible to be a humanist without having to bear the weight of sociopolitical advance on one's shoulders. There is no claim made for humanitarian goals in the present humanistic account. So far as the writer is concerned, a Nazi could be humanistic in theoretical persuasion even though he would surely not be a humanitarian by customary standards of definition. The distinction between humanism and mechanism is thus removed from anything but a comparison of the technical devices employed in generating knowledge. It does not even matter what a theorist might call himself. The determination of whether he is humanistic in orientation—just as the determination of whether he is a realist, or a drive-reduction theorist—should be possible simply by analyzing his actual statements through our technical, theory-construction issues (Rychlak, 1973).

KNOWLEDGE AS COMBINING THEORY AND METHOD

The concept of "knowledge" is elusive. If one takes a demonstrative view of its meaning he is likely to think of knowledge as something one "has," a primary and true item of information—at least, insofar as anything can be known to be "true." Yet surely we can know that we do *not* know. Is this circumstance the presence of something (knowing that one lacks knowledge), or is it the absence of something (lacking information or "not knowing")? It is also possible to know two things about something at the same time, each of which may be true even though the two items of knowledge are contradictory. The wave versus the particle theory of light or the contrasting theories of gravity proposed (and validated) by Einstein and Whitehead are cases in point (Rychlak, 1968, pp. 117–118). To the dialectician, such contradictions provide further support that our observations will never be circumscribed by one and only one theoretical formulation. But it challenges us to think of knowledge in these more complex terms.

The writer has found it profitable to construe knowledge as a more abstract term than either theory or method. A *theory* is simply a stipulated (hypothesized, suggested, believed-in, etc.) relationship between two or more constructs (items, terms, observed events, etc.). A *method* is the means or manner of testing the theoretical proposition we have formulated (Rychlak, 1968, pp. 42–43). Knowledge is the understanding of why a given theoretical proposition (construct, statement, etc.) is true or false *after* this proposition has been put to test. Precisely when someone is prepared to say he knows something always depends on the methodological test he is prepared to make, and his formulation of some stand, conclusion, or interpretation thereby. Even if we agree that truth is relative and merely true "for the time being," the point of methodological test is to bring a theoretical statement down to earth as *fact* or as likelihood to "such and such" an error probability.

There are two broad categories of methodological test, one of which we might call *cognitive* and the other *research*. If we believe something because of its plausibility and consistency with common-sense knowledge, we do so on the basis of *procedural* evidence (ibid., p. 75). This cognitive test is used by all thinkers, who must, after all, begin someplace in order to proceed with a line of thought. When one hears of "theoretical proof" or "philosophical examination," it is the cognitive method and procedural evidence which is being alluded to. Historically, this approach to the "true" has been termed a coherence theory of truth, since what one believes is based on what makes best sense in relation to all of the other things that one knows and holds to. We can see in this theory of truth a heavy reliance on formal causality. That totality within which an item is said to cohere is as a piece in a puzzle. The total pattern thus lends meaning to the individual item.

With the rise of modern science, a more stringent requirement for the exercise of evidence was called for. We noted above that William

Gilbert adapted a machine model to experimentation in natural science. Considered now strictly as a means of proof, the great benefit of this model for method was that it permitted an extraspective observer to follow the development of events in a clear, objective, step-by-step fashion. One does not have to view this flow of events—taking place "over there" (extraspectively considered)—in *only* efficient cause-effect terms. We can drop the concept of a machine and still prearrange events successively in order to predict their outcome. This is a "put up or shut up" test; if the scientist is unable to prearrange events to meet his expectations, he is not given the ear of the scientific community. There are, of course, many other reasons why he may or may not get this community's collective ear. But at a bare minimum, the values of science stress the need of such evidence in an experimental context. This more rigorous approach we have called the research method, and consider that it provides us with *validating* evidence (Rychlak, 1968, p. 77).

The term *method* is not used uniformly in psychology. It is often confounded with the meaning of experimental design, probably because of the style of writing in experimental reports where a design is outlined for the reader under a methods section. The present view draws a sharp distinction between the global concept of method and the more restricted concept of design. Although paired associates and T-mazes are alternative ways of studying learning (i.e., they are different as to design) they are identical as to method in that both result in validation. An experiment (via the research method) might thus be thought of as a trial run, *designed* to test the implications of a theory—no matter how informally this theory is framed or how narrowly it may be conceived. Many theories in psychology are no more than rough analogies. Yet, since they tie constructs (i.e., meanings) together in a stylized fashion we have every right to consider these theories or theoretical formulations. The reasoning strategy of validation is obviously demonstrative. Operational definitions frame in that "primary and true" series of experimental variables which must—"for the purposes of this study"—stand for the theoretical construct under test. Predictions are made within these controlled strictures, and data are then gathered—to be tested statistically according to the canons of yet another set of plausibilities. That is, mathematics rests ultimately on procedural evidence (especially the principle of tautology). And so the generation of scientific knowledge goes from theory to methods (cognitive, research) and back again.

Now that we recognize a distinctive role for both theory and method, it is less surprising to learn that each functions somewhat independently of the other. Phillip Frank (1957, pp. 1–45) has shown how the methodological "findings" of scientific experimentation actually outstripped mankind's common sense, so that at present we can predict things which we really do not quite understand. This demonstrates that "control and prediction" is not always an infallible guide to knowledge. It also brings up another point referred to above, to the effect that multiple views of reality in science are now and doubtless always will be possible. Indeed, most modern philosophers of science believe that for any research sequence of events (independent variable to dependent variable) there are *in principle* N potential theories to account for the observed regularity (the "law" ensuing) (ibid., p. 31). Scientists usually narrow theoretical description down to several or only a few theories, but no single theory explains everything equally well.

There is another characteristic of science we should consider in the present context, having to do with what is called "affirming the consequent" of an "If [antecedent], then [consequent]" proposition. We know from (demonstrative) logic that when a proposition like "All men are mortal" is succeeded by the affirmation "This is a man," it follows necessarily in syllogistic sequence that "This man is mortal." In this case we have affirmed the antecedent of an "If man, then mortal" proposition. In the case of succeeding "All men are mortal" with the affirmation "This is a mortal," it does *not necessarily* follow that "This is a man." Obviously, there can be several other beings besides humans designated as mortals. We have affirmed the consequent of an "If man, then mortal" proposition, resulting in a fallacious conclusion if we presume that man and *only* man will be signified by mortality.

With this error in logic before us, consider the typical sequence of reasoning by a scientist, as he moves to validate. He probably reasons, "If my theory holds, then, through controlled variables of this and that variety, such and thus can be predicted to occur." In a subsequent data collection, "such and thus" *does* occur as predicted. Even so, as Adams (1937) once made clear to Hull vis à vis the latter's hypothetico-deductive method, the strategy of reasoning and testing here is all on the side of affirming the consequent. Clearly, the predicted succession of events lends credence to the theory under test. But data can *never* signify that only the theory which delineated them is being "proven" in the results obtained. This is simply a further recognition of the fact that we must distinguish between our theories and the methods employed to test them.

The fallacy of affirming the consequent is not fatal for science. It is offset by the fact that scientists perform a host of experiments on the theoretical "paradigm" which they find helpful at the moment (Kuhn, 1970). Indeed, one of the requirements of a satisfactory scientific paradigm is that it be sufficiently prolific for the advocates to generate considerable data in its application. In this way, a consistent set of valid facts is obtained, and as the picture is filled in it is more difficult for alternative paradigms to account for the body of findings. Actually, the paradigm dictates the design of experiments so that a tailoring of method to theory takes place. All methods seek a compatibility with their theories. The hope is that the data accrued and the paradigm being enriched will prove instructive and useful to humanity, but not even this exalted aspiration need ensure that a paradigm will be rejected (or retained). The instructiveness of a paradigm can be a very restricted affair, known only to a small number of scientists, who work for each other in total disregard for the broader reaches of the scientific community, much less of mankind (Kuhn, 1970, p. 20). Yet even if a paradigm is ascendant, popular, and instructive for everyone, the logic of scientific investigation allows us to say that it can *always* be replaced by one or more alternative formulations. Theoretical paradigms must ever be suspect and subject to replacement or otherwise changed. But what of methodological paradigms? Are they ever revolutionized?

WHAT SORT OF REVOLUTION IS CALLED FOR IN PSYCHOLOGICAL SCIENCE?

Thanks in recent years to Kuhn's (1962, revised in 1970) analysis of the "scientific paradigm," we in psychology have been giving increased attention to the question of whether or not we *have* one and, if so, whether it needs changing. It is not uncommon to read that psychology lacks a formal paradigm. Robert Watson (1967) has claimed that rather than functioning under an institutionalized paradigm, psychology splits up into camps under the influence of a series of oppositionally framed "prescriptions," such as monism-dualism, functionalism-structuralism, and so forth. Giorgi (1970, p.

175) has suggested that we may be in a *preparadigmatic* stage, for surely we have much disagreement over what sort of image of humanity we are to embrace. The present writer holds that psychology does have a legitimate, Kuhnian paradigm which it consciously furthers, and that this institutionalized paradigm follows the outlines of what we have called above the mechanistic, Lockean, efficient-cause model. Furthermore, we argue that psychology has performed a kind of historical repetition in confounding its theoretical with its methodological paradigms, so that at least three generations of psychologists have mistakenly believed that evidence gathered in the methodological sphere supports this and *only* this model of behavior. In brief, we now charge that psychology as practiced in American academic centers has made a metaphysic of its methodology (Burtt, 1955).

Some of the misunderstanding over whether or not psychology has a formal paradigm stems from the many ways in which Kuhn originally used this term. In his revision, Kuhn admitted to two different usages (1970, p. 175), but Masterman (1970, pp. 59–89) has suggested that there were roughly 21 different meanings expressed by Kuhn in the paradigm concept. Yet only one or two of these 21 usages can properly be said to deal with what we have been calling method. In the most pertinent instance, Kuhn (1970, pp. 59–60) is discussing the fact that occasionally a scientist's commitment to the experimental designs of his predecessors can actually hamper his discovery of something new. If he could but shake himself free of a certain routine approach in the laboratory, he might well come upon something entirely different from what his conventional practices make possible. Kuhn then asks: "Ought we conclude from the frequency with which such instrumental [i.e., design] commitments prove misleading that science should abandon standard tests and standard instruments? That would result in an inconceivable method of research. Paradigm procedures and applications are as necessary to science as paradigm laws and theories" (ibid., p. 60).

We have suggested above that both methods and theories are based on paradigms. All notions of a theoretical model, scheme, construct, and so forth borrow from this essentially formal-cause conception of the "paradigm." Scientists used the earlier paradigm of material sound waves to think about light waves (Oppenheimer, 1956, p. 131), ferreting out in time the correct analogy from the incorrect in their developing theories. But what about methodological paradigms? What does it mean to speak of a paradigm in the context of proof? A moment's reflection will convince one that this refers to the *theory of knowledge* accepted by the scientific community in its metaphysical assumptions. We have already seen how Gilbert's machine paradigm helped cement the efficient cause into science as a major conceptualization. Machines had been under construction for centuries before Gilbert's adaptation. The eminent mathematician Bronowski (1958, pp. 23–26) has shown how the "practical" machines of a da Vinci in the fifteenth century were, by the eighteenth century, used in quite a different sense. Da Vinci willed some end, and then designed a machine to reach this goal. Newton, beginning with the realistic assumption of a world of machinelike (because God-created) precision, constructed *his* machines to prove a point.

We might now ask of Kuhn: Has there *ever* been a complete revolution in the methodological paradigms of science? The answer here is no, and as the citation above demonstrates, Kuhn himself believes that to abandon standard tests and (machinelike) instrumentation would result in chaos for science. It seems clear, therefore, that when Kuhn uses the term *paradigm* he is speaking about changes in theoretical outlook (see his recognition of this, 1970, p. 182). When we get to that most abstract of theoretical outlooks—the realm of metaphysical theory, on which methods are based—we cannot find a revolution taking place in the history of science. The scientific method has remained stable from its inception, based on the logic of validating evidence. It is the clarity, objectivity, and openhandedness of validation which makes it so necessary for science. There have been and doubtless will continue to be revolutions in the theoretical conceptualizations a scientist brings to bear in the *design* of his experiments, which is really what Kuhn is talking about in the above example.

The closest we come to a revolution in the theory of knowledge underlying scientific method has to do with the theoretical interpretation one gives to the experimental "variables" concept. When Dirichlet (Eves, 1953, p. 371) enlarged on the "function" concept of Leibniz in the nineteenth century, he did so exclusively in a formal-cause sense, as a mathematical ratio between two numerical values. The "connection" between independent and dependent variables might thus be said to occur "by definition," and the resultant patterned relationship was varied at the convenience of the mathematician. Dirichlet stipulated that whenever two variables x and y are so related that a value assigned to x results automatically (by some rule or correspondence) in an assigned value to y, then we can say that y is a (single valued) *function* of x. The variable x, to which the mathematician assigned a value *at will*, was to be called the independent variable, and the y variable was to be called the dependent variable. Nothing in this definition implied that x efficiently caused y.

If we now combine this mathematical conception with the machine paradigm of Gilbert's experimental method, what is the implication? Clearly, the point is that one need *not* view the independent-to-dependent-variable course of observed events in *only* efficient-cause (machine) terms. A theory which attempted to account for the x-y functions—often called "laws"—might take its meaning from any of our four causes. Gilbert's theory of knowledge was framed by a mechanistic (efficient-cause) paradigm and Dirichlet's theory of knowledge was framed by a mathematical (formal-cause) paradigm. The latter did not revolutionize science, however, because what occurred was a blending of the two conceptions. Newtonian science, which had already mathematized nature, now simply proclaimed that the functionally related variables *in fact* tracked the efficient-cause regularities to be seen before our experimenter's eyes. Modern physical theory was in time able to shake loose the mathematics from the method, so that today's theoretical physicist no longer views nature as "only" efficiently caused (see Russell, 1960).

However, in the case of psychology the philosophy of science which was promulgated via the Lockean biases of our institutionalized model ensured that the Newtonian identification of statistical variables with experimentally manipulated variables would continue. Psychology has permitted stimulus-response terminology to become the *only* scientific theoretical account of observed regularities between functionally related variables. The foremost spokesman for S-R laws was Spence (1956), who left no doubt that a truly functional (formal-cause) "R-R" law was "less basic" (p. 9) in essence than the more properly scientific S-R law. Never mind that the phrase "S-R law" is a mixing of terms (S-R as theoretical and law as methodological terminology). The perception of orderly and predictable relationships between experimental variables is ipso facto taken as a demonstration of *only* a stimulus-response theoretical finding. And the S-R concept is the sine qua non of efficient causality. The writer has called this the "S-R bind" (Rychlak, 1968, pp. 57–60), but it could just as easily be termed the "efficient-caused bind."

Many humanists have tried to follow the rules of science in

validation, only to be strangled by this theoretical bind. For example, a humanist might formulate some theoretical construct having teleological meanings. He designs an experiment which flows from his premising theory, properly controls variables in the light of his prediction, tests his findings with the proper statistics, and then proudly writes up his "significant findings" as evidence for his telic formulation. What does the typical toughminded referee say upon reading this humanistic write-up? From personal experience, the writer can suggest that the reviewer's cogitations run something like this: "There seems to be an S-R regularity in there, but until we delineate all of the antecedent variables controlling these measured responses, we are unable to say 'what?' is taking place. One thing for certain: all of this poppycock about mental intentions and aspirations and self-directed judgments is *not* an adequate scientific explanation of these observed S-R laws!" This often highly competent, yet foolishly overconfident, individual can reason as he does because he is used to confounding S-R with IV-DV. He slips our IV-DV *methodological* finding underneath *his* pet S-R *theoretical* construct and sees in our data support for *his*—and only his—theory.

This insufferable experience prompts many humanists to suggest that what we need in psychology is a complete revolution in method! While appreciating the reasons for this demand, the writer must insist that it is not our method which is at fault but rather the naiveté of our leading research psychologists vis à vis the role of theory in all science. *The revolution called for in psychology is entirely on the side of theory.* We must fully appreciate and continually publicize the harmful effect which the current Lockean model has on psychology when it is accepted and pressed as the *only* acceptable theoretical paradigm for a science of psychology. One can see the development of this confounding of theory and method in American psychology's history. A brief survey will make this charge clear.

In his opening call for behaviorism, John Watson (1913) set as his goal for psychology the "working out [of] a systematic scheme for the prediction and control of response in general" (pp. 162–163). As we now understand it, the phrase "control and prediction" defines validating evidence, but Watson was not saying that the experimentalist performs this activity in order to support or refute his theoretical hypotheses, which in turn might account for the observed data. He was not controlling an independent variable, but a "stimulus" (ibid., p. 163), so that he might efficiently cause the organism's movements to go the way he wanted them to go (see Kuo, 1928, for this continuing thesis). Hence, behaviorism sought lawful ties of stimuli to responses, rather than validated knowledge: "In a system of psychology completely worked out, given the response the stimuli can be predicted; given the stimuli the response can be predicted" (Watson, 1913, p. 167).

Tolman was next to confound theoretical with methodological terminology, and he did so while expressly trying to "cognize" the simplistic efficient-cause approach of Watson. Watson had removed the organism as thinker from the succession of events called behavior, but Tolman reintroduced a modest role for mentality in behavior, as a kind of "middle term" in the efficient-cause sequence: "Our system . . . conceives [of] mental processes as functional variables intervening between stimuli, initiating physiological states, and the general heredity and past training of the organism, on the one hand, and final resulting responses on the other. These *intervening* [italics added] variables it defines as behavior-determinants" (Tolman, 1967, p. 414). What this confounding of theory and method immediately suggests is that all one can *ever* prove in an experiment done on the cognitive life of humans is that these "intervening variables" have themselves been placed into the hopper of mind by past experience. And this past input is *itself* accomplished by way of efficient causation. From this time forward, a truly teleological account of behavior was made impossible, thanks to the confused rules of the scientific game being written by our leading psychologists.

S. S. Stevens (1935) next crystallized an attitude in experimental theoretical description which has continued until today, when he wrote: "Psychology regards all observations, including those which a psychologist makes upon himself, as made upon 'the other one' and thereby makes explicit the distinction between the experimenter and the thing observed" (p. 517). This extraspective principle furthered efficient-cause accounts because, as we have noted above, a more introspective perspective is required if we want to ascribe intentions and purposes to organisms. Though the psychologist thought of himself in the role of experimenter as making statistical assumptions, formulating experimental hypotheses, and testing his observed findings according to an evaluative act, the "subject" being described "over there, in the apparatus" was essentially *trapped* in the S-R bind, with his intelligence "functioning" as one of those

Tolmanian mediators. No Kantian premise, framing-in experience from the outset of life, was seen to influence the course of his life. Early inputs were stored, and when enough were there to act as current mediators, some kind of circular feedback system might be attributed to the human intellect. But in reality these mental mediators are merely old inputs, warmed over.

It was Hull (1937) who firmed up the equation of method to theory. The second rule of his hypothetico-deductive method called for what is effectively a tautological identity of theory (or postulate) and the test of that theory (in the experimental procedure). It was at this point that Adams (1937) tried without apparent success to alert Hull and the other behaviorists to see that because of "affirming the consequent" (refer above) their theoretical system must ever be only one of many possible accounts of experimental findings. Bergmann and Spence (1941) then voiced a classic confounding of terms in their reiteration of the Watsonian dream when they observed: "Like every other science, psychology conceives its problem as one of establishing the interrelations within a set of variables, most characteristically between response variables on the one hand and a manifold of environmental variables on the other" (pp. 9–10). To speak of "response variables" is blatantly to preempt the possible theoretical account of why experimental variables might be said to bear an observed relationship. This paradigmatic preemption effectively *dictates* terms to the experimenter, who must now either see his dependent variable as a "response" or risk being considered nonscientific. Meehl and MacCorquodale's (1948) subsequent paper on the distinction between a hypothetical construct (theory) and an intervening variable (method) did nothing to check the developing terminological confusion. The *point* of this classic paper was to suggest that a methodological construct—that is, the intervening variable—is somehow more meaningful (because wedded to the operations made in validation) than is a theoretical construct (which accounts for the observed data in a more "hypothetical" fashion).

Today, it is second nature for our leading psychologists to slip back and forth between terminologies. The foremost behaviorist of our time, B. F. Skinner, can be seen to do this, as in the following statement drawn from his interview with Evans (1968): "As an analyst of behavior, I want to relate the probability of response to a large number of independent variables, even when these variables are separted in time and space" (p. 12).

What sort of revolution is called for in psychological science? A revolution on the side of theory, one which will open up and even foster alternative theoretical descriptions of the *same* data collections. We do not need to supplant the Lockean-mechanistic models with Kantian-humanistic models altogether. Anyone who professes interest in Lockean formulations should be encouraged to continue his study as he now does. But it is hoped that he would be, if not humbled, then at least made contemplative by the recognition that his historical ties to the machine paradigm of scientific method are no longer mandates for a preferred position in the scientific hierarchy. Telic accounts are no longer to be dismissed as lacking parsimony or departing from the "data as observed." No one can claim objectivity in science who is unable or unwilling to take the theoretical viewpoint of another. If the concepts being used are found wanting, they can easily be refuted within the language realm of the theory under espousal. But if a critic simply refuses to comprehend a telic theory, and in some way claims the rights of preemption as a "genuine" scientist who "knows" what a proper scientific account must be like, we have something far more serious taking place. In this case, rather than with critical analysis, we are faced with *paradigmatic repression*, pure and simple.

WHY HUMANISTIC METHODOLOGIES TEND TO FAIL AS SCIENCE

There is much talk these days of "humanistic methods" in psychology. As suggested in the previous sections, the writer cannot support these moves if it means altering the necessary scientific sequencing of: (1) theoretical speculation; (2) testing the plausibility of such speculations cognitively and designing thereby an experiment which can show others the implications of this theory; (3) carrying out the projected validation. Sharp distinctions between these three steps (especially 1 and 2) are not possible, but the general logic here suggests that only those who move through step 3 "at least some of the time" are actually participating in a scientific endeavor.

Note that we elevate both theory and procedural evidence in stressing three steps. The course taken here is termed the "line of development" (Rychlak, 1968, p. 218), and by acknowledging it we can now say that it can be *stretched* somewhat in going from points 1 to 3. It is not a violation of parsimony to conduct an experiment which was implied by theory, even though this design is not testing "the" background theory per se. It is, of course, highly desirable for an experimental design to test the generating paradigm "directly." Yet, many of the more humanistic, introspectively conceived constructs are never actually circumscribed in the apparatus. We measure the presumed reflections of a concept like "aspiration" in the phantasy stories written by the subject or in the goals he sets himself on some task. This "once removed" measurement is no strike against the science which follows our three steps to validation. What is being suggested here is that some of the so-called control which becomes prominent at step 3 is already under way in the logical control being developed across points 1 and 2.

The reason the writer cannot accept "humanistic methods" is that they either stop somewhere around points 1 or 2, falling short of scientific validation altogether, or they go on to 3 with some loosely designed project, often boiling down to a discursive survey of some group of individuals. There is a rationale for such steps, which we will shortly go into, but it seems that the justifications given simply do not salvage the kind of tepid science which ensues. What is so disheartening about these efforts is that they pass by many fine opportunities to show humanistic features of behavior in the laboratory. It is the writer's conviction that humanistic behavioral descriptions are to be found relevant to the most rigidly controlled, arid realms of laboratory science imaginable. It goes without saying that if an experiment is designed specifically to *minimize* telic factors, it is going to be more difficult to adopt a humanistic explanation of the succession of events ultimately observed. This is the natural outcome of our demonstrative style of reasoning when we move to step 3 in order to prove "something" already predicated by step 1 (however informally such predications may be held to). One can only prove what he looks for, the "primary and true" features of his experimental hypotheses.

Yet it is clearly possible to take a teleological view of the work of others and find, in these studies designed to prove one point, considerable evidence for some other point. This is what we feel Rosenthal (1966) has accomplished in his excellent work on experimenter and subject influences in the research relationship. Properly considered, this line of study is a commentary on the play of teleological factors in psychological experimentation—often masquerading under rubrics like "demand characteristics" or "modeling." The same holds for the classical studies of Dulany

(1962) and DeNike and Spielberger (1963) on the role of *awarenes* in operant conditioning. This is more a telic than a mechanistic formulation. The operant-conditioning design originally took no cognizance of the introspective formulation of subject behavior (awareness of the response-reinforcement contingency). Yet we now have (via methodological study!) incontrovertible evidence that something akin to a subject-contributed "conceptualization" is essential to the operant-conditioning procedure—at least, this is the case when humans are used as subjects. A telic explanation is now possible, one which meets phenomenal experience as well as observed evidential data. Subjects are "conditioned" only when they guess the experimental design (formal cause) as being conducted by the experimenter, and then behave "for the sake of" the intended effect (final cause). Page (1972) has even designed a fascinating study in which he proves that some subjects know the experimenter's "study plan," yet *fail* to cooperate and "be conditioned." These data are meaningless in a nontelic formulation of what seems clearly to be going on in such operant studies.

It is easy to be sympathetic with the dreams of those who hope someday to find a scientific method which is capable of capturing the richness of lived, human experience. The scientific method is clearly aimed demonstratively at restricting and narrowing alternative factors down to the point that any *one* study is rather a thin soup. This is why paradigms need considerable filling in during what Kuhn (1970) has called the phase of "normal science" (pp. 23–42). But this delimitation in each study proves discouraging to many humanists, on two counts. First, there is the sense of artificiality which such "controlled" efforts lend to the theoretical account to follow. It all seems a make-believe game; either validation is sought for some trivia already known, or there is no true relevance to the "lived experience" of the man on the street. Secondly, the humanist who considers himself existentialistic or phenomenological in orientation finds the "variables" designed for in the experiment to be so far removed from what the individual is actually experiencing at "his end" of the observer-subject continuum as to be a violation of scientific objectivity on the face of things. This charge of a distortion in the arbitrarily selected dimensions of study by the extraspectionist, who then forces his schemes onto his subjects with total disregard for their actual experience, is what we mean by the *purity criticism* (Rychlak, 1968, p. 390).

It is charged that the extraspectionist in psychology has purposely neglected his responsibility to capture the more introspectively framed account of life that we all live within, each day of our existence. Based on some misguided principle of "natural" science, the extraspectionist ignores "pure, spontaneous" experience (at the level of the phenomenal field) to perpetuate the illusion of a material and efficient-cause theory of humanity as "natural products." Although quite legitimate, the unhappy result of the purity criticism is that it tends to focus on the methods of science rather than on its theories. The nemesis of our previous section—the failure to distinguish proof from theoretical description or explanation—continues to dog us. A typical derision of science is to be seen in the following quote from Boss (1963), who is commenting on his approach to psychology (i.e., *Daseinsanalysis*): " . . . analysis of *Dasein* urges all those who deal with human beings to start seeing and thinking from the beginning, so that they can remain with what they immediately perceive and do not get lost in 'scientific' abstractions, derivations, explanations, and calculations estranged from the immediate reality of the given phenomena" (pp. 29–30).

What makes such derision unfortunate is that if one merely surveys the leading figures in science over this century—men like Bridgman (1959), Bronowski (1958), Conant (1952), Eddington (1958), Einstein (1934), Oppenheimer (1956), Schrödinger (1957), and Whitehead (1958)—he would find much more support for a humanistic account of behavior than support for a mechanistic account. Modern science has become more open to Kantian-like terminology, thanks to its recognition that what one observes in the "hard reality" is due at least in part to what one presumes from the outset. This is clearly a recognition of the telic factors in the work of science. A liberal approach to scientific theorizing is more current and appropriate than is the staid and lifeless form of Newtonian science which is still dreamed of in too many psychology departments. However, it seems to us more harmful than helpful to provide our students with a humanistic outlook which is internally hostile to research design. By misplacing our guns we tend to attract students who are *in fact* disinterested in developing the necessary self-discipline and exerting the effort which a scientific career demands.

There have been two extended analyses of science in the recent literature, each of which purports to suggest a more humanistic approach to method. We refer here to van Kaam (1969) and Giorgi (1970) and would like now to look into each commentary in light of our claim that scientific methods need *not* be revised, much less revolutionized. As we shall hope to show, there is nothing in either of these two distinguished arguments to change our minds.

The van Kaam (1969) book is existential in outlook, and we are not surprised to find a purity criticism being leveled early in the presentation: " . . . human sciences will never present us with a full understanding of man so long as they are pure speculative knowledge or mere laboratory knowledge without reference to the real, lived world of man" (p. 25). The culprit is developed as more method than theory, with the suggestion that a phenomenological substitution is called for: "Phenomenology as a method in psychology thus seeks to disclose and elucidate the phenomena of behavior as they manifest themselves in their perceived immediacy" (p. 29).

A distinction between comprehensive and differential psychological theories (van Kaam's term for theory here is "modes of existence") is then drawn (ibid., pp. 114–175). The point of this distinction is to say that science tends to discriminate and break down behavior from its totality into differential pieces (Lockean-model reductionism), whereas a comprehensive psychological theory tries to retain the wholeness of lived experience. As such, comprehensive theory would retain teleological descriptions of human behavior (p. 110). Though one might suspect that van Kaam's polemic is solely on the side of theory, when he speaks of his approach as "anthropological phenomenology" he brings in the factor of method as supposedly *also* changed: "Anthropological existential phenomenology is both an attitude [in our terms, theory] and a controlled method. It leads to a comprehensive understanding of intentional behavior as a structured whole which is differentiated in many patterns of behavior" (p. 252).

Without phenomenological explication of scientific endeavors a science of psychology can be sent scurrying about on meaningless endeavors: "Empirical observation, experimentation, measurement, and accumulation of data should be fostered in all differential psychologies. From the viewpoint of comprehensive psychology, however, much of this admirable effort is wasted if there is no phenomenological explication of *what* it is that is being observed, experimented upon, measured, correlated, and applied" (ibid., p. 303). Now, one can heartily agree with the need for phenomenological explication, if what this means is something akin to our steps 1 and 2—that is, thinking about what sorts of speculations are worth making and, in light of this reflective assessment, a procedural testing of what one's scientific activity is all about. This sort of activity is absolutely essential, and it seems as if this is what van Kaam is referring to. However, in the familiar style of purity critics, he bears down rather severely on the scientific method as captured in our step 3. The foibles of method are constantly emphasized, as in the following excerpt, where he is discussing the evience of so-called differential (i.e., typical Lockean) psychology:

> . . . the hypothesis that learning is based on a process of conditioning can be verified only by differential-scientific evidence; it cannot be validated directly by either spontaneous or comprehensive-scientific evidence. The evidences of differential psychologies are only indirect evidences. They do not make behavior itself manifest; they are deduced from spontaneous evidences by means of abstract scientific methods. The latter may consist of logical, mathematical deductions or of empirical inductions, the methods of which may differ in each differential psychology. To be sure, the conclusions of differential psychology possess their own types of evidence. Yet such scientific-differential evidences are always less reliable than naïve self-evidences. [Ibid. p. 275]

We learn in the next few paragraphs that what van Kaam means by "unreliable" is "less constant" or "subject to change," as when a future scientific account based on new evidence alters our current thinking on some topic, such as "learning," for example. People 50 years from now will have the same spontaneous, phenomenal experience of learning that we have today. However, our scientific theories of the learning process, based on evidence accumulated over the next 50 years, may be vastly different from what it is today. Hence, differential scientific evidences are less reliable than the naive commentaries proffered by living subjects (ibid., p. 276). Note what has happened here: van Kaam has *also* confounded theory with method so that he is uncertain as to what is unreliable and what needs ever to be reliable in the scientific quest. Is it not likely (or at the least, possible) that the style of accruing evidence has remained highly reliable over the 50-year span, even as the theories being put to test in this fixed strategy of accruing evidence altered? In fact, these theories *could* have altered in the direction of greater congruence with the spontaneous, phenomenal accounts of today.

To say that a method (evidence source) is unreliable because it tests different theories over time is like saying an aging automobile is unreliable (or unfaithful) because it dependably carries a series of different masters over time. What van Kaam has stumbled upon here is the fact that scientific methods are *always* those last steps of our three-step sequence, which means they always have more than one theory which might account for them. Methods are those "consequents" we spoke about above, which get affirmed and to that extent are *never* in one-to-one (necessary) agreement with their antecedent theoretical backgrounds. The empirical findings of scientific method are not unreliable, they are simply subject to change in theoretical description—over time, within time, anytime! By confounding what is method with the theory accounting for the resultant findings, van Kaam, like so many humanistic critics, points his guns in the wrong direction.

In his example of the phenomenological method in action, van Kaam presents data on a survey of high school and college students who "explicated" their feelings (on a written form) when they were "really understood by somebody" (ibid., p. 331). The sample is broken down into percentages of subjects expressing various positive reactions to being understood, such as that they felt relieved and satisfied, safe in the relationship, in experiential communion with the person, accepted, and so on (p. 336). It is hard to see the difference between this study and the kind of prestudy that *any* conscientious investigator would perform in order to develop his terminology for an attitude scale, or some such. For the sake of convenience he would construct a scale following such prestudy and then search about for other samples in order to extend the range of his knowledge about the construct "feeling really understood."

For example, there is every chance that a group of prisoners might have a different sense of what it means to be really understood than high school and college students. Though the phenomenal experience is presented very positively, what about those times when we are caught in a lie or some other misbehavior and hence feel "really understood," yet hardly safe, at ease, or in experiential communion with the person or persons who understood us. The survey instructions (ibid., p. 331) do not make such circumstances clear, and there was obviously a very positive demand characteristic which the subject "behaved for the sake of" in this study. But these are precisely the kinds of questions a sagacious investigator would next seek to answer if he is sincerely interested in his construct. This is

why the paradigm continues to be filled in in "normal" science
(Kuhn, 1970). We do not wish to be unfair to van Kaam, since
presumably this study was done merely as an *example*, to show how
his approach let the subjects define their construct, rather than
providing them with a preconceived definition of the construct (a la
the purity criticism); yet we must at least point out that humanists
are frequently criticized for the paucity and superficiality of their
scientific work.

Giorgi (1970) begins his critique with a sophisticated review of
the tendency in psychology to press natural-science, efficient-cause
models onto the teleological human being. He argues that there was a
kind of choice early in the game between a humanistic theory of man
and a scientific methodological approach, with the result being that
"in the conflict between fidelity to scientific methodology and
fidelity to the phenomena (in this case man), almost all early
psychologists opted for the methodology" (p. 92). Once again,
we find a leading humanist making it appear that scientific
method is by definition anathema to humanistic theories. Yet, both
Gustav Fechner and Johannes Müller—individuals who were not
unimportant to the founding of experimental methods in psychology—took a clearly Kantian, humanistic view of mankind
(Boring, 1950, pp. 275–295). Fechner's well-known law was the
result of his desire to prove a humanistic theory—that is, that mind
functioned independently of body (inner psychophysics). It was
only later, as the Lockean thinkers Helmholtz and Wundt came on
the scene, that a confounding of efficient-cause method with efficient-
cause theory was accomplished. Rather than having an "option" in
the matter, these Lockeans were merely encouraged by the "hard
data" that complex human behavior was reducible to underlying
simple forces and motions (Cassirer, 1950, pp. 85–91).

The purity criticism plays a major role in Giorgi's (1970, p. 148)
polemic. There is perhaps no better example of this criticism than the
following:

Let us take, as an example, experiments designed to discover
the threshold time for subjects to perceive how many dots
are on a screen. This experiment is usually described as
"perception as a function of time," meaning that the experimenter is interested in finding out how long it takes the
subject to perceive what he (the experimenter) already *knows*.
Thus, the subject must acquire knowledge and express an ob-

jective fact—*x* dots—and is usually not in any way instructed to relate how he experienced the phenomenon of tachistoscopic visual presentations. The latter factor is simply presumed and never taken into account. [P. 153]

In line with our statements above, the fault here would seem to lie in the exclusively extraspective and arbitrary *theory* of the experimenter, who selected the time dimension as a base rate standard against which to claim learning "was a function of." Yet, Giorgi's continuing analysis places the fault on the side of the method used to validate such assumptions. He calls for a "phenomenological technique" (ibid., p. 162) of "reduction," which means that we should try to clarify and delineate the presuppositions which define our "perspective." By perspective is meant something akin to the Kantian spectacles that we bring to bear in formulating a precedent "slant" on things, a slant which in turn will determine sequaciously what we will say about them: "The fact of perspectivity is the main argument against all theories that posit absolute positions" (p. 163). This seems more a question of theory than method. But Giorgi also favors Merleau-Ponty's concept of "structure," which is a conceptualized "whole" that is identifiable, analyzable, and transposable. When clarified or explicated it reflects the psychological meaning a person experiences in relation to it (pp. 178–179). This formal-cause concept implies that a procedural-evidence-based examination of structure can be carried out, because of its internal consistency as a "total" (coherence theory of truth). Giorgi refers to this analysis of structure as a "method" (p. 192), but it would obviously stop short of our step 3 and thus—according to the present viewpoint—*not* constitute proper science.

An experiment by Colaizzi (1967) is then cited, in which subjects in a memory task are interrupted after one trial and asked what they were thinking about at that time (Giorgi, 1970, p. 192). It was found that—rather than "learning as a function of time" or whatever—these subjects were found to be getting accustomed to the apparatus; some mentioned the unfamiliarity of the learnable materials; others gave their reactions to the instructions; and so forth. Here again, the aim is to map the course of learning according to the (introspectively conceived) subject's actual experience rather than to the already known fact that it would take *time* (practice, rehearsal, familiarization, repetition, etc.) to acquire the materials. Giorgi calls such experimental designs "human scientific procedures"

(p. 193) and adds that they are really not totally existent today but they *are* possible. Though they may not "look scientific," they are just as scientific as any other approach to valid data.

Our reaction here would be to ask: "How does this procedure differ from the standard control and prediction sequence? Obviously, Colaizzi's design could be repeated, with the data found initially predicted to cross-validate. Hence, what makes this a *humanistic* procedure—the theoretical background, or the method of evidence pursued?" Clearly, there is no strike against scientific method in this study. What is called for is more of the same, more routine effort in the "normal science" sense to fill in the humanistic, introspectively conceived theory that prompted Colaizzi's design in the first place. We leave Giorgi's searching analysis with a feeling that he has not made a case for a shift in scientific method. Our procedural-evidence convictions say that he, like van Kaam, is misplacing his polemic.

In summary, it is our feeling that all this talk about revolutionizing the methods of science constitutes a *straw-man* argument. There is no inherent conflict between validation and humanism! Those approaches which profess to fall back on the wisdom of philosophy or on the knowledge to be gained from the arts have failed as science because of their need to rely exclusively on procedural evidence to support their theoretical points of view. This in no way denigrates the role of philosophy or art in existence, and in point of fact, one can often go directly from philosophy and art to a scientifically testable line of development. We must never forget that human beings can create or "think up" possibilities which are not now in existence but which they could indeed "make happen." To say that something is phenomenally true but not amenable to scientific validation might just mean that it has not yet reached creation in overt behavior. This ability to create can of course be studied scientifically. But to expect a scientist to run after each person's "phenomenal reality" in hopes of capturing each "possibility" that might be concocted is surely unnecessary and a waste of time. We need philosophical analysis to clarify our thinking, and artistic creations to enrich our life-alternatives. These theory-laden and procedural-evidence-based activities are necessary and important to science. Yet, so is validation important to science. Any so-called humanistic methodology which falls short of validation is therefore doomed to failure. Humanists *must* take our third step.

WHY MEDIATIONAL AND RELATED "COGNITIVE" THEORIES TEND TO FAIL AS HUMANISMS

If the humanist has committed errors in his analysis of method, then the mechanist has made equally fallacious efforts to formulate a quasi-humanistic *theory* of behavior. It is not uncommon for the humanist to learn from some colleague, or possibly a student, that all of his worries over the Lockean paradigm's grip on psychology are about to end. Thanks to some "new look" in human learning, or a new clarification of an older stand, a blending of the humanistic with the mechanistic account is just around the corner. The most recent savior-theory heard by the writer is supposedly a revivification of *cognitive* theory. In the present section we hope to show that such a solution on the side of theory is unfortunately impossible, due to the unyielding theory-construction issues which divide the mechanist and the humanist. We will also take a close look at a recent effort to make humanism scientifically respectable: that is, the reclamation of a "cognitive" paradigm by Boneau (1974).

In order to appreciate the mechanistic theorist's efforts to account for what a humanist calls the final cause, we must remember that he always reasons extraspectively. Observing the undoubted flux of efficient cause-effects "over there," the extraspectionist reasons that he must find a way of saying that the flow of causality is self-correcting, and with this theoretical maneuver all will be settled. Thus, he reasons as follows: "Let us simply acknowledge from the outset that a living organism *does* mediate between the inputs and the outputs of experience, and that thanks to a feedback mechanism of some kind, there *is* an influence being brought to bear on the new input as the human being begins to acquire earlier environmental inputs and to retain them in memory, and so forth. This is 'really' what a humanist is calling the final cause. Old inputs are the 'that' for the sake of which newer outputs are mediated. Once we accept this, and realize that any of a number of mediators may 'influence behavioral sequences' we have dealt with the heart of the humanist's objection to Lockean theorizing."

Such mediation-theory thinking simply does not get at what is separating the Kantian from the Lockean theorist. It is done in a continuing efficient-cause frame, so that the older inputs, now acting as a cybernetic bridge to the future, spring to new life as quasi-final causes in the present. Yet this is surely nothing new to the Lockean model, since John Locke himself discussed several ways in which the

mind makes use of past information to influence now the processing
of new information (see Locke, 1952, pp. 178–200). In psychology,
we tend to trace mediation theory to Tolman's (1967) sign-gestalts,
or to Woodworth's S-O-R ideas (Goss, 1961). However, even our so-
called founding fathers had conceptions which recognized an
influence from yesterday's learning on today's behavior—for
example, Helmholtz in his "unconscious inference" construct and
Wundt in his "apperception" construct (Boring, 1950, pp. 308–311
and 338–339, respectively). What then is the crux of the Lockean-
Kantian paradigmatic confrontation on the question of teleology?

The fundamental issue is, does the organism *from birth*—or even
possibly a bit before literal birth—"do anything" in a pro forma
sense to the inputs of experience? Or is the organism exclusively
tabula rasa at this first of life's protopoints (i.e., a fixed point of
reference from which the organism contributes to its experience).
Mediation theory prejudices the case in favor of Lockean
formulations, since it puts this conceptualizing ability at the
organism's disposal only *after* an initial input has been etched upon
the tabula rasa intellect. Sign-gestalts (Tolman, 1967) and related
mediational concepts such as the cue-producing response (Dollard &
Miller, 1950, p. 98) are efficient causes *first* (old input "effects"),
formal causes second (patterns which determine the new output
behavior), and *never* final causes! To think of final causality in its
pristine meaning we have to believe that the organism *truly* judges,
truly weighs alternatives, so that at least in some circumstances he
faces what amounts to an arbitrary line of behavior. This means he
can—as an identity!—make a real difference to what eventually
"happens."

In the Kantian model, formal- and final-cause meanings are given
primary emphasis to suggest that how the individual approaches a
life situation determines what will eventually take place—that is,
they literally serve as one "cause" of the string of efficient causes
that will flow forward, from *this* point onward! Indeed, the
individual realizes that he might proceed in *different* ways from now
onward. Granting "way A," such and thus will come about. Granting
"way B," another, possibly less desirable, course of action will come
about. Still, since the less desirable course of action is open to
alteration by a personal strategy of some kind, why not risk it? *This*
is the kind of development which is possible in a truly teleological
theory of behavior. It is *not* fixed by the frequencies of past inputs,
and it is *not* glued to the probabilities of an independent reality. It

recognizes a mental realm as well as a physical and an interpersonal realm. Realities within these realms can be altered, if only the human as telic organism is given a chance to behave within them. Note that the role for dialectic here is very significant. The reason we can speak of true arbitrariness in behavior is because we accept it as given that human reasoning is both demonstrative and dialectical in nature.

Mediation theory therefore falls short of a genuinely telic commentary in at least three ways: (a) mediators (signs, rules, encoders, models, etc.) are input and hence past "effects" rather than truly present "causes," which means that (b) a genuine "that for the sake of which" determination in the sequence of motion called behavior is *never* achieved (i.e., there is no arbitrariness in behavior), resulting in an exclusively (c) demonstrative way of describing the course of behavioral events.

In speaking of a pro forma influence from birth the writer might be said to embrace an "innate ideas" position. Thanks to the supremacy of the Lockean paradigm in psychology, it is often hard to make clear that an innate Kantian idea is something quite different from an innate Lockean idea. Locke looked at ideas as receptacles, as if some information that had flowed in now occupied the idea as a unipolar designation (a "bit" of information unto itself), the way water fills a glass. The idea was not a conceptualizing (organizing, lending-meaning-to, etc.) process in mind. It was an "effect" in the efficient-cause sequence. What was "in" the idea, as a meaning, was put there by the environment, just as the water is put into the glass.

Kant's (1952) categories of the understanding as so-called innate ideas are something much different from this receptacle notion (p. 233). These are more akin to conceptualizing "formal causes" for the sake of which perceived (phenomenal) reality is organized. What was innate about the idea was the ability to *lend meaning* to life experience as well as the particular dimensions along which such meaning could be induced, for example, unity-plurality, possibility-impossibility, and so forth. Kant was not saying that individuals are born with the meaning of the words *unity* and *plurality* pocketed in little receptacles. As a neo-Kantian, the humanist can claim that not until the child knows the meaning of left will he know the meaning of right. Not until he grasps up will he grasp down, or the same for good and evil, long and short, and so forth. Coming to know one side he knows the other because meanings are often bipolar and not only unipolar designations. The humanist does not have to claim—as the Lockean paradigm would force him to claim—that the child has an innate capacity to know what left, up, good, and long means— much less their opposites. The specific content of an idea waits on experience. But, at least *some* meanings as input from experience in the Lockean simple-idea sense are not so simple! They will be oppositionally complex from the very point of input, calling for an active affirmation by the organism (self, ego, I, etc.) to affirm "this" meaning or "that" in the situation which continually arises before it.

We now turn to the "cognitive behaviorism" paradigmatic innovation proposed by Boneau (1974), who sets out expressly to show that a mixture of statistical-decision theory and information-processing theory will provide a better analogue for psychology than the behavioristic thesis which has the organism under the direct control of the stimulus (p. 298). Boneau indicates that his speculations may open the door to a more humanistic form of psychology (p. 308). He is also well aware of his indebtedness to Tolman (1967, p. 301). We agree with this assessment completely, and considering the interest and even excitement which such "revivals" of cognitive theory seem to be generating these days, we think it very important to take a close look at one such theory—and this is a good one! But, is it *really* based on a paradigmatic revision, revolution, or change of any sort in the currently ascendant Lockean model? We want to keep this question before us as we examine the basic concepts of this proposed innovation.

Though teleology is not discussed directly by Boneau, there are obvious telic overtones in the effort to provide behaviorism with a more palatable conceptualization, and that frequent stand-in for a more clearly final-cause construct, the "expectancy" notion, is employed. The use of "cognitive" to describe this theory stems from Boneau's claim that human beings (all organisms, really, but we confine our comments to humans) internalize information from the environment via what he calls a "commerce" with the environment. This information is then "structured" by the organism into an *internal model of the environment* (IME), which is the real basis of behavior rather than direct stimulus control (Boneau, 1974, pp. 299–300).

The IME is said to consist of three "dimensions" corresponding roughly to the behaviorist's conceptions of stimulus, response, and reinforcement. The first dimension is *situation*, which amounts to sensory inputs which are discriminated by the individual into all sorts of meaningful things like faces, colors, symbols, and so on. The next is an *action* dimension, which is anything from a muscle twitch to the highly organized behaviors of social relations. A subdimension of action is the *internal action dimension,* by way of which humans can see potential actions in their upcoming behavior—either by recalling actions that they had performed earlier, observing the actions of others, or even by conceptualizing "new possibilities of actions that have been performed by no one" (ibid., p. 299). This sounds very much like humanistic theory, and it excites our interest all the more when we hear Boneau suggest that behavior can "become to a degree unpredictable because it is based on an internal process geared to the task of generating novel action, of restructuring the internal environment" (p. 308).

The third dimension of the IME is the *outcome,* which, like the situation, is a "sensory input" (ibid., p. 300). The outcome is essentially what occurs or fails to occur given some situation and an action following within it. If we open the refrigerator door and see there some tidbit, the situation (kitchen and refrigerator therein) has had an altered outcome (presence of food) following action (opening door). But even if nothing had taken place—no food, no change in the situation following action—we could still speak of the outcome. We thus have two sensory inputs, situation and outcome, and one output feature, the action, all of which are rolled up into a continuing model of the environment. Boneau refers to this model as a "personal construct" (p. 307), though we should not confuse this with George Kelly's (1955) usage. As a model of the environment, the IME is not necessarily a "perfect copy." It is actually a probabilistic "expectancy" framework (Boneau, 1974, p. 301) which the individual uses to order life, based on past experience and other features of its "internal processes."

Though he uses the terms "phenomenal" and even "inferential" to describe the IME, this must not be equated with gestalt-phenomenological or existentialistic-phenomenological conceptions. The latter theories view a phenomenal field as "creating the situation" or "constituting reality" for the individual. As basically idealistic theories they stress the subjective features of inference, suggesting that everyone "comes at" experience with their own subjectivities (recall the purity criticism, above). For Boneau, however, a phenomenal realm is that vale of sensory input that we must deal with in processing information from reality. And his concept of inference is purely statistical, essentially a probability estimate. Boneau candidly describes himself as a "naive realist" rather than an idealist, adding: "Things, we assume, are 'out there,' and, further, they are what they seem to be at least most of the time" (ibid., p. 299). An observer, looking out at reality, can determine the probabilities that certain actions, in certain situations, will lead to certain outcomes. Such experimenter-determined values of probability about a sequence of behavior can be more or less congruent with the internally held subjectively determined values of the individual. At least one type of learning that all organisms are engaged in involves matching up the subjectively determined probabilities with the (third person) experimenter-determined probability values of what might be termed the "reality." Thus: "A well-trained animal, for example, with long, appropriate experience, may behave as if the P_{ijk} ["reality" probability] and the p_{ijk} ["subjective" probability] have identical values. . . . Human individuals are no less capable" (p. 301).

Thus far, we have a fairly straightforward reformulation of Tolmanian thought. Tolman (1967) included inference in his theory (pp. 164–180), and his concept of means-ends hierarchies allowed for probabilities, although he spoke of "possibilities" since he likened his approach to logic rather than statistics (p. 190). Although Tolman included emotions—as sensations of pleasantness and unpleasantness—in his theory of sign-gestalts (1967, p. 264), Boneau (1974, p. 301) seems to feel that purposive behaviorism was lacking in motivation theory. Boneau proposes that *hedonic values*, or sensations of pleasure-pain, are correlated with (albeit independent of) the outcomes of developing situations. The axiom which flows from this is that "the individual will behave in order to maximize the potential hedonic value available in a situation" (p. 302).

This utilitarian principle is then brought into relationship with the IME to produce *expected hedonic values*, a multiplicative function of the subjectively determined probabilities times the hedonic value. Boneau assumes that hedonic values vary along a unidimensional scale of negative values (repellent outcomes) to zero values (neutral outcomes) to positive values (attractive outcomes), and that an individual *can* make absolute value judgments on this scale. In speaking of "maximizing hedonic values" in the above quote, Boneau therefore means that a person will seek only positive outcomes in life. Summing up his view, Boneau can now say:

Summarizing the whole theoretical machinery, it is supposed that the individual through commerce with its environment can create for itself a model of that environment containing information about known situations, about the set of known outcomes available, and about the likelihood that those outcomes occur when known actions are performed. The theory then postulates that the individual in any situation evaluates the set of possible outcomes with their various hedonic effects at that time, determines the expected hedonic value of the outcomes, and then performs the action necessary to produce the highest expected hedonic values. [P. 303]

We can now step back from this fine example of a current cognitive theory and ask: Is this theory a real paradigmatic confrontation for the established Lockean paradigm, as for example when gestalt-cognitive psychology challenged traditional psychology in the 1920s and 1930s? A reasoned answer here would surely be *no*! Boneau has given us one more Lockean model, one which is hard to distinguish from Tolman (1967), highly similar to Rotter's (1954) social-learning theory, and, in many of its details, already anticipated by Dollard and Miller (1950). For example, Boneau's (1974) call for a concept of "implicit trial and error" is already in the literature, as employed by Dollard and Miller's (1950) mediational adaption of Hull's fractional antedating goal reaction (i.e., anticipatory goal response; see p. 37, pp. 110–111, and p. 286). Psychology has had a series of such nonconfrontations in its history. It can even be shown that the celebrated "clash" between Titchenerian structuralism and the Chicago School of functionalism was a relatively minor dispute over method between two clearly Lockean theoretical camps. We should not be misled by terms like "cognitive" and "inference" and "unpredictability of human behavior" into thinking that anyone who uses these meanings is *really* calling for a change in our institutionalized paradigm. Boneau's theory, like every one of the "modern cognitive theories" the writer has taken time to look at, is just another variation on the Lockean theme. Here are some points:

1. A Kantian "cognitive" theory would stress that the individual could model "from birth," but Boneau's modeling construct—a formal-cause addition to the material and efficient-cause terminology of some behaviorisms—is said to occur later, as a sort of organization of the input from reality. Despite the claim that he is removing behavioral control from the stimulus, Boneau's input constructs of situation, outcome, and hedonic value are all sensational and, as

depicted, *determine* what is framed in action. A personal construction here is the ordering of such inputs, which get combined (somehow?) into a complex mediator. This is identical to Tolman. But if an organism can order its existence *after* sensation, maybe it can *order sensation.* Maybe "reality itself" is organized by the individual. As we know, Boneau rejects such idealistic talk and puts his trust in observed reality. Indeed, this is why he can so confidently presume that an experimenter's probabilities are a "standard" against which the animal or human's learning is to be measured. The subject is "subjective" and the extraspective observer is seeing reality "objectively, " that is, truly. An existentialist might talk of intersubjectivity here—subject and experimenter each "modeling" reality—but Boneau has not foresaken the Lockean interpretation of an idea (IME) as a mapping of reality.

2. Note the several fine reflections of demonstrative reasoning in Boneau's conceptions. Hedonic tones, which are easily conceptualized dialectically, are presumed to fall along a unidimension. We can stack up feelings and judge them from negative to positive steps. Talk of ambivalence, or loving and hating at the same time, would be either error or a sort of neutral balancing at the zero value point on this view. Humanistic theories like to capture such contradictory features of behavior, as well as the possibility of opting for self-destruction (death instincts, and so forth). Boneau's theory would not consider it possible on the face of things for an individual to opt for a harmful outcome; or, at the very least, it would be difficult to explain behaviors which seem to be clearly self-destructive.

3. Teleological humanistic accounts want to describe how it is possible for a person to express a true "choice." Although Boneau speaks of the individual "evaluating" the set of possible outcomes as weighted by expected hedonic values, a true choice is not possible because he must say that the person follows the resultant odds. Humanists are drawn to the fact that people *do* opt against the odds, standing against pressures, accepting the likelihood of death, taking the short end of a "long shot," and so forth. How could it be possible for an individual to do this unless something else is in that demonstrative and true calculation of a given outcome times a given hedonic value?

It makes no difference whether one talks about the (a) "frequency of past stimulus input" which controls behavior in the present or (b) the "probability of present action leading to a given outcome and hedonic tone" which controls behavior in the present. The former is emphasizing efficient causation, and the latter introduces formal-cause meanings in the mathematical treatment; but if, in principle, the individual being described has no option but to follow the efficient-cause frequencies of past input or the formal-cause probabilities of the record of such inputs, *there is no true choice!* Hence, there is no true teleology, and there is surely no humanistic psychology under theoretical promulgation. Boneau could have easily gone directly to John Locke (1952), who believed—after all—that thinking *was* statistical (i.e., mathematical) in nature. Locke observed in what some would probably call cognitive terms today that "probability . . . carries so much evidence with it, that it naturally determines the judgment, and leaves us as little liberty to believe or disbelieve, as a demonstration does, whether we will know or be ignorant" (Locke, 1952, p. 369).

4. Boneau has the typical disregard of a concept of *meaning* in his theory that all Lockeans do. It is the frequency (based on contiguity assumptions) of "this" behavior associated with "that" reward (outcome, drive-reduction, hedonic value, etc.) which accounts for behavior and not the meaning of a situation, the import of an action as "intentionally put into expression," and so forth. To "cognize" is to *know*, and a cognitive theory should deal with how one knows—as this one does, of course—but is it possible to speak of knowledge without at some point at least implying knowledge about some complex of meanings? Behaviorism has always taken more interest in the mechanics of learning—the fluid (efficient-cause) description of how it takes place—than in the significance which this learning has for the person in the learning situation. Boneau seems to be altering this, but actually he does not. He makes the person a kind of actuary, or a cybernetic machine, manipulating frequencies of a memory-bank recollection of past actions and hedonic tones into a "most probable" determination for the future. But meaning, as such, has no more relevance for the person than it has for the cybernetic machine.

5. Though Boneau (1974) says he can envision an individual whose "internal process" is geared to the task of generating "novel action," no real justification for true novelty exists in this model. Since meanings are not taken into consideration, and since what "happens" in behavior is a function of sensory inputs (situation, outcome, hedonic value), the novel action *must* be predicated either on serendipity or on past inputs which gave the individual a direct premise of "act in a novel fashion" (as, by observing others,

being rewarded for seeming to be novel when one was not, and so forth). Lacking a concept of arbitrariness, the nondialectical features of Boneau's theory must redefine what is meant by true psychological novelty. As with our mention of free choice above, no description of that "internal process" we have been told about by Boneau convinces us that the person as psychological identity can contribute anything to the determinate inputs. This can only result in the "look" of a humanistic account, not a real humanistic psychology. Once again: It is simply *not* a teleological theory.

6. Boneau has not even erased the time-honored behavioristic distinction between "learning" and "motivation" in his account. This distinction was called for initially because of the behaviorist's extraspective account of learning as a bonding of stimulus to response. It was necessary to say why certain S-R regularities were bonded into habit, while others were not. Hence, we can think of the associative bonding as learning, and the "reason" for this bonding taking place as "motivation." Those S-R regularities which were reinforcing became "attached," that is, resulted in a drive reduction, and so on. Phenomenological cognitivists like George Kelly (1955) rail against this arbitrary and—for them—unnecessary distinction. Kelly felt that the maximization and extension of meaning by way of construct-formation was sufficient theoretical description for how people learn. They learn because they wish to extend their phenomenal (meaningful) grasp of experience. Of course, as noted above, by seeing the "phenomenal field" as something which is input rather than as an organizer of raw sensation into a meaning complex, Boneau's theory must retain that feature of explanation which he claims Tolman's lacked, namely, *motivation*. From our perspective, Tolman's development was far more innovative in concept than Boneau's. Tolman appreciated that emotions too were actions, and hence served as sign-gestalts on a purely cognitive level, rather than as some kind of multiplicative "motivator" concurrent with an action-induced probability estimation (see Tolman, 1967, pp. 258–268). Boneau's hedonic-value construct is written more for the (extraspective) convenience of an observer than for the (introspective) convenience of a person under observation. We can believe that people assess probabilities about outcomes in situations, given the likelihood of certain actions. Introspectively this is plausible. But do they "multiply" this probability estimate times how much they like or dislike the outcome? Or do they simply include this

likability estimate in the original expectancy projected? Tolman favored this view, making him more genuinely cognitive than Boneau.

We conclude, therefore, that Boneau's cognitive psychology is not a paradigmatic innovation, much less a dramatic innovation in the already clearly established mediation line of theoretical descent. Boneau's theory is a conventional Lockean formulation. It does not advance psychology to *mean* one thing and state another. When we get down to certain rock-bottom (albeit highly abstract) notions about what it is that we "see out there" versus what we "know in here," there are always going to be differences in the theories we formulate, based as they are on bipolarity in meaningful slant. This is why in a true paradigmatic confrontation a revolution is called for. There is no way of negotiating our differences. We have either to throw one another over or live in peaceful coexistence. But how much better and honest this is than trying *formally* to "handle" things in certain language when everyone knows *informally* what is being said or implied. It is the writer's hope that all those who write on cognitive and/or humanistic psychology in the future will at least take some time to tell the reader what their views on teleological description are. If they feel that a humanistic psychology is possible without telic commentary, let them say how this is possible. Such care to make things explicit would at least reduce the tremendous misunderstanding which now develops when those in psychology who want a teleological description of behavior think they are seeing it in these repetitively Lockean "cognitive" accounts.

AN EXAMPLE OF A RIGOROUS PROGRAM OF HUMANISTIC RESEARCH

For some 15 years now the writer has been developing what he takes to be a humanistic theory of human behavior, drawn from a more Kantian frame of paradigmatic reference. A series of roughly 50 data collections have issued from this approach. In the present section we will give an overview of the theory and then survey the highlights of the research findings to date. Space requirements limit the presentation, but a full statement of the theory and research, as well as a more thorough case for humanism in psychological science, is now being drafted (Rychlak, 1977).

A Humanistic Theory

The general approach taken is called "logical learning theory," but we include under this designation dialectical as well as the more familiar demonstrative (Aristotelian) logic. We do not always expect individuals to behave or reason "rationally"—according to probability estimates or whatever—any more than we expect them to be constantly irrational. Dialectical reasoning is often the source of those unpredictable and unlikely trains of thought we term illogical, unfounded, emotional, psychotic, and so forth. We do not deny that logical errors of the classical demonstrative variety are possible, as our use of the "affirming the consequent" fallacy makes plain (refer above). But often there is a madcap, inconsistent, self-contradictory, ironic, arbitrary style to thought which is still logical, if one but recognizes the (dialectical) form of logic at play. The unpredictable fruits of such reasoning often end up in the "error variance" of our research experiments, and of course, as true scientists we are not supposed to busy ourselves with an explanation of the error variance. This is supposedly a form of "noise" in our input-gathering of information. Demonstrative science deals with what "is" (primary and true) and not with what "is not." And so the Kantian humanist who tries to capture this elusive, capricious quality in behavior is likely to be looked at with a sense of astonishment by the Lockean establishment.

In rejecting the S-R bind (and its derivatives) on psychology, logical learning theory proposes a view of behavior as telosponsive, in addition to its being simply responsive. The *telosponse* construct acknowledges a mental contribution to "observed behavior," viewing (introspectively) the human being as putting down certain conceptual premises "for the sake of which" behavior then flows. Telosponsiveness can be seen in true acts of judgment, evaluation, assessment, and the like. A purpose or intention is *always* based on some form of relational judgment. The final-cause phrase of "for the sake of" signifies that behavior does not run off directly as the S-R construct implies, with nothing but an "association" bonding the regularity (including mediated "associators" of this or that past frequency). Behavior is said now to be predicated on, aimed for, or desirous of completing (achieving, gaining) a projected end. The "goal" of such telic behavior is not down the road of time. It is held *precedently*, in the *meaning* of the premise. Meaning always reaches to some reference beyond the specific symbol that designates "what is being meant." In other words, meaning is telosponsiveness by definition. Based on the precedent meaning of a premise (model, paradigm, "idea," etc.) certain meaning extensions are not only possible, they are *sequaciously* necessary. The precedent premise is, therefore, necessarily extended, by way of what are called inductions, deductions, implications, metaphors, analogical extensions, and so forth.

Mental activity is therefore pro forma, lending meaning to experience as the individual "comes at" life with a capacity to understand. A *"psycho-"* logical principle of the *tautology* is used to explain how such meaning-extensions take place. This is viewed introspectively, as having to do with the (meaning-) relationship between the person and items of his experience. Or it is the relationship between various items as framed (introspectively) by the individual. We must always see the process of meaning extension from the point of view of the person doing the conceptualizing. A tautology implies *identity in relationship*, as in the case of "A rose is a rose," or even "A rose is a flower," if we view the actual thought-identities of people, many of whom have equated the construct *flower* with some given variety without appreciating the multiplicity of flowers. If one understands the quality of a rose, however, and now hears that "Rose is a person's name" (i.e., some people are named Rose) he can understand the *intent* of a parent wanting to extend roselike characteristics to a beloved offspring. The meaning of rose is tautologized, brought forward, extended to encompass the meaning of a child named Rose.

Without such meaning extensions learning is superficial and lacking in understanding. But even rote learning can be seen to follow tautological principles, since it relies on copying the sound of what is being communicated to one. The rehearsal in rote memory is like a running mime of "saying what is said to one" (reading what is there and repeating it subvocally, etc.) without actually bringing to bear a conceptual understanding. In most cases such mimicry is not learned well until the individual brings to bear some other precedent analogue (so-called mediators) to organize that which he cannot readily understand. Learning is thus not a question of attaching old responses to new stimuli, or of generalizing old responses to similar stimuli, but rather it involves the extension of what is conceptualized as a given (premise) to what is a possible application of the meaning so understood. Learning is not acquired, but applied. A single item of input "information" is not really "meaningful information" until that input is employed as a conceptual scheme. These are the only "practice trials" which count in learning with understanding. Logical learning theory refers to this as *affirmation* of input information. Often this affirmation is no more than an analogy.

The *analogy* is customarily defined as a "relation of likeness" between two items of experience. An example would be: "If indecisive, then like a leaf in the wind." The relation between the antecedent and consequent here is analogical because it is acknowledged that only a rough equation has taken place in the meaning extension. Highly precise tautologies occur in mathematical proofs and principles—such as the central limit theorem, or the Pythagorean theorem—but in the case of analogy we realize the equation is not perfect. Literary variations on this form of meaning extension include the metaphor (a ship plows the sea) and the allegory (an extended metaphorical story). Yet, analogies always hinge upon the *tautological identity* in meaning which is extended from one item to the other.

The mental capacity to tautologize is surely a most pervasive quality of human behavior, holding vast implications for humanistic psychological theory: Traditional logic has employed this concept in an extraspective fashion, so that relationships between items are seen to occur independently of a person who does the reasoning. As a psychologist, the writer now claims that something akin to tautologizing takes place in all those behaviors we take to be "mental." It functions independently of time factors, so that efficient cause-effects are irrelevant to this explanation of learning. Indeed, logical learning theory can account for the "learning" of a cybernetics machine—which also functions outside of time to align meanings in a preestablished pattern (program)—whereas classical S-R learning theories cannot (resulting in so-called statistical decision theories or information-processing theories as supplemental accounts).

One of the fascinating aspects of this tautologizing capacity is that, as pure mental ability to see and create relationships, tautological reasoning is not simply meaningless repetition. It borrows this seemingly repetitive quality from what we have called above its demonstrative application. Saying "that is a tree" is demonstratively to say "tree is tree" (primary and true, unequivocal, unidimensional referent). What we overlook here is that even in the demonstrative act of fixing a unipolar referent by some term or act of pointing, the individual turns this unipolarity into a bipolarity; that is, the "observed (sensory differentiation) tree" is one pole and the term used to describe it or the act which pointed to it is at the other pole. We have already discussed the question of bipolarity in meaning, above. What we now claim is that by turning unipolarities into bipolarities the human intellect makes teleological reasoning possible. There is a two-step feature to learning, whereby one pole now *predicates* (points to) the other. This removes the human understanding from direct contact with one side or the other, giving reason room for arbitrariness in what might now be affirmed, denied, qualified, and so on. Meaningful understanding is impossible without such predication (premising) and when extended, this meaning-extension is what we call "the functioning of mind."

Even more fascinating, when the bipolarity is a dialectical arrangement of opposites—that is, when one pole defines the other, or it cannot make sense without the other also being understood, etc.—we have the case of a tautology which is "identical while oppositional." Dialectical logic is therefore a logic of implication, but one which is also rooted in the tautology. From the factual given it can move to alternatives by way of the opposites these tautological givens imply "by definition." Somewhere on the scale of evolution there emerged an animal which could turn back on those unipolar input-promptings of sensory experience, see bipolarity in the *single-*determinate prompting signifying "go that way" or "eat this" or "defecate now," and formulate alternatives through the implications this unipolar "natural command" held, once a bipolarity was framed and steps might then be taken away from natural prompting through reasoning by opposition. It is *this* animal we seek to account for in a humanistic psychology. But how can such wordy speculations on human nature be translated into the laboratory?

A Program of Research

As Kuhn (1970) points out, the work of "normal science" is to fill in the (precedent) implications of an accepted paradigm, taking up those investigations which (sequaciously) arise as we contemplate the meanings of our area of interest. As a first step, it was necessary to form a line of theorectial development from logical learning theory to an experimental "variable" which might be studied in many contexts. The theoretical construct which would be measured by this variable had to be clearly teleological, dialectical in conception, and subject to idiographic measurement (so that it might capture the uniqueness of behavior), having broad implications for behavior, and open to test in literally any laboratory experiment that might be conducted on human subjects. In settling on a target laboratory design, the writer focused his attention on the procedures employed in so-called verbal-learning investigations, especially those which involved paired associates, recognition, and free-recall learning formats. This realm of laboratory investigation seemed to meet our needs most directly, since it purported to deal with conceptions of meaning and meaningfulness. Furthermore, the clear ascendance of Lockeanism in explanations of verbal learning attracted our attention. If we could establish the functioning of a more Kantian, humanistic variable in the verbal-learning area, it would surely lend encouragement to humanists who might wish to tackle a more teleological conception in other areas of so-called rigorous psychological investigation. Fifteen years have now passed, and the evidence has continued to support our initial confidence.

In extending the line of theoretical development, the tack taken was to presume that literally from birth human beings have the capacity affectively to assess their environmental circumstance (inputs). We have already noted above that assessments are telosponses, by which one item is aligned to a standard and to that extent "judged, evaluated, or put to test." A true telosponse must be envisioned as capable of going "either way" or "several ways" in coming to some directional action. In other words, it must be at some point *arbitrary* or capable of shifting grounds "for the sake of which" it then proceeds. An affective assessment is held to be of this nature, which means it is *not* an emotion. Titchener (1909) distinguished between an emotion and its affect (p. 226), claiming that affects were either pleasant or unpleasant, but the emotion identified the nature of the feeling tone being so experienced (i.e., the specific meaning of the emotion for the person; p. 277). The writer also looks at affections as dialectically expressed, so that one either likes or dislikes an experience, mood, or event in life. One can be ambivalent about such factors, but to claim "neutrality" in affect is essentially to say the person is not assessing (or he is actually making a mildly negative assessment such as boredom or disinterest).

A major telosponse in life is therefore affective assessment, and to define this behavior operationally we have employed ratings of like-dislike, termed as a measurement the reinforcement value (RV) of various items. This is viewed as a dimension of meaningfulness, that is, the extent of significance or import which an item's meaning has for the individual, disregarding the specific designate or indicant of that item. For example, a meaning could be "mother" or "spinach," but the significance and import these items have for the individual would be assessed via some metric of meaningfulness. Unlike traditional measures of meaningfulness in verbal learning, the RV of a learnable item is *not* said to reside in the (incoming) stimulus, but rather in the act of assessing that stimulus as it is input. The Lockean model presumes that such meaningfulness values lie outside the organism, in the environment. Analogizing to Kant's categories of the understanding, we now say that a capacity to assess affectively is innate, and that it is brought to bear on all entering experience, rendering it either positively or negatively meaningful.

Emotions have been referred to as physiological appraisals (see, e.g., Arnold, 1970, p. 174). But note: as physiological stimuli, emotional displays are really *not* arbitrary. An emotional reaction is always "what it is," and though they clearly help the individual define the life situation he finds himself in, emotions are more properly "having the person" than vice versa. An emotion is "in the stimulus input," and because of its lack of arbitrariness, we feel it is incorrect to apply a telic interpretation to emotional behavior. Emotions are surely material, efficient, and formal causal in nature. But they stop short of final-cause meaning, and since we wish to retain this telic emphasis of logical learning theory, we have introduced affection as a psychological accompaniment of behavior.

In those situations where input stimuli are *decidedly* one way or another, a perfect correspondence between emotion and affection is the case. It is always easy to make it appear that life is determined by past emotional experiences retained in memory. All we need do is think of the blatantly positive or negative events in our past lives. Getting hurt is clearly negative, so one can think about the times in the past when he was punished, failed a task, or was injured in an accident. Being pleased is clearly positive, so one can think of those times in the past when he was shown love, scored an academic triumph, or ate a marvelous meal. But what of all those other times, the in-between times when the valleys and peaks of emotional reaction are not so clearly discernible? This is where we usually live. Can we honestly believe that those times when we had a lot to do, met some new people, spent an evening home alone, woke up one morning, or took a day off were *clearly* positive or negative in emotional tone—as a sort of summated generalization from the past?

And if not, then we can see how the way in which we affectively approached the upcoming events lent a certain meaning to them, precedently aligning the implied significance of our assessment to the sequaciously determined "environmental stimuli" which therefore "occurred" (were created!).

The Lockean formulations of verbal learning would have it that all such meaning-extensions occur from a past memory bank of inputs, which either work as mediated responses or as mediated probability estimates (see Boneau's theory, above) to determine the judgment or assessment made in the present. Logical learning theory takes a Kantian approach to say that even if the fear a child has today of sharp objects is due to the past experience he had when his mother accidentally pricked him with a pin, the assessment made *now* is no different from the assessment made *then*. Past experience gives us information about the grounds for which today's assessment is made, but this past experience is no more the (efficient) cause of today's (final cause) judgment than is last year's taste of "sweet" candy the cause of this year's taste of "sweet" brandy. The act of assessment is separate and distinct from that which is judged.

Since we speak of RV in a telosponsive fashion, it is necessary for us to say what a reinforcement is. The term was selected initially because it appeared to be sufficiently abstract for alternative explanations. It seemed a good idea to begin the Lockean-Kantian confrontation with a widely respected term like *reinforcement*, even though no extraspective theory of efficient-cause hookups or associations was being implied. We soon learned that RV conceptions were always seen extraspectively, as a sort of experimenter's estimate of what kind of reinforcement "worked" to cement S-R regularities into habit "over there," in the apparatus. However, since we are now committed to the term it behooves us to say what reinforcement can mean in the context of logical learning theory. As suggested in the overview of our theory, above, a practice trial is not believed to be contributing to learning unless the material to be learned is conceptualized. This active conceptualization is what we would say a reinforcement amounts to. Often in experimental designs some "reward" is given to a subject, so it appears from the extraspective perspective that this reward is what "reinforces" the behavioral pattern. Logical learning theory would say that the reward is made possible by the individual's preliminary conceptualization, and that (as the "awareness" research discussed above demonstrates) only when such meaning-extensions take place is it proper to say a reinforcement occurs. Paraphrasing William James, we might say that a reinforcement is the "cash value" of a conception. The meaning extended "pays off" in attaining a goal, filling in an understanding, or makes it (dialectically) possible to *reject* some course of manipulation and behave oppositionally according to personal predilection, etc.

When a subject is asked to learn a list of consonant-vowel-consonant (CVC) trigrams (nonsense syllables) which had been prerated for RV (i.e., like-dislike), what might we expect to find? These RV preratings are always made idiographically (each subject rating material personally for likability) and on two occasions (24 hours intervening); only those trigrams rated "liked" and/or "disliked" on both occasions are used in the experimental task. Logical learning theory predicted from the principle of tautological meaning-extension (refer above) that if a subject assessed himself positively, he would extend positive meanings more readily than negative meanings in his learning task. This is what was found in the initial series of studies (Rychlak, 1966), and it has been repeated dozens of times since. The theory would also suggest that abnormals, who presumably assess themselves negatively, might extend disliked meanings more readily and hence "learn" such trigram materials readily. This prediction was immediately supported and cross-validated in independent data collections (Rychlak, McKee, Schneider, & Abramson, 1971).

The theory and Kantian paradigm lying behind it seemed to hold promise, but critics were soon to point out that likability and frequency of past contact with items in experience tended to be positively related. It was therefore necessary to show that RV was a separate dimension of meaningfulness from what might be termed an *association value* (AV) dimension of meaningfulness (the typical Lockean construct employed by verbal-learning theorists). Such AV measures are based on a frequency rationale, that is, the proportion of a group of subjects (nomothetic measure) who associate a word to a trigram (Archer, 1960), or the number of times a word appears in the standing language structure (Thorndike & Lorge, 1944). In the former procedure, it is possible to correlate the proportion of subjects who say, "Yes, the trigram is wordlike," with the proportion of subjects who say, "I like the trigram's appearance or sound." When one treats AV and RV ratings in this nomothetic fashion, it is not uncommon to find Pearsonian correlations of .54 to .84 between ratings if the range of trigrams selected is great (i.e., if they are likely to cover the range of nomothetic AV values, from near zero to 100% AV, where they become actual words, such as POP or CAN). Such findings have in the past convinced many Lockeans that affective assessments "are a function of" unnamed AV factors.

It is easy to demonstrate, however, that these are spurious correlations, due to the confounding of ratings predominantly at the lower nomothetic levels of trigrams and the excessive range which is achieved across nomothetic levels in the correlation formula. When the same data are reanalyzed via a 2×2 chi-square per trigram, it is found that at the 80% to 100% nomothetic AV level, where trigrams are easily identified as having word quality, only one trigram in five reaches significance (i.e., is rated yes-like and no-dislike by subjects) (Tenbrunsel, Nishball, & Rychlak, 1968). It would seem to follow that if two estimates of meaningfulness (RV and AV) are variations of the same dimension, then at that level where verbal materials are "most" meaningful we should witness the greatest similarity in ratings. Yet, it is actually the reverse, with three to four out of five trigrams at the very low nomothetic level (below 50%) that show such confounding. It is probable that verbal-learning studies have capitalized on RV in the past, since the probability of liking a trigram to which the subject has no association is low (which, incidentally, makes good sense!). If we now compare "low AV" material (probably disliked in general) with "high AV" material (in which positive RV is more likely) there is every reason to expect that some of the variance which shows that "increasing AV facilitates learning" is due to RV and not merely to AV! But, affective assessments continue to go uncontrolled in the experimentation of Lockean verbal-learning theory.

One week test-retest reliability for RV is comparable to AV in trigram materials—that is, with Pearsonian correlations in the .90s nomothetically and about 35 out of 100 subjects changing their ratings over the two occasions when considered idiographically by chi-square. The same independence for RV and AV is found in word materials, where just because a word is more prevalent in the language structure (e.g., *street*) does not mean it is going to be rated more positively by a subject than a word which rarely appears (e.g., *domicile*). Indeed, cross-validating factor analyses on ratings of both trigrams and words established beyond reasonable doubt the clear independence of AV and RV measures of meaningfulness (Flynn, 1967, 1969).

It has also been demonstrated that when CVC trigrams rated

differently for RV are submitted to Noble's (1952) production method, subjects do not associate more words to liked then to disliked trigrams, which is a variant on the "frequency" thesis. However, ratings for RV made on the words that are associated to these materials follow true to form. That is, liked CVC trigrams suggest liked words to a subject and disliked trigrams suggest disliked words (Rychlak, McKee, Schneider & Abramson, 1971). Experimental evidence of the independence of RV from AV in actual learning situations (as opposed to mere rating studies) was readily obtained. Liked materials were seen to reach criterion more readily than disliked materials across several nomothetic levels of AV and, within any such level (as the 50–60% level of nomothetic AV), were statistically independent of idiographic AV as well (Abramson, Tasto, & Rychlak, 1969).

The RV methodology has been used in various contexts, spanning typical verbal-learning formats (paired associates, free recall, recognition, etc.), but also adapting well to the learning of names (Rychlak & Saluri, 1973), "naming" faces (Galster, 1971), and recognizing abstract paintings and designs (McFarland, 1969). Effects have been shown across the age span, from first graders through subjects past the age of 60. In a recent doctoral, subjects were seen to cluster words and quasi-words in free recall according to the RV of these materials (Jack, 1974). We continue to proceed on the assumption that virtually any rigorous laboratory format employed in learning studies can be shown to have a contribution made by the affective assessments of those human beings who participate as subjects in the data collection.

Moving on now to some of the extensions we have made from the laboratory setting to more lifelike circumstances, an initial challenge was to account for the diminution and/or reversal of typical RV-positive effects in our learning data. Logical learning theory suggested that the individual had to base his assessment of even nonsense materials on some precedent evaluation, "for the sake of which" (telosponse) meaning extension took place tautologically. This implied that a person's self-estimate might serve such a premising role, and that diminutions or reversals might be the case when a person has made negative self-evaluations (so-called weak ego-strength), as on a test of adjustment. Studies by Lappin (1969) and Boland (1970) reflected .10 trends in this direction, and more refined studies by Carlsen (1970) and August, Rychlak, and Felker (1975) provided highly significant findings in line with predictions.

The tautology taking place here was envisioned along the lines of LIKED (Self) = LIKED (Trigram- or Word-meaningfulness). Keep in mind that the individual makes *both* estimates and so it is he (introspectively considered) who is doing this tautologizing (meaning extension). In the case of abnormals or normals with weak self-images (as assessed by independent statements answered by a subject on a test of personal adjustment), the tautological extension becomes: DISLIKED (Self) = DISLIKED (Trigram- or Word-meaningfulness).

This early formulation of what might now be termed a "normal versus abnormal" style of learning held that RV-positive or RV-negative styles were *uniform*. That is, some subjects learned (extended meanings) more readily in one direction on *all* of life's dimensions and others extended it uniformly along the other. Events were to alter this simplistic view, however. When affective assessment research was studied in relation to a subject's (independently measured) personality style, it was found that masculine females learning feminine words *reversed* their positive learning styles (Rychlak, Tasto, Andrews, & Ellis, 1973). Whereas these subjects had learned masculine word-meanings along the positive RV direction, disliked feminine word-meanings reached criterion more rapidly than liked feminine words by these *same* masculine females. A similar reversal was found in another sample of passive males, who reversed in this limited fashion *only* when learning dominant words (i.e., their passive word lists reflected the typical RV-positive effect).

Logical learning theory does not demand that global RV-styles be the case. It is entirely possible for the same individual to have a positively evaluated premise in one life area—say, baseball—yet evaluate another area—say, golf—rather negatively (even though both are sports). Premising baseball with meanings he takes to be positive, such an individual might well extend positive implications into his continuing fascination with hitting and pitching records, and so on. He readily "recalls" all that is good about the "nation's pastime" and either overlooks or minimizes the critical reports he hears or reads in the newspapers. Golf, on the other hand, is presumed to be boring at all times; he forgets the names of important golf stars and the tournaments they play in, but he does recall a few controversial incidents about golf which were featured in the sport pages of his newspaper. The theoretical line of development was therefore revised to suggest that even a delimited area of meaning could reflect RV-reversals or diminutions, and an experiment was designed to test this prediction.

Dunning (1973) obtained a sample of college students who had indicated a problem area in one of two realms—namely, either intimacy in interpersonal relations or adjusting to authority in power situations—but said that they were perfectly competent in the other area. Words were identified in pretesting which reliably reflected the meanings of intimacy and power. Subjects prerated these words (controlled for AV factors) in the typical RV fashion, and then free-recall lists were constructed for each subject. As predicted, the lists which were constructed of competency words were recalled along an RV-positive extension, but the conflict area words (of either specific meaning) reflected an RV-reversal. It would follow that to the extent an individual's affective assessments of life (including his self-image) are negative, the ratio of expanding negativity to positive assessments would be greatly disproportionate. A kind of "Malthusian principle" of geometric negativity to algebraic positiveness would be under way. In such a circumstance, the eventual likelihood of intrapersonal and interpersonal difficulties "getting out of hand" would seem probable. This more global RV-reversal might then herald a serious abnormality.

A further description of the paper referred to above is in order, involving the learning of personality-related verbal materials (Rychlak, Tasto, Andrews, & Ellis, 1973). The point of these two data collections was to demonstrate that if a person is asked to learn words having the meaning of his or her predominant personality tendencies—as measured by independent tests of personality—a tautological identity might be expected to take place from personality to word meaning. Since RV is viewed as a metric of meaningfulness, it was predicted that a masculine or ascendant-dominant individual would be especially likely to learn verbal materials with these meanings if they were also judged by him to be affectively positive. In broad outline, this is what was found, providing further evidence that affective assessment and tautological views of learning can be extended into more lifelike learning situations even though traditional laboratory procedures are used.

In another personality-related study, subjects (both sexes) rated names and pictures of faces (both sexes) for affective value (Rychlak, Galster, & McFarland, 1972). Lists of names and faces were then formed into "paired associates," with the face flashed onto a screen and the name following. Subjects had to name the face before the name appeared on the screen. After allowing subjects to overlearn the task (in which positive RV played a role) via five consecutive trials of 100% correct anticipations, subjects were presented the faces tachistoscopically. Flashes were of course unrecognizable at first, and then gradually the exposure time was increased until it was very easy to see the face under presentation. It was found that the males of the sample recognized both their liked and disliked female faces with about equal facility. The female subjects, however, after reflecting a pronounced RV-positive effect in their recognition of females, reversed on their male faces and recognized their disliked more quickly than their liked males.

This finding on females would appear to contradict logical learning theory, but we must keep in mind that not until an experimenter knows what the subject's (introspective) premise is can he speak with authority about the findings (extraspectively) observed. If one were to take a "perceptual defense" approach, it could well be that in the generation of subjects studied, and recognizing that such patterns might change over subsequent generations, a pattern of sexual aggressiveness might be more typical of males than females. If the feminine pattern is to avoid leering at sexually attractive males, then we would expect the observed results. Logical learning theory would suggest that leering behavior would be assessed negatively by the females, who, when forced into such behavior, would further the precedent disliked aspects of the task and see disliked faces as a tautological extension.

Although such behaviors are generally subsumed under a "motivational" rubric in theories of learning, logical learning theory does not need to explain why behavior literally "moves along" in one direction rather than another (via muscle actions and the like). The efficient-cause movements of behavior are about as relevant to this theory as is the fact of blood flow to operant conditioning, or as the rate of hair growth is to drive-reduction theory. It is assumed that "an experience" is only so thanks to the conceptual meanings involved, and any behavior taking place thereby is to be understood within the context of such meanings (e.g., intentions, acting as telosponses). The arbitrary distinction between motivation and learning arose because of the need to account for habitual behavior in the "blind determinisms" of mechanistic S-R theory (refer above). The determinism in logical learning theory *follows* the premise taken, in that directing and orienting meaning of a final cause. If we can account for the premise, we can predict the sequacious line of behavior to follow determinately.

As a dimension of meaningfulness, RV cannot tell us the meaning of a premise. Yet, the patterning of affective assessments vis à vis learning proficiency should result in a predictable outcome. For example, if one is working in a preferred task and eventually completes it, what is the likely effect of this "experience" or "practice" on the subsequent effectiveness in a disliked task? Would there necessarily be an improvement? Logical learning theory would say no, even when it has been established that both tasks are of equivalent difficulty level based on various AV controls (i.e., same relative frequency in language structure, same number of subjects having a word-associate, etc.). The premise for the task has shifted from "liked task, achievement" to "disliked [hard] task, effort," and the overall effectiveness of meaning extension, granting the latter premise, will simply not be as great as with the former. The reverse arrangement is like moving from a premise of "disliked [hard] task, finally completed" to a premise of "liked [easier, more meaningful] task, continuing improvement." We are speaking here in "affective syllogistic" terms, but the predictions do follow from logical learning theory.

Several data collections have now supported this theoretical development (Rychlak & Tobin, 1971; Rychlak, Tuan, & Schneider, 1974). A pronounced improvement (positive "nonspecific" transfer) was found when subjects moved from disliked to liked paired-associates lists, whereas in the reverse direction a diminished improvement or actual decrease in efficiency (negative transfer) was the case. This finding has been noted in several unrelated designs, and obtains even when a subject is carried over four learning tasks. Some of the so-called fatigue effects in learning tasks are probably due to RV assessments as the effort drags on. Also, we have wondered whether the discounted theories of "formal discipline" in education were not in some sense accurate observations of RV phenomena. If one can assume that as a rule most students disliked classical studies, then by comparison they might have indeed shown a spurt in arithmetic performance following a stint in the study of Greek or Latin.

This patterning of RV effects has served analogously to answer a recurring criticism of logical learning theory. That is, despite arguments to the contrary (see above), a critic will often claim that affective assessments are not really independent judgments in the present—using past experience as well as current circumstances as grounds to base assessment on—but are rather completely determined "effects" of past reinforcements. The claim here is that the past inputs determined today's judgment in that typical mediational sense (refer above). Yet, as humanists like to point out, there are times in emotionally upsetting or challenging situations when the individual "rises to the challenge" and meets his environmental and physically sensed input head-on to bring about a diametrically opposite eventuality. The first speech given before a group may have terrified today's accomplished speaker, who now seeks with great desire rather than avoids forensic opportunities. This is because he did not give in to the negative emotion of fear (which he disliked), but brought to bear a resolve to "do the job in spite of himself" (which he liked). The premised resolve was no more an efficiently caused "effect" of the situational (including physical-sensory) input than are today's affective assessments of speaking engagements the efficiently caused "effects" of such past life victories. Indeed, the significance of this victory was in no way "input," but gained or earned through dialectical confrontation with the negative "input" as it was literally taking place. We now have empirical evidence helping us to understand the undoubted sense of "positive reinforcement" experienced by the individual when he finally does "turn the tables" and moves from negative to positive affective circumstances. Reversing the affective sequence, we can also now see how failure in a highly valued (liked) situation can be seriously defeating. If we "learn from such mistakes," this is surely a most inefficient level of learning, a decided setback in the progression of meaning extension into the future.

Affective assessment research has been extended to other types of samples, with some provocative initial results. As predicted, it was found that underachievers maximize and overachievers minimize the RV-positive effect (Rychlak & Tobin, 1971). The picture is complicated by the fact that so many underachievers are negative self-evaluators and hence tend to add in RV-reversal effects to the variance (Boland, 1970; Jack, 1974; Lappin, 1969). Probably one of the most interesting findings to date has to do with racial factors and affective learning style. The performance of blacks in the learning of both CVC trigrams and words has been shown to be *more* sensitive to affective assessment than is the performance of whites (Rychlak, Hewitt, & Hewitt, 1973; Woodward, 1973). In those instances where black college students showed a superiority to the learning performance of whites, the material being learned by the blacks was always liked. Interesting questions arise here, since we are not yet certain whether the black performs as someone with lessened "ability" relative to the task or whether his performance is more like that of an underachiever. We have data to suggest that as a task becomes increasingly difficult for a subject relative to his ability (e.g., IQ), a more pronounced disparity between liked and disliked tasks will be seen in his performance (Laberteaux, 1968; Rychlak & Saluri, 1973). Since both circumstances can account for the increasing RV differential, we have much more work to do in isolating the relevant factor.

It should not be concluded that affective assessments have only been shown to influence verbal learning materials and the related "laboratory type" tasks discussed to this point. A recent doctoral study of seventh graders by Rumsey (1974) established that RV preratings of the Wechsler IQ subtests resulted in the predicted RV-positive effect taking place when actual IQ values were subsequently determined. Both black and white children performed better on liked than on disliked Wechsler subtests. The Full Scale IQ value is higher when calculated for liked than for disliked subtests. Formerly, this would have been dismissed lightly as due merely to "motivational" factors whereby subjects "tried harder" or "attended better" on IQ subtests which they liked than on those which they disliked. However, the numerous studies done on RV which establish that these effects take place even when difficulty is controlled for argues against such a simplistic explanation. To say that a task is *disliked* because it is *difficult*, without being able to distinguish between these two aspects of experience, is no real help to the theorist interested in explaining behavior. If difficulty level and affection were unidirectional, children would dislike all difficult tasks, and clearly this is not true. In post experimental discussions with children, we find they often say the *reason* they dislike a particular school subject is because they find it difficult, but it is rarely clear in their minds why they find it difficult. When they do proffer an explanation it is often circular—that is, the difficult subject simply is not "fun" to learn (suggesting that it is disliked from the outset, as logical learning theory would predict).

Sometimes a difficult school subject is said to be confusing and lacking in easy understanding for the person involved. The role of affection in human understanding is surely monumental. Based on theoretical considerations, our predictions were that Osgood's (1952) Evaluation dimension would not only load on a factor drawing RV in a factor analysis, but that in a subsequent free-recall learning experiment *only* Evaluation would show effects comparable to RV. That is, whereas trigram ratings of Evaluation (good-bad) *would* influence free-recall (good learned more readily than bad), such ratings of Potency (strong-weak) and Activity (fast-slow) would *not* show any differences in subjects' memory proclivities. Three data collections supported these predictions, strongly suggesting that RV and Evaluation were indeed comparable if not identical dimensions of meaningfulness (Rychlak, Flynn, Burger, & Townsend, 1974). When one considers the vast scope of Osgood's research (Snider & Osgood, 1969), it is not expansive to suggest that a dimension of affective assessment is *basic to all* human understanding, including memory, thinking, and so forth. Surely there is nothing in the most rigorously gathered body of data to weaken the humanist's conviction that human beings *do* make self-induced contributions to that "external and/or internal [sensory] stimulus" which is supposedly determining behavior directly, in the present circumstance, or indirectly via mediation from the past. We can envision an animal with this self-contribution, *from birth*, to the organization, retention, and extension of meaning in life.

One last suggestion to this effect may be seen in a recent doctoral study conducted by Muller (1974), who had subjects prerate for RV in the typical fashion, and then, while they performed the paired-associates task, "reinforced" them by sounding a bell following their anticipations of the second CVC trigram in a pair. One group of subjects was reinforced "positively" each time they correctly anticipated the second member (whether these pairs were liked or disliked). A second group was "negatively" reinforced in that each time they made an error of anticipation or neglected to call out a second member, the bell was sounded (once again, for both liked and disliked pairs). It was found as predicted that under conditions of positive reinforcement the *liked* trigram pairs were learned more readily, but under conditions of negative reinforcement the *disliked* pairs were learned more readily. This is difficult to rationalize unless one assumes that the individual—quite spontaneously—construed the reinforcement as a "signal" toward which he tautologically extended the meanings of material he was actively conceptualizing "in kind." Negative meanings were tautologized to the negative signal ("failure") while positive meanings were tautologized to the positive signal ("success"). The only concession we now wish to have from classical Lockean thought is that a contribution was made here to the input which was not itself an input, or an old input, but was part and parcel of the human being's capacity to influence even as he or she is being influenced!

This completes our survey of a sample humanistic theory and some of its research evidence to date. It has not been easy to demonstrate to students *or* colleagues the reasons for having to indulge in something so apparently far removed from the writer's specialties of clinical or personality and social psychology as is the study of nonsense syllables. One is pictured more the Don Quixote, riding into the arid land of irrelevance, than the Sir Galahad. No amount of talk about proving man to be human can assuage the shudder of horror sent up the spines of "dynamic" psychologists when they hear these words *verbal learning*. The writer can attest that paired-associates learning has been adjudged dead and buried by more than one panel of experts, sitting on review boards for psychological journals and granting agencies. Confounding methods with theories, friend and foe alike have thought it necessary for the writer to "think up a new research gimmick that *really* tests your views," as if what a method has to teach us is limited to the ways in which its originator employed it to support his floundering theories of man.

Although verbal learning was selected in 1959 (when work on affective assessment began) because it was then a highly respected arm of rigorous psychology, the writer has since pondered the wisdom of being tied to a dying experimental design. However, the *point* of the work done these past 15 years has been made. There is simply no reason why a rigorous, properly scientific methodology need contravene humanistic explanations of the data, which in turn ever call for more work to be done to fill in the background paradigm in the Kuhnian sense of "normal science." If humanism is to survive as science, it *must* generate interesting, instructive, worthwhile questions and answers. It must, because this is how a paradigm which is pregnant with meaning functions. Precedent paradigm meanings sequaciously generate ideas worth following up on. Specific experimental designs are quite secondary in this continuing pursuit of knowledge. We can let these instrumentalities fall, or revive them as we see fit. But the precious feature of the scientific quest is on the side of our theories. Here we have a right and a duty to pursue truth as we see it. We need a revolution in theory and a willingness to fight where the opposition feels it has carte blanche privileges of explanation.

A HUMANISTIC MANIFESTO

In the continuing spirit of a revolution in theory which this treatise has called for, the writer would like to close by abstracting seven points from the above sections and frame them as a "humanistic manifesto." If it were followed, it is our belief that humanistic psychology would be much easier to achieve. We therefore call on all psychologists to:

1. *Accept the distinction between theory and method, with the corollary idea that extraspective methods are compatible with theories framed introspectively.* It is when we forget the distinction between method and theory that the former tends to dictate the latter in science. The attitude of "I can only say in my scientific report what I have observed in my method" has lead to a tautological rephrase of the experimental design in the discussion to follow. By acknowledging two aspects to the scientific endeavor, psychology may develop some expertise in the theoretical introductions and discussions to match the expertise that is already apparent in the sections on methods and results in our scientific reports.

2. *Demand "parsimony" in the descriptive accounts given to both the experimenter's and the subject's behavior as coparticipants in the experiment.* Parsimony has been too long identified with attempting to explain observed events in *only* material- and efficient-cause terms, which in turn helps promote the easy equation of method and theory. The purity criticism is aimed at such reductive attempts, since rather than construing explanations from within the phenomenal reality of the subject, the experimenter turns his subject into a kind of "tail-end reinforcement history" in which past events have made him what he is today. Yet, the experimenter's account of *his* scientific behavior is said to proceed on the basis of hypotheses, which are tested by statistical devices requiring reasoned assumptions, and the mathematics of which are proven via formal-cause "self evidences" (e.g., the central limit theorem). Mechanism *clearly* drops out of this account, making our behavioral theories dualistic and hence unparsimonious. It is therefore time for the theories of behavior employed in our empirical studies to *match parsimoniously* the theories used to describe our own behavior. We need a more modern conception of parsimony, one which makes it possible for us to view the "experiment" for what it is—a conceptual exercise for *both* subject and experimenter.

3. *Recognize that there are, in principle, N possible explanations*

for any observed factual pattern—experimental or otherwise. Though almost no theoretical physicist today is naive enough to assume that an *experimentum crucis* is possible, much less desirable, too many psychologists still harbor this eighteenth-century dream. Method will never suffice for theory, and though we may put down rules of thumb for theoretical descriptions (as in the "new parsimony" called for above), no psychologist should delude himself into believing that a method can be devised which will allow him to settle, once and for all time, which theory is representative of "the" nature of anything! More than one theory can and always will be true about the same thing.

4. *Extend the conception of "control" in the phrase "control and prediction" to include logical controls.* The concept of "controlling behavior" has been given too narrow a definition in discussions of method. It is presumed that only an efficient-cause control is meant, when in fact the *logic* of scientific discovery—that is, the aligning of premises, the seeking of data, the testing of predicted results, and the drawing of conclusions—is heavily weighted with the meanings of formal and final causality. Even if the scientist denies that he reasons teleologically (using final causation), he surely cannot deny that he follows ordered steps of logic, and logic is *not* an efficiently caused succession of events. Hence, at least *some* of the control in our "control and prediction" definition of validating evidence is *logical* control. This simply means we are never observing only efficient causes in our scientific procedures. We are observing what we have logically prearranged to see, and this is a succession of events that might easily be influenced by both our own and our subject's (precedent-to-sequacious) logic.

5. *Call for "conceptual research," by lengthening the line of development from theory to methodological test.* As already suggested under point 1, psychology suffers as much from a conscious effort to *avoid* conceptualizing data as it does from so-called loose conceptualization in wild theorizing. If there was a time when psychologists theorized wildly (and we doubt it), that time is surely long past. A conceptual research effort cannot be done successfully unless the psychologist, and those who later review his work for publication outlet, accept the fact that a "logical line of development" is possible from the background conceptualization to the empirical test generated. This line can be lengthened a bit, so long as our logical controls remain clear and rigorous (point 4). By trying to see theory in method—that is, in the experimental

design—psychology has guaranteed that conceptual innovation will never take place. It is not legitimate to dismiss a study on the grounds that it failed to test its entire paradigm "at once," or that only a logical derivative of the background paradigm was tested in the actual experiment. Since validation is patterned on efficient causality, all that one can "see directly" as a paradigm in this ordering of events is the precedent Lockean model. To claim that this paradigm is the only one possible in evidence generated by scientific method is to *forego* true objectivity!

6. *Establish a "new functionalism" which would be more objective and less repressive to theory than is the functionalism currently practiced.* Though functionalism may have begun in the admirable desire to make objective statements about evidential data without prejudging the case, in point of fact it has become a new standard by which certain scientific accounts have been repressed. We have gone in psychology from "Let's not prejudge data" to "You can't say that about data" to "You can't say anything about data, except possibly repeat the fact that you found them." This move is repressive, since by claiming today that all we can say is what is functionally noted between variables X and Y, we in effect *dictate* terms to the scientist who actually had an honest and sincere hunch, leading him to conduct the experiment. He was *not* interested in the "variables" observed to vary systematically, but in the *theory* generating the definitions of these variables. It is surely ingenuine and almost dishonest for an experimenter to say, "This is what I found, without any preconceptions," when in fact we all know that he had—at the least!—some paradigmatic frame of reference, rough analogy, or interest proclivity in the area investigated. Why not get these ideas stated, clearly explicated, revamped, rejected, understood, or tossed out as unhelpful altogether? Functionalism is *not* objective when it forecloses speculations on the data. Functionalists hope that someone will come along and "put it all together" someday, but this philosophy of science has gone bankrupt. We must appreciate that data per se "add up" to nothing! Data must be organized within a paradigmatic frame, and all they add up to today in most research journals is the Lockean frame—again and again. Let us be truly functional, in *both* theory and method, and call for alternatives in theoretical formulations even as we call for multiplicity in data collection.

7. *In the realm of theory, readmit formal- and final-cause constructs.* Humanistic psychology is simply impossible without

teleological description of behavior. This requires that we return to a style of description which has been disowned and ridiculed in "natural" science for over three centuries. Scientists threw out telic description 350 years ago for good and proper reasons. It created problems it could not solve, and those it did "solve" were achieved repressively. But we are untrue to our mission as twentieth-century scientists if we must, like sheep, herded along by the weight of seventeenth-century history, continue to press a restriction on our theoretical descriptions which has been negating man's humanity in the face of rigorous evidence to the opposite. We can no longer tolerate this circumstance.

So we say, "Humanistic psychologists of the world, unite! You have nothing to lose but your second-class standing. Go into the laboratories and prove your theories on the mechanist's home ground. It is a new time, with new problems, and new theoretical solutions are called for. It is our time!"

REFERENCES

Abramson, Y., Tasto, D. L., & Rychlak, J. F. Nomothetic vs. idiographic influences of association value and reinforcement value on learning. *Journal of Experimental Research in Personality*, 1969, **4**, 65–71.

Adams, D. K. The inference of mind. *Psychological Review*, 1928, **35**, 235–252.

Adams, D. K. Note on method. *Psychological Review*, 1937, **44**, 212–218.

Allport, G. W. The psychologist's frame of reference. *Psychological Bulletin*, 1940, **37**, 1–28.

Allport, G. W. Personalistic psychology as a science: A reply. *Psychological Review*, 1946, **53**, 132–135.

Archer, E. J. Re-evaluation of the meaningfulness of all possible CVC trigrams. *Psychological Monographs*, 1960, **74**(10, Whole No. 497).

Aristotle. *Topics* and *Physics*. In R. M. Hutchins (Ed.), *Great books of the western world*, Vol. 8. Chicago: Encyclopedia Britannica, 1952. Pp. 143–223, 257–355.

Arnold, M. B. (Ed.), *Feelings and emotions*. New York: Academic Press, 1970

August, G., Rychlak, J. F., & Felker, D. W. Affective assessment, self-concept, and the verbal learning styles of fifth grade children. *Journal of Educational Psychology*, 1975, **67**, 801–806.

Bacon, F. *Advancement of Learning*. In R. M. Hutchins (Ed.), *Great books of the western world*, Vol. 30. Chicago: Encyclopedia Britannica, 1952.

Pp. 1–101.

Bakan, D. Learning and the scientific enterprise. *Psychological Review,* 1953, **60**, 45–49. (a)

Bakan, D. Learning and the principle of inverse probability. *Psychological Review,* 1953, **60**, 360–370. (b)

Bergmann, G., & Spence, K. Operationism and theory in psychology. *Psychological Review,* 1941, **48**, 1–14.

Binswanger, L. *Being-in-the-world.* Translated and with a critical introduction by J. Needleman. New York: Basic Books, 1963.

Boland, G. C. The relationship of personality adjustment to the learning of material having connotative and associative meaningfulness. Unpublished doctoral dissertation, St. Louis University, 1970.

Boneau, C. A. Paradigm regained? Cognitive behaviorism restated. *American Psychologist,* 1974, **29**, 297–309.

Boring, E. G. Mind and mechanism. *American Journal of Psychology,* 1946, **54**, 173–192.

Boring, E. G. *A history of experimental psychology.* (2nd ed.) New York: Appleton-Century-Crofts, 1950.

Boss, M. *Psychoanalysis and daseinsanalysis.* New York: Basic Books, 1963.

Bridgman, P. W. *The way things are.* Cambridge, Mass.: Harvard University Press, 1959.

Bronowski, J. *The common sense of science.* Cambridge, Mass.: Harvard University Press, 1958.

Burtt, E. A. *The metaphysical foundations of modern physical science.* (Rev. ed.) Garden City, N.Y.: Doubleday, 1955.

Calverton, V. F. The rise of objective psychology. *Psychological Review,* 1924, **31**, 418–426.

Carlsen, N. L. The effect of high and low self concept on learning along an intensity dimension of meaningfulness. Unpublished master's thesis, Purdue University, 1970.

Cassirer, E. *The problem of knowledge.* New Haven: Yale University Press, 1950.

Colaizzi, P. An analysis of the learner's perception of learning material at various phases of a learning process. *Review of Existential Psychology and Psychiatry,* 1967, **7**, 95–105.

Conant, J. B. *Modern science and modern man.* Garden City, N.Y.: Doubleday, Anchor Press, 1952.

DeNike, L., & Spielberger, C. Induced mediating states in verbal conditioning. *Journal of Verbal Learning and Verbal Behavior,* 1963, **1**, 339–345.

Dollard, J., & Miller, N. E. *Personality and psychotherapy: An analysis in terms of learning, thinking, and culture.* New York: McGraw-Hill, 1950.

Dulany, D. E., Jr. The place of hypotheses and intentions: An analysis of verbal control in verbal conditioning. In C. W. Eriksen (Ed.), *Behavior and awareness*. Durham, N.C.: Duke University Press, 1962. Pp. 102–129.

Dunning, L. P. The effects of reinforcement value on the learning of words varying in positive and negative meaning for subjects high or low in ego-strength. Unpublished master's thesis, Purdue University, 1973.

Eddington, A. *The philosophy of physical science*. Ann Arbor: University of Michigan Press, 1958.

Einstein, A. *Essays in science*. New York: Philosophical Library, 1934.

Evans, R. I. *B. F. Skinner: The man and his ideas*. New York: E. P. Dutton, 1968.

Eves, H. *An introduction to the history of mathematics*. New York: Holt, Rinehart & Winston, 1953.

Fernberger, S. W. Behavior versus introspective psychology. *Psychological Review*, 1922, **29**, 409–413.

Flynn, E. J. The factor analysis of meaning in CVC trigrams rated for association value and reinforcement value. Unpublished master's thesis, St. Louis University, 1967.

Flynn, E. J. Beyond frequency: A two-dimensional theory of verbal meaningfulness. Unpublished doctoral dissertation, St. Louis University, 1969.

Frank, P. *Philosophy of science*. Englewood Cliffs, N.J.: Prentice-Hall, 1957.

Galster, J. M. Affective factors in paired-associate acquisition and tachistoscopic recognition of faces and names. Unpublished master's thesis, Purdue University, 1972.

Giorgi, A. *Psychology as a human science: A phenomenologically based approach*. New York: Harper & Row, 1970.

Goss, A. E. Early behaviorism and verbal mediating responses. *American Psychologist*, 1961, **16**, 285–298.

Hobbes, T. *Leviathan*. In R. M. Hutchins (Ed.), *Great books of the western world*, Vol. 23. Chicago: Encyclopedia Britannica, 1952. Pp. 49–283.

Hull, C. L. Mind, mechanism, and adaptive behavior. *Psychological Review*, 1937, **44**, 1–32.

Husserl, E. *Phenomenology and the crisis of philosophy*. Trans. by Q. Lauer. New York: Harper & Row, Torchbooks, 1965.

Jack, R. M. The effect of reinforcement value in mixed and unmixed lists on the learning style of overachieving and underachieving female college students. Unpublished doctoral dissertation, Purdue University, 1974.

Jung, C. G. *Psychology and alchemy*. In H. Read, M. Fordham, & G. Adler (Eds.), *The collected works of C. G. Jung*, Vol. 12. Bollingen series XX.12. New York: Pantheon Books, 1953.

Kant, I. *The critique of pure reason*. In R. M. Hutchins (Ed.), *Great books of the western world*, Vol. 42. Chicago: Encyclopedia Britannica, 1952. Pp. 1–250.

Kelly, G. A. *The psychology of personal constructs*. 2 vols. New York: W. W. Norton, 1955.

Kuhn, T. S. *The structure of scientific revolutions*. (2nd ed.) Chicago: University of Chicago Press, 1970. (1st ed., 1962)

Kuo, Z. Y. The fundamental error of the concept of purpose and the trial and error fallacy. *Psychological Review*, 1928, **35**, 414–433.

Laberteaux, T. E. The influence of positive versus negative reinforcement value on mediated paired-associate learning. Unpublished master's thesis, St. Louis University, 1968.

Lappin, R. W. Meaningfulness, deviant achievers, and personal adjustment. Unpublished doctoral dissertation, St. Louis University, 1969.

Locke, J. *An essay concerning human understanding*. In R. M. Hutchins (Ed.), *Great books of the western world*, Vol. 35. Chicago: Encyclopedia Britannica, 1952. Pp. 85–395.

Masterman, M. The nature of a paradigm. In I. Lakatos & A. Musgrave (Eds.), *Criticism and the growth of knowledge*. Cambridge: University Press, 1970. Pp. 59–89.

McDougall, W. Prolegomena to psychology. *Psychological Review*, 1922, **29**, 1–43.

McFarland, K. K. The influence of reinforcement value and school achievement on a "pictorial-verbal" learning task. Unpublished master's thesis, St. Louis University, 1969.

Meehl, P. E., & MacCorquodale, K. On a distinction between hypothetical constructs and intervening variables. *Psychological Review*, 1948, **55**, 95–107.

Miller, D. L. The meaning of explanation. *Psychological Review*, 1946, **53**, 241–246.

Muller, J. B. The differential effects of feedback, affective learning style, and reinforcement value on the acquisition of CVC trigrams. Unpublished doctoral dissertation, Purdue University, 1974.

Noble, C. E. An analysis of meaning. *Psychological Review*, 1952, **59**, 421–430.

Oppenheimer, R. Analogy in science. *American Psychologist*, 1956, **11**, 127–135.

Osgood, C. E. The nature and measurement of meaning. *Psychological Bulletin*, 1952, **49**, 197–237.

Page, M. M. Demand characteristics and the verbal operant conditioning experiment. *Journal of Personality and Social Psychology,* 1972, **23**, 304–308.

Rogers, C. R. *On becoming a person.* Boston: Houghton Mifflin, 1961.

Rosenthal, R. *Experimenter effects in behavioral research.* New York: Appleton-Century-Crofts, 1966.

Rotter, J. B. *Social learning and clinical psychology.* Englewood Cliffs, N.J.: Prentice-Hall, 1954.

Rumsey, J. Affective assessment and intelligence testing of black and white adolescents. Unpublished doctoral dissertation, Purdue University, 1974.

Russell, B. *Our knowledge of the external world.* New York: New American Library, 1960.

Rychlak, J. F. Reinforcement value: A suggested idiographic, intensity dimension of meaningfulness for the personality theorist. *Journal of Personality,* 1966, **34**, 311–335.

Rychlak, J. F. *A philosophy of science for personality theory.* Boston: Houghton Mifflin, 1968.

Rychlak, J. F. *Introduction to personality and psychotherapy: A theory-construction approach.* Boston: Houghton Mifflin, 1973.

Rychlak, J. F. *The psychology of rigorous humanism.* New York: John Wiley & Sons, 1977.

Rychlak, J. F., Flynn, E. J., Burger, B., & Townsend, J. W. Osgoodian evaluation and reinforcement value: Identical or different dimensions of meaningfulness? Unpublished manuscript, Purdue University, 1974.

Rychlak, J. F., Galster, J., & McFarland, K. K. The role of affective assessment in associative learning: From designs and CVC trigrams to faces and names. *Journal of Experimental Research in Personality,* 1972, **6**, 186–194.

Rychlak, J. F., Hewitt, C. W., & Hewitt, J. Affective evaluation, word quality, and the verbal learning styles of black versus white junior college females. *Journal of Personality and Social Psychology,* 1973, **27**, 248–255.

Rychlak, J. F., McKee, D. B., Schneider, W. E., & Abramson, Y. Affective evaluation in the verbal learning styles of normals and abnormals. *Journal of Abnormal Psychology,* 1971, **77**, 11–16.

Rychlak, J. F., & Saluri, R. E. Affective assessment in the learning of names by fifth- and sixth-grade children. *Journal of Genetic Psychology,* 1973, **123**, 251–261.

Rychlak, J. F., Tasto, D. L., Andrews, J. E., & Ellis, H. C. The application of an affective dimension of meaningfulness to personality-related verbal learning. *Journal of Personality,* 1973, **41**, 341–360.

Rychlak, J. F., & Tobin, T. J. Order effects in the affective learning styles of overachievers and underachievers. *Journal of Educational Psychology*, 1971, **62**, 141–147.

Rychlak, J. F., Tuan, N. D., & Schneider, W. E. Formal discipline revisited: Affective assessment and nonspecific transfer. *Journal of Educational Psychology*, 1974, **66**, 139–151.

Schrödinger, E. *Science theory and man.* New York: Dover Publications, 1957.

Skaggs, E. B. The limitations of scientific psychology as an applied practical science. *Psychological Review*, 1934, **41**, 572–576.

Skinner, B. F. Are theories of learning necessary? *Psychological Review*, 1950, **57**, 193–216.

Skinner, B. F. *Cumulative record.* (3rd. ed.) New York: Appleton-Century-Crofts, 1972.

Snider, J. C., & Osgood, C. E. (Eds.) *Semantic differential technique.* Chicago: Aldine Publishing Co., 1969.

Spence, K. W. The nature of theory construction in contemporary psychology. *Psychological Review*, 1944, **51**, 47–68.

Spence, K. W. The postulates and methods of 'behaviorism.' *Psychological Review*, 1948, **55**, 95–107.

Spence, K. W. *Behavior theory and conditioning.* New Haven, Conn.: Yale University Press, 1956.

Stevens, S. S. The operational definition of psychological concepts. *Psychological Review*, 1935, **42**, 517–527.

Tenbrunsel, T. W., Nishball, E. R., & Rychlak, J. F. The idiographic relationship between association value and reinforcement value, and the nature of meaning. *Journal of Personality*, 1968, **36**, 126–137.

Thorndike, E. L., & Lorge, I. *The teacher's word book of 30,000 words.* New York: Teacher's College, Columbia University, 1944.

Titchener, E. B. *A text-book of psychology.* New York: Macmillan Co., 1909.

Tolman, E. C. *Purposive behavior in animals and men.* New York: Appleton-Century-Crofts, 1967.

van Kaam, A. *Existential foundations of psychology.* Garden City, N.Y.: Doubleday, Image Books, 1969.

Waters, R. H. Morgan's canon and anthropomorphism. *Psychological Review*, 1939, **46**, 534–540.

Waters, R. H. Mechanicomorphism: A new term for an old mode of thought. *Psychological Review*, 1948, **55**, 139–142.

Watson, J. B. Psychology as the behaviorist views it. *Psychological Review*, 1913, **20**, 158–177.

Watson, J. B. An attempted formulation of the scope of behavior psychology. *Psychological Review*, 1917, **24**, 329–352.

Watson, R. I. Psychology: A prescriptive science. *American Psychologist,* 1967, **22**, 435–443.

Weiss, A. P. The mind and the man within. *Psychological Review,* 1919, **26**, 327–334.

Whitehead, A. N. *The function of reason.* Boston: Beacon Press, 1958.

Winter, J. E. The postulates of psychology. *Psychological Review,* 1936, **43**, 130–148.

Woodward, K. E. Affective learning style across race: Group and individual identification procedures. Unpublished master's thesis, Purdue University, 1973.

Yerkes, R. M. Concerning the anthropocentrism of psychology. *Psychological Review,* 1933, **40**, 209–212.

Zilsel, E. The origins of Gilbert's scientific method. In P. P. Wiener & A. Noland (Eds.), *Roots of scientific thought.* New York: Basic Books, 1957. Pp. 219–250.

Phenomenology and the Foundations of Psychology

Amedeo Giorgi[1]
Duquesne University

Our most urgent need in psychology
is not the variety and universality
of the tenets, but rather the unity of
the doctrine. Within this framework
we must strive to attain what first
mathematics and then physics,
chemistry, and physiology have
already attained, i.e. a core of generally
accepted truths capable of attracting
to it contributions from all other
fields of scientific endeavor. We must
seek to establish a single unified
science of psychology in place of the
many psychologies we now have.
[Brentano, 1973, p. xvi]

*T*he above quotation from Franz Brentano was written in 1874. Here I am, 100 years later, still claiming that psychology lacks unity, and as you will soon see, I am not alone in making the claim today. What can it mean that psychology, after almost 100 years of existence—if we accept the tradition that the birth of psychology as an independent science took place in Leipzig in 1879 with the founding of a laboratory by Wundt—still lacks unity? What does it mean that it began an independent existence without at first securing the unity it was seeking?

This paper will deal with these issues and I do not want to get too far ahead of myself. Besides, I would agree that in many senses, since its modest beginning, psychology has come a long way and has

1. I would like to thank my assistants Jim Mandiberg and Fred Wertz for their help in researching many of the references used in this article.

justified its decision to transform itself from a branch of philosophy into an independent science. Psychology is established in practically every university in the Western world and it has thousands of practitioners working in every segment of society. It has discovered innumerable facts about man, fostered many controversial or inspiring theses, and even influenced a whole cultural epoch's interpretation of man.

Despite this proliferation and success, as noted above, the viewpoint of this paper is that psychology still has not come of age. Yet, the critique to be developed is positive in intent, for it must be realized, first, that 100 years is not very old for a scientific enterprise, and second, that psychology's praxis is not necessarily as bad as some of its theorizing would indicate. To say that psychology has not come of age means to me that it has not yet found its paradigm (Kuhn, 1970) or clarified its approach (Giorgi, 1970). Again, in and of itself, this need not be surprising, since praxis often precedes clarification of intent. The critical point is whether or not, after almost 100 years of experience, a critical interrogation of the meaning of psychology uncovers the necessity for a change in direction, or simply a reaffirmation of the direction in which it is proceeding. Ultimately the investigation will have to concern itself with foundational questions and philosophical issues. Psychology may be independent of philosophy in organization and administration, but it is still dependent in terms of ideas and presuppositions concerning man and the world. Consequently, the choice of a philosophical framework also codetermines the meaning that psychology will have.

In the language of Kuhn (1970), my position is that psychology, as a whole, is still in a preparadigmatic state of development with respect to its authentic paradigm, but obviously not with respect to the sheer de facto existence of a paradigm. I hope to demonstrate this by speaking to the lack of unity in psychology, by pointing to the ambiguous status of its relevance to the everyday world, and lastly by indicating that its own understanding of science is deficient. I shall do this at two levels: (a) at the level of the whole field and (b) at the level of a concrete phenomenon, namely, memory. My point is that the foundational problems of psychology have been with us from the beginning and that they can be clarified and rectified only by means of conceptual changes and/or theoretical advances which, in turn, have implications for methodology and practically every other phase of psychological praxis. My own bias is that phenomenological philosophy can contribute to the solution of psychology's foundational problems, and for this reason, I shall try to spell out the relevance of phenomenology for psychology and will sketch some of the implications of that relevance.

PSYCHOLOGY'S THEORETICAL CRISIS

When I was preparing my book (Giorgi, 1970) in the late sixties, I continually ran across articles in the *American Psychologist*—where psychologists speak mostly to each other and in terms that have more than a specialty interest—that were critical of the status of psychology as a science. While noting that the critiques seemed to be more prevalent, I argued at that time that the same critiques were being made in the late nineteenth century (e.g., Dilthey) and were due more to an endemic weakness concerning psychology's conceptual self-understanding than to recent developments.

As though to prove my point, a review of the *American Psychologist* since 1970 shows that matters have not changed: there is still a series of articles critiquing the institutionalization of psychology. These articles range far and wide, from the scientist-professional dichotomy (Proshansky, 1972), through questioning of the meaning of science in psychology (Tyler, 1970) and discussions concerning the identity of clinical psychology (Schneider, 1971), to future predictions concerning industrial psychology (Meyer, 1972). Typical of the kinds of challenges being presented is Rogers's (1973, p. 379) query: "Does our profession dare to develop the new conception of science which is so necessary if we are to have a true psychological science? Or will we continue as a pseudoscience?" Throughout the whole article Rogers argues in the same vein and ends up as follows:

> I have raised the question as to whether psychology will remain a narrow technological fragment of a science, tied to an outdated philosophical conception of itself, clinging to a security blanket of observable behaviors only; or whether it can possibly become a truly broad and creative science, rooted in subjective vision, open to all aspects of the human condition, worthy of the name of a mature science.

The thrust of Rogers's comments is that a different understanding of science or, if you will, a different paradigm is called for in psychology. It is no longer an unfamiliar demand, but the important implication for us is that theoretical or conceptual transformations are required to meet this demand. As has already been indicated, psychology's crisis is theoretical, and we hope to demonstrate this fact by appealing to contemporary formulations of the crisis. For the purposes of this paper I shall limit the demonstration of psychology's theoretical crisis to three aspects: (a) its lack of unity, (b) the doubts expressed concerning its relevancy, and (c) psychology's understanding of science.

The Crisis in Terms of Lack of Unity

Catania (1973, p. 434) has commented on the lack of unity in psychology in the following way:

> Students of psychology still are asked to choose theoretical sides. They see functional accounts of operant behavior pitted against ethological accounts of behavioral structure, analyses of reinforcement contingencies pitted against theories of cognitive processing, and descriptions of language as verbal behavior pitted against psycholinguistic formulations of language competence....psychologists are not yet even agreed on whether theirs is a science of behavior or a science of mental life.

Hebb (1974, p. 71), while arguing in defense of traditional psychology, still had to note the lack of unity. "It's hard to keep up," Hebb writes, "even in your own specialty. . . . psychology is not clinical psychology; it is not physiological psychology; it is not social or comparative or developmental or human experimental psychology. It is something more, comprising all those lines of approach to the central mystery." Boneau (1974) has observed that the era of epic, grand theories ended in the fifties and that today one tends rather to deal in mini-theories. Boneau himself, however, offers a model for psychology that was developed for a particular experimental situation to apply to the behavior of pigeons in a color discrimination task in a Skinner box, and writes with approval that the model may "serve as a device that allows for the viewing of psychology as a coherent, organized panorama rather than as a collection of disparate intellectual and scientific doodles valued as a whole only by those with sufficient faith or with a highly developed appreciation of abstract design to support a belief that it somehow all makes sense" (p. 303). The very proposal of a model indicates that unity in psychology is desirable but nonexistent. Sherif (1970, p. 145), reporting on a survey by McGrath and Altman on small group research, states that they arrived at discouraging conclusions concerning such research, claiming that "the problem seems to arise because research in the small group field is so segmented—in the form of idiosyncratic variables, tasks, and measures peculiar to the individual investigators—that no one has a common base from which to argue." Lastly, Coffield (1970) notes that a tension in psychology between formal experimentation and research procedures that do not follow such rigorous prescriptions has existed since the beginning of the twentieth century, although the dichotomy has been variously labelled—such as experimental versus genetic, general versus individual, experimental versus correlational, etc. The fact that Coffield's own attempt to unify the differences takes place in the seventh decade of this century indicates the obstinacy of the problem.

With respect to future development, wholly different models for psychology have been proposed: Levine (1974) has suggested an adversary model somewhat similar to that employed by the legal profession, Brown (1974) has proposed a Marxist model, von Eckartsberg (1971) a dialogal model, and as indicated above, Hebb (1974) has suggested that we simply continue doing what we have been doing.

Clearly, there is a lack of unity in psychology with respect to theories, methods, importance of data, definition of subject matter and almost every other important dimension. Moreover, the same critiques concerning the science of psychology perseverate. Why? Because somehow the organization of the field of psychology is not meeting the pervasive needs of all of its practitioners. And this, in turn, is because its organization has not yet found the central viewpoint for integrating the various facets of its field. So one meaning of lack of unity in psychology is the fact that the point of view or central perspective for integrating the disparate aspects of psychology has not yet been achieved or elaborated. This means that the perspective adopted is exhausted before one comes to the end of commonly accepted psychological phenomena. Or it means that one can comprehend the totality of psychological phenomena only by excessive abstraction or ambiguous labeling. Thus, the term *stimulus* can be applied to almost any psychological situation, but it is either so abstract that it loses psychological value, or else it is used ambiguously because it often shifts connotations as contexts differ. A science, sure of its central unity, would be able to handle these problems.

Second, precisely because the central perspective is lacking, many competing claims exist concerning the future of psychology. This is another way that lack of unity manifests itself. We have just enumerated some of the proposals for psychology's future and we have seen how varied they are. Thus a lack of unity is expressed even when it comes time to speak for the *direction* in which psychology is to move.

Third, some of the articles spoke to the fragmentation of psychology. One could point to the proliferation of divisions within APA structure, whose only organization is numbering by chronology. Or one can point to the fact that practitioners of one specialty not only do not know what is going on in certain other areas, they are not even able to keep up within their own specialty. This is not just a matter of too much information; it's also a question of how it is organized. Furthermore, it has recently been demonstrated that although there are only slightly more than 200 graduate schools of psychology, over 75 different fields of study where graduate students could specialize were listed (Mitchell, 1974).

Fourth, I mentioned earlier that we accept as part of our tradition that psychology began the day Wundt founded his lab in 1879. Yet, Allport (1968) has written that social psychology really began with Comte in 1852; Hebb (1966, p. 4) states that modern psychology really began with the founding of behaviorism in 1913; in testing, Binet's 1905 work dates the beginnings; and some psychologists justifiably point to the tradition founded by Brentano's publication in 1874 (Rancurello, 1968). When psychology is viewed in a national perspective, the dates of foundings vary even more (Sexton & Misiak, 1971). Historians, of course, are aware of the difficulties encountered in determining a founding date, but it seems to me that these differences reflect as well the disarray of present biases. Each present viewpoint can find an "origin date" consistent with its own bias and emphasis (Samelson, 1974).

As additional evidence that psychology lacks the unity of an authentic paradigm and therefore is really in a preparadigmatic phase, I would like to mention the fact that while Wundt is recognized as the official founder of psychology, the attempt to found psychology over again has persisted throughout its first 100 years. In addition to Wundt there was Brentano, Dilthey, MacDougall, Watson, Skinner, and Hebb, just to mention a few. If psychology had its paradigm, if it understood how to interpret its phenomena, then why would these successive foundings take place? Why would philosophers as disparate as Husserl (1962b) and Wittgenstein (1958) feel compelled to speak to the inadequate founding of psychology or its conceptual confusion? Presumably, only because the problems exist. It should be realized of course that a paradigm shift is not the same thing as repeated attempts at founding an authentic paradigm. The difference is in terms of intrinsic criteria whereby solutions of problems that persist over time can be ascertained. Hence, while the Einsteinian paradigm has replaced the Newtonian one, the Newtonian laws still hold for its context. No psychological paradigm gives that amount of assurance over a range of phenomena.

Lastly, one can point to the dramatically different language systems and privileged phenomena that different systems of psychology select. The language of behaviorism includes stimulus, response, reinforcement, contingency; the language of psychoanalysis contains psychosexual development, complexes, repression, the unconscious; the language of phenomenology includes phenomenon, consciousness, intentionality, meaning. Behaviorism emphasizes observable phenomena and an external viewpoint, psychoanalysis emphasizes symbolic behavior and relations with significant others, phenomenology emphasizes the internal viewpoint, experience, and meanings. How can a genuine paradigmatic unity be claimed for these three perspectives? Only by supporting a bias which, in the long run, may or may not be true. Thus, at the moment, my own claim that a phenomenologically based paradigm could be an authentic paradigm for psychology is still only a bias. When psychology achieves awareness of its authentic paradigm, arguments will be unnecessary because the fruitfulness of the paradigm should be obvious.

What are the consequences of this lack of unity? For practitioners, it seems that there are few or no consequences, except perhaps for an occasional identity crisis. Usually they will pick a frame within which to work, and if that frame meets the immediate needs of their everyday work situation, then there is no problem, and that is fair enough. But theoreticians or academicians cannot remain content with lack of unity, and their efforts to resolve this issue in turn will have important consequences for the practice of psychology. The attempt to clarify one's own practice belongs to the very meaning of science; indeed, that is what method in science is all about. Procedures without clarification can never become methods, and approaches without clarification can never become paradigms.

Two precautions concerning the lack of unity in psychology should be mentioned. First of all, perhaps it should be clarified that in attempting to discover the unity of psychology I do not mean to imply a desire for uniformity, homogeneity, or lack of problems. Physics has a more unified paradigm, and yet theoretical differences and interesting problems still exist. What I mean by unity is a commonly accepted and clarified perspective that differentiates psychology from other disciplines and enables psychologists to relate data obtained from various research projects in a meaningful way. For example, to say that psychology's subject matter is how man behaves in the world does not in and of itself differentiate it from sociology, anthropology, law, or economics. There must also be a point of view or perspective. My position is that such a unity is always implied anyway—even in eclecticism—and that the explicit clarification of the implied unity of any school or perspective will hasten the day when a commonly accepted and comprehensive unity will come into being; that will be the founding of psychology's authentic paradigm.

The second precaution deals with the interpretation that says perhaps I have proved my case too well—the history of psychology is such that it proves beyond doubt that psychology can never be a coherent science. The most recent defender of this position has been Sigmund Koch (1969, 1974). My position is that although the lack of unity (or coherence) is factually true, it is not essentially true. Koch seems to be saying that for reasons of principle, psychology cannot be a unified science. But a close examination of one article (Koch, 1969) shows that where Koch makes this point, he implicitly accepts the natural scientific conception of science, rather than seeing natural science as but one example of a more generic understanding of science. I have argued elsewhere (Giorgi, 1970) that it is precisely the natural scientific conception of science that is most responsible for psychology's fragmentation. But I also can conceive of the possibility that as a *human* science, psychology can achieve its elusive unity. In another paper Koch (1974) argues that some psychological investigations may look more like investigations in the humanities that scientific studies in the strict sense. I can even agree with this point, except that my position would be that a deeper probing into the discipline involved in such studies may show that a human scientific conception was being followed after all. My point here is simply that I am aware of the fact that the actual history of psychology could lead some to conclude that psychology can never be unified. My response is that while no unifying conception has appeared as yet, a unified psychology is imaginable or conceivable, and if so, I will hold out the hope that it will become a reality.

By way of summary I may say that psychology's lack of unity is indicated by (a) the fragmentary nature of its findings, (b) the diverse models it proposes to follow, (c) the tension that has been historically present in the selection of its methods, (d) the confusion over its future direction, (e) the multiple foundings claimed to be the origin of psychology as well as the continued attempts to found a new paradigm, and lastly, (f) the fact that different psychological viewpoints have different languages and emphasize different phenomena as foundational. My position is that this is a factual state of affairs that could be changed by adopting a proper perspective.

The Crisis in Terms of Lack of Relevance

If authentic unity is to be achieved in psychology, the principles of relevance will have to be determined, but relevancy cannot be established without considering the intentions of a human subject. What is relevant information? What is relevant activity? Abstract questions such as these can only be answered abstractly, but even then, they imply some awareness of intentions, aims, or goals on the part of a human being. Relevant information is information that helps one to know or do what he wants to do; relevant activity is activity that helps one get to where he wants to go. Thus, relevance always implies an intention, goal, or purpose.

Actually the meaning of relevance for psychology breaks down into two distinct, but ultimately related, senses. One meaning of relevance is concerned with the *approach* to the topic of research and the other with the *choice* of research topics. The latter meaning is usually implied when social critics charge psychology with irrelevancy, and the former is generally meant by those who criticize psychology's paradigm. The question of relevancy in psychology has received a surprising amount of attention in the early seventies, and psychology has been criticized and defended in both senses of the term outlined above. Some examples of the way in which the relevancy issue is being voiced in psychology are as follows.

In a survey of graduate students and faculty in psychology designed to discover the most important issue confronting psychology today, about 50% of the students and faculty named relevance as the biggest single issue and approximately 65% would point to relevance and questions concerning research and theory as the two most important issues (Lipsey, 1974). Another empirical study on the meaning of relevance was conducted with undergraduate students in which relevance was seen to be "related to personal needs and/or social applicability" (Menges & Trumpeter, 1972, p. 217). Both experimental psychology (Baron, 1971) and animal learning studies (Logan, 1972) were defended as being relevant. However, Sherif (1970, p. 144) has written that "a social psychology that is relevant must do much more than conduct research on significant social problems after they have already become urgent business to administrators, policy makers and a general public alarmed by them." He points out that the bias in social psychology has been the study of relatively stable social systems, whereas a "relevant social psychology is the study of social movements produced by social problems, for it is these movements that are groping toward the shape of the future" (p. 156). Lastly, in an article dealing with the crisis in social psychology, Silverman (1971) distinguishes between internal and external problems. He argues that relevance has to be determined from within first and that the issue of relevance must also be seen in the *"broader scientifically credible sense of the relevance of data to the construct to which they pertain"* (p. 584, italics in original).

Thus, in a way not seen before, the meaning of relevancy for psychology is being investigated, challenged, and defended. Formerly, it is safe to say, it was generally taken for granted. For us, the reason that the question of relevance is so important is that it is intimately related to the question of unity; indeed, the question of unity cannot be answered without an appreciation of relevance, which in turn presupposes a guiding interest or intention.

What, then, is psychology's guiding interest? Let us see how psychologists actually utilize their knowledge. What is their work, and how are they employed? First of all, they are in the helping professions; they try to help people live full, complete, normal, healthy lives in every sense of the term. That aim is relatively clear. Researchers try to investigate the normal, everyday processes of living. Why? In order to understand them better. Why? So that what it means to live a normal, everyday life can be understood even better and in a concrete, clarified way in order to detect and anticipate problems that may arise. Consulting psychologists offer their advice and expertise to government, businesses, industry. Why? In order to solve problems, correct abuses, and, in general, help organized groups or individuals perform better. Teachers communicate to students knowledge about man. Why? So students can understand themselves and their families and friends better and perhaps even live better. Thus psychologists help others, teach others, do research for others and consult with others. Psychology as a *science professes* to be of help to others (Tyler, 1970). If this is true, why is there a dichotomy between psychology's scientific and professional interests?

Now for strictly theoretical reasons I would say that a science is relevant to the extent to which it is of service for the *life-world*, that is, the everyday world we all experience, or some segment of it. Of course, there are degrees of relevancy, so that one may be interested in the relevance of some data for a particular theory without being explicitly concerned about the relevancy of that theory for the life-world in a factual sense, but if challenged, he should be able to show how, in principle, the theory could be so extended. Similarly, the problems of division of labor within a given science may be such that certain individuals do not in fact deal with the relevancy of their science to the life-world, but in principle they could. Thus, psychology should be relevant to the life-world, and if the nature of this relevancy could be clarified, then psychology's unity would be enhanced. Now my claim, first, is that in fact, psychology's relevance to the life-world is partial, ambiguous and contingent; thus its unity is not clear, and it remains in its preparadigmatic phase. That is why relevance with respect to *choice* of topics is so often criticized. Secondly, my claim is that psychology does not *approach* its topic in ways that are most fruitful. That is why relevance in the sense of approach to topics is often criticized. What is the main reason for this state of affairs? In my view it is the conception of science that psychology chooses to emulate and by which it understands itself.

Psychology's Understanding of Itself As a Science

If relevancy to the life-world is a constitutive part of science, how is it that psychology's relevance is askew? The problem is the conception of science that psychology began to emulate, namely, that of the natural sciences. The reasons why psychology chose to emulate the natural sciences have been delineated extensively before both by myself and others so they need not be repeated here. We shall dwell more directly on why the natural scientific conception of science leads to an irreconcilable dilemma for psychology: being faithful to the demands of the life-world and not doing justice to science, or remaining faithful to the requirements of science and precisely because of that, not doing justice to the life-world and thereby remaining irrelevant. This is the dilemma that has plagued psychology since its inception, although it was not noticed initially because only the scientific requirements were being weighed, and the assumption was that the relevancy issue would resolve itself once a sufficient number of facts were collected.

One of the main reasons that the natural scientific conception of science, perfectly legitimate within its own context, cannot lead to relevant rigorous knowledge about man in the world is that *world* and *nature* are not the same thing. By world we are referring to what everyone knows naively and is directly experienced by all men; nature, in contrast, is the world viewed under a very special attitude —one that strips all objects of their relationship to living beings—and thus nature comes to mean physical and inert matter. Physics and chemistry then assume different tasks of analysis with respect to this object "nature," which was, we must bear in mind, actually constituted by man. From the very beginning, therefore, nature is defined in terms of its exclusion of living beings.

"Worlds," on the other hand, are correlates of consciousnesses that know them as such, and in order to understand worlds, one must follow their implications back to the human subjects. Nature, too, is the correlate of a conscious attitude, but its meaning is such that the reference back to the conscious structure that knows it is not pursued. Nature is to be treated only in its relationships to other material or spatio-temporal things, but not in the way this network of relationships is supported by a special structure of consciousness. Thus, in this conception of science, the difference between the domain of "nature" and that of "world" is such that one cannot extend the concepts, procedures, and findings from one to the other without serious distortion.

Now, if the primary way of achieving unity is by means of relevance, and if relevance for psychology means to relate to others in the world and to approach phenomena as they present themselves in the world, then the kind of science psychology should be must be constructed from within the viewpoint of the "world." For the world of man, psychology has to be a human science; to have a psychology of animals, we must understand the animal world, and this would be an animal science. This would almost seem to be so self-evident as to be embarrassing, as Rollo May (1967) once stated. The fact that it is not, or that it has to be elaborated, justified, and defended is, it seems to me, the scandal of our contemporary thought.

Precisely what makes the idea of human science so difficult to grasp are deeply rooted cultural prejudices which, because of the conception of nature described above, strongly identify science with the impersonal, the anonymous, and the thinglike. As a result the mere mention of the personal, self-initiative, and the socially relevant motivates psychologists to speak of an impossible chasm. But what is forgotton is that the meaning of nature, upon which the history of science understood in that sense is based, is not the given, but a conception of nature that has been constituted by man. Nature, in other words, is derived because it is conceived by man; it is not what man finds spontaneously before him, which is, on the contrary, "world." Consequently, the operations performed upon the objects of nature are operations invented in the light of that particular conception of nature. Then by a curious switch, nature and the operations invented to study it are given greater reality than the world which is spontaneously given to us. The circle is completed and everyone wonders how we can study the varied world which man experiences in a rigorous way, or how we can transform the world that we spontaneously live in into the clean systematic regulated world of science. But since the primacy is actually with the everyday perceptual world—because that is the world we are born into and live before we are scientists—and since historically man walked on earth and coped with his world before science was invented, to achieve such an aim would be like accounting for behavioral traits of a father in terms of his son rather than the other way around. In other words, a derived, partial perspective—the scientific viewpoint—cannot wholly account for an original totality —the life-world.

Thus the history of the natural sciences is the history of man's relationship with nature whereby, within the context of certain prescribed attitudes, man deepened his understanding of nature.

However, since for such a long period of time the only science was in fact natural science, everyone assumed that, in principle, the only possible kind of science was being practiced. Consequently, with the founding of psychology, the same prescribed attitude and the same operations were maintained, only this time man was the object of study and whatever exceeded the adopted frame of reference was ignored and what remained was studied. Sometimes surface modifications of the conceptual structure ensued, but the basic presuppositions were never questioned nor radically transformed. Perhaps the most succinct expression of this whole question was provided by Koch (1959, p. 783) when he wrote, "But, at the time of *its* inception, *psychology was unique in the extent to which its institutionalization preceded its content and its methods preceded its problems*" (italics in original).

Let us analyze this statement a little more closely and see what it means. "Psychology was unique in the extent to which its institutionalization preceded its content." This means that the primary frame of reference, the key operations, and a certain understanding of method all existed before the turning toward psychological subject matter—behavior. But if we ask the further question—upon what subject matter did this institutionalization take place?—the answer once again is nature. The implicit presupposition is that behavior is like nature and therefore we can use the same attitude and procedures. Of course, applying this attitude to behavior is possible, as naive behaviorism has demonstrated, but it is not adequate in the sense that a significant residue of behavior is still left to be accounted for when one stays strictly within the natural scientific attitude, as certain forms of neobehaviorism demonstrate. What deceives us here is the fact that *something can be said* about man from a strictly natural scientific viewpoint, but it is knowledge of man as a natural object—knowledge which is only minimal and hardly exhausts him. Thus, man as a physical entity obeys laws of gravity when he falls, burns when placed in fire, and is displaced according to principles of force and inertia when he is hit by a car. But these data tell us nothing about man as social, man as creative, man as artistic, etc. Lastly it should be recalled that against a ground of no history, the initial facts obtained even within a natural scientific perspective can seem significant, but after 100 years of such data the diminishing nature of the returns becomes apparent and the need for a critical reassessment can no longer be ignored.

Now to the second part of Koch's statement: psychology's

"methods preceded its problems." What are the implications here? For one thing, the methods were developed in relation to problems connected with the natural or physical sciences and then applied to the behavioral sciences only after they were already formed. In a certain sense this means that despite psychology's claim to being empirical and positivistic, the methods employed by psychology existed prior to the problems encountered, and consequently, the problems were conceived in terms of the available methods. What deceives us here is that there is a history associated with the methods of the natural sciences, but it is a history with the domain of nature and not with man's or even animal's behavior. Thus the application of natural scientific method to man and animal is a prejudice, or prejudgment, that is then rationalized in terms of a metaphysical postulate (again despite psychology's claim to be scientific and nonphilosophical). The postulate is that there is only one nature, and the only difference between man and nature, or psychology and physics, is one of complexity so that the same techniques are valid across all strata of reality. When one points out that in terms of a radical understanding of man, psychology has not made much progress, the complexity of man is appealed to once again; but the institutionalization, the method, and the attitude themselves are not questioned.

Perhaps a concrete example from our times can highlight this point. In the early 1960s President Kennedy made the claim that the United States would land a man on the moon by the end of the decade, and indeed we did. It was vintage Americana and we were all proud and rightly marveled at the wonders of science and technology. In the 1950s, however, we also stated that we would stamp out juvenile delinquency, in the late 1960s we had the war on poverty, and in the early 1970s there was a crusade against drug abuse. Today there are still juvenile delinquents, poor people, and drug problems. No victory march was heard. What is the difference between the two cases? In racing for the moon, it was man against nature, and we have 500 years' history with a genuine paradigm for coping with that type of problem. With sufficient motivation and economic backing, we achieved our goal. But in dealing with juvenile delinquents, the poor, and drug abuse, we are dealing with relations among humans. Not only is our history with these problems shorter in the thematic sense, but we are also confused in our dealings with these problems because we are unsure of our paradigm.

Therefore, let us return to the key point. Koch's description of psychology's beginnings, in my view, is accurate. But is that the way science began? Not at all. It was not that self-conscious nor that imitative. When the natural scientific attitude was trying to express itself and differentiate itself from the dominant philosophical or theological viewpoints of its day, there was only a void to be filled, not an institution or a method to be imitated or used. Hence the natural sciences grew out of a concrete confrontation with their phenomena of interest. Over the years specific conceptualizations and specific procedures were seen to be fruitful and were finally systematized into a method. In other words, with the natural sciences the method did not precede the problems, the institution of science did not precede the content; in both cases, they emerged together in a dialectical way. Consequently, if psychology really wanted to imitate the natural sciences, it should imitate their actual growth and not some caricature thereof. In any event, that is the critical step psychology missed in its development, namely, a coming to grips with its own self-definition in dialogue with its phenomena. Psychology chose, instead, to go the short route, accept the natural scientific preinterpretation of the world, and then try to operate within that frame by merely modifying its fundamental terms rather than starting from scratch. It has been paying the price for this decision ever since.

Thus far I have given an interpretation of why psychology as a natural science renders impossible a relationship of direct relevancy with the life-world. Let me give some concrete demonstrations of what this means before I proceed further.

Boneau, for example, in the article cited previously (1974, p. 299), writes as follows: "Let us consider the situation dimension first. The processes by which external physical energy is transduced through the sensory receptors of an organism and subsequently segregated and organized is the subject matter of important chapters in psychology which are relied on here." Boneau is attempting to describe a model of behavior, and is speaking of, as he says, the situation dimension. But why does he have to begin with the situation conceived of in terms of "external physical energy" that is "transduced through sensory receptors"? I am not saying that one cannot do this, but the point is, what is the advantage to psychology of beginning this way? I have been obtaining open-ended descriptions of situations for about six years now and no one spontaneously talks about the physical energy or their own sense organs—they describe objects, individuals, tasks, meanings, etc. Why then do psychologists always feel that they must remain consistent with knowledge as obtained by physics *first*, and then work up to psychological relevance? This has become so automatic, so indigenous to the behavior of psychologists that it is no longer justified; it is merely assumed. It is part of what it means for psychology to be scientific. But beginning in such ways makes the movement back to the life-world difficult and obscures the genuinely psychological. The only way in which one could be content to begin with such an alien starting point is if one assigned to such an extraneous point of departure an exceptionally high status or an extremely important significance—such as a belief that physical description is the *really real*, or that the more psychology is like physics, the more scientific it will be. My point is that beginning in such a fashion, that is, with physical descriptions of the environment and working through physiological or anatomical descriptions of the sense organs, is simply a contingency established by the natural scientifically biased interpretation of science that psychology holds.

Allow me to cite a second example. Hebb (1974, p. 72) writes: "Man is a social *animal*. His society is complex, the experience and learning of the child growing up in it are complex, and so it is hard to trace the origins of adult human social behavior. With animals, there's a better chance." This type of argument is familiar and recurs frequently. A careful examination will show, however, that the argument rests on a bias—the analytic, atomistic bias. The reason that simple things are ostensibly easier to understand is related to the assumption that science proceeds by analysis to discover and isolate the irreducible elements of any phenomenon, and that complex phenomena differ from simple only by the increasing number of elements that are contained, or by the increased number of relationships that are entailed. This assumption, too, is a holdover from natural scientific praxis, and may or may not be true for human or animal phenomena. In many ways, research with animals is just as difficult and complex as research with humans, but only in a different way. Similarly, simple situations may indeed be easier for *conducting* research, but they are often much more difficult to relate meaningfully to the life-world, whereas complex situations may actually be more difficult to research, but if they are researched, then the relevance of the research results for the life-world is relatively straightforward. To say that the former is a better way of researching than the latter is simply a prejudice based upon a certain conception of what science means.

One last illustration of how the natural scientific bias in psychology limits the relevancy of research. Simkins (1969, p. 60) in speaking about the aims of science writes as follows:

> Scientific inquiry has two major goals. These are to understand and control its subject matter. . . . The word "control" may have two meanings. In one sense, the word is used in the experimental procedure of holding certain variables constant so that one variable can be isolated and its effects studied. The second meaning of control refers to the application of a principle established under experimental conditions to the practical control of the subject matter.

Simkins then goes on to give an example of the second meaning of control in terms of raising tulips. If we learn that certain factors help tulips to grow more quickly, then we apply that knowledge and thus "control" the growth rate of tulips.

Now it is understandable that in the man-nature relationship, man would, in the interest of is own survival, want to control some of the forces of nature. But even here, as ecologists are showing, nature should not be controlled indiscriminately or else we may be even worse off than initially. Beyond this, however, is the extension of the attitude of control, in the second meaning that Simkins gives it, to the domain of human behavior legitimate? Is it not at least problematic, or debatable? But we often find these questions are not asked, and in the name of science, attitudes and interpretations are simply soaked up and carried over to psychology. But what if control in the sense of influencing the subject matter itself were not essential to science as such, but only to the way the natural sciences are practiced, and where, indeed, it apparently raises no ethical objection?

I will return to this specific problem later, but I do believe that these three examples have illustrated my major point, namely, that the natural scientific interpretation and practice of science have influenced psychology's understanding of itself as a science in such a way as to make its relevancy to the life-world problematic. The first example revealed a physicalistic bias, the second example an atomistic bias, and the last, a "controlling" bias. The point of this paper is that science does not stand or fall with these biases; they could be eliminated and science would still be science. On the other hand, the abandonment of these biases would serve a liberating function for psychology. The elimination of the physical bias will help us zero in more quickly on the properly psychological, the elimination of the atomistic bias will enable us to find concepts and descriptions that are closer to the way humans live their situations, and the elimination of the "controlling" bias will aid the integration of psychology and ethics. In brief, the removal of these biases would increase scientific psychology's potential relevance to the life-world because one would no longer be burdened with the problem of making man "see" what he can only conceive (e.g., 450 mμ); or of trying to make man experience what can only be seen as objects in others (e.g., rods and cones); or of trying to make others experience isolated elements when perceptual organization always presents us with contextualized wholes; or finally, of trying to make one person control another, when, in speaking of human relations, control can only be used in a metaphorical and not a literal sense.

Again, others have noted that the concept of science which psychology supports is narrow and restricting. Raush (1974), for example, states flatly that the academician's interpretation of psychology simply does not hold outside of academia, claiming that "we have all been sold a parochial definition of science, and those of us who are teachers continue to foist it on students" (p. 679). Later he quotes the following statement of Bakan with approval: "In other words, the fact that the present conception of science forces honest, astute and conscientious investigators to look elsewhere for guidance must be interpreted as a shortcoming in the current conceptions of sciences" (p. 679). While defending empirical psychology, Shotter and Gauld (1971, p. 465) had to admit that "the choice that lies before psychology at present would appear to be either, on the one hand, continuing with the established theoretical presuppositions and methods of investigation and dealing only with those problems that happen to be amenable to them, or, on the other hand, taking up the fascinating and vitally important problems of human conceptual thought and rule-regulated behavior, and siding with those who, however haltingly, and with whatever difficulty, are endeavoring to find new theoretical concepts and practical methods with which the problems can be effectively tackled." Lastly, Wolman (1971) has recently asked whether psychology does not need its own philosophy of science in order to work on its own problems more adequately. All of these expressions (and more could be found) center on the need for psychology to transform its understanding of science.

A brief summary of what we have established thus far is as follows: our position is that psychology is in a preparadigmatic phase of development because it lacks the unity of a genuine paradigm, although it does follow a de facto paradigm borrowed from the natural sciences. Its de facto paradigm gave psychology autonomy, but not unity. In order to achieve unity, the claim was made that psychology's discoveries and facts have to be made more relevant to the life-world, and, furthermore, that its phenomena have to be researched from within contexts that are relevant to the way these phenomena appear in man's experience, and which would, in turn, also increase psychology's relevance to the life-world. It is psychology's implicit intent to be relevant to the life-world, and if it is not, in fact, as relevant as it could be, it is because of the interpretation of science that it chooses to adopt. Only a change in its conception of science can break the vicious circle. Can a more radical understanding of science be attained? We believe so, but before presenting the alternative notion of science, we would like to see if the picture of psychology we have presented remains consistent with concrete studies. In this investigation the phenomenon of memory will serve as an example.

THEORY AND RESEARCH IN THE PSYCHOLOGY OF MEMORY

The purpose of this section is to see if concrete studies in psychology can somehow escape the general critique we have presented above. It could be, for example, that the field of psychology as a whole is in theoretical disarray, whereas concrete studies with specific phenomena are basically problem-free in terms of theory and approach. To test this possibility we have chosen the phenomenon of memory.

All psychologists agree that the experimental investigation of memory began in 1885 with the publication of *Memory* by Ebbinghaus. If we look at the attitude with which he approached the phenomenon, we can detect an obvious natural scientific bias. Ebbinghaus (1964, p. 7) writes as follows:

The method of obtaining exact measurements—i.e. numerically exact ones—of the inner structure of causal relations is, by virtue of its nature, of general validity. This method, indeed, has been so exclusively used and so fully worked out by the natural sciences that, as a rule, it is defined as something peculiar to them, as *the* method of natural science. To repeat, however, its logical nature makes it generally applicable to all spheres of existence and phenomena. Moreover, the possibility of defining accurately and exactly the actual behavior of any process whatever, and thereby of giving a reliable basis for the direct comprehension of it depends above all upon the possibility of applying this method.

We all know of what this method consists: an attempt is made to keep constant the mass of conditions which have proven themselves causally connected with a certain result; one of these conditions is isolated from the rest and varied in a way that can be numerically described; then the accompanying change on the side of the effect is ascertained by measurement or computation.

Ebbinghaus then goes on to describe the difficulties encountered in applying the natural scientific method to memory processes and how to surmount them. Unwittingly, Ebbinghaus demonstrates exactly how method preceded content in psychology since he can describe the scientific method fully but has to argue for the application of this method in psychology.

Moreover, this passage reveals rather directly the general attitude of the early experimental psychologists to the natural scientific method. There was no questioning of the method per se; they recognized only the problem of how to apply it to psychological phenomena, and defended the universality of the method for all phenomena. As an aside, we can even agree that in the historical sense the attempt to apply the natural scientific method should have been made so that psychology could be established as an independent science; the question today is a matter of whether or not psychology should continue along the same path. Almost all sciences live through a preparadigmatic phase.

That many psychologists agree to continue with the same viewpoint can be seen by Hilgard's comments in the introduction to the English translation of Ebbinghaus's book, written in 1963, and published in 1964:

In this very first experimental study of learning and memory Ebbinghaus did at least four things, all ahead of his times, and valid today: (1) He abandoned reliance upon the testimony of introspection in favor of objective evidence of memory. . . . (2) He invented a calibrated material (nonsense syllables) to provide a new substance to be memorized. (3) He criticized the established laws of association, particularly those of contiguity and immediate succession, by introducing a quantitative study of remote associations. (4) He made use of statistical and mathematical notions to test the significance of his findings and to formulate his results in accordance with a mathematical "model." For the beginner in a new field to have done all of these things—and more—is so surprising as to baffle our understanding of how it could have happened. [Hilgard, 1964]

In brief, Hilgard praises Ebbinghaus for being so contemporary in his approach. And of what did that consist? According to Hilgard, he used objective measurements instead of introspection, he used calibrated material, that is, material that had been made discrete with known relationships to some standard rather than material with spontaneous organization, he quantified associations rather than merely describing them, and lastly, he explicitly employed statistics and mathematical "models." In other words, Ebbinghaus transformed his phenomenon in order to make it more compatible with the natural scientific conception of method, and Hilgard praises him precisely for that achievement. This praise indicates that the values of that approach are still affirmed today, while Ebbinghaus's transformations themselves indicate that the phenomenon of memory as it was lived was not the object of study. Essentially, then, the natural scientific approach studies transformed phenomena. But the transformation is justified in terms of scientific method, not in terms of demands springing from the phenomenon of memory.

In any event, that is how the scientific psychology of memory got its start and how it is continuing, at least theoretically. A quick survey of more recent literature on memory shows that while facts have changed somewhat, many specific theories have come and gone, and techniques have improved, the concepts and theories themselves show little improvement. It is not hard to find the same symptoms in memory research and theories as we have in psychology as a whole: namely, lack of unity, lack of relevance, and precommitment to a natural scientific conception of science. The latter point, of course, has already been demonstrated in our example concerning Ebbinghaus and Hilgard.

As for lack of unity, without elaborating any details we can point to the following: Adams (1967) cites three primary theories on the "fate of the stored trace"—trace decay, trace transformation, and interference theory—without being able to decide among them. Feigenbaum (1969) delineates "levels of discourse" in memory theory and research as follows: (1) behavior of neurons, (2) neural systems, (3) elementary symbol-manipulating properties and structures, (4) programs for organizing symbol-processing activity and (5) human behavior. Those levels are roughly compared to a computer, but what interests us in this perspective is that while levels one and two interact, they do not interact with any of the other three levels; levels three and four interact with each other, but not with any of the other three, and the last level does not interact with any of the four. Norman (1970) says that memory models have three different historical roots: mathematical learning theory, signal detection theory, and computer processes. In addition there are physiological models (Hebb, 1949) and biochemical models (Gurowitz, 1969) of memory. In order to appreciate the disarray, one should recall that unified research would imply different researches working on different facets of a problem; here the facets cannot be differentiated from the overall problem.

The case for lack of relevancy in both its meanings can also be made fairly easily. In the sense of an inadequate *approach* to the problem of memory, we can cite the following factors. First of all, it is interesting to note how often the "models" for memory come from other phenomena. We have noted, above, computers, mathematical learning theory, and signal detection theory, all of which spring from studies in psychophysics and sensory thresholds. How then can an adequate or relevant model for memory be designed if one does not turn to memory itself? How strange, also, that there is no experiential model for memory, that is, one based on how memory is experienced or lived! This is especially curious in the light of the fact that either life-world or behavioral phenomena are appealed to in order to account for the performance features of memory or forgetting. For example, Adams's theory of trace disappearance was couched in terms of decay—a radical change in living tissue; transformation—a process which ultimately depends on perception; or interference—a concept which comes from behavioral data related to the learning of a series of items. Thus one must appeal to either perceptual or behavioral data in order to account for memory whenever strictly mechanical, physiological, or biochemical models are used. This can only mean that an inadequate approach is being used, and therefore irrelevant findings with respect to lived memory are the inevitable outcome.

When behavioral terms are used in the approach to the problem of memory, either they are too narrow or they are not elaborated or defined except in physiological terms. For example, part of Adams's (1967, p. 10) definition of memory is "memory is the habit states of a subject that give the capability of correct occurrences of criterion responses." The definition continues in a straight operational way so that one knows that it can correspond only to an experimental situation. But no question concerning the relation of the experimental situation to the life-world is raised. Furthermore, habits turn out to be memory traces. We can also point to the inevitable fact that consciousness always appears to us as a stream, but most of the memory studies tend to emphasize discreteness. This inevitably results in a lack of contextualization as well.

What about relevance in the second sense, that is, the relevance of memory research for the life-world? That memory research and theories fail here as well can also be easily documented.

There are at least two ways in which they fail. The first has to do with the lack of temporal and social contexts for memory research. Kvale (1974), for example, shows that the conception of time underlying experimental research in psychology, drawn from traditional philosophies, "corresponds to clock time, which is divisible into separate homogeneous and substitutable moments, quantifiable and one-dimensional, to be represented spatially" (p. 8). Then he shows how this conception is presupposed in memory research: "Time atomization and spatialization of consciousness are also reflected in the concept of memory as consisting of separate memory traces, traces of the incoming sensations kept somewhere in the memory storehouse" (p. 8). This, in turn, according to Kvale, leads to the hypothesis that memory is permanent. The difficulty is that this theory of memory is too thinglike to be helpful in understanding how memory is experienced in everyday life—which is as an activity. Kvale then contrasts this conceptualization of memory with one based upon the philosophies of James and Husserl, and this leads to a temporal theory of memory in which historical and social dimensions are not missing. Because of his behavioral or experiential approach to memory, Kvale (undated) states that memory has to be studied in its temporal and social context because it is always situated. "The past may be continually changed as it is remembered from continually new presents, each with its own activities of interest. Thus the remembering of the past appears open to social influences of the remembering situation." In this approach, because the historical and social dimensions are not missing, the relevancy of memory research to everyday life is immediately apparent. Indeed, von Wright (1959) has pointed out that interference theories—usually implying a permanent memory—have been based upon rote recall of lists of independent items, whereas schema theories such as Barlett's and Piaget's—favoring a changeable memory—have been built upon investigations of complex materials, like pictures and stories, in situations closer to everyday life. Moreover, theories drawn from research based on everyday situations are also more contextual, social, and historical, and ultimately, therefore, more relevant for the life-world.

The second thing we learn from memory as it is lived is that memory always involves the awareness of the past as past from the present. One of the major difficulties with all physiological and chemical approaches is that they cannot account for the past as past from the present, and thus just how one is to make sense of these memory studies is difficult to say. Thus relevancy becomes a problem. Trace theorists are aware of this difficulty, but the research continues nonetheless. The problem, of course, is that if a present trace is reactivated, then it is present. If it is not, then how can the memory presumably contained in the trace become effective? Usually, there is an implicit appeal to an appropriate function, like coding or activating, without indicating a functioner. For example, Murdock (1974) identifies three possibilities for encoding: tagging, strength of trace, and collection. Certainly Murdock looks for physiological or chemical analogues of these processes, but the fact that he had to appeal to human categories to identify the process once again shows the weakness of models or theories that do not refer to the experience of memory. How can we have the function of tagging, strength determination, or collection without a tagger, strength determiner, or collector?

Ignoring the role of the present situation for memory also has serious effects. Van den Berg (1972) has written that there can only be distortions of memory when one's present is distorted. Similarly, when one's present is in order, one can have a well-ordered past instead of a chaotic one. That is why Freud could discover that his neurotic patients had "false memories." Confirmation for this interpretation also comes from the work of Talland (1965). It was always assumed in working with Korsakoff patients that they were confabulators—that is, they made up memories or stories to fill in the gaps due to amnesia. But it was discovered after some time that the

stories were true except that the Korsakoff patients did not recognize them *as past*. This is why their relating the stories was
pathological—the patients were unable to distinguish genuine past
events from present fictions. Since the trace theory has the same
difficulty, it would appear that it is of no help in solving this real life-
world problem.

I should mention in passing that the one exception to my critique
is Bartlett (1932), a man whose work is as significant as it is
neglected. He approached memory in a descriptive, contextualized
way and obtained data from real remembered situations. It is
significant, though, that no one has developed his approach in a
genuinely creative way. He is simply referred to as an example of a
type of memory research. The reason for this state of affairs, I am
sure you recognize by now, is the conception of science that guides
psychological research.

The power of the natural scientific conception of science cannot be
overestimated. For example, all theories of memory which suppose a
trace, of which there are many, have clarified neither their understanding of memory nor of trace. This is demonstrated by the
simple fact that researchers have looked for the trace in the neuron,
an anatomical source; in the synapse, a functinal interpretation; and
most recently, in the structure of DNA or RNA, a chemical or
molecular basis for the trace. Thus, in the history of the search, one
moves nonchalantly from anatomical, to functional, to chemical
conceptions without blinking. Even the failure to find the trace
(Lashley, 1950) has ended neither the search nor the reference to it.
What does the search for the trace mean? Why has not the lack of
success forced one to change the interpretation of memory instead?
That is, why not develop an alternative model or theory of memory,
especially since the search for a trace has so far failed? What strong
bias is being clung to? Why is a letting go of the trace concept so
threatening, as it must be, since it persists so long? I have no direct
answer to this problem, but I suspect it has a lot to do with
metaphysical assumptions concerning reality and methodological
assumptions with respect to science.

Two comments concerning the trace theory are worth mentioning.
Straus (1966) has written a critique of trace theories demonstrating
the inherent deficiencies in using an unclarified concept as the
guideline for research. Using a phenomenological analysis of a
simple event—footprints in the snow—Straus clarified the conditions
necessary for a trace to be a trace. For Straus, "the trace is an object

of historical interpretation of fragmentary residues of past events in a preserving material, as far as these relations, in their temporal interlacing, can be comprehended on the basis of certain indications" (p. 90). Traces, then, for Straus, preserve past events *as past* in the present, and they demand interpreters. The theory of traces as found in contemporary memory research does not meet these two demands. Mostly, it is assumed that traces are merely reactivated and the memory appears automatically; no effort is made to account for how the past as past appears. The important point here is that the criteria of a trace emerged from a phenomenological clarification of the meaning of how traces are experienced in everyday life.

One last point illustrates how unclarified biases can keep research efforts from genuine progress. A simple glance at psychology texts will show that while memory is one of the phenomena most studied in psychology, future-oriented temporality, such as anticipations, expectations, and intentions, is one of the least studied. Why? Once again, probably because of the strong physicalistic, empirical, and positivistic biases which hold that one cannot study what one has not experienced. Also, the fact that something has occurred in the past allows one to assume that some kind of modification has occurred in the nervous system and thus one can search for the presumed effects of the experience. In this case, most probably, the biases that have held up progress are more metaphysical than scientific, but it is worth noting that all of the metaphysical biases I have mentioned are compatible with the natural sciences. To make my point even more dramatic, allow me to venture a hypothesis. I just mentioned that studies of the future dimension of time are rarely conducted. One of the reasons for this, I am sure, is that researchers do not know how to go about studying expectations or anticipations empirically. Once this breakthrough is made, however, I am willing to venture that the same structure that is developed for future-oriented time studies should also be the model for past-oriented time studies. In other words, memory studies allow us to invoke the physicalistic and positivistic biases of the scientific method, and therefore novel approaches will be hard to come by as long as we keep with these biases. Anticipations, it is true, may seem difficult to study, but by the same token, if someone succeeds, he may have a genuine breakthrough in our understanding of temporally dependent activities.

In summary, we see that, just as in the case of psychology in general, a certain conception of science dominates the state of affairs of memory research. Because of the conception of science that is accepted, whether intentionally or not, certain metaphysical assumptions concerning reality are chosen over others. This choice, in turn, leads to certain kinds of studies that have more relevance to scientific ideology than to the phenomena as they are lived, and thus any of a number of hypotheses concerning the functioning of memory seem equally plausible. Moreover, since there is no certain way of choosing among alternative explanations except by hunch or bias, unity is lacking in psychology, and thus, however reluctantly, one is forced to conclude that psychology, as a science, is still in its preparadigmatic stage of development.

Obviously, one does not have to be a phenomenologist in order to understand this critique. As a matter of fact, a recent article on memory (Jenkins, 1974) shows how experimental psychologists are themselves transforming their inadequate conceptualizations and turning toward research prescriptions that may not appear as "scientific," yet seem to be demanded by the facts. Jenkins describes how, in order to comprehend memory better, he had to change the perspective from which he approaches memory. Essentially Jenkins moves from a more traditional associationistic perspective to a contextualist approach, and for him, "this position alters the way we interpret phenomena, emphasizes the importance of natural problems and realistic methodology, and changes what counts as an explanation" (p. 786). Jenkins makes an even more important point for our position when, in speaking of the associationistic position, he says, "*This view is so pervasive in American psychology that it is almost coextensive with being an experimentalist.* Indeed, I think many of us confuse the dicta of associationism with the grounds of empirical science itself. But associationism is only one view; it is not a necessary view" (p. 786, italics in original). Thus, both the nature of Jenkins's critique, in that he uncovers a deeply rooted bias apparently held by most researchers, and the direction of his corrective, a contextualist theory of memory, are in fact points that converge with the phenomenological critique of psychology. But phenomenology is not limited to critiques; it also has a positive program. In effect, phenomenology presents strong theoretical arguments for psychology to change its understanding of itself as a science, and if these changes are accepted, they could save many years of dubious effort. We shall try in the next section to characterize phenomenology, for I think we have demonstrated our major point of this section, namely, that the same problems present themselves at the level of concrete research as those which plague psychology as a whole.

PHENOMENOLOGY

In order to appreciate the vision of science that I am trying to communicate, some discussion of phenomenology is necessary. Phenomenology is a philosophical discipline that claims to be propaedeutic to all philosophizing and scientific praxis. Because of difficulties encountered with foundational philosophical problems, Husserl, its founder, decided that an objective and strict way of founding all knowledge would have to be discovered and he spent his own life in search of an apodictic starting point.

We as psychologists need not follow Husserl's path in all its ups and downs and interpretations and counterinterpretations, for they are essentially worked out within the context of a philosophical project. Certain key discoveries should be of interest to us, however, and I shall limit myself to the most salient points, in part to combat many misunderstandings concerning phenomenology and in part so that we can move on to the constructive alternative for psychological research.

First, phenomenology is the study of the phenomena of the world as experienced by man, and second, it is a method for studying such phenomena. When a phenomenologist uses the term *phenomenon*, he means that whatever is given in experience is to be understood simply as the correlate of awareness, of an act of consciousness. No other attribute is to be assigned to the given except the meanings that derive explicitly from what is presented in the concrete experience. Thus if I turn in my room and look at a chair, then within the special attitude called the phenomenological attitude I state that what is given to me is an object that presents itself with the meaning "a really existing chair." The fact that it may be a cardboard prop made to look like a chair does not cancel out the meaning of my experience—that it presents itself to me as a really existing chair. The phenomenologist is protected from such deceptions because he limits himself to how the given presents itself, and that does not change. Thus, to concentrate on the phenomenon, that is, on the given understood as the correlate of my act of awareness, always means to seek a clarification of the meaning of the given.

Perhaps an example from psychology would be helpful. Let us assume that I am looking at the Ames distortion room under precisely the right conditions for the illusion to take hold, and what I would see is a person who is apparently a midget at the rear of one side of the room and a person who is apparently a giant at the front end of the other side of the room. Within the phenomenological attitude, the experience would be described in the following way: "The given presents itself to me as a normal room with two persons of extreme sizes, one at the rear very small and the other up close and very big." And the statement is descriptive of the state of affairs. That is how the Ames distorted room looks under the right conditions. But now suppose the researcher walks you around the room, and places you in it so that other than merely visual modes of being present in the room are also obtained. How then could it be described? As follows: "The given presents itself to me as a distorted room with two normal persons who are standing in different places in the room." Within the phenomenological attitude, that statement is also descriptively accurate. And if I were to be put back in the right conditions so that the persons looked distorted, then the first description would hold again—even though I *knew* differently. That is the power of the phenomenological approach; one describes as precisely as one can the experience that is present to him and he brackets, or renders noninfluential, what he *knows* about it. Initially one only speaks about what he is aware of on the basis of what is given. A second step is involved when one compares what is known on the basis of a present experience with what is known from past situations. That is the meaning of phenomenon for phenomenology—namely, it is our presence to the world in an ongoing experience prior to drawing upon our knowledge of the phenomenon based on other sources.

The second valuable insight that can be gained from phenomenological philosophy is related to its understanding of consciousness. For phenomenology, consciousness is always consciousness of something that is not consciousness itself—and this is what is known as *intentionality*. Thus, consciousness is understood more as a "medium of access" (Gurwitsch, 1964) than as a container; it is understood as a *process* rather than as a substance.

To be aware is always to be aware of something that is not consciousness, since consciousness or awareness is simply the process or the medium of access by which we are present to something else. This is true regardless of the modality of consciousness, that is, whether something is presently perceived, or remembered, or imagined, or merely thought. It is equally true when something is hated, desired, lusted, or avoided. Thus, quite contrary to the notion of a passive receptacle, consciousness, for phenomenology, is a stream of activity that keeps bursting forth toward the world and needs, so to speak, objects in the world to help stop its centrifugal movement. Thus, consciousness cannot be understood without its being related to the world. It is for this reason that many problems posed by the more traditional philosophies that massed this relationship can be overcome. There is no longer a question of how consciousness, enclosed in itself, is related to something outside itself; it belongs to the very definition of consciousness to be related to that which is not itself, which is the world. Consequently we begin with relationships, not with two isolated substances whose relationship we have to establish.

Later phenomenologists have extended the notion of intentionality to behavior itself. Paraphrasing Husserl, behavior is always directed toward something that is not the behavior itself. That is why it is so difficult "to do" and "to be aware of the doing" at the same time, because the end toward which behavior and consciousness are directed is, in fact, transcendent to both of them. The implication of this discovery for psychology is tremendous, because whether psychology is defined as consciousness or behavior, all psychological phenomena are intentional, that is, intrinsically directed toward the world, and must be interpreted in that fashion. Ultimately this means that the concrete situation constituted by the intentional relationships between man and his world becomes the basic unit for psychological analysis.

Earlier, when we were discussing the nature of phenomena, we implied another important feature of phenomenology although we did not make it explicit, and that is the ideal of presuppositionless description. A phenomenological attitude requires that we bracket our knowledge about the phenomenon we are encountering in order to describe how it presents itself to us directly. The question then becomes to what extent an actual living person can be totally presuppositionless. Phenomenological philosophy tries to handle this problem by directing the describer to assume a transcendental attitude, that is, an attitude of consciousness as such and not the consciousness the describer has insofar as he is a living human subject. There is debate among phenomenological philosophers themselves as to whether or not this attitude culminates in a transcendental ego. In any event, I do not think that that step is the most fruitful one for psychology. I would agree that presuppositionless descriptions are not possible because, at the very least, one cannot totally eliminate historicity and sociality. Consequently, the first step in controlling descriptions is to make as clear as possible one's own presuppositions. Once a person's own presuppositions are clarified, the perspective from which he is making his descriptions is revealed as well as the horizonal context, and these serve as the limits within which the description holds.

Another important notion of phenomenology is that of the life-world, a term we have already utilized a number of times in this paper. The life-world, for phenomenologists, is the everyday world we all spontaneously live and experience in the course of normal living. This is the domain where obvious practical meanings are perceived and lived out by embodied persons doing mundane things with all their ambiguities, puzzlements, and obvious meanings! For phenomenology this is the primordial reality and all other attitudes that one assumes toward man or the world are derivative of this primary reality. Consequently, in the first place, no matter how derived an attitude one assumes, no matter how specialized a topic one pursues, the ultimate relevance is rooted in how the knowledge gained or the topic pursued relates back to the network of lived meanings as pursued in the life-world. Second, as Gurwitsch (1964) has shown, the dimensions that are vital in the life-world are precisely those from which we never can escape: temporality, the perceptual world, and our bodies. No matter how far our fantasies can carry us, no matter how abstract we become, we are never totally unaware of at least a segment of our stream of consciousness (temporality), our bodies, and the perceptual world. For these two reasons the reference back to the life-world becomes critical within a phenomenological approach.

The last characteristic of phenomenology that I will mention is its emphasis on meaning. Science is usually associated with facts, but phenomenology deals with meanings. However different these two are, they cannot be strictly divorced, because facts are important insofar as they are meaningful and meanings are derived with the help of facts. Phenomenologically based approaches therefore tend to keep alive the tension between meanings and facts rather than relying exclusively upon the determination of facts.

In summary, then, a phenomenologically based psychology would be interested, first, in describing in as presuppositionless a way as possible what appears within an attitude of open-ended presence to the phenomenon that is unfolding before one. An implication of this step is that one does not use language derived from explanatory systems or models in the initial description, but precisely everyday, naive language. Nor does one move toward explanation or reconstruction of the phenomenon in a second step; rather one tries to obtain a deeper understanding by interrogating the complete description. Second, one tries to clarify as much as possible, also through description, the presuppositions behind the perspective he assumes with respect to the phenomenon, as well as the context within which it appears to him. Third, one tries to capture the lived meaning of the phenomenon as revealed through the facts. Fourth, one acknowledges the initial dependence of one's attitudes on the life-world, and although all scientific attitudes are different from life-world attitudes, one develops the scientific attitude in a dialogue with the phenomena of the life-world, ultimately relating the specialized findings of science to these phenomena. Last, the intentional character of consciousness and behavior must be kept intact.

PHENOMENOLOGY AND SCIENCE

We can now summarize the main points that we made concerning phenomenology in the previous section. Phenomenology asks that we describe in as presuppositionless a way as possible the phenomena as they are presented to us in our experience in order to clarify the meaning of these phenomena. These phenomena spontaneously present themselves to us in the life-world, the same world from which science is derived. Furthermore, we have accepted phenomenology's description and understanding of consciousness and behavior as intentional, that is, as intrinsically directed toward the world. Now why should a philosophy with these characteristics be of help to psychology as a science? Precisely because these characteristics contain guidelines that will help us move toward a new understanding of science developed *in dialogue with the phenomena* rather than prior to them.

Certainly none of the characteristics mentioned can be seen as antithetical to science. To say that the scientific world view is derived from the life-world is not a negation of science but a grounding of it, and to try to emphasize meaning is not a denial of facts but a shift in emphasis that tries to go beyond sheer facts. To emphasize the intentionality of consciousness is not a bias but an affirmation of a relationship uncovered by description that promises to become the basis for resolving the age-old problems of subject-object, inner-outer, etc. Finally, the attempt to describe the appearance of phenomena in an unbiased way is not an obstacle to science but, on the contrary, the beginning of all good scientific methodology. Indeed, Binswanger once wrote that Husserl's phenomenology is "the most developed and the most pure form among methods of knowledge—which do not have as their purpose a knowledge of 'brute facts' or the elaboration of hypothetical theories, but rather—place above all else a 'respect for the phenomena'" (cited by Buytendijk, 1967, p. 355). The above comment points out a peculiar bias concerning current interpretations of scientific procedures. On the one hand, scientists limit themselves only to "facts" and refuse to speak to their horizons or contexts. On the other hand, scientists try to elaborate hypotheses and hypothetical systems or models which go beyond sheer facts. A phenomenologically based approach to science attempts both to *ascertain the facts and elaborate the horizons or contexts* within which the facts are obtained. Thus, the activities that a phenomenologically based approach to science would want a scientist to perform are not really so different—it's just that the positivistic bias in science interprets certain kinds of elaborations as hypothetical, whereas the phenomenological approach would call them descriptive of the horizons of the situation. A phenomenologically based science would not necessarily want to eliminate hypothesizing, but it would want to distinguish it from horizonal description.

It is generally agreed that the aim of science is production of knowledge (Radnitzky, 1970). Etymologically, science comes from the Latin *scientia*, meaning knowledge. But what distinguishes scientific knowledge from everyday knowledge is how it is obtained, and the formalization of the "how" is called method. An examination of the practice of scientific research shows that two things are generally necessary to guarantee a scientific procedure. In traditional parlance, one has to be objective, and some process of verification must take place. Because these terms are so closely tied up with praxis in the natural sciences, I would like to state the same aims in a slightly different way. Instead of objectivity, I would say that scientific knowledge calls for *rigor*, that is, making sure that the demands of the phenomenon as it appears in the situation is in harmony with the intentions of the researcher (whereas normal usage of objectivity in science usually implies stripping away the subjectivity of the researcher). And instead of verification, I would say that scientific knowledge calls for a *consistency of meaning that is transsituational*. Whereas verification implies that one must doubt the findings of a single piece of research until other studies "verify" them, in our approach, the meaning can be valid for a single study but not necessarily generalizable as formulated. In other words, we must be sure that the knowledge obtained has a minimum level of generality, but generality can be achieved by contexturalization and other means as well as by traditional verification procedures. Both of these suggestions derive from the primordial criterion without which no science can proceed, namely, that initially one must be faithful to the phenomenon as it appears. Because different types of phenomena appear differently, one cannot prescribe beforehand precisely what must be done to achieve rigor and consistency of meaning unless one is first sure that all types of phenomena can be comprehended by whatever specifications are made. If one has not checked for a particular possibility beforehand, then one ends up in an imperialistic attitude whereby one dictates to phenomena, telling them what they should be, rather than developing procedures in dialogue with the phenomena so that one can discover how they appear and what they mean. That is what has happened with traditional psychology; it has imitated natural scientific procedures and interpretations without first checking to see if the phenomena to which the procedures are being applied were of the same type as those which the natural sciences study. This is where either pragmatic or metaphysical assumptions are made by traditional psychology in order for its praxis to continue. Our own motive in expanding objectivity to rigor and verification to transsituational consistency of meaning was precisely to generalize the aim of the scientific procedure so as to incorporate as wide a range of phenomena types as possible.

Being faithful to the "phenomenon of man" demands this enlargement of scientific procedure, and it is this enlargement that has to be achieved all the way across scientific psychology in order to make room for human phenomena. It should be clear from this kind of correction that phenomenology is not antiscience; it is only trying to enlarge science sufficiently so that human phenomena can be studied in a way that is faithful to how they appear in our experience. This is simply an application of the general phenomenological procedure of first interrogating a fact or descriptive statement, that is, raising questions in order to awaken the general meaning contained in it, and then, from the viewpoint of the discovered meaning, seeing the particular fact or statement as simply one example of a range of facts or statements that can be comprehended by the same meaning. Thus, for example, if quantification serves as a procedure for making precise a description of a physical object, rigor in psychology would not demand automatically quantifying a psychological phenomenon, but first raising the question of what procedure one might use to describe a psychological phenomenon in a more precise and rigorous way. Once the question has been answered on its own merits, whether through the development of a new procedure or through the selection of a standard procedure, one can raise the further question of the relationship between the two "precision procedures" and obtain a deeper meaning of scientific precision. Consequently, science will be changed mildly or radically, depending upon the extent to which the procedures currently in existence have been developed in dialogue with a broad or narrow range of phenomena of a given type. But even radical changes do not change the fundamental *meaning* of science, which is to obtain knowledge concerning all phenomena experienceable by man; they only change how science might appear and how it is to be conducted. Since, however, the natural sciences developed without having to take into explicit account historicity, sociality, or internal viewpoints because their phenomena did not contain these dimensions, it seems as though the changes required by the human sciences at this stage of development are radical. And indeed they might be, although they are not outside the *intent of science*. Consequently, we shall now look at the phenomenon of science from this perspective. That is, we shall examine a phenomenologically based critique of scientific praxis as it is applied in psychology in order to see what kind of scientific praxis human psychological phenomena might demand.

MERLEAU-PONTY'S CRITIQUE OF
TRADITIONAL PSYCHOLOGY

In this discussion I will be presenting an analysis of the phenomenologically based critique of traditional psychology developed by
Merleau-Ponty. This analysis follows in outline from the work
of Antonio Muniz de Rezende (1974), a Brazilian philosopher currently teaching in Canada, whose doctoral dissertation dealt with
Merleau-Ponty's critique of scientific dogmatism in psychology. The
examples that fill out the outline were selected by me. It should be
noted that the term *dogmatic* in this context, simply means
uncritical. Actually, de Rezende goes a step beyond Merleau-Ponty,
because he shows more explicitly what Merleau-Ponty substituted
for the dogmatism he was criticizing. It is hard to say whether or not
Merleau-Ponty himself was fully aware of his own contributions.

I would first like to present all of de Rezende's main points in
schematic form and I will then elaborate these points as I discuss
them. De Rezende's argument is that Merleau-Ponty not only
criticized certain dogmatic attitudes in scientific psychology, but also
actualized concrete alternatives in his writings. De Rezende states
that Merleau-Ponty criticized (a) the scientific attitude in psychology
in the name of the term *phenomenon* and in the light of
phenomenological reduction; (b) the analysis of phenomena into
parts in the name of structure; (c) scientific realism—and then
substituted for it an interrogation of the sense of experience
from within a phenomenological attitude; (d) mechanical or causal
explanation in the name of existence; and (e) a positivism of laws,
which is then supplanted by dialectics. We shall now turn to a
discussion of these five factors.

The first point that de Rezende makes is that Merleau-Ponty
criticizes the scientific attitude in psychology in the name of the term
phenomenon and in the light of the phenomenological reduction.
What he means here is that instead of reality being known primarily in terms of scientific constructs, it should be known as a
phenomenon which is described in the attitude of the reduction.
Merleau-Ponty gives a clear example of this at the beginning of *The
Structure of Behavior* (1963). He is talking about how an ordinary
person would describe a spot of light that moves along a wall in a
darkroom. Understood from the viewpoint of the experiencer, the
experiencer's "behavior seems directed and gifted with an intention
and a meaning" (p. 7). The experiencer himself might say that the

light "has 'attracted' my attention and I have turned my eyes
'toward' it" (p. 7). Then Merleau-Ponty goes on to say the following:
"Science seems to demand that we reject these characteristics as
appearances under which a reality of another kind must be
discovered" (p. 7). In his analysis of this simple example, Merleau-
Ponty describes the transformations that take place in the name of
science (pp. 7–9). What was formerly called "a light on the wall"
becomes merely an appearance, a certain quality, and in order to
understand what was really there from now on we have to call it "a
portion of the visible spectrum." Instead of being stimulated by "a
moving light on the wall," the stimulus now is the vibratory
movement from the wall to the retina. The simple expression "seeing
the spot of light move along the wall" has to be decomposed into as
many partial processes as there are distinct anatomical elements in
the body as understood by science. Thus the vibratory movement
from the wall has to be followed through the lens system of the eye,
which is understood in terms of a mechanical model, and then to the
retina itself, which is understood anatomically in terms of rods and
cones, and then in terms of the behavior of the rods and cones
themselves, which is a chemical process, and then through the optic
chiasma and other nerve pathways, which are understood
electrically, and then to the occipital region of the cortex, whose
integrative process is understood as a gestalt; finally the cortical
synthesis somehow triggers a conscious state, which is understood
representationally, that is, the content of the consciousness of the
experiencer represents the real spot that was out on the wall. Now
why do these transformations have to take place? How can an
explanation move so facilely through mechanical, anatomical, chemical, electrical, perceptual, and epistemological contexts without
batting an eyelash? If a primitive person naively moved through five
separate contexts in order to explain a phenomenon of his world,
would we not simply smile condescendingly and be tolerantly
amused by his superstitions? Well, why not here? For one reason, we
do not experience them as superstitions, or dogmas, but as reality.
Secondly, because, in a way, I have not been totally accurate in a
descriptive sense; in the description I presented above I added
critical parenthetical remarks. Normally a person does not really
experience himself moving through five different contexts but only
one, that of science. Nevertheless, what I have pointed out is still
true—the full explanatory process does move across five separate
contexts, but the prestige of science is so great that these shifting

perspectives are not noticed. Thus, while science itself is a critical enterprise with respect to its content, it rests on doxic or dogmatic grounds to the extent that it fails to clarify its presuppositions or contexts. Now if we ask, Why do all these transformations have to take place? there is no clear-cut answer. Why can't a behavioral science begin with the sentence "I see a white dot moving along the wall" and proceed from there? Why must experience be explained in terms of the nervous system? Is this reduction simply a convention, an attitude, a habit that is uncritically accepted because it has been done before? On the other hand, to replace the scientific attitude with the phenomenological attitude, to replace scientific constructs with descriptions of phenomena, means not to prejudge them; it means rather that one is open to lived phenomena as they are experienced, and not as they are known within an abstract and specialized scientific attitude that may or may not be adequate. In this way, Merleau-Ponty opens up the possibility of a whole new approach.

Merleau-Ponty's second criticism of scientific psychology, according to de Rezende, appears as a critique of the analytical method in terms of a structural approach. The analytical method refers not only to the process of breaking down an integral experience into parts, but it also implies that the parts, once they have been so constituted, are treated as separate entities without contexts. Within a structural approach, in contrast, the parts that are constituted are perceived to follow the natural articulations of the phenomenon and thus they are understood as parts belonging to their given contexts. Furthermore, within a structural approach the parts have to be understood in terms of their already given relationships, however intermeshed, rather than posited as separate entities that begin their network of relations from a presupposed zero point. Thus, trying to understand, for example, the anger of an adolescent toward her parent because of a curfew, the anger of a revolutionary toward General Motors because of its latest profit statement, or the anger of a husband toward an unfaithful wife, in terms of a separate "anger-in-itself"—which is then related differently in three different situations—is to misunderstand the way anger is lived. Anger is always experienced as anger about something; thus, it cannot be separated from but belongs to the situation in which it is experienced. Or, turning to the example used earlier, following a spot of light moving against a dark wall cannot be comprehensively understood in terms of anonymous anatomical parts and physical stimuli alone—the intention of the experiencer has also to be considered. Again, however, if one asks why the analytical method is adhered to so rigidly in psychology, the answer is due more to factors of tradition than of critical choice. Psychology has been so intimately tied to the natural scientific attitude that a deviation from it is considered as a deviation from science itself. However, that is precisely the uncritical assumption that must be overcome if psychology is to develop its own directions.

The third dogmatic factor in traditional psychology that Merleau-Ponty criticizes is scientific realism, and he substitutes for it an analysis of the sense of the experience from the viewpoint of a modified transcendental attitude. Merleau-Ponty summarizes his points succinctly in the following passage:

> At the beginning of the century materialism made the "mental" a particular sector of the real world: . . . The counter mentalistic thesis posited consciousness as a productive cause or as a thing: first it was the realism of "states of consciousness" bound together by causal relations . . . ; then, in a more refined psychology, it was the realism of "mental energy" which substituted . . . a flowing reality for the disconnected mental facts. But consciousness remained the analogue of a force. [1963, pp. 3–4]

Thus, scientific realism means to take the world of physics as the primary model of reality and to designate as actually existing matter even those concepts or ideas that are constructed in order to render phenomena comprehensible. In offering an alternative to this scientific realism, Merleau-Ponty points out that even being able to assume the transcendental attitude means that consciousness is not to be viewed as a real datum but rather as that by means of which all real data can be known and discussed. From this perspective, the analyses that one performs are not realistic analyses, but rather analyses of the *sense* of the real. Thus, in the description of the "moving spot of light," Merleau-Ponty would analyze the total experience in terms of its meaning for the experiencing subject rather than in terms of the "causes" that are operating on the person, or of the conditions that must be fulfilled in order for a person to see a moving spot of light. This difference will be elaborated further in the next section dealing with causal analysis.

The fourth dogmatic characteristic that Merleau-Ponty criticizes is mechanical or causal explanation in the name of existence. Merleau-Ponty first demonstrates the pervasiveness of causal thinking and mechanical models in psychology, especially in the classical theory of the reflex and certain forms of behaviorism. He then shows how the very practice and findings of physiological research go beyond their own theoretical formulations. The major difficulty with causal explanation, however, is that it is not a sufficiently accurate description of the phenomena of life. Such descriptions always leave a residue or remainder that cannot be accounted for by concepts of the same type. For example, trying to account for the "prospective activity" involved in perceiving a moving light across a dark wall purely in terms of reflex theory would invoke so many added presuppositions and/or ad hoc hypotheses that the reconstruction totters and tumbles from the excess. One would have to presuppose at least the following: only linear causal relations; preestablished nerve pathways; "that the organism is passive and limits itself to executing what is prescribed for it" (Merleau-Ponty, 1963, p. 9); that motor reactions must be related to the stimuli only as ensembles of physical and chemical stimuli; and that the parts of the stimulus can only be related to each other and to the responding organism in an external way. Implicitly all these assumptions are involved in practicing a causal analysis. Merleau-Ponty, on the other hand, would rather speak of existential relations. A full explication of what Merleau-Ponty means by existence is hard to come by in a brief manner, but one way of indicating what he means is to say that existence means the totality of our behavioral and conscious relations to the world, to ourselves, and to others. Another way of expressing the same thing is to say that by *existence* Merleau-Ponty means to comprehend in an integrated way what traditional philosophy has included dichotomously and mutually exclusively under the terms *consciousness* and *nature*. In one of his more telling passages Merleau-Ponty writes, "Existence is the movement through which man is in the world and involves himself in a physical and social setting which then becomes his point of view on the world" (1964c, p. 72). Elsewhere he writes, "Existence in the modern sense refers to a certain modality of our relation to the world" (1964b, p. 62). The major emphasis is that an existential analysis, as opposed to a causal or mechanical analysis, is faithful to the phenomena of experience and is, in addition, more comprehensive and without remainder.

According to de Rezende, the last dogmatic factor in traditional psychology that Merleau-Ponty attacks is a positivism of laws which is supplanted by dialectics. Many times Merleau-Ponty (1963, p. 226) argues that causal or mechanical thinking will have to be supplanted by dialectical thinking because, as he sees it, experiencing creatures do not so much follow laws as *norms*, the difference being that experiencing creatures *contribute to the constitution of the norms they follow*. However, if one follows rules to which he has contributed, then the relationship is not linear but dialectical because it is an internally generated relationship that carries with it the possibility of further change and development in either the behavior or the norm itself. With a positivism of laws, however, no deviation or growth is possible; things must simply submit.

Thus, in essence, we have two contexts. The one, which I shall now call the natural scientific context, consists of the scientific attitude, the analytical method, scientific realism, mechanical or causal explanation, and a positivism of laws. The other, which I shall call the phenomenological context, consists of a description of phenomena as they are experienced, a structural approach, an effort after meaning within a modified transcendental attitude, existential analyses, and dialectical thinking. I have argued and demonstrated, I hope, that what Merleau-Ponty practiced was a critique of the former and an application of the latter. I have labeled the scientific context as a dogmatic one, but I have not made the same accusation of the phenomenological context. Why? What is the difference between them?

First of all, as we have been emphasizing throughout, the whole scientific attitude was carried over as a context from the natural sciences to interpret the phenomenon of man as studied by psychology without ever inquiring as to whether this was in fact the proper context in which to interpret man. The delineation of the phenomenological attitude, on the other hand, took place in direct contact with the phenomena of man's experience. It should be recalled that the phenomenological themes I presented were not explicit for Merleau-Ponty, but were drawn out by de Rezende. Merleau-Ponty was defining them as he practiced them; they were not part of an a priori list he drew up to be applied when relevant. In brief, almost all of the differences between the scientific and phenomenological attitudes with respect to the issue of dogmatism stem from the central fact that a critical attitude toward the application of a scientific context to the study of psychological man was never undertaken. Some concrete differences are as follows: for one thing, in studying the multiplicity of data that psychology produced, Merleau-Ponty was not interested in controlling man but in seeking his unity; he was looking for that meaning that rendered man's behavior intelligible. Behavioristic psychology, for example, is essentially looking for the features of the environment that control man, whereas a phenomenological psychology is trying to discover the meanings that he lives. As a further difference, the style of causal thinking in the natural scientific context is such that the attainment of knowledge is identical to possession of an inert and everlasting truth; for phenomenology, critical thinking leads to a renewal in man's knowledge (Rabil, 1967, p. 145). The classical formula for scientific thinking is: if A, then B. For dialectical thinking, every change in A is already reflected in B, and therefore the whole relationship has to be reexamined. For traditional thinking, the absence of an absolute is threatening; for the phenomenological attitude, the absence of the absolute in the traditional sense is openness to the truth. Causal thinking demands absolute evidence, otherwise how can we know things for certain? In phenomenological philosophy, certitude is discovered only within the context of interrogation. Traditional science wants to persuade its community and society in general of the validity of its doctrines; phenomenologically based social science wants to call the community into question, to awaken a critical attitude that will sensitize its members to their limits, their presuppositions, their blind side. Perhaps the whole difference in style can be summarized as follows: the traditional scientific attitude holds out *the* truth so that all men may submit to it; the phenomenological attitude presents a truth to be examined for its relevance to the examiner. Consequently, to the extent that a phenomenologically based psychology seeks renewal, openness, interrogation, and reexamination, and calls phenomena into question, it cannot be considered dogmatic.

While the description of the phenomenological context does not appear to be scientific, I submit that such an appearance is simply due to strong cultural prejudices that we have all been accepting for too long a time. The phenomenological context for practicing science still aims for rigorous knowledge that is meaningful and intersubjective. It is not the fault of the context in and of itself that certain phenomena of the world display themselves in such a way that the traditional scientific context is not applicable. Moreover, similar kinds of questions and suggestions are being raised wherever man is being studied, and that is why I feel it is time to invoke the notion of the "human sciences" as a larger frame of reference for the future development of psychology.

THE HUMAN SCIENCES

Since we have documented elsewhere (Giorgi, 1970) the history of
the effort to conceive of psychology as a human science rather than a
natural science, we do not have to repeat the details here. All of the
attempts implicitly or explicitly argue that the phenomenon of man
is not the same as the phenomenon of nature, and therefore it cannot
be presumed that the categories, concepts, methods, and procedures
of the natural sciences can automatically be applied to the phenomenon of man. Indeed, some thinkers (e.g., Sartre, 1962, p. 18)
have observed that the phenomenon of man and that of world must
be of the same type of being, although psychologists often forget
that the natural sciences have reduced the meaning of "world" to
that of an external, objective "nature" detached from man. As a
consequence, an uncritical acceptance of the natural science
framework by psychology carries with it an assumption concerning
content, namely, that the phenomenon of man is of the same type of
being as the external, objective nature of the natural sciences. It is
precisely this assumption that has been consistently rejected by
those who claim that psychology should be a human science. The
phenomenon of man is not the phenomenon of nature and we must
see how man presents himself in the world and study him
accordingly. For Husserl (1962a), the principle of all principles is
that in originary perceiving or in primordial intuition in the
philosophical sense, a phenomenon indicates not only what it is, but
also how it is to be approached. If we take advantage of this
principle, then a rigorous human science can be founded and
developed.

It is worth noting that the same crisis exists with the other
sciences of man. All the social sciences began with the assumption
that the natural sciences were true science and have gradually come
to realize that other ways of conceiving of science are not only
possible, but necessary. For example, Gouldner (1970) has spoken of
the coming crisis in sociology; Roszak (1969) has spoken of the
myth of objective consciousness; in economics we find Heilbroner
(1973, p. 32) writing, "It is understandable, then, that today's
economists, who are undergoing a kind of *crise de foi* in the light of
the myopia of neoclassical analysis, look wistfully in the direction of
a 'political economy'" because "the social universe is not a replica of
the natural universe"; and Lewis (1953) has written of the tension
between affinity to the natural sciences and affinity to the humanities

that exists in anthropology. More recently the case has been made that anthropology should be reinvented (Hymes, 1973) and even the biological sciences are looking for better contextualization (Selye, 1967).

What these books and critiques all have in common is a movement away from the natural scientific interpretation of science. It is also interesting to observe how the crisis in the sciences of man challenges different aspects of the natural scientific embodiment of science. Thus, some human sciences react against the atomism of natural sciences; others react against the attempt to quantify human phenomena; still others oppose a reductionistic bais, and even the so-called neutrality of science has been called into question (Habermas, 1971). It should be recalled, however, that the thesis of this paper is specifically that presuppositions such as atomism, quantification, etc., are only contingent to science, not essential to it. The fact that human sciences other than psychology criticize the same factors tends to support the thesis of this paper. Moreover, the fact that such critiques evoke such strong objections (e.g., Hebb, 1974) demonstrates how dogmatism has also crept into the human sciences.

The common crisis shared by the human sciences raises an important point. When psychology initially wanted to become independent, the natural sciences were already institutionalized and so psychology had only to conform to the preestablished insti-tutionalization. Now, however, when it is a question not of autonomy but of authentic paradigm, psychology finds only a void because the human sciences themselves have not been authentically institutionalized as a whole. They, too, have only declared their autonomy. Consequently, psychology, along with the other human sciences, has the double problem of clarifying its own self-understanding as a human science, and of clarifying a human scientific paradigm as such. From the viewpoint of pioneering concrete praxis, it is not an easy distinction to make.

However, it is not difficult to ascertain certain minimal char-acteristics that a human scientific paradigm ought to have. In order to appreciate these characteristics, science has to be understood as a human achievement. There was a time in the history of mankind when an institution called science did not exist and it came into existence as the consequence of the inventiveness of man. Since science is the result of human inventiveness, it can be changed, modified, or transformed by man, without a great catastrophe occurring. Only those who are forgetful of man's own role in the constitution of science can be shocked by such changes. For others, it should be clear that those institutions that are radically dependent on man share the fundamental dimensions of man such as historicity, sociality, and meaningfulness.

Thus, science is historical. This means, first, that it does not exist outside the normal human cultural history in which all human activity takes place and that, in addition, it has its own peculiar history inside the larger context of human history. Second, an examination of the history of science shows it to be both evolutionary and dialectical. This means that the theories and methods which we are currently using in science are not those which were always used, and in fact those in current usage are based upon historical examples. To claim that our current understanding of method or theory is the final one is to give an unjustifiable privilege to the present.

Science is also social. No matter how great a genius Galileo or Newton was, neither one worked strictly alone. Every thinker draws upon books, facts, researches, etc. that were the end results of others' activities and every scientist wants to communicate his knowledge to others.

But these two points are readily conceded. No one today would argue against them. However, the idea that a human science wants to make a third claim, a claim for meaningfulness, does at times meet resistance. For an authentic human science to function adequately, it must make use of the meaning that situations have for the behaving subjects. To most natural scientists this constitutes "subjective data" in the pejorative sense of the term, and thus they want no part of it. Besides, they see no necessity for it because the typical cause-effect relations that most traditional psychologists are interested in determining do not require the inclusion of the meaning of the situation for the subject.

Thus we have a curious paradox. Science, as an institution invented by man, is considered to be a historical, social, and meaningful enterprise; the individual scientist, both as a human being and as a scientist, is historical, social, and engaged in meaningful pursuits; but when man becomes the *subject* of scientific investigation, these dimensions are not considered worthy enough to be included. However, this is clearly a bias of the natural scientific interpretation of science, since its subject matter does not require the scientist to take into account the historicity, sociality, or meaningfulness of the subject matter; science was conceived after a mode of scientific praxis that ignored these dimensions. Natural scientific bias is also the reason that the initiative for behavior is seen to be on the side of the environment as understood by physics (as opposed to world), or on the side of the body as understood by anatomists or physiologists (as opposed to the body understood as a subjectivity); it is the reason for insisting upon comprehending man in terms of cause-effect relationships (as opposed to relationships of meaning). Thus a privileged position is always given to the end results of natural scientific research—and then the psychological is defined as that which is left over, or it is defined negatively, or ignored, or seen as a mere epiphenomenon. But it is not directly studied! Yet, an authentic psychology cannot emerge unless it centers specifically on the meaningful behavior initiated (not caused) by an embodied (not physiological) subject in the world (not physical environment or nature).

Hence, the institution of science partakes of the historical, the social, and the meaningful, but ironically, the subject of scientific psychological investigation is presumed to be a person who lacks these dimensions. It is no wonder that relevancy is a problem, because if this state of affaris were true, the scientist would be unable to understand himself. However, the above description pertains more to scientific ideology than to scientific practice, and we will return to this point shortly (see the following section). Right now we are merely interested in showing that the expression "human science" is not a contradiction in terms, even if the human sciences have yet to achieve the level of clarity that we find in the natural sciences. But then the human sciences are all younger. It is as if we were expecting the maturity of an Einstein's conceptions 100 years after Galileo. What the human sciences seek is knowledge about man in relation to his world and others in a rigorous and intersubjective way. Thus, their aim is to belong to the family of sciences. But since their subject matter is man, or humans, they want to indicate this fact by including the adjective *human*, just as the sciences of nature call themselves natural sciences. The motive for this inclusion is simply the desire to avoid premature metaphysical speculation that man and nature are one (man and world, as noted earlier, would be different), when in point of fact they spontaneously present themselves in such different ways in the world. Hence, there should be no theoretical obstacle to the project of psychology as a human science.

PSYCHOLOGY'S THEORETICAL CRISIS AND THE
HUMAN SCIENTIFIC CONCEPTUALIZATION
OF PSYCHOLOGY

While our analyses thus far have been important, they have also
been for the most part critical. But there is a positive program for a
phenomenologically based human scientific psychology. Critical
theoretical differentiation from traditional approaches had to come
first, then theoretical articulation of the alternative vision had to
follow before the concrete question of praxis could be taken up.
However, as we turn to this matter, it seems to me that there is
already sufficient evidence in support of the promise that an authentic
paradigm for psychology can be founded by a phenomenologically
based approach. It is impossible to detail here and now both the
achievements and problems surrounding the praxis of human
scientific psychology (for some examples, see Kracklauer, 1974;
McConville, 1974; Giorgi, 1975). However, in an effort to share this
hope with you, I shall speak to the way in which I see the questions
of the lack of unity, the lack of relevance, and the meaning of science
being resolved by a .phenomenologically based human scientific
psychology.

The Question of Unity

In a previous work (Giorgi, 1974) I argued that Merleau-Ponty's
thought can provide a theoretical unity to the somewhat scattered
viewpoints in psychology. Based upon key phenomenological
concepts such as intentionality, meaning, and structure, as they were
used in the works of Merleau-Ponty, I tried to show that three major
movements in psychology, namely, behaviorism, psychoanalysis,
and Gestalt psychology plus social psychology, could be synthesized
and unified. I do not mean this in the simplistic sense that all these
movements were really saying the same thing. Rather, I mean that if
one can discover concepts that are sufficiently descriptive and
comprehensive (which phenomenology can provide), if one
reawakens the implicit guiding intentions of the three movements
rather than limiting oneself to their explicit formulations, and if one
interprets them sympathetically, then one can see that the three
movements do have overlapping intentions and that the differentiating intentions are complementary and can be unified. The

only time serious difficulties arise is when certain phenomena studied in the past were defined with an extreme physical bias (e.g., perceptual theories relying on the constancy hypothesis), or were approached with an extreme physiological bias (e.g., the memory trace), or were studied in a highly fragmented or isolated way (e.g., reaction time). However, if each of the above types of phenomena were to be approached more behaviorally, or more experientially, or more contextually, then their inclusion in the overall metapsychological framework would be possible. Since my earlier formulation of this point is as succinct as it can be, I shall repeat it here.

Let us begin with Gestalt psychology. Firstly, Merleau-Ponty states that psychology's concern is the structure of behavior and, of course, many Gestalt experiments include behavioral components and thus the ties to behaviorism are not hard to see. However, Merleau-Ponty also wrote that Gestalts arise from polymorphism and Freud spoke of infants as "polymorphously perverse." In addition, Gestalts for Merleau-Ponty are the locale of spontaneity that arises from the body understood as a subject and of course, for Freud, the id was the unknown source of impulses, desires, and other forms of spontaneous urges. It may be that given the generally more restricted context of Gestalt investigations the only spontaneities that could emerge were the original perceptual configurations that are today identified with Gestalt psychology. Thus, Gestalt and psychoanalytic themes overlap. Lastly, social facts were best understood as structures and thus a tie-in with social psychology also occurs. Merleau-Ponty's interpretation of behaviorism affirms its intention to place man in contact with the social world and thus the relevance of social psychology is immediately evident. Secondly, he sees in behaviorism's initial project the attempt to comprehend behavior as a totality with an internal law which ties in with Gestalt psychology's project. Merleau-Ponty wants to understand behavior dialectically, which includes man's relationship to nature and biology which would then subsume the psychoanalytic project. Lastly, the dialectical approach to behavior would connote references to social and economic forces and bring in Marxist themes to the concrete analysis of behavior.

Next, if we look at his psychoanalytic comments, we see

references to Gestalt psychology because Merleau-Ponty saw as one of the tasks of psychoanalysis to comprehend the totality of the life experiences of the individual, which implies uncovering the structural context of meanings. Simultaneously, of course, Freud spoke about the "hidden meanings of behavior" and the necessity for understanding behavior as a kind of oneiric language. Moreover, Freud's interpersonal analyses were a social psychology of the family. Lastly, social psychology is concerned with the multiple interpretations of the structure of the behavior of individuals in relation to groups, or of the groups themselves. [Giorgi, 1974]

Thus, with a theoretical frame of reference that is sufficiently large, and with a dialectical interpretation of possibly conflicting concepts, a similarity among the major movements in psychology is perceptible.

A second way to demonstrate a resolution to the question of unity is to show that a phenomenologically based praxis converges with traditional psychological praxis and, furthermore, that the former would be able, in principle, to unify the latter theoretically because the phenomenological point of departure is more comprehensive. In order to demonstrate this I shall first have to describe briefly the human scientific paradigm in terms of its approach, method, and content, and then I will show the overlap with traditional viewpoints.

Within a phenomenological perspective, the content or subject matter of psychology consists in the contextualized and situated experiential-behavioral relationships of man with himself, the world, and others. Thus the basic unit of psychological analysis is the situation and one must always begin with the concrete behavior and experience of the person in a given situation, but these must not be understood merely physically. The future horizons (i.e., the intentions, anticipations, expectations, etc.) and the history (memories, habits, and past interpretations) of both behavior and experience *belong* to the concrete situation that forms the basic unit. Similarly, the network of lateral relations with significant others that influence specific behavior also belongs to the situation. Concreteness is defined by what spontaneously belongs to a situation according to the subject rather than what is merely perceptually present to the researcher. However the above statement may strike one, the state of affairs is even more complicated, for in attempting to cope with experiential-behavioral relations, one is dealing with the *relationship between relations*. From this viewpoint, experience means being present to the givens of a situation in relation to one's history and intentions; behaving refers to the ongoing functioning constantly taking place in relation to the same situation; and both already imply subject-world-other relations. A total comprehension would then imply the relation between these sets of relationships. Another term comprehending this network of relationships would be *human praxis*.

I want now to leap to the approach, for a method is the result of the exchange between the phenomenon as it appears and the attitude one adopts toward it. If we are concerned with the relationship between experience and behavior, how should we approach it? Since both the concepts of experience and behavior themselves offer difficulties, their relationships should be approached warily. Therefore the approach of the researcher should include initially the following two characteristics: (a) receptivity—one should first of all stand back and give the phenomenon time to emerge so that its intrinsic constituents can be discovered; and (b) fidelity—the phenomenon should then be described precisely as it presents itself to the researcher. The key criterion of "fidelity to the phenomenon as it appears" is critical to any science—especially in its founding phase; it is the one criterion most overlooked in psychology because we often begin by stating that we *know* certain things, but too often this knowledge is derived from extrapsychological sources.

Merleau-Ponty (1964a) has written that the only scientific method is to place in evidence the effective relationships that are lived. Usually one says that description is the method of the human sciences, whereas it is really only the point of departure. The real methodology begins only after open-ended description is completed, for then the researcher must reflect upon his descriptions, interrogate them, and come up with the key findings that will comprehend the situation of his subjects in a psychologically significant way. Reflection should not be confused with speculation; the former stays within the confines of the given, thoughtfully penetrates it, and comes up with a deeper understanding, whereas the latter takes off from the given and considers numerous possibilities. In this view, method in psychology is a movement from one type of language—naive everyday language—to another type which is psychological language—a second-order expression mediated by reflection (mathematics is only one type of second-order expression).

With that sketch of the human scientific paradigm as a

background, let me now try to show that traditional psychology considers as important the same dimensions referred to in the phenomenological analysis but either handles them differently or implicitly, or else takes them for granted.

In my discussion of approach I emphasized receptivity and fidelity to the phenomenon. Obviously receptivity is also present in traditional psychological praxis, since all psychologists are interested in being receptive to the behavior of the subjects they observe. Yet because of their philosophical outlook, traditional psychologists are receptive to a narrower and more constricted segment of behavior than the one specified above. Usually, therefore, the horizonal aspects of intention, anticipation, etc. are missing because strict empirical criteria are adhered to. Since, for example, the intentionality of behavior is not sensorily given as such, it is never spoken to, even though it could be understood when the very same behaviors are being observed. Paradoxically, neither are the "causes" of traditional psychologists merely perceived; they, too, are understood. It's a matter, therefore, of accepting a different set of presuppositions or meanings. Further, in perceptual or learning tasks the role of memories or habits is not usually sought in traditional psychological praxis unless it is the specific aim of the study to investigate the relationship between learning and memory. In the descriptive approach of a phenomenological analysis, however, the relevant factors include the dimensions revealed by the subjects' descriptions, even if any such factor was not defined a priori as an independent variable. Thus, if I am studying the ability of subjects to discriminate and recall present perceptual configurations, and one subject finds one configuration particularly easy because he has seen it before, the memory of the prior perception is not irrelevant. Trying to handle such incidents by random procedures is not necessarily the only, nor even the best, way. One could, for example, define independent variables after the experiment, based upon subjects' descriptions, and then group subjects accordingly.

Similarly, fidelity to a phenomenon is practiced by traditional psychologists, but fidelity to a certain conception *of science* is given priority over the phenomenon being investigated. In other words, the concepts, language, and techniques employed are first scrutinized to see whether or not they measure up to science; if so, they may be applied to the phenomenon under study. A lack of adequate correspondence between the concepts and the phenomenon usually results in a reduction of the latter. Thus, traditional psychology first gives allegiance to a certain conception of science, and one consequence is a prerestricted openness to human phenomena. In any event our point holds: both traditional and human scientific perspectives are following receptivity and fidelity, but differently.

In my description of content from a human scientific viewpoint, I emphasized the relation between experience and behavior. Experience, behavior, and their relationship have all been emphasized in psychology before. However, the horizonal temporalities (both past and future of behavior and experience) are given weight by traditional psychology in different ways. Most animal learning studies try to account for the history of the organism by *controlling* it along dimensions relevant for their experiments, such as food intake, water consumption, and exposure to environmental characteristics. Similarly, the future aspect is acknowledged implicitly by those developments in learning theory that stress the importance of the consequences of behavior for control of behavior. An ongoing behavior being guided by its potential consequences has to be future oriented. The difference between the paradigms, therefore, is that traditional psychology attempts to account for history by controlling it and for future consequences by knowing in advance a limited number of options that the organism has, whereas in our paradigm, access to past and future is mediated through the language of the subject, or significant others, in a more spontaneous way and with the burden of selectivity placed on the subject or the significant other. Again, the difference between the paradigms is not in the recognition of what is important—there is agreement—but rather in how the important matters are handled.

Finally, in the section on method I emphasized description and reflection. Both are taken seriously by traditional psychology, but again, implicitly or differently. If description is not an access to truth or intersubjective understanding, how is it that the description of apparatus and experimental setups in the procedure section of every publication do not fail to communicate? Hundreds of experiments have been replicated on the basis of description. However, most psychologists would probably agree that description is necessary, but not sufficient. The paths generally part at the next step, where most traditional psychologists look for an externalized operation as part of its method, while we recommend reflection. But this is only a bias, since no researcher actually avoids reflection in his praxis. How does the typical researcher decide upon his method? How does he ascertain what the independent and dependent variables are? How does he select his statistical techniques? By merely imitating others? Then how does he identify new variables? By remembering what he did in the past? Then how are new methods invented? No—the only intelligent way is for the researcher to ascertain what is available and to decide what it is that he wants to demonstrate and what aspects of the research situation will best demonstrate what he wants to prove. In other words, he must *reflect on* what is given and how it relates to what he wants to do. Thus an understanding of science that is truly comprehensive must begin with the practice of the scientist, and when it does, it includes what phenomenological analyses claim must be present.

Still, one might object, all of the above discussion relates to the *process* of research. Do psychologists also use reflection to produce *results* in a way at least similar to the one I outlined? Well, for example, how else could Piaget have come up with his stages of development, except by reflecting on the observations he made? Did he "see" sensory-motor behavior or a type of behavior that could be called sensory-motor with the special meaning he assigned to it? How did Freud discover repression? He did not "see" repression per se, but based upon certain descriptions of behavior in situations described by the client, he came to understand that a variety of behaviors expressed what he meant by repression. He arrived at the meaning of repression by reflecting upon certain givens. Again, how did Goldstein arrive at the distinction between concrete and abstract behavior? What he observed in each situation was behavior, but somehow qualitatively different. The categories were not a priori, since Goldstein had no idea that he would come up with such a distinction prior to his investigation. He discovered the distinction. But how? By reflecting upon characteristic differences between two types of behavior. That is, he came up with an idea that comprehensively and adequately subsumes under it a variety of seemingly diverse behavior. Reflection is an indispensable tool for all research and theorizing and it should be given its due.

Thus, the difference between a phenomenologically based human scientific psychological approach and the traditional psychological approach is that the former would like to go further and open itself up to more aspects of the phenomenon precisely because the phenomenon demands it and in the name of rigor. It does not want to vitiate totally what traditional psychology is doing; it only wants to realize traditional psychology's implicit intention more rigorously.

Consequently there is a convergence in praxis between the two perspectives that augurs well for an ultimate theoretical unity.

One last way of demonstrating the possibility of unity would be to show that what a human scientific approach values explicitly is valued implicitly by the traditional approach anyway. Of course this does not mean that the making explicit of what was formerly implicit requires no changes; quite the opposite. But our point is to show that implicitly shared values can lead to theoretical unity even if some changes are required.

We saw in the previous section that a brief way of characterizing the difference between the two approaches was to say that the human scientific approach wants to give full weight to historicity, sociality, and the meaning of the situation for the subject. We indicated then that in practice, if not in theory, traditional researchers value the same criteria. First, of course, all researchers value themselves as being historical social, and as dealing with situations that have meaning for them, and therefore they should not deprive their human subjects of their right to participate in the same dimensions. Second, these dimensions are valued so highly by traditional researchers that attempts are constantly made to *control* the presence of these dimensions in research. With respect to a subject's historicity, for example, a researcher always wants to know whether or not a subject has previously participated in the type of experiment he is conducting; nonsense syllables were invented so that past differences with words and letters would not be a contaminating factor; most animal researchers want laboratory-bred animals for research because their past experiences are more homogeneous and more knowable; Latin square designs were invented so that the sequence in which tasks were performed would not be a bias; all of these concerns relate, as I have indicated, to historicity. Similarly, a subject's relationships with others, that is, his sociality, are constantly monitored in research; subjects do not necessarily perform the same with others as they do alone, as the Asch (1952) experiments indicate. If indeed the psychological subject were not social, how could psychoanalysis be practiced, since it consists in uncovering the client's lived relations with others? Last, the meaning of the situation for the subject is always assumed, if not acknowledged, in traditional research if for no other reason than the fact that the experimenter wants to be sure that the subject is participating in the experiment correctly; that is one reason why instructions are necessary. In all testing situations it is assumed that the testee responds to test items according to how they appear to *him*, not the tester. We can even point to Tolman's famous expression that to understand what it is like for a rat to go through a maze, we have to understand the world of a rat! Or, in our terminology, we have to understand what the maze means to the rat.

Thus, historicity, sociality, and the meaning of the situation for the subject are valued in traditional research, or at least they are values *for* the scientist. The difficulty seems to be that these factors are seen as dimensions that have to be controlled, if not manipulated, by the researcher rather than dimensions that of necessity belong to the existing subject. Thus, they bear upon the research situation according to the researcher's intention rather than according to the way in which the subject might spontaneously choose to live these dimensions. However, can one truly control factors like historicity and sociality in this a priori way, since they are always already lived? Moreover, even if we were to control them in this fashion, can the phenomena we are researching remain the same as they were before our interference? We cannot discuss these issues fully here, but I will simply state that other ways of "controlling" or accounting for historicity, sociality, and the meaning of the situation for the subject are possible. Our only point here is that both positions acknowledge, in their own way, the values that are the explicit values of the human scientific approach to psychology. Shared awareness of this fact could lead to a convergence of research interests, which in turn would help foster the movement toward unity in psychology.

The Question of Relevance

Earlier in this paper we indicated that relevance had two separate meanings: one sense referred to the adequacy of the approach to problems and the other to the selection of topics for research. In this section I would like to demonstrate how human scientifically based research can meet the demands of both senses of relevance. Consequently, I would like to describe more concretely how explicit acknowledgment of human factors can transform the meaning of research as well as the meaning of science. In order to do this I shall draw heavily upon a dissertation conducted within a hermeneutical or interpretational perspective by one of my students, Charles Kracklauer.

Kracklauer's (1974) dissertation was primarily a study interested in investigating the meaning of the drug problem for contemporary society, but in the formulation of the problem he was also able to direct himself to certain theoretical issues that are important both for methodology and the question of relevance. The thrust of Kracklauer's theoretical points is that psychology is about to take over as a paradigm for social research certain assumptions that have already been used in a sociological context and that have failed to prove fruitful. The first assumption that Kracklauer questions is the assumption that social problems are readily identifiable. The difficulty with this assumption, as Kracklauer makes clear, is that the very people who are the experts, namely, the social psychologists and the sociologists, can only react to full-blown problems which already exist in society. They can only respond to problems and conflicts already created by factors outside of their control, and this ultimately forces the "helpers" to choose one segment of society over the other, since any recommendation for a solution would necessitate some kind of additional conflict between the segments. If academic social psychologists were more sensitive to the "social relevance" issue, that is, to relevance in terms of problem selection, they could respond to problems before they became full-blown and, conceivably, avoid the dilemma.

According to Kracklauer, the second questionable assumption guiding social research is one that posits the objective nature of social problems and is best expressed by Blumer (cited by Kracklauer, 1974, p. 8):

> Sociologists treat a social problem as if its being consisted of a series of *objective items,* such as rates of incidence, the kind of people involved in the problem, their number, their types, their social characteristics, and the relation of their condition to various selected societal factors. It is assumed that the reduction of a social problem into such objective elements catches the problem in its central character and constitutes its scientific analysis.

Precisely because the societal definition of the problem is accepted, Kracklauer notes, the social psychologist assumes that he already knows what the problem is, and this entails the assumption that the problem resides not in society but in individuals. Thus his task becomes one of discovering how the individuals themselves got that way. With respect to the problem of deviancy, for example, Kracklauer notes that the two current trends of interpretation of deviant behavior have different emphases—the positivistically oriented perspective of functional-structuralism, tending to focus primarily on the person identified as deviant, and the interactionist school, focusing on the exchange between the deviant person and the normal population.

The difficulty with the assumption as a whole is that it does not capture the problem as it is lived, and on the practical level, it does not work toward a total integration of society. For as Kracklauer (1974) observes, despite

> the difference between the statistical approach of structural positivism and the more situated task of the interactionist-labelling school, both orientations share an objectifying stance towards the phenomenon of deviancy. The first position reifies the subject, while the second frees the subject but reifies his role. . . . The result of objectifying either the deviant . . . or the process of becoming deviant . . . is the effective removal of the phenomenon in question from the sphere of social discourse and debate over the possible meaning of the behavior in question. . . . It becomes something for society either to get rid of as a menace or to preserve as a natural curiosity. In each case a segment of society has been effectively eliminated from the field of public discourse.

The third assumption underlying social problem research is that the knowledge obtained by social scientists can be used directly by society to solve its problems. The difficulties with this assumption, according to Kracklauer, are, first, that when true, the assumption becomes a self-fulfilling prophecy, and second, that some of its epistemological grounds do not hold. Furthermore, to assume uncritically that the end product of social psychological research is technically exploitable information also assumes implicity that men receive this information either neutrally or as things. This presuppositon of course flies in the face of the facts and is aptly summarized by Seeley in terms of two theorems: the inexhaustibility theorem and the freedom theorem (cited by Kracklauer, 1974). Both theorems deal with the relationship between man the researched and man the researcher, and both have to do with the illusion of being able to set up a simple one-to-one relationship within the context of the human sciences. The first theorem states, in Seeley's words, "The subject matter of something cannot be exhausted if the first description both alters and in many cases, increases the subject matter to be described" (cited by Kracklauer, 1974), and the second one states, again in Seeley's words, "If a theory regarding human behavior enters into human behavior as a 'new factor' then there is no sense in which the behavior can be said to be determined in any definite sense" (cited by Kracklauer, 1974). Kracklauer then extends this notion regarding theorems of self-interpretation by including what he calls the enslavement theorem, that is, a person can view himself in the light of the generalities that are publicized about him and then begin to behave in that way. Kracklauer concludes his critique of the current status of social problem research in the following manner:

> What both the freedom and enslavement theorem refer to is what I will call . . . the *hermeneutical character of man*. By hermeneutical I mean interpretational, and by saying that man has this character I mean that *man is the being who is and becomes the way he interprets himself and his world*. A truly human program of social problem research would have as its goal, not the production of technical information about man, but *the maximization of man's awareness of his own hermeneutical character*. It is only through increasing man's awareness of this dimension of himself, within the context of his actual historical and social situation, that he can become and remain autonomous and individual. [Kracklauer, 1974]

In a manner parallel to his critique of the traditional approach, Kracklauer goes on to suggest three alternative assumptions regarding social problem research that are formulated from within the hermeneutical approach. I can only begin to sketch the alternatives here because a full treatment would be too lengthy. Kracklauer suggests, first, that the responsible psychologist must deal with all social problems, whether recognized or unrecognized by society, and only by such an approach can research lead to an understanding of the phenomenon of the social problem as such—that is, why certain social problems become thematic and others do not. The second alternative that Kracklauer proposes is that "social problems [are] socially constructed phenomena which point to and arise from breakdowns in communication." His third assumption is that a hermeneutically based psychology would be interested in the "production of knowledge with emancipatory relevance [in order] to promote the autonomy of the individual and the solidarity of the [entire] community" (Kracklauer, 1974) rather than the production of technically exploitable information. Kracklauer then proceeds to study the drug problem according to the latter three assumptions, interviewing all relevant personnel and describing their participation in the phenomenon.

The above set of assumptions demonstrates that another way of conceiving psychological research is possible, and it is a way in which the relevance of the research and our understanding of science are more compatible. In Kracklauer's study, relevance in the sense of problem selection is clearly not in question because the drug problem was a recognized social problem. At the same time, the demands of relevance in the sense of approach to problems are met because the drug problem was conceived as a social problem involving many perspectives that called for clarification and was approached precisely with assumptions consistent with that conception so that it penetrated the phenomenon in an adequate way. This should not be surprising, since the intention was to meet the relevancy requirements without sacrificing scientific rigor. What remains to be explored is the conception of science that enables us to do this with meaningful, historical, social—in brief, human—phenomena.

A Human Scientific Self-Understanding of Psychology

Human scientific psychology is still in the process of defining itself and articulating its mode of praxis. In effect it is the synthesis of a number of traditions and influences whose only common source is that they have tried to cope with problems of man in the world. Thus, some influences came from philosophy, from the history of philosophy and sciences, and from reflection upon how a number of social sciences themselves have functioned. While I cannot detail all of the influences, I would at least like to indicate how some of these forces are converging to form an extended notion of science.

The first major influence to be considered is phenomenological philosophy. We have already discussed phenomenology extensively in this paper and the only point I wish to make here is that a phenomenologically grounded philosophy of science interprets and understands the practice of both natural and human sciences in ways very different from positivistic and empirical philosophies. Its ontological presuppositions concerning man are different and therefore its criteria for rigor also differ. The presupposition that really matters maintains that fidelity to the way any phenomenon appears must be the beginning of all science. That is why a human scientific psychology must begin descriptively and try systematically to deepen the original description in a rigorous way. It seems that a clarification of the procedures whereby one does this is perhaps the major stumbling block to greater acceptance; and while it is true that a complete systematic exposition of the theory and practice of human scientific psychology is still lacking, its internal logic, in my opinion, is convincing and the early attempts that have been made to apply this framework demonstrate, in principle, its feasibility (e.g., Colaizzi, 1967; Stevick, 1971).

In addition to the influence of phenomenology, the repeated crises in science have occasioned reflections from so many perspectives that a whole new discipline—metascience—has been created in order to clarify just how science is practiced and understood. It differs from the philosophy of science in that it is concerned not with merely the foundations of science and the principles of "good science" but also with understanding the actual way in which science is practiced and, still further, with describing the tension between ideals and practical decisions. One of the major works in this field is that of Radnitzky (1970). His study of science showed that there are at least two styles of scientific praxis, logical-empirical and hermeneutic-dialectic. While the distinction does not hold absolutely, in general the hermeneutic-dialectic context is used with human sciences and the logical-empirical one with sciences of nature. However, that is only a general trend and the reverse is not hard to find. The reason for citing this distinction here, though, is to show that the hermeneutic-dialectic context not only converges with a phenomenologically based conception of science but is, at the same time, fundamentally in harmony with the ideals of science necessary for a human scientific conception of psychology.

While Radnitzky combines the hermeneutic-dialectic tradition into a single movement, and I think it is legitimate to do so, it has actually come out of two different traditions. According to Radnitzky (1970, II, p. 20), the term *hermeneutics*, which is the name for the science of interpretation, was coined in the seventeenth century and referred to the procedures used in interpreting texts. The basic question of the hermeneutic approach is: "What meaning, i.e. meaning *significant for us today*, does this text (situation, behavior) have?" (p. 20, italics in original). Radnitzky (p. 21) then adds the following concerning hermeneutics (all italics in original):

> *Its key notions are thus meaning, language and history.* . . .
> The *early* hermeneutics was based upon the distinction be-
> tween objectivations of the human cultural activity, which can
> be understood "from the inside" . . . and natural phenomena,
> which are only explainable. This distinction was replaced by
> the distinction between such *entities with which the inquirer*
> can establish communication and *may* at *least in principle*
> *enter into a dialogue* and those with which this is not possible.
> . . . With respect to human beings the inquirer may, *at least*
> *in principle, obtain,* besides information about their objective
> situation, *also a shared experience* to which the objects of his
> study have contributed as communication partners. With respect
> to non-human entities his experience is channelized by his
> theories: guided by his prenotions, he describes them in such
> a way that certain types of explanation become possible. In
> the case of human phenomena *one of the main control*
> *mechanisms is the "answer" which the texts themselves*
> *provide.*

Of course, where human subjects are used instead of texts, the
answers of the subjects introduce a controlling factor.

The hermeneutic tradition also implies that there is a certain
precomprehension of the phenomenon being investigated, and the
process of research itself clarifies both the method and the
comprehension of the phenomenon. Thus, from a postresearch
comprehension perspective, the precomprehension of the phenomenon is transcended, and one understands more completely
the how and why of a phenomenon.

The dialectic approach, on the other hand, grew out of a
developmental perspective, especially with the development of social
ensembles (Radnitzky, 1970, II, p. 60). To apply the notion to human
sciences in general means that a dialectical model of knowledge is
being subscribed to whereby totalizations from various perspectives
occur, come into conflict, and then have to be retotalized. But it also
implies that psychological phenomena develop dialectically, or
change in a dialectical fashion over time and therefore call for a
dialectical style of thinking.

The combination of hermeneutic and dialectical traditions thus
provides a style of thinking, a frame of reference for interpreting the
meaning of phenomena, and a theory of knowledge that both meet
the requirements of science in general and are at the same time

compatible with the way human phenomena are lived in the everyday world. Moreover, it satisfies the double meaning of relevance because it approaches human phenomena according to the way they are experienced and it allies itself with the critical-emancipatory aims of social theory which want to make the world a better place for humans to live. Radnitzky (1970, II, p. 22) explains the latter point as follows: "[The hermeneutic-dialectic tradition] suggests that texts, etc. (behaviors, meanings) will be judged *important* to the degree in which they are *relevant* for the practice of life, on the ground that the heart of the human sciences is *co-understanding and possibly also consent about the possibilities and norms of being-in-the-world*." We saw earlier that psychology implicitly shares this aim of making the world a better place for man to live in.

In brief, I have suggested that human scientific psychology is still in the process of understanding and defining itself and that a number of different influences and traditions are contributing to this process. In particular, I have tried to show that the hermeneutic-dialectic tradition converges with a phenomenologically based conception of science and, furthermore, that both are compatible with the ideals of science essential to any human scientific conception of science.

SUMMARY

Thus we see that the three theoretical problems chosen as examples of psychology's crisis status—lack of unity, lack of relevance, and a deficiency in its understanding of science—can be overcome, but only by changing our style of thinking. We have argued throughout this paper that the major stumbling block to a resolution of these problems is a narrow conception of science, a conception toward which psychologists have responded, as a rule, in two disparate ways. One group has accepted the existing natural scientific conception of science uncritically and rigidly tried to impose its methodological criteria on psychological man. The other group has been sensitive to the shortcomings of natural scientific methodology with respect to man's experience and behavior, but since science meant precisely those methodological claims, they turned against science itself and tried to conceive of psychology in opposition to science.

Our own approach has been to extend the notion of science by showing that science always implies fidelity to the phenomenon under study and in no way would want to distort phenomena for the sake of ideology. Thus, our approach is, first, to discover how the phenomenon of man appears in the world, and then to try to determine ways of studying him that will yield systematic, rigorous, and intersubjective psychological knowledge, which is, of course, what science has always sought. Once it becomes clear that the notion of science can be broadened, and that the notions of verification and objectivity can be defined and practiced in ways other than those defined and practiced by the natural sciences, then the remaining theoretical problems can also be handled because they are, for the most part, a consequence of the narrow conception of science that psychology initially adopted. Thus phenomenological prescriptions concerning the "phenomenon of man" have been able to lead us to an understanding of science on the part of psychology that, in principle at least, can not only help us found psychology adequately, but also make it relevant to our world. Undoubtedly, experience in applying this program will introduce changes and modifications, but we feel that the fundamental paradigmatic insights are sound, and psychology may be able to begin its second century freed from foundational concerns and its "crisis" atmosphere.

REFERENCES

Adams, J. *Human memory.* New York: McGraw-Hill, 1967.
Allport, G. The historical background of modern social psychology. In G. Lindzey & E. Aronson (Eds.), *The handbook of social psychology,* Vol. 1. (2nd ed.) Reading, Mass.: Addison-Wesley, 1968. Pp. 1–80.
Asch, S. E. *Social psychology.* Englewood Cliffs, N.J.: Prentice-Hall, 1952.
Baron, J. Is experimental psychology relevant? *American Psychologist,* 1971, **26**, 713–716.
Bartlett, F. C. *Remembering.* Cambridge: Cambridge University Press, 1932.
Boneau, C. A. Paradigm regained? Cognitive behaviorism restated. *American Psychologist,* 1974, **29**, 297–309.
Brentano, F. *Psychology from an empirical standpoint.* 1874 (German edition). New York: Humanities Press, 1973.
Brown, P. *Toward a Marxist psychology.* New York: Harper & Row, 1974.

Buytendijk, F. J. J. Husserl's phenomenology and its significance for contemporary psychology. In N. Lawrence & D. O'Connor (Eds.), *Readings in existential phenomenology*. Englewood Cliffs, N.J.: Prentice-Hall, 1967. Pp. 352–364.

Catania, A. C. The psychologies of structure, function and development. *American Psychologist*, 1973, **28**, 434–443.

Coffield, K. E. Research methodology: A possible reconciliation. *American Psychologist*, 1970, **25**, 511–516.

Colaizzi, P. Analysis of the learner's perception of learning material at various phases of a learning process. *Review of Existential Psychology and Psychiatry*, 1967, **7**, 95–105.

de Rezende, A. M. *Le Structuralisme de Merleau-Ponty*. Unpublished doctoral dissertation, University of Louvain, Belgium, 1974.

Ebbinghaus, H. *Memory*. 1885. Trans. by H. A. Ruger & C. E. Bussenius. New York: Dover Publications, 1964.

Feigenbaum, E. A. An information-processing theory of memory. In D. Kimble (Ed.), *Readiness to remember*. Proceedings of the third Conference on Learning, Remembering, and Forgetting. New York: Gordon & Breach Science Pub., 1969. Pp. 113–210.

Giorgi, A. *Psychology as a human science*. New York: Harper & Row, 1970.

Giorgi, A. The meta-psychology of Merleau-Ponty as a possible basis for unity in psychology. *Journal of Phenomenological Psychology*, 1974, **5**, 53–74.

Giorgi, A. An application of the phenomenological method in psychology. In A. Giorgi, C. T. Fischer, & E. Murray, (Eds.), *Duquesne studies in phenomenological psychology*, Vol. 2. Pittsburgh: Duquesne University Press, 1975. Pp. 82–103.

Gouldner, A. W. *The coming crisis of western sociology*. New York: Basic Books, 1970.

Gurowitz, E. M. *The molecular basis of memory*. Englewood Cliffs, N.J.: Prentice-Hall, 1969.

Gurwitsch, A. *The field of consciousness*. Pittsburgh: Duquesne University Press, 1964.

Habermas, J. *Knowledge and human interests*. 1968 (German edition). Trans. by J. J. Shapiro. Boston: Beacon Press, 1971.

Hebb, D. O. *The organization of behavior*. New York: Wiley, 1949.

Hebb, D. O. *A textbook of psychology*. Philadelphia: W. B. Saunders, 1966.

Hebb, D. O. What psychology is about. *American Psychologist*, 1974, **29**, 71–79.

Heilbroner, R. L. Balancing the world's accounts. *New York Review of Books*, 1973, **20**(19), 31–34.

Hilgard, E. Introduction to Dover edition of *Memory*, by H. Ebbinghaus. New York: Dover Publications, 1964. Pp. vii–x.

Husserl, E. *Ideas.* Trans. by W. R. Boyce Gibson. New York: Collier Books, 1962. (a)

Husserl, E. *Phänomenologische Psychologie.* In W. Biemel (Ed.), *Husserliana*, Vol. 9. The Hague: Martinus Nijhoff, 1962. (b)

Hymes, D. (Ed.) *Re-inventing anthropology.* New York: Pantheon, 1973.

Jenkins, J. J. Remember that old theory of memory? Well, forget it! *American Psychologist*, 1974, **29**, 785–795.

Koch, S. Epilogue: Some trends of study I. In S. Koch (Ed.), *Psychology: A study of a science*, Vol. 3. New York: McGraw-Hill, 1959. Pp. 729–788.

Koch, S. Psychology cannot be a coherent science. *Psychology Today*, 1969, **3**, 14.

Koch, S. Psychology as an integral discipline: The history of an illusion. Paper presented to Divisions of Philosophical Psychology and the History of Psychology, as a contribution to their symposium, A paradigm for psychology: Perspectives and integrative proposals, at the meeting of the American Psychological Association, New Orleans, August 1974.

Kracklauer, C. The drug problem: A hermeneutical social psychological investigation. Unpublished doctoral dissertation, Duquesne University, Pittsburgh, 1974.

Kuhn, T. S. *The structure of scientific revolution.* (2nd ed.) Chicago: University of Chicago Press, 1970.

Kvale, S. The temporality of memory. *Journal of Phenomenological Psychology*, 1974, **5**, 7–31.

Kvale, S. The temporal and social constitution of the past: Working notes on a sociality of memory. Unpublished paper, University of Oslo, n.d.

Lashley, K. S. In search of the engram. *Symposium of the Society for Experimental Biology*, 1950, **4**, 454–482.

Levine, M. Scientific method and the adversary model: Some preliminary thoughts. *American Psychologist*, 1974, **29**, 661–677.

Lewis, O. Controls and experiments in field work. In A. L. Kroeber (Ed.), *Anthropology today.* Chicago: University of Chicago Press, 1953. Pp. 452–475.

Lipsey, M. W. Research and relevance: A survey of graduate students and faculty in psychology. *American Psychologist*, 1974, **29**, 541–553.

Logan, F. A. Experimental psychology of animal learning and now. *American Psychology*, 1972, **27**, 1055–1062.

May, R. *Psychology and the human dilemma.* Princeton, N.J.: Van Nostrand, 1967.

McConville, M. Perception in the horizontal dimension of space: An empirical exploration of perceptual experience. Unpublished doctoral dissertation, Duquesne University, Pittsburgh, 1974.

Menges, R. J., & Trumpeter, P. W. Toward an empirical definition of relevance in undergraduate instruction. *American Psychologist*, 1972, **27**, 213–217.

Merleau-Ponty, M. *The structure of behavior*. Trans. by Alden L. Fisher. Boston: Beacon Press, 1963.

Merleau-Ponty, M. Maurice Merleau-Ponty a la Sorbonne. *Bulletin de Psychologie*, 1964, 18 109–336. (a)

Merleau-Ponty, M. *The primacy of perception*. Ed. by J. M. Edie. Evanston, Ill.: Northwestern University Press, 1964. (b)

Merleau-Ponty, M. *Sense and non-sense*. Trans. by H. Dreyfus & P. A. Dreyfus. Evanston, Ill.: Northwestern University Press, 1964. (c)

Meyer, H. H. The future for industrial and organizational psychology: Oblivion or millenium? *American Psychologist*, 1972, **27**, 608–614.

Mitchell, C. C. On the diversification of graduate study in psychology. *American Psychologist*, 1974, **29**, 272.

Murdock, B. B. *Human memory: Theory and data*. Potomac, Md.: Lawrence Erlbaum Associates, 1974.

Norman, D. (Ed.) *Models of human memory*. New York: Academic Press, 1970.

Proshansky, H. M. For what are we training our graduate students? *American Psychologist*, 1972, **27**, 205–212.

Rabil, A., Jr. *Merleau-Ponty: Existentialist of the social world*. New York: Columbia University Press, 1967.

Radnitzky, G. *Contemporary schools of metascience*. 2 vols. in 1. Goteborg, Sweden: Scandinavian University Books, 1970.

Rancurello, A. *A Study of Franz Brentano*. New York: Academic Press, 1968.

Raush, H. L. Research, practice and accountability. *American Psychologist*, 1974, **29**, 678–681.

Rogers, C. Some new challenges. *American Psychologist*, 1973, **28**, 379–387.

Roszak, T. *The making of a counter culture*. Garden City, N.Y.: Doubleday & Co., 1969.

Samelson, F. History, origin, myth, and ideology: The "discovery" of social psychology by August Comte. *Journal for the Theory of Social Behaviour*, 1974, **4**, 217–231.

Sartre, J. P. *Sketch for a theory of the emotions*. London: Methuen & Co., 1962.

Schneider, S. F. Reply to Albee's "The uncertain future of clinical psychology." *American Psychologist*, 1971, **26**, 1058–1070.

Selye, H. *In vivo*. New York: Liveright, 1967.

Sexton, V. S., & Misiak, H. *Historical perspectives in psychology: Readings*. Belmont, Calif.: Brooks/Cole, 1971.

Sherif, M. On the relevance of social psychology. *American Psychologist*, 1970, **25**, 144–156.

Shotter, J., & Gauld, A. The defense of empirical psychology. *American Psychologist*, 1971, **26**, 460–466.

Silverman, I. Crisis in social psychology: The relevance of relevance. *American Psychologist*, 1971, **26**, 583–584.

Simkins, L. D. *The basis of psychology as a behavioral science.* Waltham, Mass.: Blaisdell, 1969.

Stevick, E. An empirical investigation of the experience of anger. In A. Giorgi, W. Fischer, & R. von Eckartsberg (Eds.), *Duquesne studies in phenomenological psychology*, Vol. 1. Pittsburgh: Duquesne University Press, 1971. Pp. 132–148.

Straus, E. Memory traces. In E. Straus (Ed.), *Phenomenological psychology.* New York: Basic Books, 1966. Pp. 75–100.

Talland, G. *Deranged memory: A psychonomic study of the amnesic syndrome.* New York: Academic Press, 1965.

Tyler, F. B. Shaping of the science. *American Psychologist*, 1970, **25**, 219–225.

van den Berg, J. H. *A different existence.* Pittsburgh: Duquesne University Press, 1972.

von Eckartsberg, R. An approach to experiential social psychology. In A. Giorgi, W. Fischer, & R. von Eckartsberg (Eds.), *Duquesne studies in phenomenological psychology*, Vol. 1. Pittsburgh: Duquesne University Press, 1971. Pp. 325–372.

von Wright, J. M. *Forgetting and interference.* Helsinki: Academic Publishers, 1959.

Wittgenstein, L. *Philosophical investigations.* Trans. by G. E. M. Anscombe. (3rd ed.) New York: Macmillan, 1958.

Wolman, B. B. Does psychology need its own philosophy of science? *American Psychologist*, 1971, **26**, 877–886.

From Traits and Equilibrium toward Developmental Dialectics

Klaus F. Riegel[1]
University of British Columbia

*I*n moving beyond the concepts of stable traits and patterns of equilibrium toward developmental dialectics, this paper will try to show that a comprehensive view of the human being can be realized only when we conceive of changing individuals as they develop in a changing social-historical world. In elaborating this dialectic conception of change and development, I will emphasize the dynamic interdependence, that is, the mutual interactions between the changes in the individuals and the changes in their social-historical world.

The following presentation consists of four parts. The first two are critical, the last two attempt to be constructive. In Part 1 I will argue for the rejection of a deeply rooted conceptual bias, that is, the preference for stable psychological entities, such as traits, abilities, and competencies. The case of intelligence and intelligence testing serves to illustrate my argument, but similar reasoning also applies to the concept of underlying psychological forces, such as drives and motivations. Instead of asking for or proclaiming abstract universal entities, we should give primary attention to concrete events interacting in temporal sequence.

In Part 2 I will argue for the rejection of another deeply rooted conceptual bias in our thinking, the preference for equilibrium and stability. In criticizing Piaget's theory of cognitive development, I will contend that the concepts of conflicts and contradictions ought to receive at least as much attention as the stabilizing concepts of

1. This paper is a result of many exchanges with friends and former students, especially during meetings in Ann Arbor, Morgantown, Rochester, and Toronto. I wish to express my friendship and gratitude to Ann Boedecker, John Broughton, Nancy Datan, Roy Freedle, Adrienne Harris, Lynn Liben, Jack Meacham, Leon Rappoport, Carol Ryff, Bob Wozniak, and Lynne Zerin. Special thanks belong to Bill and Mary Arnold and Ruth Riegel for extensive editorial help and support.

solutions and agreements. Instead of directing all our attention toward the question of how problems are solved and answers are given, at least equal emphasis should be devoted to the issue of how problems are created and questions are raised.

If we expand the search for answers to include a search for the original questions, we transform Piaget's interpretations of the growing child's intellectual operations into an analysis of cognitive development in its social and historical context. The minimal condition for such an analysis includes two individuals—for example, a mother and her child—both of which operate interactively and, thereby, grow and develop together. In Part 3 I will describe some conditions of such interactions as revealed most clearly in language dialogues.

Language dialogues, however, depict only short-term temporal patterns of interactions. In Part 4, on the dialectic of changes, I will suggest that such an analysis needs to be extended into interpretations of long-term changes in both the individual and society. In contrast to the short-term situational analysis of dialogues, such a dialectic interpretation is concerned with progressions of events along several interacting dimensions. The four dimensions discussed in this paper are referred to as the *inner-biological*, the *individual-psychological*, the *cultural-sociological*, and the *outer-physical*. To be more specific, a dialectic interpretation of development is based on the recognition that the interactions among these progressions of events are not always coordinated or synchronized. Whenever these interactions are out of step or contradictory, a conflict or crisis is said to exist. In a dialectic conception it is the discordance and tension of these contradictory interactions that become the source of new development, more specifically, of leaps in development. Through the development of coordinating and integrative actions and thoughts, synchrony will be reestablished and, thereby, progress achieved. Yet even as synchrony is attained, new discrepancies emerge and, in so doing, produce a continuous flux of contradictions and developmental change. Finally, in Part 4 I will discuss the significance of dialectic thinking for psychological research and theory.

THE ABSTRACTNESS OF ABILITIES
AND MOTIVATIONS

Psychology, like any other science, has been influenced by basic conceptions which originated in Greek philosophy. Several contrastive distinctions are important for our present discussion: the emphasis on stable entities or ceaseless changes, on general substances or analytical elements, on ideal conditions or observable states, and on universal forms or underlying forces. Needless to say, one can not exist without the other, but traditionally, preference has been given in psychology to an analytical elementalism searching for stable if not ideal entities (Riegel, 1973a).

Historical Overview

An early inquiry into stable entities is known as *Vermögenspsychologie*, or faculty psychology (Reid, 1764; Stewart, 1793; Tetens, 1777; Wolff, 1734). On the basis of common observations and introspections, a number of entities were proposed, such as passion, prudishness, courage, and intelligence, and the occurrence of observable behaviors of these types was explained by the capacity or—in modern terms—competence for such behavior. Although brought into disrepute many times, this original conception did not differ decisively from the seemingly more advanced forms of inquiry during the second half of the nineteenth century.

Because of its methodological rigor and its firm adherence to natural science conceptions, the well-known scientific psychology of this period appeared to be superior to earlier attempts. But just as before, the search was directed toward the "detection" of universal, stable entities, now, however, conceived of as indivisible mental elements (sensations, images, and simple feelings, in the formulation of Wundt, 1873–74, 1896) rather than as global potentialities of the organism and faculties of the mind.

In particular, Wundt pointedly rejected the idea of testing for individual and developmental differences and tried to eliminate short-term changes due to learning or habituation by carefully arranging his experiments. Only through the back door and in an area of concern which until now has not gained a firm foothold in psychology, namely, ethno-psychology (1900–1920), did he introduce the concept of variations or, more specifically, of cultural and historical variations. Undoubtedly, in this regard he was much more foresighted than most of his contemporary and our present-day colleagues.

Toward the end of the nineteenth century, the topic of individual and developmental differences became a dominant theme for psychological studies (Binet & Henri, 1896; Hall, 1904; Stern, 1900). While retreating from the conception of universal psychological elements, as previously studied in sensory-perceptual, psychomotor, or learning psychology, students of individual differences nevertheless aimed for the analysis of stable states (capacities, traits, skills) which, though variable in quantity from person to person, would represent general charcteristics of the human being.

More sophisticated (as well as obscure) in their formulations, personality theorists (Freud, 1917; Spranger, 1914; Stern, 1906) would often give recognition to the dynamic interdependencies of these entities, but the need for concise expressions (especially in writing) often assigned substantive and stable properties to them. And even if such was not the intent of the writer, for the readers (especially once the material was condensed into textbooks) and for the practitioners engaged in their repetitive applications, these dynamic properties became again rigidly delineated units.

In contrast to personality theories, developmental research never ventured far into more sophisticated speculations (Gesell, 1928; Hall, 1904; Terman, 1916). Instead, it readily adopted the terms and concepts from other psychological subdisciplines, such as learning, cognition, and personality research, and in its surge toward measurement and data, applied operationally their concepts in large-scale empirical investigations. With very few exceptions, the theoretical limitations were narrowly restricted to investigations of the here-and-now of performance or behavior in individuals differing in age. Neither the experienced past nor the anticipated future were considered as decisive conditions for developmental progression. This limitation, once more, reflects the static conception of psychology and, in particular, the failure of developmental psychologists to be seriously concerned with developmental changes, at least in the individual (Riegel, 1972c).

A dramatic change was seemingly introduced into psychology when theoreticians of mental testing began to distinguish "true" or potential scores from the observed data of actual performances and when they began to construct elaborate mathematical models on such a basis (Gulliksen, 1950). Unfortunately, the dualism between what theoretically could be but what practically never is—a split which reappeared in the distinction between competence and performance in modern linguistics (Chomsky, 1968) and cognitive developmental theory (Wohlwill & Flavell, 1969)—merely provided a more sophisticated cover for the old conception of psychological faculties, capacities, and traits, and their realization in observable behavior.

The same holds true for attempts to separate the forms of behavior from the forces which bring these forms to their realization. In terms of one recent proponent, Atkinson (1974), abilities and motivations are curvilinearly related to one another. When motivation is either very low or very high, abilities will not be effectively realized. Only when there is an optimal degree of motivation will abilities produce maximum scores. Maximum achievement is identified as the "true" ability which, like for the psychometricians, is produced under ideal conditions.

The distinction between forces and the forms upon which these forces act is the oldest known distinction in philosophy and can be traced back historically to Anaximander of Milet. Among the generations of philosophers guided by this distinction, one group emphasized the search for the stable, universal forms of being, and another the energizing forces that produced the continuous change of becoming. The former in their search for timeless structures looked at the fixed constellations of the stars as a prototypical case for synchronic order. The latter were concerned with changing nature, society, and, last but not least, the human being. Time and change being of central concern in their interpretations, they could but use the metaphor of fire to depict their notion about the ceaseless flux.

Psychological inquiries, by and large, have been more strongly influenced by the static views of the former conception. Whenever the processes and changes of psychological conditions were emphasized, as for example in the act psychology of Brentano (1874) and in the phenomenological or functional psychologies of Stumpf (1906) or James (1890), these attempts were always regarded as interesting but hopeless philosophical extravagancies, primarily because their proponents failed to translate their ideas into the operational language of the psychological laboratory.

For these reasons, it was hailed by many as a major breakthrough when, in the early 1950s, following the suggestions by Lewin (1935) and Murray (1938), psychologists made concrete proposals to investigate the effects of motivational and social variables in the laboratory. Thus, in addition to the dichotomy of the true and the observed (or the potential and the actual), the dichotomy between form and force was introduced. However, the conception of an elusive underlying force which made it possible for capacities to be realized at all, was not taken lightly. After all, it meant another intrusion and distortion of the ideal of stable and timeless entities.

The debates and controversies about the scientific need for such a force lasted for more than two decades and are still not laid to rest. The series of Symposia at the University of Nebraska gives ample evidence of the seriousness and depth of these debates. Nevertheless, I reject an orientation promoting such forces, just as I reject an orientation promoting stable psychological entities. There are two arguments that I have to propose. First, such a conception represents an abstraction from the concrete events and episodes which characterize human actions. Thus such a conception is bound to share a fate similar to that of the concept of stable traits or capacities, that is, of losing its dynamic character through reification and substantification. Second, this fate is likely to befall the concept of an underlying force, as it has befallen the concept of a stable capacity, because neither of the two, nor both in their interaction, are seen from a developmental-historical perspective.

Throughout this paper I will try to show that only a conception in which the individuals are seen in their developmental context, and in which, moreover, individual developmental changes are seen in their changing cultural-historical context, can lead to a comprehensive understanding of human activities. These activities are reflected neither in stable capacities or states nor in universal forces or energies but by the sequences of interacting events and episodes which—often lying plainly on the surface—provide structure and meaning to the life of the individual and society.

Capacities and Competencies

The concept of intelligence and the methods of its measurement illustrate most pointedly the limitations and problems of traditional psychology (Riegel, 1973c). Although originally conceived and constructed as a technical device to select and, eventually, to aid mentally retarded children, through its widespread adaptation the pragmatic character of the intelligence test was gradually modified by the more ambitious conception of intelligence as a capacity or

competence underlying a variety of intellectual surface performances. Admittedly, no subject and no instrument would readily
reveal these true capacities, but with increasing methodological
refinements and with strengthened theoretical sophistication, investigations would move step by step closer to this goal.

The constricted character of the instrument and the abstract
character of the postulated ability became clearly apparent when
individuals were tested who revealed anything but maximum
achievements, for example, adult and aged persons. Because these
individuals make up the largest and most important part of the
population, it proved especially troublesome to find that they
performed much less well than youngsters for whom, of course, the
whole machinery was set into motion in the first place.

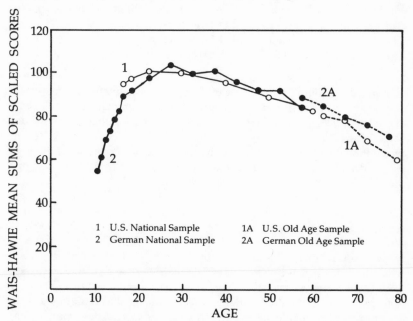

FIG. 1. A cross-national comparison of scores on an adult intelligence
test and age. Results are taken from the United States samples with the
Wechsler Adult Intelligence Scale (WAIS) (Wechsler, 1955) and from
the German samples with the translated test (HAWIE) (Wechsler, 1956).
The German old-age sample is from Riegel and Riegel (1959). Both
versions of the test are adjusted to give a maximum score of 100 between
the ages of 20 and 34 years. From J. E. Birren (Ed.), *Handbook of Aging
and the Individual* (1959), Fig. 4, p. 24. Copyright by the University of
Chicago Press. Reprinted by permission.

1. Originally, measures of intelligence were expected to yield reliable coefficients of the basic capacity or competence of individuals and, subsequently, to remain firmly stable throughout the whole lifespan. The evidence gathered did not confirm this expectation. A recent example, on the *growth and decline of intelligence,* including cross-cultural comparisons, is shown in Figure 1 (Birren, 1959).

The surprise and shock generated by these studies led to the search for alternative explanations or denials of the results. By using a test that allowed for the separate analysis of eight (presumably) different intellectual skills, Jones and Conrad (1933) substantiated the notion of *differential changes of intellectual functions.* Most notably, tasks requiring language skills and the utilization of long-established habits —occasionally called "crystallized" abilities (Cattell, 1934)—revealed a slow rate of growth, a late peak, and a high stability or slow decline in performance during the later years. Tasks requiring sensory-motor coordination, new learning, and speedy performance—occasionally called "fluid" intelligence (Cattell, 1934)—revealed a fast rate of growth, an early peak, and a rapid rate of decline during adulthood and aging.

2. According to these early test results, the intelligence of children is dominated by "fluid" rather than by "crystallized" functions. The former are already well developed; the latter are not. In contrast, the intelligence of older adults is dominated by "crystallized" rather than "fluid" performances. The findings by Jones and Conrad (1933) led to the recognition of structural changes in intelligence with age, a topic to be explored with the then new technique of factor analysis and, in spite of a multitude of inconclusive results, still not laid to its deserved rest.

By the time of Jones and Conrad's investigation, numerous new tests had appeared on the market giving selective emphasis to either of these two or many other functions. Finally the question was raised as to what, after all, the *concept of intelligence* stands for. This question was sardonically treated in a statement by Boring (1923) that "intelligence is what the intelligence test measures." Since there were many tests, there were many intelligences. However, since Jones and Conrad had shown that particular tests differentially affect persons differing in age, the above statement should have been still further extended by proclaiming that "intelligence is what a specific intelligence test measures at a specific age level."

3. Miles and Miles (1932) were among the first to explore the question of differences in the rates of changes as a function of original intelligence level, education, and socioeconomic status. The issue of the *dependency of decline on the original level of functioning* was later elaborated in longitudinal studies and led Owens (1953) to conclude that "age is kinder to the initially more able." According to his findings, bright persons not

only develop faster and reach a higher performance level than average persons, but the skills of bright persons also decline more slowly. The opposite is true for persons of below-average intelligence. The present author reported that this observation holds only for "fluid" intelligence (Riegel & Riegel, 1972). For "crystallized" functions the opposite statement holds, namely, that "the last will be first." Less able persons continue to gain in verbal performance over the whole span of the adult years. Able persons show less improvement though little decline. Consequently, the variance in scores between high and low individuals decreases with increasing age. In regard to the operational definition a further modification thus becomes necessary: "Intelligence is what a specific intelligence test measures not only at a specific age level but also within a specific group of individuals."

Since human beings are changing all the time, they can not be appropriately described by instruments that are supposed to reflect universal and stable properties. As I will show in this paper, changes in human beings can only be apprehended by studying concrete psychological events in their interactions with inner-biological events, such as illnesses, injuries, rehabilitations, and recoveries, and especially with cultural-sociological and outer-physical events, such as marriage, promotion, change of location, growth of children, loss of parents, partners, and friends, disqualification, and retirement. Undoubtedly, these inner and outer events by themselves say little about the individual-psychological status of different persons. However, by exploring the modes and efforts with which individuals try to cope with these and many other conditions, one can draw important inferences about their ever changing status during adulthood and aging as well as during childhood and adolescence.

Subject-Object Segregation

One of the fundamental assumptions for the construction of stable competencies consists in conceptual and manipulative segregation of the subject from the object. By mimicking classical natural sciences, testing procedures always aim at removing the testee intellectually, emotionally, and socially from the test administrator in order to create seemingly "objective" conditions (Riegel, 1975f). In this manner the testee serves as the object of the investigation (although he is being called "subject") and the experimenter functions as a superior subject.

These prescriptions resemble the earlier efforts to achieve objectivity in experimental psychology where they were forcefully expressed by Wundt (1907). In his four theses about the scope of psychological experiments, Wundt proposed that an experimenter should be able to (a) determine the onset of events, (b) follow the course of events with "intense attention," (c) repeat the experiment several times under identical conditions in order to validate the results, and (d) vary systematically, one after the other, the accompanying conditions.

Wundt's demands were intended as a confrontation for the psychologists at Würzburg who, for the first time, were studying thought processes. But according to Wundt's critique, the introspective analysis of these processes, as proposed by the scholars at Würzburg, would disturb if not destroy the thoughts themselves. Thus, the second (as well as the first) of his criteria could not be met and the investigation would become futile. Furthermore, ongoing thought processes could never attain the same, that is, prior, state again; they are in continuous dialectic flux. Therefore, repetitions of the experiment under the same conditions (as demanded under the third criterion) are not possible, nor are variations (as demanded under the fourth criterion) which depend, of course, on the possibility for repetitions.

Just as experimental psychologists have continued to deny or to take seriously the experimenter's participatory role, so have diagnosticians erected a screen (concretely speaking, a one-way window) between themselves and their clients. Under "objective" testing conditions, the tester is prevented from interacting with the testee in any reasonable manner. The most he is permitted to do is to smile encouragingly or to utter "Hm hm" or "It's just fine the way you are doing it." The situation is comparable to the master-slave segregation. It not only alienates the testee but creates fictitious results even for the administrator with the best intentions.

These deficiencies are created by the artificial character of the experimental and the testing conditions. In real-life situations, all performances (on the assembly line or in the executive session) are determined interactively by several and often large groups of participating members. Even if individuals appear to perform in the complete isolation of their shops or offices, they nevertheless interact with and are influenced by cohorts of other persons who are either currently engaged in similar work or have been so over many generations in the past. No individual can ever operate in complete separation from the coexisting and preexisting efforts of countless other individuals.

Furthermore, in real-life situations all of the achievements in concrete work situations are the outcome of performance dialogues in which the roles are interactively determined. Although on the assembly line the foreman, or in the executive committee meeting the director, is the "master," these masters are dependent upon the "slaves"; they cannot function without them. In psychological testing, however, the segregation is carried to a one-sided extreme and the asymmetric relationship cast into a rigid mold. The social implications of such an arrangement have been systematically criticized by Steinar Kvale (1972).

4. The difficulties of psychodiagnostic arrangements become apparent in situations in which the two-person relation is readily reversible, for example, in the testing of aged individuals. As discussed at length in the earlier literature on psychoanalytic treatments of the elderly (for reviews, see Rechtschaffen, 1959; Riegel, 1959), the test administrator is commonly much younger than the testee. In terms of his age and genealogical status he might well represent the child of his client. Thus, the relationship induced by the testing procedure is readily brought into imbalance. The tester might feel insecure and, in psychoanalytic terminology, might develop countertransference reviving his old child-parent relationship instead of playing effectively the role of the father figure (master) during the test administration. The testee, on the other hand, might feel equally insecure and afraid of revealing his deficiencies as an aged person, deficiencies about which he has heard so much since they represent one of the strongest stereotypes in our society. Consequently, neither the testers nor the testees are able to do their best and the meager degree of interaction permissable under the standard testing conditions distorts the results even further.

Elliot Stern (personal communication) has recently suggested a way to remedy the situation by treating both the tester and the testee as equals and placing them in a two-person cooperative situation. The tester would receive credit for any points that the testee makes. Thus, the tester would become a testee. At the same time the testee would receive a bonus for whatever the tester is able to elicit from him. Since the credit would not be of benefit to him alone but to the tester as well, one of the most effective means for gaining the cooperation of older persons is utilized, namely, their willingness to assist other persons, especially younger ones, in achieving their social or professional functions. Preliminary investigations have revealed considerable gains when aged subjects are brought into cooperative rather than one-way or competitive testing situations.

Our emphasis upon the mutuality of influence between the tester and the testee converts the testing situation into a performance dialogue in which not only the tester asks questions and the testee gives answers but in which, eventually, both participants ask questions and receive answers. As a further implication, such a conversion destroys the rigid barrier between the diagnostic and the therapeutic aspects of clinical interventions. Traditionally diagnosis, especially under objective testing conditions, has been dominated by a sharp subject-object separation; therapy, on the other hand, if ever successful, aims toward an interactive dialogue. With the proposed conversion of the testing situation to a dialogue of mutual influence, the sharp and artificial separation between these two parts of the intervention would disappear (see Brown, 1975).

Individual and Cultural Changes

The conversion of the subject-object segregation into a performance dialogue forces us to consider the cultural-historical background of the two individuals participating in the testing situation. An effective dialogue requires the accommodation to and the assimilation of all information exchanged between the participants prior to any given point in time. Yet, even that is not enough. Each participant enters the dialogue with certain preconceptions and experiences rooted in his own developmental history. As a result the dialogue is dependent not only upon the particular directions taken by the speakers but also upon the preconceptions brought to the dialogue by each speaker. Ultimately, their exchanges reflect both the personal histories of the speakers and significant segments of the developing cultural-sociological history within which they are participating members. While such implications may seem overwhelmingly broad to be explored concretely at this moment, the issue of cultural-historical determination must be recognized and included in any elaboration of the traditional testing situation.

5. During World War II the occasion arose for testing large groups of young adults with the same instrument that was used with similar groups in WW I. As reported by Tuddenham (1948), the median test score of the WW II recruits coincided with the 84th percentile in the distribution of scores obtained in WW I. Thus a considerable improvement in

Table 1

Years of Birth of Four Cohorts in a Demonstration of
Developmental-Historical Research Designs

Time of	Age	
Testing	10	70
1910	1900	1840
1970	1960	1900

NOTE: After Baltes, 1968, and Schaie, 1965.

performance had taken place with historical time, attributable, perhaps, to changes in education, communication, and welfare. Although not fully recognized at that time, these results revealed the fictitiousness of studies exploring developmental differences in individuals without taking due account of the concurrent social and historical changes.

6. Recent advances in developmental research designs by Schaie (1965) and Baltes (1968) have enabled us to unconfound individual and societal changes. Table 1 shows some of these possibilities. As indicated by the year of birth, each cell represents a corpus of data from one cohort. Under the conditions shown, we could make *two cross-sectional comparisons* between the 10- and 70-year-old individuals. For this purpose, we would compare the two cells within each of the two rows. As evidenced by the different birth dates of the cohorts compared, a cross-sectional design not only reflects age differences, for example, in the intelligence of 10- and 70-year-olds, but also cohort differences as well, that is, for the historical periods from 1840 to 1900, and from 1900 to 1960, respectively.

Also, *two time-lag comparisons* are embedded in our example shown in Table 1. In this case we would analyze the historical differences, for example, in intelligence between the 10-year-olds of 1910 and 1970. The same comparison can be made for the 70-year-olds. Thus, we would compare the data of two cells lying vertical to one another in either of the two columns of Table 1. Time-lag designs confound cohort differences with the time-of-testing differences, both of which are historical in nature. Age differences are not considered, or rather, are kept constant in each of the two possible comparisons.

Finally, *one longitudinal design* is embedded in the example shown in Table 1. We might analyze, for instance, the changes in intelligence between the 10-year-olds of 1910 and the same group at an age of 70 years in 1970. Any changes observed reflect both age and time-of-testing differences.

According to these arguments, none of the three approaches—

cross-sectional, time-lag, and longitudinal comparisons—provides us directly with "pure" estimates of either age, cohort, or time differences. However, by joint utilizations of all three basic designs, such estimates can be obtained. This recognition represents a true breakthrough. Now, psychology may justifiably describe individual developmental changes, sociology may describe cohort differences, and history may describe cultural changes. This analysis also makes us aware that none of these disciplines ought to remain in isolation. A true understanding of changes in the individual and in society can be achieved only if their contributions are recognized in their complementary interdependence. Each discipline alone produces fictitious results and interpretations.

Recently, an increasing number of studies have been reported in which modern developmental research designs have been applied. In many instances, cohort differences and historical changes were found to be more significant determinants of the results than developmental differences which have been commonly employed as explanations. At first, reports of supporting evidence were limited to analyses of changes during the later years of life (Riegel, Riegel & Meyer, 1967; Schaie & Strother, 1968a, 1968b; Baltes & Labouvie, 1972; Riegel & Riegel, 1972; Schaie, Labouvie & Buech, 1973; Schaie & Labouvie-Vief, 1974), but strong evidence has been reported since then on changes during childhood (Baltes, Baltes & Reinert, 1970) and adolescence (Nesselroade & Baltes, 1974). However, most of these reports failed to elaborate the specific nature of the changing historical conditions that played a key role as determinants of the observed results. In most instances, general but vague arguments were made attributing these results to changes in education, communication, transportation, urbanization, welfare, medical care, nutrition, or even more generally to changing economic and political conditions (Riegel, 1972b).

The eventual recognition of generational differences as an explanation for historical changes can be traced to the work of Karl Mannheim (1952). This explanation has since been applied to social and personality issues by Ryder (1965), Riley, Johnson and Foner (1972), and Neugarten and Datan (1973); to the topic of human memory by Meacham (1972); and to cognitive and language variables by Jenkins and Russell (1960) and Riegel (1965, 1975d). Most recently, Zajonc and Markus (1975) analyzed specific changes in interaction within families as an explanation for temporal changes in intellectual performances. Family size and birth order were proposed and confirmed as determinants of the results.

7. Intellectual development is dependent upon the cumulative interactions of the individuals in their environment which, in the model proposed by Zajonc and Markus (1975), consists of the siblings' and parents' intelligence. Mutual influences on the intellectual development of the siblings are described by a parameter which changes its value with progression through time. Five features explain the data, (originally reported by Belmont & Marolla, 1973).

First, intellectual performance decreases with birth order but only when there is close spacing between successive children [Figure 2]. Under these conditions each successive child has access to a less favorable intellectual environment. With larger gaps between children this pattern can be arrested and even reversed. . . . Second, intellectual ability decreases with family size because the larger the family the poorer the intellectual environment. . . . Third, the last child shows a larger drop in intelligence scores because of a lack of opportunity to teach. Fourth, the only child also suffers from the last child handicap. Finally, the upswing in the . . . scores found for the lower ranks in larger families occurs because lower ranks have an environment that includes fewer individuals with an intelligence level lower than their own, while this is not the case for higher birth ranks. [Zajonc & Markus, 1975, p. 85]

The main feature of the formulation is that *the individual is considered to be part of his own environment.* And this environment is conceived of not as a static and stable background condition, but as one that is dynamically interdependent with its components. The individual is continually influenced by his own environment, and being thus influenced and changed, himself brings about changes in his environment *by virture of his very own change.* [P. 86]

The conclusion of this debate, orginating in gerontological and life-span psychology, can be summarized rather pointedly: It is insufficient and distorting to study individuals unless they are studied in their developmental progression; it is also insufficient and distorting to study developing individuals unless they are studied within the developing progression of the group and society of which they are a part.

This recognition of the interdependence between individual-psychological changes and cultural-sociological changes shows once more how inappropriate it is to search for stable universal competence in a developmental-historical vacuum. Such an approach generates abstract and therefore fictitious results. In the concluding parts of my paper (see Parts 3 and 4), I will present a perspective which, by taking account of developmental-historical changes, places individual human beings back into the center of attention; human

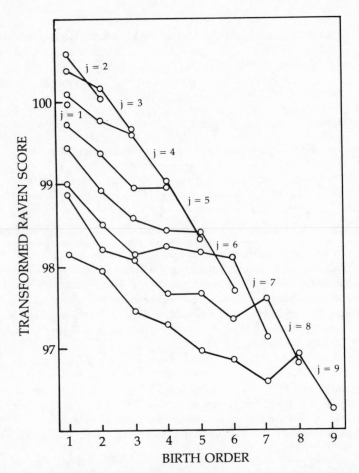

FIG. 2. Average transformed Raven scores as a function of birth order (*i*) and family size (*j*), recalculated from Belmont and Marolla (1973). The Raven scores were reported by Belmont and Marolla in terms of six categories, from 1 (high) to 6 (low). For the purposes of the present analysis a linear transformation ($\bar{X}_{tr} = 113.45 - 5.0047\bar{X}$) was performed on these scores, inverting the scale so that increasing values now indicate increasing intelligence, and setting the score of the only child at 100. From R. B. Zajonc & G. B. Markus, "Birth Order and Intellectual Development," *Psychological Review*, 1975, **82**, 74–88. Copyright 1975 by the American Psychological Association. Reprinted by permission.

beings are no longer treated as entities composed of abstract traits, a condition to which they have been degraded in experimental psychology and in the psychology of individual and developmental differences (Riegel, 1975b).

THE TRANQUILITY OF EQUILIBRIUM
AND CONSONANCE

Just as there has been a preference for describing the individual in terms of abstract traits and competencies, there has also been a long-established preference for an equilibrium model in the behavioral sciences. The reasons for such a preference have never been made clear. Without an exploration of the underlying assumptions, it has been taken for granted that a state of equilibrium, stability, and rest is more desirable than a state of upheaval, uncertainty, and change. The "tendency" toward stability has been regarded as a major force in problem solving and performance, with varying motivations as a somewhat more specific factor helping the individual to move toward such a goal.

In psychology the preference for equilibrium has found expression in balance theory, equilibrium theory, steady state theory, and, indirectly, the theory of cognitive dissonance (which deals with the individual's efforts and techniques of overcoming a state of disequilibrium). These theories (with the possible exception of cognitive dissonance theory) failed to recognize that any improvement or, more generally, any change must be preceded by a state of imbalance which serves as the basis of any future development and, in effect, makes movement possible at all. In recognizing this prerequisite, stability appears only as a transitory condition in the stream of ceaseless changes. While the conditions of stability and equilibrium might be easier to describe than the flux of contradictions and changes, the latter constitute the conditions from which everything new emerges and on which any development and growth is based. Perhaps the most clear-cut example of the treatment of stability at the expense of change or, more specifically, of the consideration of states of equilibrium rather than processes of transition, has been provided in Piaget's extensive work on the cognitive development of children.

Stability and Cognitive Development

Piaget's approach is different from the traditional, codified method for testing intelligence or other capacities. Limiting his explorations to early development, he engages the child in an appealing game or constructive task. By modifying the conditions and making pointed inquiries he determines why children fail or how they arrive at particular solutions. Piaget studies processes of intellectual operations which he interprets within a theoretical framework specifically derived from children's performances. His inquiries are limited, however, in that they explore the child's operations with objects and rarely include the child's social interactions and judgments.

Piaget starts his interpretations with the dialectic schema of assimilation and accommodation leading to new adaptation. The eating of food is perhaps the best example for explaining his schema. The hungry organism accommodates during this task by grasping, breaking, biting, chewing, salivating, and swallowing. At the same time, the food is assimilated; it is broken, disintegrated, chemically changed (through the saliva), and absorbed. This interactive process between the organism and the object continues until the former reaches a state of satisfaction (balance or equilibrium) at which he will cease eating. Significantly for this particular situation as well as for all other situations covered by Piaget's theory, only the organisms being studied are viewed as active participants. They initiate their own accommodations and thereby also produce the changes in the object. The more general case where both the organism and its object are active participants, for example, a hunter and his prey or the mother and her child, is neglected by Piaget. His analysis is restricted to the interaction between active organisms and passive objects. Much of my later efforts will consist in extending this paradigm to interactions in which the object represents another subject, that is, another active organism.

Piaget's dialectic schema of accommodation and assimilation succeeds in explaining some basic organismic functions such as eating, drinking, grasping, and holding of objects (parenthetically, it fails utterly to explain sex). Nevertheless, from the present point of view, it overemphasizes the state of satisfaction, balance, or equilibrium during which the organism's activities come to a halt (it would emphasize sexual satisfaction but not excitement). Alternatively, we should ask how organisms manage to break out of their tranquility; how do they become hungry again; when do they regain their activity; and why do they ask new questions rather than settle with old answers. By and large neither Piaget nor any other psychologist or sociologist pays much attention to these issues. All their efforts are directed toward the exploration of the balance achieved, satisfaction gained, and answers found.

In theory, the dialectic schema of accommodation and assimilation forms the basis for all other activities, including all higher forms of operations discussed by Piaget. But with each additional developmental step, less attention is given to this dialectic schema. Instead, the operations are explained in terms of the particular logic found to be appropriate for the new developmental levels, and as a consequence, the discussion of accommodation and assimilation appears to become redundant and unnecessary. With this shift in explanation, Piaget's subsequent developmental explanations successively deemphasize the dialectic basis expressed by his accommodation-assimilation schema, and as a result, his inter-pretations become increasingly formal and abstract. But beyond this, they also become psychologically empty and socially irrelevant (Wilden, 1972).

8. For a demonstration of the problems investigated in the light of Piaget's analyses, let us consider the well-known experiments on the conservation of liquids. Such an experiment requires two beakers equal in shape and equally filled with a liquid. After the child has correctly judged that both glasses contain the same amount (a task which is achieved by most children even at a young age), the content from one of them is poured into another beaker different in shape, either taller and thinner or shorter and wider. Young children when asked will reply that the amount of liquid is not the same, often arguing that it rises higher in the tall and thin beaker than in the standard container with which the children were confronted first. Later in development, they will recognize the contradiction in their judgments. Thus a disequilibrium is generated. After some reflection, the children might arrive at the correct solution and state that the amount of the liquid has remained the same and only the shape of the vessel is different.

This and the multitude of similar experiments conducted by Piaget and his followers demonstrate a basic conception directed toward the problem of how children resolve conflicting situations, contradictory evidence, or inconsistent impressions. These investigators do not address themselves to the issue of how children come to question their earlier judgments but rather how they find more advanced and consistent solutions. While, undoubtedly, Piaget's concern with the process of resolving discrepancies in experience and thought is of great importance, it disregards at least one-half of the process of operative and cognitive activity.

Piaget's preference for studying how problems are solved rather than generated, how questions are answered rather than raised, is concretely revealed by the particularity of the experimental conditions chosen for his studies. The experimenter poses the problem and expects the child to solve it. Further questioning aims at eliciting from the child answers that would allow the experimenter to draw inferences about the structure of the child's operations and thoughts. Without any noteworthy exceptions, all questions are asked by the experimenter and all answers are given by the child.

Piaget's preference for studying how problems are solved rather than generated reflects his commitment to an equilibrium model that describes the child's development as a succession of plateaus during which the operational structures are in balance. Whenever new questions and doubts arise in the child, triggered by paradoxical new experiences but not consistently explained by the theory, the balance is disturbed and new operativity is generated by the child. Eventually, a new equilibrium will be attained, and thereby the child may have moved into the next higher level of cognitive balance. While the sequence of progression described is convincing and a great step forward in comparison to earlier mechanistic inter-pretations, little attention is given to the question of how equilibria are lost and transitions are initiated. For a comprehensive analysis of development these issues need to be considered at least as seriously as the interpretations of how problems are solved.

Contradiction and Dialectic Operations

Previously I have criticized Piaget's interpretations because the consecutive equilibration of experiences and operations that occurred originally in contradictory relationships, and thereby formed the basis for generativity, leads to an intellectual alienation of individuals, that is, to the separation of their experiences and operations from their dialectic basis (Riegel, 1973b). The direction and theme of this development is quite pointedly expressed by Piaget's denotation of the fourth stage as that of *formal operational* or abstract thinking.

One of the main differences between formal and dialectic logic lies in the recognition and acceptance of contradiction as a basic operation of thinking by the latter and its firm rejection by the former. Since all interpretations in formal logic and all investigations in the classical natural sciences (which exemplify these inter-pretations) have been built upon the notion of noncontradiction and the removal of contradictions from inferences, there is little compatibility between these two types of logic. Nevertheless, dialectic logic, in being built upon fewer suppositions, can be regarded as the more general system. Of more importance, the two logics have completely different goals. Formal logic represents a system and provides methods by which unambiguous and consistent, that is, noncontradictory, inferences can be derived. Dialectic logic, in contrast, tries to depict the origin and movement of thought both in the individual and in society. In other words, formal logic is static and synchronic, dialectic logic is dynamic and developmental (see Kosok, 1972).

The importance of these distinctions becomes clear when applied to child development. Individuals who are brought up to the level of formal operational thought, usually by the time of adolescence, can reason consistently and convincingly, but they may be at a loss when faced with concrete situations full of contradictions which can not be removed through abstract analysis. If these individuals are going to succeed in a world of paradox and uncertainty, they will have to dare to be incomplete, inconsistent, and contradictive again. Formal logic, if it can be carried consistently into concrete life situations, would leave them with long lists of possibilities and options, with many *if*'s and *when*'s, but would not aid them in reaching decisions and initiating actions.

9. Various reports (see, for example, Piaget, 1962, 1965; Piaget & Inhelder, 1967) provide rich sources for demonstrating the dialectic basis of the child's thought. The following example shows shifts in the concept of identity by a child two years and seven months old: "J. seeing L. in a new bathing suit, with a cap, J. asked: *What's the baby's name?* Her mother explained that it was a bathing costume, but J. pointed to L. herself and said: *But, what's the name of that?* (indicating L's face) and repeated the question several times. But as soon as L. had her dress on again, J. exclaimed very seriously: *It's Lucienne again*, as if her sister had changed her identity in changing her clothes" (1962, p. 224).

At an early age children are not disturbed by their own contradictory judgments, as shown in the following example from a child at an age of six years and nine months: "Are there more wooden beads or more brown ones?—*More brown ones.*—If we make a necklace with the wooden beads and a necklace with the brown ones, which would be longer?—*The one with the wooden beads* (without hesitating).—Why?—*Because there are the two extra white ones*" (1965, p. 176).

Although the child apprehends increasingly complex structures which consolidate the contradictory evidence experienced, in concrete situations the contradictory conditions remain to coexist. Each new situation demands transformation of the discrete experience into the consolidated structures. Each new situation remains contradictory as each thought remains tied to its dialectic basis. Take, for example, students who are puzzled by an ambiguous multiple choice item (and which item fails to be ambiguous?). It matters little for an understanding of the process of the students' thinking whether or not they finally find the "correct" answer or even what the "correct" answer is; what matters are the ambiguity and the contradictions they experience as they move toward a choice. Thus, thinking, in the dialectic sense, is the process of transforming contradictory experience into momentary stable structures. These stable structures do in fact consolidate the contradictory evidence but they do not represent the process of thinking; they merely represent the products of thinking.

10. Recently, several studies explored the acquisition of comparative terms by children, such as *more* and *less* or *tall, taller, tallest*. These investigations have been conducted and summarized either by emphasizing a linguistic (Clark, 1970) or a perceptual-cognitive basis (Huttenlocher & Higgins, 1971).

According to the available evidence, the following stages in the development of comparative terms may be distinguished. At level 1, when children are producing single words only, expressions such as "more" are used as imperative demands without comparative implications. Paraphrasing their expression, the children seem to say, "I want this here!" At level 2, when the children operate simultaneously with two terms, they might use such words as "more" in form of a dichotomy, contrasting it with "not more" but not implying a gradation of magnitudes. At level 3, when the children operate simultaneously with three terms, transitivity is established. For instance, the children might apply terms like "tall, taller, tallest." By dropping off one of the extreme items of such a series, that is, $A < B < C$, they are able to extend it without limitation. That is, they may drop A and add an element D at the right of the series that is larger than C. Since the two retained items, B and C, also retain the order within the series, transitivity is preserved. Next, the procedure can be repeated by dropping item B and adding item E, etc.

Level 3 represents an important step in an additional sense. All earlier comparisons implied absolute anchor points. In the one-term expressions, the condition and desire of the speakers themselves serve as absolute points of reference. In the two-term comparison, the expression "more" serves as the positive instance; "not more" represents merely its negation. At level 3, the anchor point becomes variable. Applying a spatial representation, usually the left-hand term, as in "tall, taller, tallest," serves this function. Such an anchor point can always be modified, however, by adding a new element, such as "less tall," or—more radically—by extending the sequence into the opposite direction, that is, "tall, less tall, least tall."

At level 4, when children operate simultaneously with four terms, they ought to be able to make comparisons between two dichotomized variables and perform class multiplications such as between "wide and narrow versus short and tall." This performance is one of the logical prerequisites for conservation tasks. Similar performances, although they do not represent any new form of operation, consist of hierarchical comparisons. For example, the child might first classify objects into large and small items and then subdivide each class again in the same manner. This operation, when executed repeatedly and consistently, may result in a series in which all items are ordered transitively. Finally, we might expect level 5 and level 6 children to compare simultaneously items along three or more dimensions.

So far our discussion has been based upon the traditional logic of classes and relations. But development does not consist only in the continuous refinement of such comparisons nor does it consist only in the compounding of an even larger number of dimensions; it also involves an increasing relativization of the standards in comparative expressions. For example, the necessity of applying alternate evaluations in judging a particular event as fortunate from one person's view but unfortunate from another person's view characterizes the behavior of older children in role-playing activities. It characterizes even more clearly the mediating operations of adult persons, operations which include our general notions with respect to the relativity of events. If an object is fast when compared within a fixed system of coordinates but slow when compared with another moving object, we recognize, once more, the dialectic principle of contradiction. This principle implies that a thing has a given quality and, at the same time, does not have it. In regard to comparatives, the statement that something is tall and at the same time small, that is, when viewed within two different frames of reference, is equally characteristic of mature judgments. Such a statement cannot easily be captured within the formal logic of classes and relations which may provide consistent inferences within each frame of reference but, unless continuously expanded, offers no aid for comparisons between the two. In other words, formal logic is closed, dialectic logic is open; formal logic is static and synchronic, dialectic logic is dynamic and developmental.

In short, the acceptance of contradictions in dialectic logic indicates a shift of emphasis from the closure of a question to the generating roots of a question. Rather than searching for final answers, dialectic logic is concerned with the contradictory origin of the endless sequence of raising questions. Needless to say, proceeding in such a sequence requires that at various points answers be found. However, these answers are only temporary markings in the continuous process of evolving problems. Only with the cessation of thought and life itself would the process ever come to a complete rest.

Contradictions and Dialectic Maturity

In a recent publication I discussed three models of qualitative development (Riegel, 1972c). These models were derived from the earlier work by Van den Daele (1969). In both publications Piaget's theory of cognitive development was considered to represent the simplest of all three models, namely, the single-sequence model. In this model qualitatively different sets of operations of behavior succeed each other in temporal sequence; provisions are made neither for differences in progression between persons or between skills nor for the transition and accumulation of behavior across developmental stages. Undoubtedly, this representation over-simplifies the richness of Piaget's theory, but at the present time, sufficient reasons are not available for assigning either one of the other models, the multiple-sequence or the complex-sequence model, to represent Piaget's theory.

With this view of Piaget's theory, the question arises as to what happens at later stages to the behavior or operations acquired during, and representing, earlier stages? Are the schemata of the sensory-motor period lost or are they modified and transformed into those of the preoperational and higher periods? Moreover, is it conceivable that an individual operates simultaneously at different levels of cognition, perhaps switching back and forth between them or choosing one for one area of activity and another for a different area?

Recently Furth has maintained that Piaget does not "pretend that stages of thinking reached in one domain will necessarily be found in the thinking of the same person in another domain" (1973, p. 8). But Piaget does not state explicitly the conditions under which such switching across stages might or must occur. After all, such an interpretation would require an elaborated theory of task conditions and changes which determine the activation of particular operations characterizing the different developmental stages. Even if we consider a much simplified interpretation, for example, that by McLaughlin (1963), we fail to derive any definite conclusion. The progression depicted by McLaughlin's model represents successive increases in the number of attributional dimensions and, thus, in the number of concepts with which a child operates simultaneously. But if children at the level of preoperational thinking characterize items according to the presence or absence of one attribute, are they, then, also able to dismiss the attributional dimension altogether and to conceive items "as such" without any categorizing efforts, that is, in the manner of sensory-motor children?

Presumably the further children have advanced in their development, the harder it will be to "regress" to the "naive" mode of early conceptualization. For this reason the growth of cognitive organization, as depicted in any of these models, represents a movement away, an alienation, from earlier thinking. Paradoxically, dialectic operations represent a further step forward in thinking and, at the same time, a return to early modes of thinking which, in the opinion of many writers (including Piaget), are dialectic in nature. In reference to dialectic theory, we might denote (with Lawler, 1975) the more mature operations as a development of "scientific dialectics" and the earlier as "primitive dialectics".

11. An increasing number of studies of adult persons have been conducted with tasks taken from the rich repertoire of Piagetian investigations (Papalia & Bielby, 1974). Two of the earliest studies (Sanders, Laurendau, & Bergeron, 1966; Kominski & Coppinger, 1968) investigated the conservation of surface areas by means of two green cardboards that were described as meadows on which two cows could graze. As blocks were placed in various positions upon the cardboards, adult persons were asked whether equal amounts of grass were available to the cows. The evidence showed that older adults do not conserve area as we would expect them to do and as older children do. They seem rather to regress to judgments based on their immediate perceptual impressions, much like those exhibited by younger children.

These results raise puzzling questions about the "disappearance of personal knowledge." Is it conceivable that persons, once they have realized during their development that the size of an area remains the same regardless of how a number of blocks are distributed, can ever lose this insight? Don't we always keep knowing what we know?

In his theoretical discussions of cognitive changes during adulthood and aging, Flavell (1970) argues for the "disappearance of knowledge" under conditions of neurophysiological damage. According to available information, such changes do not affect all aging persons to a significant extent. Arguments against the "disappearance of knowledge," on the other hand, are based upon the distinction between competence and performance as introduced into linguistics by Chomsky and as translated into cognitive developmental psychology by Wohlwill and Flavell (1969).

For Chomsky, competence refers to the knowledge about language; it is intuitive, immediate, and ideal. Performance refers to the execution of linguistic tasks; it is acquired, incomplete, and concrete. This distinction reflects (and fails to overcome) the old mind-body dualism originating with Descartes. In its idealistic extension it argues for the immutability of competence or knowledge; in its mechanistic extension it proposes that competence is innate. When applied to the knowledge of aged persons, this interpretation maintains that only their performance has declined; their competence remains intact.

According to my earlier proposal of a final period of dialectic operations (Riegel, 1973b), neither the arguments for nor those against the "disappearance of knowledge" lead to satisfactory explanations. In both cases knowledge tends to be regarded as something fixed and completed, that is, as a commodity; but it should rather be regarded as being in ceaseless flux and change, that is, as labor. In this conception, active knowledge is the highest, most mature, and most creative form of knowledge. It consists in the continuous, ongoing process of apprehending dialectic contradictions (Lawler, 1975; Riegel, 1975e).

During their development individuals may progress directly from any earlier developmental level to its corresponding mode of dialectic operations, thereby reaching a mature stage of thinking. This provision introduces interindividual alternatives or options at the level of maturity: persons might reach dialectic maturity without ever having passed through the period of formal operations or even through that of concrete operations. This provision also introduces intraindividual options: the skills and activities in one area, for instance in sciences, might be of the type of formal dialectic operations; those in a second area, for instance in everyday business transactions, might be of the type of concrete dialectic operations; those in a third area, for instance in artistic performances, might be of the type of preoperational dialectic intelligence; finally, those of intimate personal interactions might be sensory-motor and therefore of the original or "primitive" dialectic type.

In his discussion of equilibration, Piaget touches most explicitly upon the issue of optional, multilevel operations. According to Piaget, organisms inherently tend toward equilibrated states. Disequilibrium represents conflict and contradiction which the organism tries to overcome through his activities. But if Piaget admits—as Furth (1969) has delared—that an organism might have implicit or explicit options to operate at different stages of thinking, depending upon the area of activity with which he happens to be concerned at a particular time, then the tendency toward equilibrium is weakened, if not abandoned. Any concurrent or closely successive operations at different developmental levels ought to create a state of conflict which needs to be equilibrated. Such an equilibrium can only mean the progression to the higher and later developmental level of operation. In other words, the option for multilevel operations contradicts Piaget's notion of equilibrium, since it reintroduces dialectic conflict; the emphasis upon equilibrium would tend to resolve this conflict at the expense of the operations at the earlier stage. In contrast to this viewpoint, the proposed modification of the theory recognizes dialectic conflicts and contradiction as a fundamental property of thought. At the levels of dialectic maturity, the individual does not neccessarily equilibrate these conflicts but is ready to live with them; stronger yet, the individual accepts these contradictions as a basic property of thought and action.

Finally, to raise the same argument from a different angle: Piaget considers exclusively (or almost so) the organisms, interactive operations with objects in their environments. Little consideration is given to the possibility that these objects represent other subjects who, like the child, operate actively through their accommodations and assimilations upon the other objects (or subjects) in their world. In other words, Piaget has paid little attention to the outer dialectics of interacting individuals or to the affective, motivational, and social aspects that are reflected in such interactions. By restricting his analysis to the interactions of the subject with objects, he succeeded in providing a developmental logic and stages in rational thinking but failed to elaborate the primitive basis of cognitive operations, a basis which rests on affective and social interactions and changes. In the following two parts, I will focus entirely on these social interactions and changes.

THE DIALOGIC OF INTERACTIONS

In the first of the preceding two sections, I criticized traditional psychology for its emphasis upon fixed entities, either in the form of capacities, traits, or skills or in the guise of underlying motivational forces or drives. In the second section, I criticized the firm but blind preference for stability, balance, and equilibrium which one-sidedly is concerned with the solution of problems but not with their generation, with answers but not with questions and doubts. By turning away from these abstract conceptions, I call attention in the following two sections to the concrete interactions and changes in common activities and everyday situations within which dialectic operations continuously take place.

First, emphasis will be given to short-term situational interactions represented most explicitly in dialogues. Dialogues are historically the earliest form of dialectics, having been brought to an idealized perfection in Plato's writings. However, in moving ahead to consider dialogues as the basis for gaining knowledge, it becomes apparent that long-term processes of change, both in the individual and in society, are insufficiently explored if we rely on short-term or situational dialogic interactions alone. In the second of the following sections, therefore, I elaborate long-term dialectic changes, or developmental-historical interactions.

Although the analysis of dialogues ought to be a central topic in the study of language, linguists and psychologists have rarely emphasized the communicative and social functions of language. Most of their efforts have been directed toward abstract or formal descriptions or idealized systems of language, or, even more important to most of them, toward the analysis of the elements of such a system, namely, words, morphemes, letters, and phonemes. In emphasizing the social aspects of language and, in particular, the communication of meaning, the interaction between two or more persons in the form of dialogues provides the fundamental basis for fulfilling these functions.

Situational Dialogues

A dialogue requires a shared code for communication between the participating members. Such a code consists not only of signs and elements, such as words or phonemes, but, more important, of relationships and rules which make the very occurrence and effective use of these signs possible. Moreover, the communication system utilized in dialogues presupposes some shared knowledge, ideas, and even feelings and emotions. Unquestionably, these features of communication systems are elusive but unless they are operative, exchanges, especially during the development of language, would not be possible at all. In sociolinguistics, these general features have been captured by terms such as theme, content, register, and topic of exchange (Halliday, 1973); they also reflect the attitudes, opinions, roles, and biases of the speakers and listeners.

Although I am emphasizing the "shared code" as a prerequisite for any interaction that could justifiably be called "dialogue," such a code does not preexist in the minds of the participants but is derived through developmental efforts. This issue indicates the fallacy inherent in purely synchronic descriptions. Only if we consider dialogues outside of their developmental contexts are we forced to reintroduce abstract entities such as knowledge, ideas, feelings, and emotions which, in their operational forms, I have rejected in the first section of this paper. While the issue of preestablished features has to be further elaborated, at this moment it is sufficient to recognize that the participants in dialogues may differ widely in regard to these features. In order to engage in an effective dialogue, however, they have to focus their attention jointly on some, though not all, of them. If this were not the case—for example, if there were no agreement between the participants as to theme or topic of their discussion—a dialogue would either degenerate into presentations of mere generalities or move aimlessly from one issue to the next.

Graphically, the consistency of a dialogue can be expressed by a chain of arrows linking the utterances of speaker A and B in their temporal order. Such a *dialogic chain* differs from a *monologue* or narrative in that there is a systematic alternation between the two speakers (and listeners). The complexity of both sequences increases if connections refer back beyond the utterances immediately preceding a given one—for example, from A_3 to A_1 and not only to A_2 in the narrative chain, and not only to B_2 in the dialogic chain. The following examples are of lowest degree of complexity:

Dialogic Chain

$$A_1 \longrightarrow B_1 \longrightarrow A_2 \longrightarrow B_2 \longrightarrow A_3 \longrightarrow B_3 \ldots.$$

Monologue or Narrative

$$A_1 \longrightarrow A_2 \longrightarrow A_3 \longrightarrow A_4 \longrightarrow A_5 \ldots.$$

As the above example has indicated, a dialogue has order and structure; more specifically, it has structured order. The speakers alternate in the presentation, and each successive statement must at least reflect the one immediately preceding it. Restricting the range of statements to be successively incorporated to the immediately preceding statement represents a minimum requirement. The maximum requirement would be attained if each utterance were to reflect all of the earlier statements. Each statement has to be consistent with the proponent's own previously expressed views and, simultaneously, it must represent an equally consistent or systematically modified reaction to all statements made by the other participant in the dialogue. Moreover, as mentioned above, each statement has to reflect basic issues of the theme or topic which are presupposed although not necessarily explicit in the dialogue.

Disregarding several intermediate cases, the simplest form of an exchange which can justifiably be called a dialogue is depicted below. Here, each of the two speakers (after their initial comments) always relates his new statements both to the last statement made by his opponent and to that made by the speaker himself. In other words, each statement is connected with the last two preceding ones. Such a case represents a *simple dialogue* which is defined by what I shall call a depth of two and has the structure of a truss:

Simple Dialogue   (Depth A = 2; Depth B = 2)

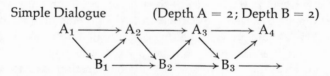

In *complex dialogues*, connections span across more than two preceding utterances (one by A and one by B). In the example below, the depth of the dialogue equals three:

Complex Dialogue   (Depth A = 3; Depth B = 3)

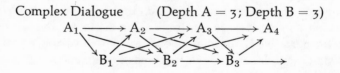

The depth of a dialogue can be conveniently determined by counting the number of converging and diverging relations for any A or B. Since the depth may increase with the length of the dialogue, one should either eliminate the first statements of both speakers or compute an average value for the whole dialogue. Since the interaction of the two speakers may differ, separate evaluations have to be made for A and B.

If a reflective coordination, as in a simple or complex dialogue, did not take place, the exchange would degenerate into alternating monologues in which each speaker would merely follow up on his earlier statements without reacting to the other speaker's elaborations. The other speaker's statements would thus appear as distractive interruptions and the only remaining dialogic feature of such a performance would consist in the alternations between the participants. If these alternations cease too, we approach a condition which Piaget (1926) has described as collective monologues. Here, two or more speakers continue their productions uninterruptedly and parallel to one another. Piaget describes such behavior as a manifestation of "egocentric" speech in young children. Undoubtedly the exchanges between adults also often reflect such egocentric tendencies and, therefore, failures in communication. Both cases are shown below; each of them has a depth of one for both speaker A and B:

Collective Monologues   (Depth A $= 1$; Depth B $= 1$)
$$A_1 \longrightarrow A_2 \longrightarrow A_3 \longrightarrow A_4$$
$$B_1 \longrightarrow B_2 \longrightarrow B_3 \longrightarrow$$

Alternating
Collective Monologues   (Depth A $= 1$; Depth B $= 1$)
$$A_1 \longrightarrow A_2 \longrightarrow A_3 \longrightarrow A_4$$
$$B_1 \longrightarrow B_2 \longrightarrow B_3 \longrightarrow$$

In a successful dialogue each speaker assimilates the other person's statements and accommodates his own productions so that they elaborate and extend the preceding viewpoints. If this were not the case, the dialogue would either degenerate into alternating collective monologues or would converge into a repetitive cycle in which each speaker merely reaffirms what has been said before. Such repetitive cycles would be indicated in the diagrams by any triangle or trapezoid with identical numerical subscripts. Like the triangular subsection in the truss of a bridge, repetitive or recursive operations are, of course, necessary for providing stability and a transitory thread to the discourse. This holds for the interactive operations of two (or more) persons as well as for the individual's own cognitive or linguistic operations. But neither of these operations can subsist on recursive production alone. The cycle has to be broken through what I have called contrastive operations (Riegel, 1975c). By means of such contrastive operations, the dialogue topic is either moved into new divergent directions or converges upon (is integrated with) previously made arguments.

Piaget identifies "pure" accommodation with imitation, and "pure" assimilation with play. The application of both concepts is even more appropriate for the analysis of dialogues than it is for the study of a single individual's operations. For example, pure accommodation or imitation in dialogues occurs if one or both speakers merely confirms, perhaps in modified phrasing, what the other participant has been saying. This case is at least partially identical with the production of repetitive or recursive cycles. Pure assimilation or play, on the other hand, is comparable to the condition of alternating collective monologues. In this case, each speaker reinterprets idiosyncratically any previous statements and, without concern for alternative viewpoints, reiterates his own interpretation.

Several intermediate dialogic conditions, or "half-dialogues," are possible that demonstrate various degrees of assimilation and accommodation. In the first of the following cases, A always assimilates the statements made by B but not his own preceding statements. Consequently, A always changes his position in reaction to B but does not remain consistent within himself. In other words, A accommodates to B and, therefore, does not participate appropriately in a simple dialogue, whereas B does. In the second of the following cases, B accommodates to A, whereas A participates appropriately in a simple dialogue:

Half-Dialogue
("pure" accommodation by A)   (Depth A $= 1$; Depth B $= 2$)

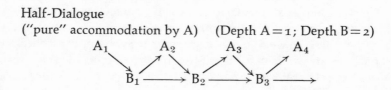

Half-Dialogue
("pure" accommodation by B)   (Depth A = 2; Depth B = 1)

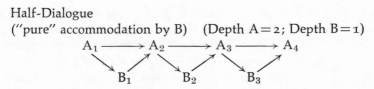

Alternative cases of half-dialogues occur when either of the two speakers engages in a monologue while the other interacts in the form of a simple dialogue. Identifying pure assimilation or play with a monologue, these half-dialogues can be depicted as follows:

Half-Dialogue
("pure" assimilation by A)   (Depth A = 1; Depth B = 2)

Half-Dialogue
("pure" assimilation by B)   (Depth A = 2; Depth B = 1)

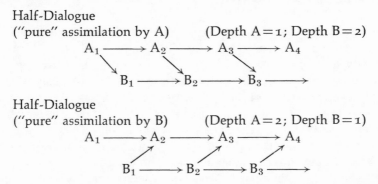

If one considers all features of language, including phonetic, syntactic, cognitive, and affective properties, the communicative basis is rather extensive. But if one considers only the criterial features, that is, those that make a difference to the participants in the dialogue, then the shared basis might be rather small. In particular, "pure" accommodation, that is, imitation or repetition, by both speakers produces maximum overlap between their messages. "Pure" assimilation or play, when applied to the interactive situation of a dialogue, represents a situation in which both speakers introduce a large amount of new information with each of their statements. Consequently, the communicative exchange may become overloaded or may break down. In the extreme case, the dialogue would degenerate into collective monologues.

Our comparison of performances in dialogues with Piaget's distinction of "pure" assimilation and "pure" accommodation also reveals that successful dialogues are dependent on the active participation of both the listener and the speaker. This proposition needs no amplification in regard to the speaker but it does, perhaps, in regard to the listener. The listener has to engage in active selection and interpretation of the information received in order to make it congruent with (assimilate) the content of former messages and, in particular, with his own conceptions. Such reinterpretations prepare him for his own rejoinder, whether confirming and elaborating or rejecting and restricting the other speaker's statements. Thus, his rejoinder is already initiated at a time when he is still listening, long before he utters the first word of his reply.

Developmental Dialogues

Comparisons of dialogue performances with children's imitation and play are not limited to activities by single persons but can be extended to interactive social games. For example, throwing and catching a ball or more complex performances in a real play, that is, on stage, reveal all of the properties of dialogues. As shown by Harris (1975), social games can be used to analyze the structural changes and development of language. The resulting comparison will be helpful because the rules of social games are often more precisely specified than those of language. This holds, especially, for field or table games with explicit rules of interactions, such as tennis, checkers, and chess. The conditions are, of course, much more complex if more than two players participate, such as in football, soccer, and card games. Explorations of the structure of children's games and their impact upon language acquisition have recently been conducted by Harris (1972) and Greenfield, Nelson, and Saltzman (1972).

Comparable to the earlier distinction between "primitive" and "scientific" dialectic (Lawler, 1975), development in general and the development of language in particular relies at the beginning on an intuitive "understanding" between the speaker and the listener, most likely between mother and child (Harris, 1975). With increasing experience in linguistic-cognitive operations the dialogue becomes explicit. Eventually, a person might be clearly aware of its conditions and might consciously select certain topics, registers, or modes of expression and apply effective ploys.

The development of the dialogue between a mother and child depends on shared extralingual knowledge, demands, and emotions. Shortly after birth such a synchronization seems to be determined by their joint physiology which, though disrupted, continues for a while to function in unison. But increasingly, temporal coordination will depend upon the mother's and the child's experience and selective operations. After just a few weeks, the child's and the mother's actions have already become finely tuned to one another. The child begins to look at the mother's face; when the mother moves, the child follows her with his eyes. Most important, when she speaks, the child might look at her mouth; when she stops, the child might vocalize and switch his attention from her mouth to her eyes. Supportive evidence for these interpretations has been provided by investigations of social interactions (Moss, 1967; Rheingold, 1961; Sameroff, 1975) and most notably by investigations of language development (Lewis, 1951; Lewis & Freedle, 1972). Interactive situations like those between the mother and her child represent the basis for subsequent sociolinguistic dialogues at more mature levels.

Early in life the dialogues between mother and child are bound to be out of balance. The mother has available a large repertoire of signs, rules, topics, and roles. The child has virtually none of these acquired forms and operations available. Consequently, the mother will have to be highly restrictive in her communication with the child; she retreats to the mode of "primitive" dialogues. But independent of her conscious interactive efforts, she will talk and sing along, and the child, eventually, will follow her activities and participate in them. On occasion she engages in directed efforts such as naming objects or giving instructions to the child. At an age between about 8 and 10 months, the linguistic sign system shared between mother and child might consist of a single sound sequence, such as MAMA. During the following weeks and months there will be a rather rapid expansion of the child's repertoire and, thus, of the sign system shared between mother and child. Over the following years, the primitive dialogue is transformed into a sociolinguistic dialogue and, potentially, a "scientific" dialogue.

The communication system shared by mother and child is at first private to both of them. As development advances—whether stepwise and in leaps or slowly and gradually—the signs become more and more congruent with the general linguistic system of the society. Seen from this point of view, the mother functions as an intermediary between her child and society. Thus the developmental dialogue is more than an exchange between two individuals. Society and history, through the mother, participate in the dialogue. Likewise in a nondevelopmental or situational dialogue, let's say between two adult speakers, each participant represents a particular social group with its particular orientations, preferences, and goals. Communication between the participants is possible only because both speakers and both groups which they represent are, in turn, part of the same large society and thus share a good many features of a common, more fundamental sign system.

Similar arguments have been made for the remote interactions between authors and their readers. In recent investigations by Marxist structuralists (see Fieguth, 1973; Mao Tse Tung, 1968; Riegel, 1975e; Schmid, 1973), the activities of authors are not merely regarded as dependent upon their personal feelings and knowledge but are also determined both by (a) the intentions and thoughts of the reader in the contemporary society and (b) the social values and ideas developed in the past through cultural-historical efforts and reflected in the present through the philosophy and ideology of the whole society. In this context, the authors' task consists in transmitting to the reader the knowledge and the direction of thought that have been generated in the society throughout its history, and their task is achieved through their participation in these cultural-historical efforts. Thus the author, like the mother, like the priest, and like the commissar, functions as an intermediary between the knowledge- and direction-seeking individuals and the values and ideas of the society—a society which throughout its history has been generated by individuals and within which, in its contemporary state, individuals remain its essential part.

Most important in the author's as well as in the mother's task is the coordination and synchronization of their efforts with those of the reader and the child respectively. Neither the reader nor the child should be overburdened or underburdened. Information has to be given at the right moment, in the right amount, and of the right kind. This is achieved through developmental interactions with the information seeker. The author may become too abstract and remote; he may progress too fast or lag behind. The mother, in a more concrete sense, has to speak as she influences her child, but she must also listen and change her own activites in accordance with the development of her child. Here, more than in the author's case, the synchronization of two time sequences, namely, the development of the child and the development of the mother, is of utmost importance. This process of synchronization is also the most important issue in any developmental description and theory. The following section is devoted to its exploration.

THE DIALECTIC OF CHANGES

A dialectic interpretation of development is concerned with simultaneous progressions of events along several complexly interacting dimensions. In the following discussion, I will distinguish between four progressions of events: (a) the inner-biological, (b) the individual-psychological, (c) the cultural-sociological, and (d) the outer-physical. A dialectic interpretation of development recognizes that the progressions of events along these interacting dimensions are not always coordinated or synchronized. Whenever the interactions between two progressions of events are out of step, a conflict or crisis is said to exist. Nevertheless, in a dialectic theory of development, conflict and crisis are rarely to be considered as destructive conditions. On the contrary, most conflicts and crises represent constructive confrontations in which the discordance of their contradictory interactions becomes the source of new development, more specifically, of leaps in development. Once generated, these new developments can transform the previously contradictory interactions of conflicting events into a coordinated, synchronized pattern of interaction and change. As synchrony is reestablished, a form of individual and social progress is achieved. And yet with each successful new development, new questions and discrepancies emerge and, in this process, produce a continuous flux of contradictions and developmental change. Below you will find a discussion of some of the conflicting and synchronized interactions that can occur among the four dimensions of developmental progression.

Inner-Biological versus Individual-Psychological Progressions

Crises originating from the inner-biological dimension, such as illness, incapacitations, and death, are rarely synchronized with events in the individual-psychological dimension, thus posing serious problems to the persons affected. Nevertheless, such a synchronization constitutes the goal of a successful life, and whenever such a crisis is resolved, retrospection reveals that a synchronizing reinterpretation of one's life situation will have taken place. Crises could be avoided if synchronization could be prospectively achieved. In this case, incapacitations and even death would become meaningful phases in one's life.

Crises and conflicts along the inner-biological and the individual-psychological dimensions can occur either within a single organism or between two organisms. The latter case includes, for example, the confrontations in preying, defending, feeding, and mating. The former condition represents conflicts between different subsystems, organs, or, ultimately, cell clusters and single cells. Modern physicists and microbiologists have argued for independent time dimensions for each of these units, frequently called time-lines or world-lines (Cohen & Riegel, 1972). Crises or conflicts—for example, the malignant growth of cells—would be described as asynchrony, in this case in the growth of specific cells or cell clusters. The cancerous cells grow at a largely accelerated rate, thereby disturbing the synchrony of the particular organ and, ultimately, of the whole organism.

Elsewhere I have described less traumatic events in the inner-biological dimension and emphasized their logic of progression (Riegel, 1975a). I have called attention to the inner-biological progression of events that leads the individual away from home, to work, marriage, and parenthood. Most of these events will be well synchronized with progressions along other dimensions; indeed they are made possible only through such a synchronization. For example, an individual marries when he is mature enough, when he has the psychological stature and intention, and when the social conditions (created in part by his own efforts) are conducive and appropriate. Of course, in many cases such a coordination is not achieved. The individual may marry without having reached an appropriate level of maturity or he may have attained the proper biological status but failed to find the right partner. All of these conditions will lead to the experience of crises.

In the above example, inner-biological and individual-psychological progressions lack coordination. Oftentimes these progressions also fail to be synchronized with conditions in the cultural-sociological or outer-physical dimension—for example, with the traditions and laws about marriage or in the case of the reduced availability of marriage partners after a war. Under successful conditions, coordinated interdependence between the progressions along all the different dimensions has to be achieved. In particular, the example of the marriage leads us to the discussion of the synchronization of two interdependent progressions along the individual-psychological plane.

Two Individual-Psychological Progressions

Within the single individual there will often be conflicts or crises between various subsystems generated by the asynchronic changes of what have come to be called wishes and duties, plans and skills, needs and actions, the unconscious and the conscious, etc. Rather than drawing attention to these issues, which constitute a traditional topic of personality theories (see Freud, 1917; Lewin, 1935; Rappoport, 1972; Rychlak, 1968, 1973), we focus upon the developmental interactions of two separate individuals.

The relations between children and their parents, brothers and sisters, husband and wife represent the most basic forms of individual interactions during the life span, but numerous others have to be considered, for example, between relatives, friends, neighbors, classmates, teachers and students, employers and employees, creditors and debtors, and venders and sellers. Familial progressions are firmly codetermined and intimately dependent upon one another. In comparison, general interindividual progressions exhibit a higher degree of flexibility and freedom in their interactions. Both types of interactive progressions may be crises-producing. For example, a child may not be wanted. This creates difficulties for the child as well as for the parents and their interactions with one another. Children may be born with defects. This is shown to result frequently in the breakdown of their parents' marriage. A student may fail or not live up to his teacher's expectations. An employee may be fired.

Individual-psychological interactions are always mutually influencing and dialectic in their progression. But the degree of mutuality or symmetry varies. For example, the synchronization of the career development of marriage partners has been traditionally achieved by subordinating the wife's progression to that of her husband. Thus, a coordination was achieved at the expense of the wife's individual-psychological development. Liberation movements are trying to change this condition. But freeing the woman and allowing her to create her own career development does not necessarily lead to a better coordination of the progressions of the two partners. At first, during its antithetical phase, it might even prevent the development of synchronized progressions. But eventually, a dialectic synthesis will be achieved (Hefner, Rebecca, & Oleshansky, 1975).

With or without liberation, a woman's development will remain more closely tied to that of her children. Thus, she may suffer more severely under the "crises" created by their departure from home. These damaging effects reflect once more the difficulties that arise within traditional society as a woman attempts to coordinate her development with the development of other individuals, especially the other members of her family. If other interpersonal tasks were required from her, as in the extended families of so-called primitive societies, or if other developmental tasks, such as a meaningful career, were more readily available to her in the modern industrial societies, no serious crises would be generated by the departure of her children.

In comparison with the career development of the married woman, a greater variety of developmental possibilities are available to her husband. As a result, he will be less affected by the changing events in his home. Nevertheless, much more attention needs to be given to well-programmed structural transformations during the adult development of both the female and the male. As I have shown elsewhere (Riegel, 1975a), a significant amount of developmental differentiation and coordination has been achieved only for academic careers.

Individual-Psychological versus Cultural-Sociological Progressions

The differentiations and coordinations demanded by individual and cultural progressions require major changes in the developmental interactions between the individual and the social group. The development and status of any social group is, of course, generated by individual efforts. But as social groups establish their means of existence (housing, communities, resources), of communication (language, trade, customs), and of organization (institutions, laws, traditions), they begin to exert a formative influence upon the individuals and their development. In a dialectic interpretation, development can be conceived of as lying neither in the individual alone nor in the social group alone but as constituted by the dialectic interactions of both. Crises will result if the progressions within the individual, within the social group, or between both are not synchronized.

It is important to note here that the whole issue of individual and social changes which has been brought into sharp focus by the elaboration of developmental research designs (Baltes, 1968; Schaie, 1965) compares changes along the inner-biological and individual-psychological dimensions, on the one hand, with those along the cultural-sociological and outer-physical, on the other. In reference to the summary presented in Table 2, it compares the two left-hand columns with the two right-hand columns, or the two upper rows with the two lower rows. Rather than elaborating the details of such comparisons in a formal manner, as Schaie, Baltes, and others have done, I am discussing the type and content of changes encountered.

Previously (Riegel, 1975a), I called attention to the coordination of individual and social progressions. In particular, I discussed the career development of "normal" scientists who participate in one paradigmatic orientation and who, consequently, suffer as this orientation fades into the background of scientific consideration. A programmed, that is, coordinated, change in their academic roles, for example, by assigning administrative and ceremonial duties to them during the later parts of their careers, would enable these scientists to resolve more smoothly the crises generated by changes in scientific orientation.

In comparison with "normal" scientists, exceptional individuals such as Wundt or Piaget are not only instrumental in generating a single paradigmatic orientation; as their orientations are implemented in laboratories and communicated through publications, these individuals move ahead by proposing new conceptualizations. Thus, their lives would appear to be most gratified and fulfilled. Nevertheless, they too may experience crises, since the scientific community is not always ready to accept their new orientations and, as a result, may either neglect or reject the contributions which these scientists have regarded as the highest achievements of their careers. In the case of Wundt, for example, his notion of transformational grammar was disregarded by the scientific community for more than 70 years and has remained neglected by modern proponents of such interpretations, most notably by Chomsky. Only the historians (Blumenthal, 1970) revived our memory for these contributions.

Two Cultural-Sociological Progressions

Although many other examples should be provided, especially for adult development in nonacademic settings, the discussion of conflicts between different paradigmatic orientations leads us to the next level of discourse, namely, the progressions through interactions of various cultural-sociological groups. More than the developmental interactions of individuals, the range of organizational units is extensive indeed. The smallest and most basic group is the family. Different families within the kin compete for leadership but they also cooperate in order to achieve welfare and security for their members. While families, kins, and tribes play a decisive role in the development of nonindustrialized societies, these functions are increasingly absorbed by interest groups and political parties, manufacturing companies, and business organizations in industrial settings. When extended to the lower limits, these groupings include teams, gangs, clubs, and classes; when extended to the upper limits, they include communities, states, nations, and civilizations. But this stratification is by no means unidimensional. It cross-cuts society in various ways, in the form of linguistic, political, occupational, religious, economic, and scientific groups, and—last but not least —generations or cohorts.

All groups are in cooperation and competition. Each develops and succeeds until it is replaced by other groups and fades into the background. Not all of the changes are coordinated in ways that lead to smooth improvements of all groups and, ultimately, of all individuals involved. Lack of synchrony creates conflicts which express themselves in revolutions, conquests, and wars, as well as depressions, inflations, bankruptcies, strikes, unemployment, etc. Without exploring these issues in any detail, I will call attention to one example in the interactive development of social groups, namely, to subcultural relations.

Just as the development of the woman in the traditional family has been subordinated to that of her husband, so has the development of minority groups been subordinated to that of the majority, at least in colonial and capitalistic societies. The liberation movement has justifiably claimed the right of the minority groups for separate developments reflecting their own cultures, languages, and institutions. Such attempts, if successful, are the prerequisites for coordinated development in the larger society. Traditionally the need for coordination has been overemphasized by the majority without due recognition of the fact that such a synthesis can only take place once the two developmental progressions have achieved a high degree of independence reflected in mutual appreciation and respect. Unfortunately, the fulfillment of these goals has rarely been supported by the majority, nor does a subsequent developmental synchronization represent the clearly recognized intention of all of the individuals and groups involved. Nevertheless, developmental synchronization on the basis of mutual recognition is the only mode by which catastrophies can be avoided and joint progress achieved.

Cultural-Sociological versus Outer-Physical Progressions

Large societies composed of well-coordinated subgroups have achieved the conquests of nature and the intellectual heights that make up the history of civilizations. These efforts, in general, have been directed toward increasing the security and welfare of the society and its individual members. Many times, however, these attempts led to conflicts with other groups, thus creating crises for the individual and catastrophes for society. In pathological cases, social groups without any apparent reasons have engaged in reckless drives for power and conquest. But in most instances, these extreme forms of expansionism were determined by catastrophic events in outer-physical nature. For example, the vast migrations leading to the destruction of the Roman Empire seem to be attributable to climatic changes which drove large masses of semicivilized tribes into Italy. In a positive sense, the rise of the Egyptian and the Greek civilizations has been attributed to the encounter of the native populations with conquering tribes which, in turn, had been forced away from their homeland by catastrophic deterioration of their living conditions.

Thus, cultural-sociological changes are frequently determined by changes in outer-physical conditions which exert their impact not only upon large organizations such as nations or civilizations, but also upon all subgroups as well as upon every individual who is a part of these subgroups. In other words, there is an interdependence between all dimensions of developmental progressions. At the upper level, outer-physical events such as earthquakes, climatic changes, droughts, and floods influence whole societies. Consequently, the cultural tasks of these societies consist in protecting themselves and their individual members from the catastrophes which they encounter. At the lowest level, these outer-physical catastrophes have a direct impact upon the single individual. In the extreme case, they destroy his biological existence. But unless such destruction is experienced in the individual-psychological dimension or is recorded at the cultural-sociological dimension, it will not achieve significance. Isolated progressions along any single dimension—it should be recognized—are empty and represent abstractions; concrete development is generated through dialectic interactions between the progressions along several different dimensions.

Crises in the most appropriate sense of the word are generated by the sheer disruption or asynchrony in the interaction between inner-biological and outer-physical progressions. Actions will be taken at the individual-psychological and cultural-sociological levels to prevent inner and outer crises (e.g., through medical treatment and through flood control) or at least to predict their occurrence well in advance (e.g., through medical checkups and through weather forecasts). But the control and coordination of these inner and outer disruptions is not always successful. So while it is true that real crises can exist, they are relatively rare compared with those generated by asynchronies in individual-psychological and cultural-sociological progressions. Events created by such discordance will also be experienced as crises. Since, however, these crises can be avoided through improved planning and coordination, they deserve their label with less justification. The constructive rearrangements which these crises generate lead to progress and new cognitive-social achievements; indeed, they represent the very basis of our individual and cultural efforts.

Schematic Summary

The crises generated through asynchronies in the developmental progressions along the four different dimensions have been summarized in Table 2. Although I have emphasized their codetermination, events occurring in one dimension can be prior, triggering, or causative for events occurring in other dimensions. In Table 2, the triggering conditions are listed along the left-hand margin, the triggered conditions along the upper margin. For example, the individual-psychological conditions listed in the second row influence the inner-biological conditions listed in the first column, leading to *disorder* or imposing *control*. All terms listed as the upper members in the cells of Table 2 indicate a negative outcome of the conflict; all those listed as the lower members indicate a positive outcome.

The cells along the main diagonal of the table represent conflicts between two progressions along the same dimension, for example,

Table 2
*Crisis with Negative (Upper Lines) and Positive (Lower Lines)
Outcomes Generated by Asynchronies along Four Planes
of Developmental Progressions*

	Inner-Biological	Individual-Psychological	Cultural-Sociological	Outer-Physical
Inner-Biological	Infection Fertilization	Illness Maturation	Epidemic Cultivation	Deterioration Vitalization
Individual-Psychological	Disorder Control	Discordance Concordance	Dissidence Organization	Destruction Creation
Cultural-Sociological	Distortion Adaptation	Exploitation Acculturation	Conflict Cooperation	Devastation Conservation
Outer-Physical	Annihilation Nutrition	Catastrophy Welfare	Disaster Enrichment	Chaos Harmony

between the individual-psychological developments of husband
and wife leading to *discordance* (upper item) or *concordance* (lower
item). All other cells of the matrix, that is, those off the main
diagonal, represent conflicts between progressions along two different dimensions, for example, between cultural-sociological and
individual-psychological developments leading to *exploitation*
(upper item) or *acculturation* (lower item). If one collapses the two
left-hand columns and the two right-hand columns and the two upper rows and the two lower rows, one ends up with comparisons
of individual (both biological and psychological) with social changes
(both cultural and physical) that have been explored in the
discussion of modern developmental research designs (Baltes, 1968;
Schaie, 1965).

Needless to say, the selection of specific terms creates ambiguities
as well as overinterpretations. The usage of most terms in common
language is more general than indicated by their assignment to a
particular cell of the matrix. All assignments are suggestive rather
than authoritative.

THE SIGNIFICANCE OF DIALECTIC THINKING FOR PSYCHOLOGICAL RESEARCH AND THEORY

In this chapter I have argued against the deeply rooted bias in favor
of stable traits and entities as well as against an overemphasis on

balance and stability in individual and historical development. I have sought to demonstrate the insufficiencies of these conceptions and the constricting effect they have imposed upon our view of man. As we have conformed to these biases without questioning the underlying assumptions, we have failed to imagine alternative possibilities. In writing this chapter, I have tried to move beyond the limitiations and restrictions of these older conceptions in order to explore the alternative of developmental dialectics.

1. Dialectic theory provides a synthesis for the many different specialities in psychology and creates constructive links with other disciplines, most notably with sociology and anthropology on the one hand, and biology on the other. By focusing upon concrete events in the life of the individual and of society, dialectic theory succeeds in overcoming one of the deepest splits in the behavioral sciences, the split between applied-clinical and academic-experimental psychology. The former, though creating abstract metastructures such as psychoanalytic theory, has been concerned with single individuals and their everyday affairs. The latter has studied abstract elements or capacities in equally abstract laboratory settings (Kvale, 1975). Dialectic theory, in contrast, describes concrete event sequences in the individual and equally concrete sequences in society, both of which it regards as interdependent and reflecting upon inner-biological and outer-physical changes. Thus, dialectic theory gets lost neither in subjective singularities nor in objective generalities. Although it remains committed to the study of real human beings, it explores them in a systematic, that is, dialectic, manner and thus provides a universal theory. The strength of dialectic theory is founded in its emphasis on change and development as well as in its ability to encompass a manifold of contradictory conceptions.

2. A dialectic theory of development regards the individual as being in a continuous process of change brought about through the successive interactions of concrete events over time. A dialectic theory recognizes that each person develops as an individual but as an individual who is an integral part of the changing society and the changing physical world. In other words, a dialectic theory of development is simultaneously concerned with the relationships of change within the individual, with the relationships of change within the world, and with the relationships between the changing individual and the changing world.

The successions of interacting events within each individual are referred to as the inner dialectics and can be illustrated by Piaget's account of the development of cognitive schemas through the operations of assimilation and accommodation. Although in this conception an individual develops his cognitive schemas as he successively interacts with the objects in his environment, the operations of assimilation and accommodation are brought about by the individual himself. Yet, in terms of a psychological theory, it is important to see that Piaget gives little attention to the possibility that the objects of these interactions can include other active organisms (Wilden, 1975). A dialectic theory, on the other hand, recognizes that when we study the successions of interactions developing between two or more active individuals, for example, a mother and her child or a scientist and his colleagues, we must also be concerned with the outer dialectics.

Outer dialectics represents the successions of interacting events in the cultural-sociological and outer-physical world. It emphasizes the existence of other active individuals and groups of individuals who are simultaneously engaged in their own process of change and development. Outer dialectics represents an aspect of development that has an importance equal to that of inner dialectics. Nevertheless, the key to a comprehensive dialectic theory of development is found in the interaction of both. To by more specific, a dialectic theory conceives of the individual as a changing being in a changing world. Development can be apprehended only by studying the successive interactions *between* the interactive events of change within the individual (inner dialectics) and the interactive events of change in the outer world (outer dialectics). In this sense, a dialectic theory of development apprehends human beings at an intersection of interactions: the changing events within individuals are interacting with and influencing the changing events in the outer world; while simultaneously, the changing events in the outer world are interacting with and influencing the changing events within individuals (Rubinsteijn, 1958, 1963; See also Payne, 1968; Riegel, 1973a; Wozniak, 1975a, 1975b).

3. In a dialectic theory of development, the successive interactions of concrete events between a changing individual and the changing world must embrace both short-term situational and long-term developmental interactions. Short-term situational interactions can be represented most explicitly in the dialectic of a dialogue (Freedle,

1975; Harris, 1975). The diagrams included in this chapter illustrate, perhaps better than words, the successions of alternating inter- actions which can occur between a changing individual and a changing representative of the outer world, that is, his dialogue partner. In this framework the dialectic of a dialogue acquires special significance when it is considered as a basis for gaining knowledge.

A dialectic theory of development is exemplified in what I have called a "complex dialogue." In a complex dialogue each speaker develops his own sequence of meaning-events (inner dialectics). This occurs as each speaker successively assimilates the other speaker's statements and accommodates his own in such a way that he selects, integrates, and transforms the existing meaning of the dialogue into a new statement of meaning. Moreover, as each new statement of meaning becomes a concrete event, an objectified product, it becomes available as a possibility for the further development of meaning within either the original speaker or his dialogue partner.

Theoretically, however, it is important to note that in a dialectic conception the development of meaning in each speaker can be understood only in its successive interactions with the developing meanings of his dialogue partner. In this dialectic succession, the meanings expressed by each speaker are inextricably linked in complementary interdependence so that neither speaker could have selected and coordinated his particular sequence of meanings in isolation from the developing meanings of his partner. In brief, each speaker in a dialogue develops and integrates his own progressions of meanings but these progressions are codetermined by the successive interactions between the changing meaning-events within the speaker himself and the changing meaning-events of his dialogue partner.

4. Although a short-term situational dialogue can serve as an example, and perhaps even a model, of a dialectic theory of development, a comprehensive view of development must include the long-term progressions of events that occur in a changing individual as he interacts with his changing cultural-sociological and outer-physical world. These long-term progressions of development have been studied most extensively within the psychology of adult development and aging. The body of data growing out of these investigations has become an argument against theories based on fixed entities or stable states. As a specific illustration, the weight of the evidence built up by the long history of intelligence testing suggests that the individual growth and decline of intelligence, once

represented as a stable entity, is determined rather by the effects of generational differences and historical change.

When research data such as these are viewed from the perspective of a dialectic theory of development, they demonstrate that it is insufficient and distorting to study an individual unless he is studied in his own progressions of change and unless, concomitantly, these individual changes are studied in their successive interactions with the socio-historical progressions of change in the group or society of which he is a part (Krüger, 1915; Mannheim, 1952). In recognizing the interdependence of individual development and social change, a dialectic theory of development has led us away from the traditional child-centered approach toward an adult or rather life-span emphasis in development.

In my discussion of developmental-historical change, I have described the long-term interactions between a mother and child as a case in point and then considered this developing relationship as a basis for other forms of individual and social activities. Throughout this developing relationship, a mother actively expresses herself to her child, but simultaneously she must accommodate her thoughts, actions, and feelings in response to the changing development of her child. As development progresses, a delicate coordination and increasing elaboration of the interactions between mother and child emerge. This process of coordinating two sequences of interactions, exemplified through this finely tuned, mutually interwoven development between a mother and child, must be considered in any interpretation of development. I would also contend that the primitive dialectics in the child and in the child-mother interactions provides a basis for the eventual development of scientific dialectics, a dialectic which finds expression in dialogues and debates—both in the thoughts of a single individual and in the exchanges among many.

5. Dialectic theory is committed to the study of activities and changes. In my discussion of the dialectics of change, I have distinguished between the simultaneous progressions of events along four complexly interacting dimensions: the inner-biological, the individual-psychological, the cultural-sociological, and the outer-physical. I have provided several examples of both conflicting and synchronizing sequences of interaction within and between these four dimensions—for example, the long-term career developments of a husband and wife, the developmental changes between minority and majority groups, and the career crises among "normal" and

"exceptional" scientists during shifts in paradigmatic orientation. Detailed examinations of such evidence reveal the significance of dialectical forms of research for our understanding of development.

The complex interactions among the changing progressions of events are not always coordinated and synchronized. Whenever synchrony breaks down, a conflict or crisis is said to exist. Nevertheless, in a dialectic theory of development, conflict and crisis are not regarded in a negative manner; on the contrary, most crises represent constructive confrontations in which the discordance and tension of their contradictory interactions can be seen as the source of every new development within both the individual and society. The contradictory and asynchronic interactions form a creative tension which generates new development, or more specifically, leaps in development. In an Aristotelian sense, the potentialities of the human being are made actual in the course of these developmental leaps. Among these new developments in thought, action, and feeling, some will be successful in transforming the previously contradictory interactions of conflicting events into coordinated and synchronized patterns of relationship and meaning.

Yet, in sharp contrast with Piaget's theory, a dialectic theory of development does not emphasize the plateaus at which equilibrium or balance is achieved. Instead, stable plateaus of balance are seen as the exception, a temporary marking or achievement, for as soon as a developmental task is completed and synchrony attained, new questions, doubts, and contradictions arise within the individual and within society. A dialectic theory places less emphasis on stable plateaus of balance and more emphasis on the contradictions and questions raised by each achievement because it is, relative to other theories, more profoundly concerned with the process of change and the conditions that keep it moving. Contradictions and questions play a central role in a dialectic theory of development because they create the discordance which provokes us to move beyond our existing achievements in a continuing progression of efforts leading to new achievements.

6. If we are to understand the critical importance of contradictions and questions in a dialectic theory of development, we must realize that such a theory sees each new product of man's thinking, action, and feeling as an integral part of a developing "reality" in the continuing process of change. In this sense there is no absolute knowledge. There are no finished products of man's thinking, no fixed and final answers that can be assembled in all their parts and

laid down once and for all. The products of man's thinking are mutable products, developing products with a potential for change. Thus each new achievement, in being a part of a developing "reality," is both an actual, objectified development relative to past achievements and, at the same time, a part of the raw material, that is, the available potential, for all future achievements. Within this process of change, a dialectic theory sees the contradictions and questions raised by each new achievement as the means by which an existing achievement can be reappraised and transformed into an achievement of still greater comprehension (Meacham, 1972; Riegel, 1972a, 1975a; Wundt, 1949).

In this succession of dialectic transformations, each new leap of achievement is a creative step in the developmental progression of the individual and society, a bench mark of psychological and social development. Step by step these products of man's thought, action, and feeling, although never anchored in fixed answers or final certainty, become selected and coordinated through a collective exchange of thought, action, and feeling into the changing structures of human knowledge. In this continuous process of transformation and change, we apprehend the dialectics of development as a ceaseless flux of contradictions and synchronizing new developmental achievements. The individual, the society, and even outer nature are never at rest, and in their restlessness, they are rarely in perfect harmony.

Development requires a delicate coordination between different progressions of events. Coordination is comparable to balance, but it is a balance in change which depends on continuous actions within and between the interacting dimensions of changing events. The dialectic theory of development is comparable to orchestral music. If there were only two instruments and if both were always to play in perfect harmony, they would merely increase the sound volume. However, orchestral arrangements, from classical music to modern jazz, create deviations. Classical music relies on counterpoint to produce deviations but retains synchrony through its harmony. Modern jazz produces deviations through dissonance but retains synchrony through rhythm and beat. Only cacophony or random alignments of notes create sounds that have neither patterns nor synchronies. They represent music as inappropriately as a series of conflicting and uncoordinated progressions of events would represent development.

7. In conclusion, a dialectic theory of development conceives of

man as a changing being in a changing world. In this relationship of change, individual and cultural changes are perceived as complementary and dynamically interdependent. Each individual coordinates and transforms the conflicting events of his experience into his own sequence of development. Within these limits, each new developmental leap of thought, action, and feeling can be seen as an individual creation. And yet in a dialectic interpretation, no individual achievement occurs in isolation from the objectified thoughts, actions, and feelings developed by other individuals. On the contrary, the creative achievements of an individual can be actualized only as the changing individual interacts successively with the changing progressions of events in the other individuals. The achievements of an individual are, in other words, individually created but created in a "collective dialogue" with the significant others of his cultural group.

Looking at individual and cultural development from a dialectic perspective, we begin to see that the thoughts, actions, and feelings of a single individual, once generated and actualized, can transform the thoughts, actions, and feelings of others who live with him or come after him; and simultaneously, the thoughts, actions, and feelings of these individuals in the outer world, perhaps enriched by the activities of the above individual, can, in their turn, interact in ways that further transform the thoughts, actions, and feelings of the single individual. And so in this dynamic conjunction of individual change and social-historical change, it becomes apparent that as man creates and transforms himself, he not only transforms the outer world in which he lives but is himself transformed by the world which he and others have created.

REFERENCES

Atkinson, J. W. Motivation and ability as interactive determinants of performance, cumulative achievement, and each other. Paper presented at 18th International Congress of Applied Psychology, Montreal, Canada, August, 1974.
Baltes, P. B. Longitudinal and cross-sectional sequences in the study of age and generation effects. *Human Development*, 1968, **11**, 145–171.
Baltes, P. B., Baltes, M. M., & Reinert, G. The relationship between time of measurement and age in cognitive development of children: An application of cross-sectional sequences. *Human Development*, 1970, **13**, 145–171.

Baltes, P. B., & Labouvie, G. V. Adult development of intellectual performance: Description, explanation, and modification. In L. Eisdorfer & M. P. Lawton (Eds.), *The psychology of adult development and aging.* Washington, D.C.: American Psychological Association, 1972. Pp. 157–219.

Belmont, L., & Marolla, F. A. Birth order, family size, and intelligence. *Science,* 1973, **182**, 1096–1101.

Binet, A., & Henri, V. La psychologie individuelle. *L'Année psychologique,* 1896, **2**, 411–465.

Birren, J. E. Principles of research on aging. In J. E. Birren (Ed.), *Handbook of aging and the individual.* Chicago: University of Chicago Press, 1959. Pp. 3–42.

Blumenthal, A. *Language and psychology.* New York: Wiley, 1970.

Boring, E. G. Intelligence as the tests test it. *New Republic,* 1923, **34**, 35–36.

Brentano, F. von. *Psychologie vom empirischen Standpunkt.* Leipzig: Meiner, 1874.

Brown, L. K. Familial dialectics in a clinical context. In K. F. Riegel (Ed.), *The development of dialectical operations.* Basel: Karger, 1975. Pp. 223–238.

Cattell, R. B. Occupational norms of intelligence and the standardization of an adult intelligence scale. *British Journal of Psychology,* 1934, **25**, 1–28.

Chomsky, N. *Language and mind.* New York: Harcourt, Brace, & World, 1968.

Clark, H. H. Comprehending comparatives. In G. B. Flores d'Arcais & W. J. M. Levelt (Eds.), *Advances in psycholinguistics.* Amsterdam: North Holland Publishing Co., 1970. Pp. 294–306.

Cohen, D., & Riegel, K. F. Time as energy: On the application of modern concepts of time to developmental sciences. Unpublished manuscript, University of Southern California, Gerontology Center, 1972.

Fieguth, R. Struktur des literarischen Wandels: Structur der Einzelwerke. Unpublished manuscript, University of Konstanz, Germany, 1973.

Flavell, J. H. Cognitive changes in adulthood. In L. R. Goulet & P. B. Baltes (Eds.), *Life-span developmental psychology: Research and theory.* New York: Academic Press, 1970. Pp. 247–253.

Freedle, R. Dialogue and inquiry systems. In K. F. Riegel (Ed.), *The development of dialectical operations.* Basel: Karger, 1975. Pp. 97–118.

Freud, S. *Vorlesungen zur Einführung in die Psychoanalyse.* Vienna: Internationaler Psychoanalytischer Verlag, 1917 (A general introduction to psychoanalysis. Garden City, N.Y.: Garden City Publishing Co., 1943).

Furth, H. G. *Piaget and knowledge.* Englewood Cliffs, N.J.: Prentice Hall, 1969.

Furth, H. G. Piaget, I. Q., and the nature-nurture controversy. *Human Development*, 1973, **16**, 61–73.

Gesell, A. *Infancy and human growth*. New York: Macmillan, 1928.

Greenfield, P. M., Nelson, H., & Saltzman, E. The development of rulebound strategies for manipulating seriated cups: A parallel between action and grammar. *Cognitive Psychology*, 1972, **3**, 291–310.

Gulliksen, H. *Theory of mental tests*. New York: Wiley, 1950.

Hall, G. S. *Adolescence*. 2 Vols. New York: Appleton, 1904.

Halliday, M. A. K. *Explorations in the functions of language*. London: Arnold, 1973.

Harris, A. E. Cognitive skills in verbal and non-verbal activity. Unpublished doctoral dissertation, University of Michigan, 1972.

Harris, A. E. Social dialectics and language: Mother and child construct the discourse. In K. F. Riegel (Ed.), *The development of dialectical operations*. Basel: Karger, 1975. Pp. 80–96.

Hefner, R., Rebecca, M., & Oleshansky, B. Development of sex role transcendence. In K. F. Riegel (Ed.), *The development of dialectical operations*. Basel: Karger, 1975. Pp. 143–158.

Huttenlocher, J., & Higgins, E. T. Adjectives, comparatives, and syllogisms. *Psychological Review*, 1971, **78**, 487–504.

James, W. *Principles of psychology*. New York: Holt, 1890.

Jenkins, J. J., & Russell, W. A. Systematic changes in word association norms: 1910–1952. *Journal of Abnormal and Social Psychology*, 1960, **60**, 293–304.

Jones, H. E., & Conrad, H. S. The growth and decline of intelligence: A study of a homogeneous group between the ages ten and sixty. *Genetic Psychological Monographs*, 1933, **13**, 223–298.

Kominski, C. A., & Coppinger, N. W. The Muller-Lyer illusion and Piaget's test for the development of the conservation of space in a group of older institutionalized veterans. Paper presented at the College of William and Mary, Williamsburg, Virginia, 1968.

Kosok, M. The formalization of Hegel's dialectic logic. In A. MacIntyre (Ed.), *Hegel: A collection of critical essays*. Garden City, N.J.: Anchor Books, 1972. Pp. 237–287.

Krüger, F. E. *Über Entwicklungspsychologie, ihre sachliche und geschichtliche Notwendigkeit*. Leipzig: W. Engelmann, 1915.

Kvale, S. *Prüfung und Herrschaft*. Weinheim: Beltz, 1972.

Kvale, S. Memory and dialectics: Some reflections on Ebbinghaus and Mao Tse-Tung. In K. F. Riegel (Ed.), *The development of dialectical operations*. Basel: Karger, 1975. Pp. 205–222.

Lawler, J. Dialectic philosophy and developmental psychology: Hegel and Piaget on contradiction. In K. F. Riegel (Ed.), *The development of dialectical operations*. Basel: Karger, 1975. Pp. 1–17.

Lewin, K. *A dynamic theory of personality*. New York: McGraw-Hill, 1935.

Lewis, M. M. *Infant speech: A study of the beginnings of language.* New York: Humanities Press, 1951.

Lewis, M., & Freedle, R. Mother-infant dyad: The cradle of meaning. *Research Bulletin 72–22.* Princeton, N.J.: Educational Testing Service, 1972.

Mannheim, K. The problem of generations. In K. Mannheim (Ed.), *Essays on the sociology of knowledge.* New York: Oxford University Press, 1952.

Mao Tse-Tung. *Four essays in philosophy.* Peking: Foreign Language Press, 1968.

McLaughlin, G. H. Psycho-logic: A possible alternative to Piaget's formulation. *British Journal of Educational Psychology,* 1963, **33**, 61–67.

Meacham, J. A. The development of memory abilities in the individual and society. *Human Development,* 1972, **15**, 205–228.

Miles, C. C., & Miles, W. R. The correlation of intelligence scores and chronological age from early to late maturity. *American Journal of Psychology,* 1932, **44**, 44–78.

Moss, H. A. Sex, age, and state as determinants of mother-infant interaction. *Merrill-Palmer Quarterly,* 1967, **13**, 19–36.

Murray, H. (and collaborators). *Explorations in personality.* New York: Oxford, 1938.

Nesselroade, J. R., & Baltes, P. B. Adolescent personality development and historical change: 1970–1972. *Monographs on the Society for Research in Child Development,* 1974, **39**, No. 154.

Neugarten, B. L., & Datan, N. Sociological perspectives on the life cycle. In P. B. Baltes & K. W. Schaie (Eds.), *Life-span developmental psychology: Personality and socialization.* New York: Academic Press, 1973. Pp. 53–69.

Owens, W. A., Jr. Age and mental abilities: A longitudinal study. *Genetic Psychological Monographs,* 1953, **48**, 3–54.

Papalia, D. A., & Bielby, D. D. V. Cognitive functioning in middle and old age adults: A review of research based on Piaget's theory. *Human Development,* 1974, **17**, 424–443.

Payne, J. R. *S. L. Rubinsteijn and the philosophical foundations of Soviet psychology.* New York: Humanities Press, 1968.

Piaget, J. *The language and thought of the child.* New York: Harcourt & Brace, 1926.

Piaget, J. *Play, dreams and imitation in childhood.* New York: Norton, 1962.

Piaget, J. *The child's conception of number.* New York: Norton, 1965.

Piaget, J., & Inhelder, B. *The child's conception of space.* New York: Norton, 1967.

Rappoport, L. *Personality development: The chronology of experience.* Glenview, Ill.: Scott, Foresman & Co., 1972.

Rechtschaffen, A. Psychotherapy with geriatric patients: A review of the literature. *Journal of Gerontology*, 1959, **14**, 73–84.

Reid, J. *Inquiry into the human mind on the principles of common sense.* London: A. Millar, 1764.

Rheingold, H. L. The effect of environmental stimulation upon social and exploratory behavior in the human infant. In B. M. Foss (Ed.), *Determinants of infant behavior*, Vol. 1. New York: Wiley, 1961. Pp. 143–177.

Riegel, K. F. Personality theory and aging. In J. E. Birren (Ed.), *Aging and the individual.* Chicago: University of Chicago Press, 1959. Pp. 797–851.

Riegel, K. F. Age and cultural differences as determinants of word associations: Suggestions for their analysis. *Psychological Reports,* 1965, **16**, 75–78.

Riegel, K. F. On the history of psychological gerontology. In C. Eisdorfer & M. P. Lawton (Eds.), *The psychology of adult development and aging.* Washington, D.C.: American Psychological Association, 1972. Pp. 37–68. (a)

Riegel, K. F. The influence of economic and political ideologies upon the development of developmental psychology. *Psychological Bulletin,* 1972, **78**, 129–141. (b)

Riegel, K. F. Time and change in the development of the individual and society. In H. Reese (Ed.), *Advances in child development and behavior*, Vol. 7. New York: Academic Press, 1972. Pp. 81–113. (c)

Riegel, K. F. Developmental psychology and society: Some historical and ethical considerations. In J. R. Nesselroade & H. W. Reese (Eds.), *Life-span developmental psychology: Methodological issues.* New York: Academic Press, 1973. Pp. 1–23. (a)

Riegel, K. F. Dialectic operations: The final period of cognitive development. *Human Development*, 1973, **16**, 346–370. (b)

Riegel, K. F. (Ed.) *Intelligence: Alternative views of a paradigm.* Basel: Karger, 1973. (c)

Riegel, K. F. Adult life crises: Toward a dialectic theory of development. In N. Datan & L. H. Ginsberg (Eds.), *Life-span developmental psychology: Normative life crises.* New York: Academic Press, 1975. Pp. 97–124. (a)

Riegel, K. F. All the trouble with linguistics. *International Journal of Psycholinguistics*, 1975, in press. (b)

Riegel, K. F. Contrastive and recursive relations. *Research Memorandum 74–23*, Princeton, N.J.: Educational Testing Service, 1975. (c)

Riegel, K. F. Semantic basis of language: Language as labor. In K. F. Riegel & G. C. Rosenwald (Eds.), *Structure and transformation: Developmental and historical aspects.* New York: Wiley, 1975. Pp. 167–192. (d)

Riegel, K. F. Structure and transformation in modern intellectual history. In K. F. Riegel & G. C. Rosenwald (Eds.), *Structure and transformation:*: Developmental and historical aspects. New York: Wiley, 1975. Pp. 3–24. (e)

Riegel, K. F. Subject-object alienation in psychological experiments and testing. In K. F. Riegel (Ed.), *The development of dialectical operations.* Basel: Karger, 1975. Pp. 181–193. (f)

Riegel, K. F., & Riegel, R. M. Development, drop and death. *Developmental Psychology,* 1972, 6, 306–319.

Riegel, K. F., Riegel, R. M., & Meyer, G. Socio-psychological factors of aging: A cohort-sequential analysis. *Human Development,* 1967, 10, 27–56.

Riegel, R. M., & Riegel, K. F. Standardisierung des Hamburg-Wechsler-Intelligenztests für Erwachsene (HAWIE) für die Altersstufen über 50 Jahre. *Diagnostica,* 1959, 5, 97–128.

Riley, M. W., Johnson, W., & Foner, A. (Eds.) *Aging and society.* Vol. 3. *A sociology of age stratification.* New York: Russell Sage Foundation, 1972.

Rubinsteijn, S. L. *Grundlagen der allgemeinen Psychologie.* Berlin: Volk und Wissen, 1958.

Rubinsteijn, S. L. *Prinzipien und Wege der Entwicklung der Psychologie.* Berlin: Akademie Verlag, 1963.

Rychlak, J. K. *A philosophy of science for personality theory.* Boston: Houghton Mifflin, 1968.

Rychlak, J. K. *Introduction to personality and psychotherapy.* New York: Houghton Mifflin, 1973.

Ryder, N. B. The cohort as a concept in the study of social changes. *American Sociological Review,* 1965, 30, 843–861.

Sameroff, A. Transactional models in early social relations. In K. F. Riegel (Ed.), *The development of dialectical operations.* Basel: Karger, 1975. Pp. 65–79.

Sanders, S., Laurendeau, M., & Bergeron, J. Aging and the concept of space: The conservation of surface. *Journal of Gerontology,* 1966, 21, 281–285.

Schaie, K. W. A general model for the study of developmental problems. *Psychological Bulletin,* 1965, 64, 92–108.

Schaie, K. W., & Labouvie Vief, G. Generational versus ontogenetic components of change in adult cognitive behavior: A fourteen-year cross-sectional sequence. *Developmental Psychology,* 1974, 10, 305–320.

Schaie, K. W., Labouvie, G. V., & Buech, B. U. Generational and cohort-specific differences in adult cognitive functioning: A fourteen-year study of independent samples. *Developmental Psychology,* 1973, 9, 151–166.

Schaie, K. W., & Strother, C. R. The cross-sequential study of age changes in cognitive behavior. *Psychological Bulletin*, 1968, **70**, 671–680. (a)

Schaie, K. W., & Strother, C. R. The effects of time and cohort differences on the interpretation of age changes in cognitive behavior. *Multivariate Behavior Research*, 1968, **3**, 259–293. (b)

Schmid, H. Anthropologische Konstanten und literarische Struktur. Unpublished manuscript, University of Bochum, Germany, 1973.

Spranger, E. *Lebensformen: Geisteswissenschaftliche Psychologie und Ethik der Persönlichkeit.* Halle/Saale: Niemeyer, 1914.

Stern, W. *Über Psychologie der individuellen Differenzen.* Leipzig: Barth, 1900.

Stern, W. *Person und Sache.* Leipzig: Barth, 1906.

Stewart, D. *Elements of the philosophy of the human mind.* Philadelphia: William Young, 1793.

Stumpf, C. Erscheinungen und Funktionen. *Abhandlungen der Preussischen Akademie der Wissenschaften, Berlin* (philosophische-historische Klasse), 1906, No. 5, 1–40.

Terman, L. M. *The measurement of intelligence.* Boston: Houghton Mifflin, 1916.

Tetens, J. N. *Philosophische Versuche ueber die menschliche Natur und ihre Entwickelung.* Leipzig: Weidmanns Erben & Reich, 1777.

Tuddenham, R. D. Soldier intelligence in World Wars I and II. *American Psychologist*, 1948, **3**, 149–159.

Van den Daele, L. D. Qualitative models in developmental analysis. *Developmental Psychology*, 1969, **1**, 305–310.

Wechsler, D. *The measurement of adult intelligence.* Baltimore: Williams & Wilkins, 1955.

Wechsler, D. *Die Messung der Intelligenz Erwachsener.* Bern: Huber, 1956.

Wilden, A. *System and structure.* London: Tavistock, 1972.

Wilden, A. Piaget and the structure as law and order. In K. F. Riegel & G. C. Rosenwald (Eds.), *Structure and transformation: Developmental and historical aspects.* New York: Wiley, 1975. Pp. 83–117.

Wohlwill, J. F., & Flavell, J. H. Formal and functional aspects of cognitive development. In D. Elking & J. H. Flavell (Eds.), *Studies in cognitive development.* New York: Oxford University Press, 1969. Pp. 67–120.

Wolff, C. von. *Psychologia rationalis.* Frankfurt: Officina Libraria Regeriana, 1734.

Wozniak, R. H. A dialectic paradigm for psychological research: Implications drawn from the history of psychology in the Soviet Union. In K. F. Riegel (Ed.), *The development of dialectical operations.* Basel: Karger, 1975. Pp. 18–34. (a)

Wozniak, R. H. Dialecticism and structuralism in Soviet philosophy and psychology. In K. F. Riegel & G. C. Rosenwald (Eds.), *Structure and transformation: Developmental and historical aspects*. New York: Wiley, 1975. Pp. 25–45. (b)

Wundt, M. *Hegel's Logik und die moderne Physik*. Cologne: Westdeutscher Verlag, 1949.

Wundt, W. *Gundzüge der physiologischen Psychologie*. Leipzig: Engelmann, 1873–74.

Wundt, W. *Grundriss der Psychologie*. Leipzig: Engelmann, 1896.

Wundt, W. *Völkerpsychologie*. 10 Vols. Leipzig: Engelmann, 1900–1920.

Wundt, W. Über Ausfrageexperimente und über die Methoden zur Psychologie des Denkens. *Psychologische Studien*, 1907, **3**, 301–360.

Zajonc, R. B., & Markus, G. B. Birth order and intellectual development. *Psychological Review*, 1975, **82**, 74–88.

Logic and
the Theory of Mind[1]

Carol Fleisher Feldman
University of Houston

Stephen Toulmin[2]
University of Chicago

THEORETICAL PROBLEMS
IN STRUCTURALIST
PSYCHOLOGY

One of the most striking features of recent discussions in cognitive theory has been the emphasis placed on "formal" or "logical" structures, systems, and relationships. Formal patterns derived from mathematics and symbolic logic have been employed at several different points, and in several different ways, to explain, account for, or represent the content and mode of development of human cognitive capacities.

Many contemporary psychologists, for instance, argue for the existence of sequences of characteristic "stages" in cognitive development. The Piagetians, for example, characterize each of these stages in terms of a set of "formal structures"; they claim that the relationships between the characteristics of successive stages are themselves logical relationships, being based on "logical inclusion." So it comes to seem as though the succession of "stages" is empirically inevitable, because it is logically "necessary." Thus, it is by now widely accepted that there is a compulsory sequence of developmental stages through which all children must pass in the same order, and that each stage in this sequence is characterized by

1. The work recorded here was supported by the National Institute of Education (DHEW/NIE–C–74–0029).

2. Also fellows of the Center for Psychosocial Studies, Chicago, to which thanks are due for research and discussion opportunities and for secretarial assistance during the preparation of this paper. We are grateful to Gerald Gratch, Sophie Haroutunian, Kenneth Kaye, Lawrence Kohlberg, Theodore Mischel, Addison Stone, and James Wertsch for their comments and help.

the existence in the child's mind of corresponding "mental structures." Piaget himself, indeed, postulates a sequence which is not merely *invariant*, but also *universal*. The terminal set of "formal operations" which constitutes the universal end-point of this sequence—namely, "mature cognition"—can as a result be used to define the central task for any "genetic epistemology" whether it is concerned with the (phylogenetic) history of ideas or with the (ontogenetic) development of any individual's mental capacities. In either case, the problem is to demonstrate how human beings come, in course of time, to develop mental operations which conform to the universal formal systems in question.

This feature of contemporary psychology has real charm, yet it also gives rise to serious epistemological obscurities and difficulties, which will be our concern in this paper. Piaget sees it as a central task of psychology to construct "a bridge between logic and genetic psychology." At the same time, problems arise if we construct any such bridge hastily or uncritically, without carefully examining the subsoil on which its two piers have to be built. Whether we consider (a) the relationships supposedly holding between elements in the mental structures characteristic of any given stage in cognitive development, or (b) the relationships linking corresponding operations or elements in successive stages, in either case there are real problems of *evidential adequacies and relevance* when we try to relate the properties of the theoretical description, or formal system, to our empirical evidence about the knowledge so represented—in particular, to the actual cognitive performances through which this knowledge is demonstrated.

So we shall be directing our attention here to the following general questions: What does it tell us about the empirical phenomena represented in cognitive psychology that they are susceptible of being cast in such formal terms at all? Can it be shown that casting them in such terms augments our scientific power to explain the phenomena? In short, what exactly is gained by casting cognitive theory in logico-mathematical form, and how do such theories relate to our empirical experience?

Mental Structures and the Problem of Empirical Corroboration

Apparently having exhausted the resources of behaviorism in the earlier part of this century, American psychology during the last ten or fifteen years has been distinguished by a concern with theories about the mind. Decades of trying to develop a "scientific" psychology, by concentrating entirely on the overt, observable performances of organisms, led to disappointment, especially in accounting for patterns in language, reasoning, and other forms of "cognitive" behavior. Although earlier theories were modified in order to accommodate an "inner life" in these cognitive areas—for example, by the addition of Pavlov's "second signal system" and the Kendlers' "mediating responses"—the results were not satisfactory. The hybrid theoretical models so created lacked the purity of the original models, but were still insufficiently rich to account adequately for the observed facts. Beginning in the early 1960s, theoretical developments in the psychology of language and thinking were dominated by the new approaches of Chomsky and Piaget: they have attempted to demonstrate the nature of human thinking *directly*, rather than indirectly, by inference from the associated behavior, and they have treated thinking as a phenomenon *qualitatively different* from behavior.

In these new theories, the basic explanatory elements are certain "mental structures" distinct from, and qualitatively unlike, "actions." The connections between these postulated mental structures and observable behavior are obscure. Mental structures cannot be related to behavioral data at all directly and straightforwardly, as could the theoretical notions of earlier periods. Whereas in the older theories theoretical statements could be construed as hypotheses and tested directly against empirical data consisting of observable behavior, this is no longer the case for statements about mental structures in the newer theories. The older theories tended to begin from the examination of relatively raw and undigested reports of behavior; if regularities were found in this behavior, they were sometimes attributed to "rules," which regulated behavior; and, insofar as mental structures were discussed, they were composed merely of such empirically derived rules. As a result, there was no gap to bridge in order to test their existence. In the newer theories, by contrast, all the basic theoretical statements tend to be presented in highly abstract terms, as describing hypothetical mental structures which are said to "underlie" behavior. Although such statements indicate in a very general way what kinds of behaviors are covered by the theory, the mental structures of these structuralist theories are in other respects problematic: it is never immediately obvious how their existence could be tested by appeal to observable behavior, nor is it even at all obvious what *kinds* of entities they are supposed to be.

What, then, is the ontological status or explanatory role of these varied mental structures? This is a matter of considerable confusion. At one extreme, mental structures might be construed as hypothetical but not directly observable entities, analogous to the electrons of modern physics. At the other extreme, they might be thought of as (so to say) simply the shadows which we cast on cognitive phenomena by adopting a particular form of theoretical representation, and reading into those phenomena formal properties which exist in reality only within theoretical analysis. These alternatives imply extreme differences in ontological status and explanatory force. The second, weaker interpretation would be, at the same time, unproblematic but merely formal: the first, stronger interpretation makes substantive claims, but raises correspondingly serious problems, for how are claims about the real existence of such abstract entities as mental structures to be tested?

The evidential problem is further complicated by the fact that the structures here claimed as real are often said to be "real" only in a psychological sense: they are supposed to exist "in the mind of" the child, without necessarily having any counterparts in his brain, in the form of physical structures or processes. In studying thinking rather than behavior, that is, we are invited to postulate "real but immaterial" structures and events. Can the cognitive psychologist rest content with a psychological reality that exists only "in the mind," or should he require evidence of a physiological structure before he is convinced of psychological reality? No answer to this question will be obvious before we know more clearly what such physiological candidates would look like. It can be said here, however, (a) that physiological data would not, by themselves, provide a satisfying explanation of structured regularities in thinking; but (b) that the functioning of the mind is truly dependent on the structure of the brain, and must ultimately be related to it in a physiologically convincing manner.

We shall try to show in this paper that certain problems of corroboration which must be faced by *any* scientific theory arise in a particularly forceful way for current structuralist theories in psychology. Specifically, we shall try to show how, by postulating abstract mental structures—structures which are neither physical objects nor actions, but which are at the same time "real," in that they regulate behavior—theoretical psychologists impose on themselves problems of corroboration of a new kind. Hypothesis testing may still go on, and empirical evidence may still be accumulated; but without further clarification, the relationship between the two will remain unclear. For, up to now, we lack any explicit statement of the supposed connection between empirical evidence and theoretical hypotheses of the kind we are familiar with both in the case of more empirically derived psychological theories and in the case of theories in the physical sciences.

In his discussions of psycholinguistics, Chomsky deals with this evidential problem in a dismissive manner. He takes the extreme position of declaring that the language behavior of laboratory subjects (Miller, 1962) can neither verify nor falsify the "psychological reality" of structures in Chomskian grammar, while insisting nonetheless that his grammar is not merely a grammar but also a model of mind. In order to make this claim plausible, Chomsky is compelled to revolutionize the ground rules of scientific inquiry—observable data about behavior are now said to be unsuitable evidence, and the "intuitions" of a native speaker are offered as the only appropriate substitute.

Piaget's attitude to the problem is less extreme; and he does indeed attempt to support his theoretical claims from behavioral data. But at this point the magnitude of the evidential problem becomes clear—the actual observed behavior of subjects has to be passed through a filter of scientific interpretation before we can see whether it in any way supports or fails to support the theoretical claims in question. First, the subject's actions must be scrutinized and classified as displaying certain systematic properties: only then can these interpreted properties be related to the theoretical mental structures. So, like Chomsky, Piaget too changes the evidential ground rules. The actions of a child cannot by themselves either corroborate or refute directly the claim that the child has any particular mental structure. For example, when the child sees a ball of clay transformed into a sausage shape and agrees that it still contains the same amount of clay, he may or may not be providing the investigator with evidence that he has a grasp of "conservation." First, the nature of the child's thinking in the situation has to be thoroughly and freely probed, and only the experimenter's interpretation of the child's collective responses to all these varied (unstandardized) manipulations are allowed to constitute potentially corroborating evidence. Piaget thus supports his theoretical claims not from the evidence of direct observation but from such interpretations. The qualitative differences between his abstract, theoretical mental structures and any empirically observable activities by the child make it impossible to relate them directly to one another.

The effects of these changes in the attitude toward "behavioral evidence" on the status of psychological theories is profound and far-reaching. Throughout the first part of the twentieth century, psychologists had been preoccupied with the problem of making psychology "scientific"—a task which they understood as requiring them to construct accounts which depended only on scientific data, that is, directly observable, uninterpreted actions. In the new theories of the 1960s, the special status of observable actions was revoked. In some quarters, the resulting theories are taken to be flatly unscientific. Others argue more cautiously that by its very nature, psychology is forced to be a less rigorously empirical science than the physical sciences that were hitherto its model, at least when the psychologist addresses certain particularly complex problems. Perhaps a level of reality exists in psychology—a level of psychological "structure"—which has no analogue in the physical sciences, and which is therefore neither reducible to physiology nor capable of being fully accounted for by the analysis of behavior. As such, psychological structures may *in principle* be unavailable to direct observation, never explicitly manifest in a child's performances (except maybe in rare cases of accurate verbal report) but at best capable of being inferred from such performances.

Yet, however loosely defined the relationship between observable performances and psychological structures may be, some such relationship must surely exist. Certain choices have to be made, depending on how much evidence (and of what kinds) we require, before we can be willing to say that such-and-such a person possesses a certain cognitive structure. As in any science, the choices will be in part arbitrary, to the extent that we are free to defend our views at any chosen level of probability. (Do we require that the subject should perform in the way predicted, given that structure, in *all* situations or only in *some*, for example, in his areas of greatest proficiency?) But if the theory of structures is to have *any determinate meaning* in empirical terms at all, we must eventually be able to explain how structures and performances are related.

Formalism and Scientific Theory

Both Piaget's and Chomsky's models make extensive use of mathematical formalism to describe the structural relations between their abstract, hypothetical mental structures. How far is it indispensable that theories of this kind should be expressed formally? Let us consider an elementary example. We might say that the Egyptians could not have built the pyramids without some understanding of geometry; but to say this does not tell us what *formal system*—if any—they used to give a theoretical organization to the various laws of geometry implicit in their practical achievements. All that we can safely say, now, is that the Egyptians acted *as if* they had a system that *we would express* as Euclidean geometry, but that they may either have expressed it in some other way or not have given it a systematic treatment at all. Ultimately, the only satisfactory evidence for declaring that they knew of a particular *system* of rules would be the historical demonstration that they gave it a systematic expression; and such historical evidence as we possess indicates, rather, that they operated in an unsystematic "rule-of-thumb" way, using a theoretically unorganized collection of pragmatic formulae.

Current cognitive theories comprise similar complex systems of structure. Such complexity is far more manageable, for theoretical purposes, if expressed in a systematic mathematical manner, precisely because the relationships between the elements in a mathematical system are carefully and explicitly defined. Thus, the development of systematic theories of mental structure has led to an increased interest in systems from outside of psychology—in particular, formal systems from mathematics that may prove suitable for capturing and expressing the systematic relations among the supposed psychological structures. Moreover, the success of mathematical physics itself has lent understandable prestige to the idea that in any fruitful natural science, explanatory power is bound up with the possibility of presenting its results in a systematic, logico-mathematical form; and even to the idea that a scientific theory, properly so called, is necessarily a *formal* theory. Certainly, there is no denying the strength of Piaget's urge to characterize his own cognitive theory in terms of formal logic: "at present perhaps the most exact of disciplines in terms of the rigor of its demonstration" (Piaget, 1973, p. 28).

But the problem of *empirical corroboration* always remains to be tackled. Formal systems—as such—are judged according to *nonempirical* criteria such as consistency, completeness, and parsimony. The employment of some one specific formal structure (or system of logical connections) in a physical science may prove, on investigation, to give us a better way of organizing our concepts and knowledge about, say, electricity than any other currently available; yet no one formal system can be *uniquely* appropriate to any given set of physical phenomena, still less can it give a *formal guarantee* of its own applicability. In itself, the construction of formal models (or patterns of possible theories) is a bare exercise for the abstract imagination. For any given "logic," there is always an unlimited number of other, alternative logics. Thus the use of formal criteria can never guarantee that a theoretical model is a good one (still less, the best possible one) for giving the most empirically apt expression to the psychological theory in question.

A logical representation may be formally coherent—that is, may be entirely free of inconsistencies—while yet being substantively inapplicable; for example, failing to lend itself to detailed comparison with actual phenomena on a specific and exact empirical level. We can check out the explanatory power of a theoretical representation adequately only if it is made clear at the outset how the formal structures existing on the abstract, theoretical level are to be related to observable regularities and/or patterns on the concrete, directly empirical level. The goal of developing systematic theories, then, leads scientists naturally to give those theories a formal expression; but the task of testing the "existence" of any postulated mental system is not the same as that of checking the formal adequacy of our theoretical representation.

Nowhere, it seems, are the differences between the problems involved in *formally representing* a theory and the problems involved in *empirically testing* it so difficult to keep separate as in the area of cognition. Just because the theoretical system in question can plausibly be presented as corresponding to some mental system in the mind of an actual child, we may be led to conclude that the formalism of the theoretical system must be directly represented by an isomorphic formalism in the mind of the child. In their account of the development of spatial knowledge, for example, Piaget and Inhelder (1956) deliberately blur the distinction between topology and Euclidean geometry as formal systems for describing (a) the spatial relations which constitute the phenomena the child copes with, and (b) the forms in the child's mind. In this way, ontological reality is assigned to the hypothetical mental structures of the theory simply on the basis of the formal expressions by which they are represented in the theory. It is this latter move—of taking logical formulae as the formal expression of empirical mental structures —that has created such danger of confusion, since (as we shall see) it confuses the character of the representation in which a theory is expressed with the character of the empirical structures which it supposedly represents.

There are, of course, special reasons why it is particularly hard to keep these two layers of reality—the representation and that which it represents—distinct in cognitive psychology. Roughly speaking: the formal systems we use to express our theories are themselves among the most striking products of human cognition, and so exemplify those very human capacities that cognitive psychologists have been most interested in studying. When we study cognition, logic is thus both the subject studied and also the medium of theoretical representation; so we are especially prone to reify the logical structures of our formal representations. For instance, when we study a child's knowledge of formal logic and express our results in terms drawn from formal logic, we must be clear that we are concerned with two ontologically distinct levels, on one of which the theoretical psychologist employs logic to give a formal representation of the child's logic existing on the other. If we slide unthinkingly from one level to the other, we may end by losing track of our own theoretical procedures and attributing to the child's mind formal characteristics that belong more properly only to our own theoretical representation.

What, then, does it tell us about actual empirical phenomena that they are susceptible of being represented in formal terms? Not as much (perhaps) as we are sometimes tempted to suppose. We select a particular formal model as an *instrument* which permits us to express ourselves clearly, precisely, and communicably; but that is all. The model will be chosen as expressing certain aspects of our theory in a particularly elegant way, but it will always have certain formal features that are irrelevant—even mismatched—to the particular theoretical application in question. Those superfluous features cannot, then, tell us anything about our own theoretical ideas, still less about the aspects of reality we are using the formal model to explain. We learn about reality by checking the consequences of our theoretical ideas against our experience; and then we choose a formal model for reasons of clarity, communicability, and scientific precision. In themselves, the properties of this formal model do not justify us in inferring anything more about reality than we could have inferred from the theoretical considerations that led us to select it in the first place.

The kinds of mismatch that can be found between formal models and the theories they represent are apparent, in the present case, if we consider how the formal system of current developmental psychology and psycholinguistics are made the basis for claims about necessary relations and sequences in cognition and language. Both Chomsky and Piaget use nonprobabilistic models which describe the relations between mental structures in terms of *formal necessities*. Indeed, these formal necessities are a crucial feature of their logico-mathematical representations. However, the status of the real-world counterparts of these formal structures—that is, the empirical relations and sequences observed in actual experience—is highly problematic: our knowledge about them is at best probabilistic, and it is not clear in what sense (if any) they can represent natural necessities.

For instance, to the extent that we can legitimately represent the patterns of thought characteristic of a given cognitive stage as conforming to a given formal structure, the *mathematical* relationships between the elements *of that formal structure* will themselves be necessary relations, in a mathematical sense. Yet what precisely can it mean to describe the *empirical* relationships between the elements *of the corresponding mental structures* as being necessary relationships? (The echoes of Kant in this question are, as we shall see, by no means accidental.) Again, it may be convenient for theoretical purposes to represent the entire sequence of cognitive stages in terms of a set of *formal* relations of logical inclusion and the like. Yet, here too, it is a great deal less clear in what sense the actual empirical process of cognitive development, by which successive synchronic stages are transformed into one another diachronically, can have any necessity about it.

In both cases—both *within* stages and *between* stages—there is a prima facie need to distinguish the formal structures of the theoretical characterization from the empirical structures they supposedly characterize: the former are logical features of theoretical representation, the latter purport to exist in empirical reality. Thus, while it may be essential to Piaget's theory that some actual cognitive structures exist in the mind of a child, in order to be responsible for such aspects of its cognitive performances as classification and seriation, it is still quite unclear how far these empirical structures must resemble the groupings that are used to give them a formal characterization. Similarly, while it may be possible to support, by empirical observations, the theoretical invariance of developmental sequences in the process of stage succession, it is again far from clear in what respects these empirical sequences must resemble the corresponding hierarchic structures in the theory, by which the formal characterizations of successive stages are linked together—so that stage S_{n-1} is presented as a logically proper part of stage S_n. While the empirical sequences may be demonstrable, the existence in psychological reality of anything corresponding to such formal inclusion is moot.

Two alternative interpretations suggest themselves. Is the force of such claims merely to underline the fact that, at any given stage, the cognitive abilities of a developing child can be represented in a logical manner? In that case, the formal or logical characteristics of the resulting theoretical exposition will be characteristic *only* of the representation itself, *not* of the phenomena represented. Alternatively, is it supposed that the inner necessities linking the various elements within the representation have direct counterparts in empirical "nature"? In that case, we should regard the theoretical representation as giving a correct isomorphic description of necessary relations actually existing in the mental lives of the children themselves, and look for some way of demonstrating the actual empirical existence of those relations.

Current theoretical models are thus faced with epistemological problems of two kinds. There are (a) those problems of evidential support, corroboration, and/or falsification that arise equally for any scientific theory, whether descriptive or formalized; and there are (b) those further problems that are created as a result of framing the theories concerned in terms of specific mathematical formalism. From the historical point of view, it is this latter group of problems that introduce new and unique considerations. Despite the earlier use of formalized theories (e.g., by Hull, 1943) it has not hitherto been supposed that the formal structures of theory were in necessary correspondence with empirical structures "in the mind." Earlier formalisms were used to summarize empirical data, without its being required also that their internal operation should be thought of as generating results *in the same way as* the human mind does in actual, empirical fact.

These new and unique problems arise, specifically, because the current formal systems are used to express relations supposedly holding also within the corresponding mental structures of the child. If the genuineness of this correspondence is merely assumed, there is then a danger of confusing the empirical with the formal issues: In the extreme form, we face the danger of taking it for granted that a *formally* satisfactory model (such as natural logic) must also be empirically applicable—so that the logical structure is ultimately taken to *be* the theory of which it is, properly speaking, only a formal representation. So, it comes to seem as though the psychologist need demonstrate only the *formal* adequacy of his theories: the quite separate need to show, also, in what respects his theoretical ideas correspond to genuine empirical realities, and to establish that they represent the resulting empirical relations correctly, may be entirely overlooked.

Piaget himself appears quite unclear about the consequences and implications of this distinction. We find him arguing sometimes one way—as though the "logical structures" of his theory corresponded directly to "mental structures" in the child—and sometimes in another way—as though these two things were quite separate and distinct. For example, in *Psychology and Epistemology* (1971), he apparently views the INRC group as a "mental entity":

By [intelligence] we mean precisely the functioning of operatory systems emanating from action (of which the main systems are those of "groups," "networks," or "lattices," and other important logico-mathematical structures). [P. 80]

Elsewhere, by contrast, he apparently assumes that logical structures exist only at the level of representation. For example, he says (Piaget, 1973):

Concerning the development of the intelligence in the child and the adolescent, we also try of course to translate into abstract language the structures of intellectual operations evidenced by the behavior of the subjects, and we use for this purpose various logico-mathematical structures coming under the head of "groups," "networks," and "groupings"; but we also try to discover the form these structures take in the minds of the subjects, insofar as their reasoning is expressed in words and is accompanied by various intentional justifications: what we discover is of course no longer an abstract structure but a set of intellectual *rules* or *norms* which take the form of *impressions* [italics added] of "logical necessity." [P. 19]

If Piaget is confused, it is not surprising that his exponents have been, also. Thus, Ginsburg and Opper (1969) write:

[The models] are abstractions which are intended to capture the essence of his thought . . . and may be said to explain and predict behavior. That is explanation in the sense that the models describe basic *processes* underlying the adolescent's approach to problems. We can say that the adolescent solved a particular problem *because* his thought can utilize the logical operations of implications or negations and so forth. [Pp. 200–201]

Here, the empirical existence of logical structures in the child's mind is apparently unquestioned; but Flavell (1963) is more cautious:

This general approach is distinctly logical rather than empirical; in itself it says nothing whatever about whether children in fact think this way. What it seems to say is that if a person fully grasps the basic nature of classes and relations and the possible operations one can perform upon them, then one can reasonably impute to him cognitive structures which approach, *as ideal patterns* [italics added] the nine groupings. Put differently, if one does what is possible to do at the purely intensive level with logical operations of class and relation one is behaving rather like a computer with a grouping program. . . . These two groupings were clearly invented because they describe *logically possible* [italics in original] cognitive structures not *empirically discovered* (as yet, at least) logical structures. [Pp. 188–189]

Stages and Stage Transitions

These two epistemological problems can be made more concrete if we consider the theoretical and empirical treatment of certain concepts within the standard Piagetian framework. Piaget's central view is that qualitatively distinct mental structures evolve in development via a process in which the active, maturing organism operates on his environment. During development, the organism's striving for "equilibrium" with his environment causes him to abandon simpler, earlier mental structures for later, more global and inclusive ones. This picture of the mechanism of development gives Piaget the means to account for his most important substantive claim, namely, that in the course of ontogenesis, the mental structures undergo major transformations, which lead to qualitatively different world views at different periods in development. Such qualitatively distinct phases in development are called "stages" in Piagetian theory; and the concept of stages involves two substantive claims. In the first place, there is the claim that such stages exist in empirical reality at all. In the second place, there is the claim that successive stages emerge in a sequence which is invariant (i.e., occurs in only one order) and also universal (i.e., occurs in all individuals).

The Existence of Stages. What, then, does it mean to characterize a child's thinking in terms of the theoretical description of a certain stage, S_n? Does it mean that all of the child's thinking in all domains will be best typified by the description of stage S_n? In an ideal case—for example, a child whose thinking is all "concrete operational"—we should expect such consistency to be found. In reality, however, few such ideal cases turn up. A child who thinks in the manner characteristic of S_n in some areas will very likely think in the way characteristic of S_{n-1} in other areas, and even in terms of S_{n+1} in a few others. While there may be grounds for speaking of a child's world view as subject to qualitative changes, accordingly, it does not seem to be the case that there are simultaneous changes in the way he views every single aspect of reality. (Piaget accounts for this state of affairs by using the notion of "horizontal *décalage*.") Individuals differ in the areas which first come under the control of any new structure, and in the age at which this occurs, as well as in the speed with which new structures attain generalized application to new areas. Furthermore, as later areas of application come into line, areas of more advanced development frequently move ahead to a further stage. As a result, the fact that any particular child is at a given age does not guarantee anything about his particular cognitive capacity, still less about the *spectrum* of cognitive abilities that he would display in different areas. Evidence of concrete operational thinking in the child will be evidence for his *being* concrete operational—that is, for his *having* the concrete operational structures in his mind—only with respect to the particular domain in which his abilities and performances are examined, and we cannot afford to assume anything about his performances in other areas on the basis of that initial observation alone.

This diversity in the actual performances of different children in different areas creates a particular difficulty for us, when it comes to deciding *at just what point* we are to say that a particular stage of cognitive development has been achieved. The stage notion is usually taken to imply that we should expect some kind of "step function" such that, over a short time span, thinking will be empirically observed to become dominated by patterns of the kind characteristic of the new stage. Given the prevalence of mixed stages within individuals, such *global* changes in any individual's reasoning appear hard to justify; and in their absence, the decision where we are to draw the line between one stage and another is indeed somewhat arbitrary. Thus, are we to say that a child has become, for example, concrete operational on the grounds that he has displayed concrete operational performances in one area, or in most areas, or in all areas and types of task? Since it is unclear what procedures would count as testing "all" areas of ability, or even "most," the best-defined point in time is probably the moment at which thinking in any *one* area first shows signs of the new stage. For instance, it is sometimes said that American children *become* concrete operational at five, while Genevan children do not give comparable evidence until age seven. Calling the five- or seven-year-old child concrete operational in this case means that *some* discriminable signs of concrete operational thinking are first evident at that age.

So we have the problem of relating a *unique* characterization of stages with a *double* populational distribution: in theory, we can represent cognitive development by a simple step function, but in empirical practice we are faced with a population of different performances for a single individual on different tasks and in different areas, and with a population of different individuals performing on any single, given task. When we confine ourselves to a single task, the implication of Piaget's theory is that many individuals must be expected to manifest the structure of a new stage at the same age. Thus, for instance, we are to expect a sharp increase, during the years from five to seven, in the number of individuals able to succeed in a particular test of concrete operational abilities. On this interpretation, the predicted step function says nothing about the comprehensiveness of a new structure as applied over all the domains of a child's thinking, but is concerned rather with the sudden inclusion of a large percentage of children in the stage concerned, as determined by a single, limited criterion.

We do not know of any satisfactory discussion, either by Piaget or by his followers, of the problems raised by the fact that the empirical material to be accounted for in their theory has this double populational character. Piagetian researchers commonly appear content with one, or a very few, performance tests. All that they usually require in order to demonstrate the existence of stages is a large number of children passing their chosen stage task at a certain age. Just how large the number of children or tasks must be remains unspecified. Yet such a procedure, arguably, does not so much *demonstrate* the existence of genuine empirical stages as *take it for granted*. Given only the current types of test, what reason have we for supposing that thinking in any one area is under the control of a universal, content-free mental structure, operative equally in all areas? And unless we are satisfied that the same step-wise transitions take place contemporaneously in all areas, what does it mean to say that any individual "possesses" such a universal, content-free structure at all? If it were clear that all of an individual's thinking was transformed at the same time, it would be the more natural to suppose that it was properly characterized in terms of a single structure; but given the empirical evidence about the prevalence of mixed stages, during which no single structure can apparently control all—or even virtually all—of a child's thinking, the question must at the very least be raised whether the current concept of cognitive stages is not itself highly problematic.

The Sequence of Stage Changes. Let us consider, also, the claims that are made about the invariance of "stage succession," namely, that every child passes through the same cognitive stages in the same invariant order, so that whatever new structures evolve to replace those characteristic of S_n will always be structures of type S_{n+1}. The claim for a sequence of stages that is invariant (and, in this sense, involves no particular assumptions about the nature of the individual stages themselves: it is supposed only (a) that *whatever* stage structures are evident in *any* of the reasoning of a given child, those universal) can take any one of three forms. The weakest form structures will make their appearance in the same developmental sequence. Both the stronger forms, by contrast, involve questionable assumptions about the universality of the stages themselves. For instance, it is sometimes claimed (b) that *all* the reasoning engaged in by children everywhere gives evidence of one or another Piagetian structure and stage. Even without the need to claim that "stage transitions" take place in a global manner, this suggestion raises serious problems: it is one thing to demonstrate that any reasoning whatever can be *characterized* in terms of the structures of *some* stage, but quite another to prove that *all* reasoning is in fact actually *governed* by such structures. On this second view, we are to expect a sequence of stages which is universal, in that the development of all reasoning in each individual everywhere will display one of several different predicted sequences of stages—namely, the sequences 1; 1,2; 1,2,3; and 1,2,3,4. On this second view, however, there is no need to claim that the topmost stage, 4, must be found universally, or indeed that it need appear in any given individual at all. Some individuals, for instance, might never reach the final stage in *any* of their areas of thinking.

The strongest claim about the universality of stage sequences (c) implies that everybody must go through the full sequence of stages—1,2,3,4—and assumes that every one of the stages is universal, and so must show up eventually in everybody's thinking. (Again, no assumption about the globality of these stages need be implied; furthermore, even if congitive stages were universal in the sense that all normal children eventually developed corresponding structures, this universality need not entail that all children *of any given age* must certainly pass *any particular set of tests*.)

Leaving aside the stronger assumptions involved in the second and third interpretations, we can limit ourselves to considering the weakest of these three claims for the universality of stage sequences, namely, that wherever and however people give evidence of developing mental structures corresponding to the various Piagetian stages, they will do so in the same more-or-less complete sequence, $S_0 \ldots S_n$, and will always pass through S_{n-1} before reaching S_n. The best available evidence for such an invariant sequence would be longitudinal in character; but some corroboration could also be obtained by sampling children from a series of age-cohorts, on a series of stage-specific tasks that are in other respects equivalent (cf. Feldman, et al., 1974). On this view about the universality of stage sequences, it would be predicted only that no child would ever pass any test involving the use of structures from stage S_n if—test errors aside—he failed in the corresponding task involving structures from stage S_{n-1}.

Agenda for This Paper. In this introductory section, we have discussed in general terms the novel epistemological difficulties that arise at the present time for developmental psychologists and psycholinguists through the use of formal representations as the basis for a theoretical account of cognitive stages. And we have done our best to indicate, in a preliminary way, how these general problems arise in specific, concrete forms when related to current accounts of cognitive stages, of the mental structures associated with them, and of the invariant sequences by which they supposedly displace one another. In the rest of this paper, we shall attempt to show how current confusions between the formal and empirical aspects of psychological theory—notably, between the problems of formal adequacy and those of empirical corroboration—can be avoided. We shall do this by drawing attention to the ways in which similar types of ambiguity and lack of clarity have arisen with respect to theoretical systems of representation in other areas of science, and to the distinctions that have been established in those other sciences in order to resolve the difficulties in question. This done, we shall draw corresponding distinctions in the field of cognitive psychology, in the hope of clarifying the legitimate use of notions like that of necessary sequence in our account of intellectual development, and suggest possible new strategies for theoretical development in these fields of inquiry.

THE GENERAL ROLE OF REPRESENTATIONS IN SCIENTIFIC EXPLANATION

So far, we have been discussing the theoretical difficulties in contemporary cognitive psychology as though they were specific to that field. This is a natural enough step, since, certainly, anything that we can do in this paper to clarify and/or solve those problems must be relevant in manifest ways to an understanding of cognitive development and language use. At the same time (we shall now argue) the best way to arrive at a better understanding of these issues may not be to push straight ahead, concentrating on the psychological details of the particular subject matters involved; rather, we should step back and place our problems in a wider context. For many of the present difficulties in fact spring substantially not from *particular details* but from the *general forms* of the problems in question, and these general forms are not unique to developmental psychology or psycholinguistics. On the contrary: again and again, over the centuries, strictly analogous general problems have arisen for scientists in other fields of inquiry, whose particular preoccupations and specific research topics appear at first sight remote from our own present concerns.

To specify some of these problems in terms that make their entirely *general* character explicit:

1. Just what explanatory power can a purely logical or formal representation give to a science? And in what respects does a *formally* satisfactory representation require further empirical corroboration, if it is to achieve genuinely scientific status?

2. To what extent do the formal structures captured in a logical representation presuppose the *actual existence* of corresponding, isomorphic empirical structures (patterns, regularities, entities) in the natural phenomena that they are used to represent? And to what extent is it legitimate to operate with theoretical representations having formal features (structures, necessities) for which *no* identifiable correlate can be found in the empirical phenomena?

3. Can we give formal descriptions, or representations, both of the *synchronic* properties and relationships (state) characteristic of any given subject matter at a given time (stage), and also of the *diachronic* processes by which that chosen subject matter develops historically from one stage and state to another over time? If so, how are these two kinds of representations related? If not, how can we relate the sequence of *formal*, synchronic "state descriptions" at successive times to the *nonformal*, historical or developmental account of the diachronic processes themselves?

Questions of these general types arise equally about theoretical representations in many different sciences. As stated here, indeed, none of them refers specifically to psychology as distinct from, say, evolutionary biology, planetary dynamics, or structural chemistry. So we can fruitfully look and see what is to be learned about the solution of these general problems by considering the experience of natural scientists who have had to tackle them in other fields, while studying and explaining phenomena of other kinds. Only by doing this at the outset, in fact, shall we be able to distinguish between, on the one hand, those theoretical quandaries in current cognitive psychology that arise out of its specific phenomena and, on the other hand, those that spring rather from general problems about the nature of logical representations, about the epistemological or ontological status of theoretical entities, and/or about the relations between "synchronic" and "diachronic" explanations. By tackling first these latter, general problems—which will arise for *any* psychological theory that claims to provide a scientific explanation of human development—we shall help to prepare the ground for a more clear-headed attack on the specifically psychological issues.

In the last 350 years, then, several branches of natural science have made the same difficult transition: from operating in a purely empirical and descriptive way, to developing theoretical concepts and representations on a formal, abstract, and/or mathematical level. In the course of the transition, most of the general problems that face us in contemporary psychology have been worked through, painfully and in detail, in relation to other kinds of subject matter. Three examples will be discussed here:

1. The creation of the first effective system of mathematical physics in the seventeenth century was a prime stimulus to epistemological controversy over the subsequent 150 years. A major topic of debate in this controversy was the question of natural necessity—i.e., the question how far the *formal* necessities characteristic of mathematical inferences and relationships reflect, and are reflected in, corresponding *physical* necessities binding on real objects and empirical phenomena in the world of nature.

2. The task of transforming zoological taxonomy, which had begun as a static account of God's Creation, into a genuinely developmental account of organic classification and evolution, compelled biologists to confront the problem of relating synchronic and diachronic representations. The methodological controversies over Darwin's theory of variation and natural selection which ensued led to the abandonment of the traditional *static* (or essentialist) definition of species, in terms of unchanging criterial features or essences, in favor of a new and more *dynamic* (or family relationship) analysis of species, in terms of the changing distribution of more-or-less general and typical properties within local populations.

3. In the late nineteenth and early twentieth centuries, the success of the atomic theory in both physics and chemistry gave the problem of *theoretical entities* a peculiar urgency. As a result, there was a lively and thorough debate about the conditions on which the existence, properties, and interactions of hypothetical structures, or particles, can be appealed to as revealing the invisible mechanisms *underlying phenomena*—as contrasted with purely theoretical structures, or formal relationships,

which reflect only the existence of regular patterns *observable in those phenomena.*

We shall try to extract from each of these episodes in turn the lessons that are relevant also to current problems in cognitive psychology. We can begin with the question of necessity.

Formal Representations in Physical Theory

The experience of physical scientists, from A.D. 1600 on, has substantially clarified some quite general points in the philosophy of science whose implications are more widespread than has yet been fully recognized. In particular, Isaac Newton's creation of the first comprehensive and effective mathematical theory for physics immediately gave rise to certain problems about "natural necessity." After a long and difficult debate, these were settled provisionally as a result of the work of David Hume and Immanuel Kant, and they were laid to rest definitively in the 1890s by Heinrich Hertz. (We refer here, specifically, to the philosophical clarifications introduced in Hertz's *Principles of Mechanics.*)

Despite Hume's claim that he was extending to the "moral and mental sciences" the methods of inquiry that had already led to success in Newtonian physics, his views on necessity were at variance with—in certain respects, almost directly opposed to—those seemingly implied by the Newtonian picture of nature. Initially, Newton's success in explaining both terrestrial and celestial happenings in dynamical terms (i.e., in terms of force and mass, acceleration and momentum) suggested that men had at last truly discovered how the planets and all other massive bodies *must move:* specifically, how the forces of impact, cohesion, pressure, and gravitational attraction, which could be identified with the help of Newton's theory, *compelled them to move.* The world of nature described by Newton was no longer a field for the operation of immaterial spirits, but it did appear to be the sphere of action for an almost equally mysterious collection of physical compulsions. Many of Newton's contemporaries complained about the occult character of these forces, notably the "force of gravitation"; and for a while the status of Newton's theory was in doubt. In particular, epistemological criticism led Hume to the conclusion that such natural necessities were not merely mysterious but downright undiscoverable. By actual empirical investigations (he argued) we can never establish with anything more than a certain probability the existence and character of the relationships holding between material bodies in fact: nothing in our experience of such physical relationships could possibly *count as* demonstrating their outright necessity.

So, for a while, it seemed that Newton had—paradoxically—succeeded in doing the very thing that Hume now proved impossible; and what were we to say about that? To claim absolute validity on behalf of Newton's dynamics would be to remove it from the realm of a rational, empirical natural science; yet to accept the Humean refutation of natural necessity would apparently weaken the intellectual claims of convinced Newtonian scientists quite drastically. This was the background against which Immanuel Kant posed one of his own most fundamental problems; namely, the question, How is a mathematical science of nature possible at all?

Kant himself had begun as an enthusiastic supporter of Newton's claims, but Hume's work subsequently made a deep impression on him. In particular, it forced him to confront the question of how it is possible, at one and the same time, for a theory of physics *both* to possess a formal, mathematical structure—complete with necessary inferences and all—*and also* to give us an empirical picture of phenomena as they in fact occur in the actual world of nature.[3] Kant saw only one way out of the deadlock between Newton and Hume; and for our purposes the significant thing about his answer is its general form. If it is possible at all for us to represent dynamical phenomena in a formal, mathematical way—he declared—this is *not* because we have discovered empirically *both* what the actual forms of physical phenomena are *and also* that these forms are necessary. (Hume had been quite right to reject that suggestion.) Rather, it is because, in our capacity as physicists, we develop systematic theoretical representations on which we confer mathematical forms, and then build the observed forms of empirical phenomena into them. In so doing, we build into the forms of our representation,

---

3. As a first hint of the significant parallels between the problems of theoretical physics and psychology, suppose that, in this question, we substitute for "a theory of physics" the words "a theory of cognitive development," and for "the actual world of nature" the words "the actual minds of children." In this way, we shall obtain the important and topical question, How is it possible, at one and the same time, for a theory of cognitive development *both* to possess a formal, mathematical structure *and also* to give us an empirical picture of phenomena as they in fact occur in the actual minds of children?

also, a novel kind of formal necessity, which has no discoverable counterpart in empirical, physical fact.

To the extent that the seeming natural necessities of physics simply mirror the formal necessities built into our mathematical representations of physical phenomena, they will be merely the shadows cast onto phenomena by these formal structures of our arguments. As such, they will not represent genuine compulsions operative within the world of nature and discoverable *independently of* those mathematical representations; rather, their status will be like that of (for example) the parallels of latitude and longitude. We may say, quite correctly, that the zero of longitude passes through the Greenwich Observatory in London, or that the Tropic of Cancer lies just two degrees south of the Florida Keys, but that in no way implies that there exist on the surface of the earth independently discoverable physical lines which can be identified and named by such phrases as "the zero of longitude." (We may *joke* about feeling a bump as our ship crosses the equator; but such a remark is quite clearly a joke.)

These distinctions, which Kant set out to establish within the framework of his "critical philosophy," were finally codified a hundred years later in Hertz's book on *The Principles of Mechanics*. In setting out his revised exposition of Newtonian dynamics, Hertz took care to discuss, separately and in succession, the *formal* (mathematical/logical) structures and relations embodied in any abstract theory of mechanics, and the *physical* (material/empirical) structures and relations considered in the concrete physical theories themselves. As he scrupulously demonstrated, we can begin by setting out the entire mathematical skeleton of Newtonian dynamics, in all its formal elegance, without giving the resulting logical structure any empirical reference at all; and in that case, we must subsequently go on to reexpound the theory, leaving its formal characteristics untouched, while showing how all the major mathematical variables in the system are to be given physical interpretation.

When dealing with any subject (such as mathematical physics) whose theories are given a formal representation, we must therefore consider the *formal characteristics* of those theories—necessities and all—as something quite apart from their *empirical reference and application*. If, within the context of any such physical theory, we recognize and state mathematically necessary connections, it does not in any way follow that corresponding physically necessary connections have been found to exist in fact, in the course of our empirical experience of nature. Rather, we are showing how physical scientists organize, and give a theoretical structure to, their understanding of this particular aspect of nature.[4] Demonstrating that the results of observation and experiment in any field of science can be organized into *formal theories*, accordingly, need not by itself reveal to us anything new about the *empirical structures* of the natural world. All that it need do, initially, is improve our theoretical/formal/conceptual grasp over the relationships between empirical structures and entities whose existence has been previously, and independently, established by empirical procedures.

We must say "initially," because further scientific investigations may subsequently suggest possible ways of observing additional empirical structures over and above those we have already succeeded in authenticating. If we do subsequently accept the existence of further structures, however, that can never be done on formal grounds alone: the correctness of this conclusion must always be established independently, by whatever kind of empirical observation is appropriate to the nature of the case. For example: it might have happened quite naturally, as a curious byproduct of, say, the earth's rotation, that a small ridge of rock or soil had formed all the way across Latin America and Africa, along the precise line of the equator; and if this had turned out to be the case, we might have fallen into the habit of using the word *equator* not just as a cartographical term but also *as a name for this ridge*. Even so, however, the existence of an equator *in our cartographical representations* would still imply nothing, either way, about the existence or nonexistence of such a ridge. Given the existence of the equator as a formal feature of our maps, the further, consequential

4. Compare the well-known passage in Wittgenstein's *Tractatus Logico-Philosophicus* (1922, pars. 6.342 ff.), which follows up Hertz's point and drives it home even more forcibly. As Wittgenstein puts the point: the bare fact that it is *possible* to use a particular formal structure—"necessities" and all—as the logical skeleton for a physical theory tells us by itself nothing about how things actually happen in the empirical world. If we want to say anything directly about how the world actually works, we must go beyond the formal structures and spell out in full detail exactly how the logical structures of the theory are interpreted empirically in different types of situation, so as to apply to different kinds of phenomena:

> The possibility of describing the world by means of Newtonian mechanics tells us nothing about the world: but what does tell us something about it is the precise *way* in which it is possible to describe it by these means.

question can indeed be raised whether any physical feature of the earth's surface corresponds to it; but this *is* a further question, requiring an independent, empirical investigation.

To sum up: the *formal structure* of any system of representation —whether a map of the earth, the mechanics of Newton, or the atomic theory—is one thing. The *physical structure* of the corresponding aspects of reality—the earth's surface, the actual constraints on physical bodies, or the submicroscopic structure of material things—is another matter. In point of history and of method alike, the task of demonstrating that a representation is adequate *simply as a representation* is temporally prior to, and logically distinct from, the task of investigating which (if any) formal features of the representation have physical counterparts in the empirical world. And it may always turn out that, although formally elegant and satisfactory, a particular system of logical structures does not lend itself appropriately to the task of representing the actual, empirical phenomena in the particular field of science concerned.

Essentialism and Populational Analysis in Evolutionary Biology

The lessons to be learned from physics about the structures, uses, and implications of scientific theory have to do only with the uses and limitations of synchronic or timeless representations. To the extent that cognitive psychology and psycholinguistics make use of formal representations, built around logical structures, these lessons will be relevant to those other sciences, too; but to the extent that we are interested in dealing with phenomena and theories that are essentially historical, or diachronic—as is clearly the case, in the study of cognitive development and language acquisition—other, rather different points need to be borne in mind. In this connection, therefore, it will be helpful to look for methodological precedents elsewhere, in other natural sciences which have had occasion to theorize about diachronic processes. We shall here concentrate on nineteenth-century biology, specifically, on the intellectual transition in the theory of organic speciation by which the Aristotelian (or typological) conception of an organic *species* was transformed into the Darwinian (or populational) conception. Lacking space to give a fully developed historico-critical analysis here, we may confine ourselves to a few crucial points.

To begin with, then: the typological view of species was an essentialist view. It set out to define species, and to distinguish them from one another, by identifying certain essential characteristics, which were supposedly universal and invariant—that is, present in all relevant members of a species, though perhaps only, say, in adult individuals, or in females. These defining characteristics were thought of as forming a unitary and unchanging structure, as being linked together by timeless or necessary connections. The fundamental nature of each distinct species was constituted by the corresponding constellation of essential characteristics, whose necessary interconnectedness supposedly maintained the stability of the species. Each distinct species then had its own distinct, unchanging *essence*: as a result, any suggestion that a species characterized by one constellation of essential characteristics might change (or evolve) into a different species, having some other distinctive essence, became strictly *unintelligible*.

The essence, or constellation of characteristics constitutive of any particular species, thus represented a specific, self-contained, and distinct formal structure. The structures characteristic of different species could not conceivably meet, still less could they evolve into, one another. Confronted with the assertion of organic evolution—whether presented in descriptive terms by Lamarck or reinforced by Darwin's explanatory theory of variations in natural selection—most French zoologists, notably the pupils and successors of Georges Cuvier such as Flourens, retorted with strictly "logical" arguments, designed to demonstrate that organic evolution, far from being plausible or explicable, was actually *inconceivable*. Having taken their own formal, systematic definition of the term *species* as a starting point, they could rigorously *prove* that any supposed evolutionary transformation of one species into another involved formal inconsistencies—nay, contradictions. And so long as they remained firmly on their own ground, the Cuvierians were of course in an impregnable position. So long as the absolute correctness of their essentialist definition of species remained unchallenged, their argument was unanswerable.

The Darwinians did not attempt to move ahead by challenging the formal validity of the Cuvierian proofs. Rather, they circumvented them. The traditional, typological definition of a species in terms of its *essence* was (they argued) merely a formal abstraction, arrived at by isolating one particular, temporal stage in the historical development of an organic *population*. The supposed existence of timeless essences was, in fact, a piece of pure speculation. The practical experience of biologists, by contrast, could not serve to justify any claim that permanent, essential constellations of characteristics were possessed universally by all individual members of any given population. Some empirically observed associations of typical features may have been very long-lasting, but there is no ground for promoting them to the status of "necessary connections." All that our practical experience shows us is the existence of widespread associations, or correlations, among many of the traits found in members of those populations which taxonomists treat as species. But these correlations represent, at most, sets of widespread "family resemblances." Any assumption of timeless, essential constellations goes far beyond the evidence of our experience.

Considered in these novel populational terms, the associations of characteristics used to distinguish species represented—in point of theory—only predominant statistical means, or peaks, within a broader distribution of characteristics acrosss the population. Within any population, certain exceptional individuals always possess unusual properties or characters which apparently deviate from the type or essence. Earlier zoologists had made a practice of ignoring these exceptions, on the grounds that they were insignificant "sports," or freaks. The Darwinians, by contrast, recognized that in some situations these untypical characters might prove advantageous; so that—given time—the traits in question might spread through later generations of the same population, and eventually achieve a statistical dominance that would tempt later taxonomists to treat them as normal, typical, or even essential. So, the idea of evolving species ceased to be a *contradiction in terms*. But it did so only at the price of abandoning the earlier formal characterization of species in terms of timeless essences.

In this way, the current characteristics of any particular specific population came to represent merely one temporary (and synchronic) cross section, or stage, arrived at by abstraction from a dynamical (or diachronic) process of development. Theoretically speaking, however, the diachronic process was fundamental. From the new populational point of view, any fixed, synchronic definition of species as possessing a timeless logical structure of characteristics (or essence), was a short-term oversimplification of that process. If we confine ourselves to formal, Aristotelian terms, it will no doubt remain impossible to conceive, still less describe, one species (or "stage" in organic evolution) being transformed into another; but that proves only what a mistake it is to confine ourselves to formal Aristotelian terms.

The point can safely be generalized. Wherever we require authentically historical explanations of developmental processes—in the case of cognitive development or language acquisition, as much as organic evolution—similar problems can arise about the relationship between the overall diachronic process and its constituent synchronic stages. It may happen that, at the outset of our investigations, we are in a position to study, analyze, and understand only selected cross sections or stages in the relevant process, and so find that we have nothing very helpful to say about the larger, developmental process. Even so, in theorizing about the separate stages, we should take care to keep in mind the longer-term need to integrate our synchronic "stage descriptions" into a subsequent diachronic account of the developmental process. For this reason, we shall do well to avoid saddling ourselves with essentialist characterizations of the individual stages, since these may place needless obstacles in our way when we later try to fit the resulting stage descriptions into a theory of historical development.[5]

Structural Explanations in Chemistry and Elsewhere

The last general concept we shall consider here is that of *structure*, and for this purpose we may conveniently glance at the history of chemistry. By now, chemistry is the preeminently structural science. There, if anywhere, we should see clearly the strengths and limitations of a structural account of things. So let us glance briefly

5. Is this to say that a *formal* representation is always, and unavoidably, a *timeless* one? Probably not. Some medieval logicians, for instance, attempted to develop a "logic of statements" (or "assertions") which differed from the standard "logic of propositions" (or "sentences") in that the truth, falsity, validity, relevance, and cogency of statements and arguments were allowed to be dependent not just on *what* they said, but also on *when and by whom* they were said. As a result, the formal properties and relations investigated by logicians themselves became, so to say, "at the mercy of history." This program has been tentatively revived during the twentieth century and may yet yield worthwhile results. Nevertheless, almost without exception, the really effective methods of formal representation available to us up to now have yielded only permanent, synchronic or "timeless" characterizations. One apparent exception to this generalization is the theory of population dynamics, which plays an important part in modern evolutionary biology; but regarded as a general branch of mathematical analysis, this theory is still comparatively young and undeveloped. Meanwhile, all the best-developed and scientifically fruitful systems of mathematical relationships are basically *ahistorical*.

at the historical transition by which chemistry *became* a structural science. Here as in evolutionary biology (we shall see), the crucial steps involved not just *empirical discoveries* but also *philosophical controversies.*

Although many of the formal patterns and relationships by which atoms combine together into molecules were already recognized in the mid–nineteenth century, the intellectual status of the concepts *atom* and *molecule* was not securely clarified and established until after the year 1900. Before the 1850s, serious ambiguities remained about the proper "molecular combinations," or chemical compositions, to be associated with different compound substances (H_2O, $NaCl$, H_2SO_4, etc.) But these disagreements were largely ironed out between 1850 and 1870. From then on, physicists and chemists alike were satisfied that water is properly described as H_2O, vitriol or sulphuric acid as H_2SO_4, common salt as $NaCl$, and so on. If active disagreements remained, these had to do not with the details of these particular descriptions but with their deeper general significance and implications. Evidently, the atomic theory accounted for many of the regularities observed in our macroscopic experience of chemical reactions, the physics of gases, and so on—chemical "combining weights," Boyle's Law, and the like. But did it give us anything more than a surface account of such macroscopic phenomena? Or was it also legitimate to interpret theoretical talk about minute atoms and molecules, in a literal-minded, empirical sense, as referring to actual physical entities? Did the theory of atoms and molecules make ontological claims about actual physical constituents and relationships, existing on an unobservably small scale of magnitude? Or was it only a convenient phenomenological model, useful in correlating and accounting for macroscopic reactions, but not to be taken in too literal-minded a way?

Considered as a formal representation, the atomic theory was evidently capable of functioning on either of two levels, or on both. On the one hand, it summarized empirical correlations in our actual macroscopic experience of physical and chemical phenomena; alternatively, it suggested tentative, hypothetical speculations about invisible entities and mechanisms underlying—and responsible for—those empirical correlations; or, finally, it could be taken in both ways at once. If we recall what we said earlier about the nature and implications of formal representations, it will be clear that the formal structure of the atomic theory, taken by itself, cannot help us to decide which of these three interpretations should be adopted:

whatever empirical interpretation we give it, *the formal structure of
the theory is the same.*

For lack of any independent empirical investigations capable of
corroborating or disproving the actual existence of atoms and
molecules, there was in fact no basis for choosing finally between these interpretations until 1905. The definitive empirical
demonstration became available only when Albert Einstein
confirmed mathematically that the so-called Brownian motion of
pollen grains in water—known for many years, but never
satisfactorily accounted for—was directly produced by *individual*
collisions between water molecules and the pollen grains, and so
manifested for the first time the actual physical existence of
individual molecules. (Hitherto, all the phenomena accounted for by
the atomic theory had manifested only *statistical averages* over multiple transactions between the hypothetical atoms and molecules.)

To put the lesson of this example at its weakest: *the general
concept of structure is not self-explanatory,* in chemistry any more
than in psychology. Any unqualified claim that the regularities
and/or correlations found in some set of phenomena—whether
physical, chemical, physiological or psychological—provide evidence
of corresponding structures, will always be initially ambiguous. We
can understand it *either* in a weaker, purely phenomenological sense
or in an alternative stronger, ontological sense. Do such theoretical
appeals to structure refer—on the empirical level—only to intelligible
patterns or regularities *within* the phenomena concerned? Or do
they alternatively imply the stronger claim, that independently
existing entities and relationships (empirical structures) will in due
course be found to *underlie* those phenomena? Or are we to interpret
the notion of structures in both a phenomenological and an
ontological sense at one and the same time? These basic questions
can legitimately be raised *whenever and wherever* new scientific
explanations are advanced in which the chief explanatory weight is
carried by the appeal to hypothetical structures.

ALTERNATIVE THEORETICAL STRATEGIES FOR
DEVELOPMENTAL PSYCHOLOGY

With these episodes from the history of science in mind, let us
return to the problems outlined in the first section of this paper. By

taking advantage of the methodological experience of scientists in other fields in dealing with the problems of formal representations and structural explanation and with the synchronic-diachronic distinction, we can open up new theoretical possibilities and indicate fresh directions of theoretical investigation along which it should be fruitful for developmental psychology to move. We shall take up three topics in turn:

1. What kinds of things are the mental structures of Piagetian theory and psycholinguistics intended to be? What exactly is meant by speaking of such structures as existing in a child's mind? And what sort of explanatory force do such structures have in accounting for the existence and character of successive developmental stages in cognitive growth?

2. Given a theory of (synchronic) cognitive stages, defined either in terms of characteristic mental structures or alternatively in terms of actual performances and/or mental processes, how are we to make the transition to a genuinely historical (diachronic) account of cognitive development?

3. What does it mean to speak of the relationships holding either within, or between, the mental capacities characteristic of successive stages as necessary or logical relationships? In what sense can empirical relationships in the mind be necessary? Similarly, how can successive developmental stages be linked together in a formal or logical manner, or constitute a unique road along which every separate individual must pass, as a matter of necessity, if his cognitive development is to achieve maturity?

The Concept of Mental Structures

As a point of return to the problem of mental structures and their role in the theory of cognitive development, we can usefully bring together the points examined in the previous section in connection with the role of formal representations in theoretical physics and the idea of structure in atomic theory. The current doctrine about mental structures seeks to combine explanatory features of both kinds. On the one hand, the Piagetian view of cognitive development gives us a representation or description of the child's mind that is quite explicitly structural: that is, it attributes his actual cognitive abilities to the possession in the mind of certain indispensable mental structures whose psychological reality and/or existence "in" any individual is supposedly a straightforward empirical fact. On the other hand, these structures are characterized for theoretical purposes in a rigorously formal manner: that is, the presence or absence of a particular structure is associated with the presumed capacity to perform any or all of a corresponding repertory of operations, represented by one or another set of logico-mathematical structures or groups—these are, for instance, the so-called lattice structure, the Klein group, and the 16-binary group.

Evidently, if we take seriously the claims of the resulting account of cognitive development to be a scientific theory, then the methodological parallels with physics and chemistry give rise to certain questions. First, in what respects, and under what conditions, can the formal features of such a theory have empirical counterparts existing in the mind of a child? Second, is the existence of the resulting structures to be understood in a phenomenological or an ontological sense? That is, is the formal theory of structures merely a roundabout way of describing regularities in cognitive performance, or are mental structures supposed to have some kind of autonomous psychological existence in their own right? Finally, in what sense can such structures be responsible—causally or in other ways—for controlling, generating, or otherwise producing actual perform- ances? These are the crucial questions to be faced if we are to see how the theoretical notion of mental structures is to be cashed in for formal structures within the cognitive theory itself or for empirical testimony about a child's actual performances.

Phenomenological or Ontological Structures? Let us begin from the implied analogy with chemical atomism. It is not hard to show ambiguities in current discussions of cognitive development parallel to those characteristic of nineteenth-century atomic theory. For instance, when a growing child's newly acquired capacity to handle certain types of problems in, say, a concrete operational manner is cited as evidence that he now possesses the corresponding mental structures, what is the force of this claim? Is it merely a *phenomenological* claim, namely, that the formal structures in the relevant theory serve to account well for the patterns manifested in children's actual cognitive performances—without any necessary implication that those performances are produced, in empirical fact, by actual mental entities isomorphic with the logical features of the relevant theory? Or is it a stronger, *ontological* claim, to the effect that the new cognitive abilities apparent in a child's performances at any age reflect the internal workings of some deeper, underlying existents in which those formal, logical features are empirically embodied—even, perhaps, that they hint at the operation of corresponding physiological or neurological structures?

As to this question of interpretation, the testimony of the current literature is unclear, and three quite distinct positions are seemingly put forward at different times. Starting with the strongest kind of ontological interpretation, (a) some writers would evidently welcome the opportunity to account for cognitive development and performances in terms of an outright "psycho-physiological parallelism." Such a position would construe the structures—that is, formal patterns—or cognitive functioning as being isomorphic with the structures—that is, physico-chemical regularities and/or physiological mechanisms—of our somatic and/or neurological processes. The existence of the mental structures appropriate to any particular stage would in this case be accounted for as the psychological counterpart of neurological structures—in the angular gyrus, the cortex, or wherever—which constitute the cerebral representation of the corresponding cognitive capacities.

At the opposite extreme, (b) one can find passages in which a much weaker, phenomenological interpretation is clearly called for. In these cases, it is implicitly—or even explicitly—denied that the theoretical appeal to mental structures entails anything of an empirical sort, either way, about underlying physiological or even psychological entities and mechanisms. On this alternative interpretation, the theory of mental structures gives us a purely descriptive account of cognitive abilities and performances, whose implications are independent of all empirical hypotheses, whether about material processes occurring on a physiological/neurological level or about the formation of specific psychological entities in the mind of a child. Faced with the stronger of these two interpretations, we are entitled to ask what corroborative evidence is available about the actual existence and character of the supposedly isomorphic neurophysiological substrate of cognitive performance. In the latter, weaker case, we need similarly to be told in detail how the formal structures within cognitive theory are to be understood empirically, as reflecting and/or representing the actual patterns of cognitive performance.

Finally, (c) there is an intermediate interpretation, which faces different problems. This interpretation avoids any neurophysiological claims, but at the same time insists that mental structures have a real empirical existence as psychological entities in the child's mind, which may or may not be manifested in performances on any actual occasion. The difficulties that arise in this third case have to do with the somewhat tenuous link between the entities in question and the actual evidence of performance. To establish the "real existence" of such mental structures, we would need—at the very least—a clear indication about the kinds (and amounts) of actual cognitive performance that will constitute satisfactory empirical evidence of their existence.

In the writings of Piaget himself, we can find hints of all three interpretations. He would like to believe that the "patterns of neurological causality" include elements analogous to his own mental structures; yet at the same time he hesitiates to equate the two things, and even leans over backwards to resist any excessively physiological interpretations. On the whole, he seems most inclined to insist that the word *structure* in his theories should be taken in a psychological, not a physiological sense. His basic distinction, between the abstract character of a structure and the concrete existence of the corresponding elements, can then be read as distinquishing the organized pattern of relationships to be found within the child's cognitive abilities from those elements in actual performance whose · structural interlinkages provide empirical embodiments of that pattern. Despite occasional hints that the child's mental structures may be embodied isomorphically on other levels (e.g., physiological), it is probably safest, accordingly, to read Piaget's version of structuralism as entailing only the existence of patterns of organization in the child's cognitive capacities, and leaving open all subsequent questions about underlying entities —whether psychological or physiological.

Even so, epistemological difficulties remain. For instance, what are we to make in this context of the distinction between capacities and performances? Even supposing that Piaget's structures represent only patterns of cognitive organization, we must still explain just what kind of evidence from actual cognitive performance is required, in order to demonstrate the existence of specific structures in a child's cognitive capacities. It must be made clear, that is, just what evidentiary force attaches to the occurrence (or nonoccurrence) of specific operations in a child's actual performances, when it comes to judging whether or not he actually possesses the corresponding mental structures or patterns of cognitive organization.

The Origins and Power of Mental Structures. In order to achieve a clearer view about what kinds of things mental structures are on this interpretation, we shall raise two particular questions. One of them is the *genetic* question: how it is supposed to be the case that the child *comes to acquire* any mental entities corresponding to the formal structures of the Piagetian theory. The other question has to do with the *mode of operation* of these mental structures: what is meant by speaking of them as generating, or controlling, or being otherwise *responsible for* the performances in which they are implicated.

As to the first question: the term "mental structures" seems to be used, at times, to cover such things as "internalized" or "interiorized" procedures of calculation and argumentation. And, indeed, there is a clear enough process by which such internalization of, say, explicit mathematical procedures can contribute recognizable elements or entities to an individual's mind. Anyone who studies, say, Euclid's geometry or Russell's "propositional calculus" may in due course learn the rules of the subject ("by heart") so effectively that he can solve problems of the corresponding kind in his head. In this case, it is clear enough what the phrase "mental structure" refers to, namely, the *internalized rules* themselves. So, in this case, accounting for the real existence of the mental structures is unproblematic. On the other hand, in this case, it is highly questionable whether the mental structures themselves "control" or "produce" the relevant cognitive performances. An internalized rule is not itself "responsible for" the relevant behavior—does not "cause" it, nor even provide a "motive" for it: rather, the individual produces, and is therefore responsible for, the performance he does, and in doing so he *chooses* to apply the internalized rule in question.

Are the mental structures of Piaget's theory intended to cover merely such internalized rules and/or formalisms? Evidently not: the Piagetian structures supposedly develop *within* the child's mind, rather than being internalizations of external formal structures, through its own natural ontogeny. Does this imply, then, that the spontaneous appearance of mental structures in the normal course of development, rather than, say, being the internalized content of education, is an immediate mental expression of the development of corresponding physical or physiological structures? In that case, we might assume that evolution had created a preestablished harmony, by which physiological structures appear quite naturally in a sequence, as required for the ontogenesis of cognitive capacities. The *existence* of mental structures, as understood in this sense, would then be bound up with the existence of the corresponding neurophysiological structures; and it would be necessary to seek external corroboration of the associated neurophysiological hypotheses before we could even accept the mental structures as authentic.

This external support might take the form either of direct neurological evidence or, alternatively, of a demonstration that such physiological structures could well have been produced by some combination of genetical mutation and natural selection which is plausible on more general evolutionary grounds. (That is to say, it will be necessary to show that the emergence of such cognitive capacities can be accounted for without the need to assume gross preadaptive "saltations," that is, sudden sweeping genetical changes whose causes are biochemically unintelligible and whose effects on the species are unaccountably beneficial.) Either way, it will again be questionable whether the resulting mental structures directly control the corresponding performances. Given such a genetical-physiological interpretation, the existence of neurophysiological and mental "structures" alike, rather than directly causing performances of one kind or another, will merely create causal preconditions for an individual's performances to exemplify, say, one cognitive stage rather than another.

Thus, on either an internalization view or a physiological-substrate view, it is not hard to see what kind of plausible basis there might be for believing in the existence of mental structures in the subject's mind, not just in the theorist's formal representation. For in either of these cases, it is clear enough what the *origin* of the corresponding mental structures would be. These accounts have the further merit of indicating—at least, roughly—what *kinds of things* such mental structures are (i.e., their ontological status), and also in what sense they can be held *responsible for* the character of an individual's resulting performances.

Unfortunately, the manner in which the concept of mental structures enters into contemporary debates about cognitive theory cannot safely be interpreted in either of these two ways; and in the absence of a clear origin for the structures—whether educational or physiological—the appeal to mental structures becomes a good deal hazier. Simply invoking the supposed existence of these structures as the hypothetical principle underlying actual cognitive performances, while disclaiming any opinions about their origins (whether educational or genetical), threatens to reduce mental structures to a kind of *virtus dormitiva*—a name without a referent—while, in the absence of any clear referent, to claim that mental structures somehow *control* performances is to beg the question. Indeed, we have no way of judging what kind of connection mental structures are supposed to have with the performances for which they are said to be responsible. Demonstrating that a theory of cognition can be built around generative principles, for instance, tells us only about the structure of the theory; it does not tell us what particular mental entities or events the theory *describes*, still less does it prove the existence of genuine mental structures causally producing *in fact* the results that are formally generated by those principles within the abstract context of the theory.

To sum up: the theorist who talks about hypothetical mental entities places on himself the burden of demonstrating *both* how these entities come into existence ("enter the child's mind") *and* how their existence can be inferred from observed performances. Unless the connection between observable performances and hypothetical mental structures can be explained unambiguously, the presence of *formal* structures in cognitive theory by itself proves nothing about the empirical existence of corresponding *mental* structures in the child's mind. Given the much looser connection often proposed between mental structures and actual cognitive performances, we are accordingly entitled to demand further corroborative evidence, whether historical, evolutionary, or physiological. Otherwise, the formal structures in question—however elegant their logico-mathematical expression—must be read as features of the theoretical model alone and not of some mental reality.

The Timeless Character of Mental Structures. The evidential problem in structuralist theory—that is, the problem of recognizing what kind of relationship is supposed to exist between actual observable performances and the structures said to underlie them—is greatly aggravated when those mental structures are said to be not merely *abstract* but also *timeless*. This is the case whenever those structures are treated as generative principles of a kind that give rise to consequences in a logical, rather than a temporal—let alone, causal—manner. For it is then doubly unclear how such principles are supposed to be manifested in the empirical facts of actual performance. Rather than building our theory of cognitive development around such static, timeless entities, we might do better to consider taking as our starting point the actual rules of procedure that are *directly* manifest in performances. These rules may be *abstract*, in the sense of not being manifested directly as behavior; but they would, at any rate, be related to the actual temporal performances through which they are expressed in a straightforward, intelligible manner. Such rules, however general, would determine the organization of actual behavior in a manner that honored the temporal realities of human action.

As matters stand, the discussion of cognitive theory is plagued by systematic ambiguities in the use of terms like "generate," "transform," "operate," and so on. Although we are continually tempted to read these words as referring to kinds of human action taking place in time, they in fact refer, instead, to sets of *timeless* mathematical relationships. The technical terminology of logical operations and mathematical transformations is introduced to characterize formal equivalences within the theory; yet, by virtue of their familiar ordinary-language associations, these terms strongly suggest a temporal interpretation, according to which the operations and transformations in question are *human activities,* and generation is a *productive process.* In this way, the rule for a mathematical operation is immediately read as implying an instruction for human action, while the formal equivalence by which an operation is defined within the theory is taken as a general description of the practical results of that action. Far from demonstrating the genuine relevance of atemporal theories of cognition to actual human cognitive processes, this use of an essentially ambiguous terminology merely sweeps the whole question of evidential relevance under the rug. It takes for granted that we understand the very thing which needs most to be experienced, namely, the relevance of the abstract rules of a timeless cognitive theory to actual, empirical thought processes and their resulting performances.

An account of cognitive development in terms of rules of procedure would eliminate these pervasive puns. And it would have the further merit, also, of lending itself to a truly developmental interpretation. Its subject matter would be actual empirical processes of mental activity and the temporal changes affecting them, rather than timeless hierarchies of hypothetical, static entities. With this in mind, let us now consider the relevance to developmental psychology of the methodological lessons drawn from our earlier discussion of evolutionary biology.

The Explanation of Cognitive Development

Whenever we set out to understand and explain the course of any diachronic process—whether organic evolution, cognitive development, or whatever—the use of static, essentialist entities to describe the individual stages in the process can create severe obstacles for us. In the case of biological evolution these obstacles were overcome by adopting a dynamical, populational conception of species in place of the earlier static, essentialist conceptions; and there are reasons for thinking that the same step could be equally fruitful now in the study of cognitive development. Just as the existence of comparatively stable forms in nature at first suggested an oversimplified picture of fixed species, so the use of formal characterizations to define cognitive stages has tended to make these stages appear more specific and more distinct than is compatible with any genuinely diachronic account of cognitive development. At best, any such static "state description" should be seen as an abstraction, arrived at by simplifying the information contained in the actual, underlying populational distribution—a simplification obtained, for instance, by averaging across that distribution and presenting the results only as an approximate generalization.

In the case of cognitive stages, there are in fact *two separate populational distributions* to be considered. When we are presented with statements about, say, the concrete operational stage, we may interpret them in the first place as referring to (a) the observed behavior not of one child only but of an entire age-cohort of children whose performances more or less exemplify the formal patterns of the stage in question. From the theoretical point of view, any particular stage may represent a phase in the lives of an entire population of *children*, rather than in the individual life of a single *child*. Even if we take each of the children separately, there is still (b) a further populational aspect to our problem. The child demonstrates his concrete operational capacities not just in one single task or type of task but in activities that display a whole spectrum of abilities, covering a great variety of performances with different materials, subject matters, etc. Our problem is to understand not just how a single, unitary capacity is displayed in a single kind of performance, but rather how, say, cognitive operational thinking is manifested and recognized in any of a varied population of performances. Part of our evidential problem thus has to do with seeing how stage-specific capacities are manifested in actual performances *at all*; but another part has to do with understanding how these capacities and the associated mental structures are related to all different *kinds* of performances in which they are supposedly expressed.

If we approach these two populational features—the *age-cohort* of children, and the *task-spectrum* of performances—from an abstract, essentialist standpoint, we shall be tempted to dismiss both kinds of variability—between different children in the same performance, and between different kinds of performance in a single child—as odd or freakish; and we may feel it necessary to invoke complementary hypotheses to explain these variations away. Drawing a lesson from evolutionary biology, we can alternatively acknowledge that such variabilities spring quite naturally from the populational nature of the case. Many of these supplementary hypotheses will then become unnecessary; and as in organic evolution, the developmental question will become a question about the processes by which individual exceptions, or novelties, gradually become typical. (Recall how biological mutations may eventually develop into species-specific features.)

Given such a populational analysis, it is at once apparent that the mental structures supposedly characteristic of any given cognitive stage will be manifested, at best, in a majority of individuals, and then only in a majority of their performances. So the characterization of a cognitive stage in terms of a fixed essence is as much of an abstraction as it is in the case of a species. The paradigmatic "concrete operational child" thus becomes an *idealized theoretical notion*—like the paradigmatic "ideal gas" of physics, or the "rational purchaser" of economics, or the "dimensionless point" of geometry. The empirical reality is always *a population of mixed individuals with mixed abilities.*

The Arbitrary Boundaries of Stages. Once evolutionists accepted a populational view of species, the decision just how broadly to apply any particular species name became *arbitrary* in a new way. So also did the decision at just what point to say that one species succeeded another—for example, at what points *Eohippus*, a three-toed precursor of the modern horse, turned into, say, *Parahippus*, and that into *Pliohippus*, and that in turn into *Equus*. Similarly, a populational analysis makes it equally clear in our own case that the boundaries between cognitive stages are determined not by nature but by *our decisions.* For some purposes, we may quite reasonably regard a child as having attained concrete operational status by virtue of performances on a single type of task, while, for other purposes, it may be just as reasonable to require that the child should display concrete operational abilities over a substantial range of performances. Correspondingly, the crucial question will now no longer be, At what point does the *mental structure* responsible for concrete-operational thinking *come into existence* in the child's mind? But rather, At what point does the *theoretical pattern* of concrete-operational thinking *become relevant and applicable* to a sufficient range of the child's actual abilities and performances? Compare the question, At what point in, say, the conversion of water to steam do the theoretical laws governing the behavior of an ideal gas *become relevant* to a sufficient range of its new empirical properties?

If we do accept the empirical reality of this double populational distribution—across cohorts of children and across spectra of tasks—it is at once clear why, in nature, no sharp stage transitions are to be expected. On the contrary: in the nature of things, we should now expect the process of cognitive development to follow the general patterns of temporal change governing organic growth and populational changes of all kinds. These patterns were analyzed long ago by D'Arcy Thompson in his classic treatise, *On Growth and Form*, and the relevance of his analysis to a much wider range of phenomena has been repeatedly confirmed in the subsequent decades in, for example, epidemiology, economics, and the sociology of science. Instead of expecting successive stages in cognitive development to follow one another in a discontinuous manner —whether by a straightforward step function, with abrupt transitions from, say, the preoperational to the concrete operational stage in every individual child, or by a series of more or less sharply and shallowly graded changes, as suggested by Flavell (1971)—we should rather expect to find the actual spread of, for example, concrete operational skills across individuals or types of tasks to follow a *sigmoid* or *logistic* growth curve.

If we consider the entire population of children in a given age-cohort, we may then expect to find a very few of them taking the step to concrete operational modes of thought unusually early, and another small group likewise taking the step very late, with a smooth increase in the rate of change among the entire population, rising to a maximum slope comparable to that of the steeper segments in Flavell's diagrams, followed by a falling away to near horizontal, as the relevant population "saturates." We should likewise expect any individual child to acquire the new type of ability first in a very small range of tasks and to be correspondingly delayed in another small range of tasks, with an intermediate phase during which he is rapidly learning to tackle more and more types of problems and materials in

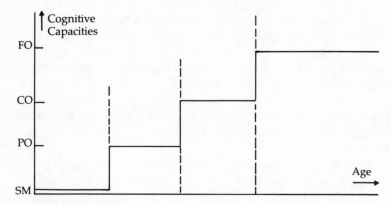

FIG. 1. Simple step function model of stage transition.

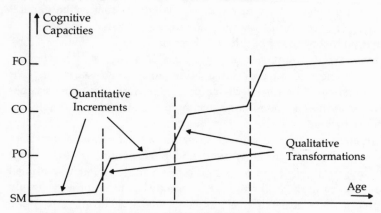

FIG. 2 Modified step function (after Flavell, 1971).

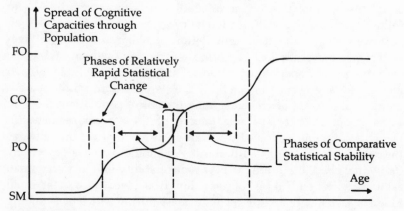

FIG. 3 Sigmoid sequence of stage transitions.

a concrete operational manner. Only if we mistake our arbitrarily imposed stage divisions for the reality of the case could we expect the graph of actual cognitive growth to be any kind of discontinuously graded step function, whether a straightforward sequence of horizontal and vertical phases or a succession of more oblique phases such as Flavell's. On the contrary, in terms of a populational approach, the family of curves best reflecting the actual realities of cognitive growth will be a succession of sigmoid or logistic curves in which all sharp transitions are smoothed off, reflecting the continuous spread of the new types of skill, either across an age-cohort of individuals or across the spectrum of tasks in a given individual.

Qualitative and Quantitative Change. The contrast between an essentialist and a populational analysis of cognitive development throws light on another vexed problem also. In the early days of zoology, a conviction that the mere quantitative multiplication of oddities or novelties in a population of one "species" (or "natural kind") could never give rise to a genuinely qualitative change from one species (or natural kind) to another prejudiced men against the very idea of organic evolution. Similar worries are evident among psychologists at the present time. There is a general division between those who would explain away all appearances of qualitative change as being inaccessible to quantitative, scientific investigation—"quantitative" here being equated with "scientific"—and those who insist on the reality of qualitative change, even at the price of abandoning quantitative methods of investigation. Yet, within evolutionary biology, it has long since been clear that there is nothing incompatible between qualitative and quantitative explanations; indeed, it is by now commonplace that populational changes in zoology can generate not merely *quantitative increments* but also *qualitative transformations* in an organic population.

The same could perfectly well be true in the case of a populational theory of cognitive development. For all the qualifications and modifications that Flavell introduces into his sensitive analysis, he continues to assume that an account based on quantitative observations will, to that extent, be unable to account for qualitative changes; but from a populational point of view, this assumption is quite simply unnecessary. However continuous the sigmoid growth curves of populational analysis may be, the plateau between them represents not merely *more extensive* but *qualitatively different* phases of development. So, qualitative changes need no more depend on discontinuities in psychology than they do in evolutionary biology, and we are not in fact obliged to choose between them. Qualitative and quantitative psychological explanations are not mutually exclusive. Whether we are dealing with cognitive development or evolutionary biology, accordingly, we can focus our theoretical attention on qualitative changes in a way that is scientifically respectable from the experimental psychologist's point of view—that is, without abandoning quantitative observation and analysis. Indeed, if we do so, the *arbitrariness* of the divisions between successive cognitive stages, far from being an *objection* to the Piagetian theory, becomes, on the contrary, a perfectly natural consequence of the populational problems that face us in reality.

The Problem of "Décalages." This same point can be carried further. So long as we regard the acquisition of a particular new mental structure as a unitary event, marking the *essential* transition to a new cognitive stage, we are confronted by the problem of explaining why this new structure does not at once make its existence apparent in *all* appropriate spheres of activity. This is the problem commonly discussed in terms of the concept of "horizontal *décalage*"; and it is a problem that is commonly stated in a way that takes for granted that once a novel stage-specific skill has appeared in one single type of performance, it should in theory be immediately available in all others also. (The relevant mental structure seemingly *exists* in the child's mind, so why is it not generally *operative?*) Currently, the fact that this simply does not happen—but that new types of capacity spread only gradually across the spectrum of a child's abilities—is taken as necessitating the hypothesis that extraneous factors (e.g., performance factors) are responsible for the variability in a range of performances that should, theoretically speaking, be all alike.

This *presumption*—that if all other things were equal, new stage-specific capacities would manifest themselves uniformly and universally in performances of all kinds—is evident in the very terminology of the theory. The French word *cale* means a wedge or block, so that the choice of the word *décalage* for the present phenomenon suggests, precisely, that the slowness in the spread of fresh capacities across a spectrum of tasks results from some active blocking, and so demands some kind of unwedging or unblocking. The use of this word suggests that once the step to a new stage has been taken—once a new mental structure has come into existence—its effects on performance can fail to appear universally only if they are positively blocked and so need to be "freed up" by counteracting the supposed inhibitory factors.

This added complication in Piagetian theory has often been criticized as *inelegant*. But the question we must now ask is, rather, whether it is not actually *unnecessary*—that is, whether the supposed blocking factors are not a fiction or artifact of the theory itself. That is what a populational analysis would in fact suggest. For such an analysis reverses the burden of the whole argument and removes the need to introduce extraneous blocking factors into our account. Rather than a unique concrete operational capacity entering the child's mind in a unitary manner, the child may very well be engaged in a succession of similar but separate learning processes. As a result, he learns to deal with every distinct type of task by using novel procedures which share sufficiently similar forms to be called by the common name, "concrete operational" procedures.

The need for horizontal *décalage* is thus a direct consequence of assuming the automatic transfer of stage-specific skills from one initial type of task to all others; and our present populational view enables us to dispense with both this assumption and the resulting implication that horizontal *décalage* is a genuine phenomenon at all. By setting aside any assumption that stage-specific mental structures operate uniformly and universally, such a view leads us to *expect* gradual rather than abrupt stage transitions; and as a result, we are spared the necessity of supposing that just because the child's new grasp of, say, concrete operational skills is slower to manifest itself in dealing with some tasks rather than others, he must have been blocked. On the contrary, such a variability in the time of appearance of novel skills, as between different types of tasks, is precisely what we should have expected and does not pose any theoretical problem about extraneous blocking factors at all. Still less do we need to speculate about any subsequent psychological process of unblocking.

(From our present point of view, the current debate involves a conceptual confusion similar to that involved in Aristotle's discussion of the flight of a projectile. Aristotle's theory of motion landed him with a theoretical puzzle about the factors supposedly responsible for keeping a projectile in motion after it had left the hand or the bow that originally launched it; and as a result, there was a notorious debate about how one might explain this supposed phenomenon of *antiperistasis*—for example, about the hypothesis that air displaced at the front of a flying stone might "rush around behind the stone and thrust it forward." Galileo at long last disposed of this problem, not by solving it but by showing that the supposed phenomenon was created by Aristotle's own theoretical expectation that had given rise to the very question of *antiperistasis* in the first place. Likewise, here, it is the mistaken presumption that novel mental structures appear in a unitary way, and should at once be manifest everywhere, that is responsible for the so-called phenomenon of horizontal *décalage*; whereas the variability in question is just what one should expect.)

Family Resemblances. The change from an essentialist view of cognitive stages to the populational one is recommended here chiefly because it permits us to develop a truly diachronic account of cognitive development; but it has one further significant consequence also. Suppose that we consider a child who is at what we would call the concrete operational stage, and pay attention to the totality of performances and procedures to be observed in this child. We can now raise afresh the question of what exactly it means to speak of all these performances and procedures as being—equally—straightforward applications of the same stage-specific mental structure. In just what respects, and to just what extent, do all these performances and procedures really have to resemble one another—that is, share a common "form"—for us to classify them all together as instances of concrete operational thinking? Once again, a populational and an essentialist view of cognitive stages will suggest quite different answers to that question.

From the essentialist standpoint, it is natural to see all concrete operational thinking as embodying *identical* formal features; and we shall then be tempted—even at the price of losing all veri-similitude—to stretch our description of the concrete operational phase so as to discover in, say, moral thinking, interpersonal behavior, the playing of games, etc., *precisely* those formal features the theory seemingly requires. From the populational standpoint, such efforts are once again quite needless. Taking biological evolution as our guide, we may take it for granted that the performances and procedures involved in tackling distinct types of tasks at the same cognitive stage will share, at most, "family resemblances." There need no longer by any *specific and unitary form*, uniquely present in all concrete operational performances as such; instead, the range of all these different procedures and performances to which, say, the name "concrete operational" can legitimately be applied will be linked by *overlapping sets of resemblances*, as we move from one type of task and one kind of performance to another.

The notion of family resemblance finds its clearest expression in Wittgenstein's *Philosophical Investigations* (1953). There, Wittgenstein argues that a great many theoretical confusions, both in traditional philosophy and elsewhere, originate in oversimplified ideas about the meaning of general terms, particularly in the assumption that all those exemplars to which any particular general term can properly be applied must share some single, common set of properties:

> Consider for example the proceedings that we call "games."
> I mean board-games, card-games, ball-games, Olympic games, and so on. What is common to them all?—Don't say "there *must* be something common or they would not be called 'games'," but *look and see* whether there is anything common at all. For, if you look at them, you will not see something that is common to *all*, but similarities, relationships, and a whole series of them at that. To repeat: don't think but look!
> . . . The result of this examination is: we see a complicated network of similarities overlapping and criss-crossing: sometimes overall similarities, sometimes similarities of detail. . . .
>
> I can think of no better expression to characterize these similarities than "family resemblances." For the various resemblances between members of a family: build, features, color of eyes, gait, temperament, etc., etc. overlap and criss-cross in the same way. —And I shall say: "games" form a family. [1973, propositions 66 and 67, pp. 31–32]

(In any particular case, the actual resemblances in virtue of which a term is applied may be many and close or few and remote: there are all kinds of family resemblances.)

The notion of family resemblances is put forward here, as elsewhere, as a substitute for that of essential defining characteristics, or criterial features. Whereas an essentialist view takes it for granted that what is true of one kind of concrete operational performance must, as a matter of logical necessity, be true of all—that is, that whatever makes it correct to describe one kind of performance as concrete operational must be identically the same for all others also—the alternative, family-resemblance view makes it a matter for *empirical investigation* to discover how far the similarities between different kinds of performance at the same cognitive stage really extend. This notion of family resemblances has great utility for the theory of cognitive development, precisely because it allows us to investigate the overlapping features of different concrete operational performances without begging any questions about the universality or necessity of this or that particular feature. All empirical gases, for instance, differ both from one another and from the theoretical physicist's paradigmatic ideal gas, to different degrees and in different respects. So, too, all the performances characteristic of, say, the concrete operational stage may of course differ from one another in significant ways; they will embody the theoretical psychologist's paradigmatic formal structure only approximately, with different exemplars deviating from it in different ways, according to the nature of the different tasks in question.

This proposal for a family-resemblance model of cognitive stages can provide us in addition with a directly empirical way of thinking about cognitive structures and/or processes. Notice that it implies nothing about the ways in which cognitive structures are to be characterized in abstract, mathematical, or logical terms: that is to say, replacing an essentialist conception of stage structures by a family-resemblance conception need not discredit the use of formal models for theoretical purposes—just so long as these formal models are recognized as theoretical idealizations, like the physicist's ideal gas or perfectly rigid body. The theoretical psychologist's formal picture may indeed serve as a useful analytical tool; but it cannot, as it stands, give us an accurate representation of all the variability actually found in the relevant mental abilities or processes.

To the extent that our formal model becomes abstract and idealized, however, its empirical relevance becomes increasingly problematic; so it becomes increasingly necessary to investigate the actual course of cognitive development in dealing with problems of different kinds empirically. Whatever formal model we adopt, its empirical relevance and application are limited by the diversity of types of tasks and contexts within which corresponding stage-specific abilities or procedures are employed. The very generality of a formal model thus guarantees its widespread applicability; but it does so only at a price. What is true of the physicist's concept of an ideal gas is true also of Piaget's formally idealized concept of a cognitive stage: to the extent that it applies to too many different things, it is inevitably more or less mismatched to them all.

Indeed, if we are to avoid theoretical confusions when using the phrase "mental structures" in *empirical* contexts, one further precaution may be forced on us. Hitherto, it has been tempting to assume that any particular cognitive stage can be defined for theoretical purposes in terms of a single formal structure, and that this *theoretical* structure has a single *empirical* counterpart (mental structure) which is embodied and operative more or less exactly in all of an individual's performances, in very different types of task. This way of looking at things naturally prompts us to question why this same mental structure is not equally effective in all kinds of tasks. (If we put it in this way, it seems as though only the *different manifestations* of any mental structure display "family resemblances" to one another: the underlying structure itself *is what it is*.) Yet the point can be put in a different way. Suppose that a child entering into, say, the concrete operational stage of development masters a whole new range of procedures, by which he deals with a wide spectrum of tasks in the novel, concrete operational manner. Might we not do better to say that the child thereby developed a *multitude* of different mental structures, and that the overlapping and criss-crossing family resemblances between those *empirical structures* may justify us in labeling them all in the same way, such as "concrete operational"?

Just as the theoretical physicist's conception of an ideal gas applies with greater or lesser exactitude to all empirical gases, without there being any single respect in which all empirical gases are necessarily and exactly alike, so we should perhaps see the different types of concrete operational performances as reflecting correspondingly many and varied mental structures—no two of which need be exactly similar, still less being perfect exemplars of the corresponding formal structure. Only some kind of Platonist hangover could force us to believe that all the different kinds of concrete operational performance must necessarily *embody identical forms*, or manifest the influence of *perfectly isomorphic empirical structures* in the mind—to say nothing of equating this supposedly universal form with the timeless, logical form in the abstract idealizations of cognitive theory.

Mental Structures or Cognitive Activities? In this subsection of our paper we began by distinguishing static (synchronic) characterizations of cognitive stages, abstracted from the actual developmental process of change, from truly developmental (diachronic) characterizations of that historical process itself; and we went on to distinguish, further, between an essentialist account of species or stages and a family-resemblance account. Although these two distinctions reinforce one another, they are in fact independent; and they are independent also of a third distinction, that between mental structures and mental processes, which was touched on at the very end of the previous subsection, and which we must discuss further here.

In the long run, any cognitive theory can yield a satisfactory overall account of cognitive development only if it lends itself to a diachronic interpretation. This requirement is essential. So we are always in a position of having to formulate cognitive theories in terms that can eventually be reconciled with such a diachronic interpretation. Given this need to prefer a diachronic over a synchronic account, we found strong arguments here for adopting also a populational view of cognitive performances and their development: conversely, we found it impossible to accept the actual existence of any hypothetical static mental entities whose origins and mode of operation were left entirely obscure. And the same arguments have now led us, in turn, to favor a family-resemblance view of stages and performances, in place of the earlier, essentialist view.

There still remains, however, the third choice: whether to formulate our theories in terms of mental structures or mental activities. Current theoretical discussions for the most part talk about mental structures—even about *timeless* logical structures—and leave the connection of these structures with actual temporal processes more or less unclear. They do so (we here argue) only because of a prior decision in favor of an essentialist account of a kind that lends itself naturally to a highly abstract kind of formal representation. Once we give up this essentialist view in favor of a family-resemblance view, the case for talking about structures rather than, say, about activities or procedures becomes correspondingly weaker. By contrast, an account in terms of family resemblances can remain much closer to the empirical facts of cognitive development—in all their variability—and accordingly gains no advantage from invoking theoretical entities any more abstract than is strictly necessary. So the timeless abstraction associated with the concept of mental structures will be foreign to such an account; rather, it will naturally be formulated in terms of temporarily organized activities and the procedures applied in the course of behavior. In short, an account of cognitive development that remains as close as possible to the actual phenomena of the field can best be formulated, not just in terms of family resemblances rather than essences, but also in terms of mental activities rather than mental structures. And it is only by making the empirical relevance and application of the theory quite clear in this way that we can discuss cognition in terms that are ultimately compatible with a properly diachronic account of cognitive development.

Opting for a diachronic/family-resemblance/activity view of cognitive activity and development does not, of course, involve calling in doubt the existence of general qualitative patterns, principles, or schemata in human cognition. On the contrary: recognizing the existence of these qualitative patterns may well be the most significant achievement of twentieth-century psychology. Hitherto, however, those psychologists who recognize such qualitative features have generally chosen to express them within the framework of theories so abstract, and so detached from the actual facts about the corresponding performances, that the resulting theories have risked becoming empirically indeterminate. (In this respect, we should add, Piaget's theoretical formulations do come somewhat nearer to being empirically testable than Chomsky's.) But this abstract detachment is not, and never was, inevitable. A theory of rules, patterns, and procedures associated with a populational view of cognitive performances and a diachronic account of cognitive development is perfectly well adapted to addressing *qualitative* differences, and so escaping any charge of associationism or behaviorism; yet at the same time, it can express the empirically discovered principles and procedures in a formal manner, and do so in *quantitative* terms which never lose touch with the empirical evidence of actual performances.

The Problem Case of "Formal Operations." The virtues of distinguishing between the *formal* entities and relationships of logic and mathematics and the *empirical* entities and relationships of actual psychological process can be most compellingly illustrated by considering the puzzling case of Piaget's "formal operations." Nowhere in current cognitive theory is the description of mental life in terms of timeless structures more plausible than it is in that case.

At the formal operational stage, it seems most plausible that the correspondence between the formal structures of cognitive theory and the empirical patterns of actual cognition is complete. So the temptation to equate the two kinds of structures becomes a strong one. The forms of abstract reasoning characteristic of the formal operational stage—with all their sophistication—may thus seem to confront our present alternative kinds of theory with a counterexample in which the timeless formalisms of logic and mathematics apparently capture precisely the empirical nature of our actual thinking.

Once again, however, this appearance rests on a failure to allow for a crucial distinction. In part, Piaget's initial concentration on formal operations seems to have been connected with his interest in our knowledge of spatial relations, which played so large a part in Kant's original discussion of concepts, categories, schemata, and other mental forms. There is thus a natural temptation to misread Piaget's discussion of formal operational knowledge and thinking as referring to our capacity to master the formalisms (i.e., formalized operations) of geometry itself. *But this is a sheer mistake.* Piaget's class of formal operations covers merely those kinds of abstract, general thinking that appear in principle to be *formalizable*, not those kinds of scholastic, mathematical deductions that become available to us only after, say, the calculus of geometry has been actually *formalized*. Paradoxically—we might say—the theory of formal operations applies directly only to those modes of thinking that have *not yet been* actually formalized!

Once again, we can see most clearly what different kinds of mental entities cognitive theory is concerned with in this case by looking first at their origins, that is, at the manner in which they are acquired in the life of any individual. Suppose, first, that a child acquires the capacity to operate in accordance with some formalized system of reasoning not as the internal product of normal ontogenetic development but through exposure to an external presentation of that system, that is, by being *taught* to operate with it. Suppose, for instance, that he studies the formal system of Euclidean geometry so effectively that he knows the rules of the system by heart and can construct proofs for new theorems on demand. In this event, a formal system originally present "in the public domain" is internalized, so that the individual may be said to have acquired a mental representation of the same system; and it can certainly be said that the mental entities associated with this internalization—and with its subsequent reapplication in the generation of new proofs—themselves "embody the rules of geometry." In this case, accordingly, "He has the mental structures in his mind" will cash in for "He has the rules of geometry by heart"; and the same kind of thing can be said of a child who masters by heart as a *theoretical* exercise, either Russell's propositional calculus or the systems of mathematics known as topology.

By contrast, consider what Piaget himself says about a child's early mastery of spatial relationships, as manifesting a *practical* grasp of toplogical relationships. On a hasty reading, Piaget may seem to suggest that the growing child displays, at a surprisingly early stage, an understanding of the exact science of *topology*—and does so in advance of his even having learned Euclidean or metrical geometry. This suggestion may well appear very puzzling to us. After all, both historically and in their own lifetimes, professional mathematicians learned to formalize, develop, and handle *topology* only after (and as a further generalization from) Euclidean or metrical geometry. However, if we break the implied link between the practical handling of elementary spatial concepts and the theoretical grasp of formalized systems of mathematics, this sense of mystery can be dissipated. There is really nothing at all surprising in the observation that children can deal in a more or less systematic manner with simple, nonmetrical properties and relationships—"big" and "small," "larger than," "to the left of," "inside," and the rest—before they have yet begun to master any metrical characteristics—"five inches long," "seven degrees of arc," "two feet higher than," and the like. But this observation in no way entails that the "premetrical" child has in any sense mastered the formalized structures of mathematical topology! All that it entails is that he has begun by mastering those very general nonmetrical procedures for recognizing and dealing with spatial relationships that have, at long last, been abstracted and formalized in the twentieth century, in mathematical topology.

In the case of formalized, mathematical systems, the presence of an isomorphism between our internal or mental structures and the external, mathematical structures which they represent is also unmysterious. In both Euclidean geometry and elementary arithmetic, the manner in which the practical operations of counting and measuring are formalized to yield systems of mathematical relationships, and the process by which these systems are subsequently internalized, have the effect of creating the very isomorphisms that it is our business here to understand. This happens as a result of not one but three successive steps. There is an initial *abstraction*, by which our first rough conceptions of spatial characteristics and relations come to be organized into general, abstract systems of practical thinking; next, there is the technical step of *formalization*, by which the practical content of metrical geometry is cast into a general, abstract mathematical form; and finally, there is a subsequent process of scholastic *learning*, by which formal calculations performed initially "in the public domain" begin to be performed, in part at least, in the head. If practical operations, geometrical theorems, and inner representations all turn out to have the same general organized patterns or structures, the reasons are clear. For the practical operations acquire a specific and definite form, by reflected glory from the mathematical system of Euclidean geometry into which they will eventually be formalized. Meanwhile, the inner representations themselves take on a specific and definite form, because it is their task to mirror the Euclidean theorems from which they have been internalized. Evidently, in this case, the form of our mental processes can indeed be the same as that of the corresponding mathematical systems. After all, that was how we created these mental processes in the first place.

How far can this conclusion be extended and generalized to cover the wider class of thought processes occurring in a child at the formal operational stage? That can be done only at great risk. Evidently, formal operational thinking is not typically learned as a scholastic exercise, that is, by internalizing public systems of formalized relationships. On the contrary, it is a kind of abstract general thinking that emerges from increasingly symbolic action-schemata. The origins of formal operational thinking are thus very different from those of scholastic calculating. So in what sense are there—as is so often supposed—genuine analogies between formal operational thinking and, say, schoolroom geometry?

One thing that gives considerable added force to this analogy is the fact that Piaget presents the formal operational system itself in the textbook symbolism of propositional logic. This leads some people to suppose that formal operational thinking in some way or other constitutes the *application* of a mentally represented system of logic. But in this respect at least, the analogy is a false one. The fact that the formalism of Piaget's theory is taken from a textbook system, just as much as that of Euclid's geometry, is merely a coincidence. In order to demonstrate that we "know geometry," in the scholastic sense, we must publicly produce proofs belonging to the public system of formal geometry; by contrast, many formal operational individuals are unaware that the propositional calculus even exists.

This is not to deny that mature abstract thinking can be said to have a logico-mathematical form, if certain rather special conditions are satisfied. That is entirely in order (a) where the *content* of the thinking itself has the structure of a logico-mathematical system—as, say, where it embodies internalized representations of textbook systems, like the propositional calculus and/or Euclidean geometry; (b) where the cognitive psychologist himself chooses to *represent* our thinking in a formal manner, for his own theoretical purposes. In these very special cases, it may be said, for example, (a) that a particular child who has learned Euclidean geometry by heart has in fact a mental representation of formal geometry, which gives logical form to his own thinking; or (b) that, for theoretical purposes, a formal representation can be developed which covers more or less exactly *all* mature abstract thinking—of which (a) above is a single, special type of case. But these two claims are completely independent.

The existence of formal representations of thought processes in psychological *theory* is one thing; the existence of "internalized representations" of mathematical formalisms in psychological *reality* is quite another. In order to think abstractly (in a formal operational manner) one does not have to have internalized the theoretical psychologist's formal representation, any more than one has to have internalized Euclidean theory in order to handle spatial relationships in a practical, nonscholastic manner. (And this would remain true even if we could learn public, formalized theories by some other process than internalization.) Knowing by heart the abstract formalizations of Piaget's cognitive theory is clearly *not* a necessary precondition for doing abstract, general thinking of a formal operational kind.

A child may indeed *happen to know* a particular formal theory—even Piaget's theory—and that same formal theory may also be known to the psychologist, and used by him, in characterizing the child's thinking. But these are entirely independent phenomena, which are most partially coincide. The fact that the child knows a formal theory whose internal logical structure is itself timeless does not entail that his own mental procedures are in general timeless; still less can we infer this from the fact that his thinking in general can be described in terms of timeless, logical statements. Even though—on occasion—the *content* of a child's knowledge may itself by (e.g.) the propositional calculus, while at the same time a psychologist may choose to explain the child's knowledge in terms of that same propositional calculus, the fundamental distinction will remain. For the *role* of the propositional calculus will be quite different in the two cases. In the first case, it will be the object of knowledge; in the other, the method of representation. Even in this strange and exceptional case—even where what the child knows, and what the psychologist says about what the child knows, can be expressed in exactly the same *formal* propositions—the two systems remain functionally and categorially distinct.

So the case of formal operations does no more to establish that our mental structures share the forms of Piaget's own theories than can be done in the case of concrete operations, or even sensory-motor and preoperational thought. The fact that the general category of formal operational thinking includes one rather special sub-variety—the fact that teenagers are able to master, and handle, formalized systems and mathematical relationships, such as those found in schoolroom geometry—can provide no basis for any *general* claim to the effect that (e.g.) the mental structures or processes involved in formal operational thinking are themselves intrinsically and essentially formal in character. On the contrary, if contemporary structuralist theories of cognition and cognitive development have so formalized a character, this reflects a historical feature of the theories themselves, not a psychological feature of our own mental performances and procedures.

In psychology as in other sciences, we are entitled to obtain the theoretical clarification that a formal representation can provide; but here as elsewhere we must take care that, in doing so, we avoid encumbering ourselves with needless metaphysical baggage. Thus, the fact that we use abstract, formal models in accounting for the empirical facts about psychological reality does not mean that we are compelled to accept equally abstract or idealized views about the empirical phenomena accounted for in this way. For instance, we might devise a formal model of mental activities, linked by family resemblances and developing in a strictly diachronic manner, quite as well as one built around the idea of static, synchronic structures, sharing some common criterial attribute or essence. Whether it will prove elegant, convenient, or otherwise advantageous to cast the resulting theory in an abstract, formalized symbolism is for us to decide; and nothing specific about the empirical world will be entailed by that decision. Yet, however our theories are formulated, one methodological demand is indispensable. They *must* permit the actual characteristics of any empirical entities to which they claim to refer to be established in an empirical manner, not merely inferred from the structure of the formalism; otherwise, these entities will have no real explanatory force.

The Idea of Necessity in Developmental Psychology

Out of all the epistemological problems we raised in the first section of this paper, one final group of issues remains for comment. That concerns the "necessary" character attributed to so many features of our cognitive functioning and development. As we remarked at the outset, these supposedly necessary features and relationships are of two kinds: relations holding between the characteristics of any single, given cognitive stage, and those supposedly characteristic of the entire sequence of successive stages. We shall discuss each of these in turn.

The salient points can be made concisely. Throughout this paper, we have emphasized the differences between the formal, logical features of the theoretical representations used in developmental psychology and the empirical features of the actual cognitive performances and abilities represented by the theory, at points where this distinction has too often been blurred. For instance, we are often tempted to talk as though actual, empirical *thinking processes* could be logical or illogical *in themselves*. But the only things that can be logical or illogical are either the propositional arguments in which the *outcome* of those processes may be expressed, or else the formal representation used by the psychologist in his *theoretical analysis* of processes. Thinking processes can be deliberate or hasty, meticulous or careless, elaborate or abbreviated; and all these *empirical* characteristics can have some influence on the more or less logical character of the resulting outcome or theoretical representation. But the thinking process itself is simply an empirical psychological phenomenon, not a formal logical entity. To project onto it the formal, logical properties that belong rather to its propositional expression or theoretical representation would be, quite simply, a "category mistake."

This observation is directly relevant to the question of necessity.

If we are going to look for *formal or logical* necessities in developmental cognitive psychology, we must do so only in those directions where such necessities can properly be found. If we claim to find necessities also in the *empirical* features of cognitive experience, these will have to be of other, *nonformal* kinds. Two varieties will be of special interest to us here, both of them being, in a broad sense, pragmatic. Thus, we may speak of two aspects (A and B) of a cognitive performance as being related in an empirically necessary manner if they are related together *instrumentally*—that is, if A is the only, the universal, or at least the typical means for bringing about B. Or, alternatively, we may speak of two different cognitive abilities (A and B) as related in an empirically necessary manner if one is the *prerequisite* of the other—that is, if a prior command of ability A is an indispensable preliminary for embarking on the task of learning B.

Much can be done to clarify the discussion of necessity in cognitive psychology merely by taking care to flag the crucial differences between *formal* necessity, *instrumental* necessity, and *prerequisiteness*. Clearly enough, all three varieties are relevant to the subject at different points, and in different ways. To the extent that the theoretical representations of Piagetian theory embody the formal structures of mathematical group and lattice theories, the *internal* connections between the different elements of the corresponding groups and lattices will be formally necessary, just because the representation in question *is* mathematical. But this particular kind of mathematical necessity is incapable of rubbing off onto the empirical processes, abilities, and performances which the theory is used to represent. It has to do *only* with the formal coherence of the theoretical structure itself, not with any empirically necessary character of the actual psychological subject matter.[6]

Likewise, to the extent that cognitive stages represent the outcome of successful accommodations, they will be correspondingly

6. If we are tempted to suppose otherwise, that may simply be a consequence of our own rhetoric. Suppose that we consider a particularly good exemplar of concrete operational thinking. It will be quite natural to infer that the empirical ability in question must possess all the corresponding formal features; and we might go on to assume that this *semantic* necessity—which applies to concrete operational abilities, simply *as* concrete operational—either embraces, or is identical with, the *formal* necessity of the corresponding theoretical representation. But this would involve a straight category confusion, like supposing the "Johnny is four" and "four is a square number" together entail "Johnny is a square number."

adaptive; thus many of their characteristic features will be as they are for *instrumental* reasons. To this extent, the fact that certain kinds of cognitive ability are uniquely efficacious, at one or another stage in the child's cognitive development, will itself give rise to empirical necessities. "Who wills the end must will the means": if a child is to obtain the functional advantages characteristic of, say, the concrete operational stage, he will have to master the correspondingly typical concrete operational means to those ends.

The relevance of *pragmatic prerequisites* to cognitive psychology is likewise clear. Think, for instance, of the relationships between successive stages in cognitive development: the abilities called into play when tackling any kind of task during, say, the formal operational stage of development may well be ones that the child could even *begin* learning only if he had previously mastered the corresponding abilities on the previous concrete operational level—and similarly for the other stage transitions. Lawrence Kohlberg (1969), for instance, takes this view in his well-known characterization of the stages in moral development. In this case, a good deal of light is thrown on the necessity for an individual to pass through Kohlberg's stages in just the order he does by establishing that the procedures characteristic of any one stage are indeed prerequisites for learning those of the next stage.

Such pragmatic instrumentalities and means-ends relationships are, however, quite distinct from formal, mathematical relationships. Rather than *equating* the resulting pragmatic necessities with formal or mathematical necessities, we shall therefore do better to respect the differences between them. This is something that Piaget himself is not always scrupulous about doing; on the contrary, he sometimes takes an almost perverse delight in doing the opposite. In explaining the self-regulating stability of mental structures, for instance, he accounts for their "equilibrium" not in *pragmatic* terms, as the outcome of an empirical interaction between the cognitively functioning organism and its environment, but rather in *mathematical* terms, as a formal consequence of "the laws governing their structure":

> There is thus no need to distinguish structures and functions (in the biological, not the mathematical sense of the term) for the functioning of the structure is reduced to its internal [formal/mathematical] transformation. [1973, p. 16]

Once *biological* structures, functions, and transformations are equated with *mathematical* structures, functions, and transformations, however, the conusion between empirical and formal necessities will be almost impossible to avoid.

Similarly, with respect to stage succession, Piaget and his followers seem to find the idea of basing all *pragmatic* necessities on underlying *formal* necessities irresistible. If the abilities characteristic of cognitive stage S_n are pragmatic prerequisites for learning those characteristics of the successive stage S_{n+1} (they insist), there is a deeper reason for that fact—namely, the fact that the cognitive structures associated with S_{n+1} logically include those associated with S_n.[7] Yet it by no means follows from this that the pragmatic relationships between successive stages can be derived from the corresponding logical relationships (e.g., logical inclusion) in the formal theory; still less, that the entire process of cognitive development is biologically adapted *because* it can be given a formal representation.

What, after all—we may ask—is the job of a formal representation in the theory of cognitive development? If we are going to take seriously Piaget's dictum "Intelligence is a biological adaptation," we shall presumably have to *start* from the presumption that later stages of cognitive development are adaptively better, functionally more efficacious, and/or pragmatically superior, when compared with earlier stages. If we can capture something of this adaptive superiority with a nice, clean logico-mathematical formalism, so much the better. In the world of abstract theory, it is an important question how far any given type of cognitive ability or performance can be represented in a formal manner. But that is as far as the claims of formalism can go. Beyond them lie the more basic claims of *functionality*. In the last resort, that is, our cognitive procedures must *prove their worth* in the competitive forum of the empirical world.

---

7. This claim surely puts the cart before the horse. If theoretical psychologists can find ways of giving structural *representations* of two such stages, S_n and S_{n+1}, which are related together by logical inclusion, that is surely because the cognitive abilities associated with S_n are indeed (pragmatic) prerequisites for those of S_{n+1}—not the other way about.

SUMMARY AND CONCLUSION

The novel theories of mental structure that have attracted so much attention in the fields of cognitive and developmental psychology and psycholinguistics during the 1960s (we have been arguing) can be credited with certain very real achievements. In particular, they have compelled psychologists to give proper weight to the *qualitative* differences between cognitive or linguistic performances, abilities, and capabilities of different kinds. Furthermore, they have introduced into the field of psychology a genuinely *theoretical* element, involving the use of precise and elaborate formal representations as a means of characterizing different stages in cognitive development, together with their associated capacities and/or structures. In this respect, the use of formalism drawn from mathematics and logic goes far beyond the *empirical* level to which earlier psychologists had confined their quantitative measurements and calculations. But these achievements have been bought at a price. By constructing their theoretical analyses around the formal calculi of logic, group theory, and the like, psychologists of this new orientation have taken upon themselves those epistemological problems that arise inescapably for any theory that aims to provide a formal representation of authentic empirical phenomena. And there are reasons for thinking that they have not yet fully faced all of these problems.

In the present paper, we have set out to do three things. In the first part of the paper, we identified the chief points at which difficulties arise in the interpretation of these modern theories (particularly, Piaget's theory of cognitive development) when we try to make explicit the manner in which the formal representations are to be checked out and corroborated against empirical observations of actual performances and/or abilities. Just because the theoretical representations employed are formal and timeless, they stand at a certain epistemological distance from the empirical phenomena they explain. In the second section, we considered some episodes in the history of other sciences in which physics, biology, and chemistry were confronted with parallel difficulties, an showed how these were overcome. Finally, in the third section, we reapplied the lessons of these historical examples, and proposed for discussion a number of possible new lines of theoretical development, designed to remove current obscurities and confusions from the contemporary debate about cognitive development. A summary of the chief results of our inquiry follows.

1. Timeless, formal structures derived from group theory, propositional logic, and similar fields of exact but abstract study can safely be put to use in the context of theoretical representations of cognitive capacities and development *only* if care is taken not to assume automatically, and without further investigation, that those formal structures must mirror exactly corresponding, empirical mental structures in the individual thinkers concerned. In the absence of further, very specific empirical evidence of such an isomorphism, we should presume that these formal structures represent at best a theoretical idealization of any corresponding empirical features, much as (e.g.) the physicist's concept of an ideal gas represents at best an idealization, not a direct description, of actual, empirical gases.

This amounts to a warning that any use we make of formalism in our attempts to develop theories about some aspect of reality—whether physical or psychological—requires us either to provide direct empirical verification of the existence of any entities referred to in the theory or else to admit frankly that no such empirical objects or structures should be expected to correspond to these entities. This warning is apt for any formally expressed theory about mental life which purports to capture the essence of psychological reality: not merely to the theoretical formulations ("mental structures," etc.) of Piagetian stage theory, which we have discussed in detail here, but equally to the theoretical formulations ("deep structures," etc.) of transformational grammar.

2. This being so, it will be necessary to examine *separately* the manners in which the cognitive abilities and performances of children change and acquire qualitatively new features, in relation to all those different types of task, subject matter, and the like with which they deal. On the face of things, *the very most* we should expect is that over a wide range of different types of tasks and ability, more or less similar qualitative changes take place at more or less the same ages, so as to yield a more or less unified stage, characterizing ways of tackling these different tasks.

Rather than take for granted that identical mental structures or organized patterns of ability characterize thinking during any single stage in different areas and for different tasks, we may initially assume that the structures and patterns involved in dealing with disparate types of task will display at most "family resemblances," in

Wittgenstein's sense of that phrase. Subsequently, of course, it may turn out that over some limited but significant spectrum of tasks, a more exact set of correspondences and isomorphisms can be demonstrated. But this is a conclusion that we can put forward only *after* separate and careful empirical investigations of children's changing abilities and performances in many significantly different types of task. Failing such empirical demonstrations, attempts to discover fresh counterparts of, say, "conservation," "decentering," "equilibration," and other Piagetian functions, in contexts remote from those in which they were originally established, can yield nothing more than loose analogies.

Thus, to provide a single, essential characterization of any set of stage-specific abilities, when these are in fact only clusters of specific abilities, more or less similar to one another in their overlapping characteristics, yields at best a simplified summary abstracted from the actual complexity and variability inherent in the real phenomena so described. All such abstractions have to be cashed in for actual human performances in one particular context or another; and there is no reason to treat the variability in these performances as more apparent than real—or to suggest, for that matter, that it is less real than the general features on which the formal theory chooses to focus. Hence, it is question-begging to treat the differences that appear across contexts simply as *distortions*, introduced by various extraneous factors operating on a common essential core.

In order to do justice to the differences as well as the similarities in the performances found at any given stage, however, we should have to take into account the contexts of the observed performances, in the most inclusive sense of the word *context*. Doing this would be as helpful in revealing the processes or procedures by which we come to organize our knowledge of *language* as it is for revealing the nature and development of the human capacity to *reason*. Once again, therefore, our present argument applies to theories of language just as much as to theories of cognitive development. Indeed, as one of us has argued elsewhere, the various formulations of transformational grammar display their greatest weakness precisely in their systematic denial of significant contextual effects (Feldman, 1971, 1974).

3. Hitherto, there is insufficient evidence that all the cognitive abilities associated with any particular stage of development really do embody strictly isomorphic features, in relation to the whole spectrum of tasks. So it is premature to raise the empirical hypothesis that all these different cognitive abilities manifest equally

the same unique underlying mental structure. Failing better evidence of such exact isomorphisms, we should assume rather that any stage transition in cognitive development is a *populational* change—doubly so, in fact, since every such transition may potentially involve both a multiplicity of children and a multiplicity of different types of task.

When we speak *in theory* about "the" change from one stage to the next, we refer therefore not to a single, abrupt temporal transition *in empirical reality* but to a more or less rapid statistical redistribution of different stage-specific abilities, both across a particular age-cohort of children and across the entire spectrum of different cognitive tasks. With this qualification, it is possible to recognize why all empirical observations of stage transition should reveal smoothed-off, sigmoid growth curves—as new types of abilities spread through the relevant cohort of children and across the relevant spectrum of tasks—rather than the discontinuous step functions implicit in more naive interpretations of stage theory.

4. A populational, family-resemblance analysis of stages and stage transitions of this kind lends itself naturally to a truly *diachronic* description of cognitive development in a way that a more formal, essentialist account of mental structures and cognitive stages is unable to do. The reasons for the superiority of such a view are the same in cognitive psychology today as they were in the biological theory of evolution a century ago. Just as distinct species characterized by fixed essences are prevented, for conceptual reasons, from *evolving* into one another, so also distinct cognitive stages characterized by formal, logico-mathematical structures are prevented, for similar reasons, from *developing* into one another. In itself, this fact does nothing to discredit the use of formal representations in the theory of cognitive development. But it does underline the need to recognize just how much epistemological distance there is between the formal structures of the theory and the empirical phenomena they are employed to describe and explain.

In short, the step-by-step *succession* of theoretical stages has as its empirical counterpart a temporal sequence of more or less rapid populational redistributions. As in Darwin's evolution theory, these populational changes involve clusters of more or less similar and related (rather than identical) features which undergo statistical redistribution among the individuals concerned. The effect of accounting for such changes in populational terms is to explain *qualitative* novelties in terms compatible with *quantitative* precision.

This said, the question arises whether, as an empirical concept, the notion of timeless, formal mental structures plays a useful part in the description of cognitive development at all, to say nothing of its being indispensable. Perhaps all the empirical burden at present borne by this notion could be carried just as well, and less misleadingly, by the temporal notion of cognitive activities or procedures, identified by their actual, empirically observable characteristics, rather than by their abstract and hypothetical "structures." Certainly, the terminology of "procedures" or "activities" enables us to bypass many of the graver epistemological obscurities in the current theory. By speaking in these terms, for instance, we can establish directly what cognitive procedure a child is employing in some situation without any of the evidential difficulties involved in the attempt to reveal his underlying mental structures. Of course, a particular individual at a particular age may quite well turn out to display no consistent pattern of activities and procedures as he moves across the whole spectrum of different types of task. Yet, if that is the way things really are, what do we gain by concealing that fact? Arguably, all we achieve by such concealment is to create for ourselves an artificial and unnecessary family of problems about "horizontal *décalage.*"

These two final points (3 and 4) are directed at theoretical problems raised in all *developmental* theories of this general type. Their bearing on stage theories of mental development—not only those of Piaget, but also those put forward by Erikson, Kohlberg, and even Freud—is straightforward and evident. They relate to the formal characterization of "language competence" provided (for example) by Chomsky rather less directly, because Chomsky does not explicitly set out to characterize the linguistic competence of children of various ages in the same kind of formal way that he does for adults. The work along these lines by other researchers, such as Klima and Bellugi (1966) and Milon (1974), has likewise provided accounts of language competence only in certain special areas, the rules regulating *negation* in the speech of five-year-olds.

Nonetheless, as we argued above—and as Chomsky himself would presumably agree—these final claims (3 and 4) are, implicitly, just as relevant to grammatical competence as to cognitive ability, since the development of any purported "deep mental structure" that manifests itself naturally during ontogenesis, rather than being produced by external factors, must ultimately be explained in a satisfactory genetical or historical manner. If adult language competence is characterized in static formal terms, akin to those of Piagetian stage theory, then any associated theory about the development of language competence in childhood must ultimately face those same problems that arise explicitly in tackling stage transition and change from the Piagetian standpoint. The fact that psycholinguists working on language competence have yet to address the problems of diachronic explanation directly may have concealed those problems hitherto; but it does not make them any the less real, or remove the theoretical need to provide an adequate *developmental* analysis of our linguistic abilities that can circumvent the difficulties facing any *formal* theory of language knowledge.

All in all, then, we conclude that as matters stand at present, the weight of the current argument is strongly *against* all naively empirical interpretations of the formal structures of Piagetian theory. What we have to deal with in actual, empirical fact is always mixed age-cohorts of children, all of whom display mixed families of cognitive abilities in dealing with different kinds of tasks. Whatever virtue the logico-mathematical characterizations of formal structures may have, when considered merely as providing theoretical representations of certain idealized cognitive stages, it does more harm than good—in the absence of quite specific empirical evidence of a kind that we now lack—to read these *theoretical* structures as mirroring internal, isomorphic mental structures underlying all the thought processes of a child at the corresponding *empirical* stage of development.

For the time being, we shall do better to attend more closely than it is customary to do at present to the epistemological distance between Piaget's formal theories and their empirical application to psychological reality. Rather than involving ourselves in question-begging assumptions and creating needless confusions and obscurities, we can avoid importing the merely *formal* features of Piagetian theory into our descriptions of *substantive* psychological phenomena; and we can recognize just how much can be done to give an adequate description of those phenomena by using a terminology and mode of description that remain much closer to the temporal and empirical realities of the phenomena in question. Failing this, there is a standing danger that empirical considerations and concepts will become irretrivably confused with theoretical ones, and that it may become quite impossible to distinguish questions about the *empirical basis* of the Piagetian theory from questions about its *formal coherence*.

Some people may object that the populational, family-resemblance view here recommended is complex and confusing, by comparison with the seeming exactness and conciseness of current theoretical terminology. To them we can only reply that this complexity has had to be accepted in other sciences—theoretical physics, structural chemistry, organic evolution—as the price of achieving a genuine measure of methodological sophistication and self-understanding. Unless we are prepared to take this step, we risk bogging ourselves down in a morass of epistemological confusion; and we shall place needless handicaps on our efforts to achieve a truly *theoretical* analysis of the qualitative transformations involved in the transitions from one cognitive stage to another, which can yield at the same time a truly *diachronic* account of the actual process of cognitive development.

REFERENCES

Feldman, C. F. The interaction of sentence characteristics and mode of presentation in recall. *Language and Speech*, 1971, **14**, 18–25.

Feldman, C. F. Pragmatic features of natural language. In A. Bruck, R. Fox, & M. LaGaly (Eds.), *Papers from the Tenth Regional Meeting, Chicago Linguistic Society.* Chicago: CLS, 1974.

Feldman, C. F., Lee, B., McLean, J. D., Pillemer, D. B., & Murray, J. R. *The development of adaptive intelligence.* San Francisco: Jossey-Bass, 1974.

Flavell, J. H. *The developmental psychology of Jean Piaget.* New York: D. Van Nostrand, 1963.

Flavell, J. H. Stage-related properties of cognitive development. *Cognitive Psychology*, 1971, **2**, 421–453.

Ginsburg, H., & Opper, S. *Piaget's theory of intellectual development: An introduction.* Englewood Cliffs, N.J.: Prentice-Hall, 1969.

Hertz, H. R. *The principles of mechanics presented in a new form.* New York: Macmillan, 1899.

Hull, C. L. *The principles of behavior.* New York: Appleton-Century-Crofts, 1943.

Klima, E. S., & Bellugi, U. Syntactic regularities in the speech of children. In J. Lyons & R. Wales (Eds.), *Psycholinguistic papers.* Edinburgh: Edinburgh University Press, 1966.

Kohlberg, L. Stage and sequence: The cognitive-development approach to socialization. In D. Goslin (Ed.), *Handbook of socialization theory and research.* New York: Rand McNally, 1969.

Miller, G. A. Some psychological studies of grammar. *American Psychologist*, 1962, **17**, 748–762.

Milon, J. The development of negations in English by a second language learner. *TESOL Quarterly*, 1974, **8**, 137–143.

Piaget, J. *Psychology and epistemology.* New York: Grossman, 1971.

Piaget, J. *Main trends in interdisciplinary research.* New York: Harper, 1973.

Piaget, J., & Inhelder, B. *The child's conception of space.* London: Routledge & Kegan Paul, 1956.

Wittgenstein, L. *Tractatus logico-philosophicus.* London: Routledge & Kegan Paul, 1922.

Wittgenstein, L. *Philosophical investigations.* Oxford: Basil Blackwell & Mott, 1953.

Language Communities, Search Cells, and the Psychological Studies

Sigmund Koch
Boston University

*T*he letter of invitation sent to the participants in this symposium refers to the "current 'crisis' with respect to alternate paradigms in psychology." If one were to try to establish the date of the letter on the basis of that phrase alone, it could have been written on any of the 36,500 days in the century-long history of "scientific" psychology. "Crisis," in the sense that the writer had in mind, is endemic to psychology; it is the inevitable fruit of the very idea of a single, conceptually coherent enterprise whose objective is the positive study of "all" consciousness, experience, organismic (or merely human) conduct, action, or behavior. It will always be thus—just as surely as it must remain forever impossible to render an unspecified universe into a universe of discourse. Perhaps that is all I have to say.

Competitive conceptual crises within knowledge-seeking groups may, of course, vary in severity in a variety of ways. The number of alternate conceptual templates competing at a given time is one of them. The frequency distribution of users (or advocates) of the respective templates is another. The crisis condition of psychology has, over its history, varied considerably in these respects. For instance, during a period which I have called the "Age of Theory" (between, roughly, 1930 and the early '50s), the gross-structure of our profession was such that the bulk of American psychologists fell into only three conceptual camps: the neobehavioristic (vastly in the ascendency), the Gestalt or field-theoretical, and—though a small and marginal camp—the psychoanalytic. (The fine-structure was considerably more intricate!) And the quality of crisis in this interval was relatively "benign" in another sense. Though the members of each group wished their own theories to achieve universal sway, the wish was tempered by at least a dim perception of the utility (from the standpoint of their group) of having a few clearly defined sets of "enemies." It was thus possible, by means of the early ritualization of a set of intergroup polemical policies, to achieve a kind of happy symbiosis. The members of each group could evade the onerous challenge of fleshing out the details of their own primitive and lacunae-ridden theoretical programs by fixing upon a few stable research contexts in which putative disagreements could be fought out. Moreover, since certain epistemological and methodic agreements transcended the theory groups, it was possible to believe that such polemical "research" was *constructive*: a policy of empirical testing of differential consequences of contending points of view would surely move the field toward conceptual unification.

That period of relatively bland "crisis" began to break down in the early to mid-fifties under the impact of a complex of "rational" and extrarational factors far too intricate to unravel at this place. The theories—most of which had claimed an unbridled range of application to "all" psychological phenomena—began to be perceived for the largely vacuous, indeterminate meta-programs that they were; it was also becoming apparent that the various programs had not moved toward any greater determinacy for periods of up to 20 years, and that the polemical research had settled virtually nothing. And some people began to sense that even if these theory-like formulations *had* been theories, the terms of most were such as to have little or no bearing on ranges of phenomena worthy of human interest. Finally, it slowly became apparent (if only dimly and partially) that the epistemic and formal procedural patterns—deriving mainly from the "rational reconstructions" of logical positivism and from operationism—which had guided the development of the more influential "theories" were utterly inappropriate to the requirements of a psychological subject matter and, indeed, based on highly inadequate generalizations of the practice of physics.

Along with the disaffection just sketched, crisis, of course, burgeoned. Beginning in the early fifties, and at an accelerating rate ever since, many new conceptual and research options were asserted, and many old ones resuscitated. "Theoretical" grandiosity contracted (regarding intended scope, claimed cognitive accomplishment, anticipated predictive specificity), and both conceptual and methodic strategies were diversified. Though many psychologists continued to promote their favored conceptual templates in the messianic spirit of converting the entire psychological research community (and, indeed, the world), it was possible, for a decade or so, to discern a new problem-centered modesty on the part of many.

Then came Thomas Kuhn. I am far from suggesting a devil theory of Thomas Kuhn. If there is anything devilish in the circumstances I am about to mention, this must be attributed to the strangely dysfunctional interaction between psychology and philosophy that has been evident during this century. It is a paradox that a "science" which for a hundred years has taken vast pride in its hard-won independence from philosophy has, over much of that interval, continued to seek out its marching orders from that queen of many edicts. That the queen is a notoriously fickle one no one can deny, but the crux of the difficulty is that most psychologists are not outstandingly precise readers, especially when it comes to philosophy. (If it be argued that Kuhn is a historian and not a philosopher, my response is that his 1962 book had philosophical objectives.) Be all this as it may, Kuhn is a strangely difficult writer. He combines a tendency to be overly pat in the main outlines of his thinking with an allusive and fluidly accretive mode of defining the conceptual elements of his framework. *The Structure of Scientific Revolutions* (1962) is, in essence, a definition *in usu* of three correlative notions: "paradigms," "normal science," and "revolutionary (or extraordinary) science." All three—and especially the central notion of paradigm—emerge as vague, though suggestive, concepts with exceedingly open meaning-horizons. It is the kind of writing that is open to easy misinterpretation by the initiate in the fields addressed by the book and to wild misinterpretation by the uninitiate.

Many psychologists took the message to be that a Kuhnian paradigm is an X (a conceptual frame, a way of "seeing," a vocabulary, a single "idea," an experimental method or situation, a mensurational device) which is somehow enormously easier to achieve than what they had thought a "theory" to be—and that a paradigm (in effect, any old paradigm), once universalized within a scientific community, would *guarantee* progress toward increasingly differentiated knowledge. Further, Kuhn seemed to be telling them, all that was necessary for "normal science" and for the easy ecstacy of "puzzle-solving" to supervene was agreement on a paradigm by the members of the community. And agreement was to be attained by "persuasion"—or quite possibly a well-intentioned unanimous vote in the interest of the social weal. (How could a guy with reservations stand in the way?) Never had the price of attaining the status of integral and progressive science appeared so cheap!

The rest of the story hardly requires summarization. At some point preceding the mid-sixties, the imagery (and associated programmatic cant) of paradigms began rapidly to replace the imagery and cant of theories and models. Paradigm promotion became the new form of psychological commerce. Every day sees the propulsion of a brand new paradigm, and every month marks a seminar or convention symposium designed to select a victorious paradigm that will render psychology one and progressive for a tidy stretch of time, if not forever. Psychology is back on the "unity" track with a vengeance—and with the ludicrous consequence that never has the field been comparably obfuscated by the babble of so vast and contentious a plurality of parochial voices.

The first echelon of this symposium falls within the tradition of paradigm-promoting just described—though I hasten to add that in important ways it lends dignity to the tradition. The voices were those of serious and able scholars (Professors Giorgi, Day, Riegel, and Rychlak) who have thought long and responsibly about their positions. Moreover, these are courageous men of unusually self-determining cast, who challenge mainstream thinking at impressive depths. Most of the newer paradigms are, after all, merely local ripples on the surface of a tide of hoary scientistic strategems. Nevertheless, in the two days of the first session of the symposium, a single audience was courted by the competing claims of a phenomenological paradigm, a "contemporary behaviorism" paradigm, a paradigm advocating "developmental dialecticism," and a paradigm urging a "telic explanation of human behavior," to be implemented within the "objective" verificational resources of traditional "logic of science." Each of these paradigm proposals solicits acceptance by the *entire* psychological community. Each urges, that is, the universalization of its own conceptual template, its own language, within the psychological community.

For some years, I have been urging that it is feckless and illusive to anticipate or search for a single paradigm for psychology, and have been inviting recognition of this by the proposal that "scientific" psychology be reconceived as *the psychological studies*. Psychology, in my view, *cannot* be a coherent discipline, howsoever "coherence" be defined: whether in terms of subject matter, methodico-strategic commitments, concrete theoretical principles or some conceivable body of such, conceptual frameworks, or even desirable common characteristics of the workforce (in respect to background, sensibility, training, etc.). Substituting the word *paradigm* for any or all of the preceding will not help! The most conspicuous trend in the *history* of psychology has been toward theoretical and substantive fractionation (and increasing insularity among the "specialties"), not integration. Psychologists have, apparently, not found this circumstance sobering. But there are many "in principle" considerations which stand in the way of any rational anticipation of coherence. In this paper, I should like to explore in depth both the historical and the principled constraints upon an integral psychology. The sequence of my analyses will be as follows:

1. A general restatement of the case for the noncohesiveness of "psychology," with an emphasis on historical considerations.

2. An analysis of the senses in which misreadings of Thomas Kuhn have given psychologists a false optimism concerning the prospects for an integral discipline—not neglecting an attempt to identify certain of the first-order vaguenesses in Kuhn himself.

3. An analysis, based on a theory of empirical definition on which I have been working for 20 years, of the conditions of meaningful communication in psychology (and in general), which shows that the psychological studies must, in principle, comprise many language communities speaking parochial and largely incommensurable languages, and thus that "paradigms," however general their intent, must remain local to the participating adept persons in given, specialized language communities. This will comprise the central section of the paper and convey the main "in principle" barriers to an integral psychology.

4. A consideration, in light of the previous analyses, of some detailed epistemic characteristics of the psychological studies in relation to those of the sciences and the humanities. And, finally, a consideration of some of the issues bearing on the *appraisal* of theories or conceptual frameworks in the psychological studies.

"PSYCHOLOGY" OR THE "PSYCHOLOGICAL STUDIES"? HISTORICAL CONSIDERATIONS

The historical evidence for the noncoherence of "psychology" at any given cross section of its history—and for the patent long-term tendency toward increasing theoretical and substantive fractionation—can be mobilized in many different ways. My account will be brief and informal, and will concentrate largely on an interval of relatively stable crisis (circa 1930–50) which marked the most ardent attempt in psychological history to achieve coherence and progressive scientific status. This was the "classic" phase of the Age of Theory, in which the neobehaviorisms were by far the most widely held formulations, but an interval also characterized by an acceptance by most of the contending theoretical forces of a common model of theoretical procedure which itself was believed to guarantee forward movement. The signal failure of the neobehaviorisms—especially if seen in relation to the essentially role-playing character of the epistemic strategies definitive of the Age—provides an unusually compelling (and poignant) historical demonstration of the elusiveness of an "integral" psychology!

Perhaps a few people of my ancient generation may recall a book, written by Grace Adams (1931), entitled *Psychology: Science or Superstition?* I read it shortly after having been appalled and insulted by my first few undergraduate courses in psychology, and found in it both amusement and solace. The idea that psychology was a congeries of weird insularities was already a cliché, but the author developed this cliché in so sprightly and compelling a fashion that the field came through to me as in some perverse way inviting. So massive an absurdity cried out for redress. Besides—an absurdity so massive could hardly hold its own against a little clear thinking.

I did not then know that Clark Hull felt pretty much the same way about this book. Toward the beginning of one of his early theoretical papers, "The Conflicting Psychologies of Learning—A Way Out" (1935), he refers to it in these words:

> The obvious implication of this general situation [the wide disagreement among psychologists] has recently called out a timely little book by Grace Adams entitled *Psychology: Science or Superstition?* In this work she points out what we all know only too well—that among psychologists there is not only a bewilderingly large diversity of opinion, but that we are divided into sects, too many of which show emotional and other signs of religious fervor. This emotionalism and this inability to progress materially toward agreement obviously do not square with the ideals of objectivity and certainty which we associate with scientific investigation; they are, on the other hand, more than a little characteristic of metaphysical and theological controversy. Such a situation leads to the suspicion that we have not yet cast off the unfortunate influences of our early associations with metaphysicians.

Somehow we have permitted ourselves to fall into essentially unscientific practices. Surely all psychologists truly interested in the welfare of psychology as a science, whatever their theoretical bias may be, should cooperate actively to correct this.

But before we can mend a condition we must discover the basis of the difficulty. A clue to this is furnished by the reassuring fact that persisting disagreements among us do not concern to any considerable extent the results of experiment, but are confined almost entirely to matters of theory. It is the thesis of this paper that such a paradoxical disparity between scientific experiment and scientific theory not only ought not to exist but that it need not and actually will not exist if the theory is truly scientific. It will be convenient in approaching this problem first to secure a little perspective by recalling the essential characteristics of some typical scientific procedures.

After these remarks, Hull proceeds to a brief and schoolmasterly discussion of the "essentials of sound scientific theory" which, of course, recapitulates the schema of a hypothetico-deductive system. Such a resumé of hypothetico-deductive procedure appears in virtually every one of Hull's earlier theoretical articles; it is always conjoined with an invitation to contending theorists that they axiomatize their nebulous thoughts and that, in the event that determinate derivations diverging from Hull's own ensued, the difference be arbitrated in the laboratory.

It is 40 years later, and the theory that Hull so diligently contrived as his answer to the massive absurdity of the "psychologies" is becoming a dim memory even to the few who still work within its tradition. And every judgment, expectation, hope, and presupposition registered in the two paragraphs just quoted has been cruelly—indeed, extravagantly—thwarted by history. We are still divided into sects, "many of which show emotional and other signs of religious fervor," but perhaps thrice as many. Far from having yet "cast off the unfortunate influences of our early associations with metaphysicians," the emergence of a large American Psychological Association Division of "Philosophical Psychology," and of a large group of discipline-hopping philosophers specializing in philosophy of mind, has reinstalled the enemy at the very center of the citadel.

Moreover, those who have most zealously practiced the rites of exorcism seem somehow to have drawn to themselves the heaviest succubi.

The judgment that "persisting disagreements . . . do not concern to any considerable extent the results of experiment" has certainly been gainsaid by the four decades of intervening history. It is rare that an experiment claimed to support a given theory is seen in that light by advocates of an alternate theory; it is rarer still that an experiment "generated" by a given theory, or merely performed in its ambience, is seen by the outgroup as defining a valid or nontrivial empirical relationship. And, more generally, the entire conception of theory and of scientific method presupposed in this passage from Hull (and explicitly developed in succeeding paragraphs in the same source) has been all but given up in those areas of scholarship from which it was imported and has been markedly attenuated even in psychology.

Somewhat before Hull wrote the quoted passage, another thinker had expressed himself in a rather similar vein. I take the liberty of changing one word in the quoted passages:

> The backward state of the [psychological] sciences can only be remedied by applying to them the methods of physical science, duly extended and generalized. . . .
>
> If there are some subjects on which the results obtained have finally received the unanimous assent of all who have attended to the proof, and others on which mankind have not yet been equally successful; on which the most sagacious minds have occupied themselves from the earliest date, and have never succeeded in establishing any considerable body of truths, so as to be beyond denial or doubt; it is by generalizing the methods successfully followed in the former inquiries, and adapting them to the latter, that we may hope to remove this blot on the face of science.

The writer was John Stuart Mill, and these words were published in 1843—almost a century before the words quoted from Hull. My one liberty in quoting Mill was to substitute "psychological sciences" for "moral sciences" in the initial sentence—a permissible substitution in that he makes it quite clear that by "moral sciences" he means the social sciences, inclusive of psychology.

Mill was no lone or pristine voice; similar strategies were advanced before him and, indeed, implemented by his master Comte and by many of the French and English philosophers of the Enlightenment. Formal institutionalization of psychology as a *science* waited upon Wundt in 1879, but by this time an endeavor called "scientific psychology" was an inevitability, if not indeed a fact.

It is worth stressing that, prior to the late nineteenth century, there are no precedents in the history of ideas for the constitution of great new fields of knowledge by edict. The institutionalization of each new field of science in the early modern period was a fait accompli of an emerging substructure in the tissue of scientific knowledge. Sciences won their way to independence, and ultimately institutional status, by achieving enough knowledge to become sciences. Physics (in the modern sense), for instance, was practiced for several hundred years by independent gentlemen scholars before it even found a niche in the universities. By the late nineteenth century, these justly discriminated fields of science had given such food to man's cognitive and material hungers that his appetite had become insatiable. And by this time, multiple lines of inquiry into the nature and trend of science itself began to focus into an apparently wholesome Victorian vision. It was a vision of a totally orderly universe, totally open to the methods of science, and a totally orderly science, totally open to the stratagems—and wants—of men. It was against such a sanguine, zealous background that psychology was stipulated into life.

At the time of its inception, psychology was unique in the extent to which its institutionalization preceded its content and its methods preceded its problems. If there are keys to history, this statement is surely a key to the history of modern psychology. Never had a group of thinkers been given so sharply specified an invitation to create. Never had inquiring men been so harried by social wish, cultural optimism, extrinsic prescription, and the advance scheduling of ways and means.

On the face of it, the nineteenth-century program for a science of psychology seems rational enough. It asks mankind to entertain a huge and wholly open hypothesis: precisely the hypothesis I have just quoted from Mill. Can the methods of natural science, "duly extended and generalized," be "adapted" to the "backward" studies of man and society (man's experiences, his actions, his artifacts, his values, his institutions, his history, his future)? To entertain such a hypothesis responsibly is no light matter. Madhouses have been populated by responses to lighter intellectual burdens. No wonder that many inheritors of this awesome challenge have protected themselves from its ravages by reinterpreting the hypothesis as an a priori truth.

For close to a century now, many psychologists have seemed to suppose that the methods of natural science are totally specifiable; that the applicability of these to social and human events is not only an established fact, but that knowledge based on inquiries not saturated with the iconology of science is worthless. From the earliest days of the experimental pioneers, man's stipulation that psychology be adequate to *science* outweighed his commitment that it be adequate to man. From the beginning, some pooled schematic image of the *form* of science was dominant; respectability held more glamor than insight, caution than curiosity, feasibility than fidelity.

The history of psychology, then, is very much a history of changing views, doctrines, images about *what* to emulate in the natural sciences—especially physics. In the nineteenth century, this meant the *extension* of experimental method to subjective phenomena on a pattern in which specifiable elements of consciousness were to be related to physically manipulable and definable input variables ("stimuli"). For early behaviorism (1913–30), it meant the *use* of experimental method exactly as in physics (i.e., "objectively")—experiential variables of any sort being regarded as unamenable to publicly verifiable specification, and thus beyond the pale of true science. The task of psychology thereby becomes one of determining correlations between *stimuli* and *responses*, and the organism or person becomes an empty area at which myriad S and R processes intersect.

By the late 1920s, there was much objective experimentation but few bodies of clearly stated predictive principles comparable to the crowning achievements of physics: its theories. Instead, experimentation sometimes seemed aimless, "theoretical" hypotheses but loosely related to data, and debate idle. Thus, beginning around 1930, we get the emulation of natural science's *theoretical method* or, at least, the emulation of an image of that method which was then being projected upon the world by the philosophy of science and gaining broad acceptance. Thus commenced the phase of *neobehaviorism* which presumed (in practice, when not in principle) that the entire, awesome domain of psychological reality could be comprehended under sets of arbitrary and lacunae-ridden postulates, based in the main on the experimental analysis of rat behavior—and not rat behavior in anything like its full richness but limited to one or another presumably prototypical response such as choice-point behavior or lever-pressing. It required close to 20 years of frenetic pursuit of such a strategy for the hypothesis to emerge that it was perhaps a bit overoptimistic.

The next stage (from about 1948 on) in the enaction of a psychological science was to presume that the synoptic theoretical conceptions of classical neobehaviorism were overambitious, and that the corrective was to curtail the scope of the objectives while pursuing precisely the same empirical and analytical tactics. This ushered in a phase of miniature theories and "models" (the period might be called "deflated neobehaviorism"), usually developed against a background of stated or unstated belief to the effect that these formulations would automatically coalesce into a supertheory of cosmic scope.

But soon many began to doubt that the analysis of arbitrarily fixed-upon aspects of animal learning was an adequate induction basis for laws bearing on all organismic achievement and process. This disabusement, gaining appreciable spread at some point in the 1950s, led to a remarkable liberalization of behaviorist "methodology." It was now permissible to restore to the psychological universe a variety of intradermal processes and events of a sort which had been extradited by the peripheralistic necessities of earlier behaviorism. Fields like perception, cognition, and psychology of language could now be readdressed, but with the quaint proviso that the internal processes and events demarcated by these fields be treated exactly as if they were at the periphery of the organism, and thus externally observable. This tour de force was effected by the inspired discovery that brain events could be *called* central responses, and sometimes even stimuli, and thus that S-R laws discovered at the surface of the organism would almost surely hold at central levels. Thus was unleashed a period that my nomenclature would allow to be called either *neo-neobehaviorism* or "post-deflated-neobehaviorism" or, if one prefers, "inflated neobehaviorism."

But the readmission of fields like perception, cognition, and language proved a dangerous maneuver. Some behavioral scientists were emboldened to conjecture that there may be a psychological subject as well as a subject matter. They became quite free, even racy, in their language. There was even talk of plans, ideas, thought, will, minds—sometimes bereft of quotation marks. To be sure, some of these bold people mitigated their verbal transgressions by calling themselves *subjective behaviorists*. Others did not. But all of them, being scientists, with the resurrected psychological *subject* upon them, saw the need to effect a more radical change of scientific strategy than any initiated by the successive phases of behaviorism. The strategy now becomes that of turning to the revered natural sciences, especially the engineering disciplines, not merely for prefabricated methods but prefabricated answers as well. Thus we get the models based on computer simulation (in some of which the computer *is* the psychological subject) or on transpositions to the events generated by actual human subjects of a variety of developments in applied mathematics, ranging from information theory to the theory of games. In this way the *science* of psychology maintains consistency with its history—by headlong retreat from the psychological subject immediately upon the long-delayed moment of reconfrontation.

I hasten to emphasize that the historical pattern just described is biased, abstract, and selective to the point of caricature. But I believe it to be both biased *and* true, selective *and* illustrative, and, as caricature, revealing. It certainly does not comprehend *all* consequences of the entertainment, over time, of the Millian hypothesis, and it does not intend to suggest that nothing has been learned.

The idea that psychology—like the natural sciences on which it is modeled—is a cumulative or progressive discipline is hardly borne out by its history. Indeed, there could be a way of writing the history of modern psychology which would have to acknowledge that most of the well-verified and solid "advances" of any generality are registered by clusters of findings that help reveal the utter inadequacy of long-flourishing analytical frameworks or so-called theories. The hard knowledge that accrues in one generation typically disenfranchises the theoretical fictions of the previous one—and any new theoretical framework this hard knowledge is believed to suggest or support typically survives only until the next. If psychology is science, it is "science" of a strange kind. Its larger generalizations are not specified and refined through time and effort; they are merely replaced. Throughout its history as "science," the *hard* knowledge it has deposited has usually been *negative* knowledge!

Examples are legion. In 1920 Lashley begins a research program designed to provide the physiological underpinnings of Watsonian conditioning theory and soon—to his astonishment—runs into findings utterly at variance with Watsonian or any other then imaginable version of associationism. After an unrelenting and often brilliant 30-year pursuit of the problems suggested by these early findings, Lashley (1950) concludes:

> This series has yielded a good bit of information about what and where the memory trace is not. It has discovered nothing of the real nature of the engram. I sometimes feel, in reviewing the evidence on the localization of the memory trace, that the necessary conclusion is that learning just is not possible.

To extend the story, it can be said that the truly impressive developments in subsequent biological psychology (after 1950), made possible by the powerful electrophysiological and other techniques then becoming available, have thus far had a similar force. As a result of dense piling up of much particulate evidence concerning such matters as graded excitation processes, central feedback to the receptors, "vertical" organization of brain process, and so on, the entire earlier history of psychophysiological theorizing can be seen as hopelessly simplistic. But again, the main *general* contribution is negative knowledge. Indeed, one reading of this knowledge is that the established complexity of C.N.S. process is such as to make the prospect of biological explanation of psychological process even more remote than Lashley tended to suggest. Furthermore, the complexity *now* apparent in neural function suggests orders of complexity in human action and experience that had been grossly slighted in the conceptualizations of behavioral and "psychological" psychology.

The experiments initiated by Gestalt psychology circa 1911 had a truly decisive significance—though this was long disputed—relative to the critique of Wundtian experimental psychology, structuralism, and, later on, behaviorism. And no one can deny that many particular findings concerning simple aspects of perceptual organization have by now been contributed. I believe these discoveries to constitute one of the few islands of solid accomplishment in this century. But it must be noted that the *positive* proposals put forward toward psychological and neurophysiological "field" theories—whether in general terms or as subtheories of restricted range, such as that of "figural aftereffects"—now appear highly inadequate.

The examples from biological psychology and the special case of Gestalt theory are far from the strongest illustrations of the negativity of psychological knowledge. For in these cases there are at least grounds for believing that particular findings of permanent value—even if not ultimate adequacy—have eventuated. But these findings give us no purchase on any "truly" science-like general analysis of the events in their domain. They give us only a means for destroying older and misconceived analyses.

Other examples of negative knowledge of a rather more curious and depressing sort could be given—too many of them. These are the "discoveries" that a preexisting framework will not do, on the basis of "findings" which, however meticulously produced, tell us nothing intrinsically illuminating. Such findings may be negative ones on *two* counts: They gainsay a given nonframework on the basis of research that, taken by itself, must be a nondiscovery. Usually they bear only a polemical and role-playing relationship to a formulation which, on other grounds, is beginning to be acknowledged for the senseless thing that it is. The twists and turns in the dominance of, or differential allegiances commanded by, the diverse behavioristic theories of learning provide relevant examples—as may easily be inferred from our earlier comments on the behaviorisms. Other illustrations might be drawn from the somewhat more complex history of conceptual realignments, and changing influence patterns, among general depth-psychological or personality theories or among the subdoctrines bearing on the psychotherapies.

A history of psychology which sought to derive the lessons for the empirical (i.e., sociological and psychological) understanding of inquiry implicit in the *negativity* of psychological "advance" would be a truly significant enterprise. But this is not the place for such an effort.

The Millian hypothesis has been under test for nearly a hundred years. It has been tested in billions of man-hours of research and of ardent theoretical thinking, scholarship, writing, planning, and administration. It has been tested in hundreds of laboratories by many thousands of investigators. There are now over 25,000 members of the American Psychological Association alone. This massive test has generated a vast literature, a vast publication apparatus, a vast organizational structure. The test has received generous support from society. The test has not been a sleazy one.

In my estimation, the Millian hypothesis has been abundantly disconfirmed. I think it by this time utterly and finally clear that psychology cannot be a coherent science, or indeed a coherent field of scholarship, in any specifiable sense of coherence that can bear upon a field of inquiry. It can certainly not expect to become *theoretically* coherent; it is already clear that no large subdivision of inquiry, including physics, can. But neither is it realistic (or desirable) to strive toward coherence—whether it be of method, linguistic and other communicative practices, size and degree of extensibility of consensus communities, or personal characteristics and training of investigators. As for the *subject matter* of psychology, it is difficult to see how it could ever have been thought to be a coherent one under any definition of the presumptive "science," whether in terms of mind, consciousness, experience, behavior, or, indeed, molecule aggregates or transistor circuits. Nothing as awesome as the total domain comprised by the functioning of all organisms can be thought the subject matter of a coherent discipline; such a belief would be tantamount to inviting into existence a *Doppelgänger* for every branch of knowledge—formal or informal, actual or potential—in the entire scattered and disorderly realm of human cognitive concerns, and expecting somehow that the *Doppelgängers* would mesh while their originals would continue to languish in chaos, each at its own station. Indeed, the picture requires that a special *Doppelgänger* be assigned to psychology itself. Urgently.

Science is perhaps the most charged, the most glittering, and—despite thermonuclear weaponry—the most reassuring word in the modern vocabulary. In the modern period, this innocent lexical unit has soaked up a meaning throughout 400 years of use in primary association with the natural sciences. During that association, the core meaning[1] of the word—and culturally its most highly prized connotation—has become connected with a special analytical pattern emerging first in classical modern astronomy, achieving more distinct fruition in Newtonian mechanics, and

---

1. It is often (and correctly) pointed out that rather different analytical or rational patterns can be discerned in the characteristic achievements of different areas of science: for instance, that parts of biology are purely taxonomic or are qualitative and still "genuine" science; that meteorology is a strangely mixed science, involving an assemblage of derivative subtheories but including large nonrationalized components. The "core meaning" I here attribute to "science" is not intended as an ultimately correct and full demarcation criterion but, rather, as the text suggests, as "culturally" the "most highly prized connotation" of the word. Moreover, I think it *historically* the case that something like the "analytic pattern" I here try to describe is what most psychologists have in mind (if only inchoately) when they claim psychology to be a science, or seek to make it one.

The question of "demarcation" between science and other forms of inquiry is rejoined, from another incidence, later in this paper.

undergoing further differentiation in postclassical physics.

That analytical pattern, though it has been the object of great interest, has not yet been successfully explicated. No one doubts that it has been implicit in the skills of great physicists. There is reason to believe that the pattern is applicable in aspects of the biological sciences. I am not deluded that I can bring this pattern much closer to explication than has, say, Michael Polanyi—and I agree with him that to set the goal of full explication of such a matter is absurd. I think it possible to bring it into finer resolution than has yet been achieved but not, as it were, in passing. What can be said here, however, is that this pattern requires: (a) the disembedding from a domain of phenomena of a small family of "variables" which demarcate important aspects of the domain's structure, when that domain is considered as an idealized, momentary static system; and (b) that this family of variables be such, by virtue of appropriate internal relations, that it can be ordered to a mathematical or formal system capable of correctly describing changes in selected aspects of the state of the system as a function of time and/or system changes describable as alterations of the "values" of specified variables.

To achieve (i.e., disembed) a family of variables having such properties is no mean feat, even in reference to rather "simple" natural systems (e.g., those constituting pressure-volume relations of a gas) having a highly "closed" character. It required a prolonged development of ancillary knowledge, culminating in an act of genius, to disembed the laws of such simple systems as those defined by the pendulum, the inclined plane, or the motions of falling bodies. Though there is currently much appreciation of the wide variability of natural systems on some such dimension as "closedness-openness" or "weakness-strength" of boundary conditions (thus, experimental isolability), insufficient concern has been given to the strong chance that at some critical point of system openness, boundary weakness, or mere internal complexity, the definitive analytic pattern may no longer apply. Von Bertalanffy has done an important service in spelling out certain implications for biology which stem from the "openness" of the systems characteristically addressed by that science, but he and other "system theorists" in his tradition have not considered the question here at issue. Rather, they tend to generate a rhetoric of confidence to the effect that the empyrean must surely contain mathematical or logical methods suitable for the analysis of systems of any degree of openness or complexity.

I do not think even the empyrean to be that well stocked. If one considers, say, the familiar estimate that the human cerebral cortex contains some ten billion neurological units, each with ramifications which may lead to as many as twenty-five thousand others—and bears in mind the complexity, density, lability, and mutual interdependencies of the process at every point, and considers further that this unbelievably differentiated piece of cyto-architecture is stuffed into a very small container—it is possible to believe that there are tight limits within which our definitive analytic pattern may be applicable. Past some limiting point of analysis, even the finest microelectrode conceivable is likely to pick up mere noise. I think that in certain areas of biological psychology that point is already being approached. When one descends to the level of molecular biology, justifiable enthusiasm over the recent advances in that field should not conceal the fact that anything analogous to the Laplacean paradigm of total specification of the state-parameters of the elements of a system (even if the "universe" be that of a single human brain) is totally beyond reach—and, indeed, beyond reason.

But biological psychology is perhaps the one area in which some approximation of the analytic pattern of science can be fruitfully applied, notwithstanding such limiting circumstances as have been mentioned. The 100-year history of what is called "scientific psychology" has established beyond doubt that most other domains that psychologists have sought to order, in the name of science and via simulations of the analytical pattern definitive of science, do not and cannot meet the conditions for meaningful application of this pattern. If this conclusion seems arbitrary, one can only submit that a hypersufficiency of grounds for it are implicit in the preceding historical rundown of the behaviorisms. Consider that the central empirical area, which was the target of all that theoretical effort, was learning. Consider the hundreds of theoretical formulations, rational equations, and mathematical models of the learning process that have accrued; the thousands of research studies. And *now* consider that there is still no wide agreement, even at the crassest descriptive level, on the empirical conditions under which learning takes place, or even on the definition of learning or its empirical and rational relations to other psychological processes or phenomena. Consider also that after all this scientistic effort, our actual *insight* into the learning process—as reflected in every humanly important context to which learning is relevant—has not improved one jot. An educator need not look far past his nose to perceive that point more clearly than he might wish.

Many legitimate and important domains of psychological *study*, then, cannot be called "science" in any significant sense, and continued application of this misleading metaphor can only vitiate, distort, or pervert research effort. When I say this, it is important that what I am *not* saying be understood. I am *not* saying that the psychological studies should not be empirical, should not strive toward the rational classification of observed events, should not essay shrewd, tough-minded, particulate, and differentiated analyses of the interdependencies among significant events. I am not saying that statistical and mathematical methods are everywhere inapplicable. I am not saying that there are no subfields of psychology, as historically constituted, that can be regarded as parts of science—although it can be argued that the most clearly discernible of these, such as "sensory psychology" and "biological psychology," might just as well (and perhaps more fruitfully) be regarded as parts of *biological* science.

I *am* saying that—in fields as close to the heart of the psychological studies as perception, cognition, motivation, and learning; and certainly social psychology, psychopathology, and personology; and, of course, aesthetics, the study of "creativity," and the empirical study of phenomena relevant to the domains of the extant humanities—in all these areas, such concepts as *law, experiment, measurement, variable, control,* and *theory* do not behave sufficiently like their homonyms in the established sciences to justify the extension to them of the term *science.* To persist in the use of this highly charged metaphor is to shackle these fields of study with exceedingly unrealistic expectations concerning generality limits of the anticipated findings, predictive specificity and confidence levels, feasible research and data-processing strategies, and modes of conceptual ordering. The inevitable heuristic effect is the enaction of imitation science rather than the generation of significant knowledge. Pursuit of imitation science, though a highly sophisticated skill, can only lead to the evasion and demeaning of subject matter and to a constriction of problematic interests. It is a deadly form of role-playing if one acknowledges that the psychological universe has something to do with persons. This kind of spurious knowledge can result in a corrupt human technology and spew forth upon man a stream of ever more degrading images of himself.

I am under no illusion that huge subcartels of the knowledge industry can be made to reorganize by rational suasion. I nevertheless propose that the essential noncohesiveness of the activities denoted by the term *psychology* be acknowledged by replacing it with some such locution as *the psychological studies.* Students should no longer be tricked by a terminological rhetoric into the belief that they are studying a single discipline or any set of specialties rendered coherent by any actual or potential principle of coherence. The current departments of psychology should be called departments of psychological studies. The change of name should mark a corresponding change in pedagogical rationale. The psychological studies, if they are really to address the historically constituted objectives of psychological thought, must range over an immense and disorderly spectrum of human activity and experience. If significant knowledge is the desideratum, problems must be approached with humility, methods must be contextual and flexible, and anticipations of synoptic breakthroughs held in check. At the very least, students should not be encouraged to believe it their responsibility to put together the pieces of a jigsaw puzzle that their professors long ago gave up trying to solve—a puzzle which is insoluble in principle, and which has the strange property of becoming more hopeless with each attempt to assemble the fragments.

There are stronger proposals that might be made, but even my weak ones will not be heeded. William McDougall firmly believed that psychological study required such resources of maturity, sensitivity, and knowledge as to make it inappropriate at the undergraduate level. In 1942, Heinrich Klüver was already looking forward with enthusiasm to what he called "the impending dismemberment of psychology." The centrifugal trends already apparent to him have continued, but most of the many specialties and cliques that have emerged have not spun away into other disciplines. I myself tend to think that most of what is solid in the psychological studies could best be pursued in association with the scientific and humanistic areas to which they are germane. Biological psychology could only profit by incorporation within biology. Psycholinguistics should certainly be happening within linguistics.

But these questions of formal association are of minor importance. What is much more vital is that broad ranges of the psychological studies (e.g., the empirical analysis of art, psychological aspects of history and philosophy, empirical analysis of inquiry) are as relevant to the humanities as they are to the psychological studies. Many of these problems are almost completely bypassed by psychology as it currently exists, and are pursued—if at all—only in the humanities.

THE KUHNIAN PARADIGM AND THE NEW
OPTIMISM CONCERNING A UNIFIED PSYCHOLOGY

Before entering this topic, it may be well to note for the benefit of
psychologists addicted to the notion of paradigms that there are
currently in the literature two Kuhns offering two very different
analyses of the character of paradigms. Some would say that there
are more than two. Indeed, one of Kuhn's critics, Margaret
Masterman (1970), distinguished 21 senses in which the word
paradigm had been used in the 1962 (original) version of *The
Structure of Scientific Revolutions*. Subsequent to this and many
other criticisms of the original position by philosophers of science,
Kuhn has published several emendations of the position (e.g., 1970a;
1970b; 1970c; 1974). Of these, the one which now should probably
be regarded as official (until further notice) is contained in a
"Postscript" to the second edition of his book (1970c). The notion of
paradigm is now developed in a radically different way from the
original treatment. If Kuhn has not achieved ultimate clarity, he at
least has altered the treatment in such a way that many of the wilder
construals and expectations engendered in psychologists and social
scientists by his initial account would *now* be less likely to be drawn.
We will confront aspects of the new Kuhn later, but it is the old
Kuhn who has had the far-reaching—and, in my opinion,
unfortunate—impact on psychologists still in evidence.

The Kuhn of 1962

Despite the vaguenesses that Kuhn now acknowledges, there is much
evidence to suggest that the old Kuhn was being read as superficially
as was Bridgman in another day. Kuhn's book, *The Structure of
Scientific Revolutions*, fell into a cluster of efforts directed toward
reassessment of the dominating positivistic views of science of this
century—a movement which, by the early '60s, when Kuhn
published, had already become so widespread and advanced as itself
to justify the adjective *revolutionary*. In my Rice Symposium paper
of 1963 (Koch, 1964), I was already able to identify that new look at
the nature of knowledge and cite an extensive bibliography. The
force of this rescrutiny relative to *scientific* knowledge was to

challenge both the sense and the utility of so-called rational reconstructions of the nature of science, and to move toward a view of the scientific enterprise more fully cognizant of the empirical particularities of inquiry. The working scientist, the historian of science, and (at least in principle) the psychological and sociological observer of science were seen to have perspectives which invited fundamental readjustment of images of science that had been arrived at through purely philosophic or logical means.

Among the important convergences already developing within this movement were the following: the scientific process was being seen as at all stages underdetermined by rule; theory was being seen as relatively independent from any strict induction base on the one side or confirmation domain on the other, while its genesis, elaboration, productiveness, reception, and fate were seen to be far more dependent on inherent aesthetic and other value-engendering properties than formerly. Perhaps the most profound member of this group was Michael Polanyi (1958), who powerfully challenged the modern tendency to *identify* the knowable and the sayable. He makes, in effect, the concept of *skill* central in his argument and analyzes in extensive detail the senses in which "knowing" must be regarded a skilled performance of a type reducible to no algorithm, resistant in principle to full specification, and governable only in loose and underdetermined ways (if at all) by "rules." For Polanyi, language use is always dependent on conjoint extra-articulate or "tacit" processes, and thus full formalization or explication of any cognitive achievement represents an impossible ideal.

Kuhn's work was a useful addition—in some ways subtle, in other ways overly pat, and in still others vague—to this incipient tradition of thought. Its special force lies in his disposition to take the history of science as criterial with respect to many of the issues concerning inquiry formerly thought to lie within the special province of the philosopher or epistemologist of science. His unifying notion of the paradigm and his bipolar typology of normal versus revolutionary science are gross but suggestive tools in this endeavor. The special quality of his contribution is his ardent and knowledgeable use of particulate examples from the history of science in such a way as to wear down the contours of traditional hyperrationalistic models of the scientific enterprise. His central notion of paradigms is thinly specified and flexibly used, to some extent deliberately so. The following is as close to an explicit definition of paradigm as he gets during the course of an entire book:

[A paradigm is an] achievement...sufficiently unprecedented to attract an enduring group of adherents away from competing modes of scientific activity. Simultaneously, it [is] sufficiently open-ended to leave all sorts of problems for the redefined group of practitioners to resolve.

Achievements that share these two characteristics I shall henceforth refer to as 'paradigms,' a term that relates closely to 'normal science.' By choosing it, I mean to suggest that some accepted examples of actual scientific practice—examples which include law, theory, application, and instrumentation together—provide models from which spring particular coherent traditions of scientific research. These are the traditions which the historian describes under such rubrics as 'Ptolemaic astronomy' (or 'Copernican'), 'Aristotelian dynamics' (or 'Newtonian'), 'corpuscular optics' (or 'wave optics'), and so on. The study of paradigms, including many that are far more specialized than those named illustratively above, is what mainly prepares the student for membership in the particular scientific community with which he will later practice. Because he there joins men who learned the bases of their field from the same concrete models, his subsequent practice will seldom evoke overt disagreement over fundamentals. Men whose research is based on shared paradigms are committed to the same rules and standards for scientific practice. That commitment and the apparent consensus it produces are prerequisites for normal science, i.e., for the genesis and continuation of a particular research tradition. [Kuhn, 1962, pp. 10–11]

Over and above this relatively explicit (though, as one can see, open-ended) definition, the meaning of the term continuously but asystematically burgeons by its application in particular contexts throughout Kuhn's book. Any *full* definition *in usu* would reveal the concept to be a vague one with an exceedingly open horizon. A paradigm is always localized in an *achievement* of some complexity but it may vary markedly in relation to scope or centering (e.g., it may center primarily on a theory, a law, an instrumental method, a pregnant system of classification or measurement, etc.). In most applications, it is clear, though, that at the core of a paradigm is a substantive idea about nature (usually conceived by Kuhn, on a perceptual-cognitive model, as a mode of seeing, a Gestalt, "a conceptual network through which scientists view the world") which is somehow highly revealing, which permits a more precise solution of older problems discriminated within an area and opens up new ones, and which commands wide assent. Though the paradigm must have broad generality relative to the area of science for which it holds, the area itself may be quite narrow.

It cannot be emphasized too strongly that Kuhn's notion of "paradigm" is not any and every construal of the standard natural language word *paradigm* ("pattern, exemplar, example," in the OED sense) but a rather special concept which seeks to desembed from the history of science a kind of theory of its special dynamic and genius. It takes Kuhn the entirety of his densely packed (if short) book (1962) to *suggest* his sense of "paradigm." *The Kuhnian paradigm is minimally a substantive cognitive achievement of sufficient differentiation and power to permit within an area corresponding to its range of application a period of "normal science." And the mark of such a period is that the entire scientific community is enabled to address a range of significant and determinate "puzzles" which are suggested by (and the solution of which facilitated by) the terms of the paradigm.*

The outlines of Kuhn's notions of "normal science" as a paradigm-dominated interval marked by "puzzle-solving," and of "revolutionary science" as an interval during which anomalies encountered by an old paradigm trigger controversial efforts toward the creation and acceptance of a new paradigm, are well known. It cannot be my intention here to review Kuhn's work, but it is necessary to hold certain other features of his position in mind. Thus, for instance, competing paradigms bearing on the same or overlapping domains are held to be "incommensurable" in ways analogous to the differential perceptual organizations induced by a fluctuating figure. Paradigm shift is seen to be a matter neither of strict verification nor falsification (on any of the formal criteria suggested by logicians of science) but, rather, a matter of gradual perception by the scientific community that the new paradigm is not only capable of removing the anomalies that invited its creation but is in other ways a more efficient and richer problem-solving instrument. Though the new paradigm is typically able to handle most of the problems dealt with by its predecessor (and often with greater precision and adequacy), it *may* be unequipped to handle certain of the problems (both solved and unsolved) within the range of the old paradigm. Because of this feature and incommensurability in other respects, a science cannot be said to progress in any *linear* way.

From all of these considerations, it follows that adoption of a new paradigm is mediated not by strict *proof* but, rather, by *persuasion*. Though Kuhn does not exempt the operation of adventitious and extrarational factors from this process of persuasion, he does recognize that the process is mainly grounded on rational considerations such as success at solving old problems and at generating and solving new ones. And he acknowledges the role of factors which correlate with such problem-solving criteria, such as the aesthetic appeal of the new paradigm. Indeed, his analysis of the conditions of paradigm shift lead him to the conclusion that *any* new paradigm that wins universal adoption in a scientific community is *necessarily* a more efficient problem-solving instrument than the one it supplants.

Finally, it should be noted that Kuhn, in his eagerness to redirect analytical attention toward the particularities of scientific inquiry rather than the generalizations and models which epistemologists have abstracted out of inquiry, makes a self-conscious point of sidestepping the notion of truth in its relation to science until almost the very end of his book. Two-and-a-half pages before his concluding line, he pridefully reports: "It is now time to notice that until the last very few pages the term 'truth' had entered this essay only in a quotation from Francis Bacon" (1962, p. 169). At this point, he embarks on a rather clumsy and irresolute coda in defense of the thesis that "we may . . . have to relinquish the notion . . . that changes of paradigm carry scientists and those who learn from them closer and closer to the truth" (p. 169). In this very same context, though, he reasserts his belief in the inevitability of progress (in the sense previously defined) in science, and acknowledges that the "developmental process described in this essay [is] . . . a process whose successive stages are characterized by an increasingly detailed and refined understanding of nature" (p. 169). Nevertheless, he rejects the view that science "draws constantly nearer to some goal set by nature in advance" (p. 170). He prefers to phrase science as an "evolution from" rather than an "evolution toward."

Unobjectionable as these points may be, they will be seen to represent a surprisingly partial and inept consideration of the intricate problem-cluster associated with the analysis of scientific truth (or of related notions such as probability). Instead of joining these issues in any differentiated way, he addresses a monolithic conception of truth (truth with a capital T) of a sort that could not, at this phase in the history of culture, be taken seriously by anyone save a participant in a fraternity seminar. Despite this, we find Kuhn saying, in the last paragraph of his book, the following:

> Anyone who has followed the argument this far will nevertheless feel the need to ask why the evolutionary process should work. What must nature, including man, be like in order that science be possible at all? Why should scientific communities be able to reach a firm consensus unattainable in other fields? Why should consensus endure across one paradigm change after another? And why should paradigm change invariably produce an instrument more perfect in any sense than those known before? From one point of view those questions, excepting the first, have already been answered. But from another they are as open as they were when this essay began. It is not only the scientific community that must be special. The world of which that community is a part must also possess quite special characteristics, and we are no closer than we were at the start to knowing what these must be. [1962, p. 172]

It should be utterly clear, then, that the 1962 Kuhn is by no means a conventionalist, a consensualist, or immune from ontological commitments. Indeed, these words and many others in the body of the essay show that his analysis invites and requires a theory of truth, and that though it is consonant with a *range* of answers, it limits that range.

I first read *The Structure of Scientific Revolutions* just a few months after it was published, at a time when I was feverishly working on a range of problems closely related to the ones it addressed. There was an apparent commonality in the drift of Kuhn's and my thinking, but I was nevertheless strangely depressed. Kuhn is not an opaque writer but his mode of exposition—the apparent black-or-whiteness of his concepts despite the gray penumbras which emerge only on close reading—is such that he can be easily misinterpreted. I predicted that his impact upon psychology could be appallingly counterproductive, and I fear that I have been confirmed. Let me indicate a few of the misuses of Kuhn that I then foresaw.

1. Because of the natural language connotations of the word *paradigm* that any reader is likely to bring with him, and because of the accretive method of definition that Kuhn employs in developing

the concept, it seemed to me that psychologists would be likely to perceive a Kuhnian paradigm as much more easily achievable than, say, an articulated theory. After all, Kuhn nowhere reconstructs in their full complexity any of the paradigms he discusses. Indeed, the force of his position is that paradigms resist full specification in principle; they are largely embedded in exceedingly intricate practices or, as Polanyi might say, tacit skills, within scientific communities. Yet so variably and fragmentarily are they addressed by Kuhn (for one illustrative purpose or another) that it is possible to believe a paradigm to be almost anything bearing an ordering relation to inquiry: a conceptual frame, a dimensional system, a descriptive grammar, a set of tentatively identified "variables," an iconic model at one or another level of specification, a classificatory system.

It should be recalled that by the early '60s psychologists had lived through a 30-year process of attenuation of their systematic expectations: the hope for immediate hypothetico-deductive theories adequate to all psychology had given way to the pursuit of "miniature" theories still of hypothetico-deductive cast; the latter had given way to the search for iconic or mathematical "models" of one or another degree of generality (and best characterized, relative to the performance of the modelers, as hypothetico-deductive formulations having more highly visible nomological holes than those put forward as of yore and asserted at lower levels of confidence). But here was Kuhn *apparently* saying that even physics is merely a matter of paradigms and that a paradigm can be almost anything. Thus was ushered in the strange phase of psychological history in which we now live: the thirst for generality can be easily slaked; psychology can become unitary, and inexorably progress throughout all future time via universal acceptance of a vocabulary, an "image of man," a method for the experimental analysis of behavior which can implement the lawful relations among three endlessly pregnant concepts or by the convenient and eminently rational adoption of a "general system theory."

2. The heady prospect of easy integration opened up by this misreading of Kuhn's primary concept of paradigm can be (and has been) shored up by many secondary misreadings. The conventionalism and nominalism once fostered by versions of logical positivism can now return in truly virulent form on the authority of a misread Kuhn. If persuasion, not proof, is the condition of paradigm change, why can't "persuasion" be read as "propaganda"

or "attitude change"? *Psychologists* know a thing or two about such matters! If cognitive advance is inevitable under conditions of normal science, and normal science happens when a paradigm is universalized within a scientific community, and, moreover, if the condition of that happy state of affairs is merely "consensus," then why can't psychologists get together and merely agree on a paradigm: any old paradigm? And, finally, if science has nothing to do with truth, then it matters little which paradigm we agree on; it is the agreement that is important, not the content of the paradigm.

In presenting these misinterpretations in short compass I have been forced toward the verge of caricature. But many paradigms pushed by the paradigm-pushing psychologists of the past decade are proof of such misreadings of Kuhn. In this abuse of his authority, Kuhn himself is not blameless. But he does not quite deserve his psychological following.

The "New" Kuhn

Coming now to the *new* Kuhn—as evinced in the second edition of his book (1970c) and in two contributions (1970a, 1970b) to a symposium volume on his views—it should immediately be noted that he takes pains to scotch the central misinterpretation that I have tried to lay bare in the preceding analysis. Apparently, Kuhn had become nervous about the rapid proliferation of paradigm proposals—each containing a built-in promise of "normal" or progressive scientific status—which had become evident in fields like psychology and the social sciences. Thus we find him saying in "Reflections on My Critics" (1970b):

> In any case, there are many fields—I shall call them pro-to-sciences—in which practice does generate testable conclusions but which nonetheless resemble philosophy and the arts rather than the established sciences in their developmental patterns. I think, for example, of fields like chemistry and electricity before the mid-eighteenth century . . . or of many of the social sciences today. In these fields, too . . . incessant criticism and continual striving for a fresh start are primary forces, and need to be. No more than in philosophy and the arts, however, do they result in clear-cut progress.
> I conclude, in short, that the proto-sciences, like the arts

and philosophy, lack some element which, in the mature sciences, permits the more obvious forms of progress. *It is not, however, anything that a methodological prescription can provide. . . .* I claim no therapy to assist the transformation of a proto-science to a science, nor do I suppose that anything of the sort is to be had. *If . . . some social scientists take from me the view that they can improve the status of their field by first legislating agreement on fundamentals and then turning to puzzle solving, they are badly misconstruing my point.* [1970b, pp. 244–245; italics added]

I hasten to note that later in the same paragraph Kuhn does say a few words which could seriously fuzz the above message in the minds of autistic proto-scientific readers:

A sentence I once used when discussing the special efficacy of mathematical theories applies equally here: 'As in individual development, so in the scientific group, maturity comes most surely to those who know how to wait.' Fortunately, though no prescription will force it, the transition to maturity does come to many fields, and it is well worth waiting and struggling to attain. [1970b, p. 245]

Lest this addendum precipitate another wild orgy of paradigm promoting, I should add that the extended context of Kuhn's discussion at this place makes it quite clear that Kuhn is making no promises but, rather, is trying to establish, for the edification of his critics, that his analysis applies only "after" the occurrence of "progress" (for the achievement of which state his theory offers no formula) "become[s] an obvious characteristic of a field." And I would presume it equally clear that even if Kuhn were meaning to reassure psychologists or some other proto-scientific group, his *intent* could have little to do with the outcome of any strategy of "waiting" or even "struggling."

Kuhn addresses the same issue (does any old paradigm bring tranquillity and progress?) in the "Postscript" to the second edition of *The Structure of Scientific Revolutions*. We here find him renouncing his 1962 distinction between the "pre-paradigm" and "post-paradigm" periods in the development of a scientific field, and saying:

The nature of that transition to maturity deserves fuller discussion than it has received in this book [meaning the original 1962 text], particularly from those concerned with the development of the contemporary social sciences. To that end it may help to point out that the transition need not (I now think should not) be associated with the first acquisition of a paradigm. The members of all scientific communities, including the schools of the "pre-paradigm" period, share the sorts of elements which I have collectively labelled "a paradigm." What changes with the transition to maturity is not the presence of a paradigm but rather its nature. *Only after the change is normal puzzle-solving research possible. Many of the attributes of a developed science which I have above associated with the acquisition of a paradigm I would therefore now discuss as consequences of the acquisition of the sort of paradigm that identifies challenging puzzles, supplies clues to their solution, and guarantees that the truly clever practitioner will succeed.* [Kuhn, 1970c, pp. 178–179; bracketed insert and italics added]

These clarifications, important though they be, represent negligible elements in the overall pattern of changes in Kuhn's current position. It is impossible to convey the entire pattern in brief compass but it is well that psychologists be apprised that the changes are far-reaching. And certain of them have a bearing on the themes of this paper. In the eight years between the two editions of Kuhn's book, philosophers and others had subjected the position to vigorous criticism. For instance: some saw the distinction between normal and revolutionary science as too stark and schematic, and some saw it as no distinction at all; some saw the notion of "puzzle-solving" as a thin and inadequate registration of what competent scientists do in periods of theoretical stability; Kuhn was criticized for "psychologism" and for oversociologizing the conception of science; there was strong criticism on many fronts concerning inadequacies of his analysis of theory choice or appraisal and of conceptual change in general (he was often accused of "irrationalism" and "subjectivity" in relation to these matters); there were many objections to Kuhn's views concerning the "incommensurability" of competing "paradigms" or theories and thus to his assessment of communicative barriers separating paradigm groups during scientific crises; overarching all these challenges and others was a barrage of complaints about the ambiguity of his presentation, especially in relation to the central notion of paradigms. The current Kuhn position is in part an accommodation to challenges of this order, in part a rejoinder to them, and, one can assume, in part a self-initiated effort to refine and develop the earlier thinking.

The notion of "paradigm" is now *dramatically* different: its sprawling reference field has been pulled back to the much more limited (though, as we shall see, still rangy) denotation of what Kuhn chooses to call "exemplars." To bring this about necessitated a complex maneuver involving the realignment of certain old ideas and the introduction of new conceptual elements. In brief, Kuhn now feels that it is circular to define a scientific community via the sharing of a paradigm. If he rewrote his book, "it would therefore open with a discussion of the community structure of science" and communities would be identified "without prior recourse to paradigms." Though the sociological methods for isolating such groups are not all "in hand," a community consists "of the practitioners of a scientific specialty. To an extent unparalleled in most other fields, they have undergone similar educations and professional initiations; in the process they have absorbed the same technical literature and drawn many of the same lessons from it" (1970c, p. 177). Again, "the members of a scientific community see themselves and are seen by others as the men uniquely responsible for the pursuit of a set of shared goals, including the training of their successors. Within such groups communication is relatively full and professional judgment relatively unanimous" (p. 177). Communities exist "at numerous levels," ranging from "the community of all natural scientists" and, at descending "levels," whole sciences and their various subfields. One arrives at something like an ultimate level with communities "of perhaps one hundred members, occasionally significantly fewer," having shared problematic interests of a delimited sort (Kuhn takes "the phage group prior to its public acclaim" as an example), and identifiable via "formal and informal communication networks" and citation patterns. Kuhn notes also that usually "individual scientists . . . will belong to several such groups." And he concludes: "communities of this sort are the units that this book has presented as the producers and validators of scientific knowledge. Paradigms are something shared by the members of such groups" (pp. 177–178).

But *what* are paradigms? The answer is intricate! One *first* isolates communities as just described. If one should then ask what "do its members share that accounts for the relative fullness of their professional communication and the relative unanimity of their professional judgments," Kuhn would answer (and does), "to that question my original text licenses the answer, a paradigm or set of paradigms" (p. 182). He *now* feels the term "inappropriate" for so general a use. Though scientists might suggest "they share a theory or set of theories," Kuhn feels that " 'theory' connotes a structure far more limited . . . than the one required here." Instead he suggests *disciplinary matrix* as the "common possession" of the community. And the matrix comprehends "all or most of the objects of group commitment that my original text makes paradigms, parts of paradigms, or paradigmatic." But *now* they are "no longer to be discussed as though they were all of a piece" (p. 182).

The disciplinary matrix is then said to comprise four sorts of component. Rapidly now:

1. *Symbolic generalizations.* These are the "formal" components of the disciplinary matrix, and Kuhn uses the logical form of a universal generalization as illustrative prototype.

2. *Beliefs in particular models.* These might include substantive theoretical models or heuristic ones. *They* supply "preferred or permissible analogies and metaphors." Kuhn points out that he would formerly have called such components "metaphysical paradigms" or "the metaphysical parts of paradigms."

3. *Values.* These are "more widely shared among different communities than either symbolic generalizations or models" (p. 184). Values have a peculiar importance, for Kuhn makes it clear that he will now lodge his account of the very sensitive issues of "crisis" identification and theory choice in the application of the group values by its members. What he says in this connection is worthy of quotation, for we are here dealing with the basis of Kuhn's theory of rational decision in science:

> Probably the most deeply held values concern predictions: they should be accurate; quantitative predictions are preferable to qualitative ones; whatever the margin of permissible error, it should be consistently satisfied in a given field; and so on. There are also, however, values to be used in judging whole theories: *they must, first and foremost, permit puzzle-formulation and solution;* where possible they should be simple, self-consistent, and plausible, compatible, that is, with other theories currently deployed. [P. 185; italics added]

4. *Exemplars.* This final "element" in the disciplinary matrix brings us to what now remains of the notion of paradigm! "For it

the term 'paradigm' would be entirely appropriate" (p. 186). Indeed, which of the two terms Kuhn proposes to use from this point on is not quite clear; in the "Postscript," his preference in the matter oscillates, though paradigm is ultimately given the edge. And again we must quote:

> By it [exemplars] I mean, initially, the concrete problem-solutions that students encounter from the start of their scientific education, whether in laboratories, on examinations, or at the ends of chapters in science texts. To these shared examples should, however, be added at least some of the technical problem-solutions found in the periodical literature that scientists encounter during their post-educational research careers and that also show them by example how their job is to be done. More than other sorts of components of the disciplinary matrix, differences between sets of exemplars provide the community fine-structure of science. All physicists, for example, begin by learning the same exemplars: problems such as the inclined plane, the conical pendulum, and Keplerian orbits; instruments such as the vernier, the calorimeter, and the Wheatstone bridge. As their training develops, however, the symbolic generalizations they share are increasingly illustrated by different exemplars. Though both solid-state and field-theoretic physicists share the Schrödinger equation, only its more elementary applications are common to both groups. [P. 187]

With the exemplar, I happily complete the formal outline of the new Kuhn.[2] I have conveyed the above amount of boresome textual

---

2. This may be a suitable point at which to express my unease over giving Kuhn's position as much attention as I have in this paper. Though I have held back from criticism of Kuhn in my effort to trace the impact of widespread misinterpretations of his position by psychologists and social scientists, it should not thereby be taken that I am a votary of the position in either of its forms (old or new).

To me, the only unarguable element in the Kuhn picture is the recognition of the *role* of "tacit knowledge" and of how this must qualify rule-saturated versions of the scientific enterprise. But, as I point out elsewhere, the *originator* of that notion, Michael Polanyi (1958), has charted its ramifications in a mode incomparably more revealing, profound, compelling, incisive, and eloquent than has Kuhn. Polanyi stands to Kuhn as does Beethoven to Bacharach!

My many demurs to Kuhn cannot be compressed into a footnote. He has, I think, a limited appreciation of the role of differential observer sensitivities in science; a limited understanding of the complexity of language use and thus detail in the wistful hope of finally exorcizing the current asssumption that the paradigm is a one-word solution to all problems of psychology. But more importantly for the present purpose, the contour of Kuhn's new view will provide a useful foil and comparison basis for issues subsequently to be discussed in this paper.

It should be noted, of course, that we have merely broached the outline of Kuhn's new position. In the "Postscript" (and other recent writing) Kuhn proceeds to develop and exploit this apparatus in the context of analyses of issues raised by his critics and, no doubt, by his own sense of the requirements for strengthening the theory. The crux of his interest in these discussions is in explicating the detailed properties of exemplars which—because of the "tacit," non-rule-subsumable perceptual information they convey—he regards as the

---

of the presence of differentially competent language appliers and sub-communities of such within the same scientific language community; a naive and outmoded sense of perceptual process, which he phrases in a lay version of a nineteenth-century language of "stimuli," "sensations," "awareness of sensations," "interpretations" upon sensations, etc. (cf. 1970c, pp. 191–198). He has a deathly fear of ontologizing and is evasive at many junctures concerning definite realist implications of his analyses. Some of these matters I address *in extenso*, though implicatively, in the text; here I wish to make my attitudes explicit, even though I cannot defend them in a footnote.

Finally, Kuhn's three primary metaphors (other than paradigm or exemplar) —normal science, revolutionary science, and puzzle-solving—are all, I think, seriously overschematic and misleading. I agree with Toulmin (1970; 1972) that the distinction between normal and revolutionary science is much too sharp— and perhaps totally unilluminating. The crux of the difficulty may be seen in the metaphor of puzzle-solving—a crass and indeed insulting characterization of what in fact goes on in the highly creative inquiry often required for the significant extension, refinement, or corroboration of frameworks. Once we give up a rule-regulated conception of science (one which assumes that scientific method is automatically self-corrective, etc.), we must perceive—and acknowledge—the intensely creative character of genuine scientific advance, however local and small by comparison with the creation of a new and powerful theory. To take the matter of experiment per se, it is important to acknowledge that a well conducted experiment is a work of art, often of a very high order. No theory uniquely determines the terms of an experiment in the sense that a puzzle, even a difficult one, uniquely determines the terms of solution. Quite aside from the essentially connoisseurlike assessment determining the choice of a significant "consequence" for test, there is the largely open-ended creative task of arriving at a relevant, sensitively discriminating, and rigorous design, and the still more artistic task of shaping, out of the world-flux, a material context which "truly" realizes the theoretical variables selected for study and their appropriate ensemble of initial conditions. And so on and on!

source of whatever uniquely differentiates his position from "rational-reconstructionist" views of science. And, in debates over theory choice, he makes a stab at spelling out in a more differentiated way what he means by "incommensurability."

DEFINITION AND PSYCHOLOGICAL LANGUAGE COMMUNITIES

In his recent concern with exploring the characteristics of exemplars—and further explicating what may be involved in the "incommensurability" of theories or conceptual frameworks—Kuhn has tended to presuppose something very much like a *perceptual* theory of definition. For instance, he tries to show that the ability to apply a scientific generalization (law or "law-schema") significantly depends on "learning from problems to see situations as like each other," and therefore: "That sort of learning is not acquired by exclusively verbal means. Rather it comes as one is given words together with concrete examples of how they function in use; nature and words are learned together. To borrow once more Michael Polanyi's useful phrase, what results from this process is 'tacit knowledge' which is learned by doing science rather than by acquiring rules for doing it" (1970c, pp. 190–191).

In a number of passages (1970c, pp. 187–206; 1970b, pp. 266–277) he develops such ideas suggestively and, at one point, issues the following invitation: "[P]hilosophers of science will need to follow other contemporary philosophers in examining, to a previously unprecedented depth, the manner in which language fits the world, asking how terms attach to nature, how those attachments are learned, and how they are transmitted from one generation to another by the members of a language community" (1970b, p. 235). Neither Kuhn, however, nor philosophers of science (nor indeed any other kinds of philosophers) are likely to do this in a way especially illuminating for the *detailed* problems and prospects of psychology. Almost 20 years ago, I began to raise precisely the complex of questions mentioned in Kuhn's invitation (in an unpublished, but frequently presented, 1956 paper entitled "Towards an Indigenous Methodology"), and though I have tapped these ideas briefly in a few publications over the years (Koch, 1961, 1964, 1973), I have never published on this work *in extenso*. The explicit notion of specialized "language communities" (whether scientific or natural) was a central part of my analysis, and my approach may be seen as providing a particulate rationale for the conditions and consequences of communicative mismatches and incommensurabilities. But, more importantly, the analysis was trained upon specific communicative problems of *psychology* and provides, I think, an "in principle" basis for the rejection of any belief that psychology can become a homogeneous or coherent discipline. A policy of "waiting" for this "proto-science" to become "mature" will be met by no other outcome than frustration, and as for "struggling," that policy may well contaminate the stream of our thinking for the next thousand years. At this point, therefore, it is well that we leave Kuhn and the philosophers and embark upon an analysis of definition which, because it sees all linguistic "meaning" as having a perceptual basis, might well be called a "psychological" theory of meaning. It is perhaps fitting that a clarification of the status of psychology should be based on a psychological mode of analysis.

A few words about the circumstances which triggered my analysis. Commencing in the early '30s, and quite possibly until this very day, psychology has been dominated by a conception of empirical definition (and meaning) which demands that all concepts be unambiguously reducible to a primitive observation language on the application conditions of which all members of a science (conceived in some large sense as, e.g., "psychology," rather than specific subfields) could readily agree. Philosophers of science had put forward various proposals—most exceedingly vague—concerning the constitutive properties of such an observation language; indeed no especially detailed treatment was ever attempted. The lore concerning "operational definition," as portrayed within psychology, was one species of such analyses of definition. Many years ago, I began to see the utterly misleading character of such reductive definitional schemata and commenced a rather simpleminded empirical analysis of the conditions of actual definitional practice, and thus communication, both in the natural languages and in science.

As an exercise in the pathology of knowledge (which has become my favorite field), a little of the relevant history may be amusing. When, in the early '30s, the Age of Theory—referred to earlier in this paper but characterized extensively in my "Epilogue" (1959a) to Study I of *Psychology: A Study of a Science*—began its search for a set of decision procedures, it could have turned to the large number of criteria for the cognitive significance of statements which logical positivism and neopragmatism had already made available. Instead, partly by historical accident, psychology focused on the early formulations of Bridgman's "operational criterion" of meaning which, by phrasing the meaning of a scientific concept in terms of corresponding *experimental* and (ultimately) observational operations, offered attractive imagery to a science at once self-conscious of its newly won experimental status and eager to get experiment into tighter relation with theory. If psychologists had done their reading in slightly different order, they might have focused on the proposals of Schlick, or of early mid-Carnap, or of the neopragmatist C. I. Lewis, or, in fact, on a variety of other criteria having an intent similar to Bridgman's. In such a case, the clang of the psychological literature regarding definition would today be different.

The lore concerning operational definition soon began to fuse with the lore concerning logical positivism. In 1936–37, Carnap published, in "Testability and Meaning," what was quickly to become the most influential analysis of meaningfulness in the history of logical positivism. Although no presentation in the psychological literature has done justice to the technical detail of Carnap's treatment, his notions of the "disposition concept," the "reduction sentence," and "chains" thereof (and, most especially, the "observable predicates" of the "thing language" as the reduction basis for the language of science) soon entered the jargon of psychological commerce. Since 1937, there has been the lushest proliferation of philosophical discussions of meaning in history. Not only have Carnap and other positivists liberalized their meaning criteria out of all recognition, but analytic philosophers and others have uncovered new vistas of subtlety. Yet, to this very day, little of this has penetrated into psychology.

Those who *have* followed recent discussions of meaning and language in the extrapsychological literature will perhaps respond to my analysis more with a feeling of *déjà vu* than of shock. In the decades since beginning to think on these lines, I have been encouraged—though sometimes grudgingly so—to note that developments in philosophic meaning theory (over a broad gamut of "positions") and, to some extent, in linguistics have moved in a similar direction. Having published so little on my views, I can at least assert an option open to all procrastinators by claiming prescience.

There are strong affinities between aspects of my position and emphases of some analytic philosophers. In its concern with the role of metaphor in natural language and in science, the present position falls into a growing cluster of analyses exemplified by work of Max Black (1954, 1962) and Mary Hesse (1954, 1966). Some of the thinking in the ambience of Chomsky's approach to linguistics—for example, Lenneberg's (1967) speculations on "reference"—is also consonant with the present views. Polanyi's (1958) analysis of word use as essentially a *skill* dependent on tacit processes which cannot, in principle, be rendered fully effable, has also a family resemblance to the present analysis. Yet all these similarities are rather more evident in certain termini of the analyses than in the routes over which they proceed. I think my route an especially instructive one for *psychology*, in that at no point does it stray far from psychological terrain.

Sketch of a Psychological Theory of Definition

To make the bearing of my analysis on the concrete problems of psychological theorists evident at the very outset, it is well that I commence with one of the principal findings of the project that eventuated in *Psychology: A Study of a Science*, Volumes 1 to 6 (Koch, 1959b, 1962b, 1963). One of my main objectives in directing that study was to invite from a large number of psychological theorists a comparison between the particularities of their conceptual and systematic practice and what the more or less "official" epistemology of the profession in those days—which was essentially a logical positivist epistemology—said they *ought* to be doing. One of the largest and most conspicuous convergences among the 36 systematists who participated in the first half of the study (Study I, Vols. 1–3) was the difficulty they reported or evinced in bringing their definitional practice into line with "operational" and cognate doctrine. This trend and others are extensively discussed in the "Epilogue" to Study I (Koch, 1959a).

The "difficulty" (really a vast and varied panoply of individual cognitive pains) might be summarized in this way: Men—whether they were learning theorists talking about intervening variables like "reaction potential," or "need-cathexis," or even specific applications of S and R; or personality theorists talking about "themas," "ego structure," "the self," or "presses"; or social psychologists talking about "constraint," "conformity," "systems of strain," "object-instrumental attitudes," or "group cohesion"—all seem to have the impression that in some sense they are talking *meaningfully*. Yet when Tolman (1959, pp. 147–148) confesses that he cannot pin down the meaning of his intervening variables to the particularities of defining experiments or empirical "pointer readings" (his final conclusion was that for him they seem to be a useful "psychologic"); or when Guthrie (1959, pp. 164–166) insists that applications of S and R depend on perceptual sensitivities of observers and must in the case of S presuppose inferences about "meaning" to the organism; or when personality and social theorists indicate in the most varied ways that their concepts are at an astronomic distance from the defining base as conventionally conceived—all are saying that the official conception of the observation base, together with the stipulated form of its linkage to scientific concepts, will not permit them to talk meaningfully. *These men feel that, at least in restricted language communities, they can communicate. Yet the official epistemology will not permit them to believe that they can communicate meaningfully.*

Such an impasse should certainly license the daring to raise questions about the *conditions* of human communication. There are, of course, many answers to such questions in a variety of disciplines—but they are in most cases precommitted answers which be absolute empiricists and raise questions about what goes on when presuppose a special theory of language. At least initially, we should words—single lexical units—are used meaningfully in ordinary discourse. How are words in the natural languages defined? What governs their meaning-transformations and accretions over time? What makes some words clear and others fuzzy, some abstract and some less so? What is involved in penetrating, revealing, or creative uses of language as against flat, obfuscating, or rote uses? What in particular are at least some of the preconditions for persons understanding each other? And so on. It cannot be overemphasized that *at the beginning* such questions should be asked in common-sense terms—that is, in the idiom of natural language itself. Even within this idiom, the questions are large questions to which we can expect only small, slow answers.[3]

3. The questions I raise here and address in the sequel will seem to the reader either stale or obvious: Stale in the sense that linguists (especially psycho-

It will perhaps be objected that one does not consult the slovenly natural languages for canons of linguistic procedure in *science*. Granted! To whatever extent possible, scientific language (by definition) is to be so forged as to give more terse, precise, salient, and unambiguous descriptions of events, and generalizations upon them, than natural language. And the cognitive and predictive aims of science will entail the dropping out of certain features and functions for which natural language has been specialized, and the appearance of other features special to the ends of science.

It should, however, be emphasized that the psychological processes which mediate communication cannot be *absolutely* different as between scientific and natural languages; whatever processes are constitutive of meaning must be the same, even if scientific languages are so constructed as to restrict their functioning in certain ways. And a second consideration must have truly decisive importance for psychology, namely: *the subject matter of psychology is such that every significant meaning that can be conveyed in a natural language must, in principle, constitute potential data for our discipline.* I do not mean merely the words (or signs) that convey these meanings, but the signs as meaningful, or even the meanings as psychological processes per se. Any theory of definition for the *psychological language* which identifies the observation base—and the rules for "constructing" terms upon it—in a way that does not meet this requirement is arbitrarily limiting the

linguists) and philosophers must surely have "dispatched" these primitive questions concerning the semantic behavior and nature of single lexical units. Have we not seen an explosion of interest in language, especially in the flurry of sophisticated activity sparked by the Chomskian era? Obvious in the sense that the circumstances of word use are surely among the most intimate and ubiquitous phenomena available to any literate person. It is my contention, however, that the detailed "behavior" of lexical units is so stupendously complex that students of language have tended, both wittingly and unwittingly, to make strong simplifying assumptions concerning "rudimentary" semantic matters as a precondition to pursuit of their often fulsome theoretical objectives. As for the matter of "obviousness," may I make the obvious point that incessant saturation in a field of phenomena is one of the strongest conceivable barriers to precise specification or analysis of those phenomena. (The elusiveness of complex psychological, and especially linguistic, events to their owners is perhaps *too* obvious a point to add!) My chief communicative difficulty in the following analyses will stem from the *familiarity* to the reader of the processes I try to explicate. I can only invite the reader to look over my shoulder and focus with me on what he and I already know; my expository task would be a breeze if the topic were utterly strange to him—and perhaps to me!

subject matter of our discipline to a corresponding degree. A psychology unafraid to face its proper universe of questions must, then, have a language sufficiently rich and free to render in some way, or admit, any meaningful discrimination that can be made in a natural language.

As a move of minimal size toward such an analysis of definition, let us consider the case of a single English word. I choose the word *dignity* partly because it has a "psychological" reference in the natural language, partly because most persons would agree that this word can be used meaningfully, and partly because it is at a level of epistemic complexity roughly comparable to such concepts of the personality theorist as trait-names.[4]

Let us first ask where we would get if we tried to "reduce" this concept to an observation base similar to that stipulated by operational or physical-thing language criteria. Does *dignity* mean a posture with a certain stiffness coefficient—or, more generously, "erect bearing"? Does it mean a "quiet voice"? Can it—still more generously—be applied to a professor such that when he has an obstreperous student in class, he freezes him with a cold glance? Or must it be a professor such that he never has obstreperous students? Note that the "reductive" or "operational symptoms" even in their initial formulation are already fairly far from an "ultimate" physical-thing observation base. We would need at least an angular criterion for "erect bearing," and a decibel cutoff point for "quiet voice." "Cold glance" and "obstreperous student" would give us still more trouble, unless we were so afflicted with physicalism as to believe that a thermometer and some such device as a windsock would solve the problem.

But these latter objections are nothing to the point. Everyone would rapidly agree that no single symptom of the type mentioned would be a reliable "index" of dignity (application rule for the term) and, moreover, that no *conjunction* or *disjunction* of such symptoms, whatever the size of the class, could give an adequate definition. People would immediately say: "Erect bearing, yes, but not stiff or haughty." "Quiet voice, probably, but not always—there are times

4. There is also a special joy in acknowledging that it is a word which B. F. Skinner finds dangerously obfuscatory. It is amusing to note that 20 years ago I fixed upon *dignity* as a prototype word for exhibiting the complexity and the remarkable richness of the "meanings" of common lexical units in a natural language. Unfortunately, I could not then know how naughty and deluded I was in so doing.

when the essence of dignity is passionate, even explosive utterance." As a matter of fact, rather subtle qualifications would now emerge. Some persons would begin to require that the erect, nonstiff, nonhaughty bearing would perhaps also be characterized by the quality of "grace." And that the quality of "grace" extend to demeanor, movement, vocalization, how one holds an object, nods, etc., etc. Matters have by now become quite complex, and "symptoms" of dignity are beginning to get specified within a subtle relational network, the terms of which are themselves epistemically no less complex than the term under definition. Soon, however, it would be perceived that no given number (whether conjunctive or disjunctive) of even such qualified and complex *symptoms* of dignity would give a really "good" (i.e., sensitively discriminating) definition.

Take, for instance, the matter of "quiet voice"—even in the qualified form which admits circumstances under which "nonquiet" voice must be interpreted as "evidence" of dignity. One easily goes further than an enumeration, so to say, of "test condition–test result" *exceptions*. One quickly perceives that "quiet voice" is *a vagrant and un-nicely bounded quality of dignity, even as a symptomatic quality having some kind of probability relationship to the trait*. One perhaps says: "Not quiet but, rather, a tone adjusted to a balanced, fitting, yet self-contained assessment of a situation." Matters are now indeed complicated. Language is directing the perception of the observer to an exceedingly subtle relational aspect of a situation, and doing this via other concepts, each of which discriminates comparably subtle relational qualities to the one being defined. Yet airy as is this relational lattice, there are unquestionably many observers who can and do agree in diagnoses of such *symptoms* of dignity as tone of voice in this way.

But note that in trying to get into proper focus and shading *symptomatic* manifestations of dignity like voice tone, we seem unwittingly to have drawn on a *quite general specification* of dignity as a relational quality of human events—*a quality the presence or absence of which would determine the symptomatic relevance of a given instance of voice quality or, indeed, a wide range of other possible symptoms*. Indeed, we begin to see that there is in some sense a "theory" of dignity in the natural language, one of extraordinary subtlety and wide involvements—and, no doubt, differentially accessible to different users and definers of language. Even at *this* point, we discover with some shock that we have barely begun to isolate the "defining properties" of dignity. Is dignity merely (one could almost say, "really") a tendency toward balanced, fitting, self-contained actions in situations? Much further and finer specification may be required for ultimate nicety. Thus dignity may involve fittingness or appropriateness, but certainly not in the sense of observing, or conforming to, *propriety*. Rather, what seems involved is a flexible appropriateness "above" propriety, in which individuality is consistently defined, yet subtly, rather than conspicuously or flambuoyantly. Matters are now horribly involved, but I am certain that individuals who apply this word sensitively (relative to the use-context at issue) presuppose a criterion no less complex and, moreover, one which, whatever the words of *their* definition—indeed, even if they can give no definition—discriminates a subtle relational quality much like the one I have sought to specify in the above formulations.

And sensitive appliers of the term would recognize many other things. For instance, there are many personal styles of dignity. And there are many partially overlapping concepts to which dignity is related in the lattice of language—for example, nobility, stateliness, gravity, worth, excellence, honorableness—which could also provide certain of the terms for an "isolation" of relevant relational characters. It should be noted, too, that a full reconstruction from usage would probably result in the discrimination of *several* relational characters—each as (so to say) specialized as the "definition" just attempted. And *these*, in actual usage, would form disjuncts so that the term might properly be used in different contexts to denote quite different relational characters.[5]

5. The above discussion of dignity has concentrated on a differentially attributive sense of the word, in which it attaches to properties of individuals in relation to their actions or to particular individual actions. Intricate as this individually attributive usage turns out to be, it may be less so than certain other meaning-disjuncts of the term.

For instance, there is a generic usage—as in such phrases as "the dignity of man"—which is so complex in reference as to prompt many tough-minded persons (or, what often comes to the same thing, simple-minded ones) to shrug off the usage as vacuous. What seems involved in this usage is a generalized ontological sense of dignity—a conception of man as the most complex and highly organized being in the known universe and, by virtue of that status, an entity of inherent *worth*. Moreover, since the constitutive condition of this worth or value is that of membership in a genus as such, all men share equally in this worth (i.e., "worth" in the sense here at issue): each individual, as human, is entitled to the respect of his fellows and to particular varieties of considera-

Other matters should be noted. It is probable that dignity—in the sense under analysis—had reference originally to a "molar" attribute of persons. But, of course, it has been extended to properties of personal actions, qualities of thought and sentiment, and characteristics of aesthetic objects (as, say, when we talk about the dignity of form, color, line, or of literary style, or, indeed, the dignity of the structures, representational or no, conveyed by a work

tion appropriate to his or her humanity. Such modalities of consideration are often localized as "rights" or "entitlements" within the ethical and legal categories of the West.

A finer analysis of this generic sense of dignity would disclose many subtheories clustering in an asystematic way about the notion and attempting more particulate specification of ontological properties deemed unique to man on grounds of which he merits one or another entitlement, form of consideration, or respect. Thus man may be seen as a being uniquely conscious of his mortality, uniquely baffled by the circumstances of his origin and *raison d'être*, uniquely terrified by the awesome extent and impenetrability of the universe, uniquely apprised of the certainty of his suffering. Hence the special kind of courage and gallantry implicit in his occupancy of the human condition, his admirable resourcefulness in wresting order from chaos, his justifiable pride in his accomplishments, however small, erratic, and infrequent. Again, there is the fact of man's "double agency": his unique reflexivity or self-consciousness; his capacity therefore for self-criticism, for assessing and revising the course and consequences of his own activities. Again, man is the only being of which tragic actions or a tragic trajectory of action may be predicated and, of course, the only natural being capable of apprehending the precise and subtle configuration of circumstances definitive of tragedy. Indeed, one possible definition of man is that he is the only *tragic being* in nature.

This limited précis of the generic theory of human dignity, of course, only scratches the surface—and hardly begins to suggest the complexity of this particular meaning-disjunct. There is indeed a vast and differentiated "literature of dignity" in the history of the humanities and in many other contexts within the history of natural and technical language. It is far from being an empty literature and, wherever meaningful, it has nothing—absolutely *nothing*—to do with the "conspicuousness [or inconspicuousness] of the causes of behavior," as one of the litterateurs of "dignity" (Skinner, 1971) would have it.

As an addendum to demonstrate further the richness of the concept of dignity, it may be noted that there is *another*, nonequalitarian sense of dignity-as-worth. The sense of "worth" here at issue registers a differential quality of achievement, of personhood. I hold back from more sustained analysis of this disjunct except to note that it is related in complex ways to both of the senses already analyzed: possession or manifestation of dignity in the sense analyzed in the text may be one of the conditions constitutive of worth in this sense; worth in the present "differential" sense seems in part metaphorically related to worth in the generic sense, and is probably the historically prior "base" for the metaphor.

of art). And we can talk meaningfully about the dignity of animals, and of aspects of animals such as personality, behavior, form, and physiognomy. It is vital to recognize that many of the so-called extensions of dignity are not *merely arbitrary* but are based, to one or another degree, on a type of *metaphor—that is, the perception in new settings of relational characters which in fact overlap with (or are similar to) the characters already tagged by an "old" term.* Such a mechanism of metaphor is fundamental to the growth—including meaning extensions, differentiations, and refinements—of natural languages.

Of course, not all extensions of word meanings are based on metaphor. Many *are* arbitrary. Some, though based on metaphor, discriminate only vaguely overlapping, or less differentiated, relational qualities of events and may thus be fairly said to constitute debased usages of the word. In truly *creative* uses of language, the meaning of a word may be sharpened and enriched by attaching it to contexts of events in which the original relational characters tagged by the term are more purely or richly exhibited, *or* by explicating a term (through "definition" or use) in a new linguistic context in such a way as to achieve the same result. Actually, the "correct" (at any level) *momentary* use of language by an individual presupposes a process very like metaphor, because the perceptual conditions for application of a term are never identical on different occasions. The limiting case of metaphor, *psychologically* speaking, would be some kind of quite habitual transposition process from one dated instance of the conditions of application to another. More discriminating uses of metaphor, as when language is used in fresh or creative ways, may involve effortful perceptual search in new contexts for subtle relational qualities which overlap with more standard meanings of words.

An important corollary of the present analysis must now be noted. Not everyone can use the words of a natural language with equal nicety or precision. Not even all literate people. There are various levels of "goodness" with which language can be applied, defined, understood. The precision and subtlety of what an individual does with a word depends on the precision, delicacy, differentiation, etc. of the perceptual discrimination which *for him* has been tagged by that word. It depends also on other factors such as his ability to make further fine discriminations of certain types—thus, his capacity for inventive metaphor. Can everyone discriminate the referent of *dignity* with equal nicety? Of course not. Some will use the word incorrectly in all circumstances. Others will use it with varying degrees of imprecision by relatively rote application to "symptomatic" contexts, at one or another of the levels that we illustrated. Subtle forms of dignity will elude them, and they will often see or assert "dignity" where it is not.

Other factors equal, the persons capable of using the term most precisely and creatively are those who, in fact, are most dignified. The truly dignified person is constantly discovering or creating new forms of dignity. He is continually solving "dignity problems." He is an artist of dignity. The relational properties controlling his behavior may not be accessible to *him* for verbalization. But if they are to be accessible for linguistic coding by *anyone*, the coder must be "sensitized" to comparable or overlapping relational properties.

It follows that *there is no single language community* for the understanding, use, or explication of *dignity*. There is a multiplicity of language communities, each at different levels of the relevant sensitivity. To insist on fixing the definition of a term by reduction, via a standard linkage relation, to some tightly restricted observation base—say, the first or second level of symptomatic statements of our illustration—would be to sacrifice the possibility of precise or subtle communication. Far worse, *it would eliminate much meaning and knowledge from the universe*. Moreover, any observation base built at the level of the "symptomatic statements" of our examples would *still* be very remote from a physical-thing or operational language, as usually conceived.

The minimum admissible size of a language community for the natural language "theory" of dignity should properly be a group of two—preferably the two people who are at once the most experientially sensitive and linguistically adept, in respect of the relevant phenomena, in the world. The only stipulation would be that these men be able to communicate reliably about their special forte.[6] All other language communities regarding dignity, by

---

6. A language community of so restricted a size as is here at issue raises, with especial insistence, the possibility of use-consistencies by imposture, by overlapping hallucinations, or even by mutual self-deception. These specters may, of course, arise in language communities of *any* size, but it is a rational presumption that the larger the community the less likely the chances of such "false reliabilities." Even so, there is a worldwide "flying saucer" community of impressive magnitude. At bottom, then, the criterion of communicative reliability that we all presuppose demands that the agreers be *competent* in a way relevant to the use-domain in question. My position in effect spells out

definition, say less when they use the word and know less about the distribution of dignity in the universe. The only way in which the richest and most differentiated conceptions of (or knowledge about) dignity could be spread more widely would be if the language community "at the summit" could devise means for communicating their knowledge to language communities at lower levels. *This, in general, could be done only by perceptual training techniques which might in the most determinate possible way guide members of less sensitive communities toward discrimination of the relevant relational characters.* In this way, the language community at the summit could be enlarged, but it is absurd to expect that it could be universalized.

Most of the suggestions I would make about a theory of definition adequate to the demands of psychology are implicit in the discussion of *dignity*. That discussion was a slovenly mode for their introduction, but perhaps quicker and more intelligible than abstract statement. I will now try to extract the bearing of that strange analysis on some problems of the theory of definition.

Definition in Natural Language. The lexical elements of a language have two aspects, a conventional one and a nonconventional. The nonconventional aspect is in fact the discriminations—perceivable "things," properties, and relations, whether simple or complex, crass or delicate, obvious or subtle—to which signs are *allocated*. It is only the allocation that is conventional—that is, the choice of sign and stipulation that it "stand for" such-and-such a thing, property, or relation. The "corresponding" discriminable qualities are in the strictest sense the "meanings" conveyed by words. In any dated instance of the meaningful use of a word, the meaning, as a

certain literal consequences of taking *competence* (relevant discriminative sensitivity) seriously as a requirement of language communities. When we suspect "summit" or small language communities, we characteristically (a) ask for the credentials of the members (if the two agreers are Einstein and von Neumann, rather than two sophomore science students, we are more likely to accredit the esoteric communication in question); (b) hopefully await evidence of successful efforts of the summit community to enlarge its membership. Neither of these "procedures" contains any *final* guarantee against nonsense. That hazard we must all accept: to promulgate the myth that nonsense can be averted *in principle* is only to augment its supply! May I suggest that presumably mature and tough-minded men in several fields of scholarship have long spent too much worry over the hazard of nonsense; they should have more confidence in their capacity to hold their own against an occasional crackpot.

psychological process, is the *perception* of some one or more of the correlated things, properties, or relations. In a loose sense it can be said that words index and, within limits, stabilize *discriminal experiences*. Natural language preserves and records the history of human sensibility (discriminal experiences) at all levels—from simple, practical discriminations among properties and relations of objects, to the most subtle and "rarefied" and creative oscillations of sensibility in which high-order relational qualities may be perceived as common to a wide range of diverse perceptual contexts.

The natural language is thus heterogeneous, and an uneven communicative tool. It may contain both "good" and "poor" concepts (in special senses of these terms). A "good" concept may involve the fixing by a conventional sign of some discriminal experience (say, of a "complex" relational quality) which is in fact common to many event matrices and that does reveal and demarcate something highly significant about the world. A "poor" concept may involve the assignment of a name to a "fuzzy" discriminal experience, one which in fact isolates trivial, vagrant, or "local" aspects of events—one which does not have the generality imputed to it, is contingent, accidental, illusory, etc. And one might distinguish also "good" and "poor" *definitions* (independent of the goodness of the concept). A glance at dictionaries of different quality will show this to be the case. Some definitions are in terms of relatively rote and symptomatic "examples"; others bound the salient properties or relations in a delicate and well-specified way.

Examination of definitional practice in natural language will show that terms are defined in three basic modes:

1. By an equivalence rule connecting the term with a *synonym*. This presupposes, of course, that the application conditions (i.e., discriminable properties or relations) for the defining term are already known by the person to whom the definition is addressed (call him the addressee). There are, incidentally, far fewer true synonyms in the natural languages than usually supposed; meaning shadings are such that partial synonymy is more often the case. A "sensitive" discussion of this point is to be found in Samuel Johnson's preface to his *Dictionary of the English Language* (1755).

2. By *metaphor*, in the sense already described. Dictionary definition by metaphor seeks to direct or guide perception to the relevant properties or relations (or system thereof) by eliciting a similar or overlapping discrimination via a configuration of words for each of which the addressee is presumed already to have the

appropriate discriminations. Note that such definition in terms of the familiar does not necessarily reduce the concept to a more crass set of discriminations. The defining terms may designate equally subtle or even more subtle properties and/or relations than the term under definition.

3. By *example*—the dictionary case being the "textual quotations" exhibiting the use of the term in various contexts. This is a mixed case in that some of the textual citations are definitions via metaphor, others specify the term *symptomatically*. It is interesting to note that the great lexicographers (like Johnson, and the authors of the *Oxford English Dictionary*) seek their examples from the works of the "best" authors and, I believe, rather favor metaphorical to symptomatic citations.

Note, finally, that no dictionary of natural language reduces its words to a standard definition base—no matter how generously defined. Dictionaries which try so far as possible to give definitions in terms of crasser discriminations, presumed to be "familiar" to the largest number of addressees, are likely to give poor definitions. Systems like "basic English," which do propose something like "reduction" to a definition base, vastly reduce the range and nicety of meanings (not *merely* "emotive," but *cognitive*) that the language can convey. Shakespeare in basic English is not basic Shakespeare—it is impoverished and garbled Shakespeare!

Dictionary practice is instructive, but locked within language. It is of more general significance to ask about definition as it takes place in the learning or teaching of language or in the adjudication of questions of usage for which dictionaries are inadequate. Here again, the three forms of definition already mentioned are used. In our discussion of *dignity*, the main types were illustrated. But there is a great difference under these circumstances. One may direct perception *outside* of language by pointing, or what has been called "ostensive definition." But if pointing be interpreted as a sightline along a finger, we will reduce language to a barren thing. Finger pointing is not a sufficiently specific identifying operation for the discrimination of embedded, subtle, or abstract relations or qualities. But the present formulation would imply that pointing, interpreted far more broadly as *perceptual guidance*, is at the basis of all definition. In this special sense, all modes of definition are ostensive.

The problem of definition is a special form of the problem of perceptual training. And any definition is at bottom an attempt to guide the addressee toward making a relevant perceptual discrimination. Thus, all methods and devices which can conceivably lead to perceptual learning are relevant to the problems of definition. In the ideal case, we reproduce the conditions which cause the relevant properties or relations to appear in the purest possible form, and the "pointing operation" is the stipulation that the experience which occurs under these conditions is a dated instance of the "meaning" of the term. Psychologists too well know that it is not easy to approximate the ideal case, even for crass discriminations. It should now be emphasized that purely verbal definition is a process of *surrogate pointing*. The defining expression can only *guide* the addressee toward contexts that "embody" the relevant property or relation (actually, a similar one), which may then be noted or not noted. *Verbal definition* per se is a most limited and imperfect medium for conveying empirical meanings.

Implications for the Observation Base of Psychology. The implications of the preceding analyses for the observation base (so-called) are obvious. *The observation base must be a far more extensive domain than is ordinarily thought. This is almost unquestionably the case for all science, but conspicuously so for psychology. Indeed, the entire conception of an observation base linked by orderly relations to concepts of higher order is called into question.* It becomes literally meaningless to talk about an observation base to or from which definitions of higher-order terms are "reduced" or "constructed." No logical combinatorial process will give us the intricately determined and highly specific "relational qualities" designated by *dignity*, from symptomatic indices even as complex as "quiet voice," no matter how varied and numerous. Nor can such relational qualities be *reduced* (in, e.g., the sense of Carnap's "reduction sentence" analysis) to symptomatic indices of this order—no matter how many reduction sentences are written. *Dignity* is no technical psychological concept, but the orders of abstraction and relational specificity which psychology must discriminate in *its* concepts are at least as great and, with respect to important or interesting problems, much greater. Moreover, whatever determinate meanings are conveyed by concepts like *dignity* represent aspects of the universe which psychology cannot fairly rule out, and which it must be willing to accept and use as *data*.

The universe of what used to be called "direct observables" must be vastly expanded. Many "theoretical" and presumably higher-order terms must be seen to discriminate definite, if perceptually highly embedded, properties and relations of events and things—to designate them in a direct way. There is a sense in which certain designations of a word like *dignity* are just as directly observable as, say, the referent of the term *red.* From this point of view, there is no distinction, in principle, between terms of the sort thought to be observation terms and those of a sort thought to be theory terms. One may talk very roughly in terms of differential degrees of abstractness, generality, subtlety, embeddedness, etc. of the properties and relations denoted by terms, but such distinctions do not fall into any systematic arrangement of "levels." If this position implies something akin to a realism, then be it said that it is one based on empirical analysis of human communication, not on metaphysical grounds.

Careful survey of definitional *practice* (as distinguished from claimed rationale) in psychology will show that it corresponds in detail to the analysis here put forward. This is so, whether at ethereal levels of personality theory or stonier levels of learning formulations. People do not construct or reduce their definitions upon an observation base, because no general meaning could be communicated in this way. When they do provide so-called operational definitions for higher-order terms, they are either not being consistent with what they really have in mind or they are providing *examples* which may, by *metaphor* or *symptom*, convey application conditions in some degree. The difficulties raised regarding definition by contributors to *Psychology: A Study of a Science* are ample evidence of this.

Examination of definitional practice shows that the definer typically attempts to direct perception toward certain discriminations by a combination of *metaphor* and a *range of examples.*[7] Communication will take place only if the addressee is equipped with the stock of discriminations called upon by the defining terms of the definition. This is a necessary, not a sufficient condition for communication. The definer must mobilize the presumptive stock of discriminations with sufficient skill to maximize the chance that perception of the intended property or relation will occur. But no amount of such skill can *guarantee* that the addressee—even if he *does* have the relevant discriminations—will perceive the intended referent. The addressee is

7. Max Black (1954, pp. 24–45) talks of "range definitions" in an analysis which is consonant, in some ways, with the present account.

beset by contingencies of much the same order as those posed by "hidden-figure" puzzles. There is an element of luck in all successful communication.

This general analysis, it should be emphasized, unites the problem of concept formation with that of concept definition and application. The theorist who has achieved an "insight" with respect to important "causal" determinants of experience or behavior has made a perception of some constant relational attribute of mental functioning, behavior, etc., which in general has not been made. The problem of definition then becomes the problem of teaching persons how to perceive that constant relational attribute. If the attribute is a highly embedded, subtle, or delicately contoured one, such a process of teaching may be very difficult indeed. The discriminations coded in extant language, technical or natural, may be entirely inadequate. The means for reproducing instances which embody the relation may not be within the control of the definer. The event matrices constitutive of instances of the relation may be provided by the world too infrequently or fleetingly for differentiated "pointing." When such event matrices do occur, the significant relation may be masked by many others more conspicuous.

In other words, we get very much the picture which the "Epilogue" to Study I (Koch, 1959a) gave of the definitional difficulties experienced with special insistence by the *personality* and *social* theorists in *Psychology: A Study of a Science.* Needless to say, the fact that such difficulties may be experienced constitutes no presumption that the relation discriminated by the theorist represents some profound regularity in the universe. *But, by the same token, the occurrence of such communicative difficulties justifies no presumption that the concept is empty or nonsensical.* It must be anticipated also that in cases of exceedingly tenuous and subtle concepts, the language community sufficiently sensitive to make or approximate the necessary discrimination may be extremely small.[8] Indeed, at this point it is well that the question of psychological language communities engage our attention.

Psychological Language Communities. On any theory of meaning, the criterion of "intersubjectivity" is, of course, basic. But the critical

---

8. Karl Zener (1958) conducts an illuminating exploration of issues concerning the qualifications of language communities relative to specific ranges of psychological phenomena in his essay "The Significance of Experience of the Individual for the Science of Psychology."

question is: intersubjectivity among whom? Who are the people who must be able to agree on the application conditions for a term or statement? It is not necessarily the business of philosophical analysis to pursue this question in detail. But the "imagery" of the more fashionable philosophical formulations has tended to suggest extraordinarily weak credentials for membership in the language community. To be sure, there is often some clause restricting membership to "competent investigators" or "adequately trained" persons. Interpretation of statements at any level "above" the ultimate definition base is usually seen as dependent upon such "training." But the usual illustrations of statements *within the definition base* are so chosen as to give to many the impression that membership in the language community may be met by the capacity to perceive pointer-scale coincidences, to see red, and perhaps to read. Of course, this was never *intended* by the philosophical analysts. But certainly their theories of definition, as imported into psychology and modified by the prevailing intellectual atmosphere, tend to represent the language community as a most accessible club.

For instance, a published "glossary" of terms used in the "objective science of behavior" (Verplanck, 1957) says of "operational definitions," "They demand agreement, and they make it possible for anyone who is able to read to reconstruct the observations to which the terms apply" (p. iii). At another place, in characterization of the "data language" (definition or observation base, as we have been speaking), the relevance of "training" is acknowledged, but in this *way:* "words . . . in the data-language . . . must be defined so that anyone after a minimum of training can use them consistently" (p. iii). Now a *minimum of training* necessary for the consistent use of a word—particularly if that word denote a highly embedded property or relation of events—may necessitate *a very great deal of training* indeed. Yet, in the psychological literature regarding empirical definition, it is quite clear that the force of such expresssions is more like *"absolute* minimum of training" than the minimum of training necessary for disciminating "so-and-so."

It is strange that the very individuals who espouse or accept such a conception of the observation base often acknowledge, in other connections, that the application conditions for observation terms, and terms close to the observation base, can only be learned and "discriminated" with sensitivity by working face-to-face with individuals who are masters of certain experimental crafts. Thus there is a large group of individuals, much interested in delicate and dramatic "shapings" of animal behavior, who are ready, even eager, to admit that the true subtleties of the art can be assimilated only by prolonged laboratory contact with one of its acknowledged masters.[9] They are right! But they have failed to generalize upon this truly profound knowledge. Language is at best a feeble instrument even among members of a highly trained language community having quite limited problematic interests.

None of the currently institutionalized sciences form single, homogeneous language communities. Physicists in one empirical area do not necessarily fully "understand" physicists in another; pathologists do not necessarily understand electro-physiologists, and so on. And within each scientific area, even when cut rather finely, one may distinguish disorderly "hierarchies" of language communities: in the extreme case, there may be quite definite and unique observable properties and relations which only two men, perhaps working in the same laboratory, may be able to perceive, and denote by some linguistic expression. Moreover, it should be stressed that the stratification of language communities within a science may reflect variations in *sensitivity* of observers just as much as differential levels or foci of *training*. There was a time when Einstein was apprised of certain invariant properties of the universe, yet could communicate these "discriminations" to few men.[10] If it be objected that Einstein did not directly "observe" these properties (which on my view he in some sense did), then take the context, say, of medical diagnosis for ready illustrations of a similar principle.

Now a language community must obviously be specified on a *psychological* criterion—a complex one demanding a certain criterial overlap of learned *discriminations* and specialized *discriminative capacities* (sensitivities) among members. Say that this criterion

9. For instance, the very same author quoted above in the capacity of behavior-science lexicographer has pointed out in an illuminating analysis of the early phase of Skinner's "system," "Those who have observed work with animal behavior in different laboratories are often struck by the remarkable degree of control which the experimental technique of Skinner and his students enables them to exert over rats, pigeons, pigs and people. . . . While it may be argued that the group has avoided problems or situations yielding poorer control, it must be pointed out that many who have tried to duplicate the procedures cannot always do so until they have had an opportunity to observe them in action" (Verplanck, 1954).

10. Stephen Toulmin (1972) has pointed out that at an early phase of what became known as the theory of relativity, Einstein had considered naming the theory "invariant theory."

defines a "discrimination pool." I think there are strong grounds to believe that the discrimination pool demanded for adequate communication in *any* area of science is far richer, more differentiated, and subtle than ordinarily supposed. One may, for instance, think of a "pointer reading" as some ultimate verifying operation (or reductive symptom). But the pointer is hooked up, both materially and inferentially, to a complex system of events, and the physicist must be attuned to relationships of great subtlety in that system if he is to interpret the pointer reading in a truly significant way. If one thinks, say, in terms of a presumably "simple" reduction sentence, the "test-result" (pointer position) may be specified via a relatively crass discrimination; the "test-condition" part may involve a most elaborate system of events which are *assumed to realize* an elaborate lattice of theoretical relationships, and the job of the physicist is to "discriminate" whether this is so. *That* is not a crass discrimination.

Yet, be all this as it may, there is little question that the discrimination pools presupposed for communication in physical science as a whole may be fewer in number and, in each case, less differentiated and "rich" than the discrimination pools presupposed in biological science as a whole, while the discrimination pools required by biology are probably less varied and (often) less internally differentiated than those ideally required by psychology. The domain of physical science is not only such as to necessitate fewer language communities than do the domains of biology or psychology, but it may well be that physical science language communities are more stable and perhaps more readily enlarged.

There are many reasons for these differences. I shall consider only one. *In psychology, problems concerning any range of human endeavor or experience can be the object of study.* No definition of our science—however restrictive its heuristic effect may have been on problem selection—has ever called into question this awesome peculiarity of our subject matter. In recent decades we have sought security by addressing only small and rather unadventurous segments of our subject matter. But problems—psychological problems—of art and morality, of scientific creativity, of human sensibility in all manifestations, of language, problem-solution, and, of course, society, personality, etc., stand before us almost untouched. If psychology is to study the conditions of the phenomena in any of these areas, it must premise its research on discrimination pools each of which overlaps to some definite extent with the "first-order" discrimination pools operative within all of those widely ranged human areas. This is not to say that, for example, the student of the psychology of science must be a creative inquirer in the given science, the psychology of which he studies. (It would not hurt!) Nor is it reasonable to demand that all psychological students of art be artists. But it is grotesque to suppose that someone totally devoid of the special discriminations and sensitivities of the natural scientist, or the artist, could make contributions to the psychology of either field—just as grotesque as to expect, say, that an illiterate could contribute to the psychology of language.

All this is shamefully obvious, but the consequences—if the history of psychology be evidence—are not. In psychology we must have many language communities, many subgroups of individuals equipped with diverse stocks of discriminations and differently specialized sensitivities. *By definition,* we must have a greater number of language communities in psychology than in any other field of inquiry currently institutionalized. We must also expect more variability, both in sensitivity and in achieved discriminations, than within other scientific language communities. As Karl Zener pointed out, psychology has long lived with a conception of its observation base such that, if a sophomore student cannot perceive a phenomenon, it is not there. And if that phenomenon be the referent of a term, the term is meaningless. The present position, however, suggests—just as has already been illustrated in the discussion of *dignity*—that the minimal acceptable size of a language community for psychology must be a community of two persons. Any formulation of a "meaning criterion" demanding a wider consensus group for *admission* of a term as meaningful would eliminate much meaning either from our universe of approachable data or from that of the scientifically (or humanly) sayable. Worse than the *amount* of meaning lost would be its altitude—for any discipline (whether scientific or other) is such that at any given time its best ideas are likely to reside in only a few of its towering sensibilities.

Relations of the Present Analysis to Some Cognate Trends in Philosophy. The force of the present position can be further clarified by comparisons with certain recent trends in the philosophical treatment of language and meaning. I restrict discussion to brief comparisons with certain emphases of analytic philosophy and with the views of Michael Polanyi.

ANALYTIC PHILOSOPHY. It will already be evident that there is a distinct consonance between certain trends of *analytic philosophy* and the point of view I have sketched. I shall suggest a few of the differences.

Until recently, most analytic philosophers have tended to regard something like *standard* "use" as adjudicative with respect to philosophic, and sometimes other, issues. They have often been criticized, and I think fairly so, for regarding "use"—as established by some combination of the *Oxford English Dictionary* and the given philosopher's linguistic sensibility (in varying proportion)—as a final court of appeal. Related to this has been an equally widespread tendency to eschew extralinguistic "considerations" in philosophic discussion: to choose to stay within language if not in fact be held within its circle by the "lingua-centric predicament."

In contradistinction, the present view would urge that anything like "standard" use would often give us a far less differentiated, subtle, delicately contoured, or nice definition of a concept than might be required for the analytic or investigative purposes at hand. If we refer back to the analysis of *dignity*—and to our comments concerning the multiplicity of language communities, each at different levels of sensitivity and/or achieved fineness of discrimination with respect to the application conditions for a term—then clearly even the best extant dictionary definition could have a leveling or "normalizing" influence, if taken as criterial in preference, say, to the definition of a "summit," or near-summit, community. Even with respect to the "ordinary language" per se, processes of inventive metaphor that can be presumed frequently to take place in the functioning of the more highly sensitive members of the overall language group can be expected to result in individual usages of greater nicety and, in some sense, fuller cognitive content than the best *dictionary* definitions.

Our perceptually oriented view of meaning directs attention to the fact that language *change* (which can, of course, be either retrograde or toward sharpening and enrichment) is, in the more fortunate cases, mediated by discovery. Users of language are *appliers* of language, and when the perceptual disposition governing a word is enriched or refined by the noting of what we have called an overlapping relational property in a new (and perhaps less masked) world context, then *knowledge* has been extended. When definition is seen in a perceptual frame, one expects meanings ever to be refined in the crucibles of at least some sensibilities, and such "refinements"

533

The Psychological Studies

are but another name for new knowledge about the universe. Thus, to the very same extent that the concept of "standard use" exerts a normalizing pressure on definition, it tends to draw attention away from the fact that much definition, and certainly the species called "empirical," is as much definition "of" the world as it is of a term. Though definition be *within language*, our "perceptual" frame constantly reminds us that language is about something—however embedded, intricately contoured, or fluidly deployed that something may be.

Most of the above divergences from what I have taken to be the tendency of analytic philosophy are no doubt related to the initial difference of problematic incidence between the approach of that "movement" and my own. I am concerned with *empirical* analysis of the *conditions* of communication, as these bear on the problem of definition; analytic philosophers are concerned with explicating the meanings of "given" communications, and exploring the rule or "use" structures of natural languages, with a view toward the resolution of philosophic perplexities. My premises bespeak the naive faith in the facts that persons perceptually interact with an external world, that aspects of that world causally related to such interactions are specifiable as stimulating energies—inclusive of distributions, gradients, and higher-order derivatives thereof, à la Gibson (1959, 1966)—of the sort open to an empirical scientist. Philosophers, however, would bring about their own technological unemployment with cataclysmic immediacy if they *began* with such premises. If philosophy is the disease of which it is the cure, it is well that it proceed slowly.

MICHAEL POLANYI. This great man is rarely acknowledged by philosophers of science—even by those who have been moving in the direction of his thinking. When mentioned at all, the acknowledgment is often grudging. For instance, Kuhn, whose views in large areas can be seen as a pallid and crude semblance of Polanyi's, cites him only in connection with his (Kuhn's) borrowing of the "useful phrase," "tacit knowledge." For such reasons—and also because he is often little more than a name to psychologists—I commence with a brief and absurdly inadequate précis of his viewpoint.

This philosopher has powerfully challenged the modern tendency to *identify* the knowable and the sayable. He has developed the most sustained and powerful argument in the history of thought to the effect that "there are things that we know but cannot tell" (1962, p. 601). He has made, in effect, the concept of *skill* central in his argument, and has analyzed in extensive and fascinating detail the senses in which "knowing" must be regarded a skilled performance of a type reducible to no algorithm, resistant in principle to full specification, governable only in loose and underdetermined ways (if at all) by "rules," and warrantable ultimately by no verificatory method other than "personal" and responsible accreditation by the knower. Such, in brief, is Polanyi's conception of *tacit knowing* on which *explicit knowledge* is always, if in varying degree, founded.

The role and "structure" of tacit knowing, in its varying interplay with the explicit, forms one of the main strands of Polanyi's work, one which he pursues with remarkable energy over much of the face of inquiry. In course of this exploration, many stereotypes concerning the nature and methods of science fall by the wayside: for example, that the scientist is a neutral and "detached" observer and applier of rules; that there is a fixed and inviolable logic of verification or evidence which, either in principle or in fact, regulates the fate of scientific ideas; that the differential adequacy of theories in the same domain is a matter merely of convenience, economy, or a kind of "fruitfulness" not grounded in truth; that presumably crucial or decisive experimental disconfirmations of a theory (e.g., the Michaelson-Morley experiment) can, per se, *enforce* a creative theoretical change; that the Laplacean paradigm is a sensible ideal for human knowledge; that "formalization" can be complete; that mathematical and logical systems are based on arbitrary assumptions and are developed via a wholly mechanical process of manipulating rules. The preceding is but a random representation of a few of the topics examined with originality, and often depth, at various places in *Personal Knowledge* (1958) and in others of Polanyi's writings (1959, 1966).

Not a few of the stereotypes questioned by Polanyi have, of course, come under fairly general criticism during the past ten or fifteen years. But Polanyi—largely by exploiting the particularities of his long and distinguished experience in science—has generated the most comprehensive and telling critique of modern scientism thus far put forward. To this task, he has brought a generous range of competences over and above his purely scientific ones: his critique of scientism is therefore linked with the elaboration of a new, "post-critical" philosophial vision. The constructive and analytic ingredients in Polanyi's thinking are, within limits, separable; it is the latter (and, in my opinion, more important) component which primarily concerns us here.

Even from the above general account, it will immediately be detected that there are strong consonances between the present theory of definition and central emphases of Polanyi. Thus, for instance, the present approach, in its own way, has all along been underlining the *limits* of purely linguistic specification. And it has emphasized the dependence of communication on extralinguistic (perceptive) processes which, by their very nature, can never be rendered fully effable. Insofar as I have suggested that the sharpness and/or delicacy of the "meaning-contour" tagged by a term for an individual will depend on such matters as his ability at "dis-embedding"—and have emphasized, in addition, that precision, subtlety, and richness of language use will depend upon capacity for inventive metaphor—I, too, have been presuming the capacity to use even a single lexical unit meaningfully to be tantamount to a *skill*.

There are many coincidences of more specific character than the above, as between the two accounts. Thus, for instance, Polanyi's observations concerning the role of tradition, connoisseurship, and apprenticeship in scientific communication and training (1958, Chaps. 4, 6, 7) are paralleled—more prosaically—in my account by its emphasis on what might be called "differentiated laboratory ostension" (via "perceptual displays") as something like a criterial paradigm for effective empirical definition within scientific language communities. Polanyi sees effective definition and meaningful use of language generally as giving knowledge about the world—and so, of course, does the present account. Polanyi sees a scientific theory as in some sense definitive of reality (e.g., 1958, pp. 3–17); the present account, in suggesting that the terms of a theory may be seen as designating "directly" highly embedded features of the universe, suggests a basis for such a position.

The Perceptual Theory of Definition: Summary

The present formulation tries to make intelligible why many terms in the natural language and in science can have general, yet *specific*, meaning in terms of the perceptual conditions of their learning and the nature of language as a psychological process. It suggests that *verification* can often be much more direct than is ordinarily supposed. It implies that a term can "tag" and preserve perceptual discriminations often of great specificity, yet highly abstract and general in the sense of being invariant for a large range of events. It supposes (at least in the typical case of *verbal* definition) that such terms are defined via other linguistic counters which have been attached to discriminations already in the repertoire of the addressee, and that definition so mobilizes these as to direct perception to the *relevant* thing, property, or relation. It supposes, further, that the ideal and often criterial case of definition is a differentiated form of "ostension" which would seek to direct perception to the relevant referent via a perceptual display that might "exhibit" the referent in its most conspicuous, sharply contoured, and pure form.

The present position presupposes that the processes of communication, as they have gone on for thousands of years in the natural languages, will have built up intricate, layered, often vastly ramified systems of *meaning* (via word interrelationships). These, though they often will be found to specify external and internal events with precision, will often require extension and differentiation in accordance with new human knowledge. The position assumes that the task of science (and of scholarship) is to devise means for making those meanings more precise, systematic, and univocal, to whatever extent its varied ranges of subject matter may permit, and thereby to isolate and discover new meanings in the universe. It proposes that the only "criterion" of *meaningfulness* be an *empirical* determination of whether two or more human beings can communicate consistently with the given *term* or *language*. It warns that requiring any number greater than two as the *minimal* size of an admissible language community is to run the risk of losing much valuable meaning and knowledge. It acknowledges that the communicative objective in science is the *maximization* of a language community, but *not* via definitional schemas that would reduce meaningful discourse to babbling, and arrogate babbling to "technically" meaningful status. It assures the practicing psychologist that he needs no permission from *any source whatsoever* to be as imaginative, penetrating, and insightful as he is able, and as contextual in his methods as his specific problems may require. Finally, it leaves many problems untouched and all of them open.

SCIENCE, THE HUMANITIES, AND THE PSYCHOLOGICAL STUDIES

The preceding account of definition should give us a purchase on the relations between the sciences and the humanities, and this, in turn, will facilitate a better understanding of endemic characteristics of the psychological studies.

The Sciences and the Humanities

It is already fairly obvious that our analysis of "empirical" definition tends to destroy certain of the traditional bases for any sharp separation between the sciences and the humanities. The distinction often presupposes that scientific and humanistic uses of language must differ in principle. It is sometimes believed that, whereas one can expect—even demand—homogeneity of use and interpretation of terms (thus "universality" of agreement) in a *science*, one must expect the very opposite in a "humanity." It is sometimes argued that, whereas many conceptualizations in the humanities require a unique integrative type of "understanding" (a species of "wholistic grasping"), the scientist may coast along on simple discriminations of a limited number of elemental "data language" referents.

A certain kind of "tough-minded" psychologist will perhaps be disturbed that distinctions of the order above illustrated are blunted by the present analysis. Amusingly, psychology is one of the few fields in the community of scholarship in which it could still seem heretical to suggest that a germ-proof curtain cannot be erected between science and the humanities. The appalling threat upon intellectual hygiene thereby created has been weathered quite heroically by the physicists, mathematicians, biologists, historians of science, and philosophers (among others) who are participating in a massive reassessment of the positivistic picture of inquiry which has now been going on for over two decades. That the methods and ends of science are continuous with those of human inquiry in any of its forms—whether in practical contexts or so-called humanistic ones—is an *empirical* generalization from which few competent students of science would any longer dissent. It is perhaps worth reminding scientistic purists in psychology that a tough-minded pragmatist like John Dewey urged precisely such a generalization upon the world over many decades of his long career (e.g., Dewey, 1910, 1917, 1938), and that he came to this generalization largely on *psychological* grounds. Like much else in Dewey, this point long went unheeded. It is now widely heeded, or at least a similar one is acknowledged, but it is a "point" which calls for continuing (indeed, permanent) development, especially along psychological lines. In recent years, some development it has received, but very little via psychological modes of analysis, and very little of *that* by psychologists. My psychologically based sketch of definition can be seen as one small step in such a tradition of analysis as is invited by Dewey's emphasis on the commonalities among all forms of human inquiry.

Even psychologists, then, will have to accept it that scientists in their best moments do not merely manipulate symbols or apparatus: they perceive *meanings*, subtle relational unities, contrasts, transitions, and recurrences, in their experience. So do poets. And artists. And creative administrators. And the methods of artistic problem-solution, of poetic problem-solution, of "practical" problem-solution can be shown to parallel in large ways those of scientific problem-solution.

What, then, are the differences? They are in fact harder to specify than the similarities. There is no single dividing line, however delicate and wavery, between *the* sciences and *the* humanities, but only wavery and delicate differences between given sciences, given areas of practical activity, given humanities. Science differs from practical problem-solution in different ways than from, say, poetry. Indeed, science "in general" may be more like poetry than it is, say, like "business." But, then again, we must face the fact that some sciences, at some phases of development, are more like business.

A possible set of differences of some generality between much of science and much work in the humanities may flow from the widely recognized interest of science in *control* of phenomena (by no means its *only* interest). This leads to the perception of different types of relations (thus meanings) in the universe than the poet or artist is likely to isolate, and results ultimately in different *modes* of communication. The scientist becomes interested in the consensus of his language community in not quite the same way that the artist is interested in consensus. The scientist seeks to maximize his language community to *whatever extent possible*. That is a necessary condition to the maximization of prediction and control. The artist (unless he is second-rate or an opportunist), being interested in the maximization of *meaning* with no practical end in view, seeks only a consensus from those equipped to see, even if it be *only* himself. Science to be efficient must be continuous, cumulative. Art to be great must be discontinuous. But even these two familiar generalizations are half-truths which emphasize the waveryness of *any* boundary. For science to be *great*, it must be discontinuous. And there are *types* of continuity and even cumulation that can be discerned in art. But the differential "aims" of science and art to which we are here pointing will at least ensure differential incidences of discontinuity.

It is this *interest in maximizing* the language community which has led to the belief that science must have a simple, almost universally comprehensible, definition base. But, as we have seen, realistic consideration of practice shows that this is not the case. *The language community of a science cannot be broadened by reducing delicate and subtle discriminations to "crasser" ones, but only by using crasser discriminations as means for directing perception toward the relevant "finer" relations and properties.* This last corollary of a perceptual theory of definition contains, I think, the key to an understanding of the empirical—and very possibly the formal—methods of science.

The characteristic methods of science—partialing out of variables, experimentation, etc.—are "devices" which can enable perception of delicate relational aspects of events (causal unities, etc.) by causing them to occur repeatedly in the purest (least embedded) possible event context. The utility of pointer readings, simple indices, etc., where possible, is essentially that these dependably mobilize crasser discriminations in such a way as to favor "perception" of the relevant, "finer" property or relation. The special extensions of language associated with science provide differentiated signs for tagging and "preserving" the new "meanings" that are discovered. Technical scientific languages develop in the first instance as differentiations of the natural language.

Theoretical terms are tags for perceptual cuts upon, or "disembeddings" from, the world-flux. There is no separate realm of "observation terms" to which they must be linked for the mediation of either application or communication. When a term is called "theoretical," there is a presumption that it enters into a network of relations with other terms having a salient bearing on some world domain. An experiment—whatever else it may be—is a device for directing the perceptual-cognitive apparatus toward the detection of the relation between two or more such concepts. *An experiment is one of many nonverbal forms of definition.*

Not having delusions of grandeur, I do not pretend to be in a position to give any final interpretation of the role of what were recently held to be the artificial languages of science, namely, logic and mathematics. So far as I can see, my position concerning "meaning" is compatible with any of the philosophical views—rationalistic *or* empiristic—which grant logic and mathematics onto-logical content. In my idiom, the formal disciplines are based in the first instance on perceptual disembeddings of structural and relational characters of the world. But so are empirical-scientific concepts, especially of the sort called "theoretical." In ontologistic views of logic or mathematics, it is usual to see the formal concepts as discriminating markedly more general characters of the world than do the concepts of empirical science. In congruent fashion, the present analysis would base logical and mathematical concepts on perceptual disembeddings of *extremely general* structural and relational invariants of experience. The disem-beddings may be thought of as second- or n-order segregations of invariants of our own "processings" of world-inputs, or as operating "directly" upon those inputs, or—what is more likely—as (in differing contexts) *either* of the preceding. Obviously, such a statement goes no further than suggesting the possibility of the translation of a range of extant alternate views into a perceptual vocabulary. But I think that differentiated thinking and research in a perception-oriented frame about logic, mathematics, and, indeed, "natural" grammar could be fruitful.

Despite the above, some psychologists will no doubt *still* be appalled by the implication that psychology in certain of its reaches (and, indeed, as regards some of its core areas like perception, cognition, motivation, learning, social psychology, psychopathology, personology, aesthetics, the analysis of creativity) must turn out to involve modes of inquiry rather more like those of the humanities than the sciences. Perhaps they will feel that humanistic knowledge is "soft" knowledge, based on soft intellectual disciplines, while scientific knowledge and research discipline is hard. But musicology is hard (in several senses), as are classics, comparative philology, biblical archeology, and responsible forms of literary criticism. And philosophy—even logic and the philosophy of science—is typically assigned to the humanities.

Return to the question of "cumulativeness"—an issue which still requires more perspicacious analysis than it has yet received in the history of thought, and one which I certainly do not hope to dispatch in passing. But it should be emphasized that no epistemologist or historian of science any longer believes that scientific knowledge moves in a linear and continuous progression, and it is dubious that any competent student of science in this century ever did. It did not wait upon Thomas Kuhn to stress the discontinuities and divigations in the temporal trajectory of science; such of his masters as Alexander Koyré, George Sarton, and, of course, Conant were sharply apprised of such matters. Cumulation means literally a "heaping up," and the heaping up of knowledge is as characteristic of the so-called humanities as it is of the sciences. It may be thought that in science this heaping up has a special force: that of a progressive refinement, differentiation, and specificity of knowledge (at least in the long run), and indeed, this may be one of the differentia between science in the strict sense and the humanities. But it must be carefully asked whether this happy property of scientific knowledge is conferred upon it by the magic of scientific methods per se or by characteristics of the world domains addressed by the established sciences which render these methods (like the "analytic pattern" of physics as discerned earlier) applicable and fertile.

Only in the pages of *Popular Mechanics* (if there) do we any longer see vestiges of a "cosmic-eye" view of science as a *durch-und-durch* impersonal and objective enterprise. Scientific inquiry and its outcome are now seen to be sensibility-dependent and perspectival in much the sense heretofore seen as definitive of humanistic modes of knowing. There are subtle differences, as we have seen, in the degree of transmissability of the knowledge achievable in the sciences as against the humanities, the sharpness and scope of the formulations that can be attained, and, perhaps, the multiplicity of significant perspectives from which the characteristic phenomena of each may be approached at any given time. But there *is* cumulation in the humanities, and it is easy to explicate the sense in which this is so.

Take, for example, the polymorphous, tenuous, ramified, and "open-horizon" concept of love, human love. The history of the humanities presents us with not a few savorers and explicators of this rather intricate context of human phenomenology, each approaching that context with his or her own special angle of vision, sensibility, and range of sensitivity. Plato has told us something about love; so have Shakespeare, Joyce, and Laurence Durrell, to pick out three other inquirers almost at random. No one would consider their perspectives as nondifferential and nonpreclusive in important respects. These four explorers have left behind four sets of spectacles through which differential modalities, contours, textures, and involvements of love may be viewed. The opportunity each of us now has to view love through each of these sets of spectacles does not mean that—by some magic of conceptual optics—they can be combined into one set of integrating spectacles, but it certainly does mean that the availability of the *four*, as against any given one, creates a potential for enriching our sense, our understanding of love. *This* is a form of cumulation, and a precious one.

Certain other circumstances should be noted. Shakespeare's theory of love does not refine the Platonic theory. Nor does Joyce refine or in some sense improve upon these two illustrious predecessors, and, most assuredly, Durrell does not represent some kind of advance upon the findings of his three predecessors. It is just that these four explorers perceive their bounded, yet inexhaustible, domain *differently*. Does it therefore follow that each is uninfluenced by his predecessors or that the perspectives and "findings" of each are genetically independent of those of his predecessors? I do not think so. The sensibility of each explorer has been enriched by the discriminations registered in the artifacts bearing the imprint of his predecessors; he can thus be enabled to arrive at his angle of search, of vision, at least in part with the help of the discriminations achieved by his intellectual forebears. That, too, is cumulation—and in a more subtle sense than mere "heaping up."

It is my contention that much of psychological inquiry and knowledge must permanently and in principle have characteristics rather more akin to such features of humanistic scholarship as I have just tried to convey than to scientific research, even when the conception of scientific research is liberalized—as it has been by Polanyi, Bronowski, and others—in such a way as to punctuate its continuities with humanistic and all other forms of knowledge seeking.

Search Cells and Language Incommensurabilities

Historically, contemporaneously, and, I submit, in principle, the psychological studies represent an assemblage of specialized language communities, research groups or, if you will, cliques, claques, application groups, action groups, interest groups, and the like. I will call such associations of inquirers pursuing roughly common problems from a common point of view, and thus sharing a specialized language, *search cells*. Each of us has been or is a member of one or more such cells. In relation to our primary or most intimate cell, one of the most poignant phenomena with which we are all at some level familiar is that we seem to know more when communicating with our fellow community members than when trying to communicate across community boundaries. And naturally, the insights provided by the conceptual net of our given community are so striking to us that we are impelled to see what its reticulations bring forth in other waters. And we almost always "lose perspective" in this process: we generously emerge with a single "paradigm" for all psychology.

Using the word *psychology* in the collective sense, it is important to see that the growth of the field involves not so much the broadening of research interests from an established base as the *multiplication* of research interests. The case is not wholly different in the natural sciences. But the polymorphous character of the phenomena that we address and their extraordinary variety, tenuousness, and subtlety are such that the assertion of significant research options increasingly forces us into not only more and more specialized search cells (thus language communities), but ones increasingly insulated by virtue of incommensurabilities of their respective discrimination pools.

Now, each of these community languages is a differentiation out of the natural language, and each "language" is only loosely systematic and of mixed composition. It is therefore not surprising that single minds can "speak" and understand several (sometimes many) such languages, in some degree. That does not mean that the speaker has integrated or can integrate these asystematically different languages. When "speaking" each (at any level) there is a change of perspective. A perspective is not the kind of thing that can fuse. Perspectival knowledge *multiplies*, but the nature of a human universe and our resources for ordering that universe are such that attempts toward large integrations or fusions can make no sense. When intentions of this sort are nevertheless asserted, we get knowledge-forms, not knowledge.

This question of the incommensurability of the discrimination pools (thus the "languages") of the nuclear search cells requires careful examination. Naturally, as between any two search cells, the incommensurability is not necessarily total. The incommensurabilities may be slight or marked, tractable or "vicious." But in a domain of such awesome range as that discriminated by the extant definitions of psychology—and one characterized by phenomena so complex and labile—many of the incommensurabilities between the languages of different search cells will be vicious ones. If the domain-segments approached by two different search cells are, in some sense, distant ones, viciousness is pretty well guaranteed. Cross-cell communication, say, between an appropriately composed (in respect to discrimination pool) cell concerned with the psychology of musical composition and a cell of rote learning investigators (or, perhaps, microelectrode analysts of brain function) is likely to be seriously muffled, if only for the fact that few members of the latter groups are likely to have any technical understanding of or refined sensitivity to music. Indeed, the musical composition cell may have difficulty communicating with, say, a cell concentrating on the psychology of visual art, and vice versa. Of course, there would be nothing counterproductive about the language incommensurabilities of such groups if they did not imperialistically presume that their respective languages were extensible to each other's domain—or, perhaps, the entire domain of "psychology." In that event, we would simply have groups of investigators pursuing different *psychological studies*.

Now consider the case of cells addressing similar or overlapping subdomains but via different languages, conceptual templates, nets, frameworks. In general, two such groups will have made different disembeddings from, different perceptual cuts upon, the world-flux. If psychological events had a kind of logical layer-cake structure, or some kind of orderly crystal-like faceting (and if the human mind were something like a camera), we could perhaps conclude that the languages might be ultimately summable, combinable into some kind of logical structure or fusible into some more general "containing" language. But psychological events tend not to be like that. Characteristically, they are multiply determined, ambiguous in their human meaning, polymorphous, contextually "environed" or embedded in complex and vaguely bounded ways, evanescent and labile in the extreme. Relative to their different analytical purposes, predictive aims, practical ends in view, metaphor-forming capacities, perceptual sensitivities, preexisting discriminaton repertoires, different *theorists* (and ultimately the search cells forming about them) will make asystematically different perceptual cuts upon the same domain. They will identify "variables" of markedly different grain and meaning-contour, selected and linked on different principles of grouping. The cuts, variables, concepts, that is, will in all likelihood establish different universes of discourse, even if loose ones.

Constraints upon Intracell Communication

Turn now to another characteristic of search cells. Insofar as a cell is a language community in my sense of the term, the community will have a "vertical" structure: it will consist of a quasi-hierarchical assemblage of subcommunities, the members of each of which "speak" and apply the language with differential competence. The fulness and precision of *intragroup* communication will thus be limited by this differential competence in the language use. Applying such considerations at the level of the individual inquirer, it can be said that there must necessarily be an idiosyncratic component in the use of the language. Such individual idiosyncrasy (and subgroup variability) is clearly by no means peculiar to *psychological* language communities. The same point may be made in relation to physics or any other natural science (or, indeed, natural language communities). But the hallmark of a science like physics is that its successful algorithmic resources and relatively univocal and precise "perceptual displays" are such as to contain communicative idiosyncrasy within narrow limits. Since—as I have tried to argue from many incidences—comparably determinate definitional devices are not available to most psychological language communities, we can expect muffled, cross-purposeful, or ambiguous *intragroup* communication within many of our search cells.

The point at issue here carries some severe entailments for the psychological studies, and some interesting ones even for the natural sciences. It is surprising, for instance, how little attention philosophers and historians of science have given to tracing out the ramifications of *leadership* in scientific communities. Be this as it may, psychological search cells are characteristically followerships (in some cases, *claques* might be the better word) in the ambience of a *leader*. The leader has forged the language and uses it with "summit" (not necessarily consummate) skill and richness. Bearing in mind the degrees of embeddedness and perceptual masking that we have seen, in the analysis of definition, to be characteristic of the referents of psychological concepts, it is clear that there must be tight limits—especially if the language be a rich one—to the leader's success at teaching or conveying the language to his followers. Even the most capable of them will internalize a rather different conceptual template than the leader's. As for the less capable, they may internalize words, slogans, but use them in rote or meaningless ways.

Such communicative difficulties will, of course, vary in severity in the different psychological studies and sometimes as between different search cells within a given one of the psychological studies. But in certain fields of psychology—as, for instance, psychopathology and social psychology—the consequences of such communicative mismatches may be far-reaching. I suspect, for instance, that not only do no two psychoanalysts *do* psychoanalysis in the same way (a fact granted by virtually everyone), but that no two of them "speak" psychoanalysis in sufficiently similar ways to warrant the conclusion that they hold the "same" theory. Yet, though Freud's formulations may be criticizable on many grounds, it is unfair to criticize him on this one. Whatever the limitations, certain of the concepts and concept relations have cut more deeply (and brought more back) than perhaps any concepts that have been formed in the history of psychology. Nevertheless, by virtue of the inevitable communicative difficulties I have tried to discriminate, it would be absurd to expect that such a theory could be *collaboratively* developed, refined in anything resembling a "progressive" way, or tested in any sense comprehended in conventional canons of research design or "formal" evidence. But this is not to say that whatever of it the followership has internalized has not enriched their professional sensibilities or in some way fed, sharpened, and guided their particular therapeutic skills.[11]

11. In stressing the inevitability of language incommensurabilities and communicative mismatches—as I have in this essay—my intent has been to delineate certain of the principled constraints upon the psychological studies which are seldom acknowledged in a sufficiently sharp way. A certain parochialism and fragmentation of search cells is necessitated by the terms of my analysis, but I do not wish to be interpreted as reveling in these circumstances or in any way discouraging efforts toward communicating *across* search cells. Nor do I advocate that the interests of all cells be trained upon domains of narrow scope. The relevant issues are intricate in the extreme, and I cannot address all of them in a single paper. But—peremptorily—the following things can be noted:

(1) Attempts to "converse" across cells should be ardently pursued—and possible knowledge overlaps, conceptual homologies, areas of translatability, potential contexts of useful borrowing (whether substantive or methodic), mutual complementations or supplementations should be identified. The force of my argument is that in most such cross-cell collating it will be unrealistic (and indeed counterproductive) to anticipate' total or any "large" degree of integrability—whether via translation, efforts to establish detailed isomorphic relations, logical subsumability in the one direction or the other, joint deducibility from a more general language, or any other type of *systematic* alignment (as, e.g., the addition, by mere logical conjunction, of the two languages in the hope that what emerges will constitute a coherent universe of discourse).

(2) If *differentiated* knowledge be the desideratum, many search cells will have to concentrate on limited (and, it can be hoped, significant) contexts of human or organismic activity. But it is proper and desirable that some cells not confine their research and explanatory objectives to tightly circumscribed phenotypic domains. May I illustratively distinguish two of the types of such cells.

(a) The traditional *process* areas of psychology—as, for example, perception, cognition, learning, motivation—are, of course, concerned with general principles of human (or organismic) functioning, whether at "psychological" or biological levels, conceived as cutting across all "phenotypic" domains. The multiple search cells in each such process area may legitimately seek knowledge of great generality. Nevertheless, the arguments in the text strongly suggest the likelihood, relative to any subject matter so complex as that discriminated by a process area, that at any time in history there will be a plurality of languages in a given area such that no single one will rationally merit preemptive allegiance. Indeed, it is already evident—cf. "Introduction to Study II" of *Psychology: A Study of a Science* (Koch, 1962a)—that there is no ultimately rational or perspective-independent basis even for demarcating or *defining* a process area.

Another epistemic peculiarity of the process areas is best shown with the aid of Kuhn's distinction (1970c, pp. 188–189) between a law schema and a law. He points out that Newton's second law, for instance, generally written as $f = ma$, is not in *that form* directly subject to "logical and mathematical manipulation." Rather, it is a schema or sketch, of which the less general (but manipulable instantiations vary markedly in different problem situations. "For the case of free fall, $f = ma$ becomes $mg = m\dfrac{d^2s}{dt^2}$; for the simple pendulum it is transformed to $mg \sin\theta = -ml\dfrac{d^2\theta}{dt^2}$; for a pair of interacting harmonic oscillators it becomes two equations, the first of which may be written $m_1\dfrac{d^2s_1}{dt^2} + k_1s_1 = k_2(s_2 - s_1 + d)$; and for more complex situations, such as the gyroscope, it takes still other forms, the family resemblance of which to $f = ma$ is still harder to discover." "Laws" of the type sought in the process areas are almost inevitably of a degree of schematism in excess of this Newtonian example selected by Kuhn. If the "law" is held to be applicable across the entire domain of psychological events, the distance between its

The Question of Community-Language or "Theory" Appraisal

It is my contention that most others of the psychological studies which address ranges of experience or action worthy of human interest face communicative problems similar to (if often less severe than) those of psychoanalysis. Though some may think this a despairing conclusion, I hasten to note that I think it liberating. Nevertheless, the great question that remains is how does one appraise a psychological "language," theory, conceptual template? And, of course, how does one choose between contending languages when they both have (or claim to have) an overlap in their range of application? Does the present theory of perceptual definition assume

---

generalized, schematic form and many of its contexts of application can only be adjudged immense. If we want *differentiated* knowledge, such schemas, per se, could have but limited guidance value. Indeed, for a long time to come, it may prove more fruitful to work toward the law-schema from particular, bounded domains than to proceed in the reverse direction. But this caution certainly does not counterindicate the value of working in the direction from process-law to phenotype. Both directions should be pursued.

(b) Another type of search cell—of which there should be many at any given time—are those concerned, in one way or another, with "the large picture." My position certainly does not denigrate or discourage comprehensive thinking within the psychological studies—endeavors which, in the light of technical-psychological and/or all other relevant sources of knowledge, seek visions, images, portraits, philosophies ("theories," if you will) of psychological man, of the human condition, of human nature, of mind. In the terms given by convention, some of this endeavor will take the form of "personality theory;" some of it "philosophy of mind;" some of it "speculative psychology;" some of it "religion" some of it the kind of textbook writing which seeks a strong organization within a wide range of material. Not a few of the seminal thinkers in the history of psychology (e.g., Aristotle, Freud, William James) fall into this category of comprehensive thinkers or visionaries.

What my position strongly urges, however, is that this mixed category of effort be seen in more accurate terms than formerly. These comprehensive explorers of man and mind do not offer us the kind of differentiated knowledge that we associate with either the mature sciences or the analytical and explicative humanities in their more rigorous forms. If what they offer can be called "theory," it is certainly not theory in the sense most prized in science— the mark of which is the capacity to mediate highly specified knowledge, whether predictive or elucidatory, of concrete phenomena. That the knowledge offered us by these explorers of comprehensive intent will be strongly perspectival and sensibility-dependent goes, of course, without saying. And it is precisely the kinds of search cells forming about such thinkers that will manifest in their more severe forms the *intragroup* communicative difficulties delineated in the text.

that all languages, theories, templates, nets, frames, or perspectives bearing on a psychological subject matter are, if not equally adequate, at least adequate in some degree? Must the "rational" attitude be that of complete libertarianism?

I do not think so. Nor do I think the answer an easy one. For it is not my position alone that raises such questions. Ever since the breakdown of what might be called "rational reconstructionism" in the philosophy of science, the entire issue of "rational grounds" for theory appraisal or selection has been conspicuously up in the air. The historico-sociologically oriented students of science have by no means given an ultimately "satisfying" answer. Kuhn's is, at least on the surface, question-begging. He says in effect that a theory will be selected because of its "puzzle-solving" power, and that scientific communities prize this property (it is perhaps their superordinate "value"), but he is vague in his specification of any independent criteria for the initial identification of the property.

It may be that there is no ultimately *satisfying* answer: the lack of closure that we feel when confronted with such apparently circular answers may in fact be the gap that has been left by the disappearance of the delusion—fortified for several thousand years by the history of philosophy—that human rationality can be rendered inviolable by a set of rules. My own delusional system is not such as to give me confidence that I can fill in this gap. But it suggests the following outline of an "answer."

My position poses fewer difficulties than most in respect to theory (or framework or concept) "appraisal." There is a sense in which both a theory of truth and a theory of error are built into the analysis of definition I have put forward. As we have seen: "Though definition be *within language*, our 'perceptual' frame constantly reminds us that language is about something—however embedded, intricately contoured, or fluidly deployed that something may be" (p. 533). Though, as we have also seen (pp. 522–524), there are "good" concepts and "poor" concepts coded within the natural language—and indeed, concepts which stabilize not only "fuzzy" discriminal experiences, but trivial, vagrant, local, or even illusory ones—the natural language may be seen as "containing" a vast, sprawling, and variably adequate ontology of the human universe. And of course, language can be *used* at varying levels of nicety, precision, or penetration—not excluding a zero level. Given terms can be applied in rote fashion (via "symptom") or in richly meaningful ways (via "creative metaphor").

Further, since language emanates from human beings, it can play the whole assemblage of deceptive games typified by "lying," it can be skewed in its bearing on reality by motive, wish, or autism; its application can be distorted or deflected by the conditions which produce perceptual illusion; or its relation to the world dimmed and realigned through psychopathological or neurological "disturbance." There are other grievous ontology-distorting factors of which psychologists are aware, and to which they might well give more investigative attention. I am, for instance, very much impressed with the endemic human need for crawling into cozy conceptual boxes—*any box*, so long as it gives promise of relieving the pains of cognitive uncertainty or easing problematic tension. This poignant human need, at any cost, for a frame, an abacus, a system, map, or set of rules which can seem to offer the wisp of a hope for resolving uncertainty makes all of us vulnerable—in one degree or another—to the claims of simplistic, reductive, hypergeneral, or in other ways ontology-distorting frames, so long as they have the appearance of "systematicity." There are many epistemic consequences of this fear-driven human propensity to seek bondage within such frames which require deep study.

There has been increasing acknowledgment in recent decades of a curious contrast between psychology and the established sciences. There is a strong sense in which psychology was already "established" before it *commenced*, whether as science or any other kind of institutionalized technical enterprise. At my previous appearance at the Nebraska Symposium (in 1956) I found myself saying:

It is often not sufficiently held in mind that psychology does not start with neutral and unmanipulated data, but that the conditions of human life are such as to force us to entertain theories of ourselves. These "theories of ourselves"—the syntax of which we seldom explore—are often, to the extent that they are acknowledged, allocated to "common sense" or "practical life" or some such limbo and then forgotten. What is not acknowledged is that such theory *itself* constitutes a most abstract and epistemologically complex ordering of the data of experience and behavior. What is truly remarkable is the degree of success that has attended such naive theoretical effort, despite evident imperfections. Nevertheless, one aim of psychological science must, by definition, be at least ultimately to supplant such "theory" with better theory. [Koch, 1956, p. 60]

Philosophers of mind have done a superb job in recent decades in asserting and implementing considerations of the above order (and through no invitation from me!). They have indeed begun to explore the "syntax" and lexicon of the "theories of ourselves" which are embedded in the ordinary language. They have traced with sensitivity the ramified meaning-contours of such mental (and intricately context-dependent) terms as *intention, emotion* (and its subspecifications), *motive, wish*, and the like. They have made progress at disembedding from the natural language the complex use structures governing the assignment of "reasons" versus "causes," and such fundamental distinctions as that between "action" and "movement." Their work has indeed begun to suggest the subtlety, complexity, and differentiation of the psychological knowledge coded within natural language. But their admirable analytic purposes are special ones, and it should not be forgotten that the subtle knowledge embedded in the natural language has been explored, clarified, and extended by every competent humanist in the history of thought and, of course, by others. I mean no disrespect to my colleagues who pursue philosophy of mind when I say that I would rather go to Shakespeare or even Durrell for an analysis of "love" than to an analytic philosopher.

Once we appreciate the vast resources of psychological knowledge coded in the natural language, and internalized in the sensibilities of those who use it well, it should become a paramount matter of intellectual responsibility for those who explore the human condition to ensure that this knowledge is not degraded, distorted, or obliterated in their technical conceptualizations. I am at one with philosophers of mind in seeing this maxim as a central *rational* decision basis for the appraisal of theories, frameworks, or concepts in the human "sciences." That it is not the *only* decision basis will emerge in a moment.

If the knowledge coded in natural language and internalized in human sensibility gives us a kind of ontology of the human universe, it then becomes possible roughly to distinguish three kinds of theories or conceptual frameworks within the human studies: some that are *ontology-distorting*, some that are *ontology-respecting*, and some that are *ontology-revealing*. My theory of definition permits me to call any technical framework which obliterates or does not permit us in some way to "recapture" the network of epistemically rich (or, in my special sense, "good") concepts in the range of natural language bearing on its domain, *ontology-distorting*. A frame which merely "respects" such distinctions but does not (by processes of metaphor as I have described them, etc.) permit the sharpening, extension, supplementation, or enrichment of the natural-language knowledge is *ontology-respecting*. A frame which *does* permit such sharpening, supplementation, or enrichment of the natural-language knowledge is *ontology-revealing*. At any given time it is, I think, possible to find, within the gamut of the psychological studies, conspicuous instances of frameworks within each of these categories. At any given time, it will also be possible to find frameworks which—because of early developmental status or other considerations—must be adjudged of *indeterminate classification*. Because of the specialized character of the languages of psychological search cells that I have taken pains to exhibit, I readily acknowledge that rational policy in respect to assigning frameworks to this *last* class obliges one to be rather generous. On the same basis, I acknowledge also that there may be instances such that *no* extant person may be truly qualified (by virtue of joint resources of relevant natural-language sensibility and mastery of the search-cell language) to make any assignment other than into the "indeterminate" category. *That* type of hazard is not confined to the psychological studies; it is present in *every* field of scholarship. However, the hazard is a terrifying one in psychology because of its oft-claimed mission to illuminate, regulate, control, or "improve" the human condition.

It may be well, at this phase, to give a few illustrations of frameworks within the psychological studies which I believe to fall into the respective categories.

Ontology-Distorting Frameworks. I think the Skinnerian framework a superb example of the ontology-distorting variety. I certainly do not hope to make this judgment plausible in a few sentences to those who reside within this framework. But consider the poverty of a conceptual abacus that would phrase the entire psychological ontology within three or four enormously general and contextually rubbery concepts (e.g., "operant behavior," "reinforcement," "contingencies of reinforcement," and "stimuli," inclusive of "private" stimuli). Yet this framework claims comprehensive applicability to the *entire* domain of significant human events by the simple strategy of obliterating most of the psychological distinctions coded in the natural language, or "translating" them into the hyperflexible schematism of the framework concepts. A set of experimental generalizations based on the analysis of the "rates" of arbitrarily selected repetitive instrumental behaviors of rats and pigeons is extrapolated—with no allowance for (or even consideration of) the local and contextual conditions of the findings—to "all" behavior. The remarkable detail in which the "schedules of reinforcement" were worked out for rate fluctuations of the bar-pressing and key-pecking behaviors studied in the foundational experiments is used to mask the astronomical analogical distances between the "laws" and their context of application. A certain plausibility is loaned to this autistic analogical leaping (in contradistinction to the leaps of other S-R theorists), in that a quasi- "purposive" connotation is built into the notion of an operant by virtue of its instrumental character serving as the defining criterion. As Skinner says:

> Possibly no charge is more often leveled against behaviorism
> or a science of behavior than that it cannot deal with purpose
> or intention. A stimulus-response formula has no answer, but
> operant behavior is the very field of purpose and intention.
> By its nature it is directed toward the future: a person acts
> *in order that* something will happen, and the order is temporal.
> [1974, p. 55]

Ontology-Respecting Frameworks. Tolman's theory, in my estimation, was in many ways an ontology-respecting formulation. His insistence, as evinced in the many successively revised formulations put forward throughout his career, that even rat behavior could not be meaningfully addressed other than through the discrimination of a large number of particulate perceptual and cognitive "variables" betokened a considerable respect for the way things are in both the rat and the human universe. His attempt to *define* such concepts objectively, in terms of "pointer-reading" experiments, he adjudged, at the very end of his career, to be a failure (1959). But all through his career, he engagingly admitted that he was at heart a "crypto-phenomenologist." It is arguable as to whether his theorizing was *ontology-revealing*. But he did shore up the dignity of rats and men during the long period when this was under severe attrition in psychology.

Ontology-Revealing Frameworks. I will cite three examples that fall into this category.

Gibson's perceptual theorizing has pointed to the possibility that there may be many dimensions of physical stimulus specification—the "higher-order variables" of stimulation—which have not been touched by classical sensory psychology. And he makes this possibility concrete and convincing by experimentally identifying certain variables "of adjacent and successive order" which seem related in orderly ways to variables of phenomenal experience and reporting behavior. To the extent that a program of this sort is successful, it supplements and refines the previously achieved discriminations of the human race bearing upon the domain not only of psychology but of physics.

Less well known than Gibson's framework—but bearing a family resemblance to it—is that of *Zener and Gaffron* (1962) which led to the isolation of "novel" dimensions of visual experience via the dedicated and patient comparison of art objects, photographs, and natural objects in their normal aspect as against their mirror-image reversals, inversions, and partial rotations. The subtle phenomenal properties which the investigators and their subjects were able to discern through such comparisons represent important extensions of human discrimination. Moreover, it was possible to show the dependence of different clusterings or organizations of these properties on variations in looking or survey behavior, quadrant of the visual field under survey, indices of hemisphere dominance, and other factors—and to make plausible inferences from these discoveries as to the character of the central processes that could mediate them. It is instructive to note that the qualifications for membership or even responsible interest in the Zener-Gaffron search cell are rather special ones: a capacity for precise analysis of visual experience, knowledge of the history of visual art and a sensitivity to its artifacts, detailed familiarity with twentieth-century perception psychology, and a considerable background in neuroanatomy and neurophysiology. It is no surprise that this particular language community is a rather small one!

Moving to a conceptual framework of markedly different cast, *Henry Murray's* (1959) remarkably differentiated anatomizing of experience and action via a range of finely discriminated concepts like *press, cathexis, dyadic system, thema, serials, ordination,* etc., provides a frame which, if "used" by an appropriately sensitive viewer, can be *ontology-revealing.*

Frameworks of Indeterminate Classification. To me, a conspicuous class of examples would be the frameworks associated with the computer modeling of mind and artificial intelligence. Obviously, the appraisal of such programs will depend upon the specific case. There is, however, a grave danger here of simplistic ontological distortion. The critical question, always, is how sensitive was the initial "job analysis" of the human process under simulation or "modeling." It is my impression that in most of the cases given us by history there is a marked oversimplification and distortion of the target process (or outcome). The history of machine-translation efforts may, perhaps, be taken as a prototypical case (cf. Bar-Hillel, 1964). Yet, in comparison to the efforts to recompose complex psychological processes from arbitrarily stipulated S-R postulates, there is in the computer theorizing at least an *intent to respect ontology.* My tendency is to come out with an answer somewhere between *ontology-distorting* and *-respecting* for this class of effort. I doubt that anything *ontology-revealing* has yet been achieved. But with respect to the still nascent efforts, the rational and fair policy is to suspend classification. It need hardly be added—in light of all I have said concerning the texture of the psychological studies—that I am *not* looking forward to a comprehensive computer theory of mind.

And *now* it will be asked *where* are the "rational" safeguards against deception, meretriciousness, obscurantism, distortion, error? Where are the rational criteria, the decision rules that *guarantee* forward movement? But, of course, there *are* none. We are *on our own*—as we always have been. Yet mankind has managed to learn a thing or two.[12]

12. Knowing something about the apperceptive equipment of psychologists, I am sure that in reading these paragraphs on framework (or theory) appraisal many of them will get the impression that I am disenfranchising all of the traditional lore concerning the corroboration of knowledge claims by experimental test, canons of evidence, and the associated statistical, mathematical, and instrumentative "methodology." I am not! I beg the reader to note my effort (pp. 538–540) to define the rationale and function of experimentation and other "characteristic methods of science" in terms of a perceptual theory of definition; my comments (pp. 491–494) concerning the applicability of the "analytic pattern of science" to fields like sensory and biological psychology; my hospitality to the use of mathematical and statistical method (and design) where significantly applicable (p. 494); and my constant emphasis on the need to gear the psychological studies to the seeking of particulate and *differentiated* knowledge, not fuzzy sloganizing, global word magic, or hypergeneral and ersatz law delivering.

My theory of definition is a theory of our capacity to define the real; it is also a theory of our capacity to detect (and indeed commit) error. We have no recourse but to follow Michael Polanyi when he says:

> I believe that we should accredit in ourselves the capacity for appraising our own articulation. Indeed, all our strivings towards precision imply our reliance on such a capacity. To deny or even doubt our possession of it would discredit any effort to express ourselves correctly, and the very conception of words as consistently used utterances would dissolve if we failed to accredit this capacity. This does not imply that this capacity is infallible, but merely that we are competent to exercise it and must ultimately rely on our exercise of it. This we must admit if we are to speak at all, which I believe to be incumbent on us to do. [1958, p. 91]

What safeguards we have, then, against irrationality, imprecision, error must be situated within ourselves. History and any individual biography will show these safeguards to be grotesquely fragile and tenuous, but they are there. It is a late date in history to report that even well-intentioned knowledge-seeking enterprises can pose a threat, can temporarily or permanently fail, can—even when partly successful—create grave hazards for the race. Because of its bearing on man's conception of himself, psychology *especially* is fraught with danger. The well-intentioned effort to emulate "successful" features of other knowledge-seeking enterprises which address quite different domains has backfired and produced much pseudo-

---

I reject no methods—however humble or however grand—the rationality of which has been established by their productiveness in mediating illuminating or useful knowledge in any context. I merely demand that method be used in appropriate and non-role-playing ways relative to the problems at issue, and that problems be chosen not wholly in terms of their amenability to particular methods considered honorific. And I emphatically argue, concerning hypothesis or theory appraisal, that even the most rigorous methods of science *enforce* no verdicts, no conclusions: it is *we*, the inquirers, who conclude or make verdicts; "verificational" methodology *suggests*, gives us *clues*, and the more rigorous and contextually apposite the method, the more dependable the clues. But the *conclusion*, the *appraisal* is a *decision* which must disembed an underlying pattern in an intricate "environment" of meanings, only one strand of which is the naked empirical finding or distribution of such, however "well verified."

knowledge. And such pseudo-knowledge now threatens to obliterate much that mankind already knows.

A view of the sort developed in this paper can do little to rectify this state of affairs. But it can do something. Should the false authority claimed by psychology in its constant flaunting of the banner of Science be stripped away, the plight of the human race might be slightly alleviated. Even nonspecialist human beings would then become less prone to relinquish to the claims of false authority what they already know or can discover. And if they learn to *trust* their capacities for intellectual appraisal, then even nonspecialists may find themselves able to detect, at least in some degree, the more flagrant *ontology-distorting* claims of psychological "scientists" or savants—not always and not everyone, just sometimes and some. And if *investigators* in the psychological studies could adopt some such modest outlook as the one I have tried to convey, then man's bane might well become man's hope.

REFERENCES

Adams, G. *Psychology: Science or superstition?* New York: Covici-Friede, 1931.

Bar-Hillel, Y. *Language and information: Selected essays on their theory and applications.* Reading, Mass.: Addison-Wesley, 1964.

Black, M. *Problems of analysis: Philosophical essays.* Ithaca, N.Y.: Cornell University Press, 1954.

Black, M. *Models and metaphors: Studies in language and philosophy.* Ithaca, N.Y.: Cornell University Press, 1962.

Carnap, R. Testability and meaning. *Philosophy of Science,* 1936, 3(4), 419–471; 1937, 4(1), 1–40.

Dewey, J. *How we think.* Boston & New York: D. C. Heath, 1910.

Dewey, J. *Essays in experimental logic.* Chicago: University of Chicago Press, 1917.

Dewey, J. *Logic: The theory of inquiry.* New York: Henry Holt, 1938.

Gibson, J. J. Perception as a function of stimulation. In S. Koch (Ed.), *Psychology: A study of a science,* Vol. 1. New York: McGraw-Hill, 1959. Pp. 456–501.

Gibson, J. J. *The senses considered as perceptual systems.* Boston: Houghton-Mifflin, 1966.

Guthrie, E. F. Association by contiguity. In S. Koch (Ed.), *Psychology: A study of a science,* Vol. 2. New York: McGraw-Hill, 1959. Pp. 158–195.

Hesse, M. B. *Science and the human imagination.* London: SCM Press, 1954.

Hesse, M. B. *Models and analogies in science.* Notre Dame, Ind.: University of Notre Dame Press, 1966.

Hull, C. L. The conflicting psychologies of learning—A way out. *Psychological Review,* 1935, 42, 491–516.

Johnson, S. *A dictionary of the English language.* London: Printed by W. Strahan for J. & P. Knapton, 1755.

Koch, S. Behavior as "intrinsically" regulated: Work notes towards a pre-theory of phenomena called "motivational." In M. R. Jones (Ed.), *Nebraska symposium on motivation,* 1956. Lincoln: University of Nebraska Press, 1956. Pp. 42–86.

Koch, S. Epilogue. In S. Koch (Ed.), *Psychology: A study of a science,* Vol. 3. New York: McGraw-Hill, 1959. Pp. 729–788. (a)

Koch, S. (Ed.) *Psychology: A study of a science.* Study I: Conceptual and systematic. Vols. 1–3. New York: McGraw-Hill, 1959. (b)

Koch, S. Psychological science versus the science-humanism antinomy: Intimations of a significant science of man. *American Psychologist,* 1961, 16, 629–639.

Koch, S. Introduction to Study II. In S. Koch (Ed.), *Psychology: A study of a science,* Vol. 4. New York: McGraw-Hill, 1962. (a)

Koch, S. (Ed.) *Psychology: A study of a science.* Study II: Empirical substructure and relations with other sciences. Vol. 4. New York: McGraw-Hill, 1962. (b)

Koch, S. (Ed.) *Psychology: A study of a science.* Study II: Empirical substructure and relations with other sciences. Vols. 5 & 6. New York: McGraw-Hill, 1963.

Koch, S. Psychology and emerging conceptions of knowledge as unitary. In T. W. Wann (Ed.), *Behaviorism and phenomenology: Contrasting bases for modern psychology.* Chicago: University of Chicago Press, 1964. Pp. 1–45.

Koch, S. Theory and experiment in psychology. *Social Research,* 1973, 40(4), 691–707.

Kuhn, T. S. *The structure of scientific revolutions.* Chicago: University of Chicago Press, 1962.

Kuhn, T. S. Logic of discovery or psychology of research? In I. Lakatos & A. Musgrave (Eds.), *Criticism and the growth of knowledge.* Cambridge, England: University Press, 1970. (a)

Kuhn, T. S. Reflections on my critics. In I. Lakatos & A. Musgrave (Eds.), *Criticism and the growth of knowledge.* Cambridge, England: University Press, 1970. (b)

Kuhn, T. S. *The structure of scientific revolutions.* (2nd ed., enlarged.) Foundations of the unity of science, Vol. 2, No. 2. Chicago: International Encyclopedia of Unified Science, 1970. (c)

Kuhn, T. S. Second thoughts on paradigms. In F. Suppe (Ed.), *The structure of scientific theories.* Urbana, Ill.: University of Illinois Press, 1974.

Lashley, K. S. In search of the engram. *Symposia of the Society for Experimental Biology,* 1950, **4,** 454–482.

Lenneberg, E. H. *Biological foundations of language.* New York: Wiley, 1967.

Masterman, M. The nature of a paradigm. In I. Lakatos & A. Musgrave (Eds.), *Criticism and the growth of knowledge.* Cambridge, England: University Press, 1970. Pp. 59–89.

Mill, J. S. *A system of logic, ratiocinative and inductive.* 1843. Vol. 1 & 2. (5th ed.) London: Parker, Son, & Bourn, 1862.

Murray, H. A. Preparations for the scaffold of a comprehensive system. In S. Koch (Ed.), *Psychology: A study of a science,* Vol. 3. New York: McGraw-Hill, 1959. Pp. 7–54.

Polanyi, M. *Personal knowledge: Towards a post-critical philosophy.* Chicago: University of Chicago Press, 1958.

Polanyi, M. *The study of man.* London: Routledge & Kegan Paul, 1959.

Polanyi, M. Tacit knowing and its bearing on some problems on philosophy. *Review of Modern Physics,* 1962, **34,** 601–616.

Polanyi, M. *The tacit dimension.* Garden City, N.Y.: Doubleday, 1966.

Skinner, B. F. *Beyond freedom and dignity.* New York: Knopf, 1971.

Skinner, B. F. *About behaviorism.* New York: Knopf, 1974.

Tolman, E. C. Principles of purposive behavior. In S. Koch (Ed.), *Psychology: A study of a science,* Vol. 2. New York: McGraw-Hill, 1959. Pp. 92–157.

Toulmin, S. E. Does the distinction between normal and revolutionary science hold water? In I. Lakatos & A. Musgrave (Eds.), *Criticism and the growth of knowledge.* Cambridge, England: University Press, 1970. Pp. 39–47.

Toulmin, S. E. *Human understanding.* Vol. 1. Princeton: Princeton University Press, 1972.

Verplanck, W. S. Burrhus F. Skinner. In W. K. Estes, S. Koch, et al., *Modern learning theory.* New York: Appleton-Century-Crofts, 1954. Pp. 267–316.

Verplanck, W. S. A glossary of some terms used in the objective science of behavior. *Psychological Review,* 1957, **64**(Supplement viii), 42.

Zener, K. The significance of experience of the individual for the science of psychology. In H. Feigl et al. (Eds.), *Minnesota studies in the philosophy of science,* Vol. 2. Minneapolis: University of Minnesota Press, 1958. Pp. 354–369.

Zener, K., & Gaffron, M. Perceptual experience: An analysis of its relations to the external world through internal processings. In S. Koch (Ed.), *Psychology: A study of a science,* Vol. 4. New York: McGraw-Hill, 1962. Pp. 515–618.

Subject Index

Author Index